America's TOP 101 COMPUTER AND TECHNICAL JOBS

Second Edition

Detailed Information on Major Jobs at All Levels of Education and Training

- ★ **Thorough, up-to-date descriptions of 101 top jobs that require computer and technical skills**

- ★ **Information on skills needed, education and training required, salaries, growth potential, and more**

- ★ **Special section providing proven career planning and job seeking advice**

- ★ **Resume examples by professional resume writers for a variety of top computer and technical jobs**

- ★ **Helpful information on labor market trends**

Part of America's Top Jobs® Series

Michael Farr

D1532937

America's Top 101 Computer and Technical Jobs, Second Edition
Detailed Information on Major Jobs at All Levels of Education and Training

Previous edition was titled *America's Top Computer and Technical Jobs*

© 2004 by JIST Publishing, Inc.

Published by JIST Works, an imprint of JIST Publishing, Inc.
8902 Otis Avenue
Indianapolis, IN 46216-1033
Phone: 800-648-JIST   Fax: 800-JIST-FAX
E-mail: info@jist.com   Web site: www.jist.com

Some other books by Michael Farr:
The Very Quick Job Search
Same-Day Resume
America's Top Resumes for America's Top Jobs
The Quick Resume & Cover Letter Book
Getting the Job You Really Want
Seven Steps to Getting a Job Fast
Best Jobs for the 21st Century (with database
    work by Laurence Shatkin, Ph.D.)

Other books in the America's Top Jobs® series:
America's Top 300 Jobs
America's 101 Fastest Growing Jobs
America's Top 101 Jobs for People Without a Four-Year Degree
America's Top 101 Jobs for College Graduates
America's Top Military Careers
Career Guide to America's Top Industries

About career materials published by JIST. Our materials encourage people to be self-directed and to take control of their destinies. We work hard to provide excellent content, solid advice, and techniques that get results. If you have questions about this book or other JIST products, call 1-800-648-JIST or visit www.jist.com.

Quantity discounts are available for JIST products. Please call 1-800-648-JIST or visit www.jist.com for a free catalog and more information.

Visit www.jist.com for information on JIST, free job search information, book excerpts, and ordering information on our many products. For free information on 14,000 job titles, visit www.careeroink.com.

Acquisition Editor: Susan Pines
Editors: Stephanie Koutek, Linda Seifert
Cover and Interior Designer: Aleata Howard
Page Layout Coordinator: Carolyn J. Newland
Proofreaders: David Faust, Jeanne Clark

Printed in Canada

Library of Congress Cataloging-in-Publication Data

Farr, J. Michael.
    America's top 101 computer and technical jobs : detailed information on
    major jobs at all levels of education and training / Michael Farr.-- 2nd ed.
            p. cm. -- (America's top jobs series)
    "Previous edition was titled America's Top Computer and Technical Jobs, 2004."
    ISBN 1-59357-073-2 (alk. paper)
    1. Computer science--Vocational guidance--United States--Dictionaries. 2. Technology--Vocational
    guidance--United States--Dictionaries. 3. Occupations--United States--Dictionaries. 4. Labor market--United States.
    5. Job hunting--United States. I. Title. II. Series.
    QA76.25.F37 2004

                                                2004012068

06 05 04   9 8 7 6 5 4 3 2 1

ISBN 1-59357-073-2

Relax—You Don't Have to Read This Whole Book!

*T*his is a big book, but you don't need to read it all. I've organized it into easy-to-use sections so you can browse just the information you want. To get started, simply scan the table of contents, where you'll find brief explanations of the major sections plus a list of the jobs described in this book. Really, this book is easy to use, and I hope it helps you.

Who Should Use This Book?

This is more than a book of job descriptions. I've spent quite a bit of time thinking about how to make its contents useful for a variety of situations, including

* **Exploring career options.** The job descriptions in Section One give a wealth of information on many of the most desirable jobs in the labor market.

* **Considering more education or training.** The information helps you avoid costly mistakes in choosing a career or deciding on additional training or education—and it increases your chances of planning a bright future.

* **Job seeking.** This book helps you identify new job targets, prepare for interviews, and write targeted resumes. The career planning and job search advice in Section Two has been proven to cut job search time in half!

* **Career planning.** The job descriptions help you explore your options, and Sections Two and Three provide career planning advice and other useful information.

Source of Information

The occupational descriptions in this book come from the good people at the U.S. Department of Labor, as published in the most recent edition of the *Occupational Outlook Handbook*. The *OOH* is the best source of career information available, and the descriptions include the latest data on earnings, growth, education required, and many other details. So, thank you to all the people at the Labor Department who gather, compile, analyze, and make sense of this information. It's good stuff, and I hope you can make good use of it.

Mike Farr

Mike Farr

Table of Contents

Summary of Major Sections

Introduction. The introduction explains what is included in each job description, gives tips on using the book for career exploration and job seeking, and provides other details. *The introduction begins on page 1.*

Section One: Descriptions of 101 Top Computer and Technical Jobs. This section presents thorough descriptions of 101 jobs that require computer skills or other technical training or experience. Education and training requirements for these jobs vary from on-the-job training to a four-year college degree or more. Each description gives information on the nature of the work, working conditions, employment, training, other qualifications, advancement, job outlook, earnings, related occupations, and sources of additional information. The jobs are presented in alphabetical order. The page numbers where specific descriptions begin are listed here in the table of contents. *Section One begins on page 11.*

Section Two: The Quick Job Search—Seven Steps to Getting a Good Job in Less Time. This brief but important section offers results-oriented career planning and job search techniques. It includes tips on identifying your key skills, defining your ideal job, using effective job search methods, writing resumes, organizing your time, improving your interviewing skills, and following up on leads. The second part of this section features professionally written and designed resumes for some of America's top computer and technical jobs. *Section Two begins on page 277.*

Section Three: Important Trends in Jobs and Industries. This section includes three well-written articles on labor market trends. The articles are short and worth your time. *Section Three begins on page 335.*

Titles of the articles in Section Three are "Tomorrow's Jobs," "Employment Trends in Major Industries," and "Training for Techies: Career Preparation in Information Technology."

The 101 Jobs Described in Section One

The titles for the 101 jobs described in Section One are listed below, in alphabetical order. The page number where each description begins is also listed. Simply find jobs that interest you, and then read those descriptions. An introduction to Section One begins on page 11 and provides additional information on how to interpret the descriptions.

Introduction

This book is about improving your life, not just about selecting a job. The career you choose will have an enormous impact on how you live your life.

While a huge amount of information is available on occupations, most people don't know where to find accurate, reliable facts to help them make good career decisions—or they don't take the time to look. Important choices such as what to do with your career and whether to get additional training or education deserve your time.

If you are considering more training or education—whether additional course work, a college degree, or an advanced degree—this book will help with solid information. Training or education beyond high school is now typically required to get better jobs, but many good jobs can be learned through on-the-job experience, informal training, and technical training or education lasting from several months to two years. The education and training needed for the jobs described in *America's Top 101 Computer and Technical Jobs* vary enormously. This book provides descriptions for major jobs requiring computer and technical skills and gives you the facts you need for exploring your options.

A certain type of work or workplace may interest you as much as a certain type of job. If your interests and values lead you to work in healthcare, for example, you can do this in a variety of work environments, in a variety of industries, and in a variety of jobs. For this reason, I suggest you begin exploring alternatives by following your interests and finding a career path that allows you to use your talents doing something you enjoy.

Also, remember that money is not everything. The time you spend in career planning can pay off in higher earnings, but being satisfied with your work—and your life—is often more important than how much you earn. This book can help you find the work that suits you best.

Keep in Mind That Your Situation Is *Not* "Average"

Projected employment growth and earnings trends are quite positive for many occupations and industries. Keep in mind, however, that the averages in this book will not be true for many individuals. Within any field, many people earn more and many earn less than the average.

My point is that **your** situation is probably not average. Some people do better than others, and some are willing to accept less pay for a more desirable work environment. Earnings vary enormously in different parts of the country, in different occupations, and in different industries. But this book's solid information is a great place to start. Good information will give you a strong foundation for good decisions.

Four Important Labor Market Trends That Will Affect Your Career

Our economy has changed in dramatic ways over the past 10 years, with profound effects on how we work and live. Section Three of this book provides more information on labor market trends, but in case you don't read it, here are four trends that you simply *must* consider.

1. Education Pays

I'm sure you won't be surprised to learn that people with higher levels of education and training have higher average earnings. The data that follows comes from the U.S. Department of Labor and the U.S. Census Bureau. I've selected data to show you the median earnings for people with various levels of education. (The median is the point where half earn more and half earn less.) Based on this information, I computed the earnings advantage of people at various education levels over those who did not graduate from high school. I've also included information showing the average percentage of people at that educational level who are unemployed.

Earnings for Year-Round, Full-Time Workers Age 25 and Over, by Educational Attainment

Level of Education	Median Annual Earnings	Premium Over High School Dropouts	Unemployment Rate
Master's degree	$56,600	$34,200	2.8%
Bachelor's degree	$47,000	$24,600	3.1%
Associate degree	$36,400	$14,000	4.0%
Some college, no degree	$34,300	$11,900	4.8%
High school graduate	$29,200	$6,800	5.3%
High school dropout	$22,400		9.2%

Source: Unemployment rate, BLS; 2002 annual avg, BLS; earnings, Census, 3/2001

As you can see in the table, the more education and training you have, the more you are likely to earn—and the less likely you are to be unemployed. These two factors can make an enormous difference in long-term earnings. For example, the earnings gap between a college graduate and someone with a high school education is now $17,800 a year. That's enough to buy a nice car, make a down payment on a house, or even take a month's vacation for two to Europe. As you see, over a lifetime, these additional earnings can make an enormous difference in the college graduate's lifestyle.

And there is more. Jobs that require education and training beyond high school are projected to grow significantly faster than jobs that do not. Research shows that people with higher educational levels are less likely to be unemployed and that they remain unemployed for shorter periods of time. Overall, the data on earnings and other criteria indicate that people with more education and training do better than those with less. There are exceptions, of course, but for most people, more education and training results in higher earnings and lower rates of unemployment.

Many jobs can be obtained without a college degree, but most better-paying jobs now require either training beyond high school or substantial work experience.

2. Knowledge of Computer and Other Technologies Is Increasingly Important

Jobs requiring computer and technical skills are projected to be among the fastest-growing jobs in America. As you look over the list of jobs in the table of contents for *America's Top 101 Computer and Technical Jobs,* you will notice the enormous variety of technical jobs. The education and training requirements for these jobs range from on-the-job experience to a four-year college degree and more. But even jobs that do not appear to be technical often call for computer literacy or technical skills. Managers, for example, are often expected to understand and use spreadsheet, word-processing, and database software.

In all fields, people without job-related technical and computer skills will have a more difficult time finding good opportunities than people who have these skills. Employers tend to hire people with the skills they need, and people without these abilities won't get the best jobs. So consider upgrading your job-related computer and technology skills if you need to—and plan to stay up-to-date on your current and future jobs.

3. Ongoing Education and Training Are Essential

School and work once were separate activities, and most people did not go back to school after they began working. But with rapid changes in technology, most people are now required to learn throughout their work lives. Jobs are constantly upgraded, and today's jobs often cannot be.handled by people who have only the knowledge and skills that were adequate for workers a few years ago. To remain competitive, people without technical or computer skills must get them. Those who do not will face increasingly limited job options.

What this means is that you should upgrade your job skills throughout your working life. This may include taking formal courses, reading work-related magazines at home, signing up for on-the-job training, or participating in other forms of education. Upgrading your work-related skills on an ongoing basis is no longer optional for most jobs, and you ignore doing so at your peril.

4. Good Career Planning Has Increased in Importance

Most people spend more time watching TV in a week than they spend on career planning during an entire year. Yet most people will change their jobs many times and make major career changes five to seven times.

While you probably picked up this book for its information on jobs, it also provides a great deal of information on career planning. For example, Section Two gives good career and job search advice, and Section Three has useful information on labor market trends. I urge you to read these and related materials because career-planning and job-seeking skills are the keys to surviving in this new economy.

Tips on Using This Book

This book is based on information from a variety of government sources and includes the most up-to-date and accurate data available. The entries are well written and pack a lot of information into short descriptions. *America's Top 101 Computer and Technical Jobs* can be used in many ways, and I've provided tips for these four major uses:

- For people exploring career, education, or training alternatives
- For job seekers
- For employers and business people
- For counselors, instructors, and other career specialists

Tips for People Exploring Career, Education, or Training Alternatives

America's Top 101 Computer and Technical Jobs is an excellent resource for anyone exploring career, education, or training alternatives. Many people do not have a good idea of what they want to do in their careers. They may be considering additional training or education but may not know what sort they should get. If you are one of these people, *America's Top 101 Computer and Technical Jobs* can help in several ways. Here are a few pointers.

Review the list of jobs. Trust yourself. Research studies indicate that most people have a good sense of their interests. Your interests can be used to guide you to career options you should consider in more detail.

Begin by looking over the occupations listed in the table of contents. Look at all the jobs, because you may identify previously overlooked possibilities. If other people will be using this book, please don't mark in it. Instead, on a separate sheet of paper, list the jobs that interest you. Or make a photocopy of the table of contents and mark the jobs that interest you.

Next, carefully read the descriptions of the jobs that most interest you. A quick review will often eliminate one or more of these jobs based on pay, working conditions, education required, or other considerations. After you have identified the three or four jobs that seem most interesting, research each one more thoroughly before making any important decisions.

Study the jobs and their training and education requirements. Too many people decide to obtain additional training or education without knowing much about the jobs the training will lead to. Reviewing the descriptions in this book is one way to learn more about an occupation before you enroll in an education or training program. If you are currently a student, the job descriptions in this book can also help you decide on a major course of study or learn more about the jobs for which your studies are preparing you.

Do not be too quick to eliminate a job that interests you. If a job requires more education or training than you currently have, you can obtain this training in many ways.

Don't abandon your past experience and education too quickly. If you have significant work experience, training, or education, these should not be abandoned too quickly. Many skills you have learned and used in previous jobs or other settings can apply to related jobs. Many times, after people carefully consider what they want to do, they change careers and find that the skills they have can still be used.

America's Top 101 Computer and Technical Jobs can help you explore career options in several ways. First, carefully review descriptions for jobs you have held in the past. On a separate sheet of paper, list the skills needed in those jobs. Then do the same for jobs that interest you now. By comparing the lists, you will be able to identify skills you used in previous jobs that you could also use in jobs that interest you for the future. These "transferable" skills form the basis for moving to a new career.

You can also identify skills you have developed or used in nonwork activities, such as hobbies, family responsibilities, volunteer work, school, military, and extracurricular interests. The descriptions can be used even if you want to stay with the same employer. For example, you may identify jobs within your organization that offer more rewarding work, higher pay, or other advantages over your present job. Read the descriptions related to these jobs, as you may be able to transfer into another job rather than leave the organization.

Tips for Job Seekers

You can use the descriptions in this book to give you an edge in finding job openings and in getting job offers—even when you are competing with people who have better credentials. Here are some ways *America's Top 101 Computer and Technical Jobs* can help you in the job search.

Identify related job targets. You may be limiting your job search to a small number of jobs for which you feel qualified, but by doing so you eliminate many jobs you could do and enjoy. Your search for a new job should be broadened to include more possibilities.

Go through the entire list of jobs in the table of contents and check any that require skills similar to those you have. Look at all the jobs, since doing so sometimes helps you identify targets you would otherwise overlook.

Many people are not aware of the many specialized jobs related to their training or experience. The descriptions in *America's Top 101 Computer and Technical Jobs* are for major job titles, but a variety of more-specialized jobs may require similar skills. The "Other Major Career Information Sources" section later in this introduction lists sources you can use to find out about more-specialized jobs.

The descriptions can also point out jobs that interest you but have higher responsibility or compensation levels. Although you may not consider yourself qualified for such jobs now, you should think about seeking jobs that are above your previous levels but within your ability to handle.

Prepare for interviews. This book's job descriptions are an essential source of information to help you prepare for interviews. If you carefully review the description of a job before an interview, you will be much better prepared to emphasize your key skills. You should also review descriptions for past jobs and identify skills needed in the new job.

Negotiate pay. The job descriptions in this book will help you know what pay range to expect. Note that local pay and other details can differ substantially from the national averages in the descriptions.

Tips for Employers and Business People

Employers, human resource professionals, and other business users can use this book's information to write job descriptions, study pay ranges, and set criteria for new employees. The information can also help you conduct more-effective interviews by providing a list of key skills needed by new hires.

Tips for Counselors, Instructors, and Other Career Specialists

Counselors, instructors, and other career specialists will find this book helpful for their clients or students exploring career options or job targets. My best suggestion to professionals is to get this book off the shelf and into the hands of the people who need it. Leave it on a table or desk and show people how the information can help them. Wear this book out—its real value is as a tool used often and well.

Additional Information About the Projections

For more information about employment change, job openings, earnings, unemployment rates, and training requirements by occupation, consult *Occupational Projections and Training Data*, published by the Bureau of Labor Statistics. For occupational information from an industry perspective, including some occupations and career paths that *America's Top 101 Computer and Technical Jobs* does not cover, consult another BLS publication, *Career Guide to Industries*. This book is also available from JIST under the title *Career Guide to America's Top Industries*.

Other Major Career Information Sources

The information in this book will be very useful, but you may want or need additional information. Keep in mind that the job descriptions here cover major jobs and not the many more-specialized jobs that are often related to them. Each job description in this book provides some sources of information related to that job, but here are additional resources to consider.

The *Occupational Outlook Handbook* (or the *OOH*): Updated every two years by the U.S. Department of Labor, this book provides descriptions for more than 270 major jobs covering more than 85 percent of the workforce. The *OOH* is the source of the job descriptions used in this book, and the book *America's Top 300 Jobs* includes all the *OOH* content plus additional information.

The *Enhanced Occupational Outlook Handbook:* Includes all descriptions in the *OOH* plus descriptions of more than 8,000 more-specialized jobs related to them.

The *O*NET Dictionary of Occupational Titles:* The only printed source of the more than 1,100 jobs described in the U.S. Department of Labor's Occupational Information Network database.

The *Guide for Occupational Exploration:* An important career reference that allows you to explore all major O*NET jobs based on your interests.

www.careerOINK.com: This Web site provides more than 14,000 job descriptions, including those mentioned in the previous books, and a variety of useful ways to explore them.

Best Jobs for the 21st Century: Includes descriptions for the 500 jobs (out of more than 1,100) with the best combination of earnings, growth, and number of openings. Useful lists make jobs easy to explore (examples: highest-paying jobs by level of education or training, best jobs overall, and best jobs for different ages, personality types, interests, and many more).

Exploring Careers—A Young Person's Guide to 1,000 Jobs: For youth exploring career and education opportunities, this book covers 1,000 job options.

Information on the Major Sections of This Book

This book was designed to be easy to use. The table of contents provides brief comments on each section, and that may be all you need. If not, here are some additional details you may find useful in getting the most out of this book.

Section One: Descriptions of 101 Top Computer and Technical Jobs

Section One is the main part of this book and is probably the reason you picked it up. It contains brief, well-written descriptions for 101 major jobs that require computer and other technical skills. The content for these job descriptions comes from the U.S. Department of Labor and is considered by many people to be the most accurate and up-to-date data available. The jobs are presented in alphabetical order. The table of contents provides a page number that shows where each description begins.

Together, the jobs in Section One provide enormous variety at all levels of earnings, training, and education. One way to explore career options is to go through the table of contents and identify those jobs that seem interesting. If you are interested in medical jobs, for example, you can quickly spot those you want to learn more about. You may also see other jobs that look interesting, and you should consider those as well.

Next, read the descriptions for the jobs that interest you and, based on what you learn, identify those that *most* interest you. These are the jobs you should consider. Sections Two and Three give you additional information on how best to do so.

Details on Each Section of the Job Descriptions

Each occupational description in this book follows a standard format, making it easier for you to compare jobs. The following overview describes the kinds of information found in each part of a description and offers tips on how to interpret the information.

Job Title

This is the title used for the job in the *Occupational Outlook Handbook*, published by the U.S. Department of Labor.

OOH O*NET Codes

This section of each job description lists one or more code numbers (for example: 11-9031.00, 11-9032.00) for related jobs in a major occupational information system used by the U.S. Department of Labor. This system, named the Occupational Information Network (or O*NET), is used by a variety of state and federal programs to classify applicants and job openings and by a variety of career information systems. You can use the O*NET code numbers to get additional information on the related O*NET titles on the Internet at www.onetcenter.org or at www.careerOINK.com. Reference books that provide O*NET descriptions include the *O*NET Dictionary of Occupational Titles* and the *Enhanced Occupational Outlook Handbook,* both published by JIST Publishing. Your librarian can help you find these books.

Significant Points

The bullet points in this part of a description highlight key characteristics for each job, such as recent trends or education and training requirements.

Nature of the Work

This part of the description discusses what workers typically do in a particular job. Individual job duties may vary by industry or employer. For instance, workers in larger firms tend to be more specialized, whereas those in smaller firms often have a wider variety of duties. Most occupations have several levels of skills and responsibilities through which workers may progress. Beginners may start as trainees performing routine tasks under close supervision. Experienced workers usually undertake more difficult tasks and are expected to perform with less supervision.

In this part of a description, you will also find information about the influence of technological advancements on the way work is done. For example, because of the Internet, reporters are now able to submit stories from remote locations with just a click of the mouse.

This part also discusses emerging specialties. For instance, Webmasters—who are responsible for all the technical aspects involved in operating a Web site—comprise a specialty within computer systems analysts, database administrators, and computer scientists.

Working Conditions

This part of the description identifies the typical hours worked, the workplace environment, physical activities, risk of injury, special equipment, and the extent of travel required. For example, stationary engineers and boiler operators are susceptible to injury, while paralegals and legal assistants have high job-related stress. Radiologic technologists and technicians may wear protective clothing or equipment, machinists do physically demanding work, and some engineers travel frequently.

In many occupations, people work regular business hours—40 hours a week, Monday through Friday. In other occupations, they do not. For example, licensed practical nurses often work evenings and weekends. The work setting can range from a hospital to a mall to an off-shore oil rig.

Information on various worker characteristics, such as the average number of hours worked per week, is obtained from the Current Population Survey (CPS), a survey of households conducted by the U.S. Census Bureau for the Bureau of Labor Statistics (BLS).

Employment

This section reports the number of jobs the occupation recently provided, the key industries where these jobs are found, and the number or proportion of self-employed workers in the occupation, if significant. Self-employed workers accounted for about 8 percent of the workforce in 2002; however, they were concentrated in a small number of occupations, such as farmers and ranchers, childcare workers, lawyers, health practitioners, and the construction trades.

When significant, the geographic distribution of jobs and the proportion of part-time (less than 35 hours a week) workers in the occupation are mentioned.

Training, Other Qualifications, and Advancement

After finding out what a job is all about, it is important to understand how to train for it. This section describes the most significant sources of education and training, including the education or training preferred by employers, the typical length of training, and the possibilities for advancement. Job skills sometimes are acquired through high school, informal on-the-job training, formal training (including apprenticeships), the U.S. Armed Forces, home study, hobbies, or previous work experience. For example, sales experience is particularly important for many sales jobs. Many professional and technical jobs, on the other hand, require formal postsecondary education—postsecondary vocational or technical training or college, postgraduate, or professional education.

This section also mentions desirable skills, aptitudes, and personal characteristics. For some entry-level jobs, personal characteristics are more important than formal training. Employers generally seek people who read, write, and speak well; compute accurately; think logically; learn quickly; get along with others; and demonstrate dependability.

Some occupations require certification or licensing to enter the field, to advance in the occupation, or to practice independently. Certification or licensing generally involves completing courses and passing examinations. Many occupations increasingly are requiring workers to participate in continuing education or training in relevant skills, either to keep up with the changes in their jobs or to improve their advancement opportunities.

Job Outlook

In planning for the future, it is important to consider potential job opportunities. This section describes the factors that will result in employment growth or decline. A number of factors are examined in developing employment projections. One factor is job growth or decline in industries that employ a significant percentage of workers in the occupation. If workers are concentrated in a rapidly growing industry, their employment will likely also grow quickly. For example, the growing need for business expertise is fueling demand for consulting services. Hence, management, scientific, and technical consulting services are projected to be among the fastest-growing industries through 2012.

Demographic changes, which affect what services are required, can influence occupational growth or decline. For example, an aging population demands more healthcare workers, from registered nurses to pharmacists. Technological change is another key factor. New technology can either create new job opportunities or eliminate jobs by making workers obsolete. The Internet has increased the demand for workers in the computer and information technology fields, such as computer support specialists and systems administrators. However, the Internet also has adversely affected travel agents, because many people now book tickets, hotels, and rental cars online.

Another factor affecting job growth or decline is changes in business practices, such as the outsourcing of work or the restructuring of businesses. In the past few years, insurance carriers have been outsourcing sales and claims adjuster jobs to large, 24-hour call centers in order to reduce costs. Corporate restructuring also has made many organizations "flatter," resulting in fewer middle management positions.

The substitution of one product or service for another can affect employment projections. For example, consumption of plastic products has grown as they have been substituted for metal goods in many consumer and manufactured products in recent years. The process is likely to continue and should result in stronger demand for machine operators in plastics than in metal.

Competition from foreign trade usually has a negative impact on employment. Often, foreign manufacturers can produce goods more cheaply than they can be produced in the United States, and the cost savings can be passed on in the form of lower prices with which U.S. manufacturers cannot compete. Increased international competition is a major reason for the decline in employment among textile, apparel, and furnishings workers.

In some cases, this book mentions that an occupation is likely to provide numerous job openings or, in others, that an occupation likely will afford relatively few openings. This information reflects the projected change in employment, as well as replacement needs. Large occupations that have high turnover, such as food and beverage serving occupations, generally provide the most job openings, reflecting the need to replace workers who transfer to other occupations or who stop working.

Some job descriptions discuss the relationship between the number of job seekers and the number of job openings. In some occupations, there is a rough balance between job seekers and job openings, resulting in good opportunities. In other occupations, employers may report difficulty finding qualified applicants, resulting in excellent job opportunities. Still other occupations are characterized by a surplus of applicants, leading to keen competition for jobs. On the one hand, limited training facilities, salary regulations, or undesirable aspects of the work—as in the case of private household workers—can result in an insufficient number of entrants to fill all job openings. On the other hand, glamorous or potentially high-paying occupations, such as actors or musicians, generally have surpluses of job seekers. Variation in job opportunities by industry, educational attainment, size of firm, or geographic location also may be discussed. Even in crowded fields, job openings do exist. Good students or highly qualified individuals should not be deterred from undertaking training for, or seeking entry into, those occupations.

KEY PHRASES USED IN THE DESCRIPTIONS

This table explains how to interpret the key phrases that describe projected changes in employment. It also explains the terms for the relationship between the number of job openings and the number of job seekers.

Changing Employment Between 2002 and 2012

If the statement reads:	Employment is projected to:
Grow much faster than average	Increase 36 percent or more
Grow faster than average	Increase 21 to 35 percent
Grow about as fast as average	Increase 10 to 20 percent
Grow more slowly than average	Increase 3 to 9 percent
Little or no change	Increase 0 to 2 percent
Decline	Decrease 1 percent or more

Job Openings Compared

If the statement reads:	Job openings compared to job seekers may be:
Very good to excellent opportunities	More numerous
Good or favorable opportunities	In rough balance
May face or can expect keen competition	Fewer

Earnings

This section discusses typical earnings and how workers are compensated—by means of annual salaries, hourly wages, commissions, piece rates, tips, or bonuses. Within every occupation, earnings vary by experience, responsibility, performance, tenure, and geographic area. Information on earnings in the major industries in which the occupation is employed may be given. Some statements contain additional earnings data from non-BLS sources. Starting and average salaries of federal workers are based on 2003 data from the U.S. Office of Personnel Management. The National Association of Colleges and Employers supplies information on average salary offers in 2003 for students graduating with a bachelor's, master's, or Ph.D. degree in certain fields. A few statements contain additional earnings information from other sources, such as unions, professional associations, and private companies. These data sources are cited in the text.

Benefits account for a significant portion of total compensation costs to employers. Benefits such as paid vacation, health insurance, and sick leave may not be mentioned because they are so widespread. Although not as common as traditional benefits, flexible hours and profit-sharing plans may be offered to attract and retain highly qualified workers. Less common benefits also include childcare, tuition for dependents, housing assistance, summers off, and free or discounted merchandise or services. For certain occupations, the percentage of workers affiliated with a union is listed.

Related Occupations

Occupations involving similar duties, skills, interests, education, and training are listed here. This allows you to look up these jobs if they also interest you.

Sources of Additional Information

No single publication can describe all aspects of an occupation. Thus, this section lists the mailing addresses of associations, government agencies, unions, and other organizations that can provide occupational information. In some cases, toll-free telephone numbers and Internet addresses also are listed. Free or relatively inexpensive publications offering more information may be mentioned; some of these publications also may be available in libraries, in school career centers, in guidance offices, or on the Internet.

Some Additional Jobs to Consider

This book includes only 101 jobs, but many other occupations have aspects that can be considered computer-oriented or technical in nature. You can look up those that interest you in one of the references mentioned in the "Other Major Career Information Sources" section.

- Accountants and auditors
- Actors, producers, and directors
- Actuaries
- Agricultural engineers
- Architects, except landscape and naval
- Audiologists
- Barbers, cosmetologists, and other personal appearance workers
- Biomedical engineers
- Boilermakers
- Bookbinders and bindery workers
- Budget analysts
- Chemical engineers
- Chemists and materials scientists
- Chiropractors
- Coin, vending, and amusement machine servicers and repairers
- Cost estimators
- Dentists
- Electricians
- Elevator installers and repairers
- Financial analysts and personal financial advisors
- Home appliance repairers
- Jewelers and precious stone and metal workers
- Landscape architects
- Millwrights
- News analysts, reporters, and correspondents
- Petroleum engineers
- Physicists and astronomers
- Printing machine operators
- Small engine mechanics
- Social scientists, other
- Veterinarians
- Writers and editors

Section Two: *The Quick Job Search*—Seven Steps to Getting a Good Job in Less Time

For more than 20 years now, I've been helping people find better jobs in less time. If you have ever experienced unemployment, you know it is not pleasant. Unemployment is something most people want to get over quickly—in fact, the quicker the better. Section Two will give you some techniques to help.

I know that most of you who read this book want to improve yourselves. You want to consider career and training options that lead to a better job and life in whatever way you define this—better pay, more flexibility, more-enjoyable or more-meaningful work, proving to your mom that you really can do anything you set your mind to, and other reasons. That is why I include advice on career planning and job search in Section Two. It's a short section, but it includes the basics that are most important in planning your career and in reducing the time it takes to get a job. I hope it will make you think about what is important to you in the long run.

The second part of Section Two showcases professionally written resumes for some of America's top computer and technical jobs. Use these as examples when creating your own resume. I know you will resist completing the activities in Section Two, but consider this: It is often not the best person who gets the job, but the best job seeker. People who do their career planning and job search homework often get jobs over those with better credentials, because they have these distinct advantages:

1. **They get more interviews**, including many for jobs that will never be advertised.

2. **They do better in interviews.**

People who understand what they want and what they have to offer employers present their skills more convincingly and are much better at answering problem questions. And, because they have learned more about job search techniques, they are likely to get more interviews with employers who need the skills they have.

Doing better in interviews often makes the difference between getting a job offer or sitting at home. And spending time planning your career can make an enormous difference to your happiness and lifestyle over time. So please consider reading Section Two and completing its activities. I suggest you schedule a time right now to at least read Section Two. An hour or so spent there can help you do just enough better in your career planning, job seeking, and interviewing to make the difference.

One other thing: If you work through Section Two and it helps you in some significant way, I'd like to hear from you. Please write or e-mail me via the publisher, whose contact information appears elsewhere in this book.

Section Three: Important Trends in Jobs and Industries

This section is made up of three very good articles on labor market trends. These articles come directly from U.S. Department of Labor sources and are interesting, well written, and short. One is on overall trends, with an emphasis on occupational groups; another is on trends in major industry groups; and the third is on training in computer-related fields. I know they sound boring, but the articles are quick reads and will give you a good idea of factors that will impact your career in the years to come.

The first article is titled "Tomorrow's Jobs." It highlights many important trends in employment and includes information on the fastest-growing jobs, jobs with high pay at various levels of education, and other details.

The second article is titled "Employment Trends in Major Industries." I included this information because you may find that you can use your skills or training in industries you have not considered. The article provides a good review of major trends with an emphasis on helping you make good employment decisions. This information can help you seek jobs in industries that offer higher pay or that are more likely to interest you. Many people overlook one important fact—the industry you work in is as important as the occupation you choose.

The third article, "Training for Techies," describes several kinds of certification and various degrees that are applicable for people interested in a career in the fields of computer science or information technology.

Section One

Descriptions of 101 Top Computer and Technical Jobs

This is the book's major section. It contains descriptions for 101 major occupations that require computer and technical skills. The jobs are arranged in alphabetical order. Refer to the table of contents for a list of the jobs and the page numbers where their descriptions begin.

The table of contents can also help you identify jobs you want to explore. If you are interested in medical jobs, for example, you can go through the list and quickly find those you want to learn more about. Also, you may spot other jobs that might be interesting, and you should consider those as well. Read the descriptions for any jobs that sound interesting.

While the descriptions in this section are easy to understand, the introduction to this book provides additional information for interpreting them. When reading the descriptions, keep in mind that they present information that is the average for the country. Conditions in your area and with specific employers may be quite different.

Also, you may come across jobs that sound interesting but require additional training or education. Don't eliminate them too soon. There are many ways to obtain training and education, and most people change jobs and careers many times. You probably have more skills than you realize that can transfer to new jobs, so consider taking some chances. Get out of your rut. Do what it takes to fulfill your dreams. Be creative. You often have more opportunities than barriers, but you have to go out and find the opportunities.

Aerospace Engineers

(O*NET 17-2011.00)

Significant Points

- Overall, job opportunities in engineering are expected to be good, but will vary by specialty.

- A bachelor's degree is required for most entry-level jobs.

- Starting salaries are significantly higher than those of college graduates in other fields.

- Continuing education is critical to keep abreast of the latest technology.

Nature of the Work

Aerospace engineers create extraordinary machines, from airplanes that weigh over a half a million pounds to spacecraft that travel over 17,000 miles an hour. They design, develop, and test aircraft, spacecraft, and missiles and supervise the manufacture of these products. Aerospace engineers who work with aircraft are called *aeronautical engineers*, and those working specifically with spacecraft are *astronautical engineers*.

Aerospace engineers develop new technologies for use in aviation, defense systems, and space exploration, often specializing in areas such as structural design, guidance, navigation and control, instrumentation and communication, or production methods. They often use computer-aided design (CAD) software, robotics, and lasers and advanced electronic optics. They also may specialize in a particular type of aerospace product, such as commercial transports, military fighter jets, helicopters, spacecraft, or missiles and rockets. Aerospace engineers may be experts in aerodynamics, thermodynamics, celestial mechanics, propulsion, acoustics, or guidance and control systems.

Aerospace engineers typically are employed in the aerospace product and parts industry, although their skills are becoming increasingly valuable in other fields. For example, in the motor vehicles manufacturing industry, aerospace engineers design vehicles that have lower air resistance and, thus, increased fuel efficiency.

Working Conditions

Most engineers work in office buildings, laboratories, or industrial plants. Others may spend time outdoors at construction sites and oil and gas exploration and production sites, where they monitor or direct operations or solve onsite problems. Some engineers travel extensively to plants or worksites.

Many engineers work a standard 40-hour week. At times, deadlines or design standards may bring extra pressure to a job, sometimes requiring engineers to work longer hours.

Employment

Aerospace engineers held about 78,000 jobs in 2002. Most worked in the aerospace product and parts manufacturing industries. Federal government agencies, primarily the U.S. Department of Defense and the National Aeronautics and Space Administration, provided 10 percent of jobs. Architectural, engineering and related services, scientific research and development services, and navigational, measuring, electromedical, and control instruments manufacturing industry firms accounted for most of the remaining jobs.

Training, Other Qualifications, and Advancement

A bachelor's degree in engineering is required for almost all entry-level engineering jobs. College graduates with a degree in a physical science or mathematics occasionally may qualify for some engineering jobs, especially in specialties in high demand. Most engineering degrees are granted in electrical, electronics, mechanical, or civil engineering. However, engineers trained in one branch may work in related branches. For example, many aerospace engineers have training in mechanical engineering. This flexibility allows employers to meet staffing needs in new technologies and specialties in which engineers may be in short supply. It also allows engineers to shift to fields with better employment prospects or to those that more closely match their interests.

Most engineering programs involve a concentration of study in an engineering specialty, along with courses in both mathematics and science. Most programs include a design course, sometimes accompanied by a computer or laboratory class or both.

In addition to the standard engineering degree, many colleges offer 2- or 4-year degree programs in engineering technology. These programs, which usually include various hands-on laboratory classes that focus on current issues, prepare students for practical design and production work, rather than for jobs that require more theoretical and scientific knowledge. Graduates of 4-year technology programs may get jobs similar to those obtained by graduates with a bachelor's degree in engineering. Engineering technology graduates, however, are not qualified to register as professional engineers under the same terms as graduates with degrees in engineering. Some employers regard technology program graduates as having skills between those of a technician and an engineer.

Graduate training is essential for engineering faculty positions and many research and development programs, but is not required for the majority of entry-level engineering jobs. Many engineers obtain graduate degrees in engineering or business administration to learn new technology and broaden their education. Many high-level executives in government and industry began their careers as engineers.

About 340 colleges and universities offer bachelor's degree programs in engineering that are accredited by the Accreditation Board for Engineering and Technology (ABET), and about 240 colleges offer accredited bachelor's degree programs in engineering technology. ABET accreditation is based on an examination of an engineering program's student achievement, program improvement, faculty, curricular content, facilities, and institutional commitment. Although most institutions offer programs in the major branches of engineering, only a few offer programs in the smaller specialties. Also, programs of the same title may vary in content. For example, some programs emphasize industrial practices, preparing students for a job in industry, whereas others are more theoretical and are designed to prepare students for graduate work. Therefore, students should investigate curricula and check accreditations carefully before selecting a college.

Admissions requirements for undergraduate engineering schools include a solid background in mathematics (algebra, geometry, trigonometry, and calculus) and science (biology, chemistry, and physics), and courses in English, social studies, humanities, and computer and information technology. Bachelor's degree programs in engineering typically are designed to last 4 years, but many students find that it takes between 4 and 5 years to complete their studies. In a typical 4-year college curriculum, the first 2 years are spent studying mathematics, basic sciences, introductory engineering, humanities, and social sciences. In the last 2 years, most courses are in engineering, usually with a concentration in one branch. For example, the last 2 years of an aerospace program might include courses in fluid mechanics, heat transfer, applied aerodynamics, analytical mechanics, flight vehicle design, trajectory dynamics, and aerospace propulsion systems. Some programs offer a general engineering curriculum; students then specialize in graduate school or on the job.

Some engineering schools and 2-year colleges have agreements whereby the 2-year college provides the initial engineering education, and the engineering school automatically admits students for their last 2 years. In addition, a few engineering schools have arrangements whereby a student spends 3 years in a liberal arts college studying preengineering subjects and 2 years in an engineering school studying core subjects, and then receives a bachelor's degree from each school. Some colleges and universities offer 5-year master's degree programs. Some 5-year or even 6-year cooperative plans combine classroom study and practical work, permitting students to gain valuable experience and to finance part of their education.

All 50 states and the District of Columbia require licensure for engineers who offer their services directly to the public. Engineers who are licensed are called Professional Engineers (PE). This licensure generally requires a degree from an ABET-accredited engineering program, 4 years of relevant work experience, and successful completion of a state examination. Recent graduates can start the licensing process by taking the examination in two stages. The initial Fundamentals of Engineering (FE) examination can be taken upon graduation. Engineers who pass this examination commonly are called Engineers in Training (EIT) or Engineer Interns (EI). After acquiring suitable work experience, EITs can take the second examination, the Principles and Practice of Engineering exam. Several states have imposed mandatory continuing education requirements for relicensure. Most states recognize licensure from other states provided that the manner in which the initial license was obtained meets or exceeds their licensure requirements. Many civil, electrical, mechanical, and chemical engineers are licensed PEs.

Engineers should be creative, inquisitive, analytical, and detail-oriented. They should be able to work as part of a team and to communicate well, both orally and in writing. Communication abilities are important because engineers often interact with specialists in a wide range of fields outside engineering.

Beginning engineering graduates usually work under the supervision of experienced engineers and, in large companies, also may receive formal classroom or seminar-type training. As new engineers gain knowledge and experience, they are assigned more difficult projects with greater independence to develop designs, solve problems, and make decisions. Engineers may advance to become technical specialists or to supervise a staff or team of engineers and technicians. Some may eventually become engineering managers or enter other managerial or sales jobs.

Job Outlook

Employment of aerospace engineers is expected to decline over the projection period. Foreign competition and the slowdown in air travel will limit the number of new jobs for aerospace engineers related to the design and production of commercial aircraft over the projection period. Despite the expected decline in employment, favorable opportunities are expected for aerospace engineers through 2012 because the number of degrees granted in aerospace engineering has declined greatly over the last decade due to the perceived lack of opportunities in this occupation. The decline in degree production has reached the point that the number trained in aerospace engineering may not be adequate to replace the large numbers of aerospace engineers who are expected to leave the occupation, especially due to retirement, over the 2002-12 period. Some employment opportunities also will occur in industries not typically associated with aerospace, such as motor vehicle manufacturing.

Earnings

Median annual earnings of aerospace engineers were $72,750 in 2002. The middle 50 percent earned between $59,520 and $88,310. The lowest 10 percent earned less than $49,640, and the highest 10 percent earned more than

$105,060. Median annual earnings in the industries employing the largest numbers of aerospace engineers in 2002 were:

Federal government $81,830

Architectural, engineering, and related services 74,890

Aerospace product and parts manufacturing 70,920

According to a 2003 salary survey by the National Association of Colleges and Employers, bachelor's degree candidates in aerospace engineering received starting salary offers averaging $48,028 a year, master's degree candidates were offered $61,162, and Ph.D. candidates were offered $68,406.

Related Occupations

Aerospace engineers apply the principles of physical science and mathematics in their work. Other workers who use scientific and mathematical principles include architects, except landscape and naval; engineering and natural sciences managers; computer and information systems managers; mathematicians; drafters; engineering technicians; sales engineers; science technicians; and physical and life scientists, including agricultural and food scientists, biological scientists, conservation scientists and foresters, atmospheric scientists, chemists and materials scientists, environmental scientists and geoscientists, and physicists and astronomers.

Sources of Additional Information

For further information about careers in the aerospace industry, contact:

- Aerospace Industries Association, 1250 Eye St. NW., Suite 1200, Washington, DC 20005-3924. Internet: http://www.aia-aerospace.org

- American Institute of Aeronautics and Astronautics, Inc., 1801 Alexander Bell Dr., Suite 500, Reston, VA 20191-4344. Internet: http://www.aiaa.org

See the introduction to the section on engineers for information on working conditions, training requirements, and other sources of additional information.

Agricultural and Food Scientists

(O*NET 19-1011.00, 19-1012.00, 19-1013.01, and 19-1013.02)

Significant Points

- Almost 4 in 10 salaried agricultural and food scientists work for federal, state, or local governments.

- A bachelor's degree in agricultural science is sufficient for some jobs in applied research; a master's or doctoral degree is required for basic research.

- Slower-than-average job growth is projected because of limited growth in the federal government and modest growth in state and local governments, the largest employers of these scientists.

Nature of the Work

The work of agricultural and food scientists plays an important part in maintaining the nation's food supply by ensuring agricultural productivity and the safety of the food supply. Agricultural scientists study farm crops and animals, and develop ways of improving their quantity and quality. They look for ways to improve crop yield with less labor, control pests and weeds more safely and effectively, and conserve soil and water. They research methods of converting raw agricultural commodities into attractive and healthy food products for consumers.

Agricultural science is closely related to biological science, and agricultural scientists use the principles of biology, chemistry, physics, mathematics, and other sciences to solve problems in agriculture. They often work with biological scientists on basic biological research and on applying to agriculture the advances in knowledge brought about by biotechnology.

In the past two decades, rapid advances in basic biological knowledge related to genetics spurred growth in the field of biotechnology. Some agricultural and food scientists use this technology to manipulate the genetic material of plants and crops, attempting to make organisms more productive or resistant to disease. These advances in biotechnology have opened up research opportunities in many areas of agricultural and food science, including commercial applications in agriculture, environmental remediation, and the food industry.

Many agricultural scientists work in basic or applied research and development. Others manage or administer research and development programs, or manage marketing or production operations in companies that produce food products or agricultural chemicals, supplies, and machinery. Some agricultural scientists are consultants to business firms, private clients, or government.

Depending on the agricultural or food scientist's area of specialization, the nature of the work performed varies.

Food science. Food scientists and technologists usually work in the food processing industry, universities, or the federal government, and help to meet consumer demand for food products that are healthful, safe, palatable, and convenient. To do this, they use their knowledge of chemistry, physics, engineering, microbiology, biotechnology, and other sciences to develop new or better ways of preserving, processing, packaging, storing, and delivering foods. Some food scientists engage in basic research, discovering new food sources; analyzing food content to determine levels of vitamins, fat, sugar, or protein; or searching for substitutes for harmful or undesirable additives, such as nitrites. They also develop ways to process, preserve, package, or store food according to industry and government regulations. Traditional food processing research into functions involving baking, blanching, canning, drying, evaporation, and pasteurization will continue to be conducted and will find new applications. Other food scientists enforce government regulations, inspecting food processing areas and ensuring that sanitation, safety, quality, and waste management standards are met. Food technologists generally work in product development, applying the findings from food science research to the selection, preservation, processing, packaging, distribution, and use of safe, nutritious, and wholesome food.

Plant science. Agronomy, crop science, entomology, and plant breeding are included in plant science. Scientists in these disciplines study plants and their growth in soils, helping producers of food, feed, and fiber crops to continue to feed a growing population while conserving natural resources and maintaining the environment. Agronomists and crop scientists not only help increase productivity, but also study ways to improve the nutritional value of crops and the quality of seed, often through biotechnology. Some crop scientists study the breeding, physiology, and management of crops and use genetic engineering to develop crops resistant to pests and drought. Entomologists conduct research to develop new technologies to control or eliminate pests in infested areas and to prevent the spread of harmful pests to new areas, as well as technologies that are compatible with the environment. They also conduct research or engage in oversight activities aimed at halting the spread of insect-borne disease.

Soil science. Soil scientists study the chemical, physical, biological, and mineralogical composition of soils as they relate to plant or crop growth. They also study the responses of various soil types to fertilizers, tillage practices, and crop rotation. Many soil scientists who work for the federal government conduct soil surveys, classifying and mapping soils. They provide information and recommendations to farmers and other landowners regarding the best use of land, plant growth, and methods to avoid or correct problems such as erosion. They may also consult with engineers and other technical personnel working on construction projects about the effects of, and solutions to, soil problems. Because soil science is closely related to environmental science, persons trained in soil science also apply their knowledge to ensure environmental quality and effective land use.

Animal science. Animal scientists work to develop better, more efficient ways of producing and processing meat, poultry, eggs, and milk. Dairy scientists, poultry scientists, animal breeders, and other scientists in related fields study the genetics, nutrition, reproduction, growth, and development of domestic farm animals. Some animal scientists inspect and grade livestock food products, purchase livestock, or work in technical sales or marketing. As extension agents or consultants, animal scientists advise agricultural producers on how to upgrade animal housing facilities properly, lower mortality rates, handle waste matter, or increase production of animal products, such as milk or eggs.

Working Conditions

Agricultural scientists involved in management or basic research tend to work regular hours in offices and laboratories. The work environment for those engaged in applied research or product development varies, depending on the discipline of agricultural science and on the type of employer. For example, food scientists in private industry may work in test kitchens while investigating new processing techniques. Animal scientists working for federal, state, or university research stations may spend part of their time at dairies, farrowing houses, feedlots, or farm animal facilities or outdoors conducting research associated with livestock. Soil and crop scientists also spend time outdoors conducting research on farms and agricultural research stations. Entomologists work in laboratories, insectories, or agricultural research stations, and also may spend time outdoors studying or collecting insects in their natural habitat.

Employment

Agricultural and food scientists held about 18,000 jobs in 2002. In addition, several thousand persons held agricultural science faculty positions in colleges and universities.

Almost 4 in 10 salaried agricultural and food scientists work for federal, state, or local governments. One out of 6 worked for the federal government in 2002, mostly in the U.S. Department of Agriculture. Another 1 in 6 worked for state governments at state agricultural colleges or agricultural research stations. Some worked for agricultural service companies; others worked for commercial research and development laboratories, seed companies, pharmaceutical companies, wholesale distributors, and food products companies. Over 1,600 agricultural scientists were self-employed in 2002, mainly as consultants.

Training, Other Qualifications, and Advancement

Training requirements for agricultural scientists depend on their specialty and on the type of work they perform. A bachelor's degree in agricultural science is sufficient for some jobs in applied research or for assisting in basic research, but a master's or doctoral degree is required for basic research. A Ph.D. in agricultural science usually is needed for college teaching and for advancement to administrative research positions. Degrees in related sciences such as biology, chemistry, or physics or in related engineering specialties also may qualify persons for some agricultural science jobs.

All states have a land-grant college that offers agricultural science degrees. Many other colleges and universities also offer agricultural science degrees or some agricultural science courses. However, not every school offers all specialties.

A typical undergraduate agricultural science curriculum includes communications, mathematics, economics, business, and physical and life sciences courses, in addition to a wide variety of technical agricultural science courses. For prospective animal scientists, these technical agricultural science courses might include animal breeding, reproductive physiology, nutrition, and meats and muscle biology. Graduate students typically specialize in a subfield of agricultural science, such as animal breeding and genetics, crop science, or horticulture science, depending on their interest and the kind of work they wish to do. For example, those interested in doing genetic and biotechnological research in the food industry need to develop a strong background in life and physical sciences, such as cell and molecular biology, microbiology, and inorganic and organic chemistry. However, students normally need not specialize at the undergraduate level. In fact, undergraduates who are broadly trained have greater flexibility when changing jobs than if they had narrowly defined their interests.

Students preparing as food scientists take courses such as food chemistry, food analysis, food microbiology, food engineering, and food processing operations. Those preparing as crop or soil scientists take courses in plant pathology, soil chemistry, entomology, plant physiology, and biochemistry, among others. Advanced degree programs include classroom and fieldwork, laboratory research, and a thesis or dissertation based on independent research.

Agricultural and food scientists should be able to work independently or as part of a team and be able to communicate clearly and concisely, both orally and in writing. Most of these scientists also need an understanding of basic business principles, and the ability to apply basic statistical techniques. Employers increasingly prefer job applicants who are able to apply computer skills to determine solutions to problems, to collect and analyze data, and to control various processes.

The American Society of Agronomy offers certification programs in crop science, agronomy, crop advising, soil science, plant pathology, and weed science. To become certified, applicants must pass designated examinations and have at least 2 years of experience with at least a bachelor's degree in agriculture or 4 years of experience with no degree. To become a certified crop advisor, however, candidates do not need a degree.

Agricultural scientists who have advanced degrees usually begin in research or teaching. With experience, they may advance to jobs such as supervisors of research programs or managers of other agriculture-related activities.

Job Outlook

Employment of agricultural and food scientists is expected to grow more slowly than the average for all occupations through 2012. This projection reflects limited growth in the federal government and modest growth in state and local governments. The need to replace agricultural and food scientists who retire or otherwise leave the occupation permanently will account for many more job openings than will projected growth.

Past agricultural research has resulted in the development of higher yielding crops, crops with better resistance to pests and plant pathogens, and chemically based fertilizers and pesticides. Research is still necessary, particularly as insects and diseases continue to adapt to pesticides and as soil fertility and water quality continue to need improvement, resulting in job opportunities in biotechnology. Agricultural scientists are using new avenues of research in biotechnology to develop plants and food crops that require less fertilizer, fewer pesticides and herbicides, and even less water for growth.

Biotechnological research, including studies and approaches relying on the tools of genomics, will continue to offer possibilities for the development of new food products. This research will allow agricultural and food scientists to develop techniques to detect and control food pathogens, and should lead to better understanding of other physiological responses of pathogens in food environments.

Agricultural scientists will be needed to balance increased agricultural output with protection and preservation of soil, water, and ecosystems. They will increasingly encourage the practice of "sustainable agriculture" by developing and implementing plans to manage pests, crops, soil fertility and erosion, and animal waste in ways that reduce the use of harmful chemicals and do little damage to the natural environment.

Further food research will result in more job opportunities for food scientists and technologists. This research will be stimulated by a heightened public focus on diet, health, and food safety, as well as domestic and global issues such as increasing world population, availability and cost of usable water, loss of arable land, deforestation, environmental pollution, and climate change.

Those with doctorates in agricultural and food science may face competition for jobs, due to an increase in the number of graduates and the limited numbers of research and teaching positions. Opportunities may be more numerous for those with a master's degree, particularly for graduates seeking basic research positions in a laboratory. Most of these positions, however, entail working under the guidance and direction of a Ph.D. scientist.

Graduates with a bachelor's degree should have opportunities, although not necessarily as an agricultural or food scientist. A bachelor's degree in agricultural science is useful for managerial jobs in businesses that deal with ranchers and farmers, such as feed, fertilizer, seed, and farm equipment manufacturers; retailers or wholesalers; and farm credit institutions. In some cases, persons with a 4-year degree can provide consulting services, or become a certified crop advisor, providing crop management recommendations to farmers to help them meet their objectives. Bachelor's degree holders also can work in some applied research and product development positions, but usually only in certain subfields, such as food science and technology, and the federal government hires bachelor's degree holders to work as soil scientists. Four-year degrees also may help persons enter occupations such as farmer, or farm or ranch manager; cooperative extension service agent; agricultural products inspector; or purchasing or sales agent for agricultural commodity or farm supply companies.

Employment of agricultural and food scientists is relatively stable during periods of economic recession. Layoffs are less likely among agricultural and food scientists than in some other occupations because food is a staple item and its demand fluctuates very little with economic activity.

Earnings

Median annual earnings of agricultural and food scientists were $48,670 in 2002. The middle 50 percent earned between $35,770 and $65,990. The lowest 10 percent earned less than $28,750, and the highest 10 percent earned more than $85,460.

The average federal salary for employees in nonsupervisory, supervisory, and managerial positions in 2003 was $82,729 in animal science and $68,846 in agronomy.

According to the National Association of Colleges and Employers, beginning salary offers in 2003 for graduates with a bachelor's degree in animal sciences averaged $30,026 a year; plant sciences, $28,203 a year; and in other agricultural sciences, $29,971 a year.

Related Occupations

The work of agricultural scientists is closely related to that of other scientists, including biological scientists, chemists and materials scientists, and conservation scientists and foresters. It also is related to the work of managers of agricultural production, such as farmers, ranchers, and agricultural managers. Certain specialties of agricultural science also are related to other occupations. For example, the work of animal scientists is related to that of veterinarians, and horticulturists perform duties similar to those of landscape architects.

Sources of Additional Information

Information on careers in agricultural science is available from:

- American Society of Agronomy, Crop Science Society of America, Soil Science Society of America, 677 S. Segoe Rd., Madison, WI 53711-1086. Internet: http://www.agronomy.org

- Food and Agricultural Careers for Tomorrow, Purdue University, 1140 Agricultural Administration Bldg., West Lafayette, IN 47907-1140.

For information on careers in food technology, write to:

- Institute of Food Technologists, Suite 300, 221 N. LaSalle St., Chicago IL 60601-1291. Internet: http://www.ift.org

Information on acquiring a job as an agricultural scientist with the federal government is available from the Office of Personnel Management through a telephone-based system.

Consult your telephone directory under U.S. government for a local number or call (703) 724-1850; Federal Relay Service: (800) 877-8339. The first number is not toll free, and charges may result. Information also is available from the Internet site http://www.usajobs.opm.gov.

Air Traffic Controllers

(O*NET 53-2021.00)

Significant Points

- Nearly all air traffic controllers are employed by the Federal Aviation Administration, part of the federal government.

- Large numbers of air traffic controllers will be eligible to retire over the next decade, potentially creating many job openings.

- Aircraft controllers earn relatively high pay and have good benefits.

Nature of the Work

The air traffic control system is a vast network of people and equipment that ensures the safe operation of commercial and private aircraft. Air traffic controllers coordinate the movement of air traffic to make certain that planes stay a safe distance apart. Their immediate concern is safety, but controllers also must direct planes efficiently to minimize delays. Some regulate airport traffic; others regulate flights between airports.

Although *airport tower* or *terminal controllers* watch over all planes traveling through the airport's airspace, their main responsibility is to organize the flow of aircraft into and out of the airport. Relying on radar and visual observation, they closely monitor each plane to ensure a safe distance between all aircraft and to guide pilots between the hangar or ramp and the end of the airport's airspace. In addition, controllers keep pilots informed about changes in weather conditions such as wind shear—a sudden change in the velocity or direction of the wind that can cause the pilot to lose control of the aircraft.

During arrival or departure, several controllers direct each plane. As a plane approaches an airport, the pilot radios ahead to inform the terminal of the plane's presence. The controller in the radar room, just beneath the control tower, has a copy of the plane's flight plan and already has observed the plane on radar. If the path is clear, the controller directs the pilot to a runway; if the airport is busy, the plane is fitted into a traffic pattern with other aircraft waiting to land. As the plane nears the runway, the pilot is asked to contact the tower. There, another controller, who also is watching the plane on radar, monitors the aircraft the last mile or so to the runway, delaying any departures that would interfere with the plane's landing. Once the plane has landed, a ground controller in the tower directs it along the taxiways to its assigned gate. The ground controller usually works entirely by sight, but may use radar if visibility is very poor.

The procedure is reversed for departures. The ground controller directs the plane to the proper runway. The local controller then informs the pilot about conditions at the airport, such as weather, speed and direction of wind, and visibility. The local controller also issues runway clearance for the pilot to take off. Once in the air, the plane is guided out of the airport's airspace by the departure controller.

After each plane departs, airport tower controllers notify *enroute controllers* who will next take charge. There are 21 air route traffic control centers located around the country, each employing 300 to 700 controllers, with more than 150 on duty during peak hours at the busier facilities. Airplanes usually fly along designated routes; each center is assigned a certain airspace containing many different routes. Enroute controllers work in teams of up to three members, depending on how heavy traffic is; each team is responsible for a section of the center's airspace. A team, for example, might be responsible for all planes that are between 30 to 100 miles north of an airport and flying at an altitude between 6,000 and 18,000 feet.

To prepare for planes about to enter the team's airspace, the radar associate controller organizes flight plans coming off a printer. If two planes are scheduled to enter the team's airspace at nearly the same time, location, and altitude, this controller may arrange with the preceding control unit for one plane to change its flight path. The previous unit may have been another team at the same or an adjacent center, or a departure controller at a neighboring terminal. As a plane approaches a team's airspace, the radar controller accepts responsibility for the plane from the previous controlling unit. The controller also delegates responsibility for the plane to the next controlling unit when the plane leaves the team's airspace.

The radar controller, who is the senior team member, observes the planes in the team's airspace on radar and communicates with the pilots when necessary. Radar controllers warn pilots about nearby planes, bad weather conditions, and other potential hazards. Two planes on a collision course will be directed around each other. If a pilot wants to change altitude in search of better flying conditions, the controller will check to determine that no other planes will be along the proposed path. As the flight progresses, the team responsible for the aircraft notifies the next team in charge of the airspace ahead. Through team coordination, the plane arrives safely at its destination.

Both airport tower and enroute controllers usually control several planes at a time; often, they have to make quick decisions about completely different activities. For example, a controller might direct a plane on its landing approach and at the same time provide pilots entering the airport's airspace with information about conditions at the airport. While instructing these pilots, the controller also would observe other planes in the vicinity, such as those in a holding pattern waiting for permission to land, to ensure that they remain well separated.

In addition to airport towers and enroute centers, air traffic controllers also work in flight service stations operated at more than 100 locations. These *flight service specialists* provide pilots with information on the station's particular area, including terrain, preflight and inflight weather information, suggested routes, and other information important to the safety of a flight. Flight service station specialists help pilots in emergency situations and initiate and coordinate searches for missing or overdue aircraft. However, they are not involved in actively managing air traffic.

Some air traffic controllers work at the Federal Aviation Administration's (FAA) Air Traffic Control Systems Command Center in Herndon, Virginia, where they oversee the entire system. They look for situations that will create bottlenecks or other problems in the system and then respond with a management plan for traffic into and out of the troubled sector. The objective is to keep traffic levels in the trouble spots manageable for the controllers working at enroute centers.

Currently, the FAA is implementing a new automated air traffic control system, called the National Airspace System (NAS) Architecture. The NAS Architecture is a long-term strategic plan that will allow controllers to more efficiently deal with the demands of increased air traffic. It encompasses the replacement of aging equipment and the introduction of new systems, technologies, and procedures to enhance safety and security and support future aviation growth.

Working Conditions

Controllers work a basic 40-hour week; however, they may work additional hours for which they receive overtime pay or equal time off. Because most control towers and centers operate 24 hours a day, 7 days a week, controllers rotate night and weekend shifts.

During busy times, controllers must work rapidly and efficiently. Total concentration is required to keep track of several planes at the same time and to make certain that all pilots receive correct instructions. The mental stress of being responsible for the safety of several aircraft and their passengers can be exhausting for some persons.

Employment

Air traffic controllers held about 26,000 jobs in 2002. The vast majority were employed by the FAA, which is part of the federal government. Air traffic controllers work at airports—in towers and flight service stations—and in air route traffic control centers. Some professional controllers conduct research at the FAA's national experimental center near Atlantic City, New Jersey. Others serve as instructors at the FAA Academy in Oklahoma City, Oklahoma. A small number of civilian controllers work for the U.S. Department of Defense. In addition to controllers employed by the federal government, some work for private air traffic control companies providing service to non-FAA towers.

Training, Other Qualifications, and Advancement

To become an air traffic controller, a person must enroll in an FAA-approved education program and pass a pre-employment test that measures his or her ability to learn the controller's duties in order to qualify for job openings in the air traffic control system. Exceptions are air traffic controllers with prior experience and military veterans. The pre-employment test is currently offered only to students in the FAA Air Traffic Collegiate Training Initiative (AT-CTI) Program or the Minneapolis Community & Technical College, Air Traffic Control Training Program. In addition, applicants must have 3 years of full-time work experience or 4 years of college, or a combination of both. In combining education and experience, 1 year of undergraduate study (30 semester or 45 quarter hours) is equivalent to 9 months of work experience.

Upon successful completion of an FAA-approved program, individuals who receive school recommendation and who meet the basic qualification requirements, including age limit and achievement of a qualifying score on the FAA authorized pre-employment test, become eligible for employment as an air traffic controller. Candidates also must pass a medical exam, drug screening, and security clearance before they can be hired.

Upon selection, employees attend the FAA Academy in Oklahoma City for 12 weeks of training, during which they learn the fundamentals of the airway system, FAA regulations, controller equipment, and aircraft performance characteristics, as well as more specialized tasks.

After graduation, it takes several years of progressively more responsible work experience, interspersed with considerable classroom instruction and independent study, to become a fully qualified controller. Controllers who fail to complete either the academy or the on-the-job portion of the training usually are dismissed. Controllers must pass a physical examination each year and a job performance examination twice each year. Failure to become certified in any position at a facility within a specified time also may result in dismissal. Controllers also are subject to drug screening as a condition of continuing employment.

Air traffic controllers must be articulate, because pilots must be given directions quickly and clearly. Intelligence and a good memory also are important because controllers constantly receive information that they must immediately grasp, interpret, and remember. Decisiveness also is required because controllers often have to make quick decisions. The ability to concentrate is crucial because controllers must make these decisions in the midst of noise and other distractions.

At airports, new controllers begin by supplying pilots with basic flight data and airport information. They then advance to the position of ground controller, then local controller, departure controller, and, finally, arrival controller. At an air route traffic control center, new controllers first deliver printed flight plans to teams, gradually advancing to radar associate controller and then radar controller.

Controllers can transfer to jobs at different locations or advance to supervisory positions, including management or staff jobs in air traffic control and top administrative jobs in the FAA. However, there are only limited opportunities for a controller to switch from a position in an enroute center to a tower.

Job Outlook

Employment of air traffic controllers is expected to grow about as fast as the average through the year 2012. Increasing air traffic will require more controllers to handle the additional work. Employment growth, however, is not expected to keep pace with growth in the number of aircraft flying because of the increasing automation of the air traffic control system and federal budget constraints. New computerized systems will assist the controller by automatically making many of the routine decisions. This will allow controllers to handle more traffic, thus increasing their productivity. Federal budget constraints also may limit hiring of air traffic controllers.

More job openings are expected due to replacement needs. The majority of today's air traffic controllers will be eligible to retire over the next decade, although not all are expected to do so. Nevertheless, replacement needs will be substantial and will result in hundreds of job opportunities each year for those graduating from the FAA training programs. Despite the increasing number of jobs coming open, competition to get into the FAA training programs is expected to remain keen, as there generally are many more applicants to get into the schools than there are openings. But those that graduate have good prospects of getting a job as a controller.

Air traffic controllers who continue to meet the proficiency and medical requirements enjoy more job security than do most workers. The demand for air travel and the workloads of air traffic controllers decline during recessions, but controllers seldom are laid off.

Earnings

Median annual earnings of air traffic controllers in 2002 were $91,600. The middle 50 percent earned between $65,480 and $112,550. The lowest 10 percent earned less than $46,410, and the highest 10 percent earned more than $131,610.

The average annual salary, excluding overtime earnings, for air traffic controllers in the federal government—which employs 90 percent of the total—in nonsupervisory, supervisory, and managerial positions was $95,700 in 2002. Both the worker's job responsibilities and the complexity of the particular facility determine a controller's pay. For example, controllers who work at the FAA's busiest air traffic control facilities earn higher pay.

Depending on length of service, air traffic controllers receive 13 to 26 days of paid vacation and 13 days of paid sick leave each year, life insurance, and health benefits. In addition, controllers can retire at an earlier age and with fewer years of service than other federal employees. Air traffic controllers are eligible to retire at age 50 with 20 years of service as an active air traffic controller or after 25 years of active service at any age. There is a mandatory retirement age of 56 for controllers who manage air traffic. However, federal law provides for exemptions to the mandatory age of 56, up to age 61, for controllers having exceptional skills and experience.

Related Occupations

Airfield operations specialists also are involved in the direction and control of traffic in air transportation.

Sources of Additional Information

For further information on how to qualify and apply for a job as an air traffic controller, contact:

- Federal Aviation Administration, 800 Independence Ave., SW, Washington, DC 20591. Internet: http://www.faa.gov

Aircraft and Avionics Equipment Mechanics and Service Technicians

(O*NET 49-2091.00, 49-3011.01, 49-3011.02, and 49-3011.03)

Significant Points

- The majority of these workers learn their job in 1 of about 200 trade schools certified by the Federal Aviation Administration.

- Opportunities should be excellent, but competition is likely for the best paying airline jobs.

Nature of the Work

To keep aircraft in peak operating condition, aircraft and avionics equipment mechanics and service technicians perform scheduled maintenance, make repairs, and complete inspections required by the Federal Aviation Administration (FAA).

Many aircraft mechanics, also called airframe, powerplant, and avionics aviation maintenance technicians, specialize in preventive maintenance. They inspect engines, landing gear, instruments, pressurized sections, accessories—brakes, valves, pumps, and air-conditioning systems, for example—

and other parts of the aircraft, and do the necessary maintenance and replacement of parts. Inspections take place following a schedule based on the number of hours the aircraft has flown, calendar days since the last inspection, cycles of operation, or a combination of these factors. Large, sophisticated planes are equipped with aircraft monitoring systems, consisting of electronic boxes and consoles that monitor the aircraft's basic operations and provide valuable diagnostic information to the mechanic. To examine an engine, aircraft mechanics work through specially designed openings while standing on ladders or scaffolds, or use hoists or lifts to remove the entire engine from the craft. After taking an engine apart, mechanics use precision instruments to measure parts for wear and use x-ray and magnetic inspection equipment to check for invisible cracks. Worn or defective parts are repaired or replaced. Mechanics may also repair sheet metal or composite surfaces, measure the tension of control cables, and check for corrosion, distortion, and cracks in the fuselage, wings, and tail. After completing all repairs, they must test the equipment to ensure that it works properly.

Mechanics specializing in repairwork rely on the pilot's description of a problem to find and fix faulty equipment. For example, during a preflight check, a pilot may discover that the aircraft's fuel gauge does not work. To solve the problem, mechanics may troubleshoot the electrical system, using electrical test equipment to make sure that no wires are broken or shorted out, and replace any defective electrical or electronic components. Mechanics work as fast as safety permits so that the aircraft can be put back into service quickly.

Some mechanics work on one or many different types of aircraft, such as jets, propeller-driven airplanes, and helicopters. Others specialize in one section of a particular type of aircraft, such as the engine, hydraulics, or electrical system. *Powerplant mechanics* are authorized to work on engines and do limited work on propellers. *Airframe mechanics* are authorized to work on any part of the aircraft except the instruments, power plants, and propellers. *Combination airframe-and-powerplant mechanics*—called A & P mechanics— work on all parts of the plane, except instruments. The majority of mechanics working on civilian aircraft today are A & P mechanics. In small, independent repair shops, mechanics usually inspect and repair many different types of aircraft.

Avionics systems are now an integral part of aircraft design and have vastly increased aircraft capability. *Avionics technicians* repair and maintain components used for aircraft navigation and radio communications, weather radar systems, and other instruments and computers that control flight, engine, and other primary functions. These duties may require additional licenses, such as a radiotelephone license issued by the U.S. Federal Communications Commission (FCC). Because of technological advances, an increasing amount of time is spent repairing electronic systems, such as computerized controls. Technicians also may be required to analyze and develop solutions to complex electronic problems.

Working Conditions

Mechanics usually work in hangars or in other indoor areas, although they can work outdoors—sometimes in unpleasant weather—when hangars are full or when repairs must be made quickly. Mechanics often work under time pressure to maintain flight schedules or, in general aviation, to keep from inconveniencing customers. At the same time, mechanics have a tremendous responsibility to maintain safety standards, and this can cause the job to be stressful.

Frequently, mechanics must lift or pull objects weighing as much as 70 pounds. They often stand, lie, or kneel in awkward positions and occasionally must work in precarious positions on scaffolds or ladders. Noise and vibration are common when engines are being tested, so ear protection is necessary. Aircraft mechanics usually work 40 hours a week on 8-hour shifts around the clock. Overtime work is frequent.

Employment

Aircraft and avionics equipment mechanics and service technicians held about 154,000 jobs in 2002; about 1 in 6 of these workers was an avionics technician. Nearly 40 percent of aircraft and avionics equipment mechanics and technicians worked for air transportation companies and close to 20 percent worked for private maintenance and repair facilities. About 20 percent worked for the federal government, and about 13 percent worked for aerospace products and parts manufacturing firms. Most of the rest worked for companies that operate their own planes to transport executives and cargo. Few mechanics and technicians were self-employed.

Most airline mechanics and service technicians work at major airports near large cities. Civilian mechanics employed by the U.S. Armed Forces work at military installations. Large proportions of mechanics who work for aerospace manufacturing firms are located in California or in Washington state. Others work for the FAA, many at the facilities in Oklahoma City, Atlantic City, Wichita, or Washington, DC. Mechanics for independent repair shops work at airports in every part of the country.

Training, Other Qualifications, and Advancement

The majority of mechanics who work on civilian aircraft are certificated by the FAA as "airframe mechanic," "powerplant mechanic," or "avionics repair specialist." Mechanics who also have an inspector's authorization can certify work completed by other mechanics and perform required inspections. Uncertificated mechanics are supervised by those with certificates.

The FAA requires at least 18 months of work experience for an airframe, powerplant, or avionics repairer's certificate. For a combined A & P certificate, at least 30 months of experience working with both engines and airframes is required.

Completion of a program at an FAA-certified mechanic school can substitute for the work experience requirement. Applicants for all certificates also must pass written and oral tests and demonstrate that they can do the work authorized by the certificate. To obtain an inspector's authorization, a mechanic must have held an A & P certificate for at least 3 years. Most airlines require that mechanics have a high school diploma and an A & P certificate.

Although a few people become mechanics through on-the-job training, most learn their job in 1 of about 200 trade schools certified by the FAA. About one-third of these schools award 2- and 4-year degrees in avionics, aviation technology, or aviation maintenance management.

FAA standards established by law require that certified mechanic schools offer students a minimum of 1,900 actual class hours. Coursework in these trade schools normally lasts from 24 to 30 months and provides training with the tools and equipment used on the job. Aircraft trade schools are placing more emphasis on technologies such as turbine engines, composite materials—including graphite, fiberglass, and boron—and aviation electronics, which are increasingly being used in the construction of new aircraft. Additionally, employers prefer mechanics who can perform a variety of tasks.

Some aircraft mechanics in the Armed Forces acquire enough general experience to satisfy the work experience requirements for the FAA certificate. With additional study, they may pass the certifying exam. In general, however, jobs in the military services are too specialized to provide the broad experience required by the FAA. Most Armed Forces mechanics have to complete the entire training program at a trade school, although a few receive some credit for the material they learned in the service. In any case, military experience is a great advantage when seeking employment; employers consider trade school graduates who have this experience to be the most desirable applicants.

Courses in mathematics, physics, chemistry, electronics, computer science, and mechanical drawing are helpful, because they demonstrate many of the principles involved in the operation of aircraft, and knowledge of these principles is often necessary to make repairs. Courses that develop writing skills also are important because mechanics are often required to submit reports.

FAA regulations require current experience to keep the A & P certificate valid. Applicants must have at least 1,000 hours of work experience in the previous 24 months or take a refresher course. As new and more complex aircraft are designed, more employers are requiring mechanics to take ongoing training to update their skills. Recent technological advances in aircraft maintenance necessitate a strong background in electronics—both for acquiring and retaining jobs in this field. FAA certification standards also make ongoing training mandatory. Every 24 months, mechanics are required to take at least 16 hours of training to keep their certificate. Many mechanics take courses offered by manufacturers or employers, usually through outside contractors.

Aircraft mechanics must do careful and thorough work that requires a high degree of mechanical aptitude. Employers seek applicants who are self-motivated, hard-working, enthusiastic, and able to diagnose and solve complex mechanical problems. Agility is important for the reaching and climbing necessary to do the job. Because they may work on the tops of wings and fuselages on large jet planes, aircraft mechanics must not be afraid of heights.

As aircraft mechanics gain experience, they may advance to lead mechanic (or crew chief), inspector, lead inspector, or shop supervisor positions. Opportunities are best for those who have an aircraft inspector's authorization. In the airlines, where promotion often is determined by examination, supervisors sometimes advance to executive positions. Those with broad experience in maintenance and overhaul might become inspectors with the FAA. With additional business and management training, some open their own aircraft maintenance facilities. Mechanics learn many different skills in their training that can be applied to other jobs, and some transfer to other skilled repairer occupations or electronics technician jobs.

Job Outlook

Opportunities for aircraft and avionics equipment mechanics and service technician jobs should be excellent for persons who have completed aircraft mechanic training programs. Employment of aircraft mechanics is expected to increase about as fast as the average for all occupations through the year 2012, and large numbers of additional job openings should arise from the need to replace experienced mechanics who retire. Avionics technicians are projected to increase at a slower than average rate. Despite the long-term forecast, these occupations are currently in a period of little to no growth. Reduced passenger traffic resulting from a weak economy and the events of September 11, 2001, have forced airlines to cut back flights and take aircraft out of service. As the economy improves and public reluctance to board aircraft decreases, a growing population should increase passenger traffic and create the need for more aircraft mechanics and service technicians over the next decade. If the number of graduates from aircraft mechanic training programs continues to fall short of employer needs, opportunities for graduates of mechanic training programs should be excellent.

Most job openings for aircraft mechanics through the year 2012 will stem from replacement needs. A large number of mechanics are expected to retire over the next decade and create several thousand job openings per year. In addition, others will leave to work in related fields, such as automobile repair, as much of their skills are transferable to other maintenance and repair occupations. Also contributing to favorable future job opportunities for mechanics is the long-term trend towards fewer students entering technical schools to learn skilled maintenance and repair trades. Many of the students who have the ability and aptitude to work on planes are choosing to go to college, work in computer-related fields, or go into other repair and maintenance

occupations with better working conditions. If the trend continues, the supply of trained aviation mechanics will not be able to keep up with air transportation industry needs when growth resumes in the industry.

Job opportunities are likely to be the best at small commuter and regional airlines, at FAA repair stations, and in general aviation. Commuter and regional airlines are the fastest growing segment of the air transportation industry, but wages in these companies tend to be lower than those in the major airlines, so they attract fewer job applicants. Also, some jobs will become available as experienced mechanics leave for higher paying jobs with the major airlines or transfer to another occupation. At the same time, general aviation aircraft are becoming increasingly sophisticated, boosting the demand for qualified mechanics. Mechanics will face more competition for jobs with large airlines because the high wages and travel benefits that these jobs offer generally attract more qualified applicants than there are openings. In spite of this, job opportunities with the airlines are expected to be better than they have been in the past. But, in general, prospects will be best for applicants with experience. Mechanics who keep abreast of technological advances in electronics, composite materials, and other areas will be in greatest demand. The number of job openings for aircraft mechanics in the federal government should decline as the government increasingly contracts out service and repair functions to private repair companies.

Earnings

Median hourly earnings of aircraft mechanics and service technicians were about $20.71 in 2002. The middle 50 percent earned between $16.94 and $25.23. The lowest 10 percent earned less than $13.16, and the highest 10 percent earned more than $28.92. Median hourly earnings in the industries employing the largest numbers of aircraft mechanics and service technicians in 2002 were:

Air transportation, scheduled $23.48
Federal government 20.59
Air transportation, nonscheduled 19.84
Aerospace product and parts manufacturing 19.68
Support activities for air transportation 17.64

Median hourly earnings of avionics technicians were about $20.21 in 2002. The middle 50 percent earned between $17.44 and $23.91. The lowest 10 percent earned less than $14.01, and the highest 10 percent earned more than $27.00.

Mechanics who work on jets for the major airlines generally earn more than those working on other aircraft. Airline mechanics and their immediate families receive reduced-fare transportation on their own and most other airlines.

Almost 4 in 10 aircraft and avionics equipment mechanics and service technicians are members of or covered by union agreements. The principal unions are the International Association of Machinists and Aerospace Workers and the

Transport Workers Union of America. Some mechanics are represented by the International Brotherhood of Teamsters.

Related Occupations

Workers in some other occupations that involve similar mechanical and electrical work are electricians, electrical and electronics installers and repairers, and elevator installers and repairers.

Sources of Additional Information

Information about jobs with a particular airline can be obtained by writing to the personnel manager of the company.

For general information about aircraft and avionics equipment mechanics and service technicians, write to:

- Professional Aviation Maintenance Association, 717 Princess St., Alexandria, VA 22314. Internet: http://www.pama.org

For information on jobs in a particular area, contact employers at local airports or local offices of the state employment service.

Aircraft Pilots and Flight Engineers

(O*NET 53-2011.00 and 53-2012.00)

Significant Points

- The best opportunities for jobs will be with the regional airlines and business aviation.

- Pilots usually start with smaller commuter and regional airlines to acquire the experience needed to qualify for higher paying jobs with national airlines.

- Most pilots traditionally have learned to fly in the military, but growing numbers have college degrees with flight training from civilian flying schools that are certified by the Federal Aviation Administration (FAA).

Nature of the Work

Pilots are highly trained professionals who fly airplanes and helicopters to carry out a wide variety of tasks. Most are *airline pilots, copilots, and flight engineers* who transport passengers and cargo, but 1 out of 5 pilots is a *commercial pilot* involved in more unusual tasks, such as dusting crops, spreading seed for reforestation, testing aircraft, flying passengers and cargo to areas not served by regular airlines, directing firefighting efforts, tracking criminals, monitoring traffic, and rescuing and evacuating injured persons.

Except on small aircraft, two pilots usually make up the cockpit crew. Generally, the most experienced pilot, the *captain*, is in command and supervises all other crew members. The pilot and the copilot, often called the first officer, share flying and other duties, such as communicating with air traffic controllers and monitoring the instruments. Some large aircraft have a third pilot—the *flight engineer*—who assists the other pilots by monitoring and operating many of the instruments and systems, making minor in-flight repairs, and watching for other aircraft. New technology can perform many flight tasks, however, and virtually all new aircraft now fly with only two pilots, who rely more heavily on computerized controls.

Before departure, pilots plan their flights carefully. They thoroughly check their aircraft to make sure that the engines, controls, instruments, and other systems are functioning properly. They also make sure that baggage or cargo has been loaded correctly. They confer with flight dispatchers and aviation weather forecasters to find out about weather conditions en route and at their destination. Based on this information, they choose a route, altitude, and speed that will provide the fastest, safest, and smoothest flight. When flying under instrument flight rules—procedures governing the operation of the aircraft when there is poor visibility—the pilot in command, or the company dispatcher, normally files an instrument flight plan with air traffic control so that the flight can be coordinated with other air traffic.

Takeoff and landing are the most difficult parts of the flight, and require close coordination between the pilot and first officer. For example, as the plane accelerates for takeoff, the pilot concentrates on the runway while the first officer scans the instrument panel. To calculate the speed they must attain to become airborne, pilots consider the altitude of the airport, outside temperature, weight of the plane, and speed and direction of the wind. The moment the plane reaches takeoff speed, the first officer informs the pilot, who then pulls back on the controls to raise the nose of the plane.

Unless the weather is bad, the actual flight is relatively easy. Airplane pilots, with the assistance of autopilot and the flight management computer, steer the plane along their planned route and are monitored by the air traffic control stations they pass along the way. They regularly scan the instrument panel to check their fuel supply, the condition of their engines, and the air-conditioning, hydraulic, and other systems. Pilots may request a change in altitude or route if circumstances dictate. For example, if the ride is rougher than expected, they may ask air traffic control if pilots flying at other altitudes have reported better conditions. If so, they may request an altitude change. This procedure also may be used to find a stronger tailwind or a weaker headwind to save fuel and increase speed.

In contrast, helicopters are used for short trips at relatively low altitude, so pilots must be constantly on the lookout for trees, bridges, powerlines, transmission towers, and other dangerous obstacles. Regardless of the type of aircraft, all pilots must monitor warning devices designed to help detect sudden shifts in wind conditions that can cause crashes.

Pilots must rely completely on their instruments when visibility is poor. On the basis of altimeter readings, they know how high above ground they are and whether they can fly safely over mountains and other obstacles. Special navigation radios give pilots precise information that, with the help of special maps, tells them their exact position. Other very sophisticated equipment provides directions to a point just above the end of a runway and enables pilots to land completely "blind." Once on the ground, pilots must complete records on their flight for their organization and the FAA report.

The number of nonflying duties that pilots have depends on the employment setting. Airline pilots have the services of large support staffs, and consequently, perform few nonflying duties. Pilots employed by other organizations such as charter operators or businesses have many other duties. They may load the aircraft, handle all passenger luggage to ensure a balanced load, and supervise refueling; other nonflying responsibilities include keeping records, scheduling flights, arranging for major maintenance, and performing minor aircraft maintenance and repairwork.

Some pilots are instructors. They teach their students the principles of flight in ground-school classes and demonstrate how to operate aircraft in dual-controlled planes and helicopters. A few specially trained pilots are "examiners" or "check pilots." They periodically fly with other pilots or pilot's license applicants to make sure that they are proficient.

Working Conditions

By law, airline pilots cannot fly more than 100 hours a month or more than 1,000 hours a year. Most airline pilots fly an average of 75 hours a month and work an additional 75 hours a month performing nonflying duties. Most pilots have a variable work schedule, working several days on, then several days off. Most spend a considerable amount of time away from home because the majority of flights involve overnight layovers. When pilots are away from home, the airlines provide hotel accommodations, transportation between the hotel and airport, and an allowance for meals and other expenses. Airlines operate flights at all hours of the day and night, so work schedules often are irregular. Flight assignments are based on seniority.

Commercial pilots also may have irregular schedules, flying 30 hours one month and 90 hours the next. Because these pilots frequently have many nonflying responsibilities, they have much less free time than do airline pilots. Except for business pilots, most do not remain away from home overnight. They may work odd hours. Flight instructors may have irregular and seasonal work schedules, depending on their students' available time and the weather. Instructors frequently work in the evening or on weekends.

Airline pilots, especially those on international routes, often suffer jet lag—fatigue caused by many hours of flying through different time zones. To guard against excessive pilot fatigue that could result in unsafe flying conditions,

the FAA requires airlines to allow pilots at least 8 hours of uninterrupted rest in the 24 hours before finishing their flight duty. The work of test pilots, who check the flight performance of new and experimental planes, may be dangerous. Pilots who are crop dusters may be exposed to toxic chemicals and seldom have the benefit of a regular landing strip. Helicopter pilots involved in rescue and police work may be subject to personal injury.

Although flying does not involve much physical effort, the mental stress of being responsible for a safe flight, regardless of the weather, can be tiring. Pilots must be alert and quick to react if something goes wrong, particularly during takeoff and landing.

Employment

Civilian aircraft pilots and flight engineers held about 100,000 jobs in 2002. About 79,000 worked as airline pilots, copilots, and flight engineers. The remainder were commercial pilots who worked as flight instructors at local airports or for large businesses that fly company cargo and executives in their own airplanes or helicopters. Some commercial pilots flew small planes for air-taxi companies, usually to or from lightly traveled airports not served by major airlines. Others worked for a variety of businesses, performing tasks such as dusting crops, inspecting pipelines, or conducting sightseeing trips. federal, state, and local governments also employed pilots. A few pilots were self-employed.

Pilots are located across the country, but airline pilots usually are based near major metropolitan airports or airports operating as hubs for the major airlines.

Training, Other Qualifications, and Advancement

All pilots who are paid to transport passengers or cargo must have a commercial pilot's license with an instrument rating issued by the FAA. Helicopter pilots must hold a commercial pilot's certificate with a helicopter rating. To qualify for these licenses, applicants must be at least 18 years old and have at least 250 hours of flight experience. The experience required can be reduced through participation in certain flight school curricula approved by the FAA. Applicants also must pass a strict physical examination to make sure that they are in good health and have 20/20 vision with or without glasses, good hearing, and no physical handicaps that could impair their performance. They must pass a written test that includes questions on the principles of safe flight, navigation techniques, and FAA regulations, and must demonstrate their flying ability to FAA or designated examiners.

To fly during periods of low visibility, pilots must be rated by the FAA to fly by instruments. Pilots may qualify for this rating by having 105 hours of flight experience, including 40 hours of experience in flying by instruments; they also must pass a written examination on procedures and FAA regulations covering instrument flying and demonstrate to an examiner their ability to fly by instruments.

Airline pilots must fulfill additional requirements. Pilots must have an airline transport pilot's license. Applicants for this license must be at least 23 years old and have a minimum of 1,500 hours of flying experience, including night and instrument flying, and must pass FAA written and flight examinations. Usually, they also have one or more advanced ratings, such as multiengine aircraft or aircraft-type ratings, dependent upon the requirements of their particular flying jobs. Because pilots must be able to make quick decisions and accurate judgments under pressure, many airline companies reject applicants who do not pass required psychological and aptitude tests. All licenses are valid so long as a pilot can pass the periodic physical and eye examinations and tests of flying skills required by federal government and company regulations.

The U.S. Armed Forces have always been an important source of trained pilots for civilian jobs. Military pilots gain valuable experience on jet aircraft and helicopters, and persons with this experience usually are preferred for civilian pilot jobs. This primarily reflects the extensive flying time military pilots receive. Persons without Armed Forces training may become pilots by attending flight schools or by taking lessons from individual FAA-certified flight instructors. The FAA has certified about 600 civilian flying schools, including some colleges and universities that offer degree credit for pilot training. Over the projection period, trained pilots leaving the military are not expected to increase very much in number as the need for pilots grows in civilian aviation. As a result, FAA-certified schools will train a larger share of pilots than in the past.

Although some small airlines will hire high school graduates, most airlines require at least 2 years of college and prefer to hire college graduates. In fact, most entrants to this occupation have a college degree. Because the number of college educated applicants continues to increase, many employers are making a college degree an educational requirement.

Depending on the type of aircraft, new airline pilots start as first officers or flight engineers. Although some airlines favor applicants who already have a flight engineer's license, they may provide flight engineer training for those who have only the commercial license. Many pilots begin with smaller regional or commuter airlines, where they obtain experience flying passengers on scheduled flights into busy airports in all weather conditions. These jobs often lead to higher paying jobs with bigger, national airlines.

Initial training for airline pilots includes a week of company indoctrination, 3 to 6 weeks of ground school and simulator training, and 25 hours of initial operating experience, including a check-ride with an FAA aviation safety inspector. Once trained and "on the line," pilots are required to attend recurrent training and simulator checks twice a year throughout their career.

Organizations other than airlines usually require less flying experience. However, a commercial pilot's license is a minimum requirement, and employers prefer applicants who have experience in the type of craft they will be flying. New employees usually start as first officers, or fly less sophisticated equipment. Test pilots often are required to have an engineering degree.

Advancement for all pilots usually is limited to other flying jobs. Many pilots start as flight instructors, building up their flying hours while they earn money teaching. As they become more experienced, these pilots occasionally fly charter planes or perhaps get jobs with small air transportation firms, such as air-taxi companies. Some advance to flying corporate planes. A small number get flight engineer jobs with the airlines.

In the airlines, advancement usually depends on seniority provisions of union contracts. After 1 to 5 years, flight engineers advance according to seniority to first officer and, after 5 to 15 years, to captain. Seniority also determines which pilots get the more desirable routes. In a nonairline job, a first officer may advance to pilot and, in large companies, to chief pilot or director of aviation in charge of aircraft scheduling, maintenance, and flight procedures.

Job Outlook

The passenger airline industry is undergoing many changes, with some airlines posting increases in passenger traffic and adding routes while others are cutting back. Overall, the employment of aircraft pilots is projected to increase about as fast as average for all occupations through 2012. In the long run, demand for air travel is expected to track increases in the population and growth of the economy. In the short run, however, employment of pilots is generally sensitive to cyclical swings in the economy. During recessions, when a decline in the demand for air travel forces airlines to curtail the number of flights, airlines may temporarily furlough some pilots.

After September 11, 2001, air travel was severely depressed. A number of the major airlines were forced to reduce schedules, layoff pilots, and even declare bankruptcy. At the same time, hiring continued at regional and low-fare airlines. It is expected that job opportunities will continue to be better with the regional airlines and low-fare carriers, which are growing faster than the more well-known major airlines. Opportunities with air cargo carriers also are expected to be good due to increasing security requirements for shipping freight on passenger airlines and growth in e-business.

Pilots attempting to get jobs at the major airlines will face strong competition, as those firms tend to attract many more applicants than they have jobs. They also will have to compete with laid off pilots for any available jobs. Pilots who have logged the greatest number of flying hours in the more sophisticated equipment typically have the best prospects. For this reason, military pilots often have an advantage over other applicants. However, prior to September 11, 2001, some airlines reported a shortage of qualified pilots to operate the most sophisticated aircraft. Thus, when hiring improves, jobseekers with the most FAA licenses will have a competitive advantage. Opportunities for pilot jobs should be better at smaller airlines and in corporate travel.

The number of flight engineers is projected to decline through 2012 as new planes needing only two pilots replace older planes that required flight engineers. Pilots also will experience some productivity improvements as airlines switch to larger planes and adopt the low-fare carrier model that emphasizes faster turnaround times for flights, keeping more pilots in the air rather than waiting on the ground.

Earnings

Earnings of aircraft pilots and flight engineers vary greatly depending whether they work as airline or commercial pilots. Earnings of airline pilots are among the highest in the nation, and depend on factors such as the type, size, and maximum speed of the plane and the number of hours and miles flown. For example, pilots who fly jet aircraft usually earn higher salaries than do pilots who fly turboprops. Airline pilots and flight engineers may earn extra pay for night and international flights. In 2002, median annual earnings of airline pilots, copilots, and flight engineers were $109,580. The lowest 10 percent earned less than $55,800. More than 25 percent earned over $145,000.

Median annual earnings of commercial pilots were $47,970 in 2002. The middle 50 percent earned between $33,830 and $70,140. The lowest 10 percent earned less than $26,100, and the highest 10 percent earned more than $101,460.

Airline pilots usually are eligible for life and health insurance plans financed by the airlines. They also receive retirement benefits and, if they fail the FAA physical examination at some point in their careers, they get disability payments. In addition, pilots receive an expense allowance, or "per diem," for every hour they are away from home. Some airlines also provide allowances to pilots for purchasing and cleaning their uniforms. As an additional benefit, pilots and their immediate families usually are entitled to free or reduced-fare transportation on their own and other airlines.

More than half of all aircraft pilots are members of unions. Most of the pilots who fly for the major airlines are members of the Airline Pilots Association, International, but those employed by one major airline are members of the Allied Pilots Association. Some flight engineers are members of the Flight Engineers' International Association.

Related Occupations

Although they are not in the cockpit, air traffic controllers and airfield operation specialists also play an important role in making sure flights are safe and on schedule, and participate in many of the decisions that pilots must make.

Sources of Additional Information

Information about job opportunities, salaries for a particular airline, and qualifications required may be obtained by writing to the personnel manager of the airline.

For information on airline pilots, contact:

● Air Line Pilots Association, 533 Herndon Parkway, Herndon, VA 22070.

● Air Transport Association of America, Inc., 1301 Pennsylvania Ave. NW., Suite 1100, Washington, DC 20004.

For information on helicopter pilots, contact:

● Helicopter Association International, 1635 Prince Street, Alexandria, VA 22314.

For information about job opportunities in companies other than airlines, consult the classified section of aviation trade magazines and apply to companies that operate aircraft at local airports.

Archivists, Curators, and Museum Technicians

(O*NET 25-4011.00, 25-4012.00, and 25-4013.00)

Significant Points

● Employment in this occupation usually requires graduate education and related work experience.

● Keen competition is expected for the most desirable job openings, which generally attract a large number of applicants.

Nature of the Work

Archivists, curators, and museum technicians acquire and preserve important documents and other valuable items for permanent storage or display. They work for museums, governments, zoos, colleges and universities, corporations, and other institutions that require experts to preserve important records. They also describe, catalogue, analyze, exhibit, and maintain valuable objects and collections for the benefit of researchers and the public. These documents and collections may include works of art, transcripts of meetings, coins and stamps, living and preserved plants and animals, and historic buildings and sites.

Archivists and curators plan and oversee the arrangement, cataloguing, and exhibition of collections and, along with technicians and conservators, maintain collections. Archivists and curators may coordinate educational and public outreach programs, such as tours, workshops, lectures, and classes, and may work with the boards of institutions to administer plans and policies. They also may research topics or items relevant to their collections. Although some duties of archivists and curators are similar, the types of items they deal with differ: curators usually handle objects with cultural, biological, or historical significance, such as sculptures, textiles, and paintings, while archivists handle mainly records and documents that are retained because of their importance and potential value in the future.

Archivists collect, organize, and maintain control over a wide range of information deemed important enough for permanent safekeeping. This information takes many forms: photographs, films, video and sound recordings, computer tapes, and video and optical disks, as well as more traditional paper records, letters, and documents. Archivists work for a variety of organizations, including government agencies, museums, historical societies, corporations, and educational institutions that use or generate records of great potential value to researchers, exhibitors, genealogists, and others who would benefit from having access to original source material.

Archivists maintain records in accordance with accepted standards and practices, that ensure the long-term preservation and easy retrieval of the documents. Records may be saved on any medium, including paper, film, videotape, audiotape, electronic disk, or computer. They also may be copied onto some other format to protect the original and to make them more accessible to researchers who use the records. As various storage media evolve, archivists must keep abreast of technological advances in electronic information storage.

Archivists often specialize in an area of history or technology so they can more accurately determine what records in that area qualify for retention and should become part of the archives. Archivists also may work with specialized forms of records, such as manuscripts, electronic records, photographs, cartographic records, motion pictures, and sound recordings.

Computers are increasingly being used to generate and maintain archival records. Professional standards for the use of computers in handling archival records are still evolving. However, computers are expected to transform many aspects of archival collections as computer capabilities and the use of multimedia and the Internet expand and allow more records to be stored and exhibited electronically.

Curators administer the affairs of museums, zoos, aquariums, botanical gardens, nature centers, and historic sites. The head curator of the museum is usually called the *museum director*. Curators direct the acquisition, storage, and exhibition of collections, including negotiating and authorizing the purchase, sale, exchange, or loan of collections. They are also responsible for authenticating, evaluating, and categorizing the specimens in a collection. Curators oversee and help conduct the institution's research projects and related educational programs. However, an increasing part of a curator's duties involves fundraising and promotion, which may include the writing and reviewing of grant proposals, journal articles, and publicity materials, as well as attendance at meetings, conventions, and civic events.

Most curators specialize in a particular field, such as botany, art, paleontology, or history. Those working in large institutions may be highly specialized. A large natural-history museum, for example, would employ separate curators for its collections of birds, fishes, insects, and mammals. Some curators maintain their collections, others do research, and others perform administrative tasks. In small institutions, with only one or a few curators, one curator may be responsible for multiple tasks, from maintaining collections to directing the affairs of the museum.

Conservators manage, care for, preserve, treat, and document works of art, artifacts, and specimens, work that may require substantial historical, scientific, and archaeological research. They use X rays, chemical testing, microscopes, special lights, and other laboratory equipment and techniques to examine objects and determine their condition, their need for treatment or restoration, and the appropriate method for preserving them. Conservators document their findings and treat items to minimize their deterioration or to restore them to their original state. Conservators usually specialize in a particular material or group of objects, such as documents and books, paintings, decorative arts, textiles, metals, or architectural material.

Museum technicians assist curators by performing various preparatory and maintenance tasks on museum items. Some museum technicians also may assist curators with research. Archives technicians help archivists organize, maintain, and provide access to historical documentary materials.

Working Conditions

The working conditions of archivists and curators vary. Some spend most of their time working with the public, providing reference assistance and educational services. Others perform research or process records, which often means working alone or in offices with only a few people. Those who restore and install exhibits or work with bulky, heavy record containers may climb, stretch, or lift. Those in zoos, botanical gardens, and other outdoor museums or historic sites frequently walk great distances.

Curators who work in large institutions may travel extensively to evaluate potential additions to the collection, organize exhibitions, and conduct research in their area of expertise. However, travel is rare for curators employed in small institutions.

Employment

Archivists, curators, and museum technicians held about 22,000 jobs in 2002. About 35 percent were employed in museums, historical sites, and similar institutions, and 15 percent worked for state and private educational institutions, mainly college and university libraries. Nearly 40 percent worked in federal, state, and local government. Most federal archivists work for the National Archives and Records Administration; others manage military archives in the U.S. Department of Defense. Most federal government curators work at the Smithsonian Institution, in the military museums of the Department of Defense, and in archaeological and other museums and historic sites managed by the U.S. Department of the Interior. All state governments have archival or historical-record sections employing archivists. State and local governments also have numerous historical museums, parks, libraries, and zoos employing curators.

Some large corporations that have archives or record centers employ archivists to manage the growing volume of records created or maintained as required by law or necessary to the firms' operations. Religious and fraternal organizations, professional associations, conservation organizations, major private collectors, and research firms also employ archivists and curators.

Conservators may work under contract to treat particular items, rather than as regular employees of a museum or other institution. These conservators may work on their own as private contractors, or they may work as an employee of a conservation laboratory or regional conservation center that contracts their services to museums.

Training, Other Qualifications, and Advancement

Employment as an archivist, conservator, or curator usually requires graduate education and related work experience. While completing their formal education, many archivists and curators work in archives or museums to gain the "hands-on" experience that many employers seek.

Although most archivists have a variety of undergraduate degrees, a graduate degree in history or library science, with courses in archival science, is preferred by most employers. Some positions may require knowledge of the discipline related to the collection, such as business or medicine. Currently, no programs offer bachelor's or master's degrees in archival science. However, approximately 65 colleges and universities offer courses or practical training in archival science as part of their history, library science, or other curriculum. The Academy of Certified Archivists offers voluntary certification for archivists. The designation "Certified Archivist" is obtained by those with at least a master's degree and a year of appropriate archival experience. The certification process requires candidates to pass a written examination, and they must renew their certification periodically.

Archivists need research and analytical ability to understand the content of documents and the context in which they were created and to decipher deteriorated or poor-quality printed matter, handwritten manuscripts, or photographs and films. A background in preservation management is often required of archivists because they are responsible for taking proper care of their records. Archivists also must be able to organize large amounts of information and write clear instructions for its retrieval and use. In addition, computer skills and the ability to work with electronic records and databases are becoming increasingly important.

Many archives, including one-person shops, are very small and have limited opportunities for promotion. Archivists typically advance by transferring to a larger unit with supervisory positions. A doctorate in history, library science, or a

related field may be needed for some advanced positions, such as director of a state archive.

For employment as a curator, most museums require a master's degree in an appropriate discipline of the museum's specialty—art, history, or archaeology—or museum studies. Many employers prefer a doctoral degree, particularly for curators in natural history or science museums. Earning two graduate degrees—in museum studies (museology) and a specialized subject—gives a candidate a distinct advantage in this competitive job market. In small museums, curatorial positions may be available to individuals with a bachelor's degree. For some positions, an internship of full-time museum work supplemented by courses in museum practices is needed.

Curatorial positions often require knowledge in a number of fields. For historic and artistic conservation, courses in chemistry, physics, and art are desirable. Since curators—particularly those in small museums—may have administrative and managerial responsibilities, courses in business administration, public relations, marketing, and fundraising also are recommended. Like archivists, curators need computer skills and the ability to work with electronic databases. Many curators are responsible for posting information on the Internet, so they also need to be familiar with digital imaging, scanning technology, and copyright law.

Curators must be flexible because of their wide variety of duties, among which are the design and presentation of exhibits. In small museums, curators need manual dexterity, to build exhibits or restore objects. Leadership ability and business skills are important for museum directors, while marketing skills are valuable in increasing museum attendance and fundraising.

In large museums, curators may advance through several levels of responsibility, eventually becoming the museum director. Curators in smaller museums often advance to larger ones. Individual research and publications are important for advancement in larger institutions.

When hiring conservators, employers look for a master's degree in conservation or in a closely related field, together with substantial experience. There are only a few graduate programs in museum conservation techniques in the United States. Competition for entry to these programs is keen; to qualify, a student must have a background in chemistry, archaeology or studio art, and art history, as well as work experience. For some programs, knowledge of a foreign language is also helpful. Conservation apprenticeships or internships as an undergraduate can enhance one's admission prospects. Graduate programs last 2 to 4 years, the latter years of which include internship training. A few individuals enter conservation through apprenticeships with museums, nonprofit organizations, and conservators in private practice. Apprenticeships should be supplemented with courses in chemistry, studio art, and history. Apprenticeship training, although accepted, usually is a more difficult route into the conservation profession.

Museum technicians usually need a bachelor's degree in an appropriate discipline of the museum's specialty, training in museum studies, or previous experience working in museums, particularly in the design of exhibits. Similarly, archives technicians usually need a bachelor's degree in library science or history, or relevant work experience. Technician positions often serve as a steppingstone for individuals interested in archival and curatorial work. Except in small museums, a master's degree is needed for advancement.

Relatively few schools grant a bachelor's degree in museum studies. More common are undergraduate minors or tracks of study that are part of an undergraduate degree in a related field, such as art history, history, or archaeology. Students interested in further study may obtain a master's degree in museum studies, offered in colleges and universities throughout the country. However, many employers feel that, while museum studies are helpful, a thorough knowledge of the museum's specialty and museum work experience are more important.

Continuing education, which enables archivists, curators, and museum technicians to keep up with developments in the field, is available through meetings, conferences, and workshops sponsored by archival, historical, and museum associations. Some larger organizations, such as the National Archives, offer such training in-house.

Job Outlook

Competition for jobs as archivists, curators, and museum technicians is expected to be keen because qualified applicants outnumber job openings. Graduates with highly specialized training, such as master's degrees in both library science and history, with a concentration in archives or records management and extensive computer skills should have the best opportunities for jobs as archivists. A curator job also is attractive to many people, and many applicants have the necessary training and knowledge of the subject, but there are only a few openings. Consequently, candidates may have to work part time, as an intern, or even as a volunteer assistant curator or research associate after completing their formal education. Substantial work experience in collection management, exhibit design, or restoration, as well as database management skills, will be necessary for permanent status. Job opportunities for curators should be best in art and history museums, since these are the largest employers in the museum industry.

The job outlook for conservators may be more favorable, particularly for graduates of conservation programs. However, competition is stiff for the limited number of openings in these programs, and applicants need a technical background. Students who qualify and successfully complete the program, have knowledge of a foreign language, and are willing to relocate will have an advantage over less qualified candidates.

Employment of archivists, curators, and museum technicians is expected to increase about as fast as the average for all occupations through 2012. Jobs are expected to grow as public and private organizations emphasize establishing archives and organizing records and information and as public interest in science, art, history, and technology increases. Museum and zoo attendance has been on the rise and is expected to continue increasing, which will generate demand for curators and museum technicians and conservators. However, museums and other cultural institutions can be subject to cuts in funding during recessions or periods of budget tightening, reducing demand for archivists and curators. Although the rate of turnover among archivists and curators is relatively low, the need to replace workers who leave the occupation or stop working will create some additional job openings.

Earnings

Median annual earnings of archivists, curators, and museum technicians in 2002 were $35,270. The middle 50 percent earned between $26,400 and $48,460. The lowest 10 percent earned less than $20,010, and the highest 10 percent earned more than $66,050.

Earnings of archivists and curators vary considerably by type and size of employer and often by specialty. Median annual earnings of archivists, curators, and museum technicians in 2002 were $33,720 in museums, historical sites, and similar institutions.. Salaries, though, of curators in large, well-funded museums can be several times higher than those in small ones. The average annual salary for archivists in the federal government in nonsupervisory, supervisory, and managerial positions was $69,706 in 2003; for museum curators, $70,100; museum specialists and technicians, $48,414; and for archives technicians, $37,067.

Related Occupations

The skills that archivists, curators, and museum technicians use in preserving, organizing, and displaying objects or information of historical interest are shared by artists and related workers; librarians; and anthropologists and archeologists, historians, and other social scientists.

Sources of Additional Information

For information on archivists and on schools offering courses in archival studies, contact

- Society of American Archivists, 527 South Wells St., 5th floor, Chicago, IL 60607-3922. Internet: http://www.archivists.org

For general information about careers as a curator and schools offering courses in museum studies, contact

- American Association of Museums, 1575 Eye St. NW., Suite 400, Washington, DC 20005. Internet: http://www.aam-us.org

For information about careers and education programs in conservation and preservation, contact

- American Institute for Conservation of Historic and Artistic Works, 1717 K St. NW., Suite 200, Washington, DC 20006. Internet: http://aic.stanford.edu

Armed Forces

(O*NET 55-1011.00, 55-1012.00, 55-1013.00, 55-1014.00, 55-1015.00, 55-1016.00, 55-1017.00, 55-1019.99, and 55-2011.00)

For specific information about careers in the Armed Forces, see the listing for Job Opportunities in the Armed Forces beginning on page 146.

Atmospheric Scientists

(O*NET 19-2021.00)

Significant Points

- Almost 4 in 10 atmospheric scientists work for the federal government, which is the largest employer of such workers.

- A bachelor's degree in meteorology, or in a closely related field with courses in meteorology, is the minimum educational requirement; a master's degree is necessary for some positions, and a Ph.D. is required for most research positions.

Nature of the Work

Atmospheric science is the study of the atmosphere—the blanket of air covering the Earth. *Atmospheric scientists*, commonly called *meteorologists*, study the atmosphere's physical characteristics, motions, and processes, and the way in which it affects the rest of our environment. The best known application of this knowledge is in forecasting the weather. Aside from predicting the weather, scientists also attempt to identify and interpret climate trends, understand past weather, and analyze today's weather. However, weather information and meteorological research also are applied in air-pollution control, agriculture, forestry, air and sea transportation, defense, and the study of possible trends in the Earth's climate, such as global warming, droughts, or ozone depletion.

Atmospheric scientists who forecast the weather, known professionally as *operational meteorologists*, are the largest group of specialists. They study information on air pressure, temperature, humidity, and wind velocity; and apply physical and mathematical relationships to make short-range and long-range weather forecasts. Their data come from weather satellites, weather radars, sensors, and weather stations in many parts of the world. Meteorologists use sophisticated computer models of the world's atmosphere to make long-term, short-term, and local-area forecasts. More accurate instruments for measuring and observing weather condi-

tions, as well as high-speed computers to process and analyze weather data, have revolutionized weather forecasting. Using satellite data, climate theory, and sophisticated computer models of the world's atmosphere, meteorologists can more effectively interpret the results of these models to make local-area weather predictions. These forecasts inform not only the general public, but also those who need accurate weather information for both economic and safety reasons, such as the shipping, air transportation, agriculture, fishing, forestry, and utilities industries.

The use of weather balloons, launched a few times a day to measure wind, temperature, and humidity in the upper atmosphere, is currently supplemented by sophisticated atmospheric monitoring equipment that transmits data as frequently as every few minutes. Doppler radar, for example, can detect airflow patterns in violent storm systems—allowing forecasters to better predict tornadoes and other hazardous winds, and to monitor the storms' direction and intensity. Combined radar and satellite observations allow meteorologists to predict flash floods.

Some atmospheric scientists work in research. *Physical meteorologists*, for example, study the atmosphere's chemical and physical properties; the transmission of light, sound, and radio waves; and the transfer of energy in the atmosphere. They also study factors affecting the formation of clouds, rain, and snow; the dispersal of air pollutants over urban areas; and other weather phenomena, such as the mechanics of severe storms. *Synoptic meteorologists* develop new tools for weather forecasting using computers and sophisticated mathematical models of atmospheric activity. *Climatologists* study climactic variations spanning hundreds or even millions of years. They also may collect, analyze, and interpret past records of wind, rainfall, sunshine, and temperature in specific areas or regions. Their studies are used to design buildings, plan heating and cooling systems, and aid in effective land use and agricultural production. Environmental problems, such as pollution and shortages of fresh water, have widened the scope of the meteorological profession. *Environmental meteorologists* study these problems and may evaluate and report on air quality for environmental impact statements. Other research meteorologists examine the most effective ways to control or diminish air pollution.

Working Conditions

Most weather stations operate around the clock, 7 days a week. Jobs in such facilities usually involve night, weekend, and holiday work, often with rotating shifts. During weather emergencies, such as hurricanes, operational meteorologists may work overtime. Operational meteorologists also are often under pressure to meet forecast deadlines. Weather stations are found everywhere—at airports, in or near cities, and in isolated and remote areas. Some atmospheric scientists also spend time observing weather conditions and collecting data from aircraft. Weather forecasters who work for radio or television stations broadcast their reports from station studios, and may work evenings and weekends. Meteorologists in smaller weather offices often work alone; in larger ones, they work as part of a team. Meteorologists not involved in forecasting tasks work regular hours, usually in offices. Those who work for private consulting firms or for companies analyzing and monitoring emissions to improve air quality usually work with other scientists or engineers; fieldwork and travel may be common for these workers.

Employment

Atmospheric scientists held about 7,700 jobs in 2002. The federal government was the largest single employer of civilian meteorologists, accounting for about 2,900. The National Oceanic and Atmospheric Administration (NOAA) employed most federal meteorologists in National Weather Service stations throughout the nation; the remainder of NOAA's meteorologists worked mainly in research and development or management. The U.S. Department of Defense employed several hundred civilian meteorologists. Others worked for professional, scientific, and technical services firms, including private weather consulting services; radio and television broadcasting; air carriers; and state government.

Although several hundred people teach atmospheric science and related courses in college and university departments of meteorology or atmospheric science, physics, earth science, or geophysics, these individuals are classified as college or university faculty, rather than atmospheric scientists.

In addition to civilian meteorologists, hundreds of Armed Forces members are involved in forecasting and other meteorological work.

Training, Other Qualifications, and Advancement

A bachelor's degree in meteorology or atmospheric science, or in a closely related field with courses in meteorology, usually is the minimum educational requirement for an entry-level position as an atmospheric scientist.

The preferred educational requirement for entry-level meteorologists in the federal government is a bachelor's degree—not necessarily in meteorology—with at least 24 semester hours of meteorology courses, including 6 hours in the analysis and prediction of weather systems, 6 hours of atmospheric dynamics and thermodynamics, 3 hours of physical meteorology, and 2 hours of remote sensing of the atmosphere or instrumentation. Other required courses include 3 semester hours of ordinary differential equations, 6 hours of college physics, and at least 9 hours of courses appropriate for a physical science major—such as statistics, chemistry, physical oceanography, physical climatology, physical hydrology, radiative transfer, aeronomy, advanced thermodynamics, advanced electricity and magnetism, light and optics, and computer science. Sometimes, a combination of education and appropriate experience may be substi-

tuted for a degree. Although positions in operational meteorology are available for those with only a bachelor's degree, obtaining a second bachelor's degree or a master's degree enhances employment opportunities and advancement potential. A master's degree usually is necessary for conducting applied research and development, and a Ph.D. is required for most basic research positions. Students planning on a career in research and development need not necessarily major in atmospheric science or meteorology as an undergraduate. In fact, a bachelor's degree in mathematics, physics, or engineering provides excellent preparation for graduate study in atmospheric science.

Because atmospheric science is a small field, relatively few colleges and universities offer degrees in meteorology or atmospheric science, although many departments of physics, earth science, geography, and geophysics offer atmospheric science and related courses. Prospective students should make certain that courses required by the National Weather Service and other employers are offered at the college they are considering. Computer science courses, additional meteorology courses, a strong background in mathematics and physics, and good communication skills are important to prospective employers. Many programs combine the study of meteorology with another field, such as agriculture, oceanography, engineering, or physics. For example, hydrometeorology is the blending of hydrology (the science of Earth's water) and meteorology, and is the field concerned with the effect of precipitation on the hydrologic cycle and the environment. Students who wish to become broadcast meteorologists for radio or television stations should develop excellent communication skills through courses in speech, journalism, and related fields. Those interested in air quality work should take courses in chemistry and supplement their technical training with coursework in policy or government affairs. Prospective meteorologists seeking opportunities at weather consulting firms should possess knowledge of business, statistics, and economics, as an increasing emphasis is being placed on long-range seasonal forecasting to assist businesses.

Beginning atmospheric scientists often do routine data collection, computation, or analysis, and some basic forecasting. Entry-level operational meteorologists in the federal government usually are placed in intern positions for training and experience. During this period, they learn about the Weather Service's forecasting equipment and procedures, and rotate to different offices to learn about various weather systems. After completing the training period, they are assigned a permanent duty station. Experienced meteorologists may advance to supervisory or administrative jobs, or may handle more complex forecasting jobs. After several years of experience, some meteorologists establish their own weather consulting services.

The American Meteorological Society offers professional certification of consulting meteorologists, administered by a Board of Certified Consulting Meteorologists. Applicants must meet formal education requirements (though not necessarily have a college degree), pass an examination to demonstrate thorough meteorological knowledge, have a minimum of 5 years of experience or a combination of experience plus an advanced degree, and provide character references from fellow professionals.

Job Outlook

Employment of atmospheric scientists is projected to increase about as fast as the average for all occupations through 2012. The National Weather Service has completed an extensive modernization of its weather forecasting equipment and finished all hiring of meteorologists needed to staff the upgraded stations. The Service has no plans to increase the number of weather stations or the number of meteorologists in existing stations. Employment of meteorologists in other federal agencies is expected to remain stable.

On the other hand, job opportunities for atmospheric scientists in private industry are expected to be better than for those in the federal government over the 2002-12 period. As research leads to continuing improvements in weather forecasting, demand should grow for private weather consulting firms to provide more detailed information than has formerly been available, especially to weather-sensitive industries. Farmers, commodity investors, radio and television stations, and utilities, transportation, and construction firms can greatly benefit from additional weather information more closely targeted to their needs than the general information provided by the National Weather Service. Additionally, research on seasonal and other long-range forecasting is yielding positive results, which should spur demand for more atmospheric scientists to interpret these forecasts and advise weather-sensitive industries. However, because many customers for private weather services are in industries sensitive to fluctuations in the economy, the sales and growth of private weather services depend on the health of the economy.

There will continue to be demand for atmospheric scientists to analyze and monitor the dispersion of pollutants into the air to ensure compliance with federal environmental regulations outlined in the Clean Air Act of 1990, but related employment increases are expected to be small. Opportunities in broadcasting are rare and highly competitive, making for very few job openings.

Earnings

Median annual earnings of atmospheric scientists in 2002 were $60,200. The middle 50 percent earned between $39,970 and $76,880. The lowest 10 percent earned less than $30,220, and the highest 10 percent earned more than $92,430.

The average salary for meteorologists in nonsupervisory, supervisory, and managerial positions employed by the federal government was about $74,528 in 2003. Meteorologists in the federal government with a bachelor's degree and no experience received a starting salary of $23,442 or $29,037, depending on their college grades. Those with a master's degree could start at $35,519 or $42,976; those with the Ph.D., at $51,508. Beginning salaries for all degree levels are slightly higher in areas of the country where the prevailing local pay level is higher.

Related Occupations

Workers in other occupations concerned with the physical environment include environmental scientists and geoscientists, physicists and astronomers, mathematicians, and civil, chemical, and environmental engineers.

Sources of Additional Information

Information about careers in meteorology is available on the Internet from:

- American Meteorological Society. Internet: http://www.ametsoc.org/AMS. Phone: (617) 227-2425.

Information on obtaining a meteorologist position with the federal government is available from the U.S. Office of Personnel Management through a telephone-based system. Consult your telephone directory under U.S. government for a local number or call (703) 724-1850; Federal Relay Service: (800) 877-8339. The first number is not toll free, and charges may result. Information also is available from the Internet site: http://www.usajobs.opm.gov.

Automotive Service Technicians and Mechanics

(O*NET 49-3023.01 and 49-3023.02)

Significant Points

- Formal automotive technician training is the best preparation for these challenging technology-based jobs.

- Opportunities should be very good for automotive service technicians and mechanics with diagnostic and problem-solving skills and knowledge of electronics and mathematics.

- Automotive service technicians and mechanics must continually adapt to changing technology and repair techniques as vehicle components and systems become increasingly sophisticated.

Nature of the Work

Anyone whose car or light truck has broken down knows the importance of the jobs of automotive service technicians and mechanics. The ability to diagnose the source of a problem quickly and accurately requires good reasoning ability and a thorough knowledge of automobiles. Many technicians consider diagnosing hard-to-find troubles one of their most challenging and satisfying duties.

The work of automotive service technicians and mechanics has evolved from mechanical repair to a high technology job. Today, integrated electronic systems and complex computers run vehicles and measure their performance while on the road. Technicians must have an increasingly broad base of knowledge about how vehicles' complex components work and interact, as well as the ability to work with electronic diagnostic equipment and computer-based technical reference materials.

Automotive service technicians and mechanics use their high-tech skills to inspect, maintain, and repair automobiles and light trucks that have gasoline engines. The increasing sophistication of automotive technology now requires workers who can use computerized shop equipment and work with electronic components while maintaining their skills with traditional handtools.

When mechanical or electrical troubles occur, technicians first get a description of the symptoms from the owner or, if they work in a large shop, the repair service estimator who wrote the repair order. To locate the problem, technicians use a diagnostic approach. First, they test to see whether components and systems are proper and secure. Then, they isolate the components or systems that could not logically be the cause of the problem. For example, if an air-conditioner malfunctions, the technician's diagnostic approach can pinpoint a problem as simple as a low coolant level or as complex as a bad drive-train connection that has shorted out the air conditioner. Technicians may have to test drive the vehicle or use a variety of testing equipment, such as onboard and hand-held diagnostic computers or compression gauges, to identify the source of the problem. These tests may indicate whether a component is salvageable or whether a new one is required to get the vehicle back in working order.

During routine service inspections, technicians test and lubricate engines and other major components. In some cases, the technician may repair or replace worn parts before they cause breakdowns that could damage critical components of the vehicle. Technicians usually follow a checklist to ensure that they examine every critical part. Belts, hoses, plugs, brake and fuel systems, and other potentially troublesome items are among those closely watched.

Service technicians use a variety of tools in their work—power tools, such as pneumatic wrenches to remove bolts quickly; machine tools like lathes and grinding machines to rebuild brakes; welding and flame-cutting equipment to remove and repair exhaust systems, and jacks and hoists to lift cars and engines. They also use common handtools, such as screwdrivers, pliers, and wrenches, to work on small parts and in hard-to-reach places.

In modern repair shops, service technicians compare the readouts from diagnostic testing devices with the benchmarked standards given by the manufacturer of the components being tested. Deviations outside of acceptable levels are an indication to the technician that further attention to an area is necessary. The testing devices diagnose problems and make precision adjustments with calculations downloaded from large computerized databases. The computerized systems provide automatic updates to technical manuals and unlimited access to manufacturers' service information, technical service bulletins, and other databases that allow technicians to keep current on problem spots and to learn new procedures.

Automotive service technicians in large shops have increasingly become specialized. For example, *transmission technicians and rebuilders* work on gear trains, couplings, hydraulic pumps, and other parts of transmissions. Extensive knowledge of computer controls, the ability to diagnose electrical and hydraulic problems, and other specialized skills are needed to work on these complex components, which employ some of the most sophisticated technology used in vehicles. *Tuneup technicians* adjust the ignition timing and valves, and adjust or replace spark plugs and other parts to ensure efficient engine performance. They often use electronic testing equipment to isolate and adjust malfunctions in fuel, ignition, and emissions control systems.

Automotive air-conditioning repairers install and repair air-conditioners and service their components, such as compressors, condensers, and controls. These workers require special training in federal and state regulations governing the handling and disposal of refrigerants. *Front-end mechanics* align and balance wheels and repair steering mechanisms and suspension systems. They frequently use special alignment equipment and wheel-balancing machines. *Brake repairers* adjust brakes, replace brake linings and pads, and make other repairs on brake systems. Some technicians and mechanics specialize in both brake and front-end work.

Working Conditions

About half of automotive service technicians work a standard 40-hour week, but almost 30 percent work more than 40 hours a week. Many of those working extended hours are self-employed technicians. To satisfy customer service needs, some service shops offer evening and weekend service. Generally, service technicians work indoors in well-ventilated and -lighted repair shops. However, some shops are drafty and noisy. Although they fix some problems with simple computerized adjustments, technicians frequently work with dirty and greasy parts, and in awkward positions. They often lift heavy parts and tools. Minor cuts, burns, and bruises are common, but technicians usually avoid serious accidents when the shop is kept clean and orderly and safety practices are observed.

Employment

Automotive service technicians and mechanics held about 818,000 jobs in 2002. The majority worked for automotive repair and maintenance shops, automobile dealers, and retailers and wholesalers of automotive parts, accessories, and supplies. Others found employment in gasoline stations; home and auto supply stores; automotive equipment rental and leasing companies; federal, state, and local governments; and other organizations. About 16 percent of service technicians were self-employed, more than twice the proportion for all installation, maintenance, and repair occupations.

Training, Other Qualifications, and Advancement

Automotive technology is rapidly increasing in sophistication, and most training authorities strongly recommend that persons seeking automotive service technician and mechanic jobs complete a formal training program in high school or in a postsecondary vocational school. However, some service technicians still learn the trade solely by assisting and learning from experienced workers.

Many high schools, community colleges, and public and private vocational and technical schools offer automotive service technician training programs. The traditional postsecondary programs usually provide a thorough career preparation that expands upon the student's high school repair experience.

Postsecondary automotive technician training programs vary greatly in format, but normally provide intensive career preparation through a combination of classroom instruction and hands-on practice. Some trade and technical school programs provide concentrated training for 6 months to a year, depending on how many hours the student attends each week. Community college programs normally spread the training over 2 years; supplement the automotive training with instruction in English, basic mathematics, computers, and other subjects; and award an associate degree or certificate. Some students earn repair certificates and opt to leave the program to begin their career before graduation. Recently, some programs have added to their curriculums training on employability skills such as customer service and stress management. Employers find that these skills help technicians handle the additional responsibilities of dealing with the customers and parts vendors.

High school programs, while an asset, vary greatly in quality. The better programs, such as the Automotive Youth Education Service (AYES), with about 150 participating schools and more than 300 participating dealers, conclude with the students receiving their technician's certification and high school diploma. Other programs offer only an introduction to automotive technology and service for the future consumer or hobbyist. Still others aim to equip graduates with enough skills to get a job as a mechanic's helper or trainee mechanic.

The various automobile manufacturers and their participating dealers sponsor 2-year associate degree programs at postsecondary schools across the nation. The Accrediting Commission of Career Schools and Colleges of Technology (ACCSCT) currently certifies a number of automotive and diesel technology schools. Schools update their curriculums frequently to reflect changing technology and equipment. Students in these programs typically spend alternate 6- to 12-week periods attending classes full time and working full time in the service departments of sponsoring dealers. At these dealerships, students get practical experience while assigned to an experienced worker who provides hands-on instruction and timesaving tips.

The National Automotive Technicians Education Foundation (NATEF), an affiliate of the National Institute for Automotive Service Excellence (ASE), establishes the standards by which training facilities become certified. Once the training facility achieves these minimal standards, NATEF recommends the facility to ASE for certification. The ASE certification is a nationally recognized standard for programs offered by high schools, postsecondary trade schools, technical institutes, and community colleges that train automobile service technicians. Automotive manufacturers provide ASE certified instruction, service equipment, and current-model cars on which students practice new skills and learn the latest automotive technology. While ASE certification is voluntary, it does signify that the program meets uniform standards for instructional facilities, equipment, staff credentials, and curriculum. To ensure that programs keep up with ever-changing technology, repair techniques, and ASE standards, the certified programs are subjected to periodic compliance reviews and mandatory recertification. NATEF program experts also review and update program standards to match the level of training and skill-level achievement necessary for success in the occupation. In 2002, about 1,200 high school and postsecondary automotive service technician training programs had been certified by ASE.

For trainee automotive service technician jobs, employers look for people with strong communication and analytical skills. Technicians need good reading, mathematics, and computer skills to study technical manuals and to keep abreast of new technology and learn new service and repair procedures and specifications. Trainees also must possess mechanical aptitude and knowledge of how automobiles work. Most employers regard the successful completion of a vocational training program in automotive service technology as the best preparation for trainee positions. Experience working on motor vehicles in the Armed Forces or as a hobby also is valuable. Because of the complexity of new vehicles, a growing number of employers require completion of high school and additional postsecondary training. Courses in automotive repair, electronics, physics, chemistry, English, computers, and mathematics provide a good educational background for a career as a service technician.

Many new cars have several onboard computers, operating everything from the engine to the radio. Some of the more advanced vehicles have global positioning systems, Internet access, and other high-tech features integrated into the functions of the vehicle. Therefore, knowledge of electronics and computers has grown increasingly important for service technicians. Engine controls and dashboard instruments were among the first components to use electronics but, now, everything from brakes to transmissions and air-conditioning systems to steering systems is run primarily by computers and electronic components. In the past, a specialist usually handled any problems involving electrical systems or electronics. Now that electronics are so common, it is essential for service technicians to be familiar with at least the basic principles of electronics. Electrical components or a series of related components account for nearly all malfunctions in modern vehicles.

In addition to electronics and computers, automotive service technicians will have to learn and understand the science behind the alternate-fuel vehicles that have begun to enter the market. The fuel for these vehicles will come from the dehydrogenization of water, electric fuel cells, natural gas, solar power, and other nonpetroleum-based sources. Some vehicles will even capture the energy from brakes and use it as fuel. As vehicles with these new technologies become more common, technicians will need additional training to learn the science and engineering that makes them possible.

Beginners usually start as trainee technicians, mechanics' helpers, lubrication workers, or gasoline service station attendants, and gradually acquire and practice their skills by working with experienced mechanics and technicians. With a few months' experience, beginners perform many routine service tasks and make simple repairs. It usually takes 2 to 5 years of experience to become a journey-level service technician, who is expected to quickly perform the more difficult types of routine service and repairs. However, some graduates of postsecondary automotive training programs are often able to earn promotion to the journey level after only a few months on the job. An additional 1 to 2 years of experience familiarizes mechanics and technicians with all types of repairs. Difficult specialties, such as transmission repair, require another year or two of training and experience. In contrast, brake specialists may learn their jobs in considerably less time because they do not need a complete knowledge of automotive repair.

In the past, many persons became automotive service technicians through 3- or 4-year formal apprenticeship programs. However, apprenticeships have become rare, as formal vocational training programs in automotive service technology have become more common.

At work, the most important possessions of technicians and mechanics are their handtools. Technicians and mechanics usually provide their own tools, and many experienced workers have thousands of dollars invested in them. Employers typically furnish expensive power tools, engine analyzers, and other diagnostic equipment, but technicians accumulate handtools with experience. Some formal training programs have alliances with tool manufacturers that help entry-level technicians accumulate tools during their training period.

Employers increasingly send experienced automotive service technicians to manufacturer training centers to learn to repair new models or to receive special training in the repair of components, such as electronic fuel injection or air-conditioners. Motor vehicle dealers also may send promising beginners to manufacturer-sponsored mechanic training programs. Employers typically furnish this additional training to maintain or upgrade employees' skills and thus increase the employees' value to the dealership. Factory representatives also visit many shops to conduct short training sessions.

Voluntary certification by the National Institute for Automotive Service Excellence (ASE) has become a standard credential for automotive service technicians. Certification is available in 1 or more of 8 different service areas, such as electrical systems, engine repair, brake systems, suspension and steering, and heating and air-conditioning. For certification in each area, technicians must have at least 2 years of experience and pass a written examination. Completion of an automotive training program in high school, vocational or trade school, or community or junior college may be substituted for 1 year of experience. In some cases, graduates of ASE-certified programs achieve certification in up to three specialties. For certification as a master automotive mechanic, technicians must be certified in all eight areas. Mechanics and technicians must retake each examination at least once every 5 years to maintain their certifications.

Experienced technicians who have leadership ability sometimes advance to shop supervisor or service manager. Those who work well with customers may become automotive repair service estimators. Some with sufficient funds open independent repair shops.

Job Outlook

Job opportunities in this occupation are expected to be very good for persons who complete automotive training programs in high school, vocational and technical schools, or community colleges. Persons with good diagnostic and problem-solving skills, and whose training includes basic electronics skills, should have the best opportunities. For well-prepared people with a technical background, automotive service technician careers offer an excellent opportunity for good pay and the satisfaction of highly skilled work with vehicles incorporating the latest in high technology. However, persons without formal automotive training are likely to face competition for entry-level jobs.

Employment of automotive service technicians and mechanics is expected to increase about as fast as the average through the year 2012. Over the 2002-12 period, population growth will boost demand for motor vehicles, which will require regular maintenance and service. Growth of the labor force and in the number of families in which both spouses need vehicles to commute to work will contribute to increased vehicle sales and employment in this industry. As personal incomes continue to rise, greater numbers of persons will be able to afford the luxury of owning multiple vehicles, which also should increase the number of passenger cars in operation. However, a slowdown in the growth of the driving-age population, as the smaller post-baby boom generation comes of age, may curb demand for cars and trucks. In addition, increasing demand due to growth in the number of vehicles in operation will be partially offset by improvements in vehicle quality and durability that improve reliability and reduce the need for extensive repair and maintenance.

Employment growth will continue to be concentrated in automobile dealerships and independent automotive repair shops. Many new jobs also will be created in small retail operations that offer after-warranty repairs, such as oil changes, brake repair, air-conditioner service, and other minor repairs generally taking less than 4 hours to complete. Employment of automotive service technicians and mechanics in gasoline service stations will continue to decline, as fewer stations offer repair services.

In addition to job openings due to growth, a substantial number of openings will be created by the need to replace experienced technicians who transfer to other occupations or who retire or stop working for other reasons. Most persons who enter the occupation can expect steady work, because changes in general economic conditions and developments in other industries have little effect on the automotive repair business.

Earnings

Median hourly earnings of automotive service technicians and mechanics, including commission, were $14.71 in 2002. The middle 50 percent earned between $10.61 and $19.84. The lowest 10 percent earned less than $8.14, and the highest 10 percent earned more than $25.21. Median annual earnings in the industries employing the largest numbers of service technicians in 2002 were as follows:

Local government	$18.04
Automobile dealers	17.66
Gasoline stations	13.04
Automotive repair and maintenance	12.77
Automotive parts, accessories, and tire stores	12.60

Many experienced technicians employed by automobile dealers and independent repair shops receive a commission related to the labor cost charged to the customer. Under this method, weekly earnings depend on the amount of work completed. Employers frequently guarantee commissioned mechanics and technicians a minimum weekly salary.

Some automotive service technicians are members of labor unions such as the International Association of Machinists and Aerospace Workers; the International Union, United Automobile, Aerospace and Agricultural Implement Workers of America; the Sheet Metal Workers' International Association; and the International Brotherhood of Teamsters.

Related Occupations

Other workers who repair and service motor vehicles include automotive body and related repairers, diesel service technicians and mechanics, and small engine mechanics.

Sources of Additional Information

For more details about work opportunities, contact local automobile dealers and repair shops or local offices of the state employment service. The state employment service also may have information about training programs.

A list of certified automotive service technician training programs can be obtained from:

- National Automotive Technicians Education Foundation, 101 Blue Seal Dr., SE., Suite 101, Leesburg, VA 20175. Internet: http://www.natef.org

For a directory of accredited private trade and technical schools that offer programs in automotive service technician training, contact:

- Accrediting Commission of Career Schools and Colleges of Technology, 2101 Wilson Blvd., Suite 302, Arlington, VA 22201. Internet: http://www.accsct.org

For a list of public automotive service technician training programs, contact:

- SkillsUSA-VICA, P.O. Box 3000, Leesburg, VA 20177-0300. Internet: http://www.skillsusa.org

Information on automobile manufacturer-sponsored programs in automotive service technology can be obtained from:

- Automotive Youth Educational Systems (AYES), 50 W. Big Beaver, Suite 145, Troy, MI 48084. Internet: http://www.ayes.org

Information on how to become a certified automotive service technician is available from:

- National Institute for Automotive Service Excellence (ASE), 101 Blue Seal Dr. SE., Suite 101, Leesburg, VA 20175. Internet: http://www.asecert.org

For general information about a career as an automotive service technician, contact:

- National Automobile Dealers Association, 8400 Westpark Dr., McLean, VA 22102. Internet: http://www.nada.org

- Automotive Retailing Today, 8400 Westpark Dr., MS #2, McLean, VA 22102. Internet: http://www.autoretailing.org

Biological Scientists

(O*NET 19-1020.01, 19-1021.01, 19-1021.02, 19-1022.00, 19-1023.00, and 19-1029.99)

Significant Points

- A Ph.D. degree usually is required for independent research, but a master's degree is sufficient for some jobs in applied research or product development; a bachelor's degree is adequate for some nonresearch jobs.

- Doctoral degree holders face considerable competition for independent research positions, particularly in universities; holders of bachelor's or master's degrees in biological science can expect better opportunities in nonresearch positions.

- Biotechnological research and development will continue to drive employment growth.

Nature of the Work

Biological scientists study living organisms and their relationship to their environment. They research problems dealing with life processes. Most specialize in some area of biology such as zoology (the study of animals) or microbiology (the study of microscopic organisms).

Many biological scientists work in research and development. Some conduct basic research to advance knowledge of living organisms, including viruses, bacteria, and other infectious agents. Basic biological research continues to provide the building blocks necessary to develop solutions to human health problems, and to preserve and repair the natural environment. Biological scientists mostly work independently in private industry, university, or government laboratories, often exploring new areas of research or expanding on specialized research started in graduate school. Those who are not wage and salary workers in private industry typically submit grant proposals to obtain funding for their projects. Colleges and universities, private industry, and federal government agencies, such as the National Institutes of Health and the National Science Foundation, contribute to the support of scientists whose research proposals are determined to be financially feasible and to have the potential to advance new ideas or processes.

Biological scientists who work in applied research or product development use knowledge provided by basic research to develop new drugs and treatments, increase crop yields, and protect and clean up the environment. They usually have less autonomy than basic researchers to choose the emphasis of their research, relying instead on market-driven directions based on the firm's products and goals. Biological scientists doing applied research and product development in private industry may be required to describe their research plans or results to nonscientists who are in a position to veto or approve their ideas, and they must understand the potential cost of their work and its impact on business. Scientists increasingly are working as part of teams, interacting with engineers, scientists of other disciplines, business managers, and technicians. Some biological scientists also work with customers or suppliers and manage budgets.

Those who conduct research usually work in laboratories and use electron microscopes, computers, thermal cyclers, or a wide variety of other equipment. Some conduct experiments using laboratory animals or greenhouse plants. This is particularly true of botanists, physiologists, and zoologists. For some biological scientists, research also is performed outside of laboratories. For example, a botanist might do research in tropical rain forests to see what plants grow there, or an ecologist might study how a forest area

recovers after a fire. Some marine biologists also work outdoors, often on research vessels from which they study various marine organisms such as marine plankton or fish.

Some biological scientists work in managerial or administrative positions, usually after spending some time doing research and learning about the firm, agency, or project. They may plan and administer programs for testing foods and drugs, for example, or direct activities at zoos or botanical gardens. Some work as consultants to business firms or to government, while others test and inspect foods, drugs, and other products.

Recent advances in biotechnology and information technology are transforming the industries in which biological scientists work. In the 1980s, swift advances in basic biological knowledge related to genetics and molecules spurred growth in the field of biotechnology. Biological scientists using this technology manipulate the genetic material of animals or plants, attempting to make organisms more productive or resistant to disease. Research using biotechnology techniques, such as recombining DNA, has led to the production of important substances, including human insulin and growth hormone. Many other substances not previously available in large quantities are starting to be produced by biotechnological means; some may be useful in treating cancer and other diseases. Today, many biological scientists are involved in biotechnology. Those who work on the Human Genome project continue to isolate genes and determine their functionality. This work continues to lead to the discovery of the genes associated with specific diseases and inherited traits, such as certain types of cancer or obesity. These advances in biotechnology have opened up research opportunities in almost all areas of biology, including commercial applications in agriculture, environmental remediation, and the food and chemical industries.

Most biological scientists are further classified by the type of organism they study or by the specific activity they perform, although recent advances in the understanding of basic life processes at the molecular and cellular levels have blurred some traditional classifications.

Aquatic biologists study micro-organisms, plants, and animals living in water. *Marine biologists* study salt water organisms, and *limnologists* study fresh water organisms. Much of the work of marine biology centers on molecular biology, the study of the biochemical processes that take place inside living cells. Marine biologists sometimes are mistakenly called oceanographers, but oceanography is the study of the physical characteristics of oceans and the ocean floor.

Biochemists study the chemical composition of living things. They analyze the complex chemical combinations and reactions involved in metabolism, reproduction, growth, and heredity. Biochemists and molecular biologists do most of their work in the field of biotechnology, which involves understanding the complex chemistry of life.

Botanists study plants and their environment. Some study all aspects of plant life, including algae, fungi, lichens, mosses, ferns, conifers, and flowering plants; others specialize in areas such as identification and classification of plants, the structure and function of plant parts, the biochemistry of plant processes, the causes and cures of plant diseases, the interaction of plants with other organisms and the environment, and the geological record of plants.

Microbiologists investigate the growth and characteristics of microscopic organisms such as bacteria, algae, or fungi. Most microbiologists specialize in environmental, food, agricultural, or industrial microbiology; virology (the study of viruses); or immunology (the study of mechanisms that fight infections). Many microbiologists use biotechnology to advance knowledge of cell reproduction and human disease.

Physiologists study life functions of plants and animals, both in the whole organism and at the cellular or molecular level, under normal and abnormal conditions. Physiologists often specialize in functions such as growth, reproduction, photosynthesis, respiration, or movement, or in the physiology of a certain area or system of the organism.

Biophysicists study the application of principles of physics, such as electrical and mechanical energy and related phenomena, to living cells and organisms.

Zoologists and wildlife biologists study animals and wildlife—their origin, behavior, diseases, and life processes. Some experiment with live animals in controlled or natural surroundings, while others dissect dead animals in order to study their structure. They also may collect and analyze biological data to determine the environmental effects of current and potential use of land and water areas. Zoologists usually are identified by the animal group studied—ornithologists (birds), mammalogists (mammals), herpetologists (reptiles), and ichthyologists (fish).

Ecologists study the relationships among organisms and between organisms and their environments, and the effects of influences such as population size, pollutants, rainfall, temperature, and altitude. Utilizing knowledge of various scientific disciplines, they may collect, study, and report data on the quality of air, food, soil, and water.

Working Conditions

Biological scientists usually work regular hours in offices or laboratories and usually are not exposed to unsafe or unhealthy conditions. Those who work with dangerous organisms or toxic substances in the laboratory must follow strict safety procedures to avoid contamination. Many biological scientists such as botanists, ecologists, and zoologists take field trips that involve strenuous physical activity and primitive living conditions. Biological scientists in the field may work in warm or cold climates, in all kinds of weather. In their research, they may dig, chip with a hammer, scoop with a net, and carry equipment in a backpack. They also may climb, stand, kneel, or dive.

The work of a marine biologist varies dramatically, depending on the type of work involved. Some work in a laboratory, while others work on research ships. Marine biologists who work underwater must practice safe diving while working around sharp coral reefs and hazardous marine life.

Although some marine biologists obtain their specimens from the sea, many still spend a good deal of their time in laboratories and offices, conducting tests, running experiments, recording results, and compiling data.

Some biological scientists depend on grant money to support their research. They may be under pressure to meet deadlines and to conform to rigid grant-writing specifications when preparing proposals to seek new or extended funding.

Employment

Biological scientists held about 75,000 jobs in 2002. Almost half of all biological scientists were employed by federal, state, and local governments. Federal biological scientists worked mainly for the U.S. Departments of Agriculture, Interior, and Defense, and for the National Institutes of Health. Most of the rest worked in scientific research and testing laboratories, the pharmaceutical and medicine manufacturing industry, or hospitals.

In addition, many biological scientists held biology faculty positions in colleges and universities.

Training, Other Qualifications, and Advancement

A Ph.D. degree usually is necessary for independent research, industrial research, and college teaching, and for advancement to administrative positions. A master's degree is sufficient for some jobs in basic research, applied research or product development, management, or inspection; it may also qualify one to work as a research technician or as a teacher in an aquarium. The bachelor's degree is adequate for some nonresearch jobs. For example, some graduates with a bachelor's degree start as biological scientists in testing and inspection, or get jobs related to biological science, such as technical sales or service representatives. In some cases, graduates with a bachelor's degree are able to work in a laboratory environment on their own projects, but this is unusual. Some may work as research assistants, while others become biological laboratory technicians or, with courses in education, high school biology teachers. Many with a bachelor's degree in biology enter medical, dental, veterinary, or other health profession schools.

In addition to required courses in chemistry and biology, undergraduate biological science majors usually study allied disciplines such as mathematics, physics, and computer science. Computer courses are essential, as employers prefer job applicants who are able to apply computer skills to modeling and simulation tasks and to operate computerized laboratory equipment. Those interested in studying the environment also should take courses in environmental studies and become familiar with current legislation and regulations. Prospective biological scientists who hope to work as marine biologists should have at least a bachelor's degree in a biological or marine science. However, students should not overspecialize in undergraduate study, as knowledge of marine biology often is acquired in graduate study. Most colleges and universities offer bachelor's degrees in biological science, and many offer advanced degrees. Curriculums for advanced degrees often emphasize a subfield such as microbiology or botany, but not all universities offer all curriculums. Larger universities frequently have separate departments specializing in different areas of biological science. For example, a program in botany might cover agronomy, horticulture, or plant pathology. Advanced degree programs include classroom and fieldwork, laboratory research, and a thesis or dissertation.

Biological scientists with a Ph.D. often take temporary postdoctoral research positions that provide specialized research experience. In private industry, some may become managers or administrators within the field of biology; others leave biology for nontechnical managerial, administrative, or sales jobs.

Biological scientists should be able to work independently or as part of a team and be able to communicate clearly and concisely, both orally and in writing. Those in private industry, especially those who aspire to management or administrative positions, should possess strong business and communication skills and be familiar with regulatory issues and marketing and management techniques. Those doing field research in remote areas must have physical stamina. Biological scientists also must have patience and self-discipline to conduct long and detailed research projects.

Job Outlook

Despite projected as fast as the average job growth for biological scientists over the 2002-12 period, doctoral degree holders can expect to face competition for basic research positions. The federal government funds much basic research and development, including many areas of medical research that relate to biological science. Recent budget increases at the National Institutes of Health have led to large increases in federal basic research and development expenditures, with research grants growing both in number and in dollar amount. At the same time, the number of newly trained scientists has continued to increase at least as fast as available research funds, so both new and established scientists have experienced difficulty winning and renewing research grants. Currently, about 1 in 3 grant proposals are approved for long-term research projects. If the number of advanced degrees awarded continues to grow, as seems likely based on enrollment trends, this competitive situation will persist. Additionally, applied research positions in private industry may become more difficult to obtain if increasing numbers of scientists seek jobs in private industry because of the competitive job market for independent research positions in universities and for college and university faculty.

Opportunities for those with a bachelor's or master's degree in biological science are expected to be better. The number of science-related jobs in sales, marketing, and research management, for which non-Ph.D.s usually qualify, is

expected to exceed the number of independent research positions. Non-Ph.D.s also may fill positions as science or engineering technicians or health technologists and technicians. Some may become high school biology teachers.

Biological scientists enjoyed very rapid gains in employment between the mid-1980s and mid-1990s, in part reflecting increased staffing requirements in new biotechnology companies. Employment growth should slow somewhat as increases in the number of new biotechnology firms slow and existing firms merge or are absorbed into larger ones. However, much of the basic biological research done in recent years has resulted in new knowledge, including the isolation and identification of genes. Biological scientists will be needed to take this knowledge to the next stage, which is the understanding of how certain genes function within an entire organism, so that gene therapies can be developed to treat diseases. Even pharmaceutical and other firms not solely engaged in biotechnology use biotechnology techniques extensively, spurring employment increases for biological scientists. Expected expansion of research related to health issues, such as AIDS, cancer, and Alzheimer's disease, also should create more jobs for these scientists. In addition, efforts to discover new and improved ways to clean up and preserve the environment will continue to add to job growth. More biological scientists, including some botanists, will be needed to determine the environmental impact of industry and government actions and to prevent or correct environmental problems, while some will find opportunities in environmental regulatory agencies. Botanists also will use their expertise to advise lawmakers on legislation for environmental protection and for ways to save environmentally sensitive areas. There will continue to be demand for biological scientists specializing in botany, zoology, and marine biology, but opportunities will be limited because of the small size of these fields.

Biological scientists are less likely to lose their jobs during recessions than are those in many other occupations because many are employed on long-term research projects. However, an economic downturn could influence the amount of money allocated to new research and development efforts, particularly in areas of risky or innovative research. An economic downturn could also limit the possibility of extension or renewal of existing projects.

Earnings

Median annual earnings of biochemists and biophysicists were $60,390 in 2002. The middle 50 percent earned between $43,110 and $82,080. The lowest 10 percent earned less than $33,930, and the highest 10 percent earned more than $102,930. Median annual earnings of microbiologists were $51,020 in 2002. The middle 50 percent earned between $39,100 and $67,420. The lowest 10 percent earned less than $31,250, and the highest 10 percent earned more than $87,060. Median annual earnings of zoologists and wildlife biologists were $47,740 in 2002. The middle 50 percent earned between $37,100 and $58,040. The lowest 10 percent earned less than $29,260, and the highest 10 percent earned more than $71,270. Median annual earnings of biochemists and biophysicists employed in scientific research and development services were $64,390 in 2002.

According to the National Association of Colleges and Employers, beginning salary offers in 2003 averaged $29,456 a year for bachelor's degree recipients in biological and life sciences; $33,600 for master's degree recipients; and $42,244 for doctoral degree recipients.

In the federal government in 2003, general biological scientists in nonsupervisory, supervisory, and managerial positions earned an average salary of $66,262; microbiologists, $73,513; ecologists, $65,207; physiologists, $85,181; geneticists, $78,652; zoologists, $90,178; and botanists, $55,727.

Related Occupations

Many other occupations deal with living organisms and require a level of training similar to that of biological scientists. These include medical scientists, agricultural and food scientists, and conservation scientists and foresters, as well as health occupations such as physicians and surgeons, dentists, and veterinarians.

Sources of Additional Information

For information on careers in the biological sciences, contact:

- American Institute of Biological Sciences, Suite 200, 1444 I St. NW, Washington, DC 20005. Internet: http://www.aibs.org

For information on careers in biochemistry or biological sciences, contact:

- Federation of American Societies for Experimental Biology, 9650 Rockville Pike, Bethesda, MD 20814. Internet: http://www.faseb.org

For information on careers in microbiology, contact:

- American Society for Microbiology, Office of Education and Training— Career Information, 1325 Massachusetts Ave. NW, Washington, DC 20005. Internet: http://www.asmusa.org

Information on obtaining a biological scientist position with the federal government is available from the U.S. Office of Personnel Management (OPM) through a telephone-based system. Consult your telephone directory under U.S. government for a local number or call (703) 724-1850; Federal Relay Service: (800) 877-8339. The first number is not toll free, and charges may result. Information also is available from the OPM Internet site: http://www.usajobs.opm.gov.

Broadcast and Sound Engineering Technicians and Radio Operators

(O*NET 27-4011.00, 27-4012.00, 27-4013.00, and 27-4014.00)

Significant Points

- Job applicants face strong competition for jobs in major metropolitan areas, where pay generally is higher; prospects are better in small cities and towns.

- Technical school, community college, or college training in electronics, computer networking, or broadcast technology provides the best preparation.

- About 32 percent work in broadcasting, mainly for radio and television stations, and 16 percent work in the motion picture and sound recording industries.

- Evening, weekend, and holiday work is common.

Nature of the Work

Broadcast and sound engineering technicians and radio operators set up, operate, and maintain a wide variety of electrical and electronic equipment involved in almost any radio or television broadcast, concert, play, musical recording, television show, or movie. With such a range of work, there are many specialized occupations within the field.

Audio and video equipment technicians set up and operate audio and video equipment, including microphones, sound speakers, video screens, projectors, video monitors, recording equipment, connecting wires and cables, sound and mixing boards, and related electronic equipment for concerts, sports events, meetings and conventions, presentations, and news conferences. They may also set up and operate associated spotlights and other custom lighting systems.

Broadcast technicians set up, operate, and maintain equipment that regulates the signal strength, clarity, and range of sounds and colors of radio or television broadcasts. They also operate control panels to select the source of the material. Technicians may switch from one camera or studio to another, from film to live programming, or from network to local programming.

Sound engineering technicians operate machines and equipment to record, synchronize, mix, or reproduce music, voices, or sound effects in recording studios, sporting arenas, theater productions, or movie and video productions.

Radio operators mainly receive and transmit communications using a variety of tools. They also are responsible for repairing equipment, using such devices as electronic testing equipment, handtools, and power tools. One of their major duties is to help to maintain communication systems in good condition.

Broadcast and sound engineering technicians and radio operators perform a variety of duties in small stations. In large stations and at the networks, technicians are more specialized, although job assignments may change from day to day. The terms "operator," "engineer," and "technician" often are used interchangeably to describe these jobs. Workers in these positions may monitor and log outgoing signals and operate transmitters; set up, adjust, service, and repair electronic broadcasting equipment; and regulate fidelity, brightness, contrast, volume, and sound quality of television broadcasts.

Technicians also work in program production. *Recording engineers* operate and maintain video and sound recording equipment. They may operate equipment designed to produce special effects, such as the illusions of a bolt of lightning or a police siren. *Sound mixers* or *rerecording mixers* produce the soundtrack of a movie or television program. After filming or recording is complete, they may use a process called "dubbing" to insert sounds. *Field technicians* set up and operate portable transmission equipment outside the studio. Television news coverage requires so much electronic equipment, and the technology is changing so rapidly, that many stations assign technicians exclusively to news.

Chief engineers, transmission engineers, and *broadcast field supervisors* oversee other technicians and maintain broadcasting equipment.

The transition to digital recording, editing, and broadcasting has greatly changed the work of broadcast and sound engineering technicians and radio operators. Software on desktop computers has replaced specialized electronic equipment in many recording and editing functions. Most radio and television stations have replaced video and audio tapes with computer hard drives and other computer data storage systems. Computer networks linked to the specialized equipment dominate modern broadcasting. This transition has forced technicians to learn computer networking and software skills.

Working Conditions

Broadcast and sound engineering technicians and radio operators generally work indoors in pleasant surroundings. However, those who broadcast news and other programs from locations outside the studio may work outdoors in all types of weather. Technicians doing maintenance may climb poles or antenna towers, while those setting up equipment do heavy lifting.

Technicians at large stations and the networks usually work a 40-hour week under great pressure to meet broadcast deadlines, and may occasionally work overtime. Technicians at small stations routinely work more than 40 hours a week. Evening, weekend, and holiday work is usual, because most stations are on the air 18 to 24 hours a day, 7 days a week.

Even though a technician may not be on duty when the station is broadcasting, some technicians may be on call during nonwork hours; that is, they must handle any problems that occur when they are on call.

Those who work on motion pictures may be on a tight schedule and may work long hours to meet contractual deadlines.

Employment

Broadcast and sound engineering technicians and radio operators held about 93,000 jobs in 2002. Their employment was distributed among the following detailed occupations:

Audio and video equipment technicians 42,000

Broadcast technicians 35,000

Sound engineering technicians 13,000

Radio operators 3,000

About 32 percent worked in broadcasting (except Internet) and 16 percent worked in the motion picture and sound recording industries. Almost 1 in 10 were self-employed. Television stations employ, on average, many more technicians than do radio stations. Some technicians are employed in other industries, producing employee communications, sales, and training programs. Technician jobs in television are located in virtually all cities, whereas jobs in radio also are found in many small towns. The highest paying and most specialized jobs are concentrated in New York City, Los Angeles, Chicago, and Washington, DC—the originating centers for most network or news programs. Motion picture production jobs are concentrated in Los Angeles and New York City.

Training, Other Qualifications, and Advancement

The best way to prepare for a broadcast and sound engineering technician job is to obtain technical school, community college, or college training in electronics, computer networking, or broadcast technology. In the motion picture industry, people are hired as apprentice editorial assistants and work their way up to more skilled jobs. Employers in the motion picture industry usually hire experienced freelance technicians on a picture-by-picture basis. Reputation and determination are important in getting jobs.

Beginners learn skills on the job from experienced technicians and supervisors. They often begin their careers in small stations and, once experienced, move on to larger ones. Large stations usually hire only technicians with experience. Many employers pay tuition and expenses for courses or seminars to help technicians keep abreast of developments in the field.

Audio and video equipment technicians generally need a high school diploma. Many recent entrants have a community college degree or various other forms of postsecondary degrees, although that is not always a requirement. They may substitute on-the-job training for formal education requirements. Working in a studio, as an assistant, is a great way of gaining experience and knowledge.

Radio operators do not usually require any formal training. This is an entry-level position that generally requires on-the-job training.

The Federal Communications Commission no longer requires the licensing of broadcast technicians, as the Telecommunications Act of 1996 eliminated this licensing requirement. Certification by the Society of Broadcast Engineers is a mark of competence and experience. The certificate is issued to experienced technicians who pass an examination.

Prospective technicians should take high school courses in math, physics, and electronics. Building electronic equipment from hobby kits and operating a "ham," or amateur, radio are good experience, as is work in college radio and television stations.

Broadcast and sound engineering technicians and radio operators must have manual dexterity and an aptitude for working with electrical, electronic, and mechanical systems and equipment.

Experienced technicians can become supervisory technicians or chief engineers. A college degree in engineering is needed in order to become chief engineer at a large television station.

Job Outlook

People seeking entry-level jobs as technicians in broadcasting are expected to face strong competition in major metropolitan areas, where pay generally is higher and the number of qualified jobseekers typically exceeds the number of openings. There, stations seek highly experienced personnel. Prospects for entry-level positions usually are better in small cities and towns for beginners with appropriate training.

Overall employment of broadcast and sound engineering technicians and radio operators is expected to grow about as fast as the average for all occupations through the year 2012. Job growth in radio and television broadcasting will be limited by consolidation of ownership of radio and television stations, and by laborsaving technical advances such as computer-controlled programming and remotely controlled transmitters. Changes to Federal Communications Commission (FCC) regulations now allow a single owner for up to eight radio stations in a single large market, and rules changes under consideration may have a similar impact on the ownership of television stations. Owners of multiple stations often consolidate the stations into a single location, reducing employment because one or a few technicians can provide support to multiple stations. Technicians who know how to install transmitters will be in demand as television stations install digital transmitters. Although most television stations are broadcasting in both analog and digital

formats and plan to switch entirely to digital, radio stations are only beginning to broadcast digital signals.

Employment of broadcast and sound engineering technicians in the cable and pay television portion of the broadcasting industry should grow as the range of services is expanded to provide, such products as cable Internet access and video-on-demand. Employment of these workers in the motion picture industry will grow rapidly. However, job prospects are expected to remain competitive because of the large number of people who are attracted by the glamour of working in motion pictures.

Projected job growth varies among detailed occupations in this field. Employment of broadcast technicians is expected to grow about as fast as the average for all occupations through 2012, as advancements in technology enhance the capabilities of technicians to produce higher quality radio and television programming. Employment of radio operators is expected to decline as more stations operate transmitters that control programming remotely. Employment of audio and video equipment technicians and sound engineering technicians is expected to grow faster than the average for all occupations. Not only will these workers have to set up audio and video equipment, but it will be necessary for them to maintain and repair this equipment.

In addition to employment growth, job openings also will result from the need to replace experienced technicians who leave this field. Some of these workers leave for other jobs that require knowledge of electronics, such as computer repairer or industrial machinery repairer.

Earnings

Television stations usually pay higher salaries than do radio stations; commercial broadcasting usually pays more than public broadcasting; and stations in large markets pay more than those in small markets.

Median annual earnings of broadcast technicians in 2002 were $27,760. The middle 50 percent earned between $18,860 and $45,200. The lowest 10 percent earned less than $14,600, and the highest 10 percent earned more than $65,970.

Median annual earnings of sound engineering technicians in 2002 were $36,970. The middle 50 percent earned between $24,330 and $57,350. The lowest 10 percent earned less than $18,540, and the highest 10 percent earned more than $82,510.

Median annual earnings of audio and video equipment technicians in 2002 were $31,110. The middle 50 percent earned between $22,670 and $43,950. The lowest 10 percent earned less than $17,710, and the highest 10 percent earned more than $61,420.

Median annual earnings of radio operators in 2002 were $31,530. The middle 50 percent earned between $24,000 and $41,430. The lowest 10 percent earned less than $17,380, and the highest 10 percent earned more than $56,340.

Related Occupations

Broadcast and sound engineering technicians and radio operators need the electronics training necessary to operate technical equipment, and they generally complete specialized postsecondary programs. Occupations with similar characteristics include engineering technicians, science technicians, and electrical and electronics installers and repairers. Broadcast and sound engineering technicians also may operate computer networks, as do computer support specialists and systems administrators. Broadcast technicians on some live radio and television programs are responsible for screening incoming calls, similar to the work of communications equipment operators.

Sources of Additional Information

For career information and links to employment resources, contact:

- National Association of Broadcasters, 1771 N St. NW, Washington, DC 20036. Internet: http://www.nab.org

For information on certification, contact:

- Society of Broadcast Engineers, 9247 North Meridian St., Suite 305, Indianapolis, IN 46260. Internet: http://www.sbe.org

Cardiovascular Technologists and Technicians

(O*NET 29-2031.00)

Significant Points

- Employment will grow faster than the average, but the number of job openings created will be low because the occupation is small.

- Employment of most specialties will grow, but fewer EKG technicians will be needed.

- About 3 out of 4 jobs were in hospitals.

Nature of the Work

Cardiovascular technologists and technicians assist physicians in diagnosing and treating cardiac (heart) and peripheral vascular (blood vessel) ailments. Cardiovascular technologists may specialize in three areas of practice—invasive cardiology, echocardiography, and vascular technology. Cardiovascular technicians who specialize in electrocardiograms (EKGs), stress testing, and Holter monitors are known as *cardiographic* or *EKG technicians*.

Cardiovascular technologists specializing in invasive procedures are called *cardiology technologists*. They assist physicians with cardiac catheterization procedures in which a small tube, or catheter, is wound through a patient's blood vessel from a spot on the patient's leg into the heart. The procedure can determine whether a blockage exists in the blood vessels that supply the heart muscle. The procedure also can help to diagnose other problems. Part of the procedure may involve balloon angioplasty, which can be used to treat blockages of blood vessels or heart valves without the need for heart surgery. Cardiology technologists assist physicians as they insert a catheter with a balloon on the end to the point of the obstruction.

Technologists prepare patients for cardiac catheterization and balloon angioplasty by first positioning them on an examining table and then shaving, cleaning, and administering anesthesia to the top of their leg near the groin. During the procedures, they monitor patients' blood pressure and heart rate with EKG equipment and notify the physician if something appears to be wrong. Technologists also may prepare and monitor patients during open-heart surgery and the implantation of pacemakers.

Cardiovascular technologists who specialize in echocardiography or vascular technology often run noninvasive tests using ultrasound instrumentation, such as Doppler ultrasound. Tests are called "noninvasive" if they do not require the insertion of probes or other instruments into the patient's body. The ultrasound instrumentation transmits high-frequency sound waves into areas of the patient's body and then processes reflected echoes of the sound waves to form an image. Technologists view the ultrasound image on a screen, and may record the image on videotape or photograph it for interpretation and diagnosis by a physician. As the instrument scans the image, technologists check the image on the screen for subtle differences between healthy and diseased areas, decide which images to include in the report to the physician, and judge if the images are satisfactory for diagnostic purposes. They also explain the procedure to patients, record any additional medical history the patient relates, select appropriate equipment settings, and change the patient's position as necessary.

Those who assist physicians in the diagnosis of disorders affecting the circulation are known as *vascular technologists* or *vascular sonographers*. They perform a medical history and evaluate pulses by listening to the sounds of the arteries for abnormalities. Then, they perform a noninvasive procedure using ultrasound instrumentation to record vascular information, such as vascular blood flow, blood pressure, limb volume changes, oxygen saturation, cerebral circulation, peripheral circulation, and abdominal circulation. Many of these tests are performed during or immediately after surgery.

Technologists who use ultrasound to examine the heart chambers, valves, and vessels are referred to as *cardiac sonographers*, or *echocardiographers*. They use ultrasound instrumentation to create images called echocardiograms. An echocardiogram may be performed while the patient is either resting or physically active. Technologists may administer medication to physically active patients to assess their heart function. Cardiac sonographers may also assist physicians who perform transesophageal echocardiography, which involves placing a tube in the patient's esophagus to obtain ultrasound images.

Cardiovascular technicians who obtain EKGs are known as *electrocardiograph* (or *EKG*) *technicians*. To take a basic EKG, which traces electrical impulses transmitted by the heart, technicians attach electrodes to the patient's chest, arms, and legs, and then manipulate switches on an EKG machine to obtain a reading. A printout is made for interpretation by the physician. This test is done before most kinds of surgery or as part of a routine physical examination, especially for persons who have reached middle age or who have a history of cardiovascular problems.

EKG technicians with advanced training perform Holter monitor and stress testing. For Holter monitoring, technicians place electrodes on the patient's chest and attach a portable EKG monitor to the patient's belt. Following 24 or more hours of normal activity by the patient, the technician removes a tape from the monitor and places it in a scanner. After checking the quality of the recorded impulses on an electronic screen, the technician usually prints the information from the tape so that a physician can interpret it later. Physicians use the output from the scanner to diagnose heart ailments, such as heart rhythm abnormalities or problems with pacemakers.

For a treadmill stress test, EKG technicians document the patient's medical history, explain the procedure, connect the patient to an EKG monitor, and obtain a baseline reading and resting blood pressure. Next, they monitor the heart's performance while the patient is walking on a treadmill, gradually increasing the treadmill's speed to observe the effect of increased exertion. Like vascular technologists and cardiac sonographers, cardiographic technicians who perform EKG, Holter monitor, and stress tests are known as "noninvasive" technicians.

Some cardiovascular technologists and technicians schedule appointments, type doctors' interpretations, maintain patient files, and care for equipment.

Working Conditions

Technologists and technicians generally work a 5-day, 40-hour week that may include weekends. Those in catheterization labs tend to work longer hours and may work evenings. They also may be on call during the night and on weekends.

Cardiovascular technologists and technicians spend a lot of time walking and standing. Those who work in catheterization labs may face stressful working conditions because they are in close contact with patients with serious heart ailments. Some patients, for example, may encounter complications from time to time that have life-or-death implications.

Employment

Cardiovascular technologists and technicians held about 43,000 jobs in 2002. About 3 out 4 jobs were in hospitals, primarily in cardiology departments. The remaining jobs were mostly in offices of physicians, including cardiologists; or in medical and diagnostic laboratories, including diagnostic imaging centers.

Training, Other Qualifications, and Advancement

Although a few cardiovascular technologists, vascular technologists, and cardiac sonographers are currently trained on the job, most receive training in 2- to 4-year programs. Cardiovascular technologists, vascular technologists, and cardiac sonographers normally complete a 2-year junior or community college program. The first year is dedicated to core courses and is followed by a year of specialized instruction in either invasive, noninvasive cardiovascular, or noninvasive vascular technology. Those who are qualified in an allied health profession need to complete only the year of specialized instruction.

Graduates from the 29 programs accredited by the Joint Review Committee on Education in Cardiovascular Technology are eligible to obtain professional certification in cardiac catheterization, echocardiography, vascular ultrasound, and cardiographic techniques from Cardiovascular Credentialing International. Cardiac sonographers and vascular technologists also may obtain certification from the American Registry of diagnostic medical sonographers.

For basic EKGs, Holter monitoring, and stress testing, 1-year certification programs exist, but most EKG technicians are still trained on the job by an EKG supervisor or a cardiologist. On-the-job training usually lasts about 8 to 16 weeks. Most employers prefer to train people already in the healthcare field—nursing aides, for example. Some EKG technicians are students enrolled in 2-year programs to become technologists, working part time to gain experience and make contact with employers.

Cardiovascular technologists and technicians must be reliable, have mechanical aptitude, and be able to follow detailed instructions. A pleasant, relaxed manner for putting patients at ease is an asset.

Job Outlook

Employment of cardiovascular technologists and technicians is expected to grow faster than the average for all occupations through the year 2012. Growth will occur as the population ages, because older people have a higher incidence of heart problems. Employment of vascular technologists and echocardiographers will grow as advances in vascular technology and sonography reduce the need for more costly and invasive procedures. However, fewer EKG technicians will be needed, as hospitals train nursing aides and others to perform basic EKG procedures. Individuals trained in Holter monitoring and stress testing are expected to have more favorable job prospects than are those who can perform only a basic EKG.

Some job openings for cardiovascular technologists and technicians will arise from replacement needs, as individuals transfer to other jobs or leave the labor force. However, job growth and replacement needs will produce relatively few job openings because the occupation is small.

Earnings

Median annual earnings of cardiovascular technologists and technicians were $36,430 in 2002. The middle 50 percent earned between $26,730 and $46,570. The lowest 10 percent earned less than $20,920, and the highest 10 percent earned more than $56,080. Median annual earnings of cardiovascular technologists and technicians in 2002 were $36,420 in offices of physicians and $35,800 in general medical and surgical hospitals.

Related Occupations

Cardiovascular technologists and technicians operate sophisticated equipment that helps physicians and other health practitioners to diagnose and treat patients. So do diagnostic medical sonographers, nuclear medicine technologists, radiation therapists, radiologic technologists and technicians, and respiratory therapists.

Sources of Additional Information

For general information about a career in cardiovascular technology, contact:

- Alliance of Cardiovascular Professionals, 4456 Thalia Landing Offices, Bldg. 2, 4356 Bonney Rd., Suite 103, Virginia Beach, VA 23452-1200. Internet: http://www.acp-online.org

For a list of accredited programs in cardiovascular technology, contact:

- Committee on Accreditation for Allied Health Education Programs, 39 East Wacker Dr., Chicago, IL 60601. Internet: http://www.caahep.org
- Joint Review Committee on Education in Cardiovascular Technology, 3525 Ellicott Mills Dr., Suite N, Ellicott City, MD 21043-4547.

For information on vascular technology, contact:

- Society of Vascular Ultrasound, 4601 Presidents Dr., Suite 260, Lanham, MD 20706-4381. Internet: http://www.svunet.org

For information on echocardiography, contact:

- American Society of Echocardiography, 1500 Sunday Dr., Suite 102, Raleigh, NC 27607. Internet: http://www.asecho.org

For information regarding registration and certification, contact:

- Cardiovascular Credentialing International, 1500 Sunday Dr., Suite 102, Raleigh, NC 27607. Internet: http://www.cci-online.org

- American Registry of diagnostic medical sonographers, 51 Monroe St., Plaza East One, Rockville, MD 20850-2400. Internet: http://www.ardms.org

Clinical Laboratory Technologists and Technicians

(O*NET 29-2011.00 and 29-2012.00)

Significant Points

- Clinical laboratory technologists usually have a bachelor's degree with a major in medical technology or in one of the life sciences; clinical laboratory technicians generally need either an associate degree or a certificate.
- Average employment growth is expected as the volume of laboratory tests increases with both population growth and the development of new types of tests.
- Job opportunities are expected to be excellent.

Nature of the Work

Clinical laboratory testing plays a crucial role in the detection, diagnosis, and treatment of disease. Clinical laboratory technologists, also referred to as clinical laboratory scientists or medical technologists, and clinical laboratory technicians, also known as medical technicians or medical laboratory technicians, perform most of these tests.

Clinical laboratory personnel examine and analyze body fluids, tissues, and cells. They look for bacteria, parasites, and other microorganisms; analyze the chemical content of fluids; match blood for transfusions; and test for drug levels in the blood to show how a patient is responding to treatment. These technologists also prepare specimens for examination, count cells, and look for abnormal cells. They use automated equipment and instruments capable of performing a number of tests simultaneously, as well as microscopes, cell counters, and other sophisticated laboratory equipment. Then they analyze the results and relay them to physicians. With increasing automation and the use of computer technology, the work of technologists and technicians has become less hands-on and more analytical.

The complexity of tests performed, the level of judgment needed, and the amount of responsibility workers assume depend largely on the amount of education and experience they have.

Clinical laboratory technologists generally have a bachelor's degree in medical technology or in one of the life sciences, or they have a combination of formal training and work experience. They perform complex chemical, biological, hematological, immunologic, microscopic, and bacteriological tests. Technologists microscopically examine blood, tissue, and other body substances. They make cultures of body fluid and tissue samples, to determine the presence of bacteria, fungi, parasites, or other microorganisms. Clinical laboratory technologists analyze samples for chemical content or a chemical reaction and determine blood glucose and cholesterol levels. They also type and cross match blood samples for transfusions.

Clinical laboratory technologists evaluate test results, develop and modify procedures, and establish and monitor programs, to ensure the accuracy of tests. Some clinical laboratory technologists supervise clinical laboratory technicians.

Technologists in small laboratories perform many types of tests, whereas those in large laboratories generally specialize. Technologists who prepare specimens and analyze the chemical and hormonal contents of body fluids are called clinical chemistry technologists. Those who examine and identify bacteria and other microorganisms are microbiology technologists. Blood bank technologists, or immunohematology technologists, collect, type, and prepare blood and its components for transfusions. Immunology technologists examine elements of the human immune system and its response to foreign bodies. Cytotechnologists prepare slides of body cells and examine these cells microscopically for abnormalities that may signal the beginning of a cancerous growth. Molecular biology technologists perform complex protein and nucleic acid testing on cell samples.

Clinical laboratory technicians perform less complex tests and laboratory procedures than technologists perform. Technicians may prepare specimens and operate automated analyzers, for example, or they may perform manual tests in accordance with detailed instructions. Like technologists, they may work in several areas of the clinical laboratory or specialize in just one. Histotechnicians cut and stain tissue specimens for microscopic examination by pathologists, and phlebotomists collect blood samples. They usually work under the supervision of medical and clinical laboratory technologists or laboratory managers.

Working Conditions

Hours and other working conditions of clinical laboratory technologists and technicians vary with the size and type of employment setting. In large hospitals or in independent laboratories that operate continuously, personnel usually work the day, evening, or night shift and may work weekends and holidays. Laboratory personnel in small facilities may work on rotating shifts, rather than on a regular shift. In some facilities, laboratory personnel are on call several nights a week or on weekends, in case of an emergency.

Clinical laboratory personnel are trained to work with infectious specimens. When proper methods of infection control and sterilization are followed, few hazards exist. Protective masks, gloves, and goggles are often necessary to ensure the safety of laboratory personnel.

Laboratories usually are well lighted and clean; however, specimens, solutions, and reagents used in the laboratory sometimes produce fumes. Laboratory workers may spend a great deal of time on their feet.

Employment

Clinical laboratory technologists and technicians held about 297,000 jobs in 2002. More than half of jobs were in hospitals. Most of the remaining jobs were in offices of physicians and in medical and diagnostic laboratories. A small proportion was in educational services; other ambulatory healthcare services, including blood and organ banks; outpatient care centers; and scientific research and development services.

Training, Other Qualifications, and Advancement

The usual requirement for an entry-level position as a clinical laboratory technologist is a bachelor's degree with a major in medical technology or in one of the life sciences; although it is possible to qualify through a combination of education, on-the-job, and specialized training. Universities and hospitals offer medical technology programs.

Bachelor's degree programs in medical technology include courses in chemistry, biological sciences, microbiology, mathematics, and statistics, as well as specialized courses devoted to knowledge and skills used in the clinical laboratory. Many programs also offer or require courses in management, business, and computer applications. The Clinical Laboratory Improvement Act requires technologists who perform highly complex tests to have at least an associate degree.

Medical and clinical laboratory technicians generally have either an associate degree from a community or junior college or a certificate from a hospital, a vocational or technical school, or one of the U.S. Armed Forces. A few technicians learn their skills on the job.

The National Accrediting Agency for Clinical Laboratory Sciences (NAACLS) fully accredits 467 programs for medical and clinical laboratory technologists, medical and clinical laboratory technicians, histotechnologists and histotechnicians, cytogenetic technologists, and diagnostic molecular scientists. NAACLS also approves 57 programs in phlebotomy and clinical assisting. Other nationally recognized accrediting agencies that accredit specific areas for clinical laboratory workers include the Commission on Accreditation of Allied Health Education Programs and the Accrediting Bureau of Health Education Schools.

Some states require laboratory personnel to be licensed or registered. Information on licensure is available from state departments of health or boards of occupational licensing. Certification is a voluntary process by which a nongovernmental organization, such as a professional society or certifying agency, grants recognition to an individual whose professional competence meets prescribed standards. Widely accepted by employers in the health industry, certification is a prerequisite for most jobs and often is necessary for advancement. Agencies certifying medical and clinical laboratory technologists and technicians include the Board of Registry of the American Society for Clinical Pathology, the American Medical Technologists, the National Credentialing Agency for Laboratory Personnel, and the Board of Registry of the American Association of Bioanalysts. These agencies have different requirements for certification and different organizational sponsors.

Clinical laboratory personnel need good analytical judgment and the ability to work under pressure. Close attention to detail is essential, because small differences or changes in test substances or numerical readouts can be crucial for patient care. Manual dexterity and normal color vision are highly desirable. With the widespread use of automated laboratory equipment, computer skills are important. In addition, technologists in particular are expected to be good at problem solving.

Technologists may advance to supervisory positions in laboratory work or may become chief medical or clinical laboratory technologists or laboratory managers in hospitals. Manufacturers of home diagnostic testing kits and laboratory equipment and supplies seek experienced technologists to work in product development, marketing, and sales. A graduate degree in medical technology, one of the biological sciences, chemistry, management, or education usually speeds advancement. A doctorate is needed to become a laboratory director; however, federal regulation allows directors of moderately complex laboratories to have either a master's degree or a bachelor's degree, combined with the appropriate amount of training and experience. Technicians can become technologists through additional education and experience.

Job Outlook

Job opportunities are expected to be excellent, because the number of job openings is expected to continue to exceed the number of job seekers. Employment of clinical laboratory workers is expected to grow about as fast as the average for all occupations through the year 2012, as the volume of laboratory tests increases with both population growth and the development of new types of tests.

Technological advances will continue to have two opposing effects on employment through 2012. On the one hand, new, increasingly powerful diagnostic tests will encourage additional testing and spur employment. On the other hand, research and development efforts targeted at simplifying routine testing procedures may enhance the ability of nonlaboratory personnel—physicians and patients in particular—to perform tests now conducted in laboratories. Although hospitals are expected to continue to be the major employer of clinical laboratory workers, employment is expected to grow faster in medical and diagnostic laboratories, offices of physicians, and other ambulatory health care services, including blood and organ banks.

Although significant, job growth will not be the only source of opportunities. As in most occupations, many openings will result from the need to replace workers who transfer to other occupations, retire, or stop working for some other reason.

Earnings

Median annual earnings of medical and clinical laboratory technologists were $42,910 in 2002. The middle 50 percent earned between $36,400 and $50,820. The lowest 10 percent earned less than $30,530, and the highest 10 percent earned more than $58,000. Median annual earnings in the industries employing the largest numbers of medical and clinical laboratory technologists in 2002 were as follows:

General medical and surgical hospitals................$43,340

Medical and diagnostic laboratories 42,020

Offices of physicians 38,690

Median annual earnings of medical and clinical laboratory technicians were $29,040 in 2002. The middle 50 percent earned between $23,310 and $35,840. The lowest 10 percent earned less than $19,070, and the highest 10 percent earned more than $43,960. Median annual earnings in the industries employing the largest numbers of medical and clinical laboratory technicians in 2002 were as follows:

General medical and surgical hospitals................$30,500

Colleges, universities, and professional schools 30,350

Offices of physicians 27,820

Medical and diagnostic laboratories 27,550

Other ambulatory health care services 26,710

According to the American Society for Clinical Pathology, median annual wages of staff clinical laboratory technologists and technicians in 2002 varied by specialty as follows:

	Lowest	Average	Highest
Cytotechnologist	$41,454	$49,920	$54,600
Histotechnologist	33,280	41,122	45,760
Medical technologist	33,280	40,186	45,760
Histotechnician	28,413	34,549	38,667
Medical laboratory technician	27,040	31,928	35,776
Phlebotomist	18,720	21,944	25,168

Related Occupations

Clinical laboratory technologists and technicians analyze body fluids, tissue, and other substances, using a variety of tests. Similar or related procedures are performed by chemists and materials scientists, science technicians, and veterinary technologists and technicians.

Sources of Additional Information

For a list of accredited and approved educational programs for clinical laboratory personnel, contact:

- National Accrediting Agency for Clinical Laboratory Sciences, 8410 W. Bryn Mawr Ave., Suite 670, Chicago, IL 60631. Internet: http://www.naacls.org

Information on certification is available from the following organizations:

- American Association of Bioanalysts, Board of Registry, 917 Locust St., Suite 1100, St. Louis, MO 63101. Internet: http://www.aab.org

- American Medical Technologists, 710 Higgins Rd., Park Ridge, IL 60068.

- American Society for Clinical Pathology, Board of Registry, 2100 West Harrison St., Chicago, IL 60612. Internet: http://www.ascp.org/bor

- National Credentialing Agency for Laboratory Personnel, P.O. Box 15945-289, Lenexa, KS 66285. Internet: http://www.nca-info.org

Additional career information is available from the following sources:

- American Association of Blood Banks, 8101 Glenbrook Rd., Bethesda, MD 20814-2749. Internet: http://www.aabb.org

- American Society for Clinical Laboratory Science, 6701 Democracy Blvd., Suite 300, Bethesda, MD 20817. Internet: http://www.ascls.org

- American Society for Clinical Pathology, 2100 West Harrison St., Chicago, IL 60612. Internet: http://www.ascp.org

- American Society for Cytopathology, 400 West 9th St., Suite 201, Wilmington, DE 19801. Internet: http://www.cytopathology.org

- Clinical Laboratory Management Association, 989 Old Eagle School Rd., Wayne, PA 19087. Internet: http://www.clma.org

Communications Equipment Operators

(O*NET 43-2011.00, 43-2021.01, 43-2021.02, and 43-2099.99)

Significant Points

- Switchboard operators hold 3 out of 4 jobs.
- Workers train on the job.
- Employment is expected to decline.

Nature of the Work

Most communications equipment operators work as *switchboard operators* for a wide variety of businesses, such as hospitals, business support services, and employment services. Switchboard operators operate private branch exchange (PBX) or voiceover Internet protocol (VoIP) switchboards to relay incoming, outgoing, and interoffice calls, usually for a single organization. They also may handle other clerical duties, such as supplying information, taking messages, and announcing visitors. Technological improvements have automated many of the tasks handled by switchboard operators. New systems automatically connect outside calls to the correct destination or automated directories, and voicemail systems take messages without the assistance of an operator.

Some communications equipment operators work as *telephone operators*, assisting customers in making telephone calls. Although most calls are connected automatically, callers sometimes require the assistance of an operator. *Central office operators* help customers to complete local and long-distance calls. *Directory assistance operators* provide customers with information such as telephone numbers or area codes.

When callers dial "0," they usually reach a central office operator, also known as a *local, long-distance,* or *call completion operator.* Most of these operators work for telephone companies, and many of their responsibilities have been automated. For example, callers can make international, collect, and credit card calls without the assistance of a central office operator. Other tasks previously handled by these operators, such as billing calls to third parties and monitoring the cost of a call, also have been automated.

Callers still need a central office operator for a limited number of tasks, including placing person-to-person calls or interrupting busy lines if an emergency warrants the disruption. When natural disasters such as storms or earthquakes occur, central office operators provide callers with emergency phone contacts. They also assist callers who are having difficulty with automated phone systems. An operator monitoring an automated system that aids a caller in placing collect calls, for example, may intervene if a caller needs assistance with the system.

Directory assistance operators provide callers with information such as telephone numbers or area codes. Most directory assistance operators work for telephone companies; increasingly, they also work for companies that provide business services. Automated systems now handle many of the responsibilities once performed by directory assistance operators. The systems prompt callers for a listing and may even connect the call after providing the telephone number. However, directory assistance operators monitor many of the calls received by automated systems. The operators listen to recordings of the customer's request and then key information into electronic directories to access the correct telephone numbers. Directory assistance operators also provide personal assistance to customers having difficulty using the automated system.

Other communications equipment operators include workers who operate satellite communications equipment, telegraph equipment, and a wide variety of other communications equipment.

Working Conditions

Most communications equipment operators work in pleasant, well-lighted surroundings. Because telephone operators spend much time seated at keyboards and video monitors, employers often provide workstations designed to decrease glare and other physical discomforts. Such improvements reduce the incidence of eyestrain, back discomfort, and injury due to repetitive motion.

Switchboard operators generally work the same hours as other clerical employees at their company. In most organizations, full-time operators work regular business hours over a 5-day workweek. Work schedules are more irregular in hotels, hospitals, and other organizations that require round-the-clock operator services. In these companies, switchboard operators may work in the evenings and on holidays and weekends.

Central office and directory assistance operators must be accessible to customers 24 hours a day; therefore, they work a variety of shifts. Some operators work split shifts, coming on duty during peak calling periods in the late morning and early evening and going off duty during the intervening hours. Telephone companies normally assign shifts by seniority, allowing the most experienced operators first choice of schedules. As a result, entry-level operators may have less desirable schedules, including late evening, split-shift, and weekend work. Telephone company operators may work overtime during emergencies.

Approximately 1 in 5 communications equipment operators works part time. Because of the irregular nature of telephone operator schedules, many employers seek part-time workers for those shifts that are difficult to fill.

An operator's work may be quite repetitive and the pace hectic during peak calling periods. To maintain operators' efficiency, supervisors at telephone companies often monitor their performance, including the amount of time they spend on each call. The rapid pace of the job and frequent monitoring may cause stress.

Employment

Communications equipment operators held about 304,000 jobs in 2002. About 3 out of 4 worked as switchboard operators. Employment was distributed as follows:

Switchboard operators, including answering service	236,000
Telephone operators	50,000
All other communications equipment operators	19,000

Most switchboard operators worked for services establishments, such as employment services, hospitals, and hotels and motels.

Training, Other Qualifications, and Advancement

Communications equipment operators receive their training on the job. At large telecommunications companies, entry-level central office and directory assistance operators may receive both classroom and on-the-job instruction that can last several weeks. At small telecommunications companies, operators usually receive shorter, less formal training. These operators may be paired with experienced personnel who provide hands-on instruction. Switchboard operators also may receive short-term, informal training, sometimes provided by the manufacturer of their switchboard equipment.

New employees are trained in the operation of their equipment and in procedures designed to maximize efficiency. They are familiarized with company policies, including the expected level of customer service. Instructors monitor both the time and quality of trainees' responses to customer requests. Supervisors may continue to monitor new employees closely after they complete their initial training session.

Employers generally require a high school diploma for operator positions. Applicants should have clear speech, good hearing, and strong reading, spelling, and numerical skills. Computer literacy and typing skills also are important, and familiarity with a foreign language is helpful because of the increasing diversity of the population. Candidates for positions may be required to take an examination covering basic language and math skills. Most companies emphasize customer service and seek operators who will remain courteous to customers while working at a fast pace.

After 1 or 2 years on the job, communications equipment operators may advance to other positions within a company. Many enter clerical occupations in which their operator experience is valuable, such as customer service representative, dispatcher, and receptionist. Operators interested in more technical work may take training classes and advance into positions having to do with installing and repairing equipment. Promotion to supervisory positions also is possible.

Job Outlook

Employment of communications equipment operators is projected to decline through 2012, due largely to new labor-saving communications technologies, the movement of jobs to foreign countries, and consolidation of telephone operator jobs into fewer locations, often staffed by business support or employment services firms. Virtually all job openings will result from the need to replace communications equipment operators who transfer to other occupations or leave the labor force.

Developments in communications technologies—in particular, voice recognition systems that are accessible and easy to use—will continue to have a significant impact on the demand for switchboard operators. Voice recognition technology allows automated telephone systems to recognize human speech. Callers speak directly to the system, which interprets the speech and then connects the call. Because voice recognition systems do not require callers to input data through a telephone keypad, they are easier to use than touch-tone systems. Voice recognition systems are increasingly able to understand sophisticated vocabulary and grammatical structures; however, many companies will continue to employ operators so that those callers who do have problems can access a "live" employee if they desire.

Electronic communication through the Internet or e-mail provides alternatives to telephone communication and requires no operators. Internet directory assistance services are reducing the need for directory assistance operators. Local telephone companies currently have the most reliable telephone directory data; however, Internet services provide information such as addresses and maps, in addition to telephone numbers. As the functions of telephones and computers converge, the convenience of Internet directory assistance is expected to attract many customers, reducing the need for telephone operators to provide this service.

Consolidations among telephone companies also will reduce the need for operators. As communications technologies improve and the prices of long-distance service fall, telephone companies will contract out and consolidate telephone operator jobs, often to other countries. Operators will be employed at fewer locations and will serve larger customer populations.

Earnings

Median hourly earnings of switchboard operators, including answering service, were $10.19 in 2002. The middle 50 percent earned between $8.41 and $12.27. The lowest 10 percent earned less than $7.13, and the highest 10 percent earned more than $14.59. Median hourly earnings in the industries employing the largest numbers of switchboard operators in 2002 are given in the following tabulation:

General medical and surgical hospitals...................$10.20

Offices of physicians 10.20

Traveler accommodation 9.69

Employment services 9.43

Business support services...8.37

Median hourly earnings of telephone operators in 2002 were $13.75. The middle 50 percent earned between $9.86 and $18.35. The lowest 10 percent earned less than $8.09, and the highest 10 percent earned more than $20.80.

Some telephone operators working at telephone companies are members of the Communications Workers of America or the International Brotherhood of Electrical Workers. For these operators, union contracts govern wage rates, wage increases, and the time required to advance from one pay step to the next. It normally takes 4 years to rise from the lowest paying nonsupervisory operator position to the highest. Contracts call for extra pay for work beyond the normal

6 1/2 to 7 1/2 hours a day or 5 days a week, for Sunday and holiday work, and for bilingual positions. A pay differential also is guaranteed for night work and split shifts. Many contracts provide for a 1-week vacation after 6 months of service, 2 weeks after 1 year, 3 weeks after 7 years, 4 weeks after 15 years, and 5 weeks after 25 years. Holidays range from 9 to 11 days a year.

Median hourly earnings of communication equipment operators, all other, in 2002 were $15.21. The middle 50 percent earned between $10.79 and $17.90. The lowest 10 percent earned less than $8.36, and the highest 10 percent earned more than $21.82.

Related Occupations

Other workers who provide information to the general public include dispatchers; hotel, motel, and resort desk clerks; information and record clerks; customer service representatives; receptionists and information clerks; and reservation and transportation ticket agents and travel clerks.

Sources of Additional Information

For more details about employment opportunities, contact a telephone company or temporary help agency, or write to either of the following unions:

- Communications Workers of America, 501 3rd St. NW, Washington, DC 20001.

- International Brotherhood of Electrical Workers, Telecommunications Department, 1125 15th St. NW., Room 807, Washington, DC 20005.

Computer and Information Systems Managers

(O*NET 11-3021.00)

Significant Points

- Projected job growth stems primarily from rapid growth among computer-related occupations.

- Employers prefer managers with formal education and advanced technical knowledge acquired through computer-related work experience.

- Job opportunities should be best for applicants with a master's degree in business administration or management information systems with technology as a core component.

Nature of the Work

The need for organizations to incorporate existing and future technologies in order to remain competitive has become a more pressing issue over the last several years. As electronic commerce becomes more common, how and when companies use technology are critical issues. Computer and information systems managers play a vital role in the technological direction of their organizations. They do everything from constructing the business plan to overseeing network security to directing Internet operations.

Computer and information systems managers plan, coordinate, and direct research and design the computer-related activities of firms. They help determine both technical and business goals in consultation with top management, and make detailed plans for the accomplishment of these goals. For example, working with their staff, they may develop the overall concepts of a new product or service, or may identify how an organization's computing capabilities can effectively aid project management.

Computer and information systems managers direct the work of systems analysts, computer programmers, support specialists, and other computer-related workers. These managers plan and coordinate activities such as installation and upgrading of hardware and software, programming and systems design, development of computer networks, and implementation of Internet and intranet sites. They are increasingly involved with the upkeep and maintenance and security of networks. They analyze the computer and information needs of their organization, from an operational and strategic perspective, and determine immediate and long-range personnel and equipment requirements. They assign and review the work of their subordinates, and stay abreast of the latest technology in order to assure the organization does not lag behind competitors.

The duties of computer and information systems managers vary with their specific titles. *Chief technology officers*, for example, evaluate the newest and most innovative technologies and determine how these can help their organization. The chief technology officer, who often reports to the organization's chief information officer, manages and plans technical standards and tends to the daily information technology issues of the firm. Because of the rapid pace of technological change, chief technology officers must constantly be on the lookout for developments that could benefit their organization. They are responsible for demonstrating to a company how information technology can be used as a competitive tool that not only cuts costs, but also increases revenue and maintains or increases competitive advantage.

Management information systems (MIS) directors manage information systems and computing resources for their entire organization. They may also work under the chief information officer and plan and direct the work of subordinate information technology employees. These managers oversee a variety of user services such as an organization's help desk, which employees can call with questions or problems. MIS directors also may make hardware and software upgrade recommendations based on their experience with an organization's technology. Helping to assure the availability, continuity, and security of data and information technology services are key responsibilities for these workers.

Project managers develop requirements, budgets, and schedules for their firm's information technology projects. They coordinate such projects from development through implementation, working with internal and external clients, vendors, consultants, and computer specialists. These managers are increasingly involved in projects that upgrade the information security of an organization.

LAN/WAN (Local Area Network/Wide Area Network) *managers* provide a variety of services, from design to administration, of an organization's local area network, which connects staff within an organization. These managers direct the network, and its related computing environment, including hardware, systems software, applications software, and all other computer-related configurations.

Computer and information system managers need strong communication skills. They coordinate the activities of their unit with those of other units or organizations. They confer with top executives; financial, production, marketing, and other managers; and contractors and equipment and materials suppliers.

Working Conditions

Computer and information systems managers spend most of their time in an office. Most work at least 40 hours a week and may have to work evenings and weekends to meet deadlines or solve unexpected problems. Some computer and information systems managers may experience considerable pressure in meeting technical goals within short timeframes or tight budgets. As networks continue to expand and more work is done remotely, computer and information system managers have to communicate with and oversee offsite employees using modems, laptops, e-mail, and the Internet.

Like other workers who sit continuously in front of a keyboard, computer and information system managers are susceptible to eyestrain, back discomfort, and hand and wrist problems such as carpal tunnel syndrome.

Employment

Computer and information systems managers held about 284,000 jobs in 2002. About 2 in 5 works in service-providing industries, mainly in computer systems design and related services. This industry provides services related to the commercial use of computers on a contract basis, including custom computer programming services; computer systems integration design services; computer facilities management services, including computer systems or data-processing facilities support services for clients; and other computer-related services, such as disaster recovery services and software installation. Other large employers include insurance and financial services firms, government agencies, and manufacturers.

Training, Other Qualifications, and Advancement

Strong technical knowledge is essential for computer and information systems managers, who must understand and guide the work of their subordinates, yet also explain the work in nontechnical terms to senior management and potential customers. Therefore, these management positions usually require work experience and formal education similar to that of other computer occupations.

Many computer and information systems managers have experience as systems analysts; others may have experience as computer support specialists, programmers, or other information technology professionals. A bachelor's degree usually is required for management positions, although employers often prefer a graduate degree, especially a master's degree in business administration (MBA) with technology as a core component. This degree differs from a traditional MBA in that there is a heavy emphasis on information technology in addition to the standard business curriculum. This is becoming important because more computer and information systems managers are making important technology decisions as well as business decisions for their organizations. Some universities specialize in offering degrees in management information systems, which blend technical core subjects with business, accounting, and communications courses. A few computer and information systems managers may have only an associate degree if they have sufficient experience and were able to learn additional skills on the job. To aid their professional advancement, though, many managers with an associate degree eventually earn a bachelor's or master's degree while working.

Computer and information systems managers need a broad range of skills. In addition to technical skills, employers also seek managers with strong business skills. Employers want managers who have experience with the specific software or technology to be used on the job, as well as a background in either consulting or business management. The expansion of electronic commerce has elevated the importance of business insight, because many managers are called upon to make important business decisions. Managers need a keen understanding of people, management processes, and customers' needs.

Computer and information systems managers must possess strong interpersonal, communication, and leadership skills because they are required to interact not only with their staff, but also with other people inside and outside their organization. They also must possess team skills to work on group projects and other collaborative efforts. Computer and information systems managers increasingly interact with persons outside their organization, reflecting their emerging role as vital parts of their firm's executive team.

Computer and information systems managers may advance to progressively higher leadership positions in their field. Some may become managers in non-technical areas such as marketing, human resources, or sales. In high technology firms, managers in non-technical areas often must possess the same specialized knowledge as do managers in technical areas.

Job Outlook

Employment of computer and information systems managers is expected to grow much faster than the average for all occupations through the year 2012. Technological advancements will boost the employment of computer-related workers; as a result, the demand for managers to direct these workers also will increase. In addition, job openings will result from the need to replace managers who retire or move into other occupations. Opportunities for obtaining a management position will be best for workers possessing an MBA with technology as a core component, or a management information systems degree, advanced technical knowledge, and strong communication and administrative skills.

Despite the recent downturn in the economy, especially in technology-related sectors, the outlook for computer and information systems managers remains strong. In order to remain competitive, firms will continue to install sophisticated computer networks and set up more complex Internet and intranet sites. Keeping a computer network running smoothly is essential to almost every organization. Firms will be more willing to hire managers who can accomplish that.

The security of computer networks will continue to increase in importance as more business is conducted over the Internet. The security of the nation's entire electronic infrastructure has come under renewed focus in light of recent threats. Organizations need to understand how their systems are vulnerable and how to protect their infrastructure and Internet sites from hackers, viruses, and other acts of cyber-terrorism. The emergence of "cyber-security" as a key issue facing most organizations should lead to strong growth for computer managers. Firms will increasingly hire cyber-security experts to fill key leadership roles in their information technology departments, because the integrity of their computing environment is of the utmost concern. As a result, there will be a high demand for managers proficient in computer security issues.

Due to the explosive growth of electronic commerce and the capacity of the Internet to create new relationships with customers, the role of computer and information systems managers will continue to evolve in the future. Persons in these jobs will continue to become more vital to their companies. The expansion of the wireless Internet will spur the need for computer and information systems managers with both business savvy and technical proficiency.

Opportunities for those who wish to become computer and information systems managers should be closely related to the growth of the occupations they supervise and the industries in which they are found.

Earnings

Earnings for computer and information systems managers vary by specialty and level of responsibility. Median annual earnings of these managers in 2002 were $85,240. The middle 50 percent earned between $64,150 and $109,950. The lowest 10 percent earned less than $47,440, and the highest 10 percent earned more than $140,440. Median annual earnings in the industries employing the largest numbers of computer and information systems managers in 2002 were:

Computer systems design and related services $94,240

Management of companies and enterprises 91,710

Insurance carriers..89,920

Depository credit intermediation 75,160

Colleges, universities, and professional schools 68,100

According to Robert Half International, average starting salaries in 2003 for high-level information technology managers ranged from $82,750 to $151,500. According to a 2003 survey by the National Association of Colleges and Employers, starting salary offers for those with an MBA, a technical undergraduate degree, and 1 year or less of experience averaged $54,643; for those with a master's degree in management information systems/business data processing, the starting salary averaged $43,750.

In addition, computer and information systems managers, especially those at higher levels, often receive more employment-related benefits—such as expense accounts, stock option plans, and bonuses—than do non-managerial workers in their organizations.

Related Occupations

The work of computer and information systems managers is closely related to that of computer programmers; computer software engineers; computer systems analysts, database administrators, and computer scientists; and computer support specialists and systems administrators. Computer and information systems managers also have some high-level responsibilities similar to those of top executives.

Sources of Additional Information

For information about a career as a computer and information systems manager, contact the sources of additional information for the various computer occupations discussed elsewhere in this book.

Computer-Control Programmers and Operators

(O*NET 51-4011.01 and 51-4012.00)

Significant Points

- Workers learn in apprenticeship programs, informally on the job, and in secondary, vocational, or postsecondary schools; many entrants have previously worked as machinists or machine setters, operators, and tenders.

- Job opportunities should be excellent, as employers are expected to continue to have difficulty finding qualified workers.

Nature of the Work

Computer-control programmers and operators use computer numerically controlled (CNC) machines to cut and shape precision products, such as automobile parts, machine parts, and compressors. CNC machines include machining tools such as lathes, multiaxis spindles, milling machines, and electrical discharge machines (EDM), but the functions formerly performed by human operators are performed by a computer-control module. CNC machines cut away material from a solid block of metal, plastic, or glass—known as a workpiece—to form a finished part. Computer-control programmers and operators normally produce large quantities of one part, although they may produce small batches or one-of-a-kind items. They use their knowledge of the working properties of metals and their skill with CNC programming to design and carry out the operations needed to make machined products that meet precise specifications.

Before CNC programmers—also referred to as numerical tool and process control programmers—machine a part, they must carefully plan and prepare the operation. First, these workers review three-dimensional computer aided/automated design (CAD) blueprints of the part. Next, they calculate where to cut or bore into the workpiece, how fast to feed the metal into the machine, and how much metal to remove. They then select tools and materials for the job and plan the sequence of cutting and finishing operations.

Next, CNC programmers turn the planned machining operations into a set of instructions. These instructions are translated into a computer aided/automated manufacturing (CAM) program containing a set of commands for the machine to follow. These commands normally are a series of numbers (hence, numerical control) that describes where cuts should occur, what type of cut should be used, and the speed of the cut. CNC programmers and operators check new programs to ensure that the machinery will function properly and that the output will meet specifications. Because a problem with the program could damage costly machinery and cutting tools, computer simulations may be used to check the program instead of a trial run. If errors are found, the program must be changed and retested until the problem is resolved. In addition, growing connectivity between CAD/CAM software and CNC machine tools is raising productivity by automatically translating designs into instructions for the computer controller on the machine tool. These new CAM technologies enable programs to be easily modified for use on other jobs with similar specifications.

After the programming work is completed, CNC operators—also referred to as computer-controlled machine tool operators, metal and plastic—perform the necessary machining operations. The CNC operators transfer the commands from the server to the CNC control module using a computer network link or floppy disk. Many advanced control modules are conversational, meaning that they ask the operator a series of questions about the nature of the task. CNC operators position the metal stock on the CNC machine tool—spindle, lathe, milling machine, or other—set the controls, and let the computer make the cuts. Heavier objects may be loaded with the assistance of other workers, autoloaders, a crane, or a forklift. During the machining process, computer-control operators constantly monitor the readouts from the CNC control module, checking to see if any problems exist. Machine tools have unique characteristics, which can be problematic. During a machining operation, the operator modifies the cutting program to account for any problems encountered. Unique, modified CNC programs are saved for every different machine that performs a task.

CNC operators detect some problems by listening for specific sounds—for example, a dull cutting tool or excessive vibration. Dull cutting tools are removed and replaced. Machine tools rotate at high speeds, which can create problems with harmonic vibrations in the workpiece. Vibrations cause the machine tools to make minor cutting errors, hurting the quality of the product. Operators listen for vibrations and then adjust the cutting speed to compensate. In older, slower machine tools, the cutting speed would be reduced to eliminate the vibrations, but the amount of time needed to finish the product would increase as a result. In newer, high-speed CNC machines, increasing the cutting speed normally eliminates the vibrations and reduces production time. CNC operators also ensure that the workpiece is being properly lubricated and cooled, because the machining of metal products generates a significant amount of heat.

Working Conditions

Most machine shops are clean, well lit, and ventilated. Most modern CNC machines are partially or totally enclosed, minimizing the exposure of workers to noise, debris, and the lubricants used to cool workpieces during machining. Nevertheless, working around high-speed machine tools presents certain dangers, and workers must follow safety precautions. Computer-controlled machine tool operators, metal and plastic, wear protective equipment, such as safety glasses to shield against bits of flying metal and earplugs to dampen machinery noise. They also must exercise caution when handling hazardous coolants and lubricants. The job requires stamina because operators stand most of the day and, at times, may need to lift moderately heavy workpieces.

Numerical tool and process control programmers work on desktop computers in offices that typically are near, but separate from, the shop floor. These work areas usually are clean, well lit, and free of machine noise. Numerical tool and process control programmers occasionally need to enter the shop floor to monitor CNC machining operations. On the shop floor, CNC programmers encounter the same hazards and exercise the same safety precautions as do CNC operators.

Most computer-control programmers and operators work a 40-hour week. CNC operators increasingly work evening and weekend shifts as companies justify investments in more expensive machinery by extending hours of operation. Overtime is common during peak production periods.

Employment

Computer-control programmers and operators held about 151,000 jobs in 2002, mostly working in machine shops, plastics products manufacturing, or machinery manufacturing. Although computer-control programmers and operators work in all parts of the country, jobs are most plentiful in the areas where manufacturing is concentrated.

Training, Other Qualifications, and Advancement

Computer-control programmers and operators train in various ways—in apprenticeship programs, informally on the job, and in secondary, vocational, or postsecondary schools. Due to a shortage of qualified applicants, many employers teach introductory courses, which provide a basic understanding of metalworking machines, safety, and blueprint reading. A basic knowledge of computers and electronics also is helpful. Experience with machine tools is extremely important. In fact, many entrants to these occupations have previously worked as machinists or machine setters, operators, and tenders. Persons interested in becoming computer-control programmers or operators should be mechanically inclined and able to work independently and do highly accurate work.

High school or vocational school courses in mathematics (trigonometry and algebra), blueprint reading, computer programming, metalworking, and drafting are recommended. Apprenticeship programs consist of shop training and related classroom instruction. In shop training, apprentices learn filing, handtapping, and dowel fitting, as well as the operation of various machine tools. Classroom instruction includes math, physics, programming, blueprint reading, CAD software, safety, and shop practices. Skilled computer-control programmers and operators need an understanding of the machining process, including the complex physics that occur at the cutting point. Thus, most training programs teach CNC operators and programmers to perform operations on manual machines prior to operating CNC machines. A growing number of computer-control programmers and operators receive most of their formal training from community or technical colleges. Less skilled CNC operators may need only a couple of weeks of on-the-job training.

To boost the skill level of all metalworkers and to create a more uniform standard of competency, a number of training facilities and colleges have recently begun implementing curriculums incorporating national skills standards developed by the National Institute of Metalworking Skills (NIMS). After completing such a curriculum and passing a performance requirement and written exam, trainees are granted a NIMS credential that provides formal recognition of competency in a metalworking field. Completion of a formal certification program provides expanded career opportunities.

Qualifications for CNC programmers vary widely depending upon the complexity of the job. Employers often prefer skilled machinists or those with technical school training. For some specialized types of programming, such as that needed to produce complex parts for the aerospace or shipbuilding industries, employers may prefer individuals with a degree in engineering.

For those entering CNC programming directly, a basic knowledge of computers and electronics is necessary, and experience with machine tools is extremely helpful. Classroom training includes an introduction to computer numerical control, the basics of programming, and more complex topics, such as computer-aided manufacturing. Trainees start writing simple programs under the direction of an experienced programmer. Although machinery manufacturers are trying to standardize programming languages, there are numerous languages in use. Because of this, computer-control programmers and operators should be able to learn new programming languages.

As new automation is introduced, computer-control programmers and operators normally receive additional training to update their skills. This training usually is provided by a representative of the equipment manufacturer or a local technical school. Many employers offer tuition reimbursement for job-related courses.

Computer-control programmers and operators can advance in several ways. Experienced CNC operators may become CNC programmers, and some are promoted to supervisory or administrative positions in their firms. A few open their own shops.

Job Outlook

Computer-control programmers and operators should have excellent job opportunities. Due to the limited number of people entering training programs, employers are expected to continue to have difficulty finding workers with the necessary skills and knowledge. Employment of computer-controlled machine tool operators is projected to grow more slowly than the average for all occupations through 2012, but employment of numerical tool and process control programmers is expected to grow about as fast as the average for all occupations through 2012. Job growth in both occupations will be driven by the increasing use of CNC machine tools. Advances in CNC machine tools and manufacturing technology will further automate production, boosting CNC operator productivity and limiting employment growth. The demand for computer-control programmers will be negatively affected by the increasing use of software that automatically translates part and product designs into CNC machine tool instructions.

Employment levels of computer-control programmers and operators are influenced by economic cycles—as the demand for machined goods falls, programmers and operators involved in production may be laid off or forced to work fewer hours.

Earnings

Median hourly earnings of computer-controlled machine tool operators, metal and plastic, were $13.97 in 2002. The middle 50 percent earned between $11.07 and $17.43. The lowest 10 percent earned less than $9.14, whereas the top 10 percent earned more than $21.27. Median hourly earnings in the manufacturing industries employing the largest numbers of computer-controlled machine tool operators, metal and plastic, in 2002 were:

Metalworking machinery manufacturing	$15.97
Other fabricated metal product manufacturing	15.14
Machine shops; turned product; and screw, nut, and bolt manufacturing	13.82
Motor vehicle parts manufacturing	13.08
Plastics product manufacturing	11.00

Median hourly earnings of numerical tool and process control programmers were $18.04 in 2002. The middle 50 percent earned between $14.52 and $22.23. The lowest 10 percent earned less than $11.53, while the top 10 percent earned more than $27.37.

Related Occupations

Occupations most closely related to computer-control programmers and operators are other metal worker occupations, which include machinists; tool and die makers; machine setters, operators, and tenders—metal and plastic; and welding, soldering, and brazing workers. Numerical tool and process control programmers apply their knowledge of machining operations, metals, blueprints, and machine programming to write programs that run machine tools. Computer programmers also write detailed programs to meet precise specifications.

Sources of Additional Information

For general information about computer-control programmers and operators, contact:

● Precision Machine Products Association, 6700 West Snowville Rd., Brecksville, OH 44141-3292. Internet: http://www.pmpa.org

For a list of training centers and apprenticeship programs, contact:

● National Tooling and Metalworking Association, 9300 Livingston Rd., Fort Washington, MD 20744. Internet: http://www.ntma.org

For general occupational information, including a list of training programs, contact:

● Precision Metalforming Association Educational Foundation, 6363 Oak Tree Blvd., Independence, OH 44131-2500. Internet: http://www.pmaef.org

Computer Hardware Engineers

(O*NET 17-2061.00)

Nature of the Work

Computer hardware engineers research, design, develop, and test computer hardware and supervise its manufacture and installation. Hardware refers to computer chips, circuit boards, computer systems, and related equipment such as keyboards, modems, and printers. The work of computer hardware engineers is very similar to that of electronics engineers, but, unlike electronics engineers, computer hardware engineers work exclusively with computers and computer-related equipment. In addition to design and development duties, computer hardware engineers may supervise the manufacture and installation of computers and computer-related equipment. The rapid advances in computer technology are largely a result of the research, development, and design efforts of computer hardware engineers. To keep up with technological advances, these engineers must continually update their knowledge.

Employment

The number of computer hardware engineers is relatively small compared with the number of computer-related workers who work with software or computer applications. Computer hardware engineers held about 74,000 jobs in 2002. Almost 40 percent worked in computer and electronic product manufacturing. Almost one-quarter worked in professional, scientific, and technical services firms, many of which provided services to the computer industry. Many of the rest were employed in the telecommunications.

Job Outlook

Computer hardware engineers may face competition for jobs because the number of degrees granted in this field has increased rapidly and because employment is expected grow more slowly than average. Although the use of information technology continues to expand rapidly, the manufacture of computer hardware is expected to be adversely affected by intense foreign competition. Also, this industry is expected to continue to experience very high levels of productivity growth, which will even affect computer hardware engineers. The utilization of foreign computer hardware engineering services also will serve to limit growth. In addition to job openings arising from employment growth, other vacancies will result from the need to replace workers who move into managerial positions, transfer to other occupations, or leave the labor force.

Earnings

Median annual earnings of computer hardware engineers were $72,150 in 2002. The middle 50 percent earned between $56,490 and $91,730. The lowest 10 percent earned less than $46,190, and the highest 10 percent earned more than $114,880. Median annual earnings in the industries employing the largest numbers of computer hardware engineers in 2002 were:

Semiconductor and other electronic component manufacturing $76,600

Computer and peripheral equipment manufacturing 75,300

Computer systems designs and related services 74,320

According to the National Association of Colleges and Employers, starting salary offers in 2003 for bachelor's degree candidates in computer engineering averaged $51,343 a year; master's degree candidates averaged $64,200.

Sources of Additional Information

For further information on careers, education, certification, publications, and conferences related to computer hardware engineers, contact:

● IEEE Computer Society, 1730 Massachusetts Ave. NW, Washington, DC 20036-1992. Internet: http://www.computer.org

See the introduction to the section on engineers for information on working conditions, training requirements, and other sources of additional information.

Computer Operators

(O*NET 43-9011.00)

Significant Points

● Computer operators usually receive on-the-job training; the length of training varies with the job and the experience of the worker.

● Employment is expected to decline sharply due to advances in technology.

- Opportunities will be best for operators who have formal computer-related education, are familiar with a variety of operating systems, and keep up-to-date with the latest technology.

Nature of the Work

Computer operators oversee the operation of computer hardware systems, ensuring that these machines are used as efficiently as possible. They may work with mainframes, minicomputers, or networks of personal computers. Computer operators must anticipate problems and take preventive action, as well as solve problems that occur during operations.

The duties of computer operators vary with the size of the installation, the type of equipment used, and the policies of the employer. Generally, operators control the console of either a mainframe digital computer or a group of minicomputers. Working from operating instructions prepared by programmers, users, or operations managers, computer operators set controls on the computer and on peripheral devices required to run a particular job.

Computer operators load equipment with tapes, disks, and paper, as needed. While the computer is running—which may be 24 hours a day for large computers—computer operators monitor the control console and respond to operating and computer messages. Messages indicate the individual specifications of each job being run. If an error message occurs, operators must locate and solve the problem or terminate the program. Operators also maintain logbooks or operating records, listing each job that is run and events, such as machine malfunctions, that occur during their shift. In addition, computer operators may help programmers and systems analysts test and debug new programs.

As the trend toward networking computers accelerates, a growing number of computer operators are working on personal computers (PCs) and minicomputers. In many offices, factories, and other work settings, PCs and minicomputers are connected in networks, often referred to as local area networks (LANs) or multi-user systems. Whereas users in the area operate some of these computers, many require the services of full-time operators. The tasks performed on PCs and minicomputers are very similar to those performed on large computers.

As organizations continue to look for opportunities to increase productivity, automation is expanding into additional areas of computer operations. Sophisticated software, coupled with robotics, enables a computer to perform many routine tasks formerly done by computer operators. Scheduling, loading and downloading programs, mounting tapes, rerouting messages, and running periodic reports can be done without the intervention of an operator. Consequently, these improvements will change what computer operators do in the future. As technology advances, the responsibilities of many computer operators are shifting to areas such as network operations, user support, and database maintenance.

Working Conditions

Computer operators generally work in well-lighted, well-ventilated, comfortable rooms. Because many organizations use their computers 24 hours a day, 7 days a week, computer operators may be required to work evening or night shifts and weekends. Shift assignments usually are made based on seniority. However, increasingly automated operations will lessen the need for shift work, because many companies can let the computer take over operations during less desirable working hours. In addition, advances in telecommuting technologies—such as faxes, modems, and e-mail—and data center automation, such as automated tape libraries, enable some operators to monitor batch processes, check systems performance, and record problems for the next shift.

Because computer operators generally spend a lot of time in front of a computer monitor, as well as performing repetitive tasks such as loading and unloading printers, they may be susceptible to eyestrain, back discomfort, and hand and wrist problems.

Employment

Computer operators held about 182,000 jobs in 2002. Jobs are found in various industries such as government, wholesale and retail trade, manufacturing, data processing services and other information industries, and finance and insurance. A number of computer operators are employed by firms in computer systems design and related services, as more companies contract out their data processing operations.

Training, Other Qualifications, and Advancement

Computer operators usually receive on-the-job training in order to become acquainted with their employer's equipment and routines. The length of training varies with the job and the experience of the worker. However, previous work experience is the key to obtaining an operator job in many large establishments. Employers generally look for specific, hands-on experience with the type of equipment and related operating systems they use. Additionally, formal computer-related training, perhaps through a community college or technical school, is recommended. Related training also can be obtained through the U.S. Armed Forces and from some computer manufacturers. As computer technology changes and data processing centers become more automated, employers will increasingly require candidates to have formal training and experience for operator jobs. And, although not required, a bachelor's degree in a computer-related field can be helpful when one is seeking employment as a computer operator or advancement to a managerial position.

Because computer technology changes so rapidly, operators must be adaptable and willing to learn. Analytical and technical expertise also are needed, particularly by operators who work in automated data centers, to deal with unique or high-level problems that a computer is not programmed to handle. Operators must be able to communicate well, and to work effectively with programmers, users, and other operators. Computer operators also must be able to work independently because they may have little or no direct supervision.

A few computer operators may advance to supervisory jobs, although most management positions within data processing or computer operations centers require advanced formal education, such as a bachelor's or higher degree. Through on-the-job experience and additional formal education, some computer operators may advance to jobs in areas such as network operations or support. As they gain experience in programming, some operators may advance to jobs as programmers or analysts. A move into these types of jobs is becoming much more difficult, as employers increasingly require candidates for more skilled computer jobs to possess at least a bachelor's degree.

Job Outlook

Employment of computer operators is expected to decline through the year 2012. Experienced operators are expected to compete for job openings that will arise each year to replace workers who transfer to other occupations or leave the labor force. Opportunities will be best for operators who have formal computer-related education, are familiar with a variety of operating systems, and keep up to date with the latest technology.

Advances in technology have reduced both the size and cost of computer equipment, while increasing the capacity for data storage and processing automation. Sophisticated computer hardware and software are now used in practically every industry, in such areas as factory and office automation, telecommunications, medicine, education, and administration. The expanding use of software that automates computer operations gives companies the option of making systems more user-friendly, greatly reducing the need for operators. Such improvements require operators to monitor a greater number of operations at the same time and be capable of solving a broader range of problems that may arise. The result is that fewer operators will be needed to perform more highly skilled work.

Computer operators who are displaced by automation may be reassigned to support staffs that maintain personal computer networks or assist other members of the organization. Operators who keep up with changing technology, by updating their skills and enhancing their training, should have the best prospects of moving into other areas such as network administration and technical support. Others may be retrained to perform different job duties, such as supervising an operations center, maintaining automation packages, or analyzing computer operations to recommend ways in which to increase productivity. In the future, operators who wish to work in the computer field will need to know more about programming, automation software, graphics

interface, client/server environments, and open systems in order to take advantage of changing job opportunities.

Earnings

Median annual earnings of computer operators were $29,650 in 2002. The middle 50 percent earned between about $23,040 and $37,950 a year. The highest 10 percent earned more than $46,780, and the lowest 10 percent earned less than $18,610. Median annual earnings in the industries employing the largest numbers of computer operators in 2002 are shown below:

Management of companies and enterprises $32,770

Computer systems design and related services 30,280

General medical and surgical hospitals..................28,130

Data processing, hosting, and related services 27,440

Depository credit intermediation 24,160

The average salary for computer operators employed by the federal government was $41,117 in 2003.

According to Robert Half International, the average starting salaries for computer operators ranged from $28,250 to $38,500 in 2003. Salaries generally are higher in large organizations than in small ones.

Related Occupations

Other occupations involving work with computers include computer software engineers; computer programmers; computer support specialists and systems administrators; and computer systems analysts, database administrators, and computer scientists. Other occupations in which workers operate electronic office equipment include data entry and information processing workers, as well as secretaries and administrative assistants.

Sources of Additional Information

For information about a career as a computer operator, contact:

- Association of Computer Operations Management (AFCOM), 722 E. Chapman Ave., Orange, CA 92860.

For information about work opportunities in computer operations, contact establishments with large computer centers, such as banks, manufacturing firms, insurance companies, colleges and universities, and data processing service organizations. The local office of the state employment service can supply information about employment and training opportunities.

Computer Programmers

(O*NET 15-1021.00)

Significant Points

- Nearly half of all computer programmers held a bachelor's degree in 2002; about 1 in 5 held a graduate degree.

- Employment is expected to grow much more slowly than that of other computer specialists.

- Prospects should be best for college graduates with knowledge of a variety of programming languages and tools; those with less formal education or its equivalent in work experience should face strong competition for programming jobs.

Nature of the Work

Computer programmers write, test, and maintain the detailed instructions, called programs, that computers must follow to perform their functions. They also conceive, design, and test logical structures for solving problems by computer. Many technical innovations in programming—advanced computing technologies and sophisticated new languages and programming tools—have redefined the role of a programmer and elevated much of the programming work done today. Job titles and descriptions may vary, depending on the organization. In this occupational statement, *computer programmer* refers to individuals whose main job function is programming; this group has a wide range of responsibilities and educational backgrounds.

Computer programs tell the computer what to do—which information to identify and access, how to process it, and what equipment to use. Programs vary widely depending upon the type of information to be accessed or generated. For example, the instructions involved in updating financial records are very different from those required to duplicate conditions on board an aircraft for pilots training in a flight simulator. Although simple programs can be written in a few hours, programs that use complex mathematical formulas, whose solutions can only be approximated, or that draw data from many existing systems may require more than a year of work. In most cases, several programmers work together as a team under a senior programmer's supervision.

Programmers write programs according to the specifications determined primarily by computer software engineers and systems analysts. After the design process is complete, it is the job of the programmer to convert that design into a logical series of instructions that the computer can follow. The programmer then codes these instructions in a conventional programming language, such as COBOL; an artificial intelligence language, such as Prolog; or one of the most advanced object-oriented languages such as Java, C++, or Smalltalk. Different programming languages are used depending on the purpose of the program. COBOL, for example, is commonly used for business applications, whereas Fortran (short for "formula translation") is used in science and engineering. C++ is widely used for both scientific and business applications. Many programmers at the enterprise level are also expected to know platform-specific languages used in database programming. Programmers generally know more than one programming language and, because many languages are similar, they often can learn new languages relatively easily. In practice, programmers often are referred to by the language they know, as are Java programmers, or the type of function they perform or environment in which they work, which is the case for database programmers, mainframe programmers, or Web programmers.

Many programmers update, repair, modify, and expand existing programs. When making changes to a section of code, called a *routine*, programmers need to make other users aware of the task that the routine is to perform. They do this by inserting comments in the coded instructions, so that others can understand the program. Many programmers use computer-assisted software engineering (CASE) tools to automate much of the coding process. These tools enable a programmer to concentrate on writing the unique parts of the program, because the tools automate various pieces of the program being built. CASE tools generate whole sections of code automatically, rather than line by line. Programmers also utilize libraries of pre-written code, which can then be modified or customized for a specific application. This also yields more reliable and consistent programs and increases programmers' productivity by eliminating some routine steps.

Programmers test a program by running it to ensure that the instructions are correct and that the program produces the desired outcome. If errors do occur, the programmer must make the appropriate change and recheck the program until it produces the correct results. This process is called testing and debugging. Programmers may continue to fix these problems throughout the life of a program. Programmers working in a mainframe environment, which involves a large centralized computer, may prepare instructions for a computer operator who will run the program. They also may contribute to a manual for persons who will be using the program.

Programmers often are grouped into two broad types—applications programmers and systems programmers. *Applications programmers* write programs to handle a specific job, such as a program to track inventory within an organization. They may also revise existing packaged software or customize generic applications called middleware. *Systems programmers*, on the other hand, write programs to maintain and control computer systems software, such as operating systems, networked systems, and database systems. These workers make changes in the sets of instructions that determine how the network, workstations, and central processing unit of the system handle the various jobs they have been given, and how they communicate with peripheral equipment such as terminals, printers, and disk drives. Because of their knowledge of the entire computer system, systems programmers often help applications programmers to determine the source of problems that may occur with their programs.

Programmers in software development companies may work directly with experts from various fields to create software—either programs designed for specific clients or packaged software for general use—ranging from games and educational software to programs for desktop publishing and financial planning. Much of this type of programming takes place in the preparation of packaged software, which constitutes one of the most rapidly growing segments of the computer services industry.

In some organizations, particularly small ones, workers commonly known as *programmer-analysts* are responsible for both the systems analysis and the actual programming work. Advanced programming languages and new object-oriented programming capabilities are increasing the efficiency and productivity of both programmers and users. The transition from a mainframe environment to one that is based primarily on personal computers (PCs) has blurred the once rigid distinction between the programmer and the user. Increasingly, adept end-users are taking over many of the tasks previously performed by programmers. For example, the growing use of packaged software, such as spreadsheet and database management software packages, allows users to write simple programs to access data and perform calculations.

Working Conditions

Programmers generally work in offices in comfortable surroundings. Many programmers may work long hours or weekends to meet deadlines or fix critical problems that occur during off hours. Given the technology available, telecommuting is becoming common for a wide range of computer professionals, including computer programmers. As computer networks expand, more programmers are able to make corrections or fix problems remotely by using modems, e-mail, and the Internet to connect to a customer's computer.

Like other workers who spend long periods in front of a computer terminal typing at a keyboard, programmers are susceptible to eyestrain, back discomfort, and hand and wrist problems, such as carpal tunnel syndrome.

Employment

Computer programmers held about 499,000 jobs in 2002. Programmers are employed in almost every industry, but the largest concentrations are in computer systems design and related services and in software publishers, which includes firms that write and sell software. Large numbers of programmers also can be found in management of companies and enterprises, telecommunications companies, manufacturers of computer and electronic equipment, financial institutions, insurance carriers, educational institutions, and government agencies.

A large number of computer programmers are employed on a temporary or contract basis or work as independent consultants, as companies demand expertise with new programming languages or specialized areas of application. Rather than hiring programmers as permanent employees and then laying them off after a job is completed, employers can contract with temporary help agencies, consulting firms, or directly with programmers themselves. A marketing firm, for example, may require the services of several programmers only to write and debug the software necessary to get a new customer resource management system running. This practice also enables companies to bring in people with a specific set of skills—usually in one of the latest technologies—as it applies to their business needs. Bringing in an independent contractor or consultant with a certain level of experience in a new or advanced programming language, for example, enables an establishment to complete a particular job without having to retrain existing workers. Such jobs may last anywhere from several weeks to a year or longer. There were 18,000 self-employed computer programmers in 2002.

Training, Other Qualifications, and Advancement

While there are many training paths available for programmers, mainly because employers' needs are so varied, the level of education and experience employers seek has been rising, due to the growing number of qualified applicants and the specialization involved with most programming tasks. Bachelor's degrees are commonly required, although some programmers may qualify for certain jobs with 2-year degrees or certificates. The associate degree is an increasingly attractive entry-level credential for prospective computer programmers. Most community colleges and many independent technical institutes and proprietary schools offer an associate degree in computer science or a related information technology field.

Employers are primarily interested in programming knowledge, and computer programmers can become certified in a programming language such as C++ or Java. College graduates who are interested in changing careers or developing an area of expertise also may return to a 2-year community college or technical school for additional training. In the absence of a degree, substantial specialized experience or expertise may be needed. Even when hiring programmers with a degree, employers appear to be placing more emphasis on previous experience.

Some computer programmers hold a college degree in computer science, mathematics, or information systems, whereas others have taken special courses in computer programming to supplement their degree in a field such as accounting, inventory control, or another area of business. As the level of education and training required by employers continues to rise, the proportion of programmers with a college degree should increase in the future. As indicated by the following tabulation, 65 percent of computer programmers had a bachelor's or higher degree in 2002.

TABLE 1

Highest level of school completed or degree received, computer programmers, 2002

Level	Percent
High school graduate or equivalent or less	7.7
Some college, no degree	15.2
Associate degree	11.6
Bachelor's degree	48.6
Graduate degree	16.7

Required skills vary from job to job, but the demand for various skills generally is driven by changes in technology. Employers using computers for scientific or engineering applications usually prefer college graduates who have degrees in computer or information science, mathematics, engineering, or the physical sciences. Graduate degrees in related fields are required for some jobs. Employers who use computers for business applications prefer to hire people who have had college courses in management information systems (MIS) and business and who possess strong programming skills. Although knowledge of traditional languages still is important, employers are placing increasing emphasis on newer, object-oriented programming languages and tools, such as C++ and Java. Additionally, employers are seeking persons familiar with fourth- and fifth-generation languages that involve graphic user interface (GUI) and systems programming. Employers also prefer applicants who have general business skills and experience related to the operations of the firm. Students can improve their employment prospects by participating in a college work-study program or by undertaking an internship.

Most systems programmers hold a 4-year degree in computer science. Extensive knowledge of a variety of operating systems is essential for such workers. This includes being able to configure an operating system to work with different types of hardware and having the skills needed to adapt the operating system to best meet the needs of a particular organization. Systems programmers also must be able to work with database systems, such as DB2, Oracle, or Sybase.

When hiring programmers, employers look for people with the necessary programming skills who can think logically and pay close attention to detail. The job calls for patience, persistence, and the ability to work on exacting analytical work, especially under pressure. Ingenuity, creativity, and imagination also are particularly important when programmers design solutions and test their work for potential failures. The ability to work with abstract concepts and to do technical analysis is especially important for systems programmers, because they work with the software that controls the computer's operation. Because programmers are expected to work in teams and interact directly with users, employers want programmers who are able to communicate with nontechnical personnel.

Entry-level or junior programmers may work alone on simple assignments after some initial instruction, or they may be assigned to work on a team with more experienced programmers. Either way, beginning programmers generally must work under close supervision. Because technology changes so rapidly, programmers must continuously update their knowledge and skills by taking courses sponsored by their employer or by software vendors, or offered through local community colleges and universities.

For skilled workers who keep up to date with the latest technology, the prospects for advancement are good. In large organizations, programmers may be promoted to lead programmer and be given supervisory responsibilities. Some applications programmers may move into systems programming after they gain experience and take courses in systems software. With general business experience, programmers may become programmer-analysts or systems analysts or be promoted to a managerial position. Other programmers, with specialized knowledge and experience with a language or operating system, may work in research and development on multimedia or Internet technology, for example. As employers increasingly contract out programming jobs, more opportunities should arise for experienced programmers with expertise in a specific area to work as consultants.

Certification is a way to demonstrate a level of competence, and may provide a jobseeker with a competitive advantage. In addition to language-specific certificates that a programmer can obtain, product vendors or software firms also offer certification and may require professionals who work with their products to be certified. Voluntary certification also is available through other various organizations.

Job Outlook

Employment of programmers is expected to grow about as fast as the average for all occupations through 2012. Jobs for both systems and applications programmers should be most plentiful in data processing service firms, software houses, and computer consulting businesses. These types of establishments are part of computer systems design and related services and software publishers, which are projected to be among the fastest growing industries in the economy over the 2002-12 period. As organizations attempt to control costs and keep up with changing technology, they will need programmers to assist in conversions to new computer languages and systems. In addition, numerous job openings will result from the need to replace programmers who leave the labor force or transfer to other occupations such as manager or systems analyst.

Employment of programmers, however, is expected to grow much more slowly than that of other computer specialists. With the rapid gains in technology, sophisticated computer software now has the capability to write basic code, eliminating the need for more programmers to do this routine work. The consolidation and centralization of systems and applications, developments in packaged software, advances in programming languages and tools, and the growing ability of users to design, write, and implement more of their own programs means that more of the programming functions can be transferred from programmers to other types of workers. Furthermore, as the level of technological innovation and sophistication increases, programmers are likely to face increasing competition from programming businesses overseas, to which much routine work can be contracted out at a lower cost.

Nevertheless, employers will continue to need programmers who have strong technical skills and who understand an employer's business and its programming requirements. This means that programmers will have to keep abreast of changing programming languages and techniques. Given the importance of networking and the expansion of client/server, Web-based, and wireless environments, organizations will look for programmers who can support data communications and help to implement electronic commerce and Intranet strategies. Demand for programmers with strong object-oriented programming capabilities and technical specialization in areas such as client/server programming, wireless applications, multimedia technology, and graphic user interface (GUI) should arise from the expansion of intranets, extranets, and Internet applications. Programmers also will be needed to create and maintain expert systems and embed these technologies in more products. Finally, growing emphasis on cyber-security will lead to increased demand for programmers who are familiar with digital security issues and skilled in using appropriate security technology.

As programming tasks become increasingly sophisticated and additional levels of skill and experience are demanded by employers, graduates of 2-year programs and people with less than a 2-year degree or its equivalent in work experience should face strong competition for programming jobs. Competition for entry-level positions, however, also can affect applicants with a bachelor's degree. Prospects should be best for college graduates with knowledge of, and experience working with, a variety of programming languages and tools—including C++ and other object-oriented languages such as Java, as well as newer, domain-specific languages that apply to computer networking, database management, and Internet application development. Obtaining vendor-specific or language-specific certification also can provide a competitive edge. Because demand fluctuates with employers' needs, jobseekers should keep up to date with the latest skills and technologies. Individuals who want to become programmers can enhance their prospects by combining the appropriate formal training with practical work experience.

Earnings

Median annual earnings of computer programmers were $60,290 in 2002. The middle 50 percent earned between $45,960 and $78,140 a year. The lowest 10 percent earned less than $35,080; the highest 10 percent earned more than $96,860. Median annual earnings in the industries employing the largest numbers of computer programmers in 2002 were:

Professional and commercial equipment and
   supplies merchant wholesalers $70,440
Software publishers 66,870

Computer systems design and related services 65,640
Management of companies and enterprises 59,850
Data processing, hosting, and related services 59,300

According to the National Association of Colleges and Employers, starting salary offers for graduates with a bachelor's degree in computer programming averaged $45,558 a year in 2003.

According to Robert Half International, a firm providing specialized staffing services, average annual starting salaries in 2003 ranged from $51,500 to $80,500 for applications development programmers/analysts, and from $55,000 to $87,750 for software developers. Average starting salaries for mainframe systems programmers ranged from $53,250 to $68,750 in 2003.

Related Occupations

Other professional workers who deal extensively with data include computer software engineers; computer systems analysts, database administrators, and computer scientists; statisticians; mathematicians; engineers; financial analysts and personal financial advisors; accountants and auditors; actuaries; and operations research analysts.

Sources of Additional Information

state employment service offices can provide information about job openings for computer programmers. Municipal chambers of commerce are an additional source of information on an area's largest employers.

Further information about computer careers is available from:

- Association for Computing Machinery (ACM), 1515 Broadway, New York, NY 10036. Internet: http://www.acm.org

- Institute of Electrical and Electronics Engineers Computer Society, Headquarters Office, 1730 Massachusetts Ave. NW, Washington, DC 20036-1992. Internet: http://www.computer.org

- National Workforce Center for Emerging Technologies, 3000 Landerholm Circle SE., Bellevue, WA 98007. Internet: http://www.nwcet.org

Computer Software Engineers

(O*NET 15-1031.00 and 15-1032.00)

Significant Points

- Computer software engineers are projected to be one of the fastest growing occupations over the 2002–12 period.

- Highly favorable opportunities are expected for college graduates with at least a bachelor's degree in computer engineering or computer science and with practical work experience.

- Computer software engineers must continually strive to acquire new skills in conjunction with the rapid changes in computer technology.

Nature of the Work

The explosive impact of computers and information technology on our everyday lives has generated a need to design and develop new computer software systems and to incorporate new technologies in a rapidly growing range of applications. The tasks performed by workers known as computer software engineers evolve quickly, reflecting new areas of specialization or changes in technology, as well as the preferences and practices of employers. Computer software engineers apply the principles and techniques of computer science, engineering, and mathematical analysis to the design, development, testing, and evaluation of the software and systems that enable computers to perform their many applications.

Software engineers working in applications or systems development analyze users' needs and design, construct, test, and maintain computer applications software or systems. Software engineers can be involved in the design and development of many types of software, including software for operating systems and network distribution, and compilers, which convert programs for execution on a computer. In programming, or coding, software engineers instruct a computer, line by line, how to perform a function. They also solve technical problems that arise. Software engineers must possess strong programming skills, but are more concerned with developing algorithms and analyzing and solving programming problems than with actually writing code.

Computer applications software engineers analyze users' needs and design, construct, and maintain general computer applications software or specialized utility programs. These workers use different programming languages, depending on the purpose of the program. The programming languages most often used are C, C++, and Java, with Fortran and COBOL used less commonly. Some software engineers develop both packaged systems and systems software or create customized applications.

Computer systems software engineers coordinate the construction and maintenance of a company's computer systems and plan their future growth. Working with a company, they coordinate each department's computer needs—ordering, inventory, billing, and payroll recordkeeping, for example—and make suggestions about its technical direction. They also might set up the company's intranets—networks that link computers within the organization and ease communication among the various departments.

Systems software engineers work for companies that configure, implement, and install complete computer systems. They may be members of the marketing or sales staff, serving as the primary technical resource for sales workers and customers. They also may be involved in product sales and in providing their customers with continuing technical support.

Computer software engineers often work as part of a team that designs new hardware, software, and systems. A core team may comprise engineering, marketing, manufacturing, and design people who work together until the product is released.

Working Conditions

Computer software engineers normally work in well-lighted and comfortable offices or computer laboratories in which computer equipment is located. Most software engineers work at least 40 hours a week; however, due to the project-oriented nature of the work, they also may have to work evenings or weekends to meet deadlines or solve unexpected technical problems. Like other workers who sit for hours at a computer, typing on a keyboard, software engineers are susceptible to eyestrain, back discomfort, and hand and wrist problems such as carpal tunnel syndrome.

As they strive to improve software for users, many computer software engineers interact with customers and coworkers. Computer software engineers who are employed by software vendors and consulting firms, for example, spend much of their time away from their offices, frequently traveling overnight to meet with customers. They call on customers in businesses ranging from manufacturing plants to financial institutions.

As networks expand, software engineers may be able to use modems, laptops, e-mail, and the Internet to provide more technical support and other services from their main office, connecting to a customer's computer remotely to identify and correct developing problems.

Employment

Computer software engineers held about 675,000 jobs in 2002. About 394,000 were computer applications software engineers, and about 281,000 were computer systems software engineers. Although they are employed in most industries, the largest concentration of computer software engineers, about 30 percent, is in computer systems design and related services. Many computer software engineers also work for establishments in other industries, such as government agencies, manufacturers of computers and related electronic equipment, and colleges and universities.

Employers of computer software engineers range from start-up companies to established industry leaders. The proliferation of Internet, e-mail, and other communications systems expands electronics to engineering firms traditionally associated with unrelated disciplines. Engineering firms specializing in building bridges and power plants, for example, hire computer software engineers to design and develop new geographic data systems and automated drafting systems.

Communications firms need computer software engineers to tap into growth in the personal communications market. Major communications companies have many job openings for both computer software applications and computer systems engineers.

An increasing number of computer software engineers are employed on a temporary or contract basis, with many being self-employed, working independently as consultants. Some consultants work for firms that specialize in developing and maintaining client companies' Web sites and intranets. Consulting opportunities for software engineers should grow as businesses need help managing, upgrading, and customizing increasingly complex computer systems. About 21,000 computer software engineers were self-employed in 2002.

Training, Other Qualifications, and Advancement

Most employers prefer to hire persons who have at least a bachelor's degree and broad knowledge of, and experience with, a variety of computer systems and technologies. Usual degree concentrations for applications software engineers are computer science or software engineering; for systems software engineers, usual concentrations are computer science or computer information systems. Graduate degrees are preferred for some of the more complex jobs.

Academic programs in software engineering emphasize software and may be offered as a degree option or in conjunction with computer science degrees. Increasing emphasis on computer security suggests that software engineers with advanced degrees that include mathematics and systems design will be sought after by software developers, government agencies, and consulting firms specializing in information assurance and security. Students seeking software engineering jobs enhance their employment opportunities by participating in internship or co-op programs offered through their schools. These experiences provide the students with broad knowledge and experience, making them more attractive candidates to employers. Inexperienced college graduates may be hired by large computer and consulting firms that train new hires in intensive, company-based programs. In many firms, new employees are mentored, and their mentors have an input into the new hires' evaluations.

For systems software engineering jobs that require workers who have a college degree, a bachelor's degree in computer science or computer information systems is typical. For systems engineering jobs that place less emphasis on workers having a computer-related degree, computer training programs leading to certification are offered by systems software vendors, including Microsoft, Novell, and Oracle. These programs usually last from 1 to 4 weeks, but the worker is not required to attend classes in order to sit for a certification exam; several study guides also are available to help prepare for the exams. Nonetheless, many training authorities feel that program certification alone is not sufficient for most software engineering jobs.

Professional certification is now offered by the Institute of Electrical and Electronics Engineers (IEEE) Computer Society. To be classified as a Certified Software Development Professional, individuals need a bachelor's degree and work experience that demonstrates that they have mastered a relevant body of knowledge, and must pass a written exam.

Persons interested in jobs as computer software engineers must have strong problem-solving and analytical skills. They also must be able to communicate effectively with team members, other staff, and the customers they meet. Because they often deal with a number of tasks simultaneously, they must be able to concentrate and pay close attention to detail.

As is the case with most occupations, advancement opportunities for computer software engineers increase with experience. Entry-level computer software engineers are likely to test and verify ongoing designs. As they become more experienced, computer software engineers may be involved in designing and developing software. Eventually, they may advance to become a project manager, manager of information systems, or chief information officer. Some computer software engineers with several years of experience or expertise find lucrative opportunities working as systems designers or independent consultants or starting their own computer consulting firms.

As technological advances in the computer field continue, employers demand new skills. Computer software engineers must continually strive to acquire such skills if they wish to remain in this extremely dynamic field. To help them keep up with the changing technology, continuing education and professional development seminars are offered by employers and software vendors, colleges and universities, private training institutions, and professional computing societies.

Job Outlook

Computer software engineers are projected to be one of the fastest growing occupations from 2002 to 2012. Rapid employment growth in the computer systems design and related services industry, which employs the greatest number of computer software engineers, should result in highly favorable opportunities for those college graduates with at least a bachelor's degree in computer engineering or computer science and practical experience working with computers. Employers will continue to seek computer professionals with strong programming, systems analysis, interpersonal, and business skills.

Despite the recent downturn in information technology, employment of computer software engineers is expected to increase much faster than the average for all occupations, as businesses and other organizations adopt and integrate new technologies and seek to maximize the efficiency of their computer systems. Job growth will not be as rapid as growth during the previous decade as the software industry begins to mature and as routine software engineering work is increasingly outsourced overseas. Competition among businesses will continue to create an incentive for increasingly sophisticated technological innovations, and organizations will need more computer software engineers to implement these changes. In addition to jobs created through employment growth, many job openings will result annually from the need to replace workers who move into managerial positions, transfer to other occupations, or leave the labor force.

Despite the recent downturn among firms specializing in information technology, demand for computer software engineers will increase as computer networking continues to grow. For example, the expanding integration of Internet technologies and the explosive growth in electronic commerce—doing business on the Internet—have resulted in rising demand for computer software engineers who can develop Internet, intranet, and World Wide Web applications. Likewise, expanding electronic data-processing systems in business, telecommunications, government, and other settings continue to become more sophisticated and complex. Growing numbers of systems software engineers will be needed to implement, safeguard, and update systems and resolve problems. Consulting opportunities for computer software engineers also should continue to grow as businesses seek help to manage, upgrade, and customize their increasingly complex computer systems.

New growth areas will continue to arise from rapidly evolving technologies. The increasing uses of the Internet, the proliferation of Web sites, and "mobile" technology such as the wireless Internet have created a demand for a wide variety of new products. As individuals and businesses rely more on hand-held computers and wireless networks, it will be necessary to integrate current computer systems with this new, more mobile technology. Also, information security concerns have given rise to new software needs. Concerns over "cyber security" should result in businesses and government continuing to invest heavily in security software that protects their networks and vital electronic infrastructure from attack. The expansion of this technology in the next 10 years will lead to an increased need for computer engineers to design and develop the software and systems to run these new applications and that will allow them to be integrated into older systems.

As with other information technology jobs, employment growth of computer software engineers may be tempered somewhat by an increase in contracting out of software development abroad. Firms may look to cut costs by shifting operations to foreign countries with highly educated workers who have strong technical skills.

Earnings

Median annual earnings of computer applications software engineers who worked full time in 2002 were about $70,900. The middle 50 percent earned between $55,510 and $88,660. The lowest 10 percent earned less than $44,830, and the highest 10 percent earned more than $109,800. Median annual earnings in the industries employing the largest numbers of computer applications software engineers in 2002 were:

Software publishers $76,450
Navigational, measuring, electromedical,
    and control instruments manufacturing..............75,890
Computer systems design and related services 71,890
Architectural, engineering, and related services 70,090
Management of companies and enterprises 67,260

Median annual earnings of computer systems software engineers who worked full time in 2002 were about $74,040. The middle 50 percent earned between $58,500 and $91,160. The lowest 10 percent earned less than $45,890, and the highest 10 percent earned more than $111,600. Median annual earnings in the industries employing the largest numbers of computer systems software engineers in 2002 are shown below:

Scientific research and development services $82,270
Software publishers 77,120
Navigational, measuring, electromedical,
    and control instruments manufacturing..............76,200
Computer systems design and related services 73,460
Wired telecommunications carriers.......................68,510

According to the National Association of Colleges and Employers, starting salary offers for graduates with a bachelor's degree in computer engineering averaged $51,343 in 2003, and those with a master's degree averaged $64,200. Starting salary offers for graduates with a bachelor's degree in computer science averaged $47,109.

According to Robert Half International, starting salaries for software engineers in software development ranged from $64,250 to $97,000 in 2003.

In addition to typical benefits, computer software engineers may be provided with profit sharing, stock options, and a company car with a mileage allowance.

Related Occupations

Other workers who use mathematics and logic extensively include computer systems analysts, database administrators, and computer scientists; computer programmers; financial analysts and personal financial advisors; computer hardware engineers; computer support specialists and systems administrators; statisticians; mathematicians; management analysts; actuaries; and operations research analysts.

Sources of Additional Information

Additional information on a career in computer software engineering is available from any of the following sources:

- Association for Computing Machinery (ACM), 1515 Broadway, New York, NY 10036. Internet: http://www.acm.org

- Institute of Electronics and Electrical Engineers Computer Society, Headquarters Office, 1730 Massachusetts Ave. NW, Washington, DC 20036-1992. Internet: http://www.computer.org

National Workforce Center for Emerging Technologies, 3000 Landerholm Circle SE., Bellevue, WA 98007. Internet: http://www.nwcet.org

Computer Support Specialists and Systems Administrators

(O*NET 15-1041.00 and 15-1071.00)

Significant Points

- Computer support specialists and systems administrators are projected to be among the fastest growing occupations over the 2002-12 period.

- There are many paths of entry to these occupations.

- Job prospects should be best for college graduates who are up to date with the latest skills and technologies; certifications and practical experience are essential for persons without degrees.

Nature of the Work

In the last decade, computers have become an integral part of everyday life, used for a variety of reasons at home, in the workplace, and at schools. And almost every computer user encounters a problem occasionally, whether it is the disaster of a crashing hard drive or the annoyance of a forgotten password. The explosion of computer use has created a high demand for specialists to provide advice to users, as well as day-to-day administration, maintenance, and support of computer systems and networks.

Computer support specialists provide technical assistance, support, and advice to customers and other users. This occupational group includes *technical support specialists* and *help-desk technicians*. These troubleshooters interpret problems and provide technical support for hardware, software, and systems. They answer telephone calls, analyze problems using automated diagnostic programs, and resolve recurrent difficulties. Support specialists may work either within a company that uses computer systems or directly for a computer hardware or software vendor. Increasingly, these specialists work for help-desk or support services firms, where they provide computer support to clients on a contract basis.

Technical support specialists are troubleshooters, providing valuable assistance to their organization's computer users. Because many nontechnical employees are not computer experts, they often run into computer problems that they cannot resolve on their own. Technical support specialists install, modify, clean, and repair computer hardware and software. They also may work on monitors, keyboards, printers, and mice.

Technical support specialists answer telephone calls from their organizations' computer users and may run automatic diagnostics programs to resolve problems. They also may write training manuals and train computer users how to properly use new computer hardware and software. In addition, technical support specialists oversee the daily performance of their company's computer systems and evaluate software programs for usefulness.

Help-desk technicians assist computer users with the inevitable hardware and software questions not addressed in a product's instruction manual. Help-desk technicians field telephone calls and e-mail messages from customers seeking guidance on technical problems. In responding to these requests for guidance, help-desk technicians must listen carefully to the customer, ask questions to diagnose the nature of the problem, and then patiently walk the customer through the problem-solving steps.

Help-desk technicians deal directly with customer issues, and companies value them as a source of feedback on their products. These technicians are consulted for information about what gives customers the most trouble, as well as other customer concerns. Most computer support specialists start out at the help desk.

Network or *computer systems administrators* design, install, and support an organization's LAN (local-area network), WAN (wide-area network), network segment, Internet, or intranet system. They provide day-to-day onsite administrative support for software users in a variety of work environments, including professional offices, small businesses, government, and large corporations. They maintain network hardware and software, analyze problems, and monitor the network to ensure its availability to system users. These workers gather data to identify customer needs and then use that information to identify, interpret, and evaluate system and network requirements. Administrators also may plan, coordinate, and implement network security measures.

Systems administrators are the information technology employees responsible for the efficient use of networks by organizations. They ensure that the design of an organization's computer site allows all of the components, including computers, the network, and software, to fit together and work properly. Furthermore, they monitor and adjust performance of existing networks and continually survey the current computer site to determine future network needs. Administrators also troubleshoot problems as reported by users and automated network monitoring systems and make recommendations for enhancements in the implementation of future servers and networks.

In some organizations, *computer security specialists* may plan, coordinate, and implement the organization's information security. These workers may be called upon to educate users on computer security, install security software, monitor the network for security breaches, respond to cyber attacks, and in some cases, gather data and evidence to be used in prosecuting cyber crime. This and other growing specialty occupations reflect the increasing emphasis on client-server applications, the expansion of Internet and intranet applications, and the demand for more end-user support.

Working Conditions

Computer support specialists and systems administrators normally work in well-lit, comfortable offices or computer laboratories. They usually work about 40 hours a week, but that may include being "on call" via pager or telephone for rotating evening or weekend work if the employer requires computer support over extended hours. Overtime may be necessary when unexpected technical problems arise. Like other workers who type on a keyboard for long periods, computer support specialists and systems administrators are susceptible to eyestrain, back discomfort, and hand and wrist problems such as carpal tunnel syndrome.

Due to the heavy emphasis on helping all types of computer users, computer support specialists and systems administrators constantly interact with customers and fellow employees as they answer questions and give valuable advice. Those who work as consultants are away from their offices much of the time, sometimes spending months working in a client's office.

As computer networks expand, more computer support specialists and systems administrators may be able to connect to a customer's computer remotely, using modems, laptops, e-mail, and the Internet, to provide technical support to computer users. This capability would reduce or eliminate travel to the customer's workplace. Systems administrators also can administer and configure networks and servers remotely, although this practice is not as common as it is with computer support specialists.

Employment

Computer support specialists and systems administrators held about 758,000 jobs in 2002. Of these, about 507,000 were computer support specialists and about 251,000 were network and computer systems administrators. Although they worked in a wide range of industries, 35 percent of all computer support specialists and systems administrators were employed in professional and business services industries, principally in computer systems design and related services. Other organizations that employed substantial numbers of these workers include banks, government agencies, insurance companies, educational institutions, and wholesale and retail vendors of computers, office equipment, appliances, and home electronic equipment. Many computer support specialists also worked for manufacturers of computers, semiconductors, and other electronic components.

Employers of computer support specialists and systems administrators range from startup companies to established industry leaders. With the continued development of the Internet, telecommunications, and e-mail, industries not typically associated with computers—such as construction—increasingly need computer-related workers. Small and large firms across all industries are expanding or developing computer systems, creating an immediate need for computer support specialists and systems administrators.

Training, Other Qualifications, and Advancement

Due to the wide range of skills required, there are many paths of entry to a job as a computer support specialist or systems administrator. While there is no universally accepted way to prepare for a job as a computer support specialist, many employers prefer to hire persons with some formal college education. A bachelor's degree in computer science or information systems is a prerequisite for some jobs; however, other jobs may require only a computer-related associate degree. For systems administrators, many employers seek applicants with bachelor's degrees, although not necessarily in a computer-related field.

Many companies are becoming more flexible about requiring a college degree for support positions because of the explosive demand for specialists. However, certification and practical experience demonstrating these skills will be essential for applicants without a degree. Completion of a certification training program, offered by a variety of vendors and product makers, may help some people to qualify for entry-level positions. Relevant computer experience may substitute for formal education.

Beginning computer support specialists usually work for organizations that deal directly with customers or in-house users. Then, they may advance into more responsible positions in which they use what they have learned from customers to improve the design and efficiency of future products. Job promotions usually depend more on performance than on formal education. Eventually, some computer support specialists become applications developers, designing products rather than assisting users. Computer support specialists at hardware and software companies often enjoy great upward mobility; advancement sometimes comes within months of initial employment.

Entry-level network and computer systems administrators are involved in routine maintenance and monitoring of computer systems, typically working behind the scenes in an organization. After gaining experience and expertise, they often are able to advance into more senior-level positions, in which they take on more responsibilities. For example, senior network and computer systems administrators may present recommendations to management on matters related to a company's network. They also may translate the needs of an organization into a set of technical requirements, based on the available technology. As with support specialists, administrators may become software engineers, actually involved in the designing of the system or network and not just the day-to-day administration.

Persons interested in becoming a computer support specialist or systems administrator must have strong problem-solving, analytical, and communication skills because troubleshooting and helping others are vital parts of the job. The constant interaction with other computer personnel, customers, and employees requires computer support specialists and systems administrators to communicate effectively on paper, via e-mail, or in person. Strong writing skills are useful when preparing manuals for employees and customers.

As technology continues to improve, computer support specialists and systems administrators must keep their skills current and acquire new ones. Many continuing education programs are offered by employers, hardware and software vendors, colleges and universities, and private training institutions. Professional development seminars offered by computing services firms also can enhance one's skills and advancement opportunities.

Job Outlook

Employment of computer support specialist is expected to increase faster than the average for all occupations through 2012, as organizations continue to adopt and integrate increasingly sophisticated technology. Job growth will continue to be driven by the continued expansion of the computer system design and related services industry, which is projected to remain one of the fastest growing industries in the U.S. economy, despite recent job losses. Job growth will not be as explosive as growth during the previous decade as these jobs are being increasingly outsourced overseas.

Employment growth among computer support specialists reflects the rapid pace of improved technology. As computers and software become more complex, support specialists will be needed to provide technical assistance to customers and other users. New mobility technologies, such as the wireless Internet, will continue to create a demand for these workers to familiarize and educate computer users. Consulting opportunities for computer support specialists also should continue to grow as businesses increasingly need help managing, upgrading, and customizing more complex computer systems. However, growth in employment of support specialists may be tempered somewhat as firms continue to cut costs by shifting more routine work abroad to countries where workers are highly skilled but labor costs are lower. Physical location is not as important for these workers as it is for others, because computer support specialists can provide assistance remotely and support services can be provided around the clock.

Employment of systems administrators is expected to increase much faster than average as firms will continue to invest heavily in securing computer networks. Companies are looking for workers knowledgeable about the function and administration of networks. Such employees have become increasingly hard to find as systems administration has moved from being a separate function within corporations to one that forms a crucial element of business in an increasingly high-technology economy. Also, demand for computer security specialists will grow as businesses and government continue to invest heavily in "cyber-security,"

protecting vital computer networks and electronic infrastructure from attack.

The growth of electronic commerce means that more establishments use the Internet to conduct their business online. This translates into a need for information technology specialists who can help organizations use technology to communicate with employees, clients, and consumers. Explosive growth in these areas also is expected to fuel demand for specialists knowledgeable about network, data, and communications security.

Job prospects should be best for college graduates who are up to date with the latest skills and technologies, particularly if they have supplemented their formal education with some relevant work experience. Employers will continue to seek computer specialists who possess a strong background in fundamental computer skills, combined with good interpersonal and communication skills. Due to the rapid growth in demand for computer support specialists and systems administrators, those who have strong computer skills but do not have a bachelor's degree should continue to qualify for some entry-level positions. However, certifications and practical experience are essential for persons without degrees.

Earnings

Median annual earnings of computer support specialists were $39,100 in 2002. The middle 50 percent earned between $29,760 and $51,680. The lowest 10 percent earned less than $23,060, and the highest 10 percent earned more than $67,550. Median annual earnings in the industries employing the largest numbers of computer support specialists in 2002 were:

Professional and commercial equipment and supplies merchant wholesalers	$46,740
Software publishers	42,870
Computer systems design and related services	41,110
Management of companies and enterprises	40,850
Elementary and secondary schools	33,480

Median annual earnings of network and computer systems administrators were $54,810 in 2002. The middle 50 percent earned between $43,290 and $69,530. The lowest 10 percent earned less than $34,460, and the highest 10 percent earned more than $86,440. Median annual earnings in the industries employing the largest numbers of network and computer systems administrators in 2002 were:

Wired telecommunications carriers	$59,710
Computer systems design and related services	58,790
Management of companies and enterprises	58,610
Data processing, hosting, and related services	56,140
Elementary and secondary schools	48,350

According to Robert Half International, starting salaries in 2003 ranged from $27,500 to $56,500 for help-desk support staff and from $51,000 to $67,250 for more senior technical support specialists. For systems administrators, starting salaries in 2003 ranged from $49,000 to $70,250.

Related Occupations

Other computer-related occupations include computer programmers; computer software engineers; and computer systems analysts, database administrators, and computer scientists.

Sources of Additional Information

For additional information about a career as a computer support specialist, contact:

- Association of Computer Support Specialists, 218 Huntington Rd., Bridgeport, CT 06608. Internet: http://www.acss.org

- Association of Support Professionals, 122 Barnard Ave., Watertown, MA 02472.

For additional information about a career as a systems administrator, contact:

- System Administrators Guild, 2560 9th St., Suite 215, Berkeley, CA 94710. Internet: http://www.sage.org

Further information about computer careers is available from:

- National Workforce Center for Emerging Technologies, 3000 Landerholm Circle SE., Bellevue, WA 98007. Internet: http://www.nwcet.org

Computer Systems Analysts, Database Administrators, and Computer Scientists

(O*NET 15-1011.00, 15-1051.00, 15-1061.00, 15-1081.00, and 15-1099.99)

Significant Points

- Education requirements range from a 2-year degree to a graduate degree.

- Employment is expected to increase much faster than the average as organizations continue to adopt increasingly sophisticated technologies.

- Job prospects are favorable.

Nature of the Work

The rapid spread of computers and information technology has generated a need for highly trained workers to design and develop new hardware and software systems and to incorporate new technologies. These workers—computer systems analysts, database administrators, and computer scientists—include a wide range of computer specialists. Job tasks and occupational titles used to describe these workers evolve rapidly, reflecting new areas of specialization or changes in technology, as well as the preferences and practices of employers.

Systems analysts solve computer problems and apply computer technology to meet the individual needs of an organization. They help an organization to realize the maximum benefit from its investment in equipment, personnel, and business processes. Systems analysts may plan and develop new computer systems or devise ways to apply existing systems' resources to additional operations. They may design new systems, including both hardware and software, or add a new software application to harness more of the computer's power. Most systems analysts work with specific types of systems—for example, business, accounting, or financial systems, or scientific and engineering systems—that vary with the kind of organization. Some systems analysts also are known as *systems developers* or *systems architects*.

Systems analysts begin an assignment by discussing the systems problem with managers and users to determine its exact nature. Defining the goals of the system and dividing the solutions into individual steps and separate procedures, systems analysts use techniques such as structured analysis, data modeling, information engineering, mathematical model building, sampling, and cost accounting to plan the system. They specify the inputs to be accessed by the system, design the processing steps, and format the output to meet users' needs. They also may prepare cost-benefit and return-on-investment analyses to help management decide whether implementing the proposed technology will be financially feasible.

When a system is accepted, systems analysts determine what computer hardware and software will be needed to set the system up. They coordinate tests and observe the initial use of the system to ensure that it performs as planned. They prepare specifications, flow charts, and process diagrams for computer programmers to follow; then, they work with programmers to "debug," or eliminate, errors from the system. Systems analysts who do more in-depth testing of products may be referred to as *software quality assurance analysts*. In addition to running tests, these individuals diagnose problems, recommend solutions, and determine whether program requirements have been met.

In some organizations, *programmer-analysts* design and update the software that a computer runs. Because they are responsible for both programming and systems analysis, these workers must be proficient in both areas. As this dual proficiency becomes more commonplace, these analysts increasingly work with databases, object-oriented programming languages, as well as client–server applications development and multimedia and Internet technology.

One obstacle associated with expanding computer use is the need for different computer systems to communicate with each other. Because of the importance of maintaining up-to-date information—accounting records, sales figures, or budget projections, for example—systems analysts work on making the computer systems within an organization, or among organizations, compatible so that information can be shared among them. Many systems analysts are involved with "networking," connecting all the computers internally—in an individual office, department, or establishment—or externally, because many organizations now rely on e-mail or the Internet. A primary goal of networking is to allow users to retrieve data from a mainframe computer or a server and use it on their desktop computer. Systems analysts must design the hardware and software to allow the free exchange of data, custom applications, and the computer power to process it all. For example, analysts are called upon to ensure the compatibility of computing systems between and among businesses to facilitate electronic commerce.

Networks come in many variations, so *network systems and data communications analysts* are needed to design, test, and evaluate systems such as local area networks (LANs), wide area networks (WANs), the Internet, intranets, and other data communications systems. Systems can range from a connection between two offices in the same building to globally distributed networks, voice mail, and e-mail systems of a multinational organization. Network systems and data communications analysts perform network modeling, analysis, and planning; they also may research related products and make necessary hardware and software recommendations. *Telecommunications specialists* focus on the interaction between computer and communications equipment. These workers design voice and data communication systems, supervise the installation of those systems, and provide maintenance and other services to clients after the system is installed.

The growth of the Internet and the expansion of the World Wide Web (the graphical portion of the Internet) have generated a variety of occupations related to the design, development, and maintenance of Web sites and their servers. For example, *webmasters* are responsible for all technical aspects of a Web site, including performance issues such as speed of access, and for approving the content of the site. *Internet developers* or *Web developers*, also called *Web designers*, are responsible for day-to-day site design and creation.

Computer scientists work as theorists, researchers, or inventors. Their jobs are distinguished by the higher level of theoretical expertise and innovation they apply to complex problems and the creation or application of new technology. Those employed by academic institutions work in areas ranging from complexity theory, to hardware, to programming-language design. Some work on multidisciplinary projects, such as developing and advancing uses of virtual reality, extending human-computer interaction, or design-

ing robots. Their counterparts in private industry work in areas such as applying theory, developing specialized languages or information technologies, or designing programming tools, knowledge-based systems, or even computer games.

With the Internet and electronic business generating large volumes of data, there is a growing need to be able to store, manage, and extract data effectively. *Database administrators* work with database management systems software and determine ways to organize and store data. They identify user requirements, set up computer databases, and test and coordinate modifications to the systems. An organization's database administrator ensures the performance of the system, understands the platform on which the database runs, and adds new users to the system. Because they also may design and implement system security, database administrators often plan and coordinate security measures. With the volume of sensitive data generated every second growing rapidly, data integrity, backup systems, and database security have become increasingly important aspects of the job of database administrators.

Working Conditions

Computer systems analysts, database administrators, and computer scientists normally work in offices or laboratories in comfortable surroundings. They usually work about 40 hours a week—the same as many other professional or office workers do. However, evening or weekend work may be necessary to meet deadlines or solve specific problems. Given the technology available today, telecommuting is common for computer professionals. As networks expand, more work can be done from remote locations through modems, laptops, electronic mail, and the Internet.

Like other workers who spend long periods in front of a computer terminal typing on a keyboard, computer systems analysts, database administrators, and computer scientists are susceptible to eyestrain, back discomfort, and hand and wrist problems such as carpal tunnel syndrome or cumulative trauma disorder.

Employment

Computer systems analysts, database administrators, and computer scientists held about 979,000 jobs in 2002; including about 89,000 who were self-employed. Employment was distributed among the following detailed occupations:

Computer systems analysts	468,000
Network systems and data communications analysts	186,000
Database administrators	110,000
Computer and information scientists, research	23,000
All other computer specialists	192,000

Although they are increasingly employed in every sector of the economy, the greatest concentration of these workers is in the computer systems design and related services industry. Firms in this industry provide services related to the commercial use of computers on a contract basis, including custom computer programming services; computer systems integration design services; computer facilities management services, including computer systems or data-processing facilities support services for clients; and other computer-related services, such as disaster recovery services and software installation. Many computer systems analysts, database administrators, and computer scientists are employed by Internet service providers, web search portals, and data-processing, hosting, and related services firms. Others work for government, manufacturers of computer and electronic products, insurance companies, financial institutions, and universities.

A growing number of computer specialists, such as systems analysts and network and data communications analysts, are employed on a temporary or contract basis; many of these individuals are self-employed, working independently as contractors or consultants. For example, a company installing a new computer system may need the services of several systems analysts just to get the system running. Because not all of the analysts would be needed once the system is functioning, the company might contract for such employees with a temporary help agency or a consulting firm or with the systems analysts themselves. Such jobs may last from several months up to 2 years or more. This growing practice enables companies to bring in people with the exact skills the firm needs to complete a particular project, rather than having to spend time or money training or retraining existing workers. Often, experienced consultants then train a company's in-house staff as a project develops.

Training, Other Qualifications, and Advancement

Rapidly changing technology requires an increasing level of skill and education on the part of employees. Companies look for professionals with an ever-broader background and range of skills, including not only technical knowledge, but also communication and other interpersonal skills. This shift from requiring workers to possess solely sound technical knowledge emphasizes workers who can handle various responsibilities. While there is no universally accepted way to prepare for a job as a systems analyst, computer scientist, or database administrator, most employers place a premium on some formal college education. A bachelor's degree is a prerequisite for many jobs; however, some jobs may require only a 2-year degree. Relevant work experience also is very important. For more technically complex jobs, persons with graduate degrees are preferred.

For systems analyst, programmer-analyst, and database administrator positions, many employers seek applicants who have a bachelor's degree in computer science, information science, or management information systems (MIS). MIS programs usually are part of the business school or college and differ considerably from computer science

ograms, emphasizing business and management-oriented course work and business computing courses. Employers are increasingly seeking individuals with a master's degree in business administration (MBA), with a concentration in information systems, as more firms move their business to the Internet. For some network systems and data communication analysts, such as webmasters, an associate's degree or certificate is sufficient, although more advanced positions might require a computer-related bachelor's degree. For computer and information scientists, a doctoral degree generally is required due to the highly technical nature of their work.

Despite employers' preference for those with technical degrees, persons with degrees in a variety of majors find employment in these computer occupations. The level of education and type of training that employers require depend on their needs. One factor affecting these needs is changes in technology. Employers often scramble to find workers capable of implementing "hot" new technologies. Those workers with formal education or experience in information security, for example, are in demand because of the growing need for their skills and services. Another factor driving employers' needs is the timeframe during which a project must be completed.

Most community colleges and many independent technical institutes and proprietary schools offer an associate's degree in computer science or a related information technology field. Many of these programs may be more geared toward meeting the needs of local businesses and are more occupation specific than are 4-year degree programs. Some jobs may be better suited to the level of training that such programs offer. Employers usually look for people who have broad knowledge and experience related to computer systems and technologies, strong problem-solving and analytical skills, and good interpersonal skills. Courses in computer science or systems design offer good preparation for a job in these computer occupations. For jobs in a business environment, employers usually want systems analysts to have business management or closely related skills, while a background in the physical sciences, applied mathematics, or engineering is preferred for work in scientifically oriented organizations. Art or graphic design skills may be desirable for webmasters or Web developers.

Jobseekers can enhance their employment opportunities by participating in internship or co-op programs offered through their schools. Because many people develop advanced computer skills in a non-computer-related occupation and then transfer those skills to a computer occupation, a background in the industry in which the person's job is located, such as financial services, banking, or accounting, can be important. Others have taken computer science courses to supplement their study in fields such as accounting, inventory control, or other business areas. For example, a financial analyst who is proficient in computers might become a computer support specialist in financial systems development, while a computer programmer might move into a systems analyst job.

Computer systems analysts, database administrators, and computer scientists must be able to think logically and have good communication skills. Because they often deal with a number of tasks simultaneously, the ability to concentrate and pay close attention to detail is important. Although these computer specialists sometimes work independently, they frequently work in teams on large projects. They must be able to communicate effectively with computer personnel, such as programmers and managers, as well as with users or other staff who may have no technical computer background.

Computer scientists employed in private industry may advance into managerial or project leadership positions. Those employed in academic institutions can become heads of research departments or published authorities in their field. Systems analysts may be promoted to senior or lead systems analyst. Those who show leadership ability also can become project managers or advance into management positions such as manager of information systems or chief information officer. Database administrators may advance into managerial positions, such as chief technology officer, on the basis of their experience managing data and enforcing security. Computer specialists with work experience and considerable expertise in a particular subject or a certain application may find lucrative opportunities as independent consultants or may choose to start their own computer consulting firms.

Technological advances come so rapidly in the computer field that continuous study is necessary to keep one's skills up to date. Employers, hardware and software vendors, colleges and universities, and private training institutions offer continuing education. Additional training may come from professional development seminars offered by professional computing societies.

Certification is a way to demonstrate a level of competence in a particular field. Some product vendors or software firms offer certification and require professionals who work with their products to be certified. Many employers regard these certifications as the industry standard. For example, one method of acquiring enough knowledge to get a job as a database administrator is to become certified in a specific type of database management. Voluntary certification also is available through various organizations associated with computer specialists. Professional certification may afford a jobseeker a competitive advantage.

Job Outlook

Computer systems analysts, database administrators, and computer scientists are expected to be among the fastest growing occupations through 2012. Employment of these computer specialists is expected to grow much faster than the average for all occupations as organizations continue to adopt and integrate increasingly sophisticated technologies. Job increases will be driven by very rapid growth in computer system design and related services, which is projected to be one of the fastest-growing industries in the U.S. economy. In addition, many job openings will arise annually from the need to replace workers who move into managerial positions or other occupations or who leave the labor force. Job growth will not be as rapid as growth during the previous decade, however, as the information technology sector begins to mature and as routine work is increasingly outsourced overseas.

Despite the recent economic downturn among information technology firms, workers in the occupation should still enjoy favorable job prospects. The demand for networking to facilitate the sharing of information, the expansion of client–server environments, and the need for computer specialists to use their knowledge and skills in a problem-solving capacity will be major factors in the rising demand for computer systems analysts, database administrators, and computer scientists. Moreover, falling prices of computer hardware and software should continue to induce more businesses to expand their computerized operations and integrate new technologies into them. In order to maintain a competitive edge and operate more efficiently, firms will keep demanding computer specialists who are knowledgeable about the latest technologies and are able to apply them to meet the needs of businesses.

Increasingly, more sophisticated and complex technology is being implemented across all organizations, which should fuel the demand for these computer occupations. There is a growing demand for system analysts to help firms maximize their efficiency with available technology. Expansion of electronic commerce—doing business on the Internet—and the continuing need to build and maintain databases that store critical information on customers, inventory, and projects are fueling demand for database administrators familiar with the latest technology. Also, the increasing importance being placed on "cybersecurity"—the protection of electronic information—will result in a need for workers skilled in information security.

The development of new technologies usually leads to demand for various kinds of workers. The expanding integration of Internet technologies into businesses, for example, has resulted in a growing need for specialists who can develop and support Internet and intranet applications. The growth of electronic commerce means that more establishments use the Internet to conduct their business online. The introduction of the wireless Internet, known as WiFi, creates new systems to be analyzed and new data to be administered. The spread of such new technologies translates into a need for information technology professionals who can help organizations use technology to communicate with employees, clients, and consumers. Explosive growth in these areas also is expected to fuel demand for specialists who are knowledgeable about network, data, and communications security.

As technology becomes more sophisticated and complex, employers demand a higher level of skill and expertise from their employees. Individuals with an advanced degree in computer science or computer engineering or with an MBA with a concentration in information systems should enjoy highly favorable employment prospects. College graduates with a bachelor's degree in computer science, computer engineering, information science, or MIS also should enjoy favorable prospects for employment, particularly if they have supplemented their formal education with practical experience. Because employers continue to seek computer specialists who can combine strong technical skills with good interpersonal and business skills, graduates with non-computer-science degrees, but who have had courses in computer programming, systems analysis, and other information technology areas, also should continue to find jobs in these computer fields. In fact, individuals with the right experience and training can work in these computer occupations regardless of their college major or level of formal education.

Earnings

Median annual earnings of computer systems analysts were $62,890 in 2002. The middle 50 percent earned between $49,500 and $78,350 a year. The lowest 10 percent earned less than $39,270, and the highest 10 percent earned more than $93,400. Median annual earnings in the industries employing the largest numbers of computer systems analysts in 2002 were as follows:

Federal government $68,370

Computer systems design and related services 67,690

Data processing, hosting, and related services 64,560

Management of companies and enterprises 63,390

Insurance carriers 59,510

Median annual earnings of database administrators were $55,480 in 2002. The middle 50 percent earned between $40,550 and $75,100. The lowest 10 percent earned less than $30,750, and the highest 10 percent earned more than $92,910. In 2002, median annual earnings of database administrators employed in computer system design and related services were $66,650, and, for those in management of companies and enterprises, earnings were $59,620.

Median annual earnings of network systems and data communication analysts were $58,420 in 2002. The middle 50 percent earned between $44,850 and $74,290. The lowest 10 percent earned less than $34,880, and the highest 10 percent earned more than $92,110. Median annual earnings in the industries employing the largest numbers of network systems and data communications analysts in 2002 were as follows:

Computer systems design and related services $65,800

Management of companies and enterprises 63,050

State government 45,110

Median annual earnings of computer and information scientists, research, were $77,760 in 2002. The middle 50 percent earned between $58,630 and $98,490. The lowest 10 percent earned less than $42,890, and the highest 10 percent earned more than $121,650. Median annual earnings of computer and information scientists employed in computer systems design and related services in 2002 were $78,730.

Median annual earnings of all other computer specialists were $54,070 in 2002. Median annual earnings of all other computer specialists employed in computer system design and related services were $49,590, and, for those in scientific research and development services, earnings were $70,150 in 2002.

According to the National Association of Colleges and Employers, starting offers for graduates with a master's degree in computer science averaged $62,806 in 2003. Starting offers averaged $47,109 for graduates with a bachelor's degree in computer science; $45,346 for those with a degree in computer programming; $41,118 for those with a degree in computer systems analysis; $40,556 for those with a degree in management information systems; and $38,282 for those with a degree in information sciences and systems.

According to Robert Half International, starting salaries in 2003 ranged from $69,750 to $101,750 for database administrators. Salaries for networking and Internet-related occupations ranged from $45,500 to $65,750 for LAN administrators and from $51,250 to $73,750 for Intranet developers. Starting salaries for security professionals ranged from $62,500 to $91,750 in 2003.

Related Occupations

Other workers who use logic and creativity to solve business and technical problems are computer programmers, computer software engineers, computer and information systems managers, financial analysts and personal financial advisors, urban and regional planners, engineers, mathematicians, statisticians, operations research analysts, management analysts, and actuaries.

Sources of Additional Information

Further information about computer careers is available from any of the following organizations:

- Association for Computing Machinery (ACM), 1515 Broadway, New York, NY 10036. Internet: http://www.acm.org

- Institute of Electrical and Electronics Engineers Computer Society, Headquarters Office, 1730 Massachusetts Ave. NW, Washington, DC 20036-1992. Internet: http://www.computer.org

- National Workforce Center for Emerging Technologies, 3000 Landerholm Circle SE., Bellevue, WA 98007. Internet: http://www.nwcet.org

Computer, Automated Teller, and Office Machine Repairers

(O*NET 49-2011.01, 49-2011.02, and 49-2011.03)

Significant Points

- Workers qualify for these jobs by receiving training in electronics from associate degree programs, the military, vocational schools, equipment manufacturers, or employers.

- Job growth reflects the increasing dependence of business and residential customers on computers and other sophisticated office machines.

- Job prospects will be best for applicants with knowledge of electronics, as well as repair experience; opportunities for computer repairers should be excellent, given that employers are reporting difficulty finding qualified applicants.

Nature of the Work

Computer repairers, also known as *computer service technicians* or *data-processing equipment repairers*, service mainframe, server, and personal computers; printers; and disc drives. These workers perform primarily hands-on repair, maintenance, and installation of computers and related equipment. Workers who provide technical assistance, in person or by telephone, to computer system users are known as computer support specialists or computer support technicians.

Automated teller machines (ATMs) allow customers to carry out bank transactions without the assistance of a teller. ATMs now provide a growing variety of other services, including stamp, phone card, and ticket sales. *Automated teller machine servicers* repair and service these machines.

Office machine and cash register servicers work on photocopiers, cash registers, mail-processing equipment, and fax machines. Newer models of office machinery increasingly include computerized components that allow them to function more effectively than earlier models.

To install large equipment, such as mainframe computers and ATMs, repairers connect the equipment to power sources and communication lines that allow the transmission of information over computer networks. For example, when an ATM dispenses cash, it transmits the withdrawal information to the customer's bank. Workers also may install operating software and peripheral equipment, checking that all components are configured to function together correctly. The installation of personal computers and other small office machines is less complex and may be handled by the purchaser.

When equipment breaks down, many repairers travel to customers' workplaces or other locations to make the necessary repairs. These workers, known as *field technicians*, often have assigned areas in which they perform preventive maintenance on a regular basis. *Bench technicians* work in repair shops located in stores, factories, or service centers. In small companies, repairers may work both in repair shops and at customer locations.

Computer repairers usually replace subsystems instead of repairing them. Replacement is common because subsystems are inexpensive and businesses are reluctant to shut down their computers for time-consuming repairs. Subsystems commonly replaced by computer repairers include video cards, which transmit signals from the computer to the monitor; hard drives, which store data; and network cards, which allow communication over the network. Defective modules may be given to bench technicians, who use software programs to diagnose the problem and who may repair the modules, if possible.

When ATMs malfunction, computer networks recognize the problem and alert repairers. Common problems include worn magnetic heads on card readers, which prevent the equipment from recognizing customers' bankcards, and "pick failures," which prevent the equipment from dispensing the correct amount of cash. Field technicians travel to the locations of ATMs and usually repair equipment by removing and replacing defective components. Broken components are brought to a repair shop, where bench technicians make the necessary repairs. Field technicians perform routine maintenance on a regular basis, replacing worn parts and running diagnostic tests to ensure that the equipment functions properly.

Office machine repairers usually work on machinery at the customer's workplace; alternatively, if the machines are small enough, customers may bring them to a repair shop for maintenance. Common malfunctions include paper misfeeds, due to worn or dirty parts, and poor-quality copy, due to problems with lamps, lenses, or mirrors. These malfunctions usually can be resolved simply by cleaning the relevant components. Breakdowns also may result from the failure of commonly used parts. For example, heavy usage of a photocopier may wear down the printhead, which applies ink to the final copy. In such cases, the repairer usually replaces the part instead of repairing it.

Workers use a variety of tools for diagnostic tests and repair. To diagnose malfunctions, they use multimeters to measure voltage, current, resistance, and other electrical properties; signal generators to provide test signals; and oscilloscopes to monitor equipment signals. To diagnose computerized equipment, repairers use software programs. To repair or adjust equipment, workers use handtools, such as pliers, screwdrivers, soldering irons, and wrenches.

Working Conditions

Repairers usually work in clean, well-lighted surroundings. Because computers and office machines are sensitive to extreme temperatures and to humidity, repair shops usually are air conditioned and well ventilated. Field repairers must travel frequently to various locations to install, maintain, or repair customers' equipment. ATM repairers may have to perform their jobs in small, confined spaces that house the equipment.

Because computers and ATMs are critical for many organizations to function efficiently, data-processing equipment repairers and ATM field technicians often work around the clock. Their schedules may include evening, weekend, and holiday shifts, sometimes assigned on the basis of seniority. Office machine and cash register servicers usually work regular business hours because the equipment they repair is not as critical.

Although their job is not strenuous, repairers must lift equipment and work in a variety of postures. Repairers of computer monitors need to discharge voltage from the equipment to avoid electrocution. Workers may have to wear protective goggles.

Employment

Computer, automated teller, and office machine repairers held about 156,000 jobs in 2002. Wholesale trade establishments employed about one-third of the workers in this occupation; most of these establishments were wholesalers of professional and commercial equipment and supplies. Many workers also were employed in electronics, appliance, and office supplies stores. Others worked in electronic and precision equipment repair shops and computer systems design firms. A small number were found in computer and peripheral equipment manufacturing, government agencies, and internet service providers. About 1 computer, automated teller, and office machine repairer in 8 was self-employed, more than twice the proportion for all installation, maintenance, and repair occupations.

Training, Other Qualifications, and Advancement

Knowledge of electronics is necessary for employment as a computer, automated teller, or office machine repairer. Employers prefer workers who are certified as repairers or who have training in electronics from associate degree programs, the military, vocational schools, or equipment manufacturers. Employers generally provide some training to new repairers on specific equipment; however, workers are expected to arrive on the job with a basic understanding of equipment repair. Employers may send experienced workers to training sessions to keep up with changes in technology and service procedures.

Most office machine and ATM repairer positions require an associate degree in electronics. A basic understanding of mechanical equipment also is important, because many of the parts that fail in office machines and ATMs are mechanical, such as paper loaders. Entry-level employees at large companies normally receive on-the-job training lasting several months. Such training may include a week of classroom instruction, followed by a period of 2 weeks to several months assisting an experienced repairer.

Field technicians work closely with customers and must have good communications skills and a neat appearance. Employers normally require that field technicians have a driver's license.

Various organizations offer certification, including ACES International, the Computing Technology Industry

Association, the Electronic Technicians Association International, and the International Society of Certified Electronics Technicians. Repairers may specialize in a variety of skill areas. To receive certification, repairers must pass qualifying examinations corresponding to their level of training and experience.

Newly hired computer repairers may work on personal computers or peripheral equipment. With experience, they can advance to positions maintaining more sophisticated systems, such as networking equipment and servers. Field repairers of ATMs may advance to bench-technician positions responsible for more complex repairs. Experienced workers may become specialists who help other repairers diagnose difficult problems or who work with engineers in designing equipment and developing maintenance procedures. Experienced workers also may move into management positions responsible for supervising other repairers.

Because of their familiarity with equipment, experienced repairers may move into customer service or sales positions. Some experienced workers open their own repair shops or become wholesalers or retailers of electronic equipment.

Job Outlook

Employment of computer, automated teller, and office machine repairers is expected to grow about as fast as the average for all occupations through 2012. Job growth will be driven by the increasing dependence of business and residential customers on computers and other sophisticated office machines. The need to maintain this equipment in working order will create new jobs for repairers. In addition, openings will result from the need to replace repairers who retire or transfer into new occupations.

Job prospects will be best for applicants with knowledge of electronics as well as repair experience; opportunities for computer repairers should be excellent, given that employers are reporting difficulty finding qualified applicants and that computers are increasingly being relied on. Although computer equipment continues to become less expensive and more reliable, malfunctions still occur and can cause severe problems for users, most of whom lack the knowledge to make repairs. Computers are critical to most businesses today and will become even more so to companies that do business on the Internet and to households that bank, pay bills, or make purchases online.

People also are becoming increasingly reliant on ATMs. Besides offering bank and retail transactions, ATMs provide an increasing number of other services, such as employee information processing and distribution of government payments. Improvements in ATM design have increased reliability and simplified repair tasks, reducing the number and extent of repairs. Opportunities for ATM repairers should be available, arising primarily from the need to replace workers who leave the specialty, rather than from employment growth.

Conventional office machines, such as calculators, are inexpensive, and often are replaced instead of repaired.

However, digital copiers and other, newer office machines are more costly and complex. This equipment often is computerized, designed to work on a network, and able to perform multiple functions. The growing need for repairers to service such sophisticated equipment should result in job opportunities for office machine repairers.

Earnings

Median hourly earnings of computer, automated teller, and office machine repairers were $15.98 in 2002. The middle 50 percent earned between $12.44 and $20.38. The lowest 10 percent earned less than $9.99, and the highest 10 percent earned more than $25.06. Median hourly earnings in the industries employing the largest numbers of computer, automated teller, and office machine repairers in 2002 were as follows:

Computer systems design and related services $17.33

Professional and commercial equipment
and supplies merchant wholesalers.........................17.28

Office supplies, stationery, and gift stores 14.79

Electronics and appliance stores 13.89

Electronic and precision equipment repair and
maintenance 13.46

Related Occupations

Workers in other occupations who repair and maintain electronic equipment include broadcast and sound engineering technicians and radio operators; electronic home entertainment equipment installers and repairers; electrical and electronics installers and repairers; industrial machinery installation, repair, and maintenance workers; and radio and telecommunications equipment installers and repairers.

Sources of Additional Information

For information on careers and certification, contact:

- ACES International, 5241 Princess Anne Rd., Suite 110, Virginia Beach, VA 23462. Internet: http://www.acesinternational.org

- Computing Technology Industry Association, 1815 S Meyers Rd., Suite 300, Oakbrook Terrace, IL 60181-5228. Internet: http://www.comptia.org

- Electronics Technicians Association International, 5 Depot St., Greencastle, IN 46135.

- International Society of Certified Electronics Technicians, 3608 Pershing Ave., Fort Worth, TX 76107-4527. Internet: http://www.iscet.org

Conservation Scientists and Foresters

(O*NET 19-1031.01, 19-1031.02, 19-1031.03, and 19-1032.00)

Significant Points

- Nearly two-thirds of salaried conservation scientists and foresters work for federal, state, or local governments.

- A bachelor's degree in forestry, range management, or a related discipline is the minimum educational requirement.

- Slower-than-average job growth is projected because of limited growth in government and in forestry and logging; most employment opportunities will be in private sector consulting.

Nature of the Work

Forests and rangelands supply wood products, livestock forage, minerals, and water; serve as sites for recreational activities; and provide habitats for wildlife. Conservation scientists and foresters manage, develop, use, and help to protect these and other natural resources.

Foresters manage forested lands for a variety of purposes. Those working in private industry may manage company forest land or procure timber from private landowners. Company forests usually are managed to produce a sustainable supply of wood for company mills. Procurement foresters contact local forest owners and gain permission to take inventory of the type, amount, and location of all standing timber on the property, a process known as timber cruising. Foresters then appraise the timber's worth, negotiate its purchase, and draw up a contract for procurement. Next, they subcontract with loggers or pulpwood cutters for tree removal, aid in road layout, and maintain close contact with the subcontractor's workers and the landowner to ensure that the work meets the landowner's requirements, as well as federal, state, and local environmental specifications. Forestry consultants often act as agents for the forest owner, performing these duties and negotiating timber sales with industrial procurement foresters.

Throughout the forest management and procurement processes, foresters consider the economics as well as the environmental impact on natural resources. To do this, they determine how to conserve wildlife habitats, creek beds, water quality, and soil stability, and how best to comply with environmental regulations. Foresters must balance the desire to conserve forested ecosystems for future generations with the need to use forest resources for recreational or economic purposes.

Through a process called regeneration, foresters also supervise the planting and growing of new trees. They choose and prepare the site, using controlled burning, bulldozers, or herbicides to clear weeds, brush, and logging debris. They advise on the type, number, and placement of trees to be planted. Foresters then monitor the seedlings to ensure healthy growth and to determine the best time for harvesting. If they detect signs of disease or harmful insects, they consult with forest pest management specialists to decide on the best course of treatment. Foresters who work for federal and state governments manage public forests and parks and work with private landowners to protect and manage forest land outside of the public domain. They may also design campgrounds and recreation areas.

Foresters use a number of tools to perform their jobs. Clinometers measure the height, diameter tapes measure the diameter, and increment borers and bark gauges measure the growth of trees so that timber volumes can be computed and growth rates estimated. Remote sensing (aerial photographs and other imagery taken from airplanes and satellites) and Geographic Information Systems (GIS) data often are used for mapping large forest areas and for detecting widespread trends of forest and land use. Once the map is generated, the data are digitized to create a computerized inventory of information required to manage the forest land and its resources. Moreover, hand-held computers, Global Positioning Satellite (GPS), and World Wide Web-based applications are used extensively.

Range managers, also called *range conservationists*, *range ecologists*, or *range scientists*, study, manage, improve, and protect rangelands to maximize their use without damaging the environment. Rangelands cover about 1 billion acres of the United States, mostly in western states and Alaska. They contain many natural resources, including grass and shrubs for animal grazing, wildlife habitats, water from vast watersheds, recreation facilities, and valuable mineral and energy resources. Range managers may inventory soils, plants, and animals, develop resource management plans, help to restore degraded ecosystems, or assist in managing a ranch. For example, they may help ranchers attain optimum livestock production by determining the number and kind of animals to graze, the grazing system to use, and the best season for grazing. At the same time, however, range managers maintain soil stability and vegetation for other uses such as wildlife habitats and outdoor recreation. They also plan and implement revegetation of disturbed sites.

Soil and water conservationists provide technical assistance to farmers, ranchers, forest managers, state and local agencies, and others concerned with the conservation of soil, water, and related natural resources. They develop programs for private landowners designed to make the most productive use of land without damaging it. Soil conservationists also assist landowners by visiting areas with erosion problems, finding the source of the problem, and helping landowners and managers develop management practices to combat it. Water conservationists also assist private landowners and federal, state, and local governments by advising on a broad range of natural resource topics—specifically, issues of water quality, preserving water supplies, groundwater contamination, and management and conservation of water resources.

Foresters and conservation scientists often specialize in one area, such as wildlife management, urban forestry, wood technology, native species, or forest economics.

Working Conditions

Working conditions vary considerably. Although some of the work is solitary, foresters and conservation scientists also deal regularly with landowners, loggers, forestry technicians and aides, farmers, ranchers, government officials, special interest groups, and the public in general. Some foresters and conservation scientists work regular hours in offices or labs. Others may split their time between fieldwork and office work, while independent consultants and especially new, less experienced workers spend the majority of their time outdoors overseeing or participating in hands-on work.

The work can be physically demanding. Some foresters and conservation scientists work outdoors in all types of weather, sometimes in isolated areas. Other foresters may need to walk long distances through densely wooded land to carry out their work. Foresters also may work long hours fighting fires. Conservation scientists often are called to prevent erosion after a forest fire, and they provide emergency help after floods, mudslides, and tropical storms.

Employment

Conservation scientists and foresters held about 33,000 jobs in 2002. Nearly one-third of all workers were employed by the federal government, many in the U.S. Department of Agriculture (USDA). Foresters were concentrated in the USDA's Forest Service; soil conservationists were employed primarily in the USDA's Natural Resource Conservation Service. Most range managers worked in the U.S. Department of the Interior's Bureau of Land Management, the Natural Resource Conservation Service, or the Forest Service. Another 20 percent of conservation scientists and foresters worked for state governments, and about 10 percent worked for local governments. The remainder worked in private industry, mainly in support activities for agriculture and forestry or in wood product manufacturing. Some were self-employed as consultants for private landowners, federal and state governments, and forestry-related businesses.

Although conservation scientists and foresters work in every state, employment of foresters is concentrated in the western and southeastern states, where many national and private forests and parks, and most of the lumber and pulpwood-producing forests, are located. Range managers work almost entirely in the western states, where most of the rangeland is located. Soil conservationists, on the other hand, are employed in almost every county in the country. Besides the jobs described above, some foresters and conservation scientists held faculty positions in colleges and universities.

Training, Other Qualifications, and Advancement

A bachelor's degree in forestry, range management, or a related discipline is the minimum educational requirement for careers in forestry or conservation science. In the federal government, a combination of experience and appropriate education occasionally may substitute for a 4-year forestry degree, but job competition makes this difficult.

Sixteen states have mandatory licensing or voluntary registration requirements that a forester must meet in order to acquire the title "professional forester" and practice forestry in the state. Of those 16 states, 7 have mandatory licensing; 5 have mandatory registration, and the remaining 4 states have optional registration. Both licensing and registration requirements usually entail completing a 4-year degree in forestry and several years of forestry work experience. Candidates pursuing licensing also must pass a comprehensive written exam.

Foresters who wish to perform specialized research or teach should have an advanced degree, preferably a Ph.D.

Most land-grant colleges and universities offer bachelor's or higher degrees in forestry; about 110 of these degree programs at around 50 educational institutions are accredited by the Society of American Foresters. Curriculums stress four components: Ecology, measurement of forest resources, management of forest resources, and public policy. Students should balance general science courses such as ecology, biology, tree physiology, taxonomy, and soil formation with technical forestry courses, such as forest inventory or wildlife habitat assessment, remote sensing, land surveying, GPS technology, integrated forest resource management, silviculture, and forest protection. In addition, communications skills, mathematics, statistics, and computer science courses also are recommended. Many forestry curriculums include advanced computer applications such as GIS and resource assessment programs. Courses in resource policy and administration, specifically forest economics and business administration, supplement the student's scientific and technical knowledge. Forestry curriculums increasingly include courses on best management practices, wetlands analysis, and sustainability and regulatory issues in response to the growing focus on protecting forested lands during timber harvesting operations. Prospective foresters should have a strong grasp of federal, state, and local policy issues and of increasingly numerous and complex environmental regulations that affect many forestry-related activities. Many colleges require students to complete a field session either in a camp operated by the college or in a cooperative work-study program with a federal or state agency or private industry. All schools encourage students to take summer jobs that provide experience in forestry or conservation work.

A bachelor's degree in range management or range science is the usual minimum educational requirement for range managers; graduate degrees usually are required for teaching and research positions. More than 30 colleges and universities offer degrees in range management that are accredited by the Society of Range Management. A number of other schools offer degree programs in range science or in a closely related discipline with a range management or range science option. Specialized range management courses combine plant, animal, and soil sciences with principles of ecology and resource management. Desirable electives include economics, statistics, forestry, hydrology, agronomy, wildlife, animal husbandry, computer science, and recreation. Selection of a minor in range management, such as wildlife ecology, watershed management, animal science, or agricultural economics, can often enhance qualifications for certain types of employment. The Society for Range Management offers certification as a professional rangeland manager (CPRM). Candidates seeking certification must have at least a bachelor's degree in range science or a closely related field, have a minimum of 5 years of full-time work experience, and pass a comprehensive written exam.

Very few colleges and universities offer degrees in soil conservation. Most soil conservationists have degrees in environmental studies, agronomy, general agriculture, hydrology, or crop or soil science; a few have degrees in related fields such as wildlife biology, forestry, and range management. Programs of study usually include 30 semester hours in natural resources or agriculture, including at least 3 hours in soil science.

In addition to meeting the demands of forestry and conservation research and analysis, foresters and conservation scientists generally must enjoy working outdoors, be physically hardy, and be willing to move to where the jobs are. They also must work well with people and have good communication skills.

Recent forestry and range management graduates usually work under the supervision of experienced foresters or range managers. After gaining experience, they may advance to more responsible positions. In the federal government, most entry-level foresters work in forest resource management. An experienced federal forester may supervise a ranger district, and may advance to forest supervisor, to regional forester, or to a top administrative position in the national headquarters. In private industry, foresters start by learning the practical and administrative aspects of the business and acquiring comprehensive technical training. They are then introduced to contract writing, timber harvesting, and decisionmaking. Some foresters work their way up to top managerial positions within their companies. Foresters in management usually leave the fieldwork behind, spending more of their time in an office, working with teams to develop management plans and supervising others. After gaining several years of experience, some foresters may become consulting foresters, working alone or with one or several partners. They contract with state or local governments, private landowners, private industry, or other forestry consulting groups.

Soil conservationists usually begin working within one county or conservation district and, with experience, may advance to the area, state, regional, or national level. Also, soil conservationists can transfer to related occupations, such as farm or ranch management advisor or land appraiser.

Job Outlook

Employment of conservation scientists and foresters is expected to grow more slowly than the average for all occupations through 2012. Growth should be strongest in private sector consulting firms and in scientific research and development services. Demand will be spurred by a continuing emphasis on environmental protection, responsible land management, and water-related issues. Job opportunities for conservation scientists will arise because government regulations, such as those regarding the management of storm water and coastlines, have created demand for persons knowledgeable about runoff and erosion on farms and in cities and suburbs. Soil and water quality experts will be needed as states design initiatives to improve water resources by preventing pollution by agricultural producers and industrial plants.

Fewer opportunities for conservation scientists and foresters are expected in federal and state government, mostly due to budgetary constraints and the trend among governments toward contracting functions out to private consulting firms. Also, federal land management agencies, such as the USDA Forest Service, have de-emphasized their timber programs and increasingly focused on wildlife, recreation, and sustaining ecosystems, thereby spurring demand for other life and social scientists rather than for foresters. However, departures of foresters who retire or leave the government for other reasons will result in some job openings between 2002 and 2012. A small number of new jobs will result from the need for range and soil conservationists to provide technical assistance to owners of grazing land through the Natural Resource Conservation Service.

Reductions in timber harvesting on public lands, most of which are located in the Northwest and California, also will dampen job growth for private industry foresters in these regions. Opportunities will be better for foresters in the Southeast, where much forested land is privately owned. Salaried foresters working for private industry—such as paper companies, sawmills, and pulpwood mills—and consulting foresters will be needed to provide technical assistance and management plans to landowners.

Scientific research and development services have increased their hiring of conservation scientists and foresters in recent years in response to demand for professionals to prepare environmental impact statements and erosion and sediment control plans, monitor water quality near logging sites, and advise on tree harvesting practices required by federal, state, or local regulations. Hiring in these firms should continue during the 2002-12 period, although at a slower rate than over the last 10 years.

Earnings

Median annual earnings of conservation scientists in 2002 were $50,340. The middle 50 percent earned between $39,300 and $61,440. The lowest 10 percent earned less than $30,630, and the highest 10 percent earned more than $70,770.

Median annual earnings of foresters in 2002 were $46,730. The middle 50 percent earned between $36,330 and $56,890. The lowest 10 percent earned less than $29,690, and the highest 10 percent earned more than $69,600.

In 2003, most bachelor's degree graduates entering the federal government as foresters, range managers, or soil conservationists started at $23,442 or $29,037, depending on academic achievement. Those with a master's degree could start at $35,519 or $42,976. Holders of doctorates could start at $51,508. Beginning salaries were slightly higher in selected areas where the prevailing local pay level was higher. In 2003, the average federal salary for foresters in nonsupervisory, supervisory, and managerial positions was $59,233; for soil conservationists, $57,084; and for rangeland managers, $53,657.

According to the National Association of Colleges and Employers, graduates with a bachelor's degree in conservation and renewable natural resources received an average starting salary offer of $29,715 in 2003.

In private industry, starting salaries for students with a bachelor's degree were comparable with starting salaries in the federal government, but starting salaries in state and local governments were usually lower.

Conservation scientists and foresters who work for federal, state, and local governments and large private firms generally receive more generous benefits than do those working for smaller firms.

Related Occupations

Conservation scientists and foresters manage, develop, and protect natural resources. Other workers with similar responsibilities include environmental engineers; agricultural and food scientists; biological scientists; environmental scientists and geoscientists; and farmers, ranchers, and agricultural managers.

Sources of Additional Information

For information about the forestry profession and lists of schools offering education in forestry, send a self-addressed, stamped business envelope to:

- Society of American Foresters, 5400 Grosvenor Lane, Bethesda, MD 20814, or visit the society's Web site: http://www.safnet.org

For information about career opportunities in forestry in the federal government, contact:

- Chief, U.S. Forest Service, U.S. Department of Agriculture, P.O. Box 96090, Washington, DC 20090-6090. Internet: http://www.fs.fed.us

Information about a career as a range manager, as well as a list of schools offering training, is available from:

- Society for Range Management, 445 Union Blvd., Suite 230, Lakewood, CO 80228-1259. Internet: http://www.rangelands.org/ScriptContent/Index.cfm.

Court Reporters

(O*NET 23-2091.00)

Significant Points

- Court reporters usually need a 2- or 4- year postsecondary school degree.

- Demand for realtime and broadcast captioning and translating will result in employment growth in the occupation.

- Job opportunities should be best for those with certification.

Nature of the Work

Court reporters typically take verbatim reports of speeches, conversations, legal proceedings, meetings, and other events when written accounts of spoken words are necessary for correspondence, records, or legal proof. Court reporters play a critical role not only in judicial proceedings, but at every meeting where the spoken word must be preserved as a written transcript. They are responsible for ensuring a complete, accurate, and secure legal record. In addition to preparing and protecting the legal record, many court reporters assist judges and trial attorneys in a variety of ways, such as organizing and searching for information in the official record or making suggestions to judges and attorneys regarding courtroom administration and procedure. Increasingly, court reporters are providing closed-captioning and realtime translating services to the deaf and hard-of-hearing community.

There are two main methods of court reporting: Stenotyping and voice writing. Using a stenotype machine, stenotypists document all statements made in official proceedings. The machine allows them to press multiple keys at a time to record combinations of letters representing sounds, words, or phrases. These symbols are then recorded on computer disks or CD-ROM, which are then translated and displayed as text in a process called computer-aided transcription. In all cases, accuracy is crucial because there is only one person creating an official transcript. In a judicial setting, for example, appeals often depend on the court reporter's transcript. Stenotype machines used for realtime captioning are linked directly to the computer. As the reporter keys in the symbols, they instantly appear as text on the screen. This process, called communications access realtime translation (CART), is used in courts, in classrooms, at meetings, and for closed captioning for the hearing-impaired on television.

The other method of court reporting is called voice writing. Using the voice-writing method, a court reporter speaks directly into a stenomask—a hand-held mask containing a microphone with a voice silencer. As the reporter repeats the testimony into the recorder, the mask and silencer prevent the reporter from being heard during testimony. Voice writers record everything that is said by judges, witnesses, attorneys, and other parties to a proceeding, including gestures and emotional reactions.

Some voice writers produce a transcript in real time, using computer speech recognition technology. Other voice writers prefer to translate their voice files after the proceeding is over, or they transcribe the files manually, without using speech recognition at all. In any event, speech recognition technology is allowing voice writers to pursue not only court reporting careers, but also careers as closed captioners, CART reporters for hearing-impaired individuals, and Internet streaming text or caption providers.

Court reporters that use either method are responsible for a number of duties both before and after transcribing events. First, they must create and maintain the computer dictionary that they use to translate stenographic strokes or voice record files into written text. They may customize the dictionary with parts of words, entire words, or terminology specific to the proceeding, program, or event—such as a religious service—they plan to transcribe. After documenting proceedings, court reporters must edit their CART translation for correct grammar, for accurate identification of proper names and places, and to ensure that the record or testimony is discernible. They usually prepare written transcripts, make copies, and provide information from the transcript to courts, counsels, parties, and the public upon request. Court reporters also develop procedures for easy storage and retrieval of all stenographic notes and files in paper or digital format.

Although many court reporters record official proceedings in the courtroom, others work outside the courtroom. For example, they may take depositions for attorneys in offices and document proceedings of meetings, conventions, and other private activities. Still others capture the proceedings taking place in government agencies at all levels, from the U.S. Congress to state and local governing bodies. Court reporters, both stenotypists and voice writers, who specialize in captioning live television programming for people with hearing loss are commonly known as *stenocaptioners*. They work for television networks or cable stations, captioning news, emergency broadcasts, sporting events, and other programming. With CART and broadcast captioning, the level of understanding gained by a person with hearing loss depends entirely on the skill of the stenocaptioner. In an emergency, such as a tornado or a hurricane, people's safety may depend entirely on the accuracy of information provided in the form of captioning.

Medical transcriptionists have similar duties, but with a different focus. They translate and edit recorded dictation by physicians and other health-care providers regarding their assessment and treatment of patients.

Working Conditions

The majority of court reporters work in comfortable settings, such as offices of attorneys, courtrooms, legislatures, and conventions. An increasing number of court reporters work from home-based offices as independent contractors, or freelancers.

Work in this occupation presents few hazards, although sitting in the same position for long periods can be tiring, and workers can suffer wrist, back, neck, or eye problems due to strain. Workers also risk repetitive motion injuries such as carpal tunnel syndrome. In addition, the pressure to be accurate and fast can be stressful.

Many official court reporters work a standard 40-hour week. Self-employed court reporters, or freelancers, usually work flexible hours, including part time, evenings, and weekends, or they can work on an on-call basis.

Employment

Court reporters held about 18,000 jobs in 2002. About 60 percent worked for state and local governments, a reflection of the large number of court reporters working in courts, legislatures, and various agencies. Most of the remaining wage and salary workers worked for court reporting agencies. Eleven percent of court reporters were self-employed.

Training, Other Qualifications, and Advancement

The amount of training required to become a court reporter varies with the type of reporting chosen. It usually takes less than a year to become a voice writer. In contrast, the average length of time it takes to become a stenotypist is 33 months. Training is offered by about 160 postsecondary vocational and technical schools and colleges. The National Court Reporters Association (NCRA) has approved about 82 programs, all of which offer courses in stenotype computer-aided transcription and realtime reporting. NCRA-approved programs require students to capture a minimum of 225 words per minute, a federal government requirement as well.

Some states require court reporters to be notary publics. Others require the certified court reporter (CCR) designation, for which a reporter must pass a state certification test administered by a board of examiners. The NCRA confers the entry-level designation "registered professional reporter" (RPR) upon those who pass a four-part examination and participate in mandatory continuing education programs. Although voluntary, the designation is recognized as a mark of distinction in the field. A reporter may obtain additional certifications that demonstrate higher levels of competency, such as "registered merit reporter" (RMR) or "registered diplomate reporter" (RDR). The RDR is the highest level of certification available to court reporters. In order to receive the designation, a court reporter must either have 5 consecutive years of experience as an RMR or be an RMR and hold a 4-year baccalaureate degree.

The NCRA also offers the designations "certified realtime reporter"(CRR), "certified broadcast captioner" (CBC), and "certified CART provider" (CCP). These designations promote and recognize competence in the specialized skill of converting the spoken word into the written word instantaneously.

Some states require voice writers to pass a test and to earn state licensure. As a substitute for state certification, the National Verbatim Reporters Association offers three national certifications to voice writers: "certified verbatim reporter" (CVR), the certificate of merit (CM), and "real-time verbatim reporter" (RVR). Earning these certifications may be sufficient to get licensed in the state. In order to get the CM or RVR, one must first earn the CVR. Candidates for the CVR must pass a written test covering punctuation, spelling, grammar, legal terminology, definitions, and more and also must pass, three five-minute dictation and transcription examinations that test for speed as well as accuracy. Passing the CM exam requires a higher level of speed and accuracy. The RVR measures the candidate's skill at realtime transcription. In order to retain these certifications, the voice writer must obtain continuing education credits. Credits are given for voice writer education courses, continuing legal education courses, and college courses.

In addition to possessing speed and accuracy, court reporters must have excellent listening skills, as well as good English grammar, vocabulary, and punctuation skills. Voice writers must learn to listen and speak simultaneously and very quickly, while also identifying speakers and describing peripheral activities in the courtroom or deposition room. They must be aware of business practices and current events as well as the correct spelling of names of people, places, and events that may be mentioned in a broadcast or in court proceedings. For those who work in courtrooms, an expert knowledge of legal terminology and criminal and appellate procedure is essential. Because capturing proceedings requires the use of computerized stenography or speech recognition equipment, court reporters must be knowledgeable about computer hardware and software applications.

With experience and education, court reporters can advance to administrative and management positions, consulting, or teaching.

Job Outlook

Employment of court reporters is projected to grow about as fast as the average for all occupations through 2012. Demand for court reporter services will be spurred by the continuing need for accurate transcription of proceedings in courts and in pretrial depositions and by the growing need to create captions for live or prerecorded television and to provide other realtime translating services for the deaf and hard-of-hearing community. Despite the good job prospects, fewer people are going into this profession, creating a shortage of court reporters—particularly stenographic typists—and making job opportunities very good to excellent. Because of this shortage, voice writers have become more widely accepted as speech recognition technology improves and error rates decline. Still, many courts hire only stenotypists to perform court reporting duties, and because of this practice, demand for these highly skilled reporters will remain high.

Federal legislation mandates that, by 2006, all new television programming must be captioned for the deaf and hard-of-hearing. In addition, the Americans with Disabilities Act gives deaf and hard-of-hearing students in colleges and universities the right to request access to realtime translation in their classes. Both of these factors are expected to increase demand for court reporters to provide realtime captioning and CART services. Although these services forgo transcripts and differ from traditional court reporting, which uses computer-aided transcription to turn spoken words into permanent text, they require the same skills that court reporters learn in their training.

Despite increasing numbers of civil and criminal cases, budget constraints are expected to limit the ability of federal, state, and local courts to expand, thereby also limiting the demand for traditional court reporting services in courtrooms and other legal venues. Further, in efforts to keep costs down, many courtrooms have installed tape recorders to maintain records of proceedings. Some jurisdictions have found the error rates associated with tape recorders to be unacceptable, bringing court reporters back to their courtrooms despite budgetary issues. Still, despite the use of audiotape and videotape technology, court reporters can quickly turn spoken words into readable, searchable, permanent text, so they will continue to be needed to produce written legal transcripts and proceedings for publication.

Earnings

Court reporters had median annual earnings of $41,550 in 2002. The middle 50 percent earned between $29,770 and $55,360. The lowest paid 10 percent earned less than $23,120, and the highest paid 10 percent earned more than $73,440. Median annual earnings in 2002 were $40,720 for court reporters working in local government.

Both compensation and compensation methods for court reporters vary with the type of reporting job, the experience of the individual reporter, the level of certification achieved, and the region of the country the reporter works in. Official court reporters earn a salary and a per-page fee for transcripts. Many salaried court reporters supplement their income by doing additional freelance work. Freelance court reporters are paid per job and receive a per-page fee for transcripts. Communication access realtime translation providers are paid hourly. Stenocaptioners receive a salary and benefits if they work as employees of a captioning company; stenocaptioners working as independent contractors are paid hourly.

Related Occupations

A number of other workers type, record information, and process paperwork. Among these are secretaries and administrative assistants, medical transcriptionists, receptionists and information clerks, and human resources assistants, except payroll and timekeeping. Other workers who provide legal support include paralegals and legal assistants.

Sources of Additional Information

State employment service offices can provide information about job openings for court reporters. For information about careers, training, and certification in court reporting, contact any of the following sources:

- National Court Reporters Association, 8224 Old Courthouse Rd., Vienna, VA 22182. Internet: http://www.ncraonline.org
- United States Court Reporters Association, P.O. Box 465, Chicago, IL 60690-0465. Internet: http://www.uscra.org
- National Verbatim Reporters Association, 207 Third Avenue, Hattiesburg, MS 39401. Internet: http://www.nvra.org

Data Entry and Information Processing Workers

(O*NET 43-9021.00 and 43-9022.00)

Significant Points

- Employers generally hire high school graduates who meet their requirements for keyboarding speed.
- Although overall employment is projected to decline, the need to replace workers who leave this large occupation each year should produce many job openings.
- Job prospects should be best for those with expertise in appropriate computer software applications.

Nature of the Work

Organizations need to process a rapidly growing amount of information. Data entry and information processing workers help ensure the smooth and efficient handling of information. By typing text, entering data into a computer, operating a variety of office machines, and performing other clerical duties, these workers help organizations keep up with the rapid changes that are characteristic of today's "Information Age." In addition to the job titles discussed below—such as word processors, typists, and data entry keyers—data entry and information processing workers are known by various other titles, including electronic data processors, keypunch technicians, and transcribers.

Word processors and typists usually set up and prepare reports, letters, mailing labels, and other textual material. Typists make neat, typed copies of materials written by other clerical, professional, or managerial workers. As entry-level workers, typists may begin by typing headings on form letters, addressing envelopes, or preparing standard forms on typewriters or computers. As they gain experience, they often are assigned tasks requiring a higher degree of accuracy and independent judgment. Senior typists may work with highly technical material, plan and type complicated statistical tables, combine and rearrange materials from different sources, or prepare master copies.

Most keyboarding is now done on word processing equipment—usually a personal computer or part of a larger computer system—which normally includes a keyboard, video display terminal, and printer, which may have "add-on" capabilities such as optical character recognition readers. Word processors use this equipment to record, edit, store, and revise letters, memos, reports, statistical tables, forms, and other printed materials. Although it is becoming less common, some word processing workers are employed on centralized word processing teams that handle transcription and typing for several departments.

In addition to fulfilling the duties mentioned above, word processors and typists often perform other office tasks, such as answering telephones, filing, and operating copiers or other office machines. Job titles of these workers frequently vary to reflect these duties. Clerk typists, for example, combine typing with filing, sorting mail, answering telephones, and other general office work. Note readers transcribe steno-typed notes of court proceedings into standard formats.

Data entry keyers usually input lists of items, numbers, or other data into computers or complete forms that appear on a computer screen. They also may manipulate existing data, edit current information, or proofread new entries to a database for accuracy. Some examples of data sources include customers' personal information, medical records, and membership lists. Usually, this information is used internally by a company and may be reformatted before other departments or customers utilize it.

Keyers use various types of equipment to enter data. Many use a machine that converts the information they type to magnetic impulses on tapes or disks for entry into a computer system. Others prepare materials for printing or publication by using data entry composing machines. Some keyers operate online terminals or personal computers. Data entry keyers increasingly also work with nonkeyboard forms of data entry, such as scanners and electronically transmitted files. When using the new character recognition systems, data entry keyers often enter only those data which cannot be recognized by machines. In some offices, keyers also operate computer peripheral equipment such as printers and tape readers, act as tape librarians, and perform other clerical duties.

Working Conditions

Data entry and information processing workers usually work a standard 40-hour week in clean offices. They sit for long periods and sometimes must contend with high noise levels caused by various office machines. These workers are susceptible to repetitive strain injuries, such as carpal tunnel syndrome, neck and back injuries, and eye strain. To help prevent these conditions, many offices have scheduled exer-cise breaks, ergonomically designed keyboards, and workstations that allow workers to stand or sit as they wish.

Employment

Data entry and information processing workers held about 633,000 jobs in 2002 and were employed in every sector of the economy; 392,000 were data entry keyers and 241,000 were word processors and typists. Some workers telecommute, working from their homes on personal computers linked by telephone lines to those in the main office. This arrangement enables them to type material at home while still being able to produce printed copy in their offices.

About 1 out of 5 data entry and information processing workers held jobs in firms providing administrative and support services, including temporary help and word processing agencies, and another 1 in 5 worked for state or local government.

Training, Other Qualifications, and Advancement

Employers generally hire high school graduates who meet their requirements for keyboarding speed. Increasingly, employers also are expecting applicants to have training or experience in word processing or data entry tasks. Spelling, punctuation, and grammar skills are important, as is familiarity with standard office equipment and procedures.

Students acquire skills in keyboarding and in the use of word processing, spreadsheet, and database management computer software packages through high schools, community colleges, business schools, temporary help agencies, or self-teaching aids such as books, tapes, and Internet tutorials.

For many people, a job as a data entry and information processing worker is their first job after graduating from high school or after a period of full-time family responsibilities. This work frequently serves as a steppingstone to higher paying jobs with increased responsibilities. Large companies and government agencies usually have training programs to help administrative employees upgrade their skills and advance to higher level positions. It is common for data entry and information processing workers to transfer to other administrative jobs, such as secretary, administrative assistant, or statistical clerk or to be promoted to a supervisory job in a word processing or data entry center.

Job Outlook

Overall employment of data entry and information processing workers is projected to decline through 2012. Nevertheless, the need to replace those who transfer to other occupations or leave this large occupation for other reasons will produce numerous job openings each year. Job prospects will be most favorable for those with the best technical skills—in particular, expertise in appropriate computer software applications. Data entry and information processing workers must be willing to upgrade their skills continuously in order to remain marketable.

Although data entry and information processing workers are affected by productivity gains stemming from organizational restructuring and the implementation of new technologies, projected growth differs among these workers. Employment of word processors and typists is expected to decline due to the proliferation of personal computers, which allows other workers to perform duties formerly assigned to word processors and typists. Most professionals and managers, for example, now use desktop personal computers to do their own word processing. However, because technologies affecting data entry keyers tend to be costlier to implement, employment of these workers will decline less than word processors and typists.

Employment growth of data entry keyers will still be dampened by productivity gains, as various data-capturing technologies, such as bar code scanners, voice recognition technologies, and sophisticated character recognition readers, become more prevalent. These technologies can be applied to a variety of business transactions, such as inventory tracking, invoicing, and placing orders. Moreover, as telecommunications technology improves, many organizations will increasingly take advantage of computer networks that allow data to be transmitted electronically. These networks will allow more data to be entered automatically into computers, reducing the demand for data entry keyers.

In addition to being affected by technology, employment of data entry and information processing workers will be adversely affected by businesses that are increasingly contracting out their work. Many organizations have reduced or even eliminated permanent in-house staff—for example, in favor of temporary employment and staffing services firms. Some large data entry and information processing firms increasingly employ workers in nations with low wages to enter data. As international trade barriers continue to fall and telecommunications technology improves, this transfer of jobs will mean reduced demand for data entry keyers in the United States.

Earnings

Median annual earnings of word processors and typists in 2002 were $26,730. The middle 50 percent earned between $21,540 and $32,950. The lowest 10 percent earned less than $17,750, while the highest 10 percent earned more than $40,450. The salaries of these workers vary by industry and by region. In 2002, median annual earnings in the industries employing the largest numbers of word processors and typists were as follows:

Local government	$27,840
State government	26,440
Elementary and secondary schools	24,960
Business support services	24,140
Employment services	24,050

Median annual earnings of data entry keyers in 2002 were $22,390. The middle 50 percent earned between $18,810 and $26,840. The lowest 10 percent earned less than $15,910, and the highest 10 percent earned more than $26,840. The following are median annual earnings for 2002 in the industries employing the largest numbers of data entry keyers:

Federal government	$25,750
Insurance carriers	22,870
Employment services	21,150
Accounting, tax preparation, bookkeeping, and payroll services	19,950
Data processing, hosting, and related services	19,720

Related Occupations

Data entry and information processing workers must transcribe information quickly. Other workers who deliver information in a timely manner are dispatchers and communications equipment operators. Data entry and information processing worker also must be comfortable working with office automation, and in this regard they are similar to court reporters, medical records and health information technicians, secretaries and administrative assistants, and computer operators.

Sources of Additional Information

For information about job opportunities for data entry and information processing workers, contact the nearest office of the state employment service.

Dental Assistants

(O*NET 31-9091.00)

Significant Points

- Job prospects should be excellent.

- Dentists are expected to hire more assistants to perform routine tasks so that they may devote their own time to more profitable procedures.

- Most assistants learn their skills on the job, although an increasing number are trained in dental-assisting programs; most programs take 1 year or less to complete.

Nature of the Work

Dental assistants perform a variety of patient care, office, and laboratory duties. They work chairside as dentists examine and treat patients. They make patients as comfortable as possible in the dental chair, prepare them for treatment, and obtain their dental records. Assistants hand instruments and materials to dentists and keep patients' mouths dry and clear by using suction or other devices. Assistants also sterilize and disinfect instruments and equipment, prepare trays of instruments for dental procedures, and instruct patients on postoperative and general oral health care.

Some dental assistants prepare materials for impressions and restorations, take dental X rays, and process X-ray film as directed by a dentist. They also may remove sutures, apply topical anesthetics to gums or cavity-preventive agents to teeth, remove excess cement used in the filling process, and place rubber dams on the teeth to isolate them for individual treatment.

Those with laboratory duties make casts of the teeth and mouth from impressions, clean and polish removable appliances, and make temporary crowns. Dental assistants with office duties schedule and confirm appointments, receive patients, keep treatment records, send bills, receive payments, and order dental supplies and materials.

Dental assistants should not be confused with dental hygienists, who are licensed to perform different clinical tasks.

Working Conditions

Dental assistants work in a well-lighted, clean environment. Their work area usually is near the dental chair so that they can arrange instruments, materials, and medication and hand them to the dentist when needed. Dental assistants must wear gloves, masks, eyewear, and protective clothing to protect themselves and their patients from infectious diseases. Following safety procedures also minimizes the risks associated with the use of X-ray machines.

About half of dental assistants have a 35- to 40-hour workweek, which may include work on Saturdays or evenings.

Employment

Dental assistants held about 266,000 jobs in 2002. Almost all jobs for dental assistants were in offices of dentists. A small number of jobs were in offices of physicians, educational services, and hospitals. About a third of dental assistants worked part time, sometimes in more than one dental office.

Training, Other Qualifications, and Advancement

Most assistants learn their skills on the job, although an increasing number are trained in dental-assisting programs offered by community and junior colleges, trade schools, technical institutes, or the Armed Forces. Assistants must be a second pair of hands for a dentist; therefore, dentists look for people who are reliable, can work well with others, and have good manual dexterity. High school students interested in a career as a dental assistant should take courses in biology, chemistry, health, and office practices.

The American Dental Association's Commission on Dental Accreditation approved 259 dental-assisting training programs in 2002. Programs include classroom, laboratory, and preclinical instruction in dental-assisting skills and related theory. In addition, students gain practical experience in dental schools, clinics, or dental offices. Most programs take 1 year or less to complete and lead to a certificate or diploma. Two-year programs offered in community and junior colleges lead to an associate degree. All programs require a high school diploma or its equivalent, and some require science or computer-related courses for admission. A number of private vocational schools offer 4- to 6-month courses in dental assisting, but the Commission on Dental Accreditation does not accredit these programs.

Most states regulate the duties that dental assistants are allowed to perform through licensure or registration. Licensure or registration may require passing a written or practical examination. States offering licensure or registration have a variety of schools offering courses—approximately 10 to 12 months in length—that meet their state's requirements. Many states require continuing education to maintain licensure or registration. A few states allow dental assistants to perform any function delegated to them by the dentist.

Individual states have adopted different standards for dental assistants who perform certain advanced duties, such as radiological procedures. The completion of the Radiation Health and Safety examination offered by the Dental Assisting National Board (DANB) meets those standards in more than 30 states. Some states require the completion of a state-approved course in radiology as well.

Certification is available through DANB and is recognized or required in more than 30 states. Other organizations offer registration, most often at the state level. Certification is an acknowledgment of an assistant's qualifications and professional competence and may be an asset when one is seeking employment. Candidates may qualify to take the DANB certification examination by graduating from an accredited training program or by having 2 years of full-time, or 4 years of part-time, experience as a dental assistant. In addition, applicants must have current certification in cardiopulmonary resuscitation. For annual recertification, individuals must earn continuing education credits.

Without further education, advancement opportunities are limited. Some dental assistants become office managers, dental-assisting instructors, or dental product sales representatives. Others go back to school to become dental hygienists. For many, this entry-level occupation provides basic training and experience and serves as a steppingstone to more highly skilled and higher paying jobs.

Job Outlook

Job prospects for dental assistants should be excellent. Employment is expected to grow much faster than the average for all occupations through the year 2012. In fact, dental assistants is expected to be one of the fastest growing occupations through the year 2012.

In addition to job openings due to employment growth, numerous job openings will arise out of the need to replace assistants who transfer to other occupations, retire, or leave the labor force for other reasons. Many opportunities are for entry-level positions offering on-the-job training.

Population growth and greater retention of natural teeth by middle-aged and older people will fuel demand for dental services. Older dentists, who have been less likely to employ assistants, are leaving the occupation and will be replaced by recent graduates, who are more likely to use one or even two assistants. In addition, as dentists' workloads increase, they are expected to hire more assistants to perform routine tasks, so that they may devote their own time to more profitable procedures.

Earnings

Median hourly earnings of dental assistants were $13.10 in 2002. The middle 50 percent earned between $10.35 and $16.20 an hour. The lowest 10 percent earned less than $8.45, and the highest 10 percent earned more than $19.41 an hour.

Benefits vary substantially by practice setting and may be contingent upon full-time employment. According to the American Dental Association, almost all full-time dental assistants employed by private practitioners received paid vacation time. The ADA also found that 9 out of 10 full-time and part-time dental assistants received dental coverage.

Related Occupations

Other workers supporting health practitioners include medical assistants, occupational therapist assistants and aides, pharmacy aides, pharmacy technicians, and physical therapist assistants and aides.

Sources of Additional Information

Information about career opportunities and accredited dental assistant programs is available from:

- Commission on Dental Accreditation, American Dental Association, 211 E. Chicago Ave., Suite 1814, Chicago, IL 60611. Internet: http://www.ada.org

For information on becoming a Certified Dental Assistant and a list of state boards of dentistry, contact:

- Dental Assisting National Board, Inc., 676 North Saint Clair, Suite 1880, Chicago, IL 60611. Internet: http://www.danb.org

For more information on a career as a dental assistant and general information about continuing education, contact:

- American Dental Assistants Association, 35 East Wacker Drive, Suite 1730, Chicago, IL 60601. Internet: http://www.dentalassistant.org

For more information about continuing education courses, contact:

- National Association of Dental Assistants, 900 S. Washington Street, Suite G-13, Falls Church, VA 22046.

Dental Hygienists

(O*NET 29-2021.00)

Significant Points

- Most dental hygiene programs grant an associate degree; others offer a certificate, a bachelor's degree, or a master's degree.
- Job prospects are expected to remain excellent.
- Opportunities for part-time work and flexible schedules are common.

Nature of the Work

Dental hygienists remove soft and hard deposits from teeth, teach patients how to practice good oral hygiene, and provide other preventive dental care. Hygienists examine patients' teeth and gums, recording the presence of diseases or abnormalities. They remove calculus, stains, and plaque from teeth; perform root planing as a periodontal therapy; take and develop dental X rays; and apply cavity-preventive agents such as fluorides and pit and fissure sealants. In some states, hygienists administer anesthetics; place and carve filling materials, temporary fillings, and periodontal dressings; remove sutures; and smooth and polish metal restorations. Although hygienists may not diagnose diseases, they can prepare clinical and laboratory diagnostic tests for the dentist to interpret. Hygienists sometimes work chairside with the dentist during treatment.

Dental hygienists also help patients develop and maintain good oral health. For example, they may explain the relationship between diet and oral health or inform patients how to select toothbrushes and show them how to brush and floss their teeth.

Dental hygienists use hand and rotary instruments and ultrasonics to clean and polish teeth, X-ray machines to take dental pictures, syringes with needles to administer local anesthetics, and models of teeth to explain oral hygiene.

Working Conditions

Flexible scheduling is a distinctive feature of this job. Full-time, part-time, evening, and weekend schedules are widely available. Dentists frequently hire hygienists to work only 2 or 3 days a week, so hygienists may hold jobs in more than one dental office.

Dental hygienists work in clean, well-lighted offices. Important health safeguards include strict adherence to proper radiological procedures, and the use of appropriate protective devices when administering anesthetic gas. Dental hygienists also wear safety glasses, surgical masks, and gloves to protect themselves and patients from infectious diseases.

Employment

Dental hygienists held about 148,000 jobs in 2002. Because multiple jobholding is common in this field, the number of jobs exceeds the number of hygienists. More than half of all dental hygienists worked part time—less than 35 hours a week.

Almost all jobs for dental hygienists were in offices of dentists. A very small number worked for employment services or in offices of physicians.

Training, Other Qualifications, and Advancement

Dental hygienists must be licensed by the state in which they practice. To qualify for licensure, a candidate must graduate from an accredited dental hygiene school and pass both a written and clinical examination. The American Dental Association Joint Commission on National Dental Examinations administers the written examination, which is accepted by all states and the District of Columbia. State or regional testing agencies administer the clinical examination. In addition, most states require an examination on the legal aspects of dental hygiene practice. Alabama allows candidates to take its examinations if they have been trained through a state-regulated on-the-job program in a dentist's office.

In 2002, the Commission on Dental Accreditation accredited about 265 programs in dental hygiene. Most dental hygiene programs grant an associate degree, although some also offer a certificate, a bachelor's degree, or a master's degree. A minimum of an associate degree or certificate in dental hygiene is required for practice in a private dental office. A bachelor's or master's degree usually is required for research, teaching, or clinical practice in public or school health programs.

About half of the dental hygiene programs prefer applicants who have completed at least 1 year of college. However, requirements vary from one school to another. Schools offer laboratory, clinical, and classroom instruction in subjects such as anatomy, physiology, chemistry, microbiology, pharmacology, nutrition, radiography, histology (the study of tissue structure), periodontology (the study of gum diseases), pathology, dental materials, clinical dental hygiene, and social and behavioral sciences.

Dental hygienists should work well with others and must have good manual dexterity, because they use dental instruments within a patient's mouth, with little room for error. High school students interested in becoming a dental hygienist should take courses in biology, chemistry, and mathematics.

Job Outlook

Employment of dental hygienists is expected to grow much faster than the average for all occupations through 2012, in response to increasing demand for dental care and the greater utilization of hygienists to perform services previously performed by dentists. Job prospects are expected to remain excellent. In fact, dental hygienists is expected to be one of the fastest growing occupations through the year 2012.

Population growth and greater retention of natural teeth will stimulate demand for dental hygienists. Older dentists, who have been less likely to employ dental hygienists, are leaving the occupation and will be replaced by recent graduates, who are more likely to employ one or even two hygienists. In addition, as dentists' workloads increase, they are expected to hire more hygienists to perform preventive dental care, such as cleaning, so that they may devote their own time to more profitable procedures.

Earnings

Median hourly earnings of dental hygienists were $26.59 in 2002. The middle 50 percent earned between $21.96 and $32.48 an hour. The lowest 10 percent earned less than $17.34, and the highest 10 percent earned more than $39.24 an hour.

Earnings vary by geographic location, employment setting, and years of experience. Dental hygienists may be paid on an hourly, daily, salary, or commission basis.

Benefits vary substantially by practice setting and may be contingent upon full-time employment. According to the American Dental Association, almost all full-time dental hygienists employed by private practitioners received paid vacation. The ADA also found that 9 out of 10 full-time and part-time dental hygienists received dental coverage. Dental hygienists who work for school systems, public health agencies, the federal government, or state agencies usually have substantial benefits.

Related Occupations

Other workers supporting health practitioners in an office setting include dental assistants, medical assistants, occupational therapist assistants and aides, physical therapist assistants and aides, physician assistants, and registered nurses.

Sources of Additional Information

For information on a career in dental hygiene, including educational requirements, contact:

- Division of Education, American Dental Hygienists' Association, 444 N. Michigan Ave., Suite 3400, Chicago, IL 60611. Internet: http://www.adha.org

For information about accredited programs and educational requirements, contact:

- Commission on Dental Accreditation, American Dental Association, 211 E. Chicago Ave., Suite 1814, Chicago, IL 60611. Internet: http://www.ada.org

The State Board of Dental Examiners in each state can supply information on licensing requirements.

Dental Laboratory Technicians

(O*NET 51-9081.00)

Significant Points

- Employment should increase slowly, as the public's improving dental health requires fewer dentures but more bridges and crowns.

- Dental laboratory technicians need artistic aptitude for detailed and precise work, a high degree of manual dexterity, and good vision.

Nature of the Work

Dental laboratory technicians fill prescriptions from dentists for crowns, bridges, dentures, and other dental prosthetics. First, dentists send a specification of the item to be manufactured, along with an impression (mold) of the patient's mouth or teeth. Then, dental laboratory technicians, also called dental technicians, create a model of the patient's mouth by pouring plaster into the impression and allowing it to set. Next, they place the model on an apparatus that mimics the bite and movement of the patient's jaw. The model serves as the basis of the prosthetic device. Technicians examine the model, noting the size and shape of the adjacent teeth, as well as gaps within the gumline. Based upon these observations and the dentist's specifications, technicians build and shape a wax tooth or teeth model, using small hand instruments called wax spatulas and wax carvers. They use this wax model to cast the metal framework for the prosthetic device.

After the wax tooth has been formed, dental technicians pour the cast and form the metal and, using small hand-held tools, prepare the surface to allow the metal and porcelain to bond. They then apply porcelain in layers, to arrive at the precise shape and color of a tooth. Technicians place the tooth in a porcelain furnace to bake the porcelain onto the metal framework, and then adjust the shape and color, with subsequent grinding and addition of porcelain to achieve a sealed finish. The final product is a nearly exact replica of the lost tooth or teeth.

In some laboratories, technicians perform all stages of the work, whereas, in other labs, each technician does only a few. Dental laboratory technicians can specialize in 1 of 5 areas: Orthodontic appliances, crowns and bridges, complete dentures, partial dentures, or ceramics. Job titles can reflect specialization in these areas. For example, technicians who make porcelain and acrylic restorations are called *dental ceramists*.

Working Conditions

Dental laboratory technicians generally work in clean, well-lighted, and well-ventilated areas. Technicians usually have their own workbenches, which can be equipped with Bunsen burners, grinding and polishing equipment, and hand instruments, such as wax spatulas and wax carvers. Some technicians have computer-aided milling equipment to assist them with creating artificial teeth.

The work is extremely delicate and time consuming. Salaried technicians usually work 40 hours a week, but self-employed technicians frequently work longer hours.

Employment

Dental laboratory technicians held about 47,000 jobs in 2002. Around 7 out of 10 jobs were in medical equipment and supply manufacturing laboratories, which usually are small, privately owned businesses with fewer than five employees. However, some laboratories are large; a few employ more than 50 technicians.

Some dental laboratory technicians work in offices of dentists. Others work for hospitals providing dental services, including U.S. Department of Veterans Affairs hospitals. Some technicians work in dental laboratories in their homes, in addition to their regular job.

Training, Other Qualifications, and Advancement

Most dental laboratory technicians learn their craft on the job. They begin with simple tasks, such as pouring plaster into an impression, and progress to more complex procedures, such as making porcelain crowns and bridges. Becoming a fully trained technician requires an average of 3 to 4 years, depending upon the individual's aptitude and ambition, but it may take a few years more to become an accomplished technician.

Training in dental laboratory technology also is available through community and junior colleges, vocational-technical institutes, and the U.S. Armed Forces. Formal training programs vary greatly both in length and in the level of skill they impart.

In 2002, 25 programs in dental laboratory technology were approved (accredited) by the Commission on Dental Accreditation in conjunction with the American Dental Association (ADA). These programs provide classroom instruction in dental materials science, oral anatomy, fabrication procedures, ethics, and related subjects. In addition, each student is given supervised practical experience in a school or an associated dental laboratory. Accredited programs normally take 2 years to complete and lead to an associate degree. A few programs take about 4 years to complete and offer a bachelor's degree in dental technology.

Graduates of 2-year training programs need additional hands-on experience to become fully qualified. Each dental laboratory owner operates in a different way, and classroom instruction does not necessarily expose students to techniques and procedures favored by individual laboratory owners. Students who have taken enough courses to learn the basics of the craft usually are considered good candidates for training, regardless of whether they have completed a formal program. Many employers will train someone without any classroom experience.

The National Board for Certification, an independent board established by the National Association of Dental Laboratories, offers certification in dental laboratory technology. Certification, which is voluntary, can be obtained in five specialty areas: Crowns and bridges, ceramics, partial dentures, complete dentures, and orthodontic appliances.

In large dental laboratories, technicians may become supervisors or managers. Experienced technicians may teach or may take jobs with dental suppliers in such areas as product development, marketing, and sales. Still, for most technicians, opening one's own laboratory is the way toward advancement and higher earnings.

A high degree of manual dexterity, good vision, and the ability to recognize very fine color shadings and variations in shape are necessary. An artistic aptitude for detailed and precise work also is important. High school students interested in becoming dental laboratory technicians should take courses in art, metal and wood shop, drafting, and sciences. Courses in management and business may help those wishing to operate their own laboratories.

Job Outlook

Job opportunities for dental laboratory technicians should be favorable, despite expected slower-than-average growth in the occupation through the year 2012. Employers have difficulty filling trainee positions, probably because entry-level salaries are relatively low and because the public is not familiar with the occupation.

The overall dental health of the population has improved because of fluoridation of drinking water, which has reduced the incidence of dental cavities, and greater emphasis on preventive dental care since the early 1960s. As a result, full dentures will be less common, as most people will need only a bridge or crown. However, during the last few years, demand has arisen from an aging public that is growing increasingly interested in cosmetic prostheses. For example, many dental laboratories are filling orders for composite fillings that are the same shade of white as natural teeth to replace older, less attractive fillings.

Earnings

Median hourly earnings of dental laboratory technicians were $13.70 in 2002. The middle 50 percent earned between $10.51 and $18.40 an hour. The lowest 10 percent earned less than $8.16, and the highest 10 percent earned more than $23.65 an hour. Median hourly earnings of dental laboratory technicians in 2002 were $13.78 in medical equipment and supplies manufacturing and $12.98 in offices of dentists.

Technicians in large laboratories tend to specialize in a few procedures, and, therefore, tend to be paid a lower wage than those employed in small laboratories who perform a variety of tasks.

Related Occupations

Dental laboratory technicians manufacture artificial teeth, crowns and bridges, and orthodontic appliances, following specifications and instructions provided by dentists. Other workers who make and repair medical devices include dispensing opticians, ophthalmic laboratory technicians, orthotists and prosthetists, and precision instrument and equipment repairers.

Sources of Additional Information

For a list of accredited programs in dental laboratory technology, contact:

- Commission on Dental Accreditation, American Dental Association, 211 E. Chicago Ave., Chicago, IL 60611. Internet: http://www.ada.org

For information on requirements for certification, contact:

- National Board for Certification in Dental Technology, 1530 Metropolitan Blvd., Tallahassee, FL 32308. Internet: http://www.nadl.org/html/certification.html

For information on career opportunities in commercial laboratories, contact:

- National Association of Dental Laboratories, 1530 Metropolitan Blvd., Tallahassee, FL 32308. Internet: http://www.nadl.org

General information on grants and scholarships is available from dental technology schools.

Designers

(O*NET 27-1021.00, 27-1022.00, 27-1023.00, 27-1024.00, 27-1025.00, 27-1026.00, 27-1027.01, and 27-1027.02)

Significant Points

- Nearly one-third of designers were self-employed—almost five times the proportion for all professional and related occupations.

- Creativity is crucial in all design occupations; most designers need a bachelor's degree, and candidates with a master's degree hold an advantage.

- Keen competition is expected for most jobs, despite average projected employment growth, because many talented individuals are attracted to careers as designers.

Nature of the Work

Designers are people with a desire to create. They combine practical knowledge with artistic ability to turn abstract ideas into formal designs for the merchandise we buy, the clothes we wear, the Web sites we use, the publications we read, and the living and office space we inhabit. Designers usually specialize in a particular area of design, such as automobiles, industrial or medical equipment, home appliances, clothing and textiles, floral arrangements, publications, Web sites, logos, signage, movie or TV credits, interiors of homes or office buildings, merchandise displays, or movie, television, and theater sets.

The first step in developing a new design or altering an existing one is to determine the needs of the client, the ultimate function for which the design is intended, and its appeal to customers or users. When creating a design, designers often begin by researching the desired design characteristics, such as size, shape, weight, color, materials used, cost, ease of use, fit, and safety.

Designers then prepare sketches or diagrams—by hand or with the aid of a computer—to illustrate the vision for the design. After consulting with the client, a creative director, or a product development team, designers create detailed designs, using drawings, a structural model, computer simulations, or a full-scale prototype. Many designers use computer-aided design (CAD) tools to create and better visualize the final product. Computer models allow ease and flexibility in exploring a greater number of design alternatives, thus reducing design costs and cutting the time it takes to deliver a product to market. Industrial designers use computer-aided industrial design (CAID) tools to create designs and machine-readable instructions that communicate with automated production tools.

Designers sometimes supervise assistants who carry out their creations. Designers who run their own businesses also may devote a considerable amount of time to developing new business contacts, examining equipment and space needs, and performing administrative tasks, such as reviewing catalogues and ordering samples. The need for up-to-date computer and communications equipment is an ongoing consideration for many designers, especially those in industrial and graphic design.

Design encompasses a number of different fields. Many designers specialize in a particular area of design, whereas others work in more than one area.

Commercial and industrial designers develop countless manufactured products, including airplanes; cars; children's toys; computer equipment; furniture; home appliances; and medical, office, and recreational equipment. They combine artistic talent with research on the use of a product, on customer needs, and on marketing, materials, and production methods to create the most functional and appealing design that will be competitive with others in the marketplace. Industrial designers typically concentrate in a subspecialty such as kitchen appliances, auto interiors, or plastic-molding machinery.

Fashion designers design clothing and accessories. Some high-fashion designers are self-employed and design for individual clients. Other high-fashion designers cater to specialty stores or high-fashion department stores. These designers create original garments, as well as clothing that follows established fashion trends. Most fashion designers, however, work for apparel manufacturers, creating designs of men's, women's, and children's fashions for the mass market.

Floral designers cut and arrange live, dried, or artificial flowers and foliage into designs, according to the customer's order. They design arrangements by trimming flowers and arranging bouquets, sprays, wreaths, dish gardens, and terrariums. They may either meet with customers to discuss the arrangement or work from a written order. Floral designers make note of the occasion, the customer's preference with regard to the color and type of flower involved, the price of the completed order, the time at which the floral arrangement or plant is to be ready, and the place to which it is to be delivered. The variety of duties performed by floral designers depends on the size of the shop and the number of designers employed. In a small operation, floral designers may own their shops and do almost everything, from growing and purchasing flowers to keeping financial records.

Graphic designers plan, analyze, and create visual solutions to communications problems. They use a variety of print, electronic, and film media and technologies to execute a design that meet clients' communication needs. They consider cognitive, cultural, physical, and social factors in planning and executing designs appropriate for a given context. Graphic designers use computer software to develop the overall layout and production design of magazines, newspapers, journals, corporate reports, and other publications. They also produce promotional displays and marketing brochures for products and services, design distinctive logos for products and businesses, and develop signs and signage systems—called environmental graphics—for business and government. An increasing number of graphic designers are developing material for Internet Web pages, computer interfaces, and multimedia projects. Graphic designers also produce the credits that appear before and after television programs and movies.

Interior designers enhance the function, safety, and quality of interior spaces of private homes, public buildings, and business or institutional facilities, such as offices, restaurants, retail establishments, hospitals, hotels, and theaters. They also plan the interiors of existing structures that are undergoing renovation or expansion. Most interior designers specialize. For example, some may concentrate on residential design, while others focus on business design. Still others may specialize further by focusing on particular rooms, such as kitchens or baths. With a client's tastes, needs, and budget in mind, interior designers prepare drawings and specifications for non-load-bearing interior construction, furnishings, lighting, and finishes. Increasingly, designers are using computers to plan layouts, because computers make it easy to change plans to include ideas received from the client. Interior designers also design lighting and architectural details—such as crown molding, built-in book-shelves, or cabinets—coordinate colors, and select furniture, floor coverings, and window treatments. Interior designers must design space to conform to federal, state, and local laws, including building codes. Designs for public areas also must meet accessibility standards for the disabled and the elderly.

Merchandise displayers and window dressers, or *visual merchandisers*, plan and erect commercial displays, such as those in windows and interiors of retail stores or at trade exhibitions. Those who work on building exteriors erect major store decorations, including building and window displays and lights. Those who design store interiors outfit store departments, arrange table displays, and dress mannequins. In large retail chains, store layouts typically are designed corporately, through a central design department. To retain the chain's visual identity and ensure that a particular image or theme is promoted in each store, designs are distributed to individual stores by e-mail, downloaded to computers equipped with the appropriate design software, and adapted to meet the size and dimension requirements of each individual store.

Set and exhibit designers create sets for movie, television, and theater productions and design special exhibition displays. Set designers study scripts, confer with directors and other designers, and conduct research to determine the historical period, fashion, and architectural styles appropriate for the production on which they work. They then produce sketches or scale models to guide in the construction of the actual sets or exhibit spaces. Exhibit designers work with curators, art and museum directors, and trade-show sponsors to determine the most effective use of available space.

Working Conditions

Working conditions and places of employment vary. Designers employed by manufacturing establishments, large corporations, or design firms generally work regular hours in well-lighted and comfortable settings. Designers in smaller design consulting firms, or those who freelance, generally work on a contract, or job, basis. They frequently adjust their workday to suit their clients' schedules and deadlines, meeting with the clients during evening or weekend hours when necessary. Consultants and self-employed designers tend to work longer hours and in smaller, more congested, environments.

Designers may transact business in their own offices or studios or in clients' homes or offices. They also may travel to other locations, such as showrooms, design centers, clients' exhibit sites, and manufacturing facilities. Designers who are paid by the assignment are under pressure to please clients and to find new ones in order to maintain a steady income. All designers sometimes face frustration when their designs are rejected or when their work is not as creative as they wish. With the increased speed and sophistication of computers and advanced communications networks, designers may form international design teams, serve a geographically more dispersed clientele, research design

alternatives by using information on the Internet, and purchase supplies electronically, all with the aid of a computer in their workplace or studio.

Occasionally, industrial designers may work additional hours to meet deadlines. Similarly, graphic designers usually work regular hours, but may work evenings or weekends to meet production schedules. In contrast, set and exhibit designers work long and irregular hours; often, they are under pressure to make rapid changes. Merchandise displayers and window trimmers may spend much of their time designing displays in their office or studio, but those who also construct and install the displays may have to move lumber and heavy materials and perform some carpentry and painting. Fashion designers may work long hours to meet production deadlines or prepare for fashion shows. In addition, fashion designers may be required to travel to production sites across the United States and overseas. Interior designers generally work under deadlines and may put in extra hours to finish a job. Also, they typically carry heavy, bulky sample books to meetings with clients. Floral designers generally work regular hours in a pleasant work environment, but holiday, wedding, and funeral orders often require overtime.

Employment

Designers held about 532,000 jobs in 2002. Approximately one-third were self-employed. Employment was distributed as follows:

Graphic designers	212,000
Floral designers	104,000
Merchandise displayers and window trimmers	77,000
Interior designers	60,000
Commercial and industrial designers	52,000
Fashion designers	15,000
Set and exhibit designers	12,000

Salaried designers worked in a number of different industries, depending on their design specialty. Graphic designers, for example, worked primarily in specialized design services; newspaper, periodical, book, and directory publishers; and advertising and related services. Floral designers were concentrated in retail florists or floral departments of grocery stores. Merchandise displayers and window trimmers were dispersed across a variety of retailers and wholesalers. Interior designers generally worked in specialized design services or in retail furniture stores. Most commercial and industrial designers were employed in manufacturing or architectural, engineering, and related services. Fashion designers generally worked in apparel manufacturing or wholesale distribution of apparel, piece goods, and notions. Set and exhibit designers worked primarily for performing arts companies, movie and video industries, and radio and television broadcasting.

In 2002, a large proportion of designers were self-employed and did freelance work—full time or part time—in addition to holding a salaried job in design or in another occupation.

Training, Other Qualifications, and Advancement

Creativity is crucial in all design occupations. People in this field must have a strong sense of the esthetic—an eye for color and detail, a sense of balance and proportion, and an appreciation for beauty. Designers also need excellent communication and problem-solving skills. Despite the advancement of computer-aided design, sketching ability remains an important advantage in most types of design, especially fashion design. A good portfolio—a collection of examples of a person's best work—often is the deciding factor in getting a job.

A bachelor's degree is required for most entry-level design positions, except for floral design and visual merchandising. Esthetic ability is important in floral design and visual merchandising, but formal preparation typically is not necessary. Many candidates in industrial design pursue a master's degree to increase their chances of selection for open positions.

Interior design is the only design field subject to government regulation. According to the American Society of Interior Designers, 22 states and the District of Columbia register or license interior designers. Passing the National Council for Interior Design qualification examination is required for registration or licensure in these jurisdictions. To be eligible to take the exam, an applicant must have at least 6 years of combined education and experience in interior design, of which at least 2 years constitute postsecondary education in design. Because registration or licensure is not mandatory in all states, membership in a professional association is an indication of an interior designer's qualifications and professional standing—and can aid in obtaining clients.

In fashion design, employers seek individuals with a 2- or 4-year degree who are knowledgeable in the areas of textiles, fabrics, and ornamentation, and about trends in the fashion world. Set and exhibit designers typically have college degrees in design. A Master of Fine Arts degree from an accredited university program further establishes one's design credentials. For set designers, membership in the United Scenic Artists, Local 829, is recognized nationally as the attainment of professional standing in the field.

Most floral designers learn their skills on the job. When employers hire trainees, they generally look for high school graduates who have a flair for arranging and a desire to learn. The completion of formal design training, however, is an asset for floral designers, particularly those interested in advancing to chief floral designer or in opening their own businesses. Vocational and technical schools offer programs in floral design, usually lasting less than a year, while 2- and 4-year programs in floriculture, horticulture, floral design, or ornamental horticulture are offered by community and junior colleges, colleges, and universities. The American Institute of Floral Designers offers an accreditation examination to its members as an indication of professional achievement in floral design.

Formal training for some design professions also is available in 2- and 3-year professional schools that award certificates or associate degrees in design. Graduates of 2-year programs normally qualify as assistants to designers, or they may enter a formal bachelor's degree program. The Bachelor of Fine Arts degree is granted at 4-year colleges and universities. The curriculum in these schools includes art and art history, principles of design, designing and sketching, and specialized studies for each of the individual design disciplines, such as garment construction, textiles, mechanical and architectural drawing, computerized design, sculpture, architecture, and basic engineering. A liberal arts education or a program that includes training in business or project management, together with courses in merchandising, marketing, and psychology, along with training in art, is recommended for designers who want to freelance. In addition, persons with training or experience in architecture qualify for some design occupations, particularly interior design.

Employers increasingly expect new designers to be familiar with computer-aided design software as a design tool. For example, industrial designers use computers extensively in the aerospace, automotive, and electronics industries. Interior designers use computers to create numerous versions of interior space designs—images can be inserted, edited, and replaced easily and without added cost—making it possible for a client to see and choose among several designs.

The National Association of Schools of Art and Design accredits more than 200 postsecondary institutions with programs in art and design. Most of these schools award a degree in art, and some award degrees in industrial, interior, textile, graphic, or fashion design. Many schools do not allow formal entry into a bachelor's degree program until a student has successfully finished a year of basic art and design courses. Applicants may be required to submit sketches and other examples of their artistic ability.

The Foundation for Interior Design Education Research also accredits interior design programs that lead to a bachelor's degree. There are about 120 accredited professional programs in the United States, located primarily in schools of art, architecture, and home economics.

Individuals in the design field must be creative, imaginative, and persistent and must be able to communicate their ideas in writing, visually, and verbally. Because tastes in style and fashion can change quickly, designers need to be well read, open to new ideas and influences, and quick to react to changing trends. Problem-solving skills and the ability to work independently and under pressure are important traits. People in this field need self-discipline to start projects on their own, to budget their time, and to meet deadlines and production schedules. Good business sense and sales ability also are important, especially for those who freelance or run their own business.

Beginning designers usually receive on-the-job training and normally need 1 to 3 years of training before they can advance to higher level positions. Experienced designers in large firms may advance to chief designer, design department head, or other supervisory positions. Some designers leave the occupation to become teachers in design schools or in colleges and universities. Many faculty members continue to consult privately or operate small design studios to complement their classroom activities. Some experienced designers open their own firms.

Job Outlook

Overall employment of designers is expected to grow about as fast as the average for all occupations through the year 2012 as the economy expands and consumers, businesses, and manufacturers continue to rely on the services provided by designers. However, designers in most fields—with the exception of floral design—are expected to face keen competition for available positions. Many talented individuals are attracted to careers as designers. Individuals with little or no formal education in design, as well as those who lack creativity and perseverance, will find it very difficult to establish and maintain a career in the occupation.

Among the design specialties, graphic designers are projected to provide the most new jobs. Demand for graphic designers should increase because of the rapidly expanding market for Web-based information and expansion of the video entertainment market, including television, movies, video, and made-for-Internet outlets.

Rising demand for interior design of private homes, offices, restaurants and other retail establishments, and institutions that care for the rapidly growing elderly population should spur employment growth of interior designers. New jobs for floral designers are expected to stem mostly from the relatively high replacement needs in retail florists that result from comparatively low starting pay and limited opportunities for advancement. The majority of new jobs for merchandise displayers and window trimmers will also result from the need to replace workers who retire, transfer to other occupations, or leave the labor force for other reasons.

Increased demand for industrial designers will stem from continued emphasis on the quality and safety of products, demand for new products that are easy and comfortable to use, and the development of high-technology products in medicine, transportation, and other fields. Demand for fashion designers should remain strong, because many consumers continue to seek new fashions and fresh styles of apparel. Employment growth for fashion designers will be slowed, however, by declines in the apparel manufacturing industries. Despite faster-than-average growth for set and exhibit designers, few job openings will result because the occupation is small.

Earnings

Median annual earnings for commercial and industrial designers were $52,260 in 2002. The middle 50 percent earned between $39,240 and $67,430. The lowest 10 percent earned less than $28,820, and the highest 10 percent earned more than $82,130. Median annual earnings were $61,530 in architectural, engineering, and related services.

Median annual earnings for fashion designers were $51,290 in 2002. The middle 50 percent earned between $35,550 and $75,970. The lowest 10 percent earned less than $25,350, and the highest 10 percent earned more than $105,280.

Median annual earnings for floral designers were $19,480 in 2002. The middle 50 percent earned between $15,880 and $23,560. The lowest 10 percent earned less than $13,440, and the highest 10 percent earned more than $29,830. Median annual earnings were $21,610 in grocery stores and $18,950 in florists.

Median annual earnings for graphic designers were $36,680 in 2002. The middle 50 percent earned between $28,140 and $48,820. The lowest 10 percent earned less than $21,860, and the highest 10 percent earned more than $64,160. Median annual earnings in the industries employing the largest numbers of graphic designers were as follows:

Advertising and related services $39,510
Specialized design services.....................................38,710
Printing and related support activities 31,800
Newspaper, periodical, book, and directory
   publishers...31,670

Median annual earnings for interior designers were $39,180 in 2002. The middle 50 percent earned between $29,070 and $53,060. The lowest 10 percent earned less than $21,240, and the highest 10 percent earned more than $69,640. Median annual earnings in the industries employing the largest numbers of interior designers were as follows:

Architectural, engineering, and related services $41,680
Specialized design services.....................................39,870
Furniture stores 36,320

Median annual earnings of merchandise displayers and window dressers were $22,550 in 2002. The middle 50 percent earned between $18,320 and $29,070. The lowest 10 percent earned less than $15,100, and the highest 10 percent earned more than $40,020. Median annual earnings were $22,130 in department stores.

Median annual earnings for set and exhibit designers were $33,870 in 2000. The middle 50 percent earned between $24,780 and $46,350. The lowest 10 percent earned less than $17,830, and the highest 10 percent earned more than $63,280.

The American Institute of Graphic Arts reported 2002 median annual earnings for graphic designers with increasing levels of responsibility. Staff-level graphic designers earned $40,000, while senior designers, who may supervise junior staff or have some decisionmaking authority that reflects their knowledge of graphic design, earned $55,000. Solo designers, who freelanced or worked under contract to another company, reported median earnings of $55,000. Design directors, the creative heads of design firms or in-house corporate design departments, earned $85,000. Graphic designers with ownership or partnership interests in a firm or who were principals of the firm in some other capacity earned $93,000.

Related Occupations

Workers in other occupations who design or arrange objects, materials, or interiors to enhance their appearance and function include artists and related workers; architects, except landscape and naval; engineers; landscape architects; and photographers. Some computer-related occupations, including computer software engineers and desktop publishers, require design skills.

Sources of Additional Information

For general information about art and design and a list of accredited college-level programs, contact:

- National Association of Schools of Art and Design, 11250 Roger Bacon Dr., Suite 21, Reston, VA 20190. Internet: http://nasad.arts-accredit.org

For information about graphic, communication, or interaction design careers, contact:

- American Institute of Graphic Arts, 164 Fifth Ave., New York, NY 10010. Internet: http://www.aiga.org

For information on degree, continuing education, and licensure programs in interior design and interior design research, contact:

- American Society for Interior Designers, 608 Massachusetts Ave. NE, Washington, DC 20002-6006. Internet: http://www.asid.org

For a list of schools with accredited programs in interior design, contact:

- Foundation for Interior Design Education Research, 146 Monroe Center NW., Suite 1318, Grand Rapids, MI 49503. Internet: http://www.fider.org

For information on careers, continuing education, and certification programs in the interior design specialty of residential kitchen and bath design, contact:

- National Kitchen and Bath Association, 687 Willow Grove St., Hackettstown, NJ 07840. Internet: http://www.nkba.org/student

For information about careers in floral design, contact:

- Society of American Florists, 1601 Duke St., Alexandria, VA 22314. Internet: http://www.safnow.org

Desktop Publishers

(O*NET 43-9031.00)

Significant Points

- Desktop publishers are expected to experience faster than average employment growth.

- Two out of three worked in firms that handle newspaper, periodical, book, and directory publishing, or printing and related support activities.

- Although formal training is not always required, those with certificates or degrees will have the best job opportunities.

Nature of the Work

Using computer software, desktop publishers format and combine text, numerical data, photographs, charts, and other visual graphic elements to produce publication-ready material. Depending on the nature of a particular project, desktop publishers may write and edit text, create graphics to accompany text, convert photographs and drawings into digital images and then manipulate those images, design page layouts, create proposals, develop presentations and advertising campaigns, typeset and do color separation, and translate electronic information onto film or other traditional forms. Materials produced by desktop publishers include books, business cards, calendars, magazines, newsletters and newspapers, packaging, slides, and tickets. As companies have brought the production of marketing, promotional, and other kinds of materials in-house, they increasingly have employed people who can produce such materials.

Desktop publishers use a keyboard to enter and select formatting properties, such as the size and style of type, column width, and spacing, and store them in the computer, which then displays and arranges columns of type on a video display terminal or computer monitor. An entire newspaper, catalog, or book page, complete with artwork and graphics, can be created on the screen exactly as it will appear in print. Operators transmit the pages for production either into film and then into printing plates, or directly into plates.

Desktop publishing is a rapidly changing field that encompasses a number of different kinds of jobs. Personal computers enable desktop publishers to perform publishing tasks that would otherwise require complicated equipment and human effort. Advances in computer software and printing technology continue to change and enhance desktop-publishing work. Instead of receiving simple typed text from customers, desktop publishers get the material over the Internet or on a computer disk. Other innovations in the occupation include digital color page-makeup systems, electronic page-layout systems, and off-press color-proofing systems. In addition, because most materials today often are published on the Internet, desktop publishers may need to know electronic-publishing technologies, such as Hypertext Markup Language (HTML), and may be responsible for converting text and graphics to an Internet-ready format.

Typesetting and page layout have been affected by the technological changes shaping desktop publishing. Increasingly, desktop publishers are using computers to do much of the typesetting and page-layout work formerly done by prepress workers, posing new challenges for the printing industry.

The old "hot type" method of text composition—which used molten lead to create individual letters, paragraphs, and full pages of text—is nearly extinct. Today, composition work is done primarily with computers. Improvements in desktop-publishing software also allow customers to do much more of their own typesetting.

Desktop publishers use scanners to capture photographs, images, or art as digital data that can be either incorporated directly into electronic page layouts or further manipulated with the use of computer software. The desktop publisher then can correct mistakes or compensate for deficiencies in the original color print or transparency. Digital files are used to produce printing plates. Like photographers and multimedia artists and animators, desktop publishers also can create special effects or other visual images, using film, video, computers, or other electronic media.

Depending on the establishment employing these workers, desktop publishers also may be referred to as publications specialists, electronic publishers, DTP operators, desktop-publishing editors, electronic prepress technicians, electronic-publishing specialists, image designers, typographers, compositors, layout artists, and web publications designers.

Working Conditions

Desktop publishers usually work in clean, air-conditioned office areas with little noise. They generally work an 8-hour day, 5 days a week. Some workers work night shifts, weekends, and holidays.

Desktop publishers often are subject to stress and the pressures of short deadlines and tight work schedules. Like other workers who spend long hours working in front of a computer monitor, they may be susceptible to eyestrain, back discomfort, and hand and wrist problems.

Employment

Desktop publishers held about 35,000 jobs in 2002. Two out of three worked in the newspaper, periodical, book, and directory publishing and printing and related support activities; the rest worked in a wide variety of industries.

Firms in the publishing industry employ most desktop publishers. These firms publish newspapers, periodicals, books, directory and mailing lists, and greeting cards. A large number of desktop publishers also work for printing and related support activities firms, which print a wide range of products—newspapers, books, labels, business cards, stationary, inserts, catalogs, pamphlets, and advertisements—while business form establishments print material such as sales receipts and business forms and perform support activities such as data imaging and bookbinding. Establishments in printing and related support activities typically perform custom composition, platemaking, and related prepress services. Other desktop publishers print or publish materials in-house or in-plant for business services firms, government agencies, hospitals, or universities, typically in a reproduction or publications department that operates within the organization.

The printing and publishing industries are two of the most geographically dispersed industries in the United States, and desktop-publishing jobs are found throughout the country. However, most jobs are in large metropolitan cities.

Training, Other Qualifications, and Advancement

Most workers qualify for jobs as desktop publishers by taking classes or completing certificate programs at vocational schools, universities, and colleges or through the Internet. Programs range in length, but the average certificate program takes approximately 1 year. However, some desktop publishers train on the job to develop the necessary skills. The length of on-the-job training varies by company. An internship or part-time desktop-publishing assignment is another way to gain experience as a desktop publisher.

Students interested in pursuing a career in desktop publishing may obtain an associate's degree in applied science or a bachelor's degree in graphic arts, graphic communications, or graphic design. Graphic arts programs are a good way to learn about desktop publishing software used to format pages, assign type characteristics, and import text and graphics into electronic page layouts to produce printed materials such as advertisements, brochures, newsletters, and forms. Applying this knowledge of graphic arts techniques and computerized typesetting usually is intended for students who may eventually move into management positions, while 2-year associate's degree programs are designed to train skilled workers. Students also develop finely tuned skills in typography, print media, packaging, branding and identity, Web-site design, and motion graphics. The programs teach print and graphic design fundamentals and provide an extensive background in imaging, prepress operations, print reproduction, and emerging media. Courses in other aspects of printing also are available at vocational-technical institutes, industry-sponsored update and retraining programs, and private trade and technical schools.

Although formal training is not always required, those with certificates or degrees will have the best job opportunities. Most employers prefer to hire people who have at least a high school diploma and who possess good communication skills, basic computer skills, and a strong work ethic. Desktop publishers should be able to deal courteously with people, because, in small shops, they may have to take customers' orders. They also may have to add, subtract, multiply, divide, and compute ratios to estimate job costs. Persons interested in working for firms using advanced printing technology need to know the basics of electronics and computers.

Desktop publishers need good manual dexterity, and they must be able to pay attention to detail and work independently. Good eyesight, including visual acuity, depth perception, a wide field of view, color vision, and the ability to focus quickly also are assets. Artistic ability often is a plus. Employers also seek persons who are even tempered and adaptable—important qualities for workers who often must meet deadlines and learn how to operate new equipment.

Workers with limited training and experience may start as helpers. They begin with instruction from an experienced desktop publisher and advance on the basis of their demonstrated mastery of skills at each level. All workers should expect to be retrained from time to time to handle new, improved software and equipment. As workers gain experience, they advance to positions with greater responsibility. Some move into supervisory or management positions. Other desktop publishers may start their own company or work as independent consultants, while those with more artistic talent and further education may find opportunities in graphic design or commercial art.

Job Outlook

Employment of desktop publishers is expected to grow faster than the average for all occupations through 2012, as more page layout and design work is performed in-house using computers and sophisticated publishing software. Desktop publishing is replacing much of the prepress work done by compositors and typesetters, enabling organizations to reduce costs while increasing production speeds. Many new jobs for desktop publishers are expected to emerge in commercial printing and publishing establishments. However, more companies also are turning to in-house desktop publishers, as computers with elaborate text and graphics capabilities have become common, and desktop publishing software has become cheaper and easier to use. In addition to employment growth, many job openings for desktop publishers also will result from the need to replace workers who move into managerial positions, transfer to other occupations, or who leave the labor force.

Printing and publishing costs represent a significant portion of a corporation's expenses, and firms are finding it more profitable to print their own newsletters and other reports than to send them out to trade shops. Desktop publishing reduces the time needed to complete a printing job and allows commercial printers to make inroads into new markets that require fast turnaround.

Most employers prefer to hire experienced desktop publishers. As more people gain desktop-publishing experience, however, competition for jobs may increase. Among persons without experience, opportunities should be best for those with computer backgrounds who are certified or who have completed postsecondary programs in desktop publishing or graphic design. Many employers prefer graduates of these programs because the comprehensive training they receive helps them learn the page-layout process and adapt more rapidly to new software and techniques.

Earnings

Earnings for desktop publishers vary according to level of experience, training, location, and size of firm. Median annual earnings of desktop publishers were $31,620 in 2002. The middle 50 percent earned between $24,030 and $41,280. The lowest 10 percent earned less than $18,670, and the highest 10 percent earned more than $52,540 a year. Median annual earnings in the industries employing the largest numbers of these workers in 2002 are presented in the following tabulation:

Printing and related support activities $35,140

Newspaper, periodical, book, and directory
    publishers...28,050

Related Occupations

Desktop publishers use artistic and editorial skills in their work. These skills also are essential for artists and related workers; designers; news analysts, reporters, and correspondents; prepress technicians and workers; public relations specialists; and writers and editors.

Sources of Additional Information

Details about apprenticeship and other training programs may be obtained from local employers such as newspapers and printing shops or from local offices of the state employment service.

For information on careers and training in printing, desktop publishing, and graphic arts, write to either of the following sources:

- Graphic Communications Council, 1899 Preston White Dr., Reston, VA 20191. Internet: http://www.npes.org/education/index.html

- Graphic Arts Technical Foundation, 200 Deer Run Rd., Sewickley, PA 15143. Internet: http://www.gatf.org

For information on benefits and compensation in desktop publishing, write to:

- Printing Industries of America, Inc., 100 Daingerfield Rd., Alexandria, VA 22314. Internet: http://www.gain.org

Diagnostic Medical Sonographers

(O*NET 29-2032.00)

Significant Points

- More than half of all sonographers were employed by hospitals, and most of the rest worked in offices of physicians or in medical and diagnostic laboratories, including diagnostic imaging centers.

- Sonographers may train in hospitals, vocational-technical institutions, colleges and universities, and the Armed Forces.

- Sonographers should experience favorable job opportunities, as sonography becomes an increasingly attractive alternative to radiologic procedures.

Nature of the Work

Diagnostic imaging embraces several procedures that aid in diagnosing ailments. Besides the familiar X ray, another common diagnostic imaging method is magnetic resonance imaging, which uses giant magnets that create radio waves, rather than radiation, to form an image. Not all imaging technologies use ionizing radiation or radio waves, however. Sonography, or ultrasonography, is the use of sound waves to generate an image for the assessment and diagnosis of various medical conditions. Many people associate sonography with obstetrics and the viewing of the fetus in the womb, but this technology has many other applications in the diagnosis and treatment of medical conditions.

Diagnostic medical sonographers, also known as *ultrasonographers*, use special equipment to direct nonionizing, high frequency sound waves into areas of the patient's body. Sonographers operate the equipment, which collects reflected echoes and forms an image that may be videotaped, transmitted, or photographed for interpretation and diagnosis by a physician.

Sonographers begin by explaining the procedure to the patient and recording any medical history that may be relevant to the condition being viewed. They then select appropriate equipment settings and direct the patient to move into positions that will provide the best view. To perform the exam, sonographers use a transducer, which transmits sound waves in a cone- or rectangle-shaped beam. Although techniques vary with the area being examined, sonographers usually spread a special gel on the skin to aid the transmission of sound waves.

Viewing the screen during the scan, sonographers look for subtle visual cues that contrast healthy areas with unhealthy ones. They decide whether the images are satisfactory for diagnostic purposes and select which ones to show to the physician.

Diagnostic medical sonographers may specialize in obstetric and gynecologic sonography (the female reproductive system), abdominal sonography (the liver, kidneys, gallbladder, spleen, and pancreas), neurosonography (the brain), or ophthalmologic sonography (the eyes). In addition, sonographers may specialize in vascular technology or echocardiography.

Obstetric and gynecologic sonographers specialize in the study of the female reproductive system. Included in the discipline is one of the more well-known uses of sonography: examining the fetus of a pregnant woman to track its growth and health.

Abdominal sonographers inspect a patient's abdominal cavity to help diagnose and treat conditions involving primarily the gallbladder, bile ducts, kidneys, liver, pancreas, and spleen. Abdominal sonographers also are able to scan parts of the chest, although studies of the heart using sonography usually are done by echocardiographers.

Neurosonographers focus on the nervous system, including the brain. In neonatal care, neurosonographers study and diagnose neurological and nervous system disorders in premature infants. They also may scan blood vessels to check for abnormalities indicating a stroke in infants diagnosed with sickle-cell anemia. Like other sonographers, neurosonographers operate transducers to perform the sonogram, but use frequencies and beam shapes different from those used by obstetric and abdominal sonographers.

Ophthalmologic sonographers use sonography to study the eyes. Sonography aids in the insertion of prosthetic lenses by allowing accurate measurement of the eyes. Ophthalmologic sonography also helps diagnose and track tumors, blood supply conditions, separated retinas, and other ailments of the eye and the surrounding tissue. Ophthalmologic sonographers use high-frequency transducers, made exclusively to study the eyes, which are much smaller than those used in other specialties.

In addition to working directly with patients, diagnostic medical sonographers keep patient records and adjust and maintain equipment. They also may prepare work schedules, evaluate equipment purchases, or manage a sonography or diagnostic imaging department.

Working Conditions

Most full-time sonographers work about 40 hours a week. Hospital-based sonographers may have evening and weekend hours and times when they are on call and must be ready to report to work on short notice.

Sonographers typically work in healthcare facilities that are clean and well lighted. Some travel to patients in large vans equipped with sophisticated diagnostic equipment. Sonographers are on their feet for long periods and may have to lift or turn disabled patients. They work at diagnostic imaging machines, but also may perform some procedures at patients' bedsides.

Employment

Diagnostic medical sonographers held about 37,000 jobs in 2002. More than half of all sonographer jobs were in hospitals. Most of the rest were in offices of physicians or in medical and diagnostic laboratories, including diagnostic imaging centers. According to data from the Sonography Benchmark Survey conducted by the Society of Diagnostic Medical Sonography, about 3 out of 4 sonographers worked in urban areas.

Training, Other Qualifications, and Advancement

There are several avenues for entry into the field of diagnostic medical sonography. Sonographers may train in hospitals, vocational-technical institutions, colleges and universities, and the Armed Forces. Some training programs prefer applicants with a background in science or experience in other health professions, but also will consider high school graduates with courses in mathematics and science, as well as applicants with liberal arts backgrounds.

Colleges and universities offer formal training in both 2- and 4-year programs, culminating in an associate or a bachelor's degree. Two-year programs are most prevalent. Course work includes classes in anatomy, physiology, instrumentation, basic physics, patient care, and medical ethics. The Commission on Accreditation for Allied Health Education Programs accredits most formal training programs—about 102 programs in 2003.

Some health workers, such as obstetric nurses and radiologic technologists, increase their marketability by seeking training in fields such as sonography. This usually requires completion of an additional 1-year program that may result in a certificate. In addition, sonographers specializing in one particular discipline often seek competency in others; for example, obstetric sonographers might seek training in, and exposure to, abdominal sonography to broaden their opportunities.

Although no state requires licensure in diagnostic medical sonography, organizations such as the American Registry of Diagnostic Medical Sonographers (ARDMS) certify the competency of sonographers through registration. Because registration provides an independent, objective measure of an individual's professional standing, many employers prefer to hire registered sonographers. Registration with ARDMS requires passing a general physics and instrumentation examination, in addition to passing an exam in a specialty such as obstetric and gynecologic sonography, abdominal sonography, or neurosonography. To keep their registration current, sonographers must complete continuing education to stay abreast of technological advances related to the occupation.

Sonographers need good communication and interpersonal skills because they must be able to explain technical procedures and results to their patients, some of whom may be nervous about the exam or the problems it may reveal. Sonographers also should have a background in mathematics and science.

Job Outlook

Employment of diagnostic medical sonographers is expected to grow faster than the average for all occupations through 2012 as the population grows and ages, increasing the demand for diagnostic imaging and therapeutic technology. In addition to job openings due to growth, some job openings will arise from the need to replace sonographers who leave the occupation permanently.

Opportunities should be favorable because sonography is becoming an increasingly attractive alternative to radiologic procedures, as patients seek safer treatment methods. Unlike most diagnostic imaging methods, sonography does not involve radiation, so harmful side effects and complications from repeated use are rarer for both the patient and the sonographer. Sonographic technology is expected to evolve rapidly and to spawn many new sonography procedures, such as 3D-sonography for use in obstetric and ophthalmologic diagnosis. However, high costs may limit the rate at which some promising new technologies are adopted.

Hospitals will remain the principal employer of diagnostic medical sonographers. However, employment is expected to grow more rapidly in offices of physicians and in medical and diagnostic laboratories, including diagnostic imaging centers. Health facilities such as these are expected to grow very rapidly through 2012 due to the strong shift toward outpatient care, encouraged by third-party payers and made possible by technological advances that permit more procedures to be performed outside the hospital.

Earnings

Median annual earnings of diagnostic medical sonographers were $48,660 in 2002. The middle 50 percent earned between $41,420 and $56,020 a year. The lowest 10 percent earned less than $35,800, and the highest 10 percent earned more than $66,680. Median annual earnings of diagnostic medical sonographers in 2002 were $50,390 in offices of physicians and $47,530 in hospitals.

Related Occupations

Diagnostic medical sonographers operate sophisticated equipment to help physicians and other health practitioners diagnose and treat patients. Workers in related occupations include cardiovascular technologists and technicians, clinical laboratory technologists and technicians, nuclear medicine technologists, radiologic technologists and technicians, and respiratory therapists.

Sources of Additional Information

For information on a career as a diagnostic medical sonographer, contact:

- Society of Diagnostic Medical Sonography, 2745 Dallas Pkwy., Suite 350, Plano, TX 75093-8730. Internet: http://www.sdms.org

For information on becoming a registered diagnostic medical sonographer, contact:

- American Registry of Diagnostic Medical Sonographers, 51 Monroe St., Plaza East I, Rockville, MD 20850-2400. Internet: http://www.ardms.org

For a current list of accredited education programs in diagnostic medical sonography, contact:

- Joint Review Committee on Education in Diagnostic Medical Sonography, 2025 Woodlane Dr., St. Paul, MN 55125-2998. Internet: http://www.jrcdms.org

- Commission on Accreditation for Allied Health Education Programs, 39 East Wacker Dr., Chicago, IL 60601. Internet: http://www.caahep.org

Diesel Service Technicians and Mechanics

(O*NET 49-3031.00)

Significant Points

- A career as a diesel service technician or mechanic offers relatively high wages and the challenge of skilled repair work.

- Opportunities are expected to be good for persons who complete formal training programs.

- National certification is the recognized standard of achievement for diesel service technicians and mechanics.

Nature of the Work

The diesel engine is the workhorse powering the nation's trucks and buses, because it delivers more power and is more durable than its gasoline-burning counterpart. Diesel-powered engines also are becoming more prevalent in light vehicles, including pickups and other work trucks.

Diesel service technicians and mechanics, also known as *bus and truck mechanics* and *diesel engine specialists*, repair and maintain the diesel engines that power transportation equipment such as heavy trucks, buses, and locomotives. Some diesel technicians and mechanics also work on heavy vehicles and mobile equipment, including bulldozers, cranes, road graders, farm tractors, and combines. A small number of technicians repair diesel-powered passenger automobiles, light trucks, or boats.

Technicians who work for organizations that maintain their own vehicles spend most of their time doing preventive maintenance, to ensure that equipment will operate safely. These workers also eliminate unnecessary wear on, and damage to, parts that could result in costly breakdowns. During a routine maintenance check on a vehicle, technicians follow a checklist that includes inspecting brake systems, steering mechanisms, wheel bearings, and other important parts. Following inspection, technicians repair or adjust parts that do not work properly or remove and replace parts that cannot be fixed.

Increasingly, technicians must be flexible, in order to adapt to customers' needs and new technologies. It is common for technicians to handle all kinds of repairs, from working on a vehicle's electrical system one day to doing major engine repairs the next. Diesel maintenance is becoming increasingly complex, as more electronic components are used to control the operation of an engine. For example, microprocessors now regulate and manage fuel timing, increasing the engine's efficiency. In modern shops, diesel service technicians use hand-held computers to diagnose problems and adjust engine functions. Technicians must continually learn about new techniques and advanced materials.

Diesel service technicians use a variety of tools in their work, including power tools, such as pneumatic wrenches, to remove bolts quickly; machine tools, such as lathes and grinding machines, to rebuild brakes; welding and flame-cutting equipment, to remove and repair exhaust systems; and jacks and hoists, to lift and move large parts. Common handtools—screwdrivers, pliers, and wrenches—are used to work on small parts and get at hard-to-reach places. Diesel service technicians and mechanics also use a variety of computerized testing equipment to pinpoint and analyze malfunctions in electrical systems and engines.

In large shops, technicians generally receive their assignments from shop supervisors or service managers. Most supervisors and managers are experienced technicians who also assist in diagnosing problems and maintaining quality standards. Technicians may work as a team or be assisted by an apprentice or helper when doing heavy work, such as removing engines and transmissions.

Working Conditions

Diesel technicians usually work indoors, although they occasionally make repairs to vehicles on the road. Diesel technicians may lift heavy parts and tools, handle greasy and dirty parts, and stand or lie in awkward positions to repair vehicles and equipment. Minor cuts, burns, and bruises are common, although serious accidents can usually be avoided if the shop is kept clean and orderly and if safety procedures are followed. Technicians normally work in well-lighted, heated, and ventilated areas; however, some shops are drafty and noisy. Many employers provide lockers and shower facilities.

Employment

Diesel service technicians and mechanics held about 267,000 jobs in 2002. About 20 percent serviced buses, trucks, and other diesel-powered equipment for customers of automotive repair and maintenance shops, motor vehicle and parts wholesalers, or automotive equipment rental and leasing agencies. About 19 percent maintained the buses, trucks, and other equipment of buslines, public transit companies, school systems, or state and local governments, and another 17 percent worked for freight trucking companies. The remaining technicians maintained vehicles and other equipment for manufacturing, construction, or other companies. A relatively small number were self-employed. Nearly every section of the country employs diesel service technicians and mechanics, although most work in towns and cities where trucking companies, buslines, and other fleet owners have large operations.

Training, Other Qualifications, and Advancement

Although many persons qualify for diesel service technician and mechanic jobs through years of on-the-job training, authorities recommend the completion of a formal diesel engine training program. Employers prefer to hire graduates of formal training programs because those workers often have a head start in training and are able to advance quickly to the journey level.

Many community colleges and trade and vocational schools offer programs in diesel repair. These programs, lasting 6 months to 2 years, lead to a certificate of completion or an associate degree. Programs vary in the degree of hands-on training they provide on equipment. Some offer about 30 hours per week on equipment, whereas others offer more lab or classroom instruction. Training provides a foundation in the latest diesel technology and instruction in the service and repair of the vehicles and equipment that technicians will encounter on the job. Training programs also improve the skills needed to interpret technical manuals and to communicate with coworkers and customers. In addition to the hands-on aspects of the training, many institutions teach communication skills, customer service, basic understanding of physics, and logical thought. Increasingly, employers work closely with representatives of training programs, providing instructors with the latest equipment, techniques, and tools and offering jobs to graduates.

Whereas most employers prefer to hire persons who have completed formal training programs, some technicians and mechanics continue to learn their skills on the job. Unskilled beginners generally are assigned tasks such as cleaning parts, fueling and lubricating vehicles, and driving vehicles into and out of the shop. Beginners usually are promoted to trainee positions as they gain experience and as vacancies become available. In some shops, beginners with experience in automobile service start as trainee technicians.

Most trainees perform routine service tasks and make minor repairs after a few months' experience. These workers advance to increasingly difficult jobs as they prove their ability and competence. After technicians master the repair and service of diesel engines, they learn to work on related components, such as brakes, transmissions, and electrical systems. Generally, technicians with at least 3 to 4 years of on-the-job experience will qualify as journey-level diesel technicians. The completion of a formal training program speeds advancement to the journey level.

For unskilled entry-level jobs, employers usually look for applicants who have mechanical aptitude and strong problem-solving skills and who are at least 18 years of age and in good physical condition. Nearly all employers require the completion of high school. Courses in automotive repair, electronics, English, mathematics, and physics provide a strong educational background for a career as a diesel service technician or mechanic. Technicians need a state commercial driver's license to test-drive trucks or buses on public roads. Many companies also require applicants to pass a drug test. Practical experience in automobile repair at a gasoline service station, in the Armed Forces, or as a hobby is valuable as well.

Employers often send experienced technicians and mechanics to special training classes conducted by manufacturers and vendors, in which workers learn the latest technology and repair techniques. Technicians constantly receive updated technical manuals and instructions outlining changes in techniques and standards for repair. It is essential for technicians to read, interpret, and comprehend service manuals in order to keep abreast of engineering changes.

Voluntary certification by the National Institute for Automotive Service Excellence (ASE) is recognized as the standard of achievement for diesel service technicians and mechanics. Technicians may be certified as master truck technicians or in specific areas of truck repair, such as gasoline engines, drivetrains, brakes, suspension and steering, electrical and electronic systems, or preventive maintenance and inspection.

For certification in each area, a technician must pass one or more of the ASE-administered exams and present proof of 2 years of relevant hands-on work experience. Two years of relevant formal training from a high school, vocational or trade school, or community or junior college program may be substituted for up to 1 year of the work experience requirement. To remain certified, technicians must be retested every 5 years. Retesting ensures that service technicians and mechanics keep up with changing technology. Diesel service technicians and mechanics also may opt for ASE certification as master school bus technicians or master truck equipment technicians.

The most important work possessions of technicians and mechanics are their handtools. Technicians and mechanics usually provide their own tools, and many experienced workers have thousands of dollars invested in them. Employers typically furnish expensive power tools, computerized engine analyzers, and other diagnostic equipment, but individual workers ordinarily accumulate handtools with experience.

Experienced technicians and mechanics with leadership ability may advance to shop supervisor or service manager. Technicians and mechanics with sales ability sometimes become sales representatives. Some open their own repair shops.

Job Outlook

Employment of diesel service technicians and mechanics is expected to grow about as fast as the average for all occupations through the year 2012. Besides openings resulting from employment growth, opportunities will be created by the need to replace workers who retire or transfer to other occupations.

Employment of diesel service technicians and mechanics is expected to grow as freight transportation by truck increases. Additional trucks will be needed to keep pace with the increasing volume of freight shipped nationwide. Trucks also serve as intermediaries for other forms of transportation, such as rail and air. Due to the greater durability and economy of the diesel engine relative to the gasoline engine, buses and trucks of all sizes are expected to be increasingly powered by diesels. In addition, diesel service technicians will be needed to maintain and repair the growing number of schoolbuses in operation.

Careers as diesel service technicians attract many because they offer relatively high wages and the challenge of skilled repair work. Opportunities should be good for persons who complete formal training in diesel mechanics at community and junior colleges or vocational and technical schools. Applicants without formal training may face stiffer competition for entry-level jobs.

Most persons entering this occupation can expect relatively steady work, because changes in economic conditions have less of an effect on the diesel repair business than on other sectors of the economy. During a downturn in the economy, however, some employers may lay off workers or be reluctant to hire new workers.

Earnings

Median hourly earnings of bus and truck mechanics and diesel engine specialists, including incentive pay, were $16.53 in 2002. The middle 50 percent earned between $13.13 and $20.54 an hour. The lowest 10 percent earned less than $10.66, and the highest 10 percent earned more than $24.61 an hour. Median hourly earnings in the industries employing the largest numbers of bus and truck mechanics and diesel engine specialists in 2002 were as follows:

Local government	$19.58
Motor vehicle and motor vehicle parts and supplies merchant wholesalers	16.80
General freight and trucking	15.62
Automotive repair and maintenance	15.36
Elementary and secondary schools	15.10

Because many experienced technicians employed by truck fleet dealers and independent repair shops receive a commission related to the labor cost charged to the customer, weekly earnings depend on the amount of work completed. Beginners usually earn from 50 to 75 percent of the rate of skilled workers and receive increases as they become more skilled, until they reach the rates of skilled service technicians.

The majority of service technicians work a standard 40-hour week, although some work longer hours, particularly if they are self-employed. A growing number of shops have expanded their hours, either to perform repairs and routine service in a more timely fashion or as a convenience to customers. Those technicians employed by truck and bus firms providing service around the clock may work evenings, nights, and weekends, usually at a higher rate of pay than those working traditional hours.

Many diesel service technicians and mechanics are members of labor unions, including the International Association of Machinists and Aerospace Workers; the Amalgamated Transit Union; the International Union, United Automobile, Aerospace and Agricultural Implement Workers of America; the Transport Workers Union of America; the Sheet Metal Workers' International Association; and the International Brotherhood of Teamsters.

Related Occupations

Diesel service technicians and mechanics repair trucks, buses, and other diesel-powered equipment. Related technician and mechanic occupations include aircraft and avionics equipment mechanics and service technicians, automotive service technicians and mechanics, heavy vehicle and mobile equipment service technicians and mechanics, and small engine mechanics.

Sources of Additional Information

More details about work opportunities for diesel service technicians and mechanics may be obtained from local employers such as trucking companies, truck dealers, or buslines; locals of the unions previously mentioned; and local offices of your state employment service. Local state employment service offices also may have information about training programs. State boards of postsecondary career schools have information on licensed schools with training programs for diesel service technicians and mechanics.

For general information about a career as a diesel service technician or mechanic, write:

- Detroit Diesel, Personnel Director, MS B39, 13400 West Outer Dr., Detroit, MI 48239.

Information on how to become a certified diesel technician of medium to heavy-duty vehicles or a certified bus technician is available from:

- National Institute for Automotive Service Excellence (ASE), 101 Blue Seal Dr. SE, Suite 101, Leesburg, VA 20175. Internet: http://www.asecert.org

For a directory of accredited private trade and technical schools with training programs for diesel service technicians and mechanics, contact:

- Accrediting Commission of Career Schools and Colleges of Technology, 2101 Wilson Blvd., Suite 302, Arlington, VA 22201. Internet: http://www.accsct.org
- National Automotive Technicians Education Foundation, 101 Blue Seal Dr., SE., Suite 101, Leesburg, VA 20175. Internet: http://www.natef.org

For a list of public training programs for diesel service technicians and mechanics, contact:

- SkillsUSA-VICA, P.O. Box 3000, Leesburg, VA 20177-0300. Internet: http://www.skillsusa.org

Dietitians and Nutritionists

(O*NET 29-1031.00)

Significant Points

- Most jobs were in hospitals, nursing care facilities, and offices of physicians or other health practitioners.

- Dietitians and nutritionists need at least a bachelor's degree in dietetics, foods and nutrition, food service systems management, or a related area.

- Average employment growth is expected; however, growth may be constrained if employers substitute other workers for dietitians and if limitations are placed on insurance reimbursement for dietetic services.

Nature of the Work

Dietitians and nutritionists plan food and nutrition programs and supervise the preparation and serving of meals. They help to prevent and treat illnesses by promoting healthy eating habits and recommending dietary modifications, such as the use of less salt for those with high blood pressure or the reduction of fat and sugar intake for those who are overweight.

Dietitians manage food service systems for institutions such as hospitals and schools, promote sound eating habits through education, and conduct research. Major areas of practice include clinical, community, management, and consultant dietetics.

Clinical dietitians provide nutritional services for patients in institutions such as hospitals and nursing care facilities. They assess patients' nutritional needs, develop and implement nutrition programs, and evaluate and report the results. They also confer with doctors and other healthcare professionals in order to coordinate medical and nutritional needs. Some clinical dietitians specialize in the management of overweight patients or the care of critically ill or renal (kidney) and diabetic patients. In addition, clinical dietitians in nursing care facilities, small hospitals, or correctional facilities may manage the food service department.

Community dietitians counsel individuals and groups on nutritional practices designed to prevent disease and promote health. Working in places such as public health clinics, home health agencies, and health maintenance organizations, community dietitians evaluate individual needs, develop nutritional care plans, and instruct individuals and their families. Dietitians working in home health agencies provide instruction on grocery shopping and food preparation to the elderly, individuals with special needs, and children.

Increased public interest in nutrition has led to job opportunities in food manufacturing, advertising, and marketing. In these areas, dietitians analyze foods, prepare literature for distribution, or report on issues such as the nutritional content of recipes, dietary fiber, or vitamin supplements.

Management dietitians oversee large-scale meal planning and preparation in healthcare facilities, company cafeterias, prisons, and schools. They hire, train, and direct other dietitians and food service workers; budget for and purchase food, equipment, and supplies; enforce sanitary and safety regulations; and prepare records and reports.

Consultant dietitians work under contract with healthcare facilities or in their own private practice. They perform nutrition screenings for their clients and offer advice on diet-related concerns such as weight loss or cholesterol reduction. Some work for wellness programs, sports teams, supermarkets, and other nutrition-related businesses. They may consult with food service managers, providing expertise in sanitation, safety procedures, menu development, budgeting, and planning.

Working Conditions

In 2002, most full-time dietitians and nutritionists worked a regular 40-hour week, although some worked weekends. About 1 in 4 worked part time.

Dietitians and nutritionists usually work in clean, well-lighted, and well-ventilated areas. However, some dietitians work in warm, congested kitchens. Many dietitians and nutritionists are on their feet for much of the workday.

Employment

Dietitians and nutritionists held about 49,000 jobs in 2002. More than half of all jobs were in hospitals, nursing care facilities, outpatient care centers, or offices of physicians and other health practitioners. State and local government agencies provided about 1 job in 5—mostly in correctional facilities, health departments, and other public health-related areas. Some dietitians and nutritionists were employed in special food services, an industry which includes firms that provide food services on contract to facilities such as colleges and universities, airlines, correctional facilities, and company cafeterias. Other jobs were in public and private educational services, community care facilities for the elderly (which includes assisted-living facilities), individual and family services, home healthcare services, and the federal government—mostly in the U.S. Department of Veterans Affairs.

Some dietitians were self-employed, working as consultants to facilities such as hospitals and nursing care facilities or providing dietary counseling to individual clients.

Training, Other Qualifications, and Advancement

High school students interested in becoming a dietitian or nutritionist should take courses in biology, chemistry, mathematics, health, and communications. Dietitians and nutritionists need at least a bachelor's degree in dietetics, foods and nutrition, food service systems management, or a related area. College students in these majors take courses in foods, nutrition, institution management, chemistry, biochemistry, biology, microbiology, and physiology. Other suggested courses include business, mathematics, statistics, computer science, psychology, sociology, and economics.

Of the 46 states and jurisdictions with laws governing dietetics, 30 require licensure, 15 require certification, and 1 requires registration. The Commission on Dietetic Registration of the American Dietetic Association (ADA) awards the Registered Dietitian credential to those who pass a certification exam after completing their academic coursework and supervised experience. Because practice requirements vary by state, interested candidates should determine the requirements of the state in which they want to work before sitting for any exam.

As of 2003, there were about 230 bachelor's and master's degree programs approved by the ADA's Commission on Accreditation for Dietetics Education (CADE). Supervised practice experience can be acquired in two ways. The first requires the completion of a CADE-accredited coordinated program. As of 2003, there were more than 50 accredited programs, which combined academic and supervised practice experience and generally lasted 4 to 5 years. The second option requires the completion of 900 hours of supervised practice experience in any of the 264 CADE-accredited/approved internships. These internships may be full-time programs lasting 6 to 12 months or part-time programs lasting 2 years. Students interested in research, advanced clinical positions, or public health may need an advanced degree.

Experienced dietitians may advance to assistant director, associate director, or director of a dietetic department or may become self-employed. Some dietitians specialize in areas such as renal or pediatric dietetics. Others may leave the occupation to become sales representatives for equipment, pharmaceutical, or food manufacturers.

Job Outlook

Employment of dietitians is expected to grow about as fast as the average for all occupations through 2012 as a result of increasing emphasis on disease prevention through improved dietary habits. A growing and aging population will boost the demand for meals and nutritional counseling in hospitals, nursing care facilities, schools, prisons, community health programs, and home healthcare agencies. Public interest in nutrition and increased emphasis on health education and prudent lifestyles will also spur demand, especially in management. In addition to employment growth, job openings will result from the need to replace experienced workers who leave the occupation.

On the one hand, the number of dietitian positions in nursing care facilities and in state government is expected to decline slightly, as these establishments continue to contract out food service operations. On the other hand, employment is expected to grow rapidly in contract providers of food services, outpatient care centers, and offices of physicians and other health practitioners.

Employment growth for dietitians and nutritionists may be constrained if some employers substitute other workers, such as health educators, food service managers, and dietetic technicians. Growth also may be curbed by limitations on insurance reimbursement for dietetic services.

Earnings

Median annual earnings of dietitians and nutritionists were $41,170 in 2002. The middle 50 percent earned between $33,210 and $49,830. The lowest 10 percent earned less than $25,520, and the highest 10 percent earned more than $58,700. In 2002, median annual earnings in general medical and surgical hospitals, the industry employing the largest number of dietitians and nutritionists, were $41,910.

According to the American Dietetic Association, median annual income for registered dietitians in 2002 varied by practice area as follows: $60,000 in consultation and business; $55,000 in food and nutrition management; $54,800 in education and research; $44,000 in clinical nutrition/ambulatory care; $43,300 in clinical nutrition/long-term care; $43,200 in community nutrition; and $40,800 in clinical nutrition/acute care. Salaries also vary by years in practice, educational level, geographic region, and size of the community.

Related Occupations

Workers in other occupations who may apply the principles of food and nutrition include food service managers, health educators, and registered nurses.

Sources of Additional Information

For a list of academic programs, scholarships, and other information about dietetics, contact:

* The American Dietetic Association, 120 South Riverside Plaza, Suite 2000, Chicago, IL 60606-6995. Internet: http://www.eatright.org

Drafters

(O*NET 17-3011.01, 17-3011.02, 17-3012.01, 17-3012.02, and 17-3013.00)

Significant Points

- The type and quality of postsecondary drafting programs vary considerably; prospective students should be careful in selecting a program.

- Opportunities should be best for individuals with at least 2 years of postsecondary training in drafting and considerable skill and experience using computer-aided design and drafting (CADD) systems.

- Demand for particular drafting specialties varies geographically, depending on the needs of local industry.

Nature of the Work

Drafters prepare technical drawings and plans used by production and construction workers to build everything from manufactured products, such as toys, toasters, industrial machinery, and spacecraft, to structures, such as houses, office buildings, and oil and gas pipelines. Their drawings provide visual guidelines, show the technical details of the products and structures, and specify dimensions, materials, and procedures. Drafters fill in technical details, using drawings, rough sketches, specifications, codes, and calculations previously made by engineers, surveyors, architects, or scientists. For example, they use their knowledge of standardized building techniques to draw in the details of a structure. Some drafters use their knowledge of engineering and manufacturing theory and standards to draw the parts of a machine in order to determine design elements, such as the numbers and kinds of fasteners needed to assemble the machine. Drafters use technical handbooks, tables, calculators, and computers to complete their work.

Traditionally, drafters sat at drawing boards and used pencils, pens, compasses, protractors, triangles, and other drafting devices to prepare a drawing manually. Most drafters now use computer-aided design and drafting (CADD) systems to prepare drawings. Consequently, some drafters are referred to as *CADD operators*. CADD systems employ computer workstations to create a drawing on a video screen. The drawings are stored electronically to facilitate revisions and create duplications easily. These systems also permit drafters to quickly prepare variations of a design. Although drafters use CADD extensively, it is only a tool: Persons who produce technical drawings with CADD still function as drafters and need the knowledge of traditional drafters, in addition to CADD skills. Despite the near-universal use of CADD systems, manual drafting and sketching still is used in certain applications.

Drafting work has many specialties, and titles may denote a particular discipline of design or drafting.

Aeronautical drafters prepare engineering drawings detailing plans and specifications used in the manufacture of aircraft, missiles, and related parts.

Architectural drafters draw architectural and structural features of buildings and other structures. These workers may specialize in a type of structure, such as residential or commercial, or in a kind of material used, such as reinforced concrete, masonry, steel, or timber.

Civil drafters prepare drawings and topographical and relief maps used in major construction or civil engineering projects, such as highways, bridges, pipelines, flood control projects, and water and sewage systems.

Electrical drafters prepare wiring and layout diagrams used by workers who erect, install, and repair electrical equipment and wiring in communication centers, power plants, electrical distribution systems, and buildings.

Electronics drafters draw wiring diagrams, circuit board assembly diagrams, schematics, and layout drawings used in the manufacture, installation, and repair of electronic devices and components.

Mechanical drafters prepare detail and assembly drawings of a wide variety of machinery and mechanical devices, indicating dimensions, fastening methods, and other requirements.

Process piping or *pipeline drafters* prepare drawings used in the layout, construction, and operation of oil and gas fields, refineries, chemical plants, and process piping systems.

Working Conditions

Most drafters work a standard 40-hour week; only a small number work part time. Drafters usually work in comfortable offices furnished to accommodate their tasks. They may sit at adjustable drawing boards or drafting tables when doing manual drawings, although most drafters work at computer terminals much of the time. Because they spend long periods in front of computer terminals doing detailed work, drafters may be susceptible to eyestrain, back discomfort, and hand and wrist problems.

Employment

Drafters held about 216,000 jobs in 2002. Architectural and civil drafters held about half of all jobs for drafters, mechanical drafters held about a third of all jobs, and the rest of all jobs were held by electrical and electronics drafters.

Almost half of all jobs for drafters were in architectural, engineering, and related services firms that design construction projects or do other engineering work on a contract basis for other industries. More than a quarter of jobs were in manufacturing industries, such as machinery manufacturing, including metalworking and other general machinery; fabricated metal products manufacturing, including architectural and structural metals; computer and electronic products manufacturing, including navigational, measuring, electromedical, and control instruments; and transportation equipment manufacturing, including aerospace products and parts manufacturing, as well as ship and boat building. Most of the rest were employed in construction, government, wholesale trade, utilities, and employment services. Only a small number were self-employed in 2002.

Training, Other Qualifications, and Advancement

Employers prefer applicants who have completed post-secondary school training in drafting, which is offered by technical institutes, community colleges, and some 4-year colleges and universities. Employers are most interested in applicants with well-developed drafting and mechanical-drawing skills; knowledge of drafting standards, mathematics, science, and engineering technology; and a solid background in computer-aided design and drafting techniques. In addition, communication and problem-solving skills are important.

Training and course work differ somewhat within the drafting specialties. The initial training for each specialty is similar. All incorporate math and communication skills, for example, but course work relating to the specialty varies. In an electronics drafting program, for example, students learn how to depict electronic components and circuits in drawings.

Many types of publicly and privately operated schools provide some form of training in drafting. The kind and quality of programs vary considerably; therefore, prospective students should be careful in selecting a program. They should contact prospective employers regarding their preferences and ask schools to provide information about the kinds of jobs that are obtained by the school's graduates, the types and conditions of the instructional facilities and equipment, and the faculty's qualifications.

Technical institutes offer intensive technical training, but less general education than do junior and community colleges. Certificates or diplomas based on the completion of a certain number of course hours may be awarded. Many technical institutes offer 2-year associate degree programs, which are similar to, or part of, the programs offered by community colleges or state university systems. Their programs vary considerably in both length and type of courses offered. Some area vocational-technical schools are post-secondary public institutions that serve local students and emphasize the type of training preferred by local employers. Many offer introductory drafting instruction. Most require a high school diploma or its equivalent for admission. Other technical institutes are run by private, often for-profit, organizations, sometimes called proprietary schools.

Community colleges offer curricula similar to those in technical institutes, but include more courses on theory and liberal arts. Often, there is little or no difference between technical institute and community college programs. However, courses taken at community colleges are more likely than those given at technical institutes to be accepted for credit at 4-year colleges. After completing a 2-year associate degree program, graduates may obtain jobs as drafters or continue their education in a related field at 4-year colleges. Most 4-year colleges usually do not offer training in drafting, but college courses in engineering, architecture, and mathematics are useful for obtaining a job as a drafter.

Technical training obtained in the Armed Forces also can be applied in civilian drafting jobs. Some additional training may be necessary, depending on the technical area or military specialty.

The American Design Drafting Association (ADDA) has established a certification program for drafters. Although employers usually do not require drafters to be certified, certification demonstrates an understanding of nationally recognized practices and standards of knowledge. Individuals who wish to become certified must pass the Drafter Certification Test, which is administered periodically at ADDA-authorized sites. Applicants are tested on their knowledge and understanding of basic drafting concepts, such as geometric construction, working drawings, and architectural terms and standards.

Individuals planning careers in drafting should take courses in mathematics, science, computer technology, design, and computer graphics, as well as any high school drafting courses available. Mechanical ability and visual aptitude also are important. Prospective drafters should be able to draw well and perform detailed work accurately and neatly. Artistic ability is helpful in some specialized fields, as is knowledge of manufacturing and construction methods. In addition, prospective drafters should have good interpersonal skills, because they work closely with engineers, surveyors, architects, other professionals, and, sometimes, customers.

Entry-level or junior drafters usually do routine work under close supervision. After gaining experience, they may become intermediate-level drafters and progress to more difficult work with less supervision. At the intermediate level, they may need to exercise more judgment and perform calculations when preparing and modifying drawings. Drafters may eventually advance to senior drafter, designer, or supervisor. Many employers pay for continuing education, and, with appropriate college degrees, drafters may go on to become engineering technicians, engineers, or architects.

Job Outlook

Employment of drafters is expected to grow more slowly than the average for all occupations through 2012. Industrial growth and increasingly complex design problems associated with new products and manufacturing processes will increase the demand for drafting services. Further, drafters are beginning to break out of the traditional drafting role and increasingly do work traditionally performed by engineers and architects, thus also increasing demand for drafters. However, the greater use of CADD equipment by drafters, as well as by architects and engineers, should limit demand for lesser skilled drafters, resulting in slower-than-average overall employment growth. Most job openings are expected to arise from the need to replace drafters who transfer to other occupations, leave the labor force, or retire.

Opportunities should be best for individuals with at least 2 years of postsecondary training in a drafting program that provides strong technical skills, as well as considerable experience with CADD systems. CADD has increased the complexity of drafting applications while enhancing the productivity of drafters. It also has enhanced the nature of drafting by creating more possibilities for design and drafting. As technology continues to advance, employers will look for drafters with a strong background in fundamental drafting principles, a higher level of technical sophistication, and an ability to apply their knowledge to a broader range of responsibilities.

Demand for particular drafting specialties varies throughout the country because employment usually is contingent upon the needs of local industry. Employment of drafters remains highly concentrated in industries that are sensitive to cyclical changes in the economy, such as manufacturing and architectural and engineering services. During recessions, drafters may be laid off. However, a growing number of drafters should continue to find employment on a temporary or contract basis as more companies turn to the employment services industry to meet their changing needs.

Earnings

Earnings for drafters vary by specialty and level of responsibility. Median annual earnings of architectural and civil drafters were $37,330 in 2002. The middle 50 percent earned between $30,170 and $45,500. The lowest 10 percent earned less than $24,570, and the highest 10 percent earned more than $56,260. Median annual earnings for architectural and civil drafters in architectural, engineering, and related services were $36,780.

Median annual earnings of mechanical drafters were $40,730 in 2002. The middle 50 percent earned between $32,100 and $51,950. The lowest 10 percent earned less than $25,950, and the highest 10 percent earned more than $64,780. Median annual earnings for mechanical drafters in architectural, engineering, and related services were $41,170.

Median annual earnings of electrical and electronics drafters were $41,090 in 2002. The middle 50 percent earned between $32,060 and $53,440. The lowest 10 percent earned less than $25,710, and the highest 10 percent earned more than $68,000. In architectural, engineering, and related services, median annual earnings for electrical and electronics drafters were $39,760.

Related Occupations

Other workers who prepare or analyze detailed drawings and make precise calculations and measurements include architects, except landscape and naval; landscape architects; designers; engineers; engineering technicians; science technicians; and surveyors, cartographers, photogrammetrists, and surveying technicians.

Sources of Additional Information

Information on schools offering programs in drafting and related fields is available from:

- Accrediting Commission of Career Schools and Colleges of Technology, 2101 Wilson Blvd., Suite 302, Arlington, VA 22201. Internet: http://www.accsct.org

Information about certification is available from:

- American Design Drafting Association, 105 E. Main St., Newbern, TN 38059. Internet: http://www.adda.org

Economists

(O*NET 19-3011.00)

Significant Points

- Quantitative skills are important in all economics specialties.

- Employment of economists is expected to grow about as fast as the average; most new jobs will arise in private industry, including economic research and consulting firms.

- Candidates who hold a master's or Ph.D. degree in economics will have the best employment prospects and advancement opportunities.

Nature of the Work

Economists study how society distributes scarce resources such as land, labor, raw materials, and machinery to produce goods and services. They conduct research, collect and analyze data, monitor economic trends, and develop forecasts. They research issues such as energy costs, inflation, interest rates, exchange rates, business cycles, taxes, or employment levels.

Economists devise methods and procedures for obtaining the data they need. For example, sampling techniques may be used to conduct a survey, and various mathematical modeling techniques may be used to develop forecasts. Preparing reports, including tables and charts, on research results is an important part of an economist's job. Presenting economic and statistical concepts in a clear and meaningful way is particularly important for economists whose research is directed toward making policies for an organization. Some economists might also provide economic analysis to the media.

Many economists specialize in a particular area of economics, although general knowledge of basic economic principles is useful in each area. *Microeconomists* study the supply and demand decisions of individuals and firms, such as how profits can be maximized and how much of a good or service consumers will demand at a certain price. *Industrial/organizational economists* study the market structure of particular industries in terms of the number of competitors, and the market decisions of competitive firms and monopolies. These economists may also be concerned with antitrust policy and its impact on market structure. *Macroeconomists* study historical trends in the whole economy and forecast future trends in areas such as unemployment, inflation, economic growth, productivity, and investment. Closely related to macroeconomists are *monetary* or *financial economists*, who study the money and banking system and the effects of rising interest rates. *International economists* study international financial markets, exchange rates, and the effects of various trade policies such as tariffs. *Labor* or *demographic economists* study the supply and demand for labor and the determination of wages. These economists also try to explain the reasons for unemployment, and the effects on labor markets of changing demographic trends such as an aging population and increasing immigration. *Public finance* economists primarily are involved in studying the role of the government in the economy and the effects of tax cuts, budget deficits, and welfare policies. *Econometricians* are involved in all areas of economics and use mathematical techniques such as calculus, game theory, and regression analysis to formulate economic models. These models help to explain economic relationships and are used to develop forecasts related to the nature and length of business cycles, the effects of a specific rate of inflation on the economy, the effects of tax legislation on unemployment levels, and other economic phenomena. Many economists have applied these fundamental areas of economics to more narrow areas with specific applications such as health, education, agriculture, urban and regional economics, law, history, energy, and the environment.

Most economists are concerned with practical applications of economic policy and work for a variety of organizations. Economists working for corporations are involved primarily in microeconomic issues, such as forecasting consumer demand and sales of the firm's products. Economists working for corporations might also analyze their competitors' growth and market share and advise their company on how to handle the competition. Other economists working for corporations monitor legislation passed by Congress, such as environmental and worker safety regulations, and assess its impact on their business. Corporations with many international branches or subsidiaries might employ economists to monitor the economic situations in countries where they do business, or to provide a risk assessment of a country into which the company might expand.

Corporations that are too small or that do not have sufficient funding might hire economists working in economic consulting or research firms to perform the same tasks as staff economists. Economists in consulting firms also perform much of the macroeconomic analysis and forecasting that is completed in the United States. These economists collect data on various indicators, maintain databases, analyze historical trends, and develop models to forecast growth, inflation, unemployment, or interest rates. These analyses and forecasts are frequently published in newspapers and journal articles.

Another large employer of economists is government. Economists in the federal government administer most of the surveys and collect most of the economic data in the United States. For example, economists in the U.S. Department of Commerce collect and analyze data on the production, distribution, and consumption of commodities produced in the United States and overseas, while economists employed by the U.S. Department of Labor collect and analyze data on the domestic economy, including those having to do with prices, wages, employment, productivity, and safety and health. Economists who work for government agencies also assess economic conditions in the United States or abroad in order to estimate the economic effects of specific changes in legislation or public policy. Government economists advise policy makers in areas such as telecommunications deregulation, Social Security revamping, the effects of tax cuts on the budget deficit, and the effectiveness of imposing tariffs on imported steel. An economist working in state or local government might analyze data on the growth of school-age or prison populations, and on employment and unemployment rates, in order to project future spending needs.

Working Conditions

Economists have structured work schedules. They often work alone, writing reports, preparing statistical charts, and using computers, but they also may be an integral part of a research team. Most work under pressure of deadlines and tight schedules, which may require overtime. Their routine may be interrupted by special requests for data, and by the need to attend meetings or conferences. Frequent travel may be necessary.

Employment

Economists held about 16,000 jobs in 2002. Private industry employed 53 percent of salaried economists, particularly in scientific research and development firms; management, scientific, and technical consulting firms; banks and securities firms, and business, professional, labor, and political organizations. A wide range of government agencies provided the remaining jobs. The U.S. Departments of Labor, Agriculture, and state are the largest federal employers of economists. A number of economists combine a full-time job in government, academia, or business with part-time or consulting work in another setting. A little over 11 percent of economists are self-employed.

Employment of economists is concentrated in large cities. Some work abroad for companies with major international operations, for U.S. government agencies, and for international organizations, such as the World Bank, International Monetary fund, and United Nations.

Besides the jobs described here, many economists hold faculty positions in colleges and universities. Economics faculties have flexible work schedules, and may divide their time among teaching, research, consulting, and administration.

Training, Other Qualifications, and Advancement

A master's or Ph.D. degree in economics is required for many private sector economist jobs, and for advancement to more responsible positions. Economics includes many specialties at the graduate level, such as advanced economic theory, econometrics, international economics, and labor economics. Students should select graduate schools strong in specialties in which they are interested. Undergraduate economics majors can choose from a variety of courses, ranging from microeconomics, macroeconomics, and econometrics, to more philosophical courses, such as the history of economic thought. Because of the importance of quantitative skills to economists, courses in mathematics, statistics, econometrics, sampling theory and survey design, and computer science are extremely helpful. Some schools help graduate students find internships or part-time employment in government agencies, economic consulting or research firms, or financial institutions prior to graduation.

In the federal government, candidates for entry-level economist positions must have a bachelor's degree with a minimum of 21 semester hours of economics and 3 hours of statistics, accounting, or calculus.

Whether working in government, industry, research organizations, or consulting firms, economists with a bachelor's degree usually qualify for most entry-level positions as a research assistant, for administrative or management trainee positions, or for various sales jobs. A master's degree usually is required to qualify for more responsible research and administrative positions. Many businesses, research and consulting firms, and government agencies seek individuals who have strong computer and quantitative skills and can perform complex research. A Ph.D. is necessary for top economist positions in many organizations. Many corporation and government executives have a strong background in economics.

A master's degree is usually the minimum requirement for a job as an instructor in junior and community colleges. In most colleges and universities, however, a Ph.D. is necessary for appointment as an instructor. A Ph.D. and extensive publications in academic journals are required for a professorship, tenure, and promotion.

Aspiring economists should gain experience gathering and analyzing data, conducting interviews or surveys, and writing reports on their findings while in college. This experience can prove invaluable later in obtaining a full-time position in the field, because much of the economist's work, especially in the beginning, may center on these duties. With experience, economists eventually are assigned their own research projects. Related job experience, such as work as a stock or bond trader, might be advantageous.

Those considering careers as economists should be able to pay attention to details, because much time is spent on precise data analysis. Patience and persistence are necessary qualities because economists must spend long hours on independent study and problem solving. Economists must be able to present their findings, both orally and in writing, in a clear, concise manner.

Job Outlook

Employment of economists is expected to grow about as fast as the average for all occupations through 2012. Many job openings are likely to result from the need to replace experienced workers who transfer to other occupations or who retire or leave the labor force for other reasons.

Opportunities for economists should be best in private industry, especially in scientific research and development, and consulting firms, as more companies contract out for economic research services. Rising demand for economists should stem from the growing complexity of the global economy, competition, and increased reliance on quantitative methods for analyzing and forecasting business, sales, and other economic trends. A greater need for economic analyses in virtually every industry could result in additional jobs for economists, although some corporations are eliminating some or all of their economist positions in favor of hiring economic consultants. Employment of economists in the federal government should decline, but not by as much as other occupations in the federal workforce. Average employment growth is expected among economists in state and local government.

A master's or Ph.D. degree, coupled with a strong background in economic theory, mathematics, statistics, and econometrics, provides the basis for acquiring any specialty within the economics field. Those skilled in quantitative techniques and their application to economic modeling and forecasting, and who have good communications skills, should have the best job opportunities. Like those in many other disciplines, however, Ph.D. holders are likely to face keen competition for tenured teaching positions in colleges and universities.

Bachelor's degree holders may face competition for the limited number of economist positions for which they qualify. They will qualify for a number of other positions, however, in which they can take advantage of their economic knowledge by conducting research, developing surveys, or analyzing data. Many graduates with bachelor's degrees will find jobs in industry and business as management or sales trainees, or as administrative assistants. Bachelor's degree holders with good quantitative skills and a strong background in mathematics, statistics, survey design, and computer science also may be hired by private firms as researchers. Some will find jobs in government.

Candidates who meet state certification requirements may become high school economics teachers. The demand for secondary school economics teachers is expected to grow, as economics becomes an increasingly important and popular course.

Earnings

Median annual wage and salary earnings of economists were $68,550 in 2002. The middle 50 percent earned between $50,560 and $90,710. The lowest 10 percent earned less than $38,690, and the highest 10 percent earned more than $120,440.

The federal government recognizes education and experience in certifying applicants for entry-level positions. The entrance salary for economists having a bachelor's degree was about $23,442 a year in 2003; however, those with superior academic records could begin at $29,037. Those having a master's degree could qualify for positions at an annual salary of $35,519. Those with a Ph.D. could begin at $42,976, while some individuals with experience and an advanced degree could start at $51,508. Starting salaries were slightly higher in selected areas where the prevailing local pay was higher. The average annual salary for economists employed by the federal government was $81,852 a year in 2003.

Related Occupations

Economists are concerned with understanding and interpreting financial matters, among other subjects. Other jobs in this area include accountants and auditors; actuaries; budget analysts; financial analysts and personal financial advisors; financial managers; insurance underwriters; loan counselors and officers; and purchasing managers, buyers, and purchasing agents. Other occupations involved in market research and data collection are management analysts, as well as market and survey researchers.

Sources of Additional Information

For information on careers in business economics, contact:

- National Association for Business Economics, 1233 20th St. NW., Suite 505, Washington, DC 20036.

Information on obtaining a position as an economist with the federal government is available from the U.S. Office of Personnel Management (OPM) through a telephone-based system. Consult your telephone directory under U.S. government for a local number or call (703) 724-1850; Federal Relay Service: (800) 877-8339. The first number is not toll free, and charges may result. Information also is available from the OPM Internet site: http://www.usajobs.opm.gov.

Electrical and Electronics Engineers, Except Computer

(O*NET 17-2071.00 and 17-2072.00)

Significant Points

- Overall, job opportunities in engineering are expected to be good, but will vary by specialty.

- A bachelor's degree is required for most entry-level jobs.

- Starting salaries are significantly higher than those of college graduates in other fields.

- Continuing education is critical to keep abreast of the latest technology.

Nature of the Work

From the global positioning system that can continuously provide the location of a vehicle to giant electric power generators, electrical and electronics engineers are responsible for a wide range of technologies. Electrical and electronics engineers design, develop, test, and supervise the manufacture of electrical and electronic equipment. Some of this equipment includes broadcast and communications systems; electric motors, machinery controls, lighting, and wiring in buildings, automobiles, aircraft, and radar and navigation systems; and power generating, controlling, and transmission devices used by electric utilities. Many electrical and electronics engineers also work in areas closely related to computers. However, engineers whose work is related exclusively to computer hardware are considered computer hardware engineers.

Electrical and electronics engineers specialize in different areas such as power generation, transmission, and distribution; communications; and electrical equipment manufacturing, or a specialty within one of these areas—industrial robot control systems or aviation electronics, for example. Electrical and electronics engineers design new products, write performance requirements, and develop maintenance schedules. They also test equipment, solve operating problems, and estimate the time and cost of engineering projects.

Working Conditions

Most engineers work in office buildings, laboratories, or industrial plants. Others may spend time outdoors at construction sites and oil and gas exploration and production sites, where they monitor or direct operations or solve onsite problems. Some engineers travel extensively to plants or worksites.

Many engineers work a standard 40-hour week. At times, deadlines or design standards may bring extra pressure to a job, sometimes requiring engineers to work longer hours.

Employment

Electrical and electronics engineers held about 292,000 jobs in 2002, making up the largest branch of engineering. Most jobs were in professional, scientific, and technical services firms, government agencies, and manufacturers of computer and electronic products and machinery. Wholesale trade, communications, and utilities firms accounted for most of the remaining jobs.

Training, Other Qualifications, and Advancement

A bachelor's degree in engineering is required for almost all entry-level engineering jobs. College graduates with a degree in a physical science or mathematics occasionally may qualify for some engineering jobs, especially in specialties in high demand. Most engineering degrees are granted in electrical, electronics, mechanical, or civil engineering. However, engineers trained in one branch may work in related branches. For example, many aerospace engineers have training in mechanical engineering. This flexibility allows employers to meet staffing needs in new technologies and specialties in which engineers may be in short supply. It also allows engineers to shift to fields with better employment prospects or to those that more closely match their interests.

Most engineering programs involve a concentration of study in an engineering specialty, along with courses in both mathematics and science. Most programs include a design course, sometimes accompanied by a computer or laboratory class or both.

In addition to the standard engineering degree, many colleges offer 2- or 4-year degree programs in engineering technology. These programs, which usually include various hands-on laboratory classes that focus on current issues, prepare students for practical design and production work, rather than for jobs that require more theoretical and scientific knowledge. Graduates of 4-year technology programs may get jobs similar to those obtained by graduates with a bachelor's degree in engineering. Engineering technology graduates, however, are not qualified to register as professional engineers under the same terms as graduates with degrees in engineering. Some employers regard technology program graduates as having skills between those of a technician and an engineer.

Graduate training is essential for engineering faculty positions and many research and development programs, but is not required for the majority of entry-level engineering jobs. Many engineers obtain graduate degrees in engineering or business administration to learn new technology and broaden their education. Many high-level executives in government and industry began their careers as engineers.

About 340 colleges and universities offer bachelor's degree programs in engineering that are accredited by the Accreditation Board for Engineering and Technology (ABET), and about 240 colleges offer accredited bachelor's degree programs in engineering technology. ABET accreditation is based on an examination of an engineering program's student achievement, program improvement, faculty, curricular content, facilities, and institutional commitment. Although most institutions offer programs in the major branches of engineering, only a few offer programs in the smaller specialties. Also, programs of the same title may vary in content. For example, some programs emphasize industrial practices, preparing students for a job in industry, whereas others are more theoretical and are designed to prepare students for graduate work. Therefore, students should investigate curricula and check accreditations carefully before selecting a college.

Admissions requirements for undergraduate engineering schools include a solid background in mathematics (algebra, geometry, trigonometry, and calculus) and science (biology, chemistry, and physics), and courses in English, social studies, humanities, and computer and information technology. Bachelor's degree programs in engineering typically are designed to last 4 years, but many students find that it takes between 4 and 5 years to complete their studies. In a typical 4-year college curriculum, the first 2 years are spent studying mathematics, basic sciences, introductory engineering, humanities, and social sciences. In the last 2 years, most courses are in engineering, usually with a concentration in one branch. For example, the last 2 years of an aerospace program might include courses in fluid mechanics, heat transfer, applied aerodynamics, analytical mechanics, flight vehicle design, trajectory dynamics, and aerospace propulsion systems. Some programs offer a general engineering curriculum; students then specialize in graduate school or on the job.

Some engineering schools and 2-year colleges have agreements whereby the 2-year college provides the initial engineering education, and the engineering school automatically admits students for their last 2 years. In addition, a few engineering schools have arrangements whereby a student spends 3 years in a liberal arts college studying pre-engineering subjects and 2 years in an engineering school studying core subjects, and then receives a bachelor's degree from each school. Some colleges and universities offer 5-year master's degree programs. Some 5-year or even 6-year cooperative plans combine classroom study and practical work, permitting students to gain valuable experience and to finance part of their education.

All 50 states and the District of Columbia require licensure for engineers who offer their services directly to the public. Engineers who are licensed are called Professional Engineers (PE). This licensure generally requires a degree from an ABET-accredited engineering program, 4 years of relevant work experience, and successful completion of a state examination. Recent graduates can start the licensing process by taking the examination in two stages. The initial Fundamentals of Engineering (FE) examination can be taken upon graduation. Engineers who pass this examination commonly are called Engineers in Training (EIT) or Engineer Interns (EI). After acquiring suitable work experience, EITs can take the second examination, the Principles and Practice of Engineering exam. Several states have imposed mandatory continuing education requirements for relicensure. Most states recognize licensure from other states provided that the manner in which the initial license was obtained meets or exceeds their licensure requirements. Many civil, electrical, mechanical, and chemical engineers are licensed PEs.

Engineers should be creative, inquisitive, analytical, and detail-oriented. They should be able to work as part of a team and to communicate well, both orally and in writing. Communication abilities are important because engineers often interact with specialists in a wide range of fields outside engineering.

Beginning engineering graduates usually work under the supervision of experienced engineers and, in large companies, also may receive formal classroom or seminar-type training. As new engineers gain knowledge and experience, they are assigned more difficult projects with greater independence to develop designs, solve problems, and make decisions. Engineers may advance to become technical specialists or to supervise a staff or team of engineers and technicians. Some may eventually become engineering managers or enter other managerial or sales jobs.

Job Outlook

Electrical and electronics engineering graduates should have favorable employment opportunities. The number of job openings resulting from employment growth and the need to replace electrical engineers who transfer to other occupations or leave the labor force is expected to be in rough balance with the supply of graduates.

Employment of electrical and electronics engineers is expected to grow more slowly than the average for all occupations through 2012. Although rising demand for electrical and electronic goods, including advanced communications equipment, defense-related electronic equipment, and consumer electronics products should increase, foreign competition for electronic products and increasing use of engineering services performed in other countries will act to limit employment growth Job growth is expected to be fastest in services industries—particularly consulting firms that provide electronic engineering expertise.

Continuing education is important for electrical and electronics engineers. Engineers who fail to keep up with the rapid changes in technology risk becoming more susceptible to layoffs or, at a minimum, more likely to be passed over for advancement.

Earnings

Median annual earnings of electrical engineers were $68,180 in 2002. The middle 50 percent earned between $54,550

and $84,670. The lowest 10 percent earned less than $44,780, and the highest 10 percent earned more than $100,980. Median annual earnings in the industries employing the largest numbers of electrical engineers in 2002 were:

Scientific research and development services	$77,410
Semiconductor and other electronic component manufacturing	72,670
Electric power generation, transmission, and distribution	71,640
Navigational, measuring, electromedical, and control instruments manufacturing	70,430
Architectural, engineering, and related services	66,980

Median annual earnings of electronics engineers, except computer, were $69,930 in 2002. The middle 50 percent earned between $55,930 and $85,980. The lowest 10 percent earned less than $46,310, and the highest 10 percent earned more than $103,860. Median annual earnings in the industries employing the largest numbers of electronics engineers in 2002 were:

Federal government	$78,830
Architectural, engineering, and related services	72,850
Navigational, measuring, electromedical, and control instruments manufacturing	70,950
Semiconductor and other electronic component manufacturing	70,800
Wired telecommunications carriers	62,670

According to a 2003 salary survey by the National Association of Colleges and Employers, bachelor's degree candidates in electrical/electronics and communications engineering received starting offers averaging $49,794 a year; master's degree candidates averaged $64,556; and Ph.D. candidates averaged $74,283.

Related Occupations

Electrical and electronics engineers apply the principles of physical science and mathematics in their work. Other workers who use scientific and mathematical principles include architects, except landscape and naval; engineering and natural sciences managers; computer and information systems managers; mathematicians; drafters; engineering technicians; sales engineers; science technicians; and physical and life scientists, including agricultural and food scientists, biological scientists, conservation scientists and foresters, atmospheric scientists, chemists and materials scientists, environmental scientists and geoscientists, and physicists and astronomers.

Sources of Additional Information

Information on careers and employment, education, publications, and conferences related to electrical and electronics engineers is available from:

- Institute of Electrical and Electronics Engineers, 445 Hoes Lane, Piscataway, NJ 08855-1331. Internet: http://www.ieee.org

See the introduction to the section on engineers for information on working conditions, training requirements, and other sources of additional information.

Electrical and Electronics Installers and Repairers

(O*NET 49-2092.01, 49-2092.02, 49-2092.04, 49-2092.05, 49-2092.06, 49-2093.00, 49-2094.00, 49-2095.00, and 49-2096.00)

Significant Points

- Knowledge of electrical equipment and electronics is necessary for employment; many applicants complete 1 to 2 years at vocational schools and community colleges, although some less skilled repairers may have only a high school diploma.

- Employment is projected to grow more slowly than average, but will vary by occupational specialty.

- Job opportunities will be best for applicants with a thorough knowledge of electrical and electronic equipment, as well as repair experience.

Nature of the Work

Businesses and other organizations depend on complex electronic equipment for a variety of functions. Industrial controls automatically monitor and direct production processes on the factory floor. Transmitters and antennae provide communication links for many organizations. Electric power companies use electronic equipment to operate and control generating plants, substations, and monitoring equipment. The federal government uses radar and missile control systems to provide for the national defense and to direct commercial air traffic. These complex pieces of electronic equipment are installed, maintained, and repaired by electrical and electronics installers and repairers.

Electrical equipment and electronic equipment are two distinct types of industrial equipment, although much equipment contains both electrical and electronic components. In general, electrical portions provide the power for the equipment, while electronic components control the device, although many types of equipment still are controlled with electrical devices. Electronic sensors monitor the equipment and the manufacturing process, providing feedback to the programmable logic control (PLC), which controls the equipment. The PLC processes the information provided by the sensors and makes adjustments to optimize output. To adjust the output, the PLC sends signals to the electrical, hydraulic, and pneumatic devices that power the machine—

changing feed rates, pressures, and other variables in the manufacturing process. Many installers and repairers, known as *field technicians*, travel to factories or other locations to repair equipment. These workers often have assigned areas in which they perform preventive maintenance on a regular basis. When equipment breaks down, field technicians go to a customer's site to repair the equipment. *Bench technicians* work in repair shops located in factories and service centers, fixing components that cannot be repaired on the factory floor.

Some industrial electronic equipment is self-monitoring and alerts repairers to malfunctions. When equipment breaks down, repairers first check for common causes of trouble, such as loose connections or obviously defective components. If routine checks do not locate the trouble, repairers may refer to schematics and manufacturers' specifications that show connections and provide instructions on how to locate problems. Automated electronic control systems are increasing in complexity, making diagnosis more challenging. Repairers use software programs and testing equipment to diagnose malfunctions. Among their diagnostic tools are multimeters, which measure voltage, current, and resistance; and advanced multimeters, which measure capacitance, inductance, and current gain of transistors. Repairers also use signal generators, which provide test signals, and oscilloscopes, which display signals graphically. Finally, repairers use handtools such as pliers, screwdrivers, soldering irons, and wrenches to replace faulty parts and adjust equipment.

Because repairing components is a complex activity and factories cannot allow production equipment to stand idle, repairers on the factory floor usually remove and replace defective units, such as circuit boards, instead of fixing them. Defective units are discarded or returned to the manufacturer or a specialized shop for repair. Bench technicians at these locations have the training, tools, and parts needed to thoroughly diagnose and repair circuit boards or other complex components. These workers also locate and repair circuit defects, such as poorly soldered joints, blown fuses, or malfunctioning transistors.

Electrical and electronics installers often fit older manufacturing equipment with new automated control devices. Older manufacturing machines are frequently in good working order, but are limited by inefficient control systems for which replacement parts are no longer available. Installers replace old electronic control units with new PLCs. Setting up and installing a new PLC involves connecting it to different sensors and electrically powered devices (electric motors, switches, and pumps) and writing a computer program to operate the PLC. Electronics installers coordinate their efforts with those of other workers who are installing and maintaining equipment.

Electrical and electronics installers and repairers, transportation equipment install, adjust, or maintain mobile electronic communication equipment, including sound, sonar, security, navigation, and surveillance systems on trains, watercraft, or other mobile equipment. *Electrical and electronics repairers, powerhouse, substation, and relay* inspect, test, repair, or maintain electrical equipment in generating stations, substations, and in-service relays. These workers may be known as powerhouse electricians, relay technicians, or power transformer repairers. *Electric motor, power tool, and related repairers*—such as armature winders, generator mechanics, and electric golf cart repairers—specialize in repairing, maintaining, or installing electric motors, wiring, or switches.

Electronic equipment installers and repairers, motor vehicles have a significantly different job. They install, diagnose, and repair communication, sound, security, and navigation equipment in motor vehicles. Most installation work involves either new alarm or sound systems. New sound systems vary significantly in cost and complexity of installation. Replacing a head unit (radio) with a new computer disc (CD) player is quite simple, requiring the removal of a few screws and the connection of a few wires. Installing a new sound system with a subwoofer, amplifier, and fuses is far more complicated. The installer builds a fiberglass or wood box designed to hold the subwoofer and to fit inside the unique dimensions of the automobile. Installing sound-deadening material, which often is necessary with more powerful speakers, requires an installer to remove many parts of a car (for example, seats, carpeting, or interiors of doors), add sound-absorbing material in empty spaces, and reinstall the interior parts. The installer also runs new speaker and electrical cables. The new system may require additional fuses, a new electrical line to be run from the battery through a newly drilled hole in the firewall into the interior of the vehicle, or an additional or more powerful alternator or battery. Motor vehicle installers and repairers work with an increasingly complex range of electronic equipment, including DVD players, satellite navigation equipment, passive-security tracking systems, and active-security systems.

Working Conditions

Many electrical and electronics installers and repairers work on factory floors, where they are subject to noise, dirt, vibration, and heat. Bench technicians work primarily in repair shops, where the surroundings are relatively quiet, comfortable, and well lighted.

Installers and repairers may have to do heavy lifting and work in a variety of positions. They must follow safety guidelines and often wear protective goggles and hardhats. When working on ladders or on elevated equipment, repairers must wear harnesses to prevent falls. Before repairing a piece of machinery, these workers must follow procedures to ensure that others cannot start the equipment during the repair process. They also must take precautions against electric shock by locking off power to the unit under repair.

Motor vehicle electronic equipment installers and repairers normally work indoors in well-ventilated and well-lighted repair shops. Minor cuts and bruises are common, but serious accidents usually are avoided when safety practices are observed.

Employment

Electrical and electronics installers and repairers held about 172,000 jobs in 2002. The following tabulation breaks down their employment by occupational specialty:

Electrical and electronics repairers, commercial and industrial equipment	85,000
Electric motor, power tool, and related repairers	31,000
Electrical and electronics repairers, powerhouse, substation, and relay	21,000
Electronic equipment installers and repairers, motor vehicles	18,000
Electrical and electronics installers and repairers, transportation equipment	18,000

Many repairers worked for utilities, building equipment contractors, machinery and equipment repair shops, wholesalers, the federal government, retailers of automotive parts and accessories, rail transportation companies, and manufacturers of electrical, electronic, and transportation equipment.

Training, Other Qualifications, and Advancement

Knowledge of electrical equipment and electronics is necessary for employment. Many applicants gain this knowledge through programs lasting 1 to 2 years at vocational schools or community colleges, although some less skilled repairers may have only a high school diploma. Entry-level repairers may work closely with more experienced technicians who provide technical guidance.

Installers and repairers should have good eyesight and color perception in order to work with the intricate components used in electronic equipment. Field technicians work closely with customers and should have good communication skills and a neat appearance. Employers also may require that field technicians have a driver's license.

Various organizations offer certification, including ACES International, the Consumer Electronics Association, the Electronics Technicians Association International, and the International Society of Certified Electronics Technicians. Repairers may specialize—in industrial electronics, for example. To receive certification, repairers must pass qualifying exams corresponding to their level of training and experience.

Experienced repairers with advanced training may become specialists or troubleshooters who help other repairers diagnose difficult problems. Workers with leadership ability may become supervisors of other repairers. Some experienced workers open their own repair shops.

Job Outlook

Job opportunities should be best for applicants with a thorough knowledge of electrical equipment and electronics, as well as with repair experience. Overall employment of electrical and electronics installers and repairers is expected to grow more slowly than the average for all occupations over the 2002–12 period, but varies by occupational specialty. In addition to employment growth, many job openings should result from the need to replace workers who transfer to other occupations or leave the labor force.

Average employment growth is projected for electrical and electronics installers and repairers of commercial and industrial equipment. This equipment will become more sophisticated and will be used more frequently as businesses strive to lower costs by increasing and improving automation. Companies will install electronic controls, robots, sensors, and other equipment to automate processes such as assembly and testing. As prices decline, applications will be found across a number of industries, including services, utilities, and construction, as well as manufacturing. Improved reliability of equipment should not constrain employment growth, however: companies increasingly will rely on repairers because any malfunction that idles commercial and industrial equipment is costly.

Employment of motor vehicle electronic equipment installers and repairers also is expected to grow as fast as the average. However, motor vehicle manufacturers will install more and better sound, security, entertainment, and navigation systems in new vehicles, limiting employment growth for aftermarket electronic equipment installers. In addition, newer electronic systems are more reliable and require less maintenance.

Employment of electric motor, power tool, and related repairers is expected to grow more slowly than average. Improvements in electrical and electronic equipment design should limit job growth by simplifying repair tasks. More parts are being designed to be easily disposable, further reducing employment growth.

Employment of electrical and electronic installers and repairers of transportation equipment is expected to grow more slowly than the average, due to declining industry employment in rail transportation, aerospace product and parts manufacturing, and ship- and boatbuilding.

Employment of electrical and electronics installers and repairers, powerhouse, substation, and relay is expected to decline slightly. Consolidation and privatization in utilities industries should improve productivity, reducing employment. Newer equipment will be more reliable and easier to repair, further limiting employment.

Earnings

Median hourly earnings of electrical and electronics repairers, commercial and industrial equipment were $19.77 in 2002. The middle 50 percent earned between $15.13 and $24.03. The lowest 10 percent earned less than $11.71, and the highest 10 percent earned more than $27.08. In 2002, median hourly earnings were $23.68 in the federal government and $16.87 in building equipment contractors, the industries employing the largest numbers of electrical and electronics repairers, commercial and industrial equipment.

Median hourly earnings of electric motor, power tool, and related repairers were $15.49 in 2002. The middle 50 percent earned between $11.82 and $19.99. The lowest 10 percent earned less than $9.32, and the highest 10 percent earned more than $25.34. In 2002, median hourly earnings were $14.05 in commercial and industrial machinery and equipment (except automotive and electronic) repair and maintenance, the industry employing the largest number of electronic motor, power tool, and related repairers.

Median hourly earnings of electrical and electronics repairers, powerhouse, substation, and relay were $24.85 in 2002. The middle 50 percent earned between $20.81 and $27.90. The lowest 10 percent earned less than $15.92, and the highest 10 percent earned more than $32.08. In 2002, median hourly earnings were $25.69 in electric power generation, transmission, and distribution—the industry employing the largest number of electrical and electronics repairers, powerhouse, substation, and relay.

Median hourly earnings of electronics installers and repairers, motor vehicles were $12.51 in 2002. The middle 50 percent earned between $9.97 and $16.02. The lowest 10 percent earned less than $8.47, and the highest 10 percent earned more than $19.45.

Median hourly earnings of electrical and electronics repairers, transportation equipment were $18.56 in 2002. The middle 50 percent earned between $13.85 and $22.96. The lowest 10 percent earned less than $10.68, and the highest 10 percent earned more than $26.87.

Related Occupations

Workers in other occupations who install and repair electronic equipment include broadcast and sound technicians and radio operators; computer, automated teller, and office machine repairers; electronic home entertainment equipment installers and repairers; and radio and telecommunications equipment installers and repairers. Industrial machinery installation, repair, and maintenance workers also install, maintain, and repair industrial machinery.

Sources of Additional Information

For information on careers and certification, contact any of the following organizations:

- ACES International, 5241 Princess Anne Rd., Suite 110, Virginia Beach, VA 23462. Internet: http://www.acesinternational.org

- Consumer Electronics Association, 2500 Wilson Blvd., Arlington, VA 22201-3834. Internet: http://www.ce.org

- Electronics Technicians Association International, 5 Depot St., Greencastle, IN 46135.

● International Society of Certified Electronics Technicians, 3608 Pershing Ave., Fort Worth, TX 76107- 4527. Internet: http://www.iscet.org

Electronic Home Entertainment Equipment Installers and Repairers

(O*NET 49-2097.00)

Significant Points

- Employment is expected to grow more slowly than the average for all occupations, because it often is cheaper to replace equipment than to repair it.

- Job opportunities will be best for applicants with knowledge of electronics and with related hands-on experience.

Nature of the Work

Electronic home entertainment equipment installers and repairers, also called *service technicians*, repair a variety of equipment, including televisions and radios, stereo components, video and audio disc players, video cameras, and video recorders. They also install and repair home security systems, intercom equipment, satellite television dishes, and home theater systems, which consist of large-screen televisions and sophisticated surround-sound audio components.

Customers usually bring small, portable equipment to repair shops for servicing. Repairers at these locations, known as *bench technicians*, are equipped with a full array of electronic tools and parts. When larger, less mobile equipment breaks down, customers may pay repairers to come to their homes. These repairers, known as *field technicians*, travel with a limited set of tools and parts, and attempt to complete the repair at the customer's location. If the job is complex, technicians may bring defective components back to the shop for thorough diagnosis and repair.

When equipment breaks down, repairers check for common causes of trouble, such as dirty or defective components. Many repairs consist simply of cleaning and lubricating equipment. If routine checks do not locate the trouble, repairers may refer to schematics and manufacturers' specifications that provide instructions on how to locate problems. Repairers use a variety of test equipment to diagnose and identify malfunctions. Multimeters detect short circuits, failed capacitors, and blown fuses by measuring voltage, current, and resistance. Color-bar and dot generators provide onscreen test patterns, signal generators to test signals, and oscilloscopes and digital storage scopes to measure complex waveforms produced by electronic equipment. Repairs may involve removing and replacing a failed capacitor, transistor, or fuse. Repairers use handtools such as pliers, screwdrivers, soldering irons, and wrenches to replace faulty parts. They also make adjustments to equipment, such as focusing and converging the picture of a television set or balancing the audio on a surround-sound system.

Improvements in technology have miniaturized and digitized many audio and video recording devices. Miniaturization has made repairwork significantly more difficult, because both the components and the acceptable tolerances are smaller. For example, an analog video camera operates at 1800 revolutions per minute (rpm), while a digital video camera may operate at 9,000 rpm. Also, components now are mounted on the surface of circuit boards, instead of plugged into slots, requiring more precise soldering when a new part is installed. Improved technologies have lowered the price of electronic home entertainment equipment, to the point where customers often replace broken equipment instead of repairing it.

Working Conditions

Most repairers work in well-lighted electrical repair shops. Field technicians, however, spend much time traveling in service vehicles and working in customers' residences.

Repairers may have to work in a variety of positions and carry heavy equipment. Although the work of repairers is comparatively safe, they must take precautions against minor burns and electric shock. Because television monitors carry high voltage even when they are turned off, repairers need to discharge the voltage before servicing such equipment.

Employment

Electronic home entertainment equipment installers and repairers held about 43,000 jobs in 2002. Most repairers worked in electronics and appliance stores that sell and service electronic home entertainment products or in electronic and precision equipment repair and maintenance shops. About 1 electronic home entertainment equipment installer and repairer in 4 was self-employed, more than 4 times the proportion for all installation, maintenance, and repair occupations.

Training, Other Qualifications, and Advancement

Employers prefer applicants who have basic knowledge and skills in electronics. Applicants should be familiar with schematics and have some hands-on experience repairing electronic equipment. Many applicants gain these skills at vocational training programs and community colleges. Training programs should include both hands-on experience and theoretical education in digital consumer electronics. Entry-level repairers may work closely with more experienced technicians, who provide technical guidance.

Field technicians work closely with customers and must have good communication skills and a neat appearance. Employers also may require that field technicians have a driver's license.

Various organizations offer certification for electronic home entertainment equipment installers and repairers, including ACES International, the Custom Electronic Design and Installation Association, the Electronic Technicians Association International, and the International Society of Certified Electronics Technicians. Repairers may specialize in a variety of skill areas, including consumer electronics. To receive certification, repairers must pass qualifying exams corresponding to their level of training and experience.

Experienced repairers with advanced training may become specialists or troubleshooters, helping other repairers diagnose difficult problems. Workers with leadership ability may become supervisors of other repairers. Some experienced workers open their own repair shops.

Job Outlook

Employment of electronic home entertainment equipment installers and repairers is expected to grow more slowly than the average through 2012, due to decreased demand for repair work. In addition to job openings arising from employment growth, some will also result from the need to replace workers who retire or who transfer to higher paying jobs in other occupations requiring electronics experience. Opportunities will be best for applicants with hands-on experience and knowledge of electronics.

The need for repairers is expected to grow slowly because home entertainment equipment is less expensive than in the past. As technological developments have lowered the price and improved the reliability of equipment, the demand for repair services has slackened. When malfunctions do occur, it often is cheaper for consumers to replace equipment rather than to pay for repairs.

Employment growth will be spurred somewhat by the introduction of sophisticated digital equipment, such as DVDs, digital televisions, and digital camcorders. So long as the price of such equipment remains high, purchasers will be willing to hire repairers when malfunctions occur.

Earnings

Median hourly earnings of electronic home entertainment equipment installers and repairers were $13.08 in 2002. The middle 50 percent earned between $10.20 and $17.00. The lowest 10 percent earned less than $8.18, and the highest 10 percent earned more than $21.48. In 2002, median hourly earnings of electronic home entertainment equipment installers and repairers were $12.73 in electronics and appliance stores and $11.99 in electronic and precision equipment repair and maintenance.

Related Occupations

Other workers who repair and maintain electronic equipment include broadcast and sound engineering technicians and radio operators; computer, automated teller, and office machine repairers; electrical and electronics installers and repairers; and radio and telecommunications equipment installers and repairers.

Sources of Additional Information

For information on careers and certification, contact:

- ACES International, 5241 Princess Anne Rd., Suite 110, Virginia Beach, VA 23462. Internet: http://www.acesinternational.org

- Custom Electronic Design and Installation Association, 7150 Winton Dr., Suite 300, Indianapolis, IN 46268. Internet: http://www.cedia.org

- Electronics Technicians Association International, 5 Depot St., Greencastle, IN 46135.

- International Society of Certified Electronics Technicians, 3608 Pershing Ave., Fort Worth, TX 76107-4527. Internet: http://www.iscet.org

Emergency Medical Technicians and Paramedics

(O*NET 29-2041.00)

Significant Points

- Job stress is common because hours of work are irregular and workers often must treat patients in life-or-death situations.

- Formal training and certification are required, but state requirements vary.

- Employment is projected to grow faster than average as paid emergency medical technician positions replace unpaid volunteers.

- Competition will be greater for jobs in local fire, police, and rescue squad departments than in private ambulance services; opportunities will be best for those who have advanced certification.

Nature of the Work

People's lives often depend on the quick reaction and competent care of emergency medical technicians (EMTs) and paramedics—EMTs with additional advanced training to perform more difficult prehospital medical procedures. Incidents as varied as automobile accidents, heart attacks, drownings, childbirth, and gunshot wounds all require immediate medical attention. EMTs and paramedics provide this vital attention as they care for and transport the sick or injured to a medical facility.

In an emergency, EMTs and paramedics typically are dispatched to the scene by a 911 operator, and often work with police and fire department personnel. Once they arrive, they determine the nature and extent of the patient's condition while trying to ascertain whether the patient has preexisting medical problems. Following strict rules and guidelines, they give appropriate emergency care and, when necessary, transport the patient. Some paramedics are trained to treat patients with minor injuries on the scene of an accident or at their home without transporting them to a medical facility. Emergency treatment for more complicated problems is carried out under the direction of medical doctors by radio preceding or during transport.

EMTs and paramedics may use special equipment, such as backboards, to immobilize patients before placing them on stretchers and securing them in the ambulance for transport to a medical facility. Usually, one EMT or paramedic drives while the other monitors the patient's vital signs and gives additional care as needed. Some EMTs work as part of the flight crew of helicopters that transport critically ill or injured patients to hospital trauma centers.

At the medical facility, EMTs and paramedics help transfer patients to the emergency department, report their observations and actions to emergency room staff, and may provide additional emergency treatment. After each run, EMTs and paramedics replace used supplies and check equipment. If a transported patient had a contagious disease, EMTs and paramedics decontaminate the interior of the ambulance and report cases to the proper authorities.

Beyond these general duties, the specific responsibilities of EMTs and paramedics depend on their level of qualification and training. To determine this, the National Registry of Emergency Medical Technicians (NREMT) registers emergency medical service (EMS) providers at four levels: First Responder, EMT-Basic, EMT-Intermediate, and EMT-Paramedic. Some states, however, do their own certification and use numeric ratings from 1 to 4 to distinguish levels of proficiency.

The lowest-level workers—First Responders—are trained to provide basic emergency medical care because they tend to be the first persons to arrive at the scene of an incident. Many firefighters, police officers, and other emergency workers have this level of training. The EMT-Basic, also known as EMT-1, represents the first component of the emergency medical technician system. An EMT-1 is trained to care for patients at the scene of an accident and while transporting patients by ambulance to the hospital under medical direction. The EMT-1 has the emergency skills to assess a patient's condition and manage respiratory, cardiac, and trauma emergencies.

The EMT-Intermediate (EMT-2 and EMT-3) has more advanced training that allows the administration of intravenous fluids, the use of manual defibrillators to give life-saving shocks to a stopped heart, and the application of advanced airway techniques and equipment to assist patients experiencing respiratory emergencies. EMT-Paramedics (EMT-4) provide the most extensive prehospital care. In addition to carrying out the procedures already described, paramedics may administer drugs orally and intravenously, interpret electrocardiograms (EKGs), perform endotracheal intubations, and use monitors and other complex equipment.

Working Conditions

EMTs and paramedics work both indoors and outdoors, in all types of weather. They are required to do considerable kneeling, bending, and heavy lifting. These workers risk noise-induced hearing loss from sirens and back injuries from lifting patients. In addition, EMTs and paramedics may be exposed to diseases such as hepatitis-B and AIDS, as well as violence from drug overdose victims or mentally unstable patients. The work is not only physically strenuous, but also stressful, involving life-or-death situations and suffering patients. Nonetheless, many people find the work exciting and challenging and enjoy the opportunity to help others.

EMTs and paramedics employed by fire departments work about 50 hours a week. Those employed by hospitals frequently work between 45 and 60 hours a week, and those in private ambulance services, between 45 and 50 hours. Some of these workers, especially those in police and fire departments, are on call for extended periods. Because emergency services function 24 hours a day, EMTs and paramedics have irregular working hours that add to job stress.

Employment

EMTs and paramedics held about 179,000 jobs in 2002. Most career EMTs and paramedics work in metropolitan areas. There are many more volunteer EMTs and paramedics, especially in smaller cities, towns, and rural areas. These individuals volunteer for fire departments, emergency medical services (EMS), or hospitals, and may respond to only a few calls for service per month or may answer the majority of calls, especially in smaller communities. EMTs and paramedics work closely with firefighters, who often are certified as EMTs as well and act as first responders.

Full-time and part-time paid EMTs and paramedics were employed in a number of industries. About 4 out of 10 worked as employees of private ambulance services. About 3 out of 10 worked in local government for fire departments, public ambulance services, and EMS. Another 2 out 10 were found in hospitals, working full time within the medical facility or responded to calls in ambulances or helicopters to transport critically ill or injured patients. The remainder worked in various industries providing emergency services.

Training, Other Qualifications, and Advancement

Formal training and certification is needed to become an EMT or paramedic. All 50 states have a certification procedure. In most states and the District of Columbia, registration with the NREMT is required at some or all levels of certification. Other states administer their own certification examination or provide the option of taking the NREMT examination. To maintain certification, EMTs and paramedics must reregister, usually every 2 years. In order to reregister, an individual must be working as an EMT or paramedic and meet a continuing education requirement.

Training is offered at progressive levels: EMT-Basic, also known as EMT-1; EMT-Intermediate, or EMT-2 and EMT-3; and EMT-Paramedic, or EMT-4. EMT-Basic coursework typically emphasizes emergency skills, such as managing respiratory, trauma, and cardiac emergencies, and patient assessment. Formal courses are often combined with time in an emergency room or ambulance. The program also provides instruction and practice in dealing with bleeding, fractures, airway obstruction, cardiac arrest, and emergency childbirth. Students learn how to use and maintain common emergency equipment, such as backboards, suction devices, splints, oxygen delivery systems, and stretchers. Graduates of approved EMT basic training programs who pass a written and practical examination administered by the state certifying agency or the NREMT earn the title "Registered EMT-Basic." The course also is a prerequisite for EMT-Intermediate and EMT-Paramedic training.

EMT-Intermediate training requirements vary from state to state. Applicants can opt to receive training in EMT-Shock Trauma, wherein the caregiver learns to start intravenous fluids and give certain medications, or in EMT-Cardiac, which includes learning heart rhythms and administering advanced medications. Training commonly includes 35 to 55 hours of additional instruction beyond EMT-Basic coursework, and covers patient assessment as well as the use of advanced airway devices and intravenous fluids. Prerequisites for taking the EMT-Intermediate examination include registration as an EMT-Basic, required classroom work, and a specified amount of clinical experience.

The most advanced level of training for this occupation is EMT-Paramedic. At this level, the caregiver receives additional training in body function and learns more advanced skills. The Technology program usually lasts up to 2 years and results in an associate degree in applied science. Such education prepares the graduate to take the NREMT examination and become certified as an EMT-Paramedic. Extensive related coursework and clinical and field experience is required. Due to the longer training requirement, almost all EMT-Paramedics are in paid positions, rather than being volunteers. Refresher courses and continuing education are available for EMTs and paramedics at all levels.

EMTs and paramedics should be emotionally stable, have good dexterity, agility, and physical coordination, and be able to lift and carry heavy loads. They also need good eyesight (corrective lenses may be used) with accurate color vision.

Advancement beyond the EMT-Paramedic level usually means leaving fieldwork. An EMT-Paramedic can become a supervisor, operations manager, administrative director, or executive director of emergency services. Some EMTs and paramedics become instructors, dispatchers, or physician assistants, while others move into sales or marketing of emergency medical equipment. A number of people become EMTs and paramedics to assess their interest in healthcare, and then decide to return to school and become registered nurses, physicians, or other health workers.

Job Outlook

Employment of emergency medical technicians and paramedics is expected to grow faster than the average for all occupations through 2012. Population growth and urbanization will increase the demand for full-time paid EMTs and paramedics rather than for volunteers. In addition, a large segment of the population—the aging baby boomers—will further spur demand for EMT services as they become more likely to have medical emergencies. There will still be demand for part-time, volunteer EMTs and paramedics in rural areas and smaller metropolitan areas. In addition to those arising from job growth, openings will occur because of replacement needs; some workers leave the occupation because of stressful working conditions, limited potential for advancement, and the modest pay and benefits in private-sector jobs.

Most opportunities for EMTs and paramedics are expected to found in private ambulance services. Competition will be greater for jobs in local government, including fire, police, and independent third-service rescue squad departments, in which salaries and benefits tend to be slightly better. Opportunities will be best for those who have advanced certifications, such as EMT-Intermediate and EMT-Paramedic, as clients and patients demand higher levels of care before arriving at the hospital.

Earnings

Earnings of EMTs and paramedics depend on the employment setting and geographic location as well as the individual's training and experience. Median annual earnings of EMTs and paramedics were $24,030 in 2002. The middle 50 percent earned between $19,040 and $31,600. The lowest 10 percent earned less than $15,530, and the highest 10 percent earned more than $41,980. Median annual earnings in the industries employing the largest numbers of EMTs and paramedics in 2002 were:

Local government $27,440
General medical and surgical hospitals..................24,760
Other ambulatory health care services 22,180

Those in emergency medical services who are part of fire or police departments receive the same benefits as firefighters or police officers. For example, many are covered by pension plans that provide retirement at half pay after 20 or 25 years of service or if the worker is disabled in the line of duty.

Related Occupations

Other workers in occupations that require quick and level-headed reactions to life-or-death situations are air traffic controllers, firefighting occupations, physician assistants, police and detectives, and registered nurses.

Sources of Additional Information

General information about emergency medical technicians and paramedics is available from:

- National Association of Emergency Medical Technicians, P.O. Box 1400, Clinton, MS 39060-1400. Internet: http://www.naemt.org

- National Registry of Emergency Medical Technicians, Rocco V. Morando Bldg., 6610 Busch Blvd., P.O. Box 29233, Columbus, OH 43229. Internet: http://www.nremt.org

- National Highway Transportation Safety Administration, EMS Division, 400 7th St. SW., NTS-14, Washington, DC 20590. Internet: http://www.nhtsa.dot.gov/people/injury/ems

Engineering and Natural Sciences Managers

(O*NET 11-9041.00 and 11-9121.00)

Significant Points

- Most engineering and natural sciences managers have previous experience as engineers, scientists, or mathematicians.

- Projected employment growth for engineering and natural sciences managers should be closely related to those for the engineers and scientists they supervise and the industries in which they are found.

- Opportunities will be best for workers with advanced technical knowledge and strong communication and business management skills.

Nature of the Work

Engineering and natural sciences managers plan, coordinate, and direct research, design, and production activities. They may supervise engineers, scientists, and technicians, along with support personnel. These managers use advanced technical knowledge of engineering and science to oversee a variety of activities. They determine scientific and technical goals within broad outlines provided by top executives. These goals may include improving manufacturing processes, advancing scientific research, or developing new products. Managers make detailed plans to accomplish these goals—for example, they may develop the overall concepts of a new product or identify technical problems preventing the completion of a project.

To perform effectively, they also must possess knowledge of administrative procedures, such as budgeting, hiring, and supervision. These managers propose budgets for projects and programs and determine staff, training, and equipment needs. They hire and assign scientists, engineers, and support personnel to carry out specific parts of each project. They also supervise the work of these employees, review their output, and establish administrative procedures and policies—including environmental standards, for example.

In addition, these managers use communication skills extensively. They spend a great deal of time coordinating the activities of their unit with those of other units or organizations. They confer with higher levels of management; with financial, production, marketing, and other managers; and with contractors and equipment and materials suppliers.

Engineering managers supervise people who design and develop machinery, products, systems, and processes; or direct and coordinate production, operations, quality assurance, testing, or maintenance in industrial plants. Many are plant engineers, who direct and coordinate the design, installation, operation, and maintenance of equipment and machinery in industrial plants. Others manage research and development teams that produce new products and processes or improve existing ones.

Natural sciences managers oversee the work of life and physical scientists, including agricultural scientists, chemists, biologists, geologists, medical scientists, and physicists. These managers direct research and development projects and coordinate activities such as testing, quality control, and production. They may work on basic research projects or on commercial activities. Science managers sometimes conduct their own research in addition to managing the work of others.

Working Conditions

Engineering and natural sciences managers spend most of their time in an office. Some managers, however, also may work in laboratories, where they may be exposed to the same conditions as research scientists, or in industrial plants, where they may be exposed to the same conditions as production workers. Most managers work at least 40 hours a week and may work much longer on occasion to meet project deadlines. Some may experience considerable pressure to meet technical or scientific goals on a short deadline or within a tight budget.

Employment

Engineering and natural sciences managers held about 257,000 jobs in 2002. About 26 percent worked in professional, scientific, and technical services industries, primarily for firms providing architectural, engineering, and related services; computer systems design and related services; and scientific research and development services. Manufacturing industries employed 35 percent of engineering and natural sciences managers. Manufacturing industries with the largest employment include those producing computer and electronic equipment, machinery, transportation equipment, including aerospace products and parts, and chemicals, including pharmaceuticals. Other large employers include government agencies and telecommunications and utilities companies.

Training, Other Qualifications, and Advancement

Strong technical knowledge is essential for engineering and natural sciences managers, who must understand and guide the work of their subordinates and explain the work in nontechnical terms to senior management and potential customers. Therefore, these management positions usually require work experience and formal education similar to those of engineers, scientists, or mathematicians.

Most engineering managers begin their careers as engineers, after completing a bachelor's degree in the field. To advance to higher level positions, engineers generally must assume management responsibility. To fill management positions, employers seek engineers who possess administrative and communications skills in addition to technical knowledge in their specialty. Many engineers gain these skills by obtaining a master's degree in engineering management or a master's degree in business administration (MBA). Employers often pay for such training. In large firms, some courses required in these degree programs may be offered on site. Engineers who prefer to manage in technical areas should get a master's degree in engineering management, while those interested in nontechnical management should get an MBA.

Many science managers begin their careers as scientists, such as chemists, biologists, geologists, or mathematicians. Most scientists or mathematicians engaged in basic research have a Ph.D.; some in applied research and other activities may have a bachelor's or master's degree. Science managers must be specialists in the work they supervise. In addition, employers prefer managers with good communication and administrative skills. Graduate programs allow scientists to augment their undergraduate training with instruction in other fields, such as management or computer technology. Given the rapid pace of scientific developments, science managers must continuously upgrade their knowledge.

Engineering and natural sciences managers may advance to progressively higher leadership positions within their discipline. Some may become managers in nontechnical areas such as marketing, human resources, or sales. In high technology firms, managers in nontechnical areas often must possess the same specialized knowledge as do managers in technical areas. For example, employers in an engineering firm may prefer to hire experienced engineers as sales workers because the complex services offered by the firm can be marketed only by someone with specialized engineering knowledge. Such sales workers could eventually advance to jobs as sales managers.

Job Outlook

Employment of engineering and natural sciences managers is expected to grow about as fast as the average through the year 2012—in line with projected employment growth in engineering and most sciences. However, many additional jobs will result from the need to replace managers who retire or move into other occupations. Opportunities for obtaining a management position will be best for workers with advanced technical knowledge and strong communication skills. In addition, business management skills are important because engineering and natural sciences managers are involved in their firm's financial, production, and marketing activities.

Projected employment growth for engineering and natural sciences managers should be closely related to the growth of the occupations they supervise and the industries in which they are found. For example, opportunities for managers should be better in rapidly growing areas of engineering—such as electrical, computer, and biomedical engineering—than in more slowly growing areas of engineering or physical science, such as aerospace and petroleum engineering. In addition, many employers are finding it more efficient to contract engineering and science management services to outside companies and consultants, creating good opportunities for managers in management services and management, scientific, and technical consulting firms.

Earnings

Earnings for engineering and natural sciences managers vary by specialty and level of responsibility. Median annual earnings of engineering managers were $90,930 in 2002. The middle 50 percent earned between $72,480 and $114,050. The lowest 10 percent earned less than $57,840, and the highest 10 percent earned more than $141,380. Median annual earnings in the industries employing the largest numbers of engineering managers in 2002 were:

Navigational, measuring, electromedical, and
    control instruments manufacturing $101,290

Management of companies and enterprises 98,000

Aerospace product and parts manufacturing 97,420

Federal government 90,030

Architectural, engineering, and related
    services 89,520

Median annual earnings of natural sciences managers were $82,250 in 2002. The middle 50 percent earned between $60,000 and $111,070. The lowest 10 percent earned less than $45,640, and the highest 10 percent earned more than $144,590. Median annual earnings in the industries employing the largest numbers of natural sciences managers in 2002 were:

Scientific research and development
services $101,690

Federal government 77,020

A survey of manufacturing firms, conducted by Abbot, Langer & Associates, found that engineering department managers and superintendents earned a median annual income of $89,271 in 2003, while research and development managers earned $86,412.

In addition, engineering and natural sciences managers, especially those at higher levels, often receive more benefits—such as expense accounts, stock option plans, and bonuses—than do nonmanagerial workers in their organizations.

Related Occupations

The work of engineering and natural sciences managers is closely related to that of engineers; mathematicians; and physical and life scientists, including agricultural and food scientists, biological and medical scientists, conservation scientists and foresters, atmospheric scientists, chemists and materials scientists, environmental scientists and geoscientists, and physicists and astronomers. It also is related to the work of other managers, especially top executives.

Sources of Additional Information

For information about a career as an engineering and natural sciences manager, contact the sources of additional information for engineers, life scientists, and physical scientists.

Engineering Technicians

(O*NET 17-3021.00, 17-3022.00, 17-3023.01, 17-3023.02, 17-3023.03, 17-3024.00, 17-3025.00, 17-3026.00, and 17-3027.00)

Significant Points

- Electrical and electronic engineering technicians make up 42 percent of all engineering technicians.

- Because the type and quality of training programs vary considerably, prospective students should carefully investigate training programs before enrolling.

- Opportunities will be best for individuals with an associate degree or extensive job training in engineering technology.

Nature of the Work

Engineering technicians use the principles and theories of science, engineering, and mathematics to solve technical problems in research and development, manufacturing, sales, construction, inspection, and maintenance. Their work is more limited in scope and more practically oriented than that of scientists and engineers. Many engineering technicians assist engineers and scientists, especially in research and development. Others work in quality control—inspecting products and processes, conducting tests, or collecting data. In manufacturing, they may assist in product design, development, or production. Many workers who repair or maintain various types of electrical, electronic, or mechanical equipment are called technicians.

Engineering technicians who work in research and development build or set up equipment, prepare and conduct experiments, collect data, calculate or record results, and help engineers or scientists in other ways, such as making prototype versions of newly designed equipment. They also assist in design work, often using computer-aided design (CAD) equipment.

Most engineering technicians specialize in certain areas, learning skills and working in the same disciplines as engineers. Occupational titles, therefore, tend to reflect those of engineers.

Aerospace engineering and operations technicians install, construct, maintain, and test systems used to test, launch, or track aircraft and space vehicles. They may calibrate test equipment and determine causes of equipment malfunctions. Using computer and communications systems, aerospace engineering and operations technicians often record and interpret test data.

Chemical engineering technicians usually are employed in industries producing pharmaceuticals, chemicals, and petroleum products, among others. They work in laboratories as well as processing plants. They help to develop new chemical products and processes, test processing equipment and instrumentation, gather data, and monitor quality.

Civil engineering technicians help civil engineers to plan and build highways, buildings, bridges, dams, wastewater treatment systems, and other structures, and to do related research. Some estimate construction costs and specify materials to be used, and some may even prepare drawings or perform land-surveying duties. Others may set up and monitor instruments used to study traffic conditions.

Electrical and electronics engineering technicians help to design, develop, test, and manufacture electrical and electronic equipment such as communication equipment, radar, industrial and medical measuring or control devices, navigational equipment, and computers. They may work in product evaluation and testing, using measuring and diagnostic devices to adjust, test, and repair equipment. (Workers whose jobs are limited to repairing electrical and electronic equipment are referred to as electronics technicians.)

Electrical and electronic engineering technology also is applied to a wide variety of systems such as communication and process controls. *Electromechanical engineering technicians* combine fundamental principles of mechanical engineering technology with knowledge of electrical and electronic circuits to design, develop, test, and manufacture electrical and computer-controlled mechanical systems.

Environmental engineering technicians work closely with environmental engineers and scientists in developing methods and devices used in the prevention, control, or correction of environmental hazards. They inspect and maintain equipment affecting air pollution and recycling. Some inspect water and wastewater treatment systems to ensure that pollution control requirements are met.

Industrial engineering technicians study the efficient use of personnel, materials, and machines in factories, stores, repair shops, and offices. They prepare layouts of machinery and equipment, plan the flow of work, make statistical studies, and analyze production costs.

Mechanical engineering technicians help engineers to design, develop, test, and manufacture industrial machinery, consumer products, and other equipment. They may assist in product tests—by setting up instrumentation for auto crash tests, for example. They may make sketches and rough layouts, record data, make computations, analyze results, and write reports. When planning production, mechanical engineering technicians prepare layouts and drawings of the assembly process and of parts to be manufactured. They estimate labor costs, equipment life, and plant space. Some test and inspect machines and equipment or work with engineers to eliminate production problems.

Working Conditions

Most engineering technicians work at least 40 hours a week in laboratories, offices, or manufacturing or industrial plants, or on construction sites. Some may be exposed to hazards from equipment, chemicals, or toxic materials.

Employment

Engineering technicians held 478,000 jobs in 2002. 204,000 of these were electrical and electronics engineering technicians, as indicated by the following tabulation.

Electrical and electronic engineering
   technicians 204,000

Civil engineering technicians 92,000

Industrial engineering technicians 62,000

Mechanical engineering technicians......................55,000

Electro-mechanical technicians.............................31,000

Environmental engineering technicians...............19,000

Aerospace engineering and operations
   technicians...15,000

About 39 percent of all engineering technicians worked in manufacturing, mainly in the computer and electronic equipment, transportation equipment, and machinery manufacturing industries. Another 20 percent worked in professional, scientific, and technical service industries, mostly in engineering or business services companies that do engineering work on contract for government, manufacturing firms, or other organizations.

In 2002, the federal government employed 11,000 engineering technicians. State governments employed 34,000, and local governments employed 24,000.

Training, Other Qualifications, and Advancement

Although it may be possible to qualify for certain engineering technician jobs without formal training, most employers prefer to hire someone with at least a 2-year associate degree in engineering technology. Training is available at technical institutes, community colleges, extension divisions of colleges and universities, and public and private vocational-technical schools, and in the Armed Forces. Persons with college courses in science, engineering, and mathematics may qualify for some positions but may need additional specialized training and experience. Although employers usually do not require engineering technicians to be certified, such certification may provide jobseekers a competitive advantage.

Prospective engineering technicians should take as many high school science and math courses as possible to prepare for postsecondary programs in engineering technology. Most 2-year associate degree programs accredited by the Technology Accreditation Commission of the Accreditation Board for Engineering and Technology (TAC/ABET) require, at a minimum, college algebra and trigonometry, and one or two basic science courses. Depending on the specialty, more math or science may be required.

The type of technical courses required also depends on the specialty. For example, prospective mechanical engineering technicians may take courses in fluid mechanics, thermodynamics, and mechanical design; electrical engineering technicians may need classes in electric circuits, microprocessors, and digital electronics; and those preparing to work in environmental engineering technology need courses in environmental regulations and safe handling of hazardous materials.

Because many engineering technicians assist in design work, creativity is desirable. Because these workers often are part of a team of engineers and other technicians, good communication skills and the ability to work well with others also are important.

Engineering technicians usually begin by performing routine duties under the close supervision of an experienced technician, technologist, engineer, or scientist. As they gain experience, they are given more difficult assignments with only general supervision. Some engineering technicians eventually become supervisors.

Many publicly and privately operated schools provide technical training; the type and quality of training varies considerably. Therefore, prospective students should be careful in selecting a program. They should contact prospective employers regarding their preferences and ask schools to provide information about the kinds of jobs obtained by graduates, instructional facilities and equipment, and faculty qualifications. Graduates of ABET-accredited programs usually are recognized to have achieved an acceptable level of competence in the mathematics, science, and technical courses required for this occupation.

Technical institutes offer intensive technical training through application and practice, but less theory and general education than do community colleges. Many offer 2-year associate degree programs, and are similar to or part of a community college or state university system. Other technical institutes are run by private, often for-profit organizations, sometimes called proprietary schools. Their programs vary considerably in length and types of courses offered, although some are 2-year associate degree programs.

Community colleges offer curriculums that are similar to those in technical institutes, but that may include more theory and liberal arts. There may be little or no difference between programs at technical institutes and community colleges, as both offer associate degrees. After completing the 2-year program, some graduates get jobs as engineering technicians, while others continue their education at 4-year colleges. However, there is a difference between an associate degree in pre-engineering and one in engineering technology. Students who enroll in a 2-year pre-engineering program may find it very difficult to find work as an engineering technician should they decide not to enter a 4-year engineering program, because pre-engineering programs usually focus less on hands-on applications and more on academic preparatory work. Conversely, graduates of 2-year engineering technology programs may not receive credit for some of the courses they have taken if they choose to transfer to a 4-year engineering program. Colleges with these 4-year programs usually do not offer engineering technician training, but college courses in science, engineering, and mathematics are useful for obtaining a job as an engineering technician. Many 4-year colleges offer bachelor's degrees in engineering technology, but graduates of these programs often are hired to work as technologists or applied engineers, not technicians.

Area vocational-technical schools, another source of technical training, include postsecondary public institutions that serve local students and emphasize training needed by local employers. Most require a high school diploma or its equivalent for admission.

Other training in technical areas may be obtained in the Armed Forces. Many military technical training programs are highly regarded by employers. However, skills acquired in military programs are often narrowly focused, so they may not be useful in civilian industry, which often requires broader training. Therefore, some additional training may be needed, depending on the acquired skills and the kind of job.

The National Institute for Certification in Engineering Technologies (NICET) has established a voluntary certification program for engineering technicians. Certification is available at various levels, each level combining a written examination in 1 of about 30 specialties with a certain amount of job-related experience, a supervisory evaluation, and a recommendation.

Job Outlook

Opportunities will be best for individuals with an associate degree or extensive job training in engineering technology. As technology becomes more sophisticated, employers will continue to look for technicians who are skilled in new technology and require a minimum of additional job training. An increase in the number of jobs related to public health and safety should create job opportunities for engineering technicians with the appropriate certification.

Overall employment of engineering technicians is expected to increase about as fast as the average for all occupations through 2012. Competitive pressures will force companies to improve and update manufacturing facilities and product designs, resulting in more jobs for engineering technicians. However, the growing use of advanced technologies, such as computer simulation and computer-aided design and drafting will continue to increase productivity and limit job growth. In addition to growth, many job openings will stem from the need to replace technicians who retire or leave the labor force.

As is the case for engineers, employment of engineering technicians is influenced by local and national economic conditions. As a result, the employment outlook varies with industry and specialization. Growth in the largest specialty—electrical and electronics engineering technicians—is expected to be about as fast as the average, and there will also be many jobs created by the need to replace technicians who retire or leave the labor force. Employment of environmental engineering technicians is expected to grow faster than average, partly due to increased demand for environmental protection and partly due to recognition of environmental engineering technicians as a separate occupation.

Earnings

Median annual earnings of engineering technicians by specialty is shown in the following tabulation.

Aerospace engineering and operations
   technicians $51,650

Electrical and electronic engineering
   technicians 42,950

Industrial engineering technicians 41,910

Mechanical engineering technicians......................41,280

Electro-mechanical technicians.............................38,120

Civil engineering technicians 37,720

Environmental engineering technicians 36,850

Median annual earnings of electrical and electronics engineering technicians were $42,950 in 2002. The middle 50 percent earned between $33,760 and $53,200. The lowest 10 percent earned less than $26,770, and the highest 10 percent earned more than $64,070. Median annual earnings in the industries employing the largest numbers of electrical and electronics engineering technicians in 2002 are shown below.

Federal government $58,520

Wired telecommunications carriers.......................49,610

Architectural, engineering, and related services 43,670

Semiconductor and other electronic component
  manufacturing 40,110

Navigational, measuring, electromedical, and
  control instruments manufacturing 39,760

Median annual earnings of civil engineering technicians were $37,720 in 2002. The middle 50 percent earned between $29,030 and $47,260. The lowest 10 percent earned less than $23,080, and the highest 10 percent earned more than $56,910. Median annual earnings in the industries employing the largest numbers of civil engineering technicians in 2002 are shown below.

Local government 42,120

Architectural, engineering, and related services 36,930

State government...34,800

In 2002, the average annual salary for aerospace engineering and operations technicians in the aerospace products and parts manufacturing industry was $54,530, and the average annual salary for environmental engineering technicians in the architectural, engineering, and related services industry was $32,690. The average annual salary for industrial engineering technicians in the semiconductor and other electronic component manufacturing industry was $38,230. In the architectural, engineering, and related services industry, the average annual salary for mechanical engineering technicians was $42,090.

Related Occupations

Engineering technicians apply scientific and engineering principles usually acquired in postsecondary programs below the baccalaureate level. Similar occupations include science technicians; drafters; surveyors, cartographers, photogrammetrists, and surveying technicians; and broadcast and sound engineering technicians and radio operators.

Sources of Additional Information

High school students interested in obtaining information about careers in engineering technology should visit the JETS Web site:

● JETS-Guidance, 1420 King St., Suite 405, Alexandria, VA 22314-2794. Internet: http://www.jets.org

Information on ABET-accredited engineering technology programs is available from:

● Accreditation Board for Engineering and Technology, Inc., 111 Market Place, Suite 1050, Baltimore, MD 21202. Internet: http://www.abet.org

Information on certification of engineering technicians as well as job and career information is available from:

● National Institute for Certification in Engineering Technologies (NICET), 1420 King St., Alexandria, VA 22314-2794. Internet: http://www.nicet.org

Engineers

(O*NET 17-2011.00, 17-2021.00, 17-2031.00, 17-2041.00, 17-2051.00, 17-2061.00, 17-2071.00, 17-2072.00, and 17-2081.00)

Significant Points

● Overall, job opportunities in engineering are expected to be good, but will vary by specialty.

● A bachelor's degree is required for most entry-level jobs.

● Starting salaries are significantly higher than those of college graduates in other fields.

● Continuing education is critical to keep abreast of the latest technology.

Nature of the Work

Engineers apply the theories and principles of science and mathematics to research and develop economical solutions to technical problems. Their work is the link between perceived social needs and commercial applications. Engineers design products, machinery to build those products, plants in which those products are made, and the systems that ensure the quality of the products and the efficiency of the workforce and manufacturing process. Engineers design, plan, and supervise the construction of buildings, highways, and transit systems. They develop and implement improved ways to extract, process, and use raw materials, such as petroleum and natural gas. They develop new materials that both improve the performance of products and take advantage of advances in technology. They harness the power of the sun, the Earth, atoms, and electricity for use in supplying the nation's power needs, and create millions of products using power. They analyze the impact of the products they develop or the systems they design on the environment and on people using them. Engineering knowledge is applied to improving many things, including the quality of healthcare, the safety of food products, and the operation of financial systems.

Engineers consider many factors when developing a new product. For example, in developing an industrial robot, engineers determine precisely what function the robot needs to perform; design and test the robot's components; fit the components together in an integrated plan; and evaluate the design's overall effectiveness, cost, reliability, and safety. This process applies to many different products, such as chemicals, computers, gas turbines, helicopters, and toys.

In addition to design and development, many engineers work in testing, production, or maintenance. These engineers supervise production in factories, determine the causes of breakdowns, and test manufactured products to maintain quality. They also estimate the time and cost to complete projects. Some move into engineering management or into sales. In sales, an engineering background enables them to discuss technical aspects and assist in product planning, installation, and use.

Most engineers specialize. More than 25 major specialties are recognized by professional societies, and the major branches have numerous subdivisions. Some examples include structural and transportation engineering, which are subdivisions of civil engineering; and ceramic, metallurgical, and polymer engineering, which are subdivisions of materials engineering. Engineers also may specialize in one industry, such as motor vehicles, or in one field of technology, such as turbines or semiconductor materials.

This statement, which contains an overall discussion of engineering, is followed by separate statements on 14 branches of engineering: Aerospace; agricultural; biomedical; chemical; civil; computer hardware; electrical and electronics, except computer; environmental; industrial, including health and safety; materials; mechanical; mining and geological, including mining safety; nuclear; and petroleum engineering.

Engineers in each branch have a base of knowledge and training that can be applied in many fields. Electronics engineers, for example, work in the medical, computer, communications, and missile guidance fields. Because there are many separate problems to solve in a large engineering project, engineers in one field often work closely with specialists in other scientific, engineering, and business occupations.

Engineers use computers to produce and analyze designs; to simulate and test how a machine, structure, or system operates; and to generate specifications for parts. Using the Internet or related communications systems, engineers can collaborate on designs with other engineers around the country or even abroad. Many engineers also use computers to monitor product quality and control process efficiency. They spend a great deal of time writing reports and consulting with other engineers, as complex projects often require an interdisciplinary team of engineers. Supervisory engineers are responsible for major components or entire projects.

Working Conditions

Most engineers work in office buildings, laboratories, or industrial plants. Others may spend time outdoors at construction sites and oil and gas exploration and production sites, where they monitor or direct operations or solve onsite problems. Some engineers travel extensively to plants or worksites.

Many engineers work a standard 40-hour week. At times, deadlines or design standards may bring extra pressure to a job, sometimes requiring engineers to work longer hours.

Employment

In 2002 engineers held 1.5 million jobs. The following tabulation shows the distribution of employment by engineering specialty.

Total, all engineers	1,478,000	100
Electrical and electronics	292,000	19.8
Civil	228,000	15.4
Mechanical	215,000	14.5
Industrial, including health and safety	194,000	13.1
Aerospace	78,000	5.3
Computer hardware	74,000	5.0
Environmental	47,000	3.2
Chemical	33,000	2.2
Materials	24,000	1.6
Nuclear	16,000	1.1
Petroleum	14,000	0.9
Biomedical	7,600	0.5
Mining and geological, including mining safety engineers	5,200	0.4
Marine engineers and naval architects	4,900	0.3
Agricultural	2,900	0.2
All other engineers	243,000	16.4

Almost 4 in 10 of all engineering jobs were found in manufacturing industries, such as transportation and equipment manufacturing and computer and electronic product manufacturing. About 354,000 wage and salary jobs were in the professional, scientific, and technical service industry, primarily in architectural, engineering, and related services and in scientific research and development services, where firms designed construction projects or did other engineering work on a contractual basis. Engineers also worked in the construction and transportation, telecommunications, and utilities industries.

Federal, state, and local governments employed about 192,000 engineers in 2002. About 88,000 of these were in the federal government, mainly in the U.S. Departments of Defense, Transportation, Agriculture, Interior, and Energy, and in the National Aeronautics and Space Administration.

Most engineers in state and local government agencies worked in highway and public works departments. In 2002, about 55,000 engineers were self-employed, many as consultants.

Engineers are employed in every state, in small and large cities, and in rural areas. Some branches of engineering are concentrated in particular industries and geographic areas, as discussed later in this chapter.

Training, Other Qualifications, and Advancement

A bachelor's degree in engineering is required for almost all entry-level engineering jobs. College graduates with a degree in a physical science or mathematics occasionally may qualify for some engineering jobs, especially in specialties in high demand. Most engineering degrees are granted in electrical, electronics, mechanical, or civil engineering. However, engineers trained in one branch may work in related branches. For example, many aerospace engineers have training in mechanical engineering. This flexibility allows employers to meet staffing needs in new technologies and specialties in which engineers may be in short supply. It also allows engineers to shift to fields with better employment prospects or to those that more closely match their interests.

Most engineering programs involve a concentration of study in an engineering specialty, along with courses in both mathematics and science. Most programs include a design course, sometimes accompanied by a computer or laboratory class or both.

In addition to the standard engineering degree, many colleges offer 2- or 4-year degree programs in engineering technology. These programs, which usually include various hands-on laboratory classes that focus on current issues, prepare students for practical design and production work, rather than for jobs that require more theoretical and scientific knowledge. Graduates of 4-year technology programs may get jobs similar to those obtained by graduates with a bachelor's degree in engineering. Engineering technology graduates, however, are not qualified to register as professional engineers under the same terms as graduates with degrees in engineering. Some employers regard technology program graduates as having skills between those of a technician and an engineer.

Graduate training is essential for engineering faculty positions and many research and development programs, but is not required for the majority of entry-level engineering jobs. Many engineers obtain graduate degrees in engineering or business administration to learn new technology and broaden their education. Many high-level executives in government and industry began their careers as engineers.

About 340 colleges and universities offer bachelor's degree programs in engineering that are accredited by the Accreditation Board for Engineering and Technology (ABET), and about 240 colleges offer accredited bachelor's degree programs in engineering technology. ABET accreditation is based on an examination of an engineering program's student achievement, program improvement, faculty, curricular content, facilities, and institutional commitment. Although most institutions offer programs in the major branches of engineering, only a few offer programs in the smaller specialties. Also, programs of the same title may vary in content. For example, some programs emphasize industrial practices, preparing students for a job in industry, whereas others are more theoretical and are designed to prepare students for graduate work. Therefore, students should investigate curricula and check accreditations carefully before selecting a college.

Admissions requirements for undergraduate engineering schools include a solid background in mathematics (algebra, geometry, trigonometry, and calculus) and science (biology, chemistry, and physics), and courses in English, social studies, humanities, and computer and information technology. Bachelor's degree programs in engineering typically are designed to last 4 years, but many students find that it takes between 4 and 5 years to complete their studies. In a typical 4-year college curriculum, the first 2 years are spent studying mathematics, basic sciences, introductory engineering, humanities, and social sciences. In the last 2 years, most courses are in engineering, usually with a concentration in one branch. For example, the last 2 years of an aerospace program might include courses in fluid mechanics, heat transfer, applied aerodynamics, analytical mechanics, flight vehicle design, trajectory dynamics, and aerospace propulsion systems. Some programs offer a general engineering curriculum; students then specialize in graduate school or on the job.

Some engineering schools and 2-year colleges have agreements whereby the 2-year college provides the initial engineering education, and the engineering school automatically admits students for their last 2 years. In addition, a few engineering schools have arrangements whereby a student spends 3 years in a liberal arts college studying pre-engineering subjects and 2 years in an engineering school studying core subjects, and then receives a bachelor's degree from each school. Some colleges and universities offer 5-year master's degree programs. Some 5-year or even 6-year cooperative plans combine classroom study and practical work, permitting students to gain valuable experience and to finance part of their education.

All 50 states and the District of Columbia require licensure for engineers who offer their services directly to the public. Engineers who are licensed are called Professional Engineers (PE). This licensure generally requires a degree from an ABET-accredited engineering program, 4 years of relevant work experience, and successful completion of a state examination. Recent graduates can start the licensing process by taking the examination in two stages. The initial Fundamentals of Engineering (FE) examination can be taken upon graduation. Engineers who pass this examination commonly are called Engineers in Training (EIT) or Engineer Interns (EI). After acquiring suitable work experience, EITs can take the second examination, the Principles and Practice of Engineering exam. Several states have imposed mandatory continuing education requirements for relicensure. Most states recognize licensure from other states provided that the manner in which the initial license was obtained meets or exceeds their licensure requirements. Many civil, electrical, mechanical, and chemical engineers are licensed PEs.

Engineers should be creative, inquisitive, analytical, and detail-oriented. They should be able to work as part of a team and to communicate well, both orally and in writing. Communication abilities are important because engineers often interact with specialists in a wide range of fields outside engineering.

Beginning engineering graduates usually work under the supervision of experienced engineers and, in large companies, also may receive formal classroom or seminar-type training. As new engineers gain knowledge and experience, they are assigned more difficult projects with greater independence to develop designs, solve problems, and make decisions. Engineers may advance to become technical specialists or to supervise a staff or team of engineers and technicians. Some may eventually become engineering managers or enter other managerial or sales jobs.

Job Outlook

Overall engineering employment is expected to grow more slowly than the average for all occupations over the 2002-12 period. Engineers tend to be concentrated in slow-growing manufacturing industries, a factor which tends to hold down their employment growth. Also, many employers are increasing their use of engineering services performed in other countries. Despite this, overall job opportunities in engineering are expected to be good because the number of engineering graduates should be in rough balance with the number of job openings over this period. Expected changes in employment and, thus, job opportunities vary by specialty. Projections range from a decline in employment of mining and geological engineers, petroleum engineers, and nuclear engineers to much faster than average growth among environmental engineers.

Competitive pressures and advancing technology will force companies to improve and update product designs and to optimize their manufacturing processes. Employers will rely on engineers to further increase productivity, as investment in plant and equipment increases to expand output of goods and services. New computer and communications systems have improved the design process, enabling engineers to produce and analyze various product designs much more rapidly than in the past and to collaborate on designs with other engineers throughout the world. Despite these widespread applications, computer technology is not expected to limit employment opportunities. Finally, additional engineers will be needed to improve or build new roads, bridges, water and pollution control systems, and other public facilities.

There is a large number of well-trained, often English-speaking engineers available in many countries who are willing to work at much lower salaries than U.S. engineers. The rise of the Internet and other electronic communications systems has made it relatively easy for much of the engineering work previously done by engineers in this country to be done by engineers in other countries, a factor that will tend to hold down employment growth.

Compared with most other workers, a smaller proportion of engineers leave their jobs each year. Nevertheless, many job openings will arise from replacement needs, reflecting the large size of this profession. Numerous job openings will be created by engineers who transfer to management, sales, or other professional occupations; additional openings will arise as engineers retire or leave the labor force for other reasons.

Many engineers work on long-term research and development projects or in other activities that continue even during economic slowdowns. In industries such as electronics and aerospace, however, large cutbacks in defense expenditures and government research and development funds in the past, as well as the trend toward contracting out engineering work to engineering services firms, both domestic and foreign, have resulted in significant layoffs of engineers.

It is important for engineers, like those working in other technical occupations, to continue their education throughout their careers because much of their value to their employer depends on their knowledge of the latest technology. Although the pace of technological change varies by engineering specialty and industry, advances in technology have significantly affected every engineering discipline. Engineers in high-technology areas, such as advanced electronics or information technology, may find that technical knowledge can become outdated rapidly. Even those who continue their education are vulnerable to layoffs if the particular technology or product in which they have specialized becomes obsolete. By keeping current in their field, engineers are able to deliver the best solutions and greatest value to their employers. Engineers who have not kept current in their field may find themselves passed over for promotions or vulnerable to layoffs, should they occur. On the other hand, it often is these high-technology areas that offer the greatest challenges, the most interesting work, and the highest salaries. Therefore, the choice of engineering specialty and employer involves an assessment not only of the potential rewards but also of the risk of technological obsolescence.

Related Occupations

Engineers apply the principles of physical science and mathematics in their work. Other workers who use scientific and mathematical principles include architects, except landscape and naval; engineering and natural sciences managers; computer and information systems managers; mathematicians; drafters; engineering technicians; sales engineers; science technicians; and physical and life scientists, including agricultural and food scientists, biological scientists, conservation scientists and foresters, atmospheric scientists, chemists and materials scientists, environmental scientists and geoscientists, and physicists and astronomers.

Sources of Additional Information

High school students interested in obtaining information about careers in engineering should visit the JETS Web site:

- JETS-Guidance, 1420 King St., Suite 405, Alexandria, VA 22314-2794. Internet: http://www.jets.org

Information on ABET-accredited engineering programs is available from:

- The Accreditation Board for Engineering and Technology, Inc., 111 Market Place, Suite 1050, Baltimore, MD 21202-4012. Internet: http://www.abet.org

Those interested in information on the Professional Engineer licensure should contact:

- The National Society of Professional Engineers, 1420 King St., Alexandria, VA 22314-2794. Internet: http://www.nspe.org
- National Council of Examiners for Engineers and Surveying, P.O. Box 1686, Clemson, SC 29633-1686. Internet: http://www.ncees.org

Information on general engineering education and career resources is available from:

- American Society for Engineering Education, 1818 N St. NW., Suite 600, Washington, DC 20036-2479. Internet: http://www.asee.org

Information on obtaining an engineering position with the federal government is available from the Office of Personnel Management (OPM) through a telephone-based system. Consult your telephone directory under U.S. government for a local number or call (703) 724-1850; Federal Relay Service: (800) 877-8339. The first number is not toll free, and charges may result. Information also is available from the OPM Internet site: http://www.usajobs.opm.gov.

Non-high school students wanting more detailed information on an engineering specialty should contact societies representing the individual branches of engineering. Each can provide information about careers in the particular branch. The individual statements that follow also provide other detailed information on aerospace; agricultural; biomedical; chemical; civil; computer hardware; electrical and electronics, except computer; environmental; industrial, including health and safety; materials; mechanical; mining and geological, including mining safety; nuclear; and petroleum engineering.

Environmental Engineers

(O*NET 17-2081.00)

Significant Points

- Overall, job opportunities in engineering are expected to be good, but will vary by specialty.
- A bachelor's degree is required for most entry-level jobs.

- Starting salaries are significantly higher than those of college graduates in other fields.
- Continuing education is critical to keep abreast of the latest technology.

Nature of the Work

Using the principles of biology and chemistry, environmental engineers develop solutions to environmental problems. They are involved in water and air pollution control, recycling, waste disposal, and public health issues. Environmental engineers conduct hazardous-waste management studies in which they evaluate the significance of the hazard, offer analysis on treatment and containment, and develop regulations to prevent mishaps. They design municipal water supply and industrial wastewater treatment systems. They conduct research on proposed environmental projects, analyze scientific data, and perform quality control checks.

Environmental engineers are concerned with local and worldwide environmental issues. They study and attempt to minimize the effects of acid rain, global warming, automobile emissions, and ozone depletion. They also are involved in the protection of wildlife.

Many environmental engineers work as consultants, helping their clients to comply with regulations and to clean up hazardous sites.

Working Conditions

Most engineers work in office buildings, laboratories, or industrial plants. Others may spend time outdoors at construction sites and oil and gas exploration and production sites, where they monitor or direct operations or solve onsite problems. Some engineers travel extensively to plants or worksites.

Many engineers work a standard 40-hour week. At times, deadlines or design standards may bring extra pressure to a job, sometimes requiring engineers to work longer hours.

Employment

Environmental engineers held about 47,000 jobs in 2002. Almost half worked in professional, scientific, and technical services and about 15,000 were employed in federal, state, and local government agencies. Most of the rest worked in various manufacturing industries.

Training, Other Qualifications, and Advancement

A bachelor's degree in engineering is required for almost all entry-level engineering jobs. College graduates with a degree in a physical science or mathematics occasionally may qualify for some engineering jobs, especially in specialties in high demand. Most engineering degrees are granted in electrical, electronics, mechanical, or civil engineering. However, engineers trained in one branch may work in related branches. For example, many aerospace engineers have training in mechanical engineering. This flexibility allows employers to meet staffing needs in new technologies and specialties in which engineers may be in short supply. It also allows engineers to shift to fields with better employment prospects or to those that more closely match their interests.

Most engineering programs involve a concentration of study in an engineering specialty, along with courses in both mathematics and science. Most programs include a design course, sometimes accompanied by a computer or laboratory class or both.

In addition to the standard engineering degree, many colleges offer 2- or 4-year degree programs in engineering technology. These programs, which usually include various hands-on laboratory classes that focus on current issues, prepare students for practical design and production work, rather than for jobs that require more theoretical and scientific knowledge. Graduates of 4-year technology programs may get jobs similar to those obtained by graduates with a bachelor's degree in engineering. Engineering technology graduates, however, are not qualified to register as professional engineers under the same terms as graduates with degrees in engineering. Some employers regard technology program graduates as having skills between those of a technician and an engineer.

Graduate training is essential for engineering faculty positions and many research and development programs, but is not required for the majority of entry-level engineering jobs. Many engineers obtain graduate degrees in engineering or business administration to learn new technology and broaden their education. Many high-level executives in government and industry began their careers as engineers.

About 340 colleges and universities offer bachelor's degree programs in engineering that are accredited by the Accreditation Board for Engineering and Technology (ABET), and about 240 colleges offer accredited bachelor's degree programs in engineering technology. ABET accreditation is based on an examination of an engineering program's student achievement, program improvement, faculty, curricular content, facilities, and institutional commitment. Although most institutions offer programs in the major branches of engineering, only a few offer programs in the smaller specialties. Also, programs of the same title may vary in content. For example, some programs emphasize industrial practices, preparing students for a job in industry, whereas others are more theoretical and are designed to prepare students for graduate work. Therefore, students should investigate curricula and check accreditations carefully before selecting a college.

Admissions requirements for undergraduate engineering schools include a solid background in mathematics (algebra, geometry, trigonometry, and calculus) and science (biology, chemistry, and physics), and courses in English, social studies, humanities, and computer and information technology. Bachelor's degree programs in engineering typically are designed to last 4 years, but many students find that it takes between 4 and 5 years to complete their studies. In a typical 4-year college curriculum, the first 2 years are spent studying mathematics, basic sciences, introductory engineering, humanities, and social sciences. In the last 2 years, most courses are in engineering, usually with a concentration in one branch. For example, the last 2 years of an aerospace program might include courses in fluid mechanics, heat transfer, applied aerodynamics, analytical mechanics, flight vehicle design, trajectory dynamics, and aerospace propulsion systems. Some programs offer a general engineering curriculum; students then specialize in graduate school or on the job.

Some engineering schools and 2-year colleges have agreements whereby the 2-year college provides the initial engineering education, and the engineering school automatically admits students for their last 2 years. In addition, a few engineering schools have arrangements whereby a student spends 3 years in a liberal arts college studying pre-engineering subjects and 2 years in an engineering school studying core subjects, and then receives a bachelor's degree from each school. Some colleges and universities offer 5-year master's degree programs. Some 5-year or even 6-year cooperative plans combine classroom study and practical work, permitting students to gain valuable experience and to finance part of their education.

All 50 states and the District of Columbia require licensure for engineers who offer their services directly to the public. Engineers who are licensed are called Professional Engineers (PE). This licensure generally requires a degree from an ABET-accredited engineering program, 4 years of relevant work experience, and successful completion of a state examination. Recent graduates can start the licensing process by taking the examination in two stages. The initial Fundamentals of Engineering (FE) examination can be taken upon graduation. Engineers who pass this examination commonly are called Engineers in Training (EIT) or Engineer Interns (EI). After acquiring suitable work experience, EITs can take the second examination, the Principles and Practice of Engineering exam. Several states have imposed mandatory continuing education requirements for relicensure. Most states recognize licensure from other states provided that the manner in which the initial license was obtained meets or exceeds their licensure requirements. Many civil, electrical, mechanical, and chemical engineers are licensed PEs.

Engineers should be creative, inquisitive, analytical, and detail-oriented. They should be able to work as part of a team and to communicate well, both orally and in writing. Communication abilities are important because engineers often interact with specialists in a wide range of fields outside engineering.

Beginning engineering graduates usually work under the supervision of experienced engineers and, in large companies, also may receive formal classroom or seminar-type training. As new engineers gain knowledge and experience, they are assigned more difficult projects with greater independence to develop designs, solve problems, and make decisions. Engineers may advance to become technical specialists or to supervise a staff or team of engineers and technicians. Some may eventually become engineering managers or enter other managerial or sales jobs.

Job Outlook

Environmental engineering graduates should have favorable job opportunities. Employment of environmental engineers is expected to increase much faster than the average for all occupations through 2012. Much of the expected growth will be due to the emergence of this occupation as a widely recognized engineering specialty rather than as an area that other engineering specialties, such as civil engineers, specialize in. More environmental engineers will be needed to comply with environmental regulations and to develop methods of cleaning up existing hazards. A shift in emphasis toward preventing problems rather than controlling those that already exist, as well as increasing public health concerns, also will spur demand for environmental engineers. However, political factors determine the job outlook for environmental engineers more than that for other engineers. Looser environmental regulations would reduce job opportunities; stricter regulations would enhance opportunities.

Even though employment of environmental engineers should be less affected by economic conditions than that of most other types of engineers, a significant economic downturn could reduce the emphasis on environmental protection, reducing employment opportunities. Environmental engineers need to keep abreast of a range of environmental issues to ensure their steady employment because their area of focus may change frequently—for example, from hazardous waste cleanup to the prevention of water pollution.

Earnings

Median annual earnings of environmental engineers were $61,410 in 2002. The middle 50 percent earned between $47,650 and $77,360. The lowest 10 percent earned less than $38,640, and the highest 10 percent earned more than $91,510. Median annual earnings in the industries employing the largest numbers of environmental engineers in 2002 were:

Architectural, engineering, and related services	$58,620
Management, scientific, and technical consulting services	57,800
State government	54,160

According to a 2003 salary survey by the National Association of Colleges and Employers, bachelor's degree candidates in environmental/environmental health engineering received starting offers averaging $44,702 a year.

Related Occupations

Environmental engineers apply the principles of physical science and mathematics in their work. Other workers who use scientific and mathematical principles include architects, except landscape and naval; engineering and natural sciences managers; computer and information systems managers; mathematicians; drafters; engineering technicians; sales engineers; science technicians; and physical and life scientists, including agricultural and food scientists, biological scientists, conservation scientists and foresters, atmospheric scientists, chemists and materials scientists, environmental scientists and geoscientists, and physicists and astronomers.

Sources of Additional Information

Further information about environmental engineering careers, training, and certification can be obtained from:

- American Academy of Environmental Engineers, 130 Holiday Court, Suite 100, Annapolis, MD 21401. Internet: http://www.aaee.net

See the introduction to the section on engineers for information on working conditions, training requirements, and other sources of additional information.

Environmental Scientists and Geoscientists

(O*NET 19-2041.00, 19-2042.01, and 19-2043.00)

Significant Points

- Work at remote field sites is common.

- Federal, state, and local governments employ nearly one-half of all environmental scientists and geoscientists.

- A bachelor's degree is adequate for a few entry-level jobs, but a master's degree is usually the minimum educational requirement; a Ph.D. degree is required for most high-level research positions.

- Employment of geoscientists is expected to grow as fast as average, while environmental scientists and hydrologists will experience faster than average growth.

Nature of the Work

Environmental scientists and geoscientists use their knowledge of the physical makeup and history of the Earth to protect the environment; locate water, mineral, and energy resources; predict future geologic hazards; and offer advice on construction and land-use projects.

Environmental scientists conduct research to identify and abate or eliminate sources of pollutants that affect people, wildlife, and their environments. These workers analyze and report measurements and observations of air, water, soil, and other sources and make recommendations on how best to clean and preserve the environment. Understanding the issues involved in protecting the environment—degradation, conservation, recycling, and replenishment—is central to the work of environmental scientists, who often use their skills and knowledge to design and monitor waste disposal sites, preserve water supplies, and reclaim contaminated land and water to comply with federal environmental regulations.

Many environmental scientists do work and have training that is similar to other physical or life scientists, but is applied to environmental areas. Many specialize in some specific area, such as environmental ecology and conservation, environmental chemistry, environmental biology, or fisheries science. Most environmental scientists are further classified by the specific activity they perform (although recent advances in the understanding of basic life processes within the ecosystem have blurred some traditional classifications). For example, *environmental ecologists* study the relationships between organisms and their environments and the effects of influences such as population size, pollutants, rainfall, temperature, and altitude. Utilizing their knowledge of various scientific disciplines, they may collect, study, and report data on air, food, soil, and water. *Ecological modelers* study ecosystems, the control of environmental pollution, and the management of resources. These environmental scientists may use mathematical modeling, systems analysis, thermodynamics, and computer techniques. *Environmental chemists* may study the toxicity of various chemicals—how those chemicals affect plants, animals, and people. *Geochemists* study the nature and distribution of chemical elements in ground water and Earth materials.

Some environmental scientists work in managerial positions, usually after spending some time performing research or learning about environmental laws and regulations. Many work as consultants to business firms or to government agencies, helping them comply with environmental policy, particularly with regard to ground-water contamination and flood control. Environmental scientists who determine policy may help identify how human behavior can be modified in the future to avoid such problems as ground-water contamination and depletion of the ozone layer.

Geoscientists study the composition, structure, and other physical aspects of the Earth. With the use of sophisticated instruments and by analyzing the composition of the earth and water, geoscientists study the Earth's geologic past and present. Many geoscientists are involved in searching for oil and gas, while others work closely with environmental scientists in preserving and cleaning up the environment.

Geoscientists usually study, and are subsequently classified into, one of several closely related fields of geoscience. *Geologists* study the composition, processes, and history of the Earth. They try to find out how rocks were formed and what

has happened to them since their formation. They also study the evolution of life by analyzing plant and animal fossils. *Geophysicists* use the principles of physics, mathematics, and chemistry to study not only the Earth's surface, but also its internal composition; ground and surface waters; atmosphere; oceans; and magnetic, electrical, and gravitational forces.

Oceanographers use their knowledge of geology and geophysics, in addition to biology and chemistry, to study the world's oceans and coastal waters. They study the motion and circulation of the ocean waters; the physical and chemical properties of the oceans; and how these properties affect coastal areas, climate, and weather. Oceanographers are further broken down according to their areas of expertise. For example, *physical oceanographers* study the ocean tides, waves, currents, temperatures, density, and salinity. They examine the interaction of various forms of energy, such as light, radar, sound, heat, and wind, with the sea, in addition to investigating the relationship between the sea, weather, and climate. *Chemical oceanographers* study the distribution of chemical compounds and chemical interactions that occur in the ocean and on the sea floor. They may investigate how pollution affects the chemistry of the ocean. *Geological and geophysical oceanographers* study the topographic features and the physical makeup of the ocean floor. Their knowledge can help companies find oil and gas off coastal waters. (*Biological oceanographers*, often called marine biologists, study the distribution and migration patterns of the many diverse forms of sea life in the ocean, but because they are considered biological scientists, they are not covered in this statement on environmental scientists and geoscientists.)

Geoscientists can spend a large part of their time in the field, identifying and examining rocks, studying information collected by remote sensing instruments in satellites, conducting geological surveys, constructing field maps, and using instruments to measure the Earth's gravity and magnetic field. For example, they often perform seismic studies, which involve bouncing energy waves off buried rock layers, to search for oil and gas or to understand the structure of subsurface rock layers. Seismic signals generated by an earthquake are used to determine the earthquake's location and intensity. In laboratories, geologists and geophysicists examine the chemical and physical properties of specimens. They study fossil remains of animal and plant life or experiment with the flow of water and oil through rocks.

Numerous specialties that further differentiate the type of work geoscientists do fall under the two major disciplines of geology and geophysics. For example, *petroleum geologists* explore for oil and gas deposits by studying and mapping the subsurface of the ocean or land. They use sophisticated geophysical instrumentation and computers to interpret geological information. *Engineering geologists* apply geologic principles to the fields of civil and environmental engineering, offering advice on major construction projects and assisting in environmental remediation and natural hazard reduction projects. *Mineralogists* analyze and classify minerals and precious stones according to their composition and structure. They study the environment surrounding rocks in order to find new mineral resources. *Paleontologists* study fossils found in geological formations to trace the evolution of plant and animal life and the geologic history of the Earth. *Stratigraphers* examine the formation and layering of rocks to understand the environment in which they were formed. *Volcanologists* investigate volcanoes and volcanic phenomena to try to predict the potential for future eruptions and possible hazards to human health and welfare. *Hydrologists* study the quantity, distribution, circulation, and physical properties of underground and surface waters. They examine the form and intensity of precipitation, its rate of infiltration into the soil, its movement through the earth, and its return to the ocean and atmosphere. The work hydrologists do is particularly important in environmental preservation, remediation, and flood control.

Geophysicists specialize in areas such as geodesy, seismology, or magnetic geophysics. *Geodesists* study the Earth's size, shape, gravitational field, tides, polar motion, and rotation. *Seismologists* interpret data from seismographs and other geophysical instruments to detect earthquakes and locate earthquake-related faults. *Geomagnetists* measure the Earth's magnetic field and use measurements taken over the past few centuries to devise theoretical models that explain the Earth's origin. *Paleomagnetists* interpret fossil magnetization in rocks and sediments from the continents and oceans to record the spreading of the sea floor, the wandering of the continents, and the many reversals of polarity that the Earth's magnetic field has undergone through time. Other geophysicists study atmospheric sciences and space physics.

Working Conditions

Some environmental scientists and geoscientists spend the majority of their time in an office, but many others divide their time between fieldwork and office or laboratory work. Many environmental scientists, such as environmental ecologists, environmental chemists, and hydrologists, often take field trips that involve physical activity. Environmental scientists in the field may work in warm or cold climates, in all kinds of weather. In their research, they may dig or chip with a hammer, scoop with a net, and carry equipment in a backpack. Oceanographers may spend considerable time at sea on academic research ships. Fieldwork often requires working long hours. Geologists frequently travel to remote field sites by helicopter or four-wheel-drive vehicles and cover large areas on foot. An increasing number of exploration geologists and geophysicists work in foreign countries, sometimes in remote areas and under difficult conditions. Travel often is required to meet with prospective clients or investors.

Environmental scientists and geoscientists in research positions with the federal government or in colleges and universities frequently are required to design programs and write grant proposals in order to continue their data collection and research. Environmental scientists and geoscientists in consulting jobs face similar pressures to market their skills and write proposals so that they will have steady work.

Employment

Environmental scientists and geoscientists held about 101,000 jobs in 2002. Environmental scientists accounted for 65,000 of the total; geoscientists, 28,000; and hydrologists, 8,000. Many more individuals held environmental science and geoscience faculty positions in colleges and universities, but they are classified as college and university faculty.

About 47 percent of environmental scientists were employed in state and local governments, 14 percent in architectural, engineering and related services, 13 percent in management, scientific, and technical consulting services, and 9 percent in the federal government. About 1,900 were self-employed.

Among geoscientists, 30 percent were employed in architectural, engineering, and related services, and 15 percent worked for oil and gas extraction companies. In 2002, the federal government employed about 3,000 geoscientists, including geologists, geophysicists, and oceanographers, mostly within the U.S. Department of the Interior for the U.S. Geological Survey (USGS) and within the U.S. Department of Defense. Another 3,400 worked for state agencies, such as state geological surveys and state departments of conservation. Nearly 3 percent of geoscientists were self-employed, most as consultants to industry or government.

Approximately 32 percent of hydrologists worked in the federal government in 2002, another 21 percent in architectural, engineering, and related services, 17 percent worked in management, scientific, and technical consulting services, and 16 percent for state governments.

Training, Other Qualifications, and Advancement

A bachelor's degree is adequate for a few entry-level positions, but environmental scientists and geoscientists increasingly need a master's degree in a natural science. A master's degree also is the minimum educational requirement for most entry-level research positions in private industry, federal agencies, and state geological surveys. A doctoral degree is necessary for most high-level research positions.

Many environmental scientists earn degrees in life science, chemistry, geology, geophysics, atmospheric science, or physics and then, either through further education or through their research interests and work experience, apply their education to environmental areas. Others earn a degree in environmental science. A bachelor's degree in environmental science offers an interdisciplinary approach to the natural sciences, with an emphasis on biology, chemistry, and geology. In addition, undergraduate environmental science majors should focus on data analysis and physical geography, particularly if they are interested in studying pollution abatement, water resources, or ecosystem protection, restoration, or management. Those students interested in working in the environmental or regulatory fields, either in environmental consulting firms or for federal or state governments, should take courses in hydrology, hazardous waste management, environmental legislation, chemistry, fluid mechanics, and geologic logging. An understanding of environmental regulations and government permit issues also is valuable for those planning to work in mining and oil and gas extraction. Hydrologists and environmental scientists should have some knowledge of the potential liabilities associated with some environmental work. Students interested in the field of hydrology should take courses in the physical sciences, geophysics, chemistry, engineering science, soils, mathematics, aquatic biology, atmospheric science, meteorology, geology, oceanography, or the management or conservation of water resources. In some cases, graduates with a bachelor's degree in a hydrologic science are qualified for positions in environmental consulting and planning regarding water quality or waste-water treatment. Curricula for advanced degrees often emphasize the natural sciences, but not all universities offer all curricula.

Traditional geoscience courses emphasizing classical geologic methods and topics (such as mineralogy, petrology, paleontology, stratigraphy, and structural geology) are important for all geoscientists. Persons studying physics, chemistry, biology, mathematics, engineering, or computer science may also qualify for some geoscience positions if their course work includes study in geology or natural sciences.

Computer skills are essential for prospective environmental scientists and geoscientists; students who have some experience with computer modeling, data analysis and integration, digital mapping, remote sensing, and geographic information systems will be the most prepared entering the job market. A knowledge of the Global Information System (GIS) and Global Positioning System (GPS)—a locator system that uses satellites—also is very helpful. Some employers seek applicants with field experience, so a summer internship may be beneficial to prospective geoscientists.

Environmental scientists and geoscientists must have excellent interpersonal skills, because they usually work as part of a team with other scientists, engineers, and technicians. Strong oral and written communication skills also are important, because writing technical reports and research proposals, as well as communicating research results to others, are important aspects of the work. Because many jobs require foreign travel, knowledge of a second language is becoming an important attribute to employers. Geoscientists must be inquisitive, be able to think logically, and have an open mind. Those involved in fieldwork must have physical stamina.

Environmental scientists and geoscientists often begin their careers in field exploration or as research assistants or technicians in laboratories or offices. They are given more difficult assignments as they gain experience. Eventually, they may be promoted to project leader, program manager, or some other management and research position.

Job Outlook

Overall employment of environmental scientists and geoscientists is expected to grow about as fast as the average for all occupations through 2012. Driving job growth will be public policy, which will force companies and organizations to comply with environmental laws and regulations, particularly those regarding ground-water contamination, clean air, and flood control.

Projected employment growth varies by occupational specialty. Environmental scientists and hydrologists are expected to grow faster than average. A general heightened awareness regarding the need to monitor the quality of the environment, to interpret the impact of human actions on terrestrial and aquatic ecosystems, and to develop strategies for ecosystem restoration are all increasingly important issues that will drive demand for environmental scientists. Issues related to water conservation, deteriorating coastal environments, and rising sea levels also will stimulate employment growth of these workers. As the population increases and moves to more environmentally sensitive locations, environmental scientists and hydrologists will be needed to assess building sites for potential geologic hazards, to mitigate the effects of natural hazards such as floods, tornadoes, and earthquakes, and to address issues related to pollution control and waste disposal. Hydrologists and environmental scientists also will be needed to conduct research on hazardous-waste sites in order to determine the impact of hazardous pollutants on soil and ground water so that engineers can design remediation systems. Demand is growing for environmental scientists who understand both the science and engineering aspects of waste remediation.

In contrast to employment of environmental scientists and hydrologists, that of geoscientists is expected to grow about as fast as the average for all occupations. In the past, employment of geologists and some other geoscientists has been cyclical and largely affected by the price of oil and gas. When prices were low, oil and gas producers curtailed exploration activities and laid off geologists. When prices were higher, companies had the funds and incentive to renew exploration efforts and hire geoscientists in large numbers. In recent years, a growing worldwide demand for oil and gas and for new exploration and recovery techniques—particularly in deep water and previously inaccessible sites—has returned a modicum of stability to the petroleum industry. Growth in this area, though, will be limited due to increasing efficiencies in finding oil and gas. Geoscientists who speak a foreign language and who are willing to work abroad should enjoy the best opportunities. An expected increase in highway building and other infrastructure projects will be a source of jobs for engineering geologists. The need to replace geoscientists who retire also will result in job openings over the next decade.

Earnings

Median annual earnings of environmental scientists were $47,600 in 2002. The middle 50 percent earned between

$36,820 and $62,400. The lowest 10 percent earned less than $29,920, and the highest 10 percent earned more than $78,200.

Median annual earnings of geoscientists were $67,470 in 2002. The middle 50 percent earned between $48,370 and $102,120; the lowest 10 percent, less than $36,580 and the highest 10 percent more than $133,310.

Median annual earnings of hydrologists were $56,530 in 2002, with the middle 50 percent earning between $44,080 and $70,160, the lowest 10 percent less than $36,790, and the highest 10 percent more than $86,620.

Median annual earnings in the industries employing the largest number of environmental scientists in 2002 were as follows:

Federal government	$66,190
Management, scientific, and technical consulting services	45,560
Local government	45,270
Architectural, engineering, and related services	44,590
State government	44,580

According to the National Association of Colleges and Employers, beginning salary offers in 2003 for graduates with bachelor's degrees in geology and related sciences averaged about $32,828 a year; graduates with a master's degree averaged $47,981, and graduates with a doctoral degree averaged $61,050.

In 2003, the federal government's average salary for geologists in managerial, supervisory, and nonsupervisory positions was $76,389 for geologists, $86,809 for geophysicists, $70,525 for hydrologists, and $79,023 for oceanographers.

The petroleum, mineral, and mining industries are vulnerable to recessions and to changes in oil and gas prices, among other factors, and usually release workers when exploration and drilling slow down. Consequently, they offer higher salaries, but less job security, than do other industries.

Related Occupations

Many geoscientists work in the petroleum and natural gas industry, an industry that also employs many other workers in the scientific and technical aspects of petroleum and natural gas exploration and extraction. Among these other workers are engineering technicians, science technicians, petroleum engineers, surveyors, cartographers, photogrammetrists, and surveying technicians. Also, some physicists and astronomers, chemists and materials scientists, and atmospheric scientists—as well as mathematicians, computer systems analysts, database administrators, and computer scientists—perform related work both in petroleum and natural gas exploration and extraction and in environment-related activities.

Sources of Additional Information

Information on training and career opportunities for geologists is available from either of the following organizations:

● American Geological Institute, 4220 King St., Alexandria, VA 22302-1502. Internet: http://www.agiweb.org

● American Association of Petroleum Geologists, P.O. Box 979, Tulsa, OK 74101. Internet: http://www.aapg.org

A packet of free career information and a list of education and training programs in oceanography and related fields, priced at $6.00, is available from:

● Marine Technology Society, 5565 Sterrett Place, Suite 108, Columbia, MD 21004. Telephone: (410) 884-5330. Internet: http://www.mtsociety.org

Information on applying for a job as a geologist, a geophysicist, a hydrologist, or an oceanographer with the federal government may be obtained through a telephone-based system from the Office of Personnel Management. Consult your telephone directory under U.S. government for a local number, or call (703) 724-1850 or Federal Relay Service (800) 877-8339. This number is not toll free, and charges may accrue. Information also is available from the Internet site http://www.usajobs.opm.gov.

Heating, Air-Conditioning, and Refrigeration Mechanics and Installers

(O*NET 49-9021.01 and 49-9021.02)

Significant Points

● Job prospects for heating, air-conditioning, and refrigeration mechanics and installers are expected to be good, particularly for those with technical school or formal apprenticeship training.

● The Air-Conditioning Excellence program, offered through North American Technician Excellence, is the standard for certification of experienced technicians.

Nature of the Work

What would those living in Chicago do without heating, those in Miami do without air-conditioning, or blood banks all over the country do without refrigeration? Heating and air-conditioning systems control the temperature, humidity, and the total air quality in residential, commercial, industrial, and other buildings. Refrigeration systems make it possible to store and transport food, medicine, and other perishable items. Heating, air-conditioning, and refrigeration mechanics and installers—also called technicians—

install, maintain, and repair such systems. Because heating, ventilation, air-conditioning, and refrigeration systems often are referred to as HVACR systems, these workers also may be called HVACR technicians.

Heating, air-conditioning, and refrigeration systems consist of many mechanical, electrical, and electronic components, such as motors, compressors, pumps, fans, ducts, pipes, thermostats, and switches. In central heating systems, for example, a furnace heats air that is distributed throughout the building via a system of metal or fiberglass ducts. Technicians must be able to maintain, diagnose, and correct problems throughout the entire system. To do this, they adjust system controls to recommended settings and test the performance of the entire system using special tools and test equipment.

Technicians often specialize in either installation or maintenance and repair, although they are trained to do both. Some specialize in one type of equipment—for example, oil burners, solar panels, or commercial refrigerators. Technicians may work for large or small contracting companies or directly for a manufacturer or wholesaler. Those working for smaller operations tend to do both installation and servicing, and work with heating, cooling, and refrigeration equipment. Service contracts—which involve heating, air-conditioning, and refrigeration work for particular customers on a regular basis—are becoming more common. Service agreements help to reduce the seasonal fluctuations of this work.

Heating and air-conditioning mechanics install, service, and repair heating and air-conditioning systems in both residences and commercial establishments. *Furnace installers*, also called *heating equipment technicians*, follow blueprints or other specifications to install oil, gas, electric, solid-fuel, and multiple-fuel heating systems. *Air-conditioning mechanics* install and service central air-conditioning systems. After putting the equipment in place, they install fuel and water supply lines, air ducts and vents, pumps, and other components. They may connect electrical wiring and controls and check the unit for proper operation. To ensure the proper functioning of the system, furnace installers often use combustion test equipment, such as carbon dioxide and oxygen testers.

After a furnace has been installed, heating equipment technicians often perform routine maintenance and repair work to keep the system operating efficiently. During the fall and winter, for example, when the system is used most, they service and adjust burners and blowers. If the system is not operating properly, they check the thermostat, burner nozzles, controls, or other parts to diagnose and then correct the problem.

During the summer, when the heating system is not being used, heating equipment technicians do maintenance work, such as replacing filters, ducts, and other parts of the system that may accumulate dust and impurities during the operating season. During the winter, air-conditioning mechanics inspect the systems and do required maintenance, such as overhauling compressors.

Refrigeration mechanics install, service, and repair industrial and commercial refrigerating systems and a variety of refrigeration equipment. They follow blueprints, design specifications, and manufacturers' instructions to install motors, compressors, condensing units, evaporators, piping, and other components. They connect this equipment to the ductwork, refrigerant lines, and electrical power source. After making the connections, they charge the system with refrigerant, check it for proper operation, and program control systems.

When heating, air-conditioning, and refrigeration mechanics service equipment, they must use care to conserve, recover, and recycle chlorofluorocarbon (CFC) and hydrochlorofluorocarbon (HCFC) refrigerants used in air-conditioning and refrigeration systems. The release of CFCs and HCFCs contributes to the depletion of the stratospheric ozone layer, which protects plant and animal life from ultraviolet radiation. Technicians conserve the refrigerant by making sure that there are no leaks in the system; they recover it by venting the refrigerant into proper cylinders; and they recycle it for reuse with special filter-dryers.

Heating, air-conditioning, and refrigeration mechanics and installers are adept at using a variety of tools, including hammers, wrenches, metal snips, electric drills, pipe cutters and benders, measurement gauges, and acetylene torches, to work with refrigerant lines and air ducts. They use voltmeters, thermometers, pressure gauges, manometers, and other testing devices to check airflow, refrigerant pressure, electrical circuits, burners, and other components.

Other craftworkers sometimes install or repair cooling and heating systems. For example, on a large air-conditioning installation job, especially where workers are covered by union contracts, ductwork might be done by sheet metal workers and duct installers; electrical work by electricians; and installation of piping, condensers, and other components by pipelayers, plumbers, pipefitters, and steamfitters. Home appliance repairers usually service room air-conditioners and household refrigerators.

Working Conditions

Heating, air-conditioning, and refrigeration mechanics and installers work in homes, stores of all kinds, hospitals, office buildings, and factories—anywhere there is climate-control equipment. They may be assigned to specific jobsites at the beginning of each day, or if they are making service calls, they may be dispatched to jobs by radio, telephone, or pager. Increasingly, employers are using cell phones to coordinate technicians' schedules.

Technicians may work outside in cold or hot weather or in buildings that are uncomfortable because the air-conditioning or heating equipment is broken. In addition, technicians might have to work in awkward or cramped positions and sometimes are required to work in high places. Hazards include electrical shock, burns, muscle strains, and other injuries from handling heavy equipment. Appropriate safety equipment is necessary when handling refrigerants because contact can cause skin damage, frostbite, or blindness. Inhalation of refrigerants when working in confined spaces also is a possible hazard.

The majority of mechanics and installers work at least a 40-hour week. During peak seasons they often work overtime or irregular hours. Maintenance workers, including those who provide maintenance services under contract, often work evening or weekend shifts and are on call. Most employers try to provide a full workweek year-round by scheduling both installation and maintenance work, and many manufacturers and contractors now provide or even require service contracts. In most shops that service both heating and air-conditioning equipment, employment is stable throughout the year.

Heating, air-conditioning, and refrigeration mechanics and installers held about 249,000 jobs in 2002; almost half worked for cooling and heating contractors. The remainder was employed in a variety of industries throughout the country, reflecting a widespread dependence on climate-control systems. Some worked for fuel oil dealers, refrigeration and air-conditioning service and repair shops, schools, and stores that sell heating and air-conditioning systems. Local governments, the federal government, hospitals, office buildings, and other organizations that operate large air-conditioning, refrigeration, or heating systems employed others. About 15 percent of mechanics and installers were self-employed.

Employment

Heating, air-conditioning, and refrigeration mechanics and installers held about 249,000 jobs in 2002; almost half worked for cooling and heating contractors. The remainder was employed in a variety of industries throughout the country, reflecting a widespread dependence on climate-control systems. Some worked for fuel oil dealers, refrigeration and air-conditioning service and repair shops, schools, and stores that sell heating and air-conditioning systems. Local governments, the federal government, hospitals, office buildings, and other organizations that operate large air-conditioning, refrigeration, or heating systems employed others. About 15 percent of mechanics and installers were self-employed.

Training, Other Qualifications, and Advancement

Because of the increasing sophistication of heating, air-conditioning, and refrigeration systems, employers prefer to hire those with technical school or apprenticeship training. Many mechanics and installers, however, still learn the trade informally on the job.

Many secondary and postsecondary technical and trade schools, junior and community colleges, and the U.S. Armed Forces offer 6-month to 2-year programs in heating, air-conditioning, and refrigeration. Students study theory,

design, and equipment construction, as well as electronics. They also learn the basics of installation, maintenance, and repair.

Apprenticeship programs frequently are run by joint committees representing local chapters of the Air-Conditioning Contractors of America, the Mechanical Contractors Association of America, the National Association of Plumbing-Heating-Cooling Contractors, and locals of the Sheet Metal Workers' International Association or the United Association of Journeymen and Apprentices of the Plumbing and Pipefitting Industry of the United States and Canada. Other apprenticeship programs are sponsored by local chapters of the Associated Builders and Contractors and the National Association of Home Builders. Formal apprenticeship programs normally last 3 to 5 years and combine on-the-job training with classroom instruction. Classes include subjects such as the use and care of tools, safety practices, blueprint reading, and the theory and design of heating, ventilation, air-conditioning, and refrigeration systems. Applicants for these programs must have a high school diploma or equivalent. Math and reading skills are essential.

Those who acquire their skills on the job usually begin by assisting experienced technicians. They may begin by performing simple tasks such as carrying materials, insulating refrigerant lines, or cleaning furnaces. In time, they move on to more difficult tasks, such as cutting and soldering pipes and sheet metal and checking electrical and electronic circuits.

Courses in shop math, mechanical drawing, applied physics and chemistry, electronics, blueprint reading, and computer applications provide a good background for those interested in entering this occupation. Some knowledge of plumbing or electrical work also is helpful. A basic understanding of electronics is becoming more important because of the increasing use of this technology in equipment controls. Because technicians frequently deal directly with the public, they should be courteous and tactful, especially when dealing with an aggravated customer. They also should be in good physical condition because they sometimes have to lift and move heavy equipment.

All technicians who purchase or work with refrigerants must be certified in their proper handling. To become certified to purchase and handle refrigerants, technicians must pass a written examination specific to the type of work in which they specialize. The three possible areas of certification are: Type I—servicing small appliances, Type II—high-pressure refrigerants, and Type III—low-pressure refrigerants. Exams are administered by organizations approved by the U.S. Environmental Protection Agency, such as trade schools, unions, contractor associations, or building groups.

Several organizations have begun to offer basic self-study, classroom, and Internet courses for individuals with limited experience. In addition to understanding how systems work, technicians must be knowledgeable about refrigerant products and the legislation and regulations that govern their use. The Air-Conditioning Excellence program, which is offered through North American Technician Excellence (NATE), generally has been adopted as the standard for certification of experienced technicians.

Advancement usually takes the form of higher wages. Some technicians, however, may advance to positions as supervisor or service manager. Others may move into areas such as sales and marketing. Still others may become building superintendents, cost estimators, or, with the necessary certification, teachers. Those with sufficient money and managerial skill can open their own contracting business.

Job Outlook

Job prospects for heating, air-conditioning, and refrigeration mechanics and installers are expected to be good, particularly for those with technical school or formal apprenticeship training. Employment of heating, air-conditioning, and refrigeration mechanics and installers is expected to grow faster than the average for all occupations through the year 2012. As the population and economy grow, so does the demand for new residential, commercial, and industrial climate-control systems. Technicians who specialize in installation work may experience periods of unemployment when the level of new construction activity declines, but maintenance and repair work usually remains relatively stable. People and businesses depend on their climate-control systems and must keep them in good working order, regardless of economic conditions.

Renewed concern for energy conservation should continue to prompt the development of new energy-saving heating and air-conditioning systems. An emphasis on better energy management should lead to the replacement of older systems and the installation of newer, more efficient systems in existing homes and buildings. Also, demand for maintenance and service work should increase as businesses and homeowners strive to keep systems operating at peak efficiency. Regulations prohibiting the discharge of CFC and HCFC refrigerants took effect in 1993, and regulations banning CFC production became effective in 2000. Consequently, these regulations should continue to result in demand for technicians to replace many existing systems, or modify them to use new environmentally safe refrigerants. In addition, the continuing focus on improving indoor air quality should contribute to the creation of more jobs for heating, air-conditioning, and refrigeration technicians. Also, growth of business establishments that use refrigerated equipment—such as supermarkets and convenience stores—will contribute to a growing need for technicians. In addition to job openings created by employment growth, thousands of openings will result from the need to replace workers who transfer to other occupations or leave the labor force.

Earnings

Median hourly earnings of heating, air-conditioning, and refrigeration mechanics and installers were $16.78 in 2002. The middle 50 percent earned between $12.95 and $21.37 an hour. The lowest 10 percent earned less than $10.34, and the top 10 percent earned more than $26.20. Median hourly earnings in the industries employing the largest numbers of heating, air-conditioning, and refrigeration mechanics and installers in 2002 were as follows:

Hardware, and plumbing and heating equipment and supplies merchant wholesalers	$18.78
Commercial and industrial machinery and equipment (except automotive and electronic) repair and maintenance	17.16
Direct selling establishments	17.14
Elementary and secondary schools	16.80
Building equipment contractors	16.03

Apprentices usually begin at about 50 percent of the wage rate paid to experienced workers. As they gain experience and improve their skills, they receive periodic increases until they reach the wage rate of experienced workers.

Heating, air-conditioning, and refrigeration mechanics and installers enjoy a variety of employer-sponsored benefits. In addition to typical benefits such as health insurance and pension plans, some employers pay for work-related training and provide uniforms, company vans, and tools.

About 20 percent of heating, air-conditioning, and refrigeration mechanics and installers are members of a union. The unions to which the greatest numbers of mechanics and installers belong are the Sheet Metal Workers' International Association and the United Association of Journeymen and Apprentices of the Plumbing and Pipefitting Industry of the United States and Canada.

Related Occupations

Heating, air-conditioning, and refrigeration mechanics and installers work with sheet metal and piping, and repair machinery, such as electrical motors, compressors, and burners. Other workers who have similar skills include boilermakers; home appliance repairers; electricians; sheet metal workers; and pipelayers, plumbers, pipefitters, and steamfitters.

Sources of Additional Information

For more information about opportunities for training, certification, and employment in this trade, contact local vocational and technical schools; local heating, air-conditioning, and refrigeration contractors; a local of the unions or organizations previously mentioned; a local joint union-management apprenticeship committee; or the nearest office of the state employment service or apprenticeship agency.

For information on career opportunities, training, and technician certification, contact:

- Air-Conditioning Contractors of America (ACCA), 2800 Shirlington Rd., Suite 300, Arlington, VA 22206. Internet: http://www.acca.org
- Refrigeration Service Engineers Society (RSES), 1666 Rand Rd., Des Plaines, IL 60016-3552. Internet: http://www.rses.org

- Plumbing-Heating-Cooling Contractors (PHCC), 180 S. Washington St., P.O. Box 6808, Falls Church, VA 22046. Internet: http://www.phccweb.org

- Sheet Metal and Air-Conditioning Contractors' National Association, 4201 Lafayette Center Dr., Chantilly, VA 20151-1209. Internet: http://www.smacna.org

For information on technician testing and certification, contact:

- North American Technician Excellence (NATE), 4100 North Fairfax Dr., Suite 210, Arlington, VA 22203. Internet: http://www.natex.org

For information on career opportunities and training, contact:

- Associated Builders and Contractors, Workforce Development Department, 4250 North Fairfax Dr., 9th Floor, Arlington, VA 22203.

- Home Builders Institute, 1201 15th St. NW., 6th Floor, Washington, DC 20005-2800. Internet: http://www.hbi.org

- Mechanical Contractors Association of America, 1385 Piccard Dr., Rockville, MD 20850-4329. Internet: http://www.mcaa.org

- Air-Conditioning and Refrigeration Institute, 4100 North Fairfax Dr., Suite 200, Arlington, VA 22203. Internet: http://www.ari.org

There are more than 500 occupations registered by the U.S. Department of Labor's National Apprenticeship System. For more information on the Labor Department's registered apprenticeship system and links to state apprenticeship programs, check their Web site: http://www.doleta.gov.

Heavy Vehicle and Mobile Equipment Service Technicians and Mechanics

(O*NET 49-3041.00, 49-3042.00, and 49-3043.00)

Significant Points

- Opportunities should be good for persons with formal postsecondary training in diesel or heavy equipment mechanics, especially if they also have training in basic electronics and hydraulics.

- This occupation offers relatively high wages and the challenge of skilled repair work.

- Skill in using computerized diagnostic equipment is becoming more important.

Nature of the Work

Heavy vehicles and mobile equipment are indispensable to many industrial activities, from construction to railroads. Various types of equipment move materials, till land, lift beams, and dig earth to pave the way for development and production. *Heavy vehicle and mobile equipment service technicians and mechanics* repair and maintain engines and hydraulic, transmission, and electrical systems powering farm equipment, cranes, bulldozers, and railcars.

Service technicians perform routine maintenance checks on diesel engines and on fuel, brake, and transmission systems to ensure peak performance, safety, and longevity of the equipment. Maintenance checks and comments from equipment operators usually alert technicians to problems. With many types of modern heavy and mobile equipment, technicians can plug hand-held diagnostic computers into onboard computers to diagnose any component needing adjustment or repair. After locating the problem, these technicians rely on their training and experience to use the best possible technique to solve the problem. If necessary, they may partially dismantle the component to examine parts for damage or excessive wear. Then, using hand-held tools, they repair, replace, clean, and lubricate parts as necessary. In some cases, technicians calibrate systems by typing codes into the onboard computer. After reassembling the component and testing it for safety, they put it back into the equipment and return the equipment to the field.

Many types of heavy and mobile equipment use hydraulics, to raise and lower movable parts. When hydraulic components malfunction, technicians examine them for fluid leaks, ruptured hoses, or worn gaskets on fluid reservoirs. Occasionally, the equipment requires extensive repairs, as when a defective hydraulic pump is replaced.

In addition to conducting routine maintenance checks, service technicians perform a variety of other repairs. They diagnose electrical problems and adjust or replace defective components. They also disassemble and repair undercarriages and track assemblies. Occasionally, technicians weld broken equipment frames and structural parts, using electric or gas welders.

It is common for technicians in large shops to specialize in one or two types of repair. For example, a shop may have individual specialists in major engine repair, transmission work, electrical systems, and suspension or brake systems. The technology used in heavy equipment is becoming more sophisticated with the increased use of electronic and computer-controlled components. Training in electronics is essential for these technicians to make engine adjustments and diagnose problems. Training in the use of hand-held computers also is necessary, because computers help technicians diagnose problems and adjust the functions of components.

Service technicians use a variety of tools in their work: power tools, such as pneumatic wrenches, to remove bolts quickly; machine tools, like lathes and grinding machines, to rebuild brakes; welding and flame-cutting equipment, to remove and repair exhaust systems; and jacks and hoists, to lift and move large parts. Service technicians also use common handtools—screwdrivers, pliers, and wrenches—to work on small parts and to get at hard-to-reach places. They may use a variety of computerized testing equipment to pinpoint and analyze malfunctions in electrical systems and other essential systems. For example, tachometers and dynamometers serve to locate engine malfunctions. Service technicians also use ohmmeters, ammeters, and voltmeters when working on electrical systems.

Mobile heavy equipment mechanics and service technicians keep construction and surface mining equipment, such as bulldozers, cranes, crawlers, draglines, graders, excavators, and other equipment, in working order. Typically, these workers are employed by equipment wholesale distribution and leasing firms, large construction and mining companies, local and federal governments, and other organizations operating and maintaining heavy machinery and equipment fleets. Service technicians employed by the federal government may work on tanks and other armored equipment.

Farm equipment mechanics service, maintain, and repair farm equipment, as well as smaller lawn and garden tractors sold to suburban homeowners. What typically was a general repairer's job around the farm has evolved into a specialized technical career. Farmers have increasingly turned to farm equipment dealers to service and repair their equipment because the machinery has grown in complexity. Modern equipment uses more electronics and hydraulics, making it difficult to perform repairs without some specialized training.

Farm equipment mechanics work mostly on equipment brought into the shop for repair and adjustment. During planting and harvesting seasons, they may travel to farms to make emergency repairs to minimize delays in farm operations.

Railcar repairers specialize in servicing railroad locomotives and other rolling stock, streetcars and subway cars, or mine cars. Most work for railroads, public and private transit companies, and railcar manufacturers.

Working Conditions

Service technicians usually work indoors, although many make repairs at the worksite. To repair vehicles and equipment, technicians often lift heavy parts and tools, handle greasy and dirty parts, and stand or lie in awkward positions. Minor cuts, burns, and bruises are common; serious accidents normally are avoided when the shop is kept clean and orderly and when safety practices are observed. Technicians usually work in well-lighted, heated, and ventilated areas. However, some shops are drafty and noisy. Many employers provide uniforms, locker rooms, and shower facilities.

When heavy or mobile equipment breaks down at a construction site, it may be too difficult or expensive to bring it into a repair shop, so the shop often sends a field service technician to the site to make repairs. Field service technicians work outdoors and spend much of their time away from the shop. Generally, the more experienced service technicians specialize in field service. They usually drive trucks specially equipped with replacement parts and tools. On occasion, they must travel many miles to reach disabled

machinery. Field technicians normally earn a higher wage than their counterparts, because they are required to make on-the-spot decisions that are necessary to serve their customers.

The hours of work for farm equipment mechanics vary according to the season of the year. During the busy planting and harvesting seasons, mechanics often work 6 or 7 days a week, 10 to 12 hours daily. In slow winter months, however, mechanics may work fewer than 40 hours a week.

Employment

Heavy vehicle and mobile equipment service technicians and mechanics held about 176,000 jobs in 2002. Approximately 126,000 were mobile heavy equipment mechanics, 35,000 were farm equipment mechanics, and 15,000 were railcar repairers. About a third were employed by machinery, equipment, and supplies merchant wholesalers. More than 12 percent were employed by federal, state, and local governments, and another 12 percent worked in construction, primarily for specialty trade contractors and highway, street, and bridge construction companies. Other service technicians worked in agriculture; mining; rail transportation and support activities; and commercial and industrial machinery and equipment rental, leasing, and repair. A small number repaired equipment for machinery and railroad rolling stock manufacturers or lawn and garden equipment and supplies stores. Less than 5 percent of service technicians were self-employed.

Nearly every section of the country employs heavy and mobile equipment service technicians and mechanics, although most work in towns and cities where equipment dealers, equipment rental and leasing companies, and construction companies have repair facilities.

Training, Other Qualifications, and Advancement

Many persons qualify for service technician jobs through years of on-the-job training, but most employers prefer that applicants complete a formal diesel or heavy equipment mechanic training program after graduating from high school. They seek persons with mechanical aptitude who are knowledgeable about the fundamentals of diesel engines, transmissions, electrical systems, and hydraulics. In addition, the constant change in equipment technology makes it necessary for technicians to be flexible and have the capacity to learn new skills quickly.

Many community colleges and vocational schools offer programs in diesel technology. Some tailor programs to heavy equipment mechanics. These programs educate the student in the basics of analytical and diagnostic techniques, electronics, and hydraulics. The increased use of electronics and computers makes training in the fundamentals of electronics essential for new heavy and mobile equipment mechanics. Some 1- to 2-year programs lead to a certificate of completion, whereas others lead to an associate degree in diesel or heavy equipment mechanics. These programs not only provide a foundation in the components of diesel and heavy equipment technology, but also enable trainee technicians to advance more rapidly to the journey, or experienced worker, level.

A combination of formal and on-the-job training prepares trainee technicians with the knowledge to service and repair equipment handled by a shop. After a few months' experience, most beginners perform routine service tasks and make minor repairs. As they prove their ability and competence, they advance to harder jobs. After trainees master the repair and service of diesel engines, they learn to work on related components, such as brakes, transmissions, and electrical systems. Generally, a service technician with at least 3 to 4 years of on-the-job experience is accepted as fully qualified.

Many employers send trainee technicians to training sessions conducted by heavy equipment manufacturers. The sessions, which typically last up to 1 week, provide intensive instruction in the repair of the manufacturer's equipment. Some sessions focus on particular components found in the equipment, such as diesel engines, transmissions, axles, and electrical systems. Other sessions focus on particular types of equipment, such as crawler-loaders and crawler-dozers. As they progress, trainees may periodically attend additional training sessions. When appropriate, experienced technicians attend training sessions to gain familiarity with new technology or equipment.

High school courses in automobile repair, physics, chemistry, and mathematics provide a strong foundation for a career as a service technician or mechanic. It is also essential for technicians to be able to read and interpret service manuals in order to keep abreast of engineering changes. Experience working on diesel engines and heavy equipment acquired in the Armed Forces is valuable as well.

Voluntary certification by the National Institute for Automotive Service Excellence is recognized as the standard of achievement for heavy vehicle and mobile equipment service technicians, who may be certified as a master heavy-duty diesel technician or in a specific area of heavy-duty equipment repair, such as brakes, gasoline engines, diesel engines, drivetrains, electrical systems, or suspension and steering. For certification in each area, technicians must pass a written examination and have at least 2 years' experience. High school, vocational or trade school, or community or junior college training in gasoline or diesel engine repair may substitute for up to 1 year's experience. To remain certified, technicians must be retested every 5 years. Retesting ensures that service technicians keep up with changing technology. However, there are currently no certification programs for other heavy vehicle and mobile equipment repair specialties.

The most important work possessions of technicians are their handtools. Service technicians typically buy their own handtools, and many experienced technicians have thousands of dollars invested in them. Employers typically furnish expensive power tools, computerized engine analyzers, and other diagnostic equipment, but handtools are normally accumulated with experience.

Experienced technicians may advance to field service jobs, wherein they have a greater opportunity to tackle problems independently and earn additional pay. Technicians with leadership ability may become shop supervisors or service managers. Some technicians open their own repair shops or invest in a franchise.

Job Outlook

Opportunities for heavy vehicle and mobile equipment service technicians and mechanics should be good for those who have completed formal training programs in diesel or heavy equipment mechanics. Persons without formal training are expected to encounter growing difficulty entering these jobs.

Employment of heavy vehicle and mobile equipment service technicians and mechanics is expected to grow slower than the average for all occupations through the year 2012. Most job openings will arise from the need to replace experienced repairers who retire. Employers report difficulty finding candidates with formal postsecondary training to fill available service technician positions, because many young people with mechanic training and experience opt to take jobs as automotive service technicians, diesel service technicians, or industrial machinery repairers—jobs that offer more openings and a wider variety of locations in which to work.

Faster employment growth is expected for mobile heavy equipment mechanics than for farm equipment mechanics or railcar repairers. Increasing numbers of heavy duty and mobile equipment service technicians will be required to support growth in the construction industry, equipment dealers, and rental and leasing companies. Because of the nature of construction activity, demand for service technicians follows the nation's economic cycle. As the economy expands, construction activity increases, resulting in the use of more mobile heavy equipment to grade construction sites, excavate basements, and lay water and sewer lines. The increased use of such equipment increases the need for periodic service and repair. In addition, the construction and repair of highways and bridges requires more technicians to service equipment. As equipment becomes more complicated, repairs increasingly must be made by specially trained technicians. Job openings for farm equipment mechanics and railcar repairers are expected to arise mostly because of replacement needs.

Construction and mining are particularly sensitive to changes in the level of economic activity; therefore, heavy and mobile equipment may be idled during downturns. In addition, winter is traditionally the slow season for construction and farming activity, particularly in cold regions. Few technicians may be needed during periods when equipment is used less; however, employers usually try to retain experienced workers. Employers may be reluctant to hire inexperienced workers during slow periods.

Earnings

Median hourly earnings of mobile heavy equipment mechanics were $17.29 in 2002. The middle 50 percent earned between $14.13 and $20.88. The lowest 10 percent earned less than $11.54, and the highest 10 percent earned more than $24.90. Median hourly earnings in the industries employing the largest numbers of mobile heavy equipment mechanics in 2002 were as follows:

Federal government	$19.44
Local government	18.03
Other specialty trade contractors	17.72
Machinery, equipment, and supplies merchant wholesalers	17.10
Commercial and industrial machinery and equipment rental and leasing	15.81

Median hourly earnings of farm equipment mechanics were $13.03 in 2002. The middle 50 percent earned between $10.50 and $16.01. The lowest 10 percent earned less than $8.73, and the highest 10 percent earned more than $18.86.

Median hourly earnings of railcar repairers were $18.78 in 2002. The middle 50 percent earned between $15.65 and $21.18. The lowest 10 percent earned less than $12.07, and the highest 10 percent earned more than $23.76. In 2002, median hourly earnings were $19.72 in rail transportation, the industry employing the largest number of railcar repairers.

Many heavy vehicle and mobile equipment service technicians and mechanics are members of unions, including the International Association of Machinists and Aerospace Workers, the International Union of Operating Engineers, and the International Brotherhood of Teamsters.

Related Occupations

Workers in related repair occupations include aircraft and avionics equipment mechanics and service technicians; automotive service technicians and mechanics; diesel service technicians and mechanics; heating, air-conditioning, and refrigeration mechanics and installers; and small engine mechanics.

Sources of Additional Information

More details about job openings for heavy vehicle and mobile equipment service technicians and mechanics may be obtained from local heavy and mobile equipment dealers and distributors, construction contractors, and government agencies. Local offices of the state employment service also may have information on job openings and training programs.

For general information about a career as a heavy vehicle and mobile equipment service technician or mechanic, contact:

- Association of Equipment Management Professionals, P.O. Box 1368, Glenwood Springs, CO 81602. Internet: http://www.equipment.org

- The AED Foundation (Associated Equipment Distributors affiliate), 615 W. 22nd St., Oak Brook, IL 60523. Internet: http://www.aednet.org/aed_foundation

For a directory of public training programs in heavy and mobile equipment mechanics, contact:

- SkillsUSA-VICA, P.O. Box 3000, Leesburg, VA 20177-0300. Internet: http://www.skillsusa.org

A list of certified diesel service technician training programs can be obtained from:

- National Automotive Technician Education Foundation (NATEF), 101 Blue Seal Dr., Suite 101, Leesburg, VA 20175. Internet: http://www.natef.org

Information on certification as a heavy-duty diesel service technician is available from:

- National Institute for Automotive Service Excellence (ASE), 101 Blue Seal Dr. SE., Suite 101, Leesburg, VA 20175. Internet: http://www.ase-cert.org

Industrial Engineers, Including Health and Safety

(O*NET 17-2111.01, 17-2111.02, 17-2111.03, and 17-2112.00)

Significant Points

- Overall, job opportunities in engineering are expected to be good, but will vary by specialty.

- A bachelor's degree is required for most entry-level jobs.

- Starting salaries are significantly higher than those of college graduates in other fields.

- Continuing education is critical to keep abreast of the latest technology.

Nature of the Work

Industrial engineers determine the most effective ways to use the basic factors of production—people, machines, materials, information, and energy—to make a product or to provide a service. They are the bridge between management goals and operational performance. They are more concerned with increasing productivity through the management of people, methods of business organization, and technology than are engineers in other specialties, who generally work more with products or processes. Although most industrial engineers work in manufacturing industries, they may also work in consulting services, healthcare, and communications.

To solve organizational, production, and related problems most efficiently, industrial engineers carefully study the product and its requirements, use mathematical methods such as operations research to meet those requirements, and design manufacturing and information systems. They develop management control systems to aid in financial planning and cost analysis and design production planning and control systems to coordinate activities and ensure product quality. They also design or improve systems for the physical distribution of goods and services. Industrial engineers determine which plant location has the best combination of raw materials availability, transportation facilities, and costs. Industrial engineers use computers for simulations and to control various activities and devices, such as assembly lines and robots. They also develop wage and salary administration systems and job evaluation programs. Many industrial engineers move into management positions because the work is closely related.

The work of health and safety engineers is similar to that of industrial engineers in that it deals with the entire production process. Health and safety engineers promote worksite or product safety and health by applying knowledge of industrial processes, as well as mechanical, chemical, and psychological principles. They must be able to anticipate, recognize, and evaluate hazardous conditions as well as develop hazard control methods. They also must be familiar with the application of health and safety regulations.

Working Conditions

Most engineers work in office buildings, laboratories, or industrial plants. Others may spend time outdoors at construction sites and oil and gas exploration and production sites, where they monitor or direct operations or solve onsite problems. Some engineers travel extensively to plants or worksites.

Many engineers work a standard 40-hour week. At times, deadlines or design standards may bring extra pressure to a job, sometimes requiring engineers to work longer hours.

Training, Other Qualifications, and Advancement

A bachelor's degree in engineering is required for almost all entry-level engineering jobs. College graduates with a degree in a physical science or mathematics occasionally may qualify for some engineering jobs, especially in specialties in high demand. Most engineering degrees are granted in electrical, electronics, mechanical, or civil engineering. However, engineers trained in one branch may work in related branches. For example, many aerospace engineers have training in mechanical engineering. This flexibility allows employers to meet staffing needs in new technologies and specialties in which engineers may be in short supply. It also allows engineers to shift to fields with better employment prospects or to those that more closely match their interests.

Most engineering programs involve a concentration of study in an engineering specialty, along with courses in both mathematics and science. Most programs include a design course, sometimes accompanied by a computer or laboratory class or both.

In addition to the standard engineering degree, many colleges offer 2- or 4-year degree programs in engineering technology. These programs, which usually include various hands-on laboratory classes that focus on current issues, prepare students for practical design and production work, rather than for jobs that require more theoretical and scientific knowledge. Graduates of 4-year technology programs may get jobs similar to those obtained by graduates with a bachelor's degree in engineering. Engineering technology graduates, however, are not qualified to register as professional engineers under the same terms as graduates with degrees in engineering. Some employers regard technology program graduates as having skills between those of a technician and an engineer.

Graduate training is essential for engineering faculty positions and many research and development programs, but is not required for the majority of entry-level engineering jobs. Many engineers obtain graduate degrees in engineering or business administration to learn new technology and broaden their education. Many high-level executives in government and industry began their careers as engineers.

About 340 colleges and universities offer bachelor's degree programs in engineering that are accredited by the Accreditation Board for Engineering and Technology (ABET), and about 240 colleges offer accredited bachelor's degree programs in engineering technology. ABET accreditation is based on an examination of an engineering program's student achievement, program improvement, faculty, curricular content, facilities, and institutional commitment. Although most institutions offer programs in the major branches of engineering, only a few offer programs in the smaller specialties. Also, programs of the same title may vary in content. For example, some programs emphasize industrial practices, preparing students for a job in industry, whereas others are more theoretical and are designed to prepare students for graduate work. Therefore, students should investigate curricula and check accreditations carefully before selecting a college.

Admissions requirements for undergraduate engineering schools include a solid background in mathematics (algebra, geometry, trigonometry, and calculus) and science (biology, chemistry, and physics), and courses in English, social studies, humanities, and computer and information technology. Bachelor's degree programs in engineering typically are designed to last 4 years, but many students find that it takes between 4 and 5 years to complete their studies. In a typical 4-year college curriculum, the first 2 years are spent studying mathematics, basic sciences, introductory engineering, humanities, and social sciences. In the last 2 years, most courses are in engineering, usually with a concentration in one branch. For example, the last 2 years of an aerospace program might include courses in fluid mechanics, heat transfer, applied aerodynamics, analytical mechanics, flight vehicle design, trajectory dynamics, and aerospace propulsion systems. Some programs offer a general engineering curriculum; students then specialize in graduate school or on the job.

Some engineering schools and 2-year colleges have agreements whereby the 2-year college provides the initial engineering education, and the engineering school automatically admits students for their last 2 years. In addition, a few engineering schools have arrangements whereby a student spends 3 years in a liberal arts college studying pre-engineering subjects and 2 years in an engineering school studying core subjects, and then receives a bachelor's degree from each school. Some colleges and universities offer 5-year master's degree programs. Some 5-year or even 6-year cooperative plans combine classroom study and practical work, permitting students to gain valuable experience and to finance part of their education.

All 50 states and the District of Columbia require licensure for engineers who offer their services directly to the public. Engineers who are licensed are called Professional Engineers (PE). This licensure generally requires a degree from an ABET-accredited engineering program, 4 years of relevant work experience, and successful completion of a state examination. Recent graduates can start the licensing process by taking the examination in two stages. The initial Fundamentals of Engineering (FE) examination can be taken upon graduation. Engineers who pass this examination commonly are called Engineers in Training (EIT) or Engineer Interns (EI). After acquiring suitable work experience, EITs can take the second examination, the Principles and Practice of Engineering exam. Several states have imposed mandatory continuing education requirements for relicensure. Most states recognize licensure from other states provided that the manner in which the initial license was obtained meets or exceeds their licensure requirements. Many civil, electrical, mechanical, and chemical engineers are licensed PEs.

Engineers should be creative, inquisitive, analytical, and detail-oriented. They should be able to work as part of a team and to communicate well, both orally and in writing. Communication abilities are important because engineers often interact with specialists in a wide range of fields outside engineering.

Beginning engineering graduates usually work under the supervision of experienced engineers and, in large companies, also may receive formal classroom or seminar-type training. As new engineers gain knowledge and experience, they are assigned more difficult projects with greater independence to develop designs, solve problems, and make decisions. Engineers may advance to become technical specialists or to supervise a staff or team of engineers and technicians. Some may eventually become engineering managers or enter other managerial or sales jobs.

Employment

Industrial engineers, including health and safety, held about 194,000 jobs in 2002. Six in 10 of these jobs were in manufacturing industries, and an additional 1 in 10 worked in professional, scientific, and technical services firms, many of whom provide consulting services to manufacturing firms. Because their skills can be used in almost any type of organization, industrial engineers are more widely distributed among industries than are other engineers.

Job Outlook

Overall employment of industrial engineers, including health and safety, is projected to grow about as fast as the average for all occupations through 2012. In addition, many openings will be created by the need to replace industrial engineers who transfer to other occupations or leave the labor force. Employment of industrial engineers is expected to increase as fast as the average while that of health and safety engineers is expected to grow more slowly than average.

Because the main function of industrial and health and safety engineers is to make a higher quality product as efficiently and as safely as possible, their services should be in demand in the manufacturing sector as firms seek to reduce costs and increase productivity. The concern for health and safety within work environments should increase the need for health and safety engineers.

Earnings

Median annual earnings of industrial engineers were $62,150 in 2002. The middle 50 percent earned between $50,160 and $75,440. The lowest 10 percent earned less than $40,380, and the highest 10 percent earned more than $90,420. Median annual earnings in the manufacturing industries employing the largest numbers of industrial engineers in 2002 were:

Semiconductor and other electronic
    component manufacturing $67,460
Navigational, measuring, electromedical, and
    control instruments manufacturing 65,470
Architectural, engineering, and related
    services 64,020
Aerospace products and parts manufacturing........63,630
Motor vehicle parts manufacturing......................62,610

Median annual earnings of health and safety engineers were $58,010 in 2002. The middle 50 percent earned between $46,580 and $71,980. The lowest 10 percent earned less than $37,230, and the highest 10 percent earned more than $87,250.

According to a 2003 salary survey by the National Association of Colleges and Employers, bachelor's degree candidates in industrial/manufacturing engineering received starting offers averaging about $47,051 a year and master's degree candidates averaged $54,565 a year.

Related Occupations

Industrial engineers apply the principles of physical science and mathematics in their work. Other workers who use scientific and mathematical principles include architects, except landscape and naval; engineering and natural sciences managers; computer and information systems managers; mathematicians; drafters; engineering technicians; sales engineers; science technicians; and physical and life scientists, including agricultural and food scientists, biological scientists, conservation scientists and foresters, atmospheric scientists, chemists and materials scientists, environmental scientists and geoscientists, and physicists and astronomers.

Sources of Additional Information

For further information about industrial engineering careers, education, and training, contact:

- Institute of Industrial Engineers, 3577 Parkway Lane, Suite 200, Norcross, GA 30092. Internet: http://www.iienet.org

Information on careers, education, accreditation and certification, and salaries of safety engineers is available from:

- American Society of Safety Engineers, 1800 E Oakton St., Des Plaines, IL 60018. Internet: http://www.asse.org

Information on certification, accreditation, careers, and safety-related degree programs for safety professionals, including safety engineers, is available from:

- Board of Certified Safety Professionals, 208 Burwash Ave., Savoy, IL 61874. Internet: http://www.bcsp.org

See the introduction to the section on engineers for information on working conditions, training requirements, and other sources of additional information.

Industrial Machinery Installation, Repair, and Maintenance Workers, Except Millwrights

(O*NET 49-9041.00 and 49-9043.00)

Significant Points

- Highly skilled mechanics usually learn their trade through a 4-year apprenticeship program, while lower skilled maintenance workers receive short-term on-the-job training.

- Employment is projected to grow more slowly than average, but applicants with broad skills in machine repair and maintenance should have favorable job prospects.

- Unlike many other manufacturing occupations, these workers usually are not affected by seasonal changes in production.

Nature of the Work

A wide range of employees is required to keep sophisticated industrial machinery running smoothly—from highly skilled industrial machinery mechanics to lower skilled machinery maintenance workers who perform routine tasks. Their work is vital to the success of industrial facilities, not only because an idle machine will delay production, but also because a machine that is not properly repaired and maintained may damage the final product or injure an operator.

The most basic tasks in this process are performed by *machinery maintenance workers*. These employees are responsible for cleaning and lubricating machinery, performing basic diagnostic tests, checking performance, and testing damaged machine parts to determine whether major repairs are necessary. In carrying out these tasks, maintenance workers must follow machine specifications and adhere to maintenance schedules. Maintenance workers may perform minor repairs, but major repairs are generally left to machinery mechanics.

Industrial machinery mechanics, also called industrial machinery repairers or maintenance machinists, are highly skilled workers who maintain and repair machinery in a plant or factory. To do this effectively, they must be able to detect minor problems and correct them before they become major problems. For example, after hearing a vibration from a machine, the mechanic must decide whether it is due to worn belts, weak motor bearings, or some other problem. Computerized maintenance, vibration analysis techniques, and self-diagnostic systems are aiding in this task, but mechanics still need years of training and experience to perform effectively.

After diagnosing the problem, the industrial machinery mechanic disassembles the equipment to repair or replace the necessary parts. When repairing electronically controlled machinery, mechanics may work closely with electronic repairers or electricians who maintain the machine's electronic parts. Increasingly, mechanics need electronic and computer skills in order to repair sophisticated equipment on their own. Once a repair is made, mechanics perform tests to ensure that the machine is running smoothly.

Although repairing machines is the primary responsibility of industrial machinery mechanics, they also may perform preventive maintenance and install new machinery. For example, they adjust and calibrate automated manufacturing equipment, such as industrial robots. As plants retool and invest in new equipment, they increasingly rely on mechanics to properly situate and install the machinery. In many plants, this has traditionally been the job of millwrights, but mechanics are increasingly called upon to carry out this task.

Industrial machinery mechanics and machinery maintenance workers use a variety of tools to perform repairs and preventive maintenance. They may use a screwdriver and wrench to adjust a motor, or a hoist to lift a printing press off the ground. When replacements for broken or defective parts are not readily available, or when a machine must be quickly returned to production, mechanics may sketch a part to be fabricated by the plant's machine shop. Mechanics use catalogs to order replacement parts and often follow blueprints and engineering specifications to maintain and fix equipment. By keeping complete and up-to-date records, mechanics try to anticipate trouble and service equipment before factory production is interrupted.

Working Conditions

In production facilities, these workers are subject to common shop injuries such as cuts, bruises, and strains. They also may work in awkward positions, including on top of ladders or in cramped conditions under large machinery, which exposes them to additional hazards. They often use protective equipment such as hardhats, safety glasses, steel-tipped shoes, hearing protectors, and belts.

Because factories and other facilities cannot afford to have industrial machinery out of service for long periods, mechanics may be called to the plant at night or on weekends for emergency repairs. Overtime is common among industrial machinery mechanics; about 33 percent work over 40 hours a week.

Employment

Industrial machinery installation, repair, and maintenance workers, except millwrights held about 289,200 jobs in 2002. Of these, 197,300 were held by the more highly skilled industrial machinery mechanics, while machinery maintenance workers accounted for 91,900 jobs. Two out of three workers were employed in the manufacturing sector, in industries such as food processing, textile mills, chemicals, fabricated metal products, motor vehicles, and primary metals. Others worked for government agencies, public utilities, mining companies, and other establishments in which industrial machinery is used.

Training, Other Qualifications, and Advancement

Machinery maintenance workers typically receive short-term on-the-job training in order to perform routine tasks, such as setting up, cleaning, lubricating, and starting machinery. This training may be offered by experienced workers, professional trainers, or product representatives.

Industrial machinery mechanics, on the other hand, often learn their trade through 4-year apprenticeship programs that combine classroom instruction with on-the-job-training. These programs usually are sponsored by a local trade union. Other mechanics start as helpers and learn the skills

of the trade informally or by taking courses offered by machinery manufacturers and community colleges.

Mechanics learn from experienced repairers how to operate, disassemble, repair, and assemble machinery. Classroom instruction focuses on subjects such as shop mathematics, blueprint reading, welding, electronics, and computer training.

Employers prefer to hire those who have completed high school or technical college and have taken courses in mechanical drawing, mathematics, blueprint reading, computers, and electronics. Mechanical aptitude and manual dexterity are important characteristics for workers in this trade. Good physical conditioning and agility also are necessary because repairers sometimes have to lift heavy objects or climb to reach equipment.

Opportunities for advancement are limited. Machinery maintenance workers may gain additional skills to make more complex repairs to machinery or work as supervisors. Industrial machinery mechanics also may advance either by working with more complicated equipment or by becoming supervisors. The most highly skilled repairers can be promoted to master mechanic or can become machinists, millwrights, or tool and die makers.

Job Outlook

Employment of industrial machinery installation, repair, and maintenance workers, except millwrights is projected to grow more slowly than the average for all occupations through 2012. Nevertheless, applicants with broad skills in machine repair and maintenance should have favorable job prospects. Many mechanics are expected to retire in coming years, and employers have reported difficulty in recruiting young workers with the necessary skills to be industrial machinery mechanics. Most job openings will stem from the need to replace workers who transfer to other occupations or who retire or leave the labor force for other reasons.

As more firms introduce automated production equipment, these workers will be needed to ensure that these machines are properly maintained and consistently in operation. However, many new machines are capable of self-diagnosis, increasing their reliability and somewhat reducing the need for repairers. Increasing imports and the relocation of production facilities abroad also are expected to dampen employment growth for these workers.

Unlike many other manufacturing occupations, industrial machinery installation, repair, and maintenance workers, except millwrights are not usually affected by seasonal changes in production. During slack periods, when some plant workers are laid off, mechanics often are retained to do major overhaul jobs and to keep expensive machinery in working order. Although these workers may face layoff or a reduced workweek when economic conditions are particularly severe, they usually are less affected than other workers because machines have to be maintained regardless of production level.

Earnings

Median hourly earnings of industrial machinery mechanics were $18.26 in 2002. The middle 50 percent earned between $14.62 and $22.95. The lowest 10 percent earned less than $11.91, and the highest 10 percent earned more than $27.48.

Machinery maintenance workers earned less than the higher skilled machinery mechanics. Median hourly earnings of machinery maintenance workers were $15.63 in 2002. The middle 50 percent earned between $12.11 and $19.81. The lowest 10 percent earned less than $9.57, and the highest 10 percent earned more than $24.19.

Earnings vary by industry and geographic region. Median hourly earnings in the industries employing the largest numbers of industrial machinery mechanics in 2002 are shown below:

Electric power generation, transmission,
  and distribution $26.25
Motor vehicle parts manufacturing..........................22.02
Local government 19.14
Converted paper products manufacturing 18.04
Machinery, equipment, and supplies merchant
  wholesalers...15.93

About 26 percent of industrial machinery installation, repair, and maintenance workers, except millwrights are union members. Labor unions that represent these workers include the United Steelworkers of America; the United Automobile, Aerospace, and Agricultural Implement Workers of America; the International Association of Machinists and Aerospace Workers; the United Brotherhood of Carpenters and Joiners of America; and the International Union of Electronic, Electrical, Salaried, Machine, and Furniture Workers.

Related Occupations

Other occupations that involve repairing and maintaining machinery include aircraft and avionics equipment mechanics and service technicians; automotive service technicians and mechanics; diesel service technicians and mechanics; elevator installers and repairers; heating, air-conditioning, and refrigeration mechanics and installers; heavy vehicle and mobile equipment service technicians and mechanics; machinists; maintenance and repair workers, general; millwrights; and small engine mechanics.

Sources of Additional Information

Information about employment and apprenticeship opportunities may be obtained from local employers, from local offices of the state employment service, or from:

● United Brotherhood of Carpenters and Joiners of America, 101 Constitution Ave. NW, Washington, DC 20001. Internet: http://www.carpenters.org

● National Tooling and Machining Association, 9300 Livingston Rd., Fort Washington, MD 20744. Internet: http://www.ntma.org

Job Opportunities in the Armed Forces

(O*NET 55-1011.00, 55-1012.00, 55-1013.00, 55-1014.00, 55-1015.00, 55-1016.00, 55-1017.00, 55-1019.99, and 55-2011.00)

Significant Points

● Opportunities should be good in all branches of the Armed Forces for applicants who meet designated standards.

● Most enlisted personnel need at least a high school diploma, while officers need a bachelor's or an advanced degree.

● Hours and working conditions can be arduous and vary substantially.

● Some training and duty assignments are hazardous, even in peacetime.

Nature of the Work

Maintaining a strong national defense encompasses such diverse activities as running a hospital, commanding a tank, programming computers, operating a nuclear reactor, or repairing and maintaining a helicopter. The military provides training and work experience in these and many other fields for more than 2.5 million people. More than 1.4 million people serve in the active Army, Navy, Marine Corps, and Air Force, and more than 1.1 million serve in their Reserve components, and the Air and Army National Guard. The Coast Guard, which is also discussed in this job description, is now part of the U.S. Department of Homeland Security.

The military distinguishes between enlisted and officer careers. Enlisted personnel, who make up about 85 percent of the Armed Forces, carry out the fundamental operations of the military in areas such as combat, administration, construction, engineering, health care, and human services. Officers, who make up the remaining 15 percent of the Armed Forces, are the leaders of the military, supervising and managing activities in every occupational specialty of the Armed Forces.

The sections that follow discuss the major occupational groups for enlisted personnel and officers.

Enlisted occupational groups:
Administrative careers include a wide variety of positions. The military must keep accurate information for planning and managing its operations. Both paper and electronic

records are kept on personnel and on equipment, funds, supplies, and other property of the military. Enlisted administrative personnel record information, type reports, maintain files, and review information to assist military officers. Personnel may work in a specialized area such as finance, accounting, legal affairs, maintenance, supply, or transportation. Some examples of administrative specialists are recruiting specialists, who recruit and place qualified personnel and provide information about military careers to young people, parents, schools, and local communities; training specialists and instructors, who provide the training programs necessary to help people perform their jobs effectively; and personnel specialists, who collect and store information about individuals in the military, including information on their training, job assignments, promotions, and health.

Combat specialty occupations refer to enlisted specialties, such as infantry, artillery, and special forces, whose members operate weapons or execute special missions during combat. Persons in these occupations normally specialize by the type of weapon system or combat operation. These personnel maneuver against enemy forces and position and fire artillery, guns, and missiles to destroy enemy positions. They also may operate tanks and amphibious assault vehicles in combat or scouting missions. When the military has difficult and dangerous missions to perform, they call upon special-operations teams. These elite combat forces maintain a constant state of readiness to strike anywhere in the world on a moment's notice. Team members from the special-operations forces conduct offensive raids, demolitions, intelligence, search-and-rescue missions, and other operations from aboard aircraft, helicopters, ships, or submarines.

Construction occupations in the military include personnel who build or repair buildings, airfields, bridges, foundations, dams, bunkers, and the electrical and plumbing components of these structures. Enlisted personnel in construction occupations operate bulldozers, cranes, graders, and other heavy equipment. Construction specialists also may work with engineers and other building specialists as part of military construction teams. Some personnel specialize in areas such as plumbing or electrical wiring. Plumbers and pipefitters install and repair the plumbing and pipe systems needed in buildings and on aircraft and ships. Building electricians install and repair electrical-wiring systems in offices, airplane hangars, and other buildings on military bases.

Electronic and electrical equipment repair personnel repair and maintain electronic and electrical equipment used in the military. Repairers normally specialize by type of equipment, such as avionics, computer, optical, communications, or weapons systems. For example, electronic instrument repairers install, test, maintain, and repair a wide variety of electronic systems, including navigational controls and biomedical instruments. Weapons maintenance technicians maintain and repair weapons used by combat forces; most of these weapons have electronic components and systems that assist in locating targets and in aiming and firing the weapon.

The military has many *engineering, science, and technical occupations*, whose members require specific knowledge to operate technical equipment, solve complex problems, or provide and interpret information. Enlisted personnel normally specialize in one area, such as space operations, emergency management, environmental health and safety, or intelligence. Space operations specialists use and repair ground-control command equipment having to do with spacecraft, including electronic systems that track the location and operation of a craft. Emergency management specialists prepare emergency procedures for all types of disasters, such as floods, tornadoes, and earthquakes. Environmental health and safety specialists inspect military facilities and food supplies for the presence of disease, germs, or other conditions hazardous to health and the environment. Intelligence specialists gather and study information by means of aerial photographs and various types of radar and surveillance systems.

Health-care personnel assist medical professionals in treating and providing services for men and women in the military. They may work as part of a patient-service team in close contact with doctors, dentists, nurses, and physical therapists to provide the necessary support functions within a hospital or clinic. Health-care specialists normally specialize in a particular area—emergency medical treatment, the operation of diagnostic tools such as x-ray and ultrasound equipment, laboratory testing of tissue and blood samples, or maintaining pharmacy supplies or patients' records, among others.

Human resources development specialists recruit and place qualified personnel and provide the training programs necessary to help people perform their jobs effectively. Personnel in this career area normally specialize by activity. For example, recruiting specialists provide information about military careers to young people, parents, schools, and local communities and explain the Armed Service's employment and training opportunities, pay and benefits, and service life. Personnel specialists collect and store information about the people in the military, including information on their previous and current training, job assignments, promotions, and health. Training specialists and instructors teach classes and give demonstrations to provide military personnel with the knowledge they need to perform their jobs.

Armed Forces personnel in *machine operator and production occupations* operate industrial equipment, machinery, and tools to fabricate and repair parts for a variety of items and structures. They may operate engines, turbines, nuclear reactors, and water pumps. Often, they specialize by type of work performed. Welders and metalworkers, for instance, work with various types of metals to repair or form the structural parts of ships, submarines, buildings, or other equipment. Survival equipment specialists inspect, maintain, and repair survival equipment such as parachutes and aircraft life support equipment. Dental and optical laboratory technicians construct and repair dental equipment and eyeglasses for military personnel.

Media and public affairs occupations deal with the public presentation and interpretation of military information and events. Enlisted media and public affairs personnel take and develop photographs; film, record, and edit audio and video programs; present news and music programs; and produce graphic artwork, drawings, and other visual displays. Other public affairs specialists act as interpreters and translators to convert written or spoken foreign languages into English or other languages.

Protective service personnel include those who enforce military laws and regulations, provide emergency response to natural and human-made disasters, and maintain food standards. These personnel normally specialize by function. For example, military police control traffic, prevent crime, and respond to emergencies. Other law enforcement and security specialists investigate crimes committed on military property and guard inmates in military correctional facilities. Firefighters put out, control, and help prevent fires in buildings, on aircraft, and aboard ships. Food service specialists prepare all types of food in dining halls, hospitals, and ships.

Transportation and material handling specialists ensure the safe transport of people and cargo. Most personnel within this occupational group are classified according to mode of transportation, such as aircraft, motor vehicle, or ship. Aircrew members operate equipment on board aircraft during operations. Vehicle drivers operate all types of heavy military vehicles, including fuel or water tank trucks, semi-trailers, heavy troop transports, and passenger buses. Quartermasters and boat operators navigate and pilot many types of small watercraft, including tugboats, gunboats, and barges. Cargo specialists load and unload military supplies, using equipment such as forklifts and cranes.

Vehicle and machinery mechanics conduct preventive and corrective maintenance on aircraft, ships, automotive and heavy equipment, heating and cooling systems, marine engines, and powerhouse station equipment. These workers typically specialize by the type of equipment that they maintain. For example, aircraft mechanics inspect, service, and repair helicopters and airplanes. Automotive and heavy-equipment mechanics maintain and repair vehicles such as jeeps, cars, trucks, tanks, self-propelled missile launchers, and other combat vehicles. They also repair bulldozers, power shovels, and other construction equipment. Heating and cooling mechanics install and repair air-conditioning, refrigeration, and heating equipment. Marine engine mechanics repair and maintain gasoline and diesel engines on ships, boats, and other watercraft. They also repair shipboard mechanical and electrical equipment. Powerhouse mechanics install, maintain, and repair electrical and mechanical equipment in power-generating stations.

Officer occupational groups:

Combat specialty officers plan and direct military operations, oversee combat activities, and serve as combat leaders. This category includes officers in charge of tanks and other armored assault vehicles, artillery systems, special opera-

tions forces, and infantry. Combat specialty officers normally specialize by the type of unit that they lead. Within the unit, they may specialize by the type of weapon system. Artillery and missile system officers, for example, direct personnel as they target, launch, test, and maintain various types of missiles and artillery. Special-operations officers lead their units in offensive raids, demolitions, intelligence gathering, and search-and-rescue missions.

Engineering, science, and technical officers have a wide range of responsibilities based on their area of expertise. They lead or perform activities in areas such as space operations, environmental health and safety, and engineering. These officers may direct the operations of communications centers or the development of complex computer systems. Environmental health and safety officers study the air, ground, and water to identify and analyze sources of pollution and its effects. They also direct programs to control safety and health hazards in the workplace. Other personnel work as aerospace engineers to design and direct the development of military aircraft, missiles, and spacecraft.

Executive, administrative, and managerial officers oversee and direct military activities in key functional areas such as finance, accounting, health administration, international relations, and supply. Health services administrators, for instance, are responsible for the overall quality of care provided at the hospitals and clinics they operate. They must ensure that each department works together to provide the highest quality of care. As another example, purchasing and contracting managers negotiate and monitor contracts for the purchase of the billions of dollars worth of equipment, supplies, and services that the military buys from private industry each year.

Health-care officers provide health services at military facilities, on the basis of their area of specialization. Officers who assist in examining, diagnosing, and treating patients with illness, injury, or disease include physicians, registered nurses, and dentists. Other health-care officers provide therapy, rehabilitative treatment, and additional services for patients. Physical and occupational therapists plan and administer therapy to help patients adjust to disabilities, regain independence, and return to work. Speech therapists evaluate and treat patients with hearing and speech problems. Dietitians manage food service facilities and plan meals for hospital patients and for outpatients who need special diets. Pharmacists manage the purchase, storage, and dispensation of drugs and medicines. Physicians and surgeons in this occupational group provide the majority of medical services to the military and their families. Dentists treat diseases and disorders of the mouth. Optometrists treat vision problems by prescribing eyeglasses or contact lenses. Psychologists provide mental health care and also conduct research on behavior and emotions.

Media and affairs officers oversee the development, production, and presentation of information or events for the public. These officers may produce and direct motion pictures, videotapes, and television and radio broadcasts that are used for training, news, and entertainment. Some plan, develop, and direct the activities of military bands. Public information officers respond to inquiries about military activities and prepare news releases and reports to keep the public informed.

Protective service officers are responsible for the safety and protection of individuals and property on military bases and vessels. Emergency management officers plan and prepare for all types of natural and human-made disasters. They develop warning, control, and evacuation plans to be used in the event of a disaster. Law enforcement and security officers enforce all applicable laws on military bases and investigate crimes when the law has been broken.

Support services officers manage food service activities and perform services in support of the morale and well-being of military personnel and their families. Food services managers oversee the preparation and delivery of food services within dining facilities located on military installations and vessels. Social workers focus on improving conditions that cause social problems such as drug and alcohol abuse, racism, and sexism. Chaplains conduct worship services for military personnel and perform other spiritual duties covering the beliefs and practices of all religious faiths

Officers in *transportation occupations* manage and perform activities related to the safe transport of military personnel and material by air and water. Officers normally specialize by mode of transportation or area of expertise, because, in many cases, they must meet licensing and certification requirements. Pilots in the military fly various types of specialized airplanes and helicopters to carry troops and equipment and to execute combat missions. Navigators use radar, radio, and other navigation equipment to determine their position and plan their route of travel. Officers on ships and submarines work as a team to manage the various departments aboard their vessels. Ships' engineers direct engineering departments aboard ships and submarines, including engine operations, maintenance, repair, heating, and power generation.

Employment

In 2003, more than 2.5 million people served in the Armed Forces. More than 1.4 million individuals were on active duty in the Armed Forces—about 490,000 in the Army, 377,000 in the Navy, 368,000 in the Air Force, and 179,000 in the Marine Corps. In addition, more than 1.1 million people served in their Reserve components, and the Air and Army National Guard. In addition, 38,000 individuals served in the Coast Guard, which is now part of the U.S. Department of Homeland Security. Table 1 shows the occupational composition of the 1.2 million active-duty enlisted personnel in 2003; Table 2 presents similar information for the 216,000 active-duty officers.

Table 1. Military enlisted personnel by broad occupational category and branch of military service, June 2003

Occupational Group - Enlisted	Army	Air Force	Coast Guard	Marine Corps	Navy	Total, all services
Administrative occupations	15,175	25,674	1,775	8,642	21,225	72,491
Combat specialty occupations	104,876	253	745	33,070	3,316	142,260
Construction occupations	15,340	6,261		5,145	5,397	32,143
Electronic and electrical repair occupations	14,035	37,155	3,530	16,082	52,094	122,896
Engineering, science, and technical occupations	63,531	43,422	720	35,237	41,003	183,913
Health care occupations	26,660	17,108	685		23,818	68,271
Human resource development occupations	16,202	12,715		6,784	5,510	41,211
Machine operator and precision work occupations	4,528	7,783	2,079	1,710	23,485	39,585
Media and public affairs occupations	4,552	5,921	131	1,556	5,255	17,415
Protective service occupations	24,831	29,516	893	6,086	10,630	71,956
Support services occupations	13,687	1,535	1,213	3,704	11,570	31,709
Transportation and material handling occupations	54,140	33,835	6,423	23,908	39,272	157,578
Vehicle machinery mechanic occupations	48,043	48,433	5,654	18,473	50,266	170,869
Total, by service	405,600	269,611	23,848	160,397	292,841	1,152,297

Source: U.S. Department of Defense, Defense Manpower Data Center East

Table 2. Military officer personnel by broad occupational category and branch of service, June 2003

Occupational Group - Officer	Army	Air Force	Coast Guard	Marine Corps	Navy	Total, all services
Combat specialty occupations	18,306	5,422	2	3,990	5,626	33,346
Engineering, science, and technical occupations	17,368	15,902	1,715	3,044	15,413	53,442
Executive, administrative, and managerial occupations	10,139	9,579	388	2,398	8,234	30,738
Health care occupations...	9,775	9,247	10		6,531	25,563
Human resource development occupations	1,369	2,406	247	23	3,807	7,852
Media and public affairs occupations	177	503	15	131	932	1,758
Protective service occupations	2,174	1,838	172	174	855	5,213
Support services occupations	1,500	836		40	1,654	4,030
Transportation occupations	12,612	19,710	3,244	6,258	12,679	54,503
Total, by service	73,420	65,443	5,793	16,058	55,731	216,445

Source: U.S. Department of Defense, Defense Manpower Data Center East

Military personnel are stationed throughout the United States and in many countries around the world. More than half of all military jobs are located in California, Texas, North Carolina, Virginia, Florida, and Georgia. About 395,000 individuals were stationed outside the United States in 2002, including those assigned to ships at sea. Approximately 104,000 of these were stationed in Europe, mainly in Germany, and another 85,000 were assigned to East Asia and the Pacific area, mostly in Japan and the Republic of Korea.

Qualifications, Training, and Advancement

Enlisted personnel. In order to join the services, enlisted personnel must sign a legal agreement called an enlistment contract, which usually involves a commitment to 8 years of service. Depending on the terms of the contract, 2 to 6 years are spent on active duty, and the balance is spent in the reserves. The enlistment contract obligates the service to provide the agreed-upon job, rating, pay, cash bonuses for enlistment in certain occupations, medical and other benefits, occupational training, and continuing education. In return, enlisted personnel must serve satisfactorily for the period specified.

Requirements for each service vary, but certain qualifications for enlistment are common to all branches. In order to enlist, one must be between 17 and 35 years old, be a U.S. citizen or an alien holding permanent resident status, not have a felony record, and possess a birth certificate. Applicants who are aged 17 must have the consent of a parent or legal guardian before entering the service. Coast Guard enlisted personnel must enter active duty before their 28th birthday, whereas Marine Corps enlisted personnel must not be over the age of 29. Applicants must both pass a written examination—the Armed Services Vocational Aptitude Battery—and meet certain minimum physical standards, such as height, weight, vision, and overall health. All branches of the Armed Forces require high school graduation or its equivalent for certain enlistment options. In 2003, nearly 9 out of 10 recruits were high school graduates.

People thinking about enlisting in the military should learn as much as they can about military life before making a decision. Doing so is especially important if you are thinking about making the military a career. Speaking to friends and relatives with military experience is a good idea. Find out what the military can offer you and what it will expect in return. Then, talk to a recruiter, who can determine whether you qualify for enlistment, explain the various enlistment options, and tell you which military occupational specialties currently have openings. Bear in mind that the recruiter's job is to recruit promising applicants into his or her branch of military service, so the information that the recruiter gives you is likely to stress the positive aspects of military life in the branch in which he or she serves.

Ask the recruiter for the branch you have chosen to assess your chances of being accepted for training in the occupation of your choice, or, better still, take the aptitude exam to see how well you score. The military uses this exam as a placement exam, and test scores largely determine an individual's chances of being accepted into a particular training program. Selection for a particular type of training depends on the needs of the service, your general and technical aptitudes, and your personal preference. Because all prospective recruits are required to take the exam, those who do so before committing themselves to enlist have the advantage of knowing in advance whether they stand a good chance of being accepted for training in a particular specialty. The recruiter can schedule you for the Armed Services Vocational Aptitude Battery without any obligation. Many high schools offer the exam as an easy way for students to explore the possibility of a military career, and the test also affords an insight into career areas in which the student has demonstrated aptitudes and interests.

If you decide to join the military, the next step is to pass the physical examination and sign an enlistment contract. Negotiating the contract involves choosing, qualifying for, and agreeing on a number of enlistment options, such as the length of active-duty time, which may vary according to the option. Most active-duty programs have first-term enlistments of 4 years, although there are some 2-, 3-, and 6-year programs. The contract also will state the date of enlistment and other options—for example, bonuses and the types of training to be received. If the service is unable to fulfill any of its obligations under the contract, such as providing a certain kind of training, the contract may become null and void.

All branches of the Armed Services offer a "delayed-entry program" by which an individual can delay entry into active duty for up to 1 year after enlisting. High school students can enlist during their senior year and enter a service after graduation. Others choose this program because the job training they desire is not currently available, but will be within the coming year, or because they need time to arrange their personal affairs.

Women are eligible to enter most military specialties; for example, they may become mechanics, missile maintenance technicians, heavy-equipment operators, and fighter pilots, or they may enter into medical care, administrative support, and intelligence specialties. Generally, only occupations involving direct exposure to combat are excluded.

People planning to apply the skills gained through military training to a civilian career should first determine how good the prospects are for civilian employment in jobs related to the military specialty that interests them. Second, they should know the prerequisites for the related civilian job. Because many civilian occupations require a license, certification, or minimum level of education, it is important to determine whether military training is sufficient for a person to enter the civilian equivalent or, if not, what additional training will be required. Other job descriptions discuss the job outlook, training requirements, and other aspects of some civilian occupations for which military training and experience are helpful. Additional information often can be obtained from school counselors.

Following enlistment, new members of the Armed Forces undergo recruit training, better known as "basic" training. Through courses in military skills and protocol recruit training provides a 6- to 12-week introduction to military life. Days and nights are carefully structured and include rigorous physical exercise designed to improve strength and endurance and build each unit's cohesion.

Following basic training, most recruits take additional training at technical schools that prepare them for a particular military occupational specialty. The formal training period generally lasts from 10 to 20 weeks, although training for certain occupations—nuclear power plant operator, for example—may take as long as a year. Recruits not assigned to classroom instruction receive on-the-job training at their first duty assignment.

Many service people get college credit for the technical training they receive on duty, which, combined with off-duty courses, can lead to an associate degree through programs in community colleges such as the Community College of the Air Force. In addition to on-duty training, military personnel may choose from a variety of educational programs. Most military installations have tuition assistance programs for people wishing to take courses during off-duty hours. The courses may be correspondence courses or courses in degree programs offered by local colleges or universities. Tuition assistance pays up to 75 percent of college costs. Also available are courses designed to help service personnel earn high school equivalency diplomas. Each branch of the service provides opportunities for full-time study to a limited number of exceptional applicants. Military personnel accepted into these highly competitive programs—in law or medicine, for example—receive full pay, allowances, tuition, and related fees. In return, they must agree to serve an additional amount of time in the service. Other highly selective programs enable enlisted personnel to qualify as commissioned officers through additional military training.

Warrant officers. Warrant officers are technical and tactical leaders who specialize in a specific technical area; for example, Army aviators make up one group of warrant officers. The Army Warrant Officer Corps constitutes less than 5 percent of the total Army. Although the Corps is small in size, its level of responsibility is high. Its members receive extended career opportunities, worldwide leadership assignments, and increased pay and retirement benefits. Selection to attend the Warrant Officer Candidate School is highly competitive and restricted to those with the rank of E5 or higher (Table 3).

Table 3. Military rank and employment for active duty personnel, June 2003

Grade

	Army	Navy and Coast Guard	Air Force	Marine Corps	Total Employment
Commissioned officers:					
O-10	General	Admiral	General	General	35
O-9	Lieutenant General	Vice Admiral	Lieutenant General	Lieutenant General	126
O-8	Major General	Rear Admiral Upper	Major General	Major General	282
O-7	Brigadier General	Rear Admiral Lower	Brigadier General	Brigadier General	446
O-6	Colonel	Captain	Colonel	Colonel	11,884
O-5	Lieutenant Colonel	Commander	Lieutenant Colonel	Lieutenant Colonel	28,565
O-4	Major	Lieutenant Commander	Major	Major	44,501
O-3	Captain	Lieutenant	Captain	Captain	69,184
O-2	1st Lieutenant	Lieutenant (JG)	1st Lieutenant	1st Lieutenant	29,416
O-1	2nd Lieutenant	Ensign	2nd Lieutenant	2nd Lieutenant	28,597
Warrant officers:					
W-5	Chief Warrant Officer	Chief Warrant Officer	—	Chief Warrant Officer	504
W-4	Chief Warrant Officer	Chief Warrant Officer	—	Chief Warrant Officer	2,082
W-3	Chief Warrant Officer	Chief Warrant Officer	—	Chief Warrant Officer	4,385
W-2	Chief Warrant Officer	Chief Warrant Officer	—	Chief Warrant Officer	6,118
W-1	Warrant Officer	Warrant Officer	—	Warrant Officer	2,603
Enlisted personnel:					
E-9	Sergeant Major	Master Chief Petty Officer	Chief Master Sergeant	Sergeant Major	10,869
E-8	1st Sergeant/Master Sergeant	Senior Chief Petty Officer	Senior Master Sergeant	Master Sergeant/1st Sergeant	26,545
E-7	Sergeant First Class	Chief Petty Officer	Master Sergeant	Gunnery Sergeant	100,002
E-6	Staff Sergeant	Petty Officer 1st Class	Technical Sergeant	Staff Sergeant	175,281
E-5	Sergeant	Petty Officer 2nd Class	Staff Sergeant	Sergeant	251,122
E-4	Corporal/Specialist	Petty Officer 3rd Class	Senior Airman	Corporal	268,606
E-3	Private First Class	Seaman	Airman 1st Class	Lance Corporal	218,219
E-2	Private	Seaman Apprentice	Airman	Private 1st Class	83,423
E-1	Private	Seaman Recruit	Airman Basic	Private	53,211

Source: U.S. Department of Defense

Officers. Officer training in the Armed Forces is provided through the federal service academies (Military, Naval, Air Force, and Coast Guard); the Reserve Officers Training Corps (ROTC) program offered at many colleges and universities; Officer Candidate School (OCS) or Officer Training School (OTS); the National Guard (State Officer Candidate School programs); the Uniformed Services University of Health Sciences; and other programs. All are highly selective and are good options for those wishing to make the military a career. Persons interested in obtaining training through the federal service academies must be single to enter and graduate, while those seeking training through OCS, OTS, or ROTC need not be single. Single parents with one or more minor dependents are not eligible to become commissioned officers.

Federal service academies provide a 4-year college program leading to a bachelor-of-science degree. Midshipmen or cadets are provided free room and board, tuition, medical and dental care, and a monthly allowance. Graduates receive regular or reserve commissions and have a 5-year active-duty obligation, or more if they are entering flight training.

To become a candidate for appointment as a cadet or midshipman in one of the service academies, applicants are required to obtain a nomination from an authorized source, usually a member of Congress. Candidates do not need to know a member of Congress personally to request a nomination. Nominees must have an academic record of the requisite quality, college aptitude test scores above an established minimum, and recommendations from teachers or school officials; they also must pass a medical examination. Appointments are made from the list of eligible nominees. Appointments to the Coast Guard Academy, however, are based strictly on merit and do not require a nomination.

ROTC programs train students in about 950 Army, approximately 70 Navy and Marine Corps, and around 1,000 Air Force units at participating colleges and universities. Trainees take 2 to 5 hours of military instruction a week, in addition to regular college courses. After graduation, they may serve as officers on active duty for a stipulated period. Some may serve their obligation in the Reserves or National Guard. In the last 2 years of a ROTC program, students receive a monthly allowance while attending school, as well as additional pay for summer training. ROTC scholarships for 2, 3, and 4 years are available on a competitive basis. All scholarships pay for tuition and have allowances for subsistence, textbooks, supplies, and other costs.

College graduates can earn a commission in the Armed Forces through OCS or OTS programs in the Army, Navy, Air Force, Marine Corps, Coast Guard, and National Guard. These officers generally must serve their obligation on active duty. Those with training in certain health professions may qualify for direct appointment as officers. In the case of persons studying for the health professions, financial assistance and internship opportunities are available from the military in return for specified periods of military service. Prospective medical students can apply to the Uniformed Services University of Health Sciences, which offers free tuition in a program leading to a doctor-of-medicine (M.D.) degree. In return, graduates must serve for 7 years in either the military or the U.S. Public Health Service. Direct appointments also are available for those qualified to serve in other specialty areas, such as the judge advocate general (legal) or chaplain corps. Flight training is available to commissioned officers in each branch of the Armed Forces. In addition, the Army has a direct enlistment option to become a warrant officer aviator.

Each service has different criteria for promoting personnel. Generally, the first few promotions for both enlisted and officer personnel come easily; subsequent promotions are much more competitive. Criteria for promotion may include time in service and in grade, job performance, a fitness report (supervisor's recommendation), and the passing of written examinations. People who are passed over for promotion several times generally must leave the military. Table 3 shows the officer, warrant officer, and enlisted ranks by service.

Job Outlook

Opportunities should be good for qualified individuals in all branches of the Armed Forces through 2012. Many military personnel retire with a pension after 20 years of service, while they still are young enough to start a new career. More than 365,000 enlisted personnel and officers must be recruited each year to replace those who complete their commitment or retire. Since the end of the draft in 1973, the military has met its personnel requirements with volunteers. When the economy is good and civilian employment opportunities generally are more favorable, it is more difficult for all the services to meet their recruitment quotas. By contrast, it is much easier to do so during a recession.

America's strategic position is stronger than it has been in decades. Despite reductions in personnel due to the elimination of the threat from Eastern Europe and Russia, the number of active-duty personnel is expected to remain roughly constant through 2012. However, recent conflicts in other countries and the resulting strain on the Armed Forces may lead to an increasing number of active-duty personnel. The Armed Forces' current goal is to maintain a sufficient force to fight and win two major regional conflicts at the same time. Political events, however, could cause these plans to change.

Educational requirements will continue to rise as military jobs become more technical and complex. High school graduates and applicants with a college background will be sought to fill the ranks of enlisted personnel, while virtually all officers will need at least a bachelor's degree and, in some cases, an advanced degree as well.

Earnings

The earnings structure for military personnel is shown in Table 4. Most enlisted personnel started as recruits at Grade E-1 in 2003; however, those with special skills or above-average education started as high as Grade E-4. Most warrant officers had started at Grade W-1 or W-2, depending upon their occupational and academic qualifications and the branch of service of which they were a member, but warrant officer is not an entry-level occupation and, consequently, these individuals all had previous military service. Most commissioned officers started at Grade O-1; some with advanced education started at Grade O-2, and some highly trained officers—for example, physicians and dentists—started as high as Grade O-3. Pay varies by total years of service as well as rank. Because it usually takes many years to reach the higher ranks, most personnel in higher ranks receive the higher pay rates awarded to those with many years of service.

In addition to receiving their basic pay, military personnel are provided with free room and board (or a tax-free housing and subsistence allowance), free medical and dental care, a military clothing allowance, military supermarket and department store shopping privileges, 30 days of paid vacation a year (referred to as leave), and travel opportunities. In many duty stations, military personnel may receive a housing allowance that can be used for off-base housing. This allowance can be substantial, but varies greatly by rank and duty station. For example, in July 2003, the housing allowance for an E-4 with dependents was $505 per month; for a comparable individual without dependents, it was $353. The allowance for an O-4 with dependents was $961 per month; for a person without dependents, it was $836. Other allowances are paid for foreign duty, hazardous duty, submarine and flight duty, and employment as a medical officer. Athletic and other facilities—such as gymnasiums, tennis courts, golf courses, bowling centers, libraries, and movie theaters—are available on many military installations. Military personnel are eligible for retirement benefits after 20 years of service.

The Veterans Administration (VA) provides numerous benefits to those who have served at least 2 years in the Armed Forces. Veterans are eligible for free care in VA hospitals for all service-related disabilities, regardless of time served; those with other medical problems are eligible for free VA care if they are unable to pay the cost of hospitalization elsewhere. Admission to a VA medical center depends on the availability of beds, however. Veterans also are eligible for certain loans, including loans to purchase a home. Veterans, regardless of health, can convert a military life insurance policy to an individual policy with any participating company in the veteran's state of residence. In addition, job counseling, testing, and placement services are available.

Veterans who participate in the New Montgomery GI Bill Program receive educational benefits. Under this program, Armed Forces personnel may elect to deduct up to $100 a month from their pay during the first 12 months of active duty, putting the money toward their future education. Veterans who serve on active duty for more than 2 years or who put in 2 years' active duty plus 4 years in the Selected Reserve will receive $528 a month in basic benefits for 36 months. Those who enlist and serve for 2 years will receive $429 a month for 36 months. In addition, each service provides its own contributions to the enlistee's future education. The sum of the amounts from all these sources becomes the service member's educational fund. Upon separation from active duty, the fund can be used to finance educational costs at any VA-approved institution. Among those institutions which are approved by the VA are many vocational, correspondence, certification, business, technical, and flight-training schools; community and junior colleges; and colleges and universities.

Table 4. Military basic monthly pay by grade for active duty personnel, June 1, 2003

| Grade | *Years of service* | | | | | |
	Less than 2	Over 4	Over 8	Over 12	Over 16	Over 20
O-10	—	—	—	—	—	$11,874.90
O-9	—	—	—	—	—	10,563.60
O-8	$7,474.50	$7,927.20	$8,468.70	$8,868.90	$9,238.20	10,008.90
O-7	6,210.90	6,739.20	7,120.80	7,559.40	8,468.70	9,051.30
O-6	4,603.20	5388.9	5,641.20	5672.1	6,564.30	7,233.30
O-5	3,837.60	4,678.50	4,977.00	5,403.00	5,991.90	6,329.10
O-4	3,311.10	4,145.70	4,637.70	5,201.40	5,471.10	—
O-3	2,911.20	3,883.50	4,273.50	4,623.30	—	—
O-2	2,515.20	3,410.00	—	—	—	—
O-1	2,183.70	2,746.80	—	—	—	—
W-5	—	—	—	—	—	5,169.30
W-4	3,088.10	3,420.60	3,733.50	4,044.60	4,356.00	4,664.40
W-3	2,747.10	3,017.70	3,281.70	3,580.50	3,915.60	4,201.50
W-2	2,416.50	2,763.00	2,993.10	3,264.00	3,453.90	3,705.90
W-1	2,133.90	2,501.10	2,782.20	3,006.90	3,203.40	3,409.50
E-9	—	—	—	3,645.00	3,687.00	4,180.80
E-8	—	—	2,975.40	3,141.30	3,342.00	3,625.50
E-7	2,068.50	2,428.20	2,667.90	2,838.30	3,066.30	3,182.70
E-6	1,770.60	2,117.10	2,400.90	2,562.30	2,663.10	2709.60
E-5	1,625.40	1,903.50	2,151.90	2,283.30	2,283.30	—
E-4	1,502.70	1,749.30	1824.00	—	—	—
E-3	1,356.90	1,528.80	—	—	—	—
E-2	1,290.00	—	—	—	—	—
E-1 4mos+	1,150.80	—	—	—	—	—
E-1 <4mos	1,064.70	—	—	—	—	—

Source: U.S. Department of Defense, Defense Finance and Accounting Service

Sources of Additional Information

Each of the military services publishes handbooks, fact sheets, and pamphlets describing entrance requirements, training and advancement opportunities, and other aspects of military careers. These publications are widely available at all recruiting stations, at most state employment service offices, and in high schools, colleges, and public libraries. Information on educational and other veterans' benefits is available from VA offices located throughout the country.

In addition, the Defense Manpower Data Center, an agency of the U.S. Department of Defense, publishes Military Career Guide Online, a compendium of military occupational, training, and career information designed for use by students and jobseekers. This information is available on the Internet: http://www.todaysmilitary.com

Librarians

(O*NET 25-4021.00)

Significant Points

- A master's degree in library science usually is required; special librarians often need an additional graduate or professional degree.

- A large number of retirements in the next decade is expected to result in many job openings for librarians to replace those who leave.

Nature of the Work

The traditional concept of a library is being redefined from a place to access paper records or books to one that also houses the most advanced media, including CD-ROM, the Internet, virtual libraries, and remote access to a wide range of resources. Consequently, librarians, or information professionals, increasingly are combining traditional duties with tasks involving quickly changing technology. Librarians assist people in finding information and using it effectively for personal and professional purposes. Librarians must have knowledge of a wide variety of scholarly and public information sources and must follow trends related to publishing, computers, and the media in order to oversee the selection and organization of library materials. Librarians manage staff and develop and direct information programs and systems for the public, to ensure that information is organized in a manner that meets users' needs.

Most librarian positions incorporate three aspects of library work: User services, technical services, and administrative services. Still, even librarians specializing in one of these areas have other responsibilities. Librarians in user services, such as reference and children's librarians, work with

patrons to help them find the information they need. The job involves analyzing users' needs to determine what information is appropriate, as well as searching for, acquiring, and providing the information. The job also includes an instructional role, such as showing users how to access information. For example, librarians commonly help users navigate the Internet so they can search for relevant information efficiently. Librarians in technical services, such as acquisitions and cataloguing, acquire and prepare materials for use and often do not deal directly with the public. Librarians in administrative services oversee the management and planning of libraries: negotiate contracts for services, materials, and equipment; supervise library employees; perform public-relations and fundraising duties; prepare budgets; and direct activities to ensure that everything functions properly.

In small libraries or information centers, librarians usually handle all aspects of the work. They read book reviews, publishers' announcements, and catalogues to keep up with current literature and other available resources, and they select and purchase materials from publishers, wholesalers, and distributors. Librarians prepare new materials by classifying them by subject matter and describe books and other library materials to make them easy to find. Librarians supervise assistants, who prepare cards, computer records, or other access tools that direct users to resources. In large libraries, librarians often specialize in a single area, such as acquisitions, cataloguing, bibliography, reference, special collections, or administration. Teamwork is increasingly important to ensure quality service to the public.

Librarians also compile lists of books, periodicals, articles, and audiovisual materials on particular subjects; analyze collections; and recommend materials. They collect and organize books, pamphlets, manuscripts, and other materials in a specific field, such as rare books, genealogy, or music. In addition, they coordinate programs such as storytelling for children and literacy skills and book talks for adults; conduct classes; publicize services; provide reference help; write grants; and oversee other administrative matters.

Librarians are classified according to the type of library in which they work: A public library; school library media center; college, university, or other academic library; or special library. Some librarians work with specific groups, such as children, young adults, adults, or the disadvantaged. In school library media centers, librarians—often called school media specialists—help teachers develop curricula, acquire materials for classroom instruction, and sometimes team teach.

Librarians also work in information centers or libraries maintained by government agencies, corporations, law firms, advertising agencies, museums, professional associations, medical centers, hospitals, religious organizations, and research laboratories. They acquire and arrange an organization's information resources, which usually are limited to subjects of special interest to the organization. These special librarians can provide vital information services by preparing abstracts and indexes of current periodicals, organizing bibliographies, or analyzing background information and preparing reports on areas of particular interest. For example, a special librarian working for a corporation could provide the sales department with information on competitors or new developments affecting the field. A medical librarian may provide information about new medical treatments, clinical trials, and standard procedures to health professionals, patients, consumers, and corporations. Government document librarians, who work for government agencies and depository libraries in each of the states, preserve government publications, records, and other documents that make up a historical record of government actions and decisionmaking.

Many libraries have access to remote databases and maintain their own computerized databases. The widespread use of automation in libraries makes database-searching skills important to librarians. Librarians develop and index databases and help train users to develop searching skills for the information they need. Some libraries are forming consortiums with other libraries through electronic mail. This practice allows patrons to submit information requests to several libraries simultaneously. The Internet also is expanding the amount of available reference information. Librarians must be aware of how to use these resources in order to locate information.

Librarians with computer and information systems skills can work as automated-systems librarians, planning and operating computer systems, and information architect librarians, designing information storage and retrieval systems and developing procedures for collecting, organizing, interpreting, and classifying information. These librarians analyze and plan for future information needs. The increasing use of automated information systems is enabling librarians to focus on administrative and budgeting responsibilities, grant writing, and specialized research requests, while delegating more technical and user services responsibilities to technicians.

More and more, librarians are applying their information management and research skills to arenas outside of libraries—for example, database development, reference tool development, information systems, publishing, Internet coordination, marketing, web content management and design, and training of database users. Entrepreneurial librarians sometimes start their own consulting practices, acting as freelance librarians or information brokers and providing services to other libraries, businesses, or government agencies.

Working Conditions

Librarians spend a significant portion of time at their desks or in front of computer terminals; extended work at video display terminals can cause eyestrain and headaches. Assisting users in obtaining information or books for their jobs, homework, or recreational reading can be challenging and satisfying, but working with users under deadlines can be demanding and stressful. Some librarians lift and carry books, and some climb ladders to reach high stacks. Librarians in small organizations sometimes shelve books themselves.

More than 2 out of 10 librarians work part time. Public and college librarians often work weekends and evenings, as well as some holidays. School librarians usually have the same workday and vacation schedules as classroom teachers. Special librarians usually work normal business hours, but in fast-paced industries—such as advertising or legal services—they can work longer hours when needed.

Employment

Librarians held about 167,000 jobs in 2002. Most worked in school and academic libraries, but nearly a third worked in public libraries. The remainder worked in special libraries or as information professionals for companies and other organizations.

Training, Other Qualifications, and Advancement

A master's degree in library science (MLS) is necessary for librarian positions in most public, academic, and special libraries and in some school libraries. The federal government requires an MLS or the equivalent in education and experience. Many colleges and universities offer MLS programs, but employers often prefer graduates of the approximately 56 schools accredited by the American Library Association. Most MLS programs require a bachelor's degree; any liberal arts major is appropriate.

Most MLS programs take 1 year to complete; some take 2. A typical graduate program includes courses in the foundations of library and information science, including the history of books and printing, intellectual freedom and censorship, and the role of libraries and information in society. Other basic courses cover the selection and processing of materials, the organization of information, reference tools and strategies, and user services. Courses are adapted to educate librarians to use new resources brought about by advancing technology, such as online reference systems, Internet search methods, and automated circulation systems. Course options can include resources for children or young adults; classification, cataloguing, indexing, and abstracting; library administration; and library automation. Computer-related course work is an increasingly important part of an MLS degree. Some programs offer interdisciplinary degrees combining technical courses in information science with traditional training in library science.

The MLS degree provides general preparation for library work, but some individuals specialize in a particular area, such as reference, technical services, or children's services. A Ph.D. degree in library and information science is advantageous for a college teaching position or for a top administrative job in a college or university library or large library system.

Usually, an MLS also is required of librarians working in special libraries. In addition, most special librarians supplement their education with knowledge of the subject in which they are specializing, sometimes earning a master's, doctoral, or professional degree in the subject. Areas of specialization include medicine, law, business, engineering, and the natural and social sciences. For example, a librarian working for a law firm may also be a licensed attorney, holding both library science and law degrees. In some jobs, knowledge of a foreign language is needed.

State certification requirements for public school librarians vary widely. Most states require school librarians, often called library media specialists, to be certified as teachers and to have had courses in library science. An MLS is needed in some cases, perhaps with a library media specialization, or a master's in education with a specialty in school library media or educational media. Some states require certification of public librarians employed in municipal, county, or regional library systems.

Librarians participate in continuing education and training once they are on the job, in order to keep abreast of new information systems brought about by changing technology.

Experienced librarians can advance to administrative positions, such as department head, library director, or chief information officer.

Job Outlook

Employment of librarians is expected to grow about as fast as the average for all occupations over the 2002–12 period. However, job opportunities are expected to be very good because a large number of librarians are expected to retire in the coming decade, creating many job openings. Also, the number of people going into this profession has fallen in recent years, resulting in more jobs than applicants in some cases. Colleges and universities report the greatest difficulty in hiring librarians, because the pay is often less than the prospective employees can get elsewhere.

Offsetting the need for librarians are government budget cuts and the increasing use of computerized information storage and retrieval systems. Both will result in the hiring of fewer librarians and the replacement of librarians with less costly library technicians. Computerized systems make cataloguing easier, allowing library technicians to perform the work. In addition, many libraries are equipped for users to access library computers directly from their homes or offices. That way, users can bypass librarians altogether and conduct research on their own. However, librarians will still be needed to manage staff, help users develop database-searching techniques, address complicated reference requests, and define users' needs.

Jobs for librarians outside traditional settings will grow the fastest over the decade. Nontraditional librarian jobs include working as information brokers and working for private corporations, nonprofit organizations, and consulting firms. Many companies are turning to librarians because of their research and organizational skills and their knowledge of computer databases and library automation systems. Librarians can review vast amounts of information and analyze, evaluate, and organize it according to a company's specific needs. Librarians also are hired by organizations to set up information on the Internet. Librarians working in these settings may be classified as systems analysts, database specialists and trainers, webmasters or web developers, or local area network (LAN) coordinators.

Earnings

Salaries of librarians vary according to the individual's qualifications and the type, size, and location of the library. Librarians with primarily administrative duties often have greater earnings. Median annual earnings of librarians in 2002 were $43,090. The middle 50 percent earned between $33,560 and $54,250. The lowest 10 percent earned less than $24,510, and the highest 10 percent earned more than $66,590. Median annual earnings in the industries employing the largest numbers of librarians in 2002 were as follows:

Elementary and secondary schools $45,660

Colleges, universities, and professional
   schools 45,600

Local government 37,970

Other information services 37,770

The average annual salary for all librarians in the federal government in nonsupervisory, supervisory, and managerial positions was $70,238 in 2003.

Nearly one in three librarians is a member of a union or is covered under a union contract.

Related Occupations

Librarians play an important role in the transfer of knowledge and ideas by providing people with access to the information they need and want. Jobs requiring similar analytical, organizational, and communicative skills include archivists, curators, and museum technicians; and computer and information scientists, research. School librarians have many duties similar to those of schoolteachers. Librarians are increasingly storing, cataloguing, and accessing information with computers. Other jobs that use similar computer skills include systems analysts, computer scientists, and database administrators.

Sources of Additional Information

For information on a career as a librarian and information on accredited library education programs and scholarships, contact:

● American Library Association, Office for Human Resource Development and Recruitment, 50 East Huron St., Chicago, IL 60611. Internet: http://www.ala.org

For information on a career as a special librarian, write to:

- Special Libraries Association, 1700 18th St. NW, Washington, DC 20009. Internet: http://www.sla.org

Information on graduate schools of library and information science can be obtained from:

- Association for Library and Information Science Education, 1009 Commerce Park Dr., Suite 150, PO Box 4219, Oak Ridge, TN 37839. Internet: http://www.alise.org

For information on a career as a law librarian, scholarship information, and a list of ALA-accredited schools offering programs in law librarianship, contact:

- American Association of Law Libraries, 53 West Jackson Blvd., Suite 940, Chicago, IL 60604. Internet: http://www.aallnet.org

For information on employment opportunities for health sciences librarians and for scholarship information, credentialing information, and a list of MLA-accredited schools offering programs in health sciences librarianship, contact:

- Medical Library Association, 65 E Wacker Place, Suite 1900, Chicago, IL 60601. Internet: http://www.mlanet.org

Information on acquiring a job as a librarian with the federal government may be obtained from the Office of Personnel Management through a telephone-based system. Consult your telephone directory under U.S. government for a local number, or call (703) 724-1850 (Federal Relay Service (800) 877-8339). The first number is not toll free, and charges may result. Information also is available on the Internet at http://www.usajobs.opm.gov.

Information concerning requirements and application procedures for positions in the Library of Congress can be obtained directly from:

- Human Resources Office, Library of Congress, 101 Independence Ave. SE, Washington, DC 20540-2231.

State library agencies can furnish information on scholarships available through their offices, requirements for certification, and general information about career prospects in the particular state of interest. Several of these agencies maintain job hot lines reporting openings for librarians.

State departments of education can furnish information on certification requirements and job opportunities for school librarians.

Library Technicians

(O*NET 25-4031.00)

Significant Points

- Training requirements range from a high school diploma to an associate's or bachelor's degree, but computer skills are needed for many jobs.

- Increasing use of computerized circulation and information systems should continue to spur job growth, but many libraries' budget constraints should moderate growth.

- Employment should grow rapidly in special libraries because growing numbers of professionals and other workers use those libraries.

Nature of the Work

Library technicians both help librarians acquire, prepare, and organize material and assist users in finding information. Library technicians usually work under the supervision of a librarian, although they work independently in certain situations. Technicians in small libraries handle a range of duties; those in large libraries usually specialize. As libraries increasingly use new technologies—such as CD-ROM, the Internet, virtual libraries, and automated databases—the duties of library technicians will expand and evolve accordingly. Library technicians are assuming greater responsibilities, in some cases taking on tasks previously performed by librarians.

Depending on the employer, library technicians can have other titles, such as library technical assistant or media aide. Library technicians direct library users to standard references, organize and maintain periodicals, prepare volumes for binding, handle interlibrary loan requests, prepare invoices, perform routine cataloguing and coding of library materials, retrieve information from computer databases, and supervise support staff.

The widespread use of computerized information storage and retrieval systems has resulted in technicians handling technical services—such as entering catalogue information into the library's computer—that were once performed by librarians. Technicians assist with customizing databases. In addition, technicians instruct patrons in how to use computer systems to access data. The increased automation of recordkeeping has reduced the amount of clerical work performed by library technicians. Many libraries now offer self-service registration and circulation areas with computers, decreasing the time library technicians spend manually recording and inputting records.

Some library technicians operate and maintain audiovisual equipment, such as projectors, tape recorders, and videocassette recorders, and assist users with microfilm or microfiche readers. They also design posters, bulletin boards, or displays.

Library technicians in school libraries encourage and teach students to use the library and media center. They also help teachers obtain instructional materials, and they assist students with special assignments. Some work in special libraries maintained by government agencies, corporations, law firms, advertising agencies, museums, professional societies, medical centers, and research laboratories, where they conduct literature searches, compile bibliographies, and prepare abstracts, usually on subjects of particular interest to the organization.

To extend library services to more patrons, many libraries operate bookmobiles, often run by library technicians. The technicians take trucks stocked with books, or bookmobiles, to designated sites on a regular schedule, frequently stopping at shopping centers, apartment complexes, schools, and nursing homes. Bookmobiles also may be used to extend library service to patrons living in remote areas. Depending on local conditions, the technicians may operate a bookmobile alone or may be accompanied by another library employee.

Library technicians who drive bookmobiles, answer patrons' questions, receive and check out books, collect fines, maintain the book collection, shelve materials, and occasionally operate audiovisual equipment to show slides or films. They participate, and may assist, in planning programs sponsored by the library, such as reader advisory programs, used-book sales, or outreach programs. Technicians who drive the bookmobile keep track of their mileage, the materials lent out, and the amount of fines collected. In some areas, they are responsible for maintenance of the vehicle and any photocopiers or other equipment in it. They record statistics on circulation and the number of people visiting the bookmobile. Technicians also may record requests for special items from the main library and arrange for the materials to be mailed or delivered to a patron during the next scheduled visit. Many bookmobiles are equipped with personal computers and CD-ROM systems linked to the main library system, allowing technicians to reserve or locate books immediately. Some bookmobiles now offer Internet access to users.

Working Conditions

Technicians answer questions and provide assistance to library users. Those who prepare library materials sit at desks or computer terminals for long periods and can develop headaches or eyestrain from working with the terminals. Some duties, like calculating circulation statistics, can be repetitive and boring. Others, such as performing computer searches with the use of local and regional library networks and cooperatives, can be interesting and challenging. Library technicians may lift and carry books, climb ladders to reach high stacks, and bend low to shelve books on bottom shelves.

Library technicians in school libraries work regular school hours. Those in public libraries and college and university (academic) libraries also work weekends, evenings and some holidays. Library technicians in special libraries usually work normal business hours, although they often work overtime as well.

The schedules of library technicians who drive bookmobiles depend on the size of the area being served. Some bookmobiles operate every day, while others go only on certain days. Some bookmobiles operate in the evenings and weekends, to give patrons as much access to the library as possible. Because library technicians who operate bookmobiles may be the only link some people have to the library, much of

their work consists of helping the public. They may assist handicapped or elderly patrons to the bookmobile or shovel snow to ensure their safety. They may enter hospitals or nursing homes to deliver books to patrons who are bedridden.

Employment

Library technicians held about 119,000 jobs in 2002. Most worked in school, academic, or public libraries. Some worked in hospitals and for religious organizations, mainly parochial schools. The federal government—primarily the U.S. Department of Defense and the U.S. Library of Congress—and state and local governments also employed library technicians.

Training, Other Qualifications, and Advancement

Training requirements for library technicians vary widely, ranging from a high school diploma to specialized postsecondary training. Some employers hire individuals with work experience or other training; others train inexperienced workers on the job. Still other employers require that technicians have an associate's or bachelor's degree. Given the rapid spread of automation in libraries, computer skills are needed for many jobs. Knowledge of databases, library automation systems, online library systems, online public access systems, and circulation systems is valuable. Many bookmobile drivers are required to have a commercial driver's license.

Some 2-year colleges offer an associate-of-arts degree in library technology. Programs include both liberal arts and library-related study. Students learn about library and media organization and operation, as well as how to order, process, catalogue, locate, and circulate library materials and work with library automation. Libraries and associations offer continuing education courses to keep technicians abreast of new developments in the field.

Library technicians usually advance by assuming added responsibilities. For example, technicians often start at the circulation desk, checking books in and out. After gaining experience, they may become responsible for storing and verifying information. As they advance, they may become involved in budget and personnel matters in their departments. Some library technicians advance to supervisory positions and are in charge of the day-to-day operation of their departments.

Job Outlook

Employment of library technicians is expected to grow about as fast as the average for all occupations through 2012. In addition to jobs opening up through employment growth, some job openings will result from the need to replace library technicians who transfer to other fields or leave the labor force.

The increasing use of library automation is expected to continue to spur job growth among library technicians. Computerized information systems have simplified certain tasks, such as descriptive cataloguing, which can now be handled by technicians instead of librarians. For example, nowadays technicians can easily retrieve information from a central database and store it in the library's computer. Although efforts to contain costs could dampen employment growth of library technicians in school, public, and college and university libraries, cost containment efforts could also result in more hiring of library technicians than librarians. Growth in the number of professionals and other workers who use special libraries should result in good job opportunities for library technicians in those settings.

Earnings

Median annual earnings of library technicians in 2002 were $24,090. The middle 50 percent earned between $18,150 and $31,140. The lowest 10 percent earned less than $14,410, and the highest 10 percent earned more than $38,000. Median annual earnings in the industries employing the largest numbers of library technicians in 2002 were as follows:

Colleges, universities, and professional
schools $27,280
Local government 23,310
Elementary and secondary schools 21,770
Other information services 20,950

Salaries of library technicians in the federal government averaged $36,788 in 2003.

Related Occupations

Library technicians perform organizational and administrative duties. Workers in other occupations with similar duties include library assistants, clerical; information and record clerks; and medical records and health information technicians.

Sources of Additional Information

For information on training programs for library/media technical assistants, write to:

● American Library Association, Office for Human Resource Development and Recruitment, 50 East Huron St., Chicago, IL 60611. Internet: http://www.ala.org

Information on acquiring a job as a library technician with the federal government may be obtained from the Office of Personnel Management through a telephone-based system. Consult your telephone directory under U.S. government for a local number, or call (703) 724-1850 (Federal Relay Service (800) 877-8339. The first number is not toll free, and charges may result. Information also is available on the Internet at http://www.usajobs.opm.gov.

Information concerning requirements and application procedures for positions in the Library of Congress can be obtained directly from:

● Human Resources Office, Library of Congress, 101 Independence Ave. SE, Washington, DC 20540-2231.

State library agencies can furnish information on requirements for technicians and general information about career prospects in the state. Several of these agencies maintain job hot lines reporting openings for library technicians.

State departments of education can furnish information on requirements and job opportunities for school library technicians.

Licensed Practical and Licensed Vocational Nurses

(O*NET 29-2061.00)

Significant Points

● Training lasting about 1 year is available in about 1,100 state-approved programs, mostly in vocational or technical schools.

● Nursing care facilities will offer the most new jobs.

● Applicants for jobs in hospitals may face competition as the number of hospital jobs for LPNs declines.

Nature of the Work

Licensed practical nurses (LPNs), or licensed vocational nurses (LVNs), care for the sick, injured, convalescent, and disabled under the direction of physicians and registered nurses.

Most LPNs provide basic bedside care, taking vital signs such as temperature, blood pressure, pulse, and respiration. They also prepare and give injections and enemas, monitor catheters, apply dressings, treat bedsores, and give alcohol rubs and massages. LPNs monitor their patients and report adverse reactions to medications or treatments. They collect samples for testing, perform routine laboratory tests, feed patients, and record food and fluid intake and output. To help keep patients comfortable, LPNs assist with bathing, dressing, and personal hygiene. In states where the law allows, they may administer prescribed medicines or start intravenous fluids. Some LPNs help deliver, care for, and feed infants. Experienced LPNs may supervise nursing assistants and aides.

In addition to providing routine beside care, LPNs in nursing care facilities help evaluate residents' needs, develop care plans, and supervise the care provided by nursing aides. In doctors' offices and clinics, they also may make appointments, keep records, and perform other clerical duties. LPNs who work in private homes may prepare meals and teach family members simple nursing tasks.

Working Conditions

Most licensed practical nurses in hospitals and nursing care facilities work a 40-hour week, but because patients need around-the-clock care, some work nights, weekends, and holidays. They often stand for long periods and help patients move in bed, stand, or walk.

LPNs may face hazards from caustic chemicals, radiation, and infectious diseases such as hepatitis. They are subject to back injuries when moving patients and shock from electrical equipment. They often must deal with the stress of heavy workloads. In addition, the patients they care for may be confused, irrational, agitated, or uncooperative.

Employment

Licensed practical nurses held about 702,000 jobs in 2002. About 28 percent of LPNs worked in hospitals, 26 percent in nursing care facilities, and another 12 percent in offices of physicians. Others worked for home healthcare services, employment services, community care facilities for the elderly, public and private educational services, outpatient care centers, and federal, state, and local government agencies; about 1 in 5 worked part time.

Training, Other Qualifications, and Advancement

All states and the District of Columbia require LPNs to pass a licensing examination after completing a state-approved practical nursing program. A high school diploma or its equivalent usually is required for entry, although some programs accept candidates without a diploma or are designed as part of a high school curriculum.

In 2002, approximately 1,100 state-approved programs provided training in practical nursing. Almost 6 out of 10 students were enrolled in technical or vocational schools, while 3 out of 10 were in community and junior colleges. Others were in high schools, hospitals, and colleges and universities.

Most practical nursing programs last about 1 year and include both classroom study and supervised clinical practice (patient care). Classroom study covers basic nursing concepts and patient care-related subjects, including anatomy, physiology, medical-surgical nursing, pediatrics, obstetrics, psychiatric nursing, the administration of drugs, nutrition, and first aid. Clinical practice usually is in a hospital, but sometimes includes other settings.

LPNs should have a caring, sympathetic nature. They should be emotionally stable, because work with the sick and

injured can be stressful. They also should have keen observational, decisionmaking, and communication skills. As part of a healthcare team, they must be able to follow orders and work under close supervision.

Job Outlook

Employment of LPNs is expected to grow about as fast as the average for all occupations through 2012 in response to the long-term care needs of an increasing elderly population and the general growth of healthcare. Replacement needs will be a major source of job openings, as many workers leave the occupation permanently.

Applicants for jobs in hospitals may face competition as the number of hospital jobs for LPNs declines. An increasing proportion of sophisticated procedures, which once were performed only in hospitals, is being performed in physicians' offices and in outpatient care centers such as ambulatory surgical and emergency medical centers, due largely to advances in technology. Consequently, employment of LPNs is projected to grow faster than average in these sectors as healthcare expands outside the traditional hospital setting.

Employment of LPNs in nursing care facilities is expected to grow faster than the average. Such facilities will offer the most new jobs for LPNs as the number of aged and disabled persons in need of long-term care rises. In addition to caring for the aged and the disabled, LPNs in nursing care facilities will care for the increasing number of patients who will have been discharged from the hospital, but have not recovered enough to return home.

Employment of LPNs is expected to grow much faster than average in home healthcare services. This growth is in response to an increasing number of older persons with functional disabilities, consumer preference for care in the home, and technological advances that make it possible to bring increasingly complex treatments into the home.

Earnings

Median annual earnings of licensed practical nurses were $31,440 in 2002. The middle 50 percent earned between $26,430 and $37,050. The lowest 10 percent earned less than $22,860, and the highest 10 percent earned more than $44,040. Median annual earnings in the industries employing the largest numbers of licensed practical nurses in 2002 were as follows:

Employment services	$40,550
Home health care services	32,850
Nursing care facilities	32,220
General medical and surgical hospitals	30,310
Offices of physicians	28,710

Related Occupations

LPNs work closely with people while helping them. So do emergency medical technicians and paramedics, social and human service assistants, surgical technologists, and teacher assistants.

Sources of Additional Information

For information about practical nursing, contact any of the following organizations:

- National League for Nursing, 61 Broadway, New York, NY 10006. Internet: http://www.nln.org

- National Federation of Licensed Practical Nurses, Inc., 605 Poole Dr., Garner, NC 27529.

Machinists

(O*NET 51-4041.00)

Significant Points

- Machinists learn in apprenticeship programs, informally on the job, and in high schools, vocational schools, or community or technical colleges.

- Many entrants previously have worked as machine setters, operators, or tenders.

- Job opportunities are expected to be excellent.

Nature of the Work

Machinists use machine tools, such as lathes, milling machines, and machining centers, to produce precision metal parts. Although they may produce large quantities of one part, precision machinists often produce small batches or one-of-a-kind items. They use their knowledge of the working properties of metals and their skill with machine tools to plan and carry out the operations needed to make machined products that meet precise specifications.

Before they machine a part, machinists must carefully plan and prepare the operation. These workers first review blueprints or written specifications for a job. Next, they calculate where to cut or bore into the workpiece (the piece of metal that is being shaped), how fast to feed the metal into the machine, and how much metal to remove. They then select tools and materials for the job, plan the sequence of cutting and finishing operations, and mark the metal stock to show where cuts should be made.

After this layout work is completed, machinists perform the necessary machining operations. They position the metal stock on the machine tool—drill press, lathe, milling machine, or other type of machine—set the controls, and make the cuts. During the machining process, they must constantly monitor the feed rate and speed of the machine. Machinists also ensure that the workpiece is being properly lubricated and cooled, because the machining of metal products generates a significant amount of heat. The temperature of the workpiece is a key concern because most metals expand when heated; machinists must adjust the size of their cuts relative to the temperature. Some rare but increasingly popular metals, such as titanium, are machined at extremely high temperatures.

Machinists detect some problems by listening for specific sounds—for example, a dull cutting tool or excessive vibration. Dull cutting tools are removed and replaced. Cutting speeds are adjusted to compensate for harmonic vibrations, which can decrease the accuracy of cuts, particularly on newer high-speed spindles and lathes. After the work is completed, machinists use both simple and highly sophisticated measuring tools to check the accuracy of their work against blueprints.

Some machinists, often called production machinists, may produce large quantities of one part, especially parts requiring the use of complex operations and great precision. Many modern machine tools are computer numerically controlled (CNC). Frequently, machinists work with computer-control programmers to determine how the automated equipment will cut a part. The programmer may determine the path of the cut, while the machinist determines the type of cutting tool, the speed of the cutting tool, and the feed rate. Because most machinists train in CNC programming, they may write basic programs themselves and often modify programs in response to problems encountered during test runs. After the production process is designed, relatively simple and repetitive operations normally are performed by machine setters, operators, and tenders.

Some manufacturing techniques employ automated parts loaders, automatic tool changers, and computer controls, allowing machine tools to operate without anyone present. One production machinist, working 8 hours a day, might monitor equipment, replace worn cutting tools, check the accuracy of parts being produced, and perform other tasks on several CNC machines that operate 24 hours a day (lights-out manufacturing). During lights-out manufacturing, a factory may need only a few machinists to monitor the entire factory.

Other machinists do maintenance work—repairing or making new parts for existing machinery. To repair a broken part, maintenance machinists may refer to blueprints and perform the same machining operations that were needed to create the original part.

Working Conditions

Today, most machine shops are relatively clean, well lit, and ventilated. Many computer-controlled machines are partially or totally enclosed, minimizing the exposure of workers to noise, debris, and the lubricants used to cool workpieces during machining. Nevertheless, working around machine tools presents certain dangers, and workers must follow safety precautions. Machinists wear protective equipment, such as safety glasses to shield against bits of flying metal and earplugs to dampen machinery noise. They also must exercise caution when handling hazardous coolants and lubricants, although many common water-based lubricants present little hazard. The job requires stamina, because machinists stand most of the day and, at times, may need to lift moderately heavy workpieces. Modern factories extensively employ autoloaders and overhead cranes, reducing heavy lifting.

Most machinists work a 40-hour week. Evening and weekend shifts are becoming more common as companies justify investments in more expensive machinery by extending hours of operation. However, this trend is somewhat offset by the increasing use of lights-out manufacturing. Overtime is common during peak production periods.

Employment

Machinists held about 387,000 jobs in 2002. Most machinists work in small machining shops or in manufacturing industries, such as machinery manufacturing and transportation equipment manufacturing (motor vehicle parts and aerospace products and parts). Maintenance machinists work in most industries that use production machinery.

Training, Other Qualifications, and Advancement

Machinists train in apprenticeship programs, informally on the job, and in high schools, vocational schools, or community or technical colleges. Experience with machine tools is helpful. In fact, many entrants previously have worked as machine setters, operators, or tenders. Persons interested in becoming machinists should be mechanically inclined, have good problem-solving abilities, be able to work independently, and be able to do highly accurate work (tolerances may reach 1/10,000th of an inch) that requires concentration and physical effort.

High school or vocational school courses in mathematics (especially trigonometry), blueprint reading, metalworking, and drafting are highly recommended. Apprenticeship programs consist of shop training and related classroom instruction lasting up to 4 years. In shop training, apprentices work almost full time, and are supervised by an experienced machinist while learning to operate various machine tools. Classroom instruction includes math, physics, materials science, blueprint reading, mechanical drawing, and quality and safety practices. In addition, as machine shops have increased their use of computer-controlled equipment, training in the operation and programming of CNC machine tools has become essential. Apprenticeship classes are taught in cooperation with local community or vocational colleges. A growing number of machinists learn the trade through 2-year associate degree programs at community or technical colleges. Graduates of these programs still need significant on-the-job experience before they are fully qualified.

To boost the skill level of machinists and to create a more uniform standard of competency, a number of training facilities and colleges are implementing curriculums that incorporate national skills standards developed by the National Institute of Metalworking Skills (NIMS). After completing such a curriculum and passing a performance requirement and written exam, trainees are granted a NIMS credential, which provides formal recognition of competency in a metalworking field. Completing a recognized certification program provides a machinist with better career opportunities.

As new automation is introduced, machinists normally receive additional training to update their skills. This training usually is provided by a representative of the equipment manufacturer or a local technical school. Some employers offer tuition reimbursement for job-related courses.

Machinists can advance in several ways. Experienced machinists may become CNC programmers, tool and die makers, or mold makers, or be promoted to supervisory or administrative positions in their firms. A few open their own shops.

Job Outlook

Despite projected slower-than-average employment growth, job opportunities for machinists should continue to be excellent. Many young people with the necessary educational and personal qualifications needed to obtain machining skills may prefer to attend college or may not wish to enter production occupations. Therefore, the number of workers obtaining the skills and knowledge necessary to fill machinist jobs is expected to be less than the number of job openings arising each year from employment growth and from the need to replace experienced machinists who transfer to other occupations or retire.

Employment of machinists is expected to grow more slowly than the average for all occupations over the 2002-12 period because of rising productivity among these workers. Machinists will become more efficient as a result of the expanded use of and improvements in technologies such as CNC machine tools, autoloaders, and high-speed machining. This allows fewer machinists to accomplish the same amount of work previously performed by more workers. Technology is not expected to affect the employment of machinists as significantly as that of most other production occupations, however, because machinists monitor and maintain many automated systems. Due to modern production techniques, employers prefer workers, such as machinists, who have a wide range of skills and are capable of performing almost any task in a machine shop.

Employment levels in this occupation are influenced by economic cycles—as the demand for machined goods falls, machinists involved in production may be laid off or forced to work fewer hours. Employment of machinists involved in plant maintenance, however, often is more stable because proper maintenance and repair of costly equipment remain critical to manufacturing operations, even when production levels fall.

Earnings

Median hourly earnings of machinists were $15.66 in 2002. The middle 50 percent earned between $12.15 and $19.45. The lowest 10 percent earned less than $9.57, while the top 10 percent earned more than $23.17. Median hourly earnings in the manufacturing industries employing the largest number of machinists in 2002 were:

Metalworking machinery manufacturing $16.75

Other general purpose machinery
manufacturing 15.91

Machine shops; turned product; and screw,
nut, and bolt manufacturing 15.45

Motor vehicle parts manufacturing.........................15.18

Employment services 9.41

Related Occupations

Occupations most closely related to that of machinist are other machining occupations, which include tool and die makers; machine setters, operators, and tenders—metal and plastic; and computer-control programmers and operators. Another occupation that requires precision and skill in working with metal is welding, soldering, and brazing.

Sources of Additional Information

For general information about machinists, contact:

- Precision Machine Products Association, 6700 West Snowville Rd., Brecksville, OH 44141-3292. Internet: http://www.pmpa.org

For a list of training centers and apprenticeship programs, contact:

- National Tooling and Machining Association, 9300 Livingston Rd., Fort Washington, MD 20744. Internet: http://www.ntma.org

For general occupational information and a list of training programs, contact:

- Precision Metalforming Association Educational Foundation, 6363 Oak Tree Blvd., Independence, OH 44131-2500. Internet: http://www.pmaef.org

Management Analysts

(O*NET 13-1111.00)

Significant Points

- Thirty percent are self-employed, about one and a half times the average for other management, business, and financial occupations.

- Most positions in private industry require a master's degree and additional years of specialized experience; a bachelor's degree is sufficient for entry-level government jobs.

- Despite projected faster-than-average employment growth, intense competition is expected for jobs.

Nature of the Work

As business becomes more complex, the nation's firms are continually faced with new challenges. Firms increasingly rely on management analysts to help them remain competitive amidst these changes. Management analysts, often referred to as *management consultants* in private industry, analyze and propose ways to improve an organization's structure, efficiency, or profits. For example, a small but rapidly growing company that needs help improving the system of control over inventories and expenses may decide to employ a consultant who is an expert in just-in-time inventory management. In another case, a large company that has recently acquired a new division may hire management analysts to help reorganize the corporate structure and eliminate duplicate or nonessential jobs. In recent years, information technology and electronic commerce have provided new opportunities for management analysts. Companies hire consultants to develop strategies for entering and remaining competitive in the new electronic marketplace.

Firms providing management analysis range in size from a single practitioner to large international organizations employing thousands of consultants. Some analysts and consultants specialize in a specific industry, such as healthcare or telecommunications, while others specialize by type of business function, such as human resources, marketing, logistics, or information systems. In government, management analysts tend to specialize by type of agency. The work of management analysts and consultants varies with each client or employer, and from project to project. Some projects require a team of consultants, each specializing in one area. In other projects, consultants work independently with the organization's managers. In all cases, analysts and consultants collect, review, and analyze information in order to make recommendations to managers.

Both public and private organizations use consultants for a variety of reasons. Some lack the internal resources needed to handle a project, while others need a consultant's expertise to determine what resources will be required and what problems may be encountered if they pursue a particular opportunity. To retain a consultant, a company first solicits proposals from a number of consulting firms specializing in the area in which it needs assistance. These proposals include the estimated cost and scope of the project, staffing requirements, references from a number of previous clients, and a completion deadline. The company then selects the proposal that best suits its needs.

After obtaining an assignment or contract, management analysts first define the nature and extent of the problem.

During this phase, they analyze relevant data, which may include annual revenues, employment, or expenditures, and interview managers and employees while observing their operations. The analyst or consultant then develops solutions to the problem. In the course of preparing their recommendations, they take into account the nature of the organization, the relationship it has with others in the industry, and its internal organization and culture. Insight into the problem often is gained by building and solving mathematical models.

Once they have decided on a course of action, consultants report their findings and recommendations to the client. These suggestions usually are submitted in writing, but oral presentations regarding findings also are common. For some projects, management analysts are retained to help implement the suggestions they have made.

Management analysts in government agencies use the same skills as their private-sector colleagues to advise managers on many types of issues, most of which are similar to the problems faced by private firms. For example, if an agency is planning to purchase personal computers, it must first determine which type to buy, given its budget and data processing needs. In this case, management analysts would assess the prices and characteristics of various machines and determine which best meets the agency's needs.

Working Conditions

Management analysts usually divide their time between their offices and the client's site. In either situation, much of an analyst's time is spent indoors in clean, well-lit offices. Because they must spend a significant portion of their time with clients, analysts travel frequently.

Analysts and consultants generally work at least 40 hours a week. Uncompensated overtime is common, especially when project deadlines are approaching. Analysts may experience a great deal of stress as a result of trying to meet a client's demands, often on a tight schedule.

Self-employed consultants can set their workload and hours and work at home. On the other hand, their livelihood depends on their ability to maintain and expand their client base. Salaried consultants also must impress potential clients to get and keep clients for their company.

Employment

Management analysts held about 577,000 jobs in 2002. Thirty percent of these workers were self-employed, about one and a half times the average for other management, business, and financial occupations. Management analysts are found throughout the country, but employment is concentrated in large metropolitan areas. Most work in management, scientific, and technical consulting firms, in computer systems design and related services firms, and for federal, state, and local governments. The majority of those working for the federal government are in the U.S. Department of Defense.

Training, Other Qualifications, and Advancement

Educational requirements for entry-level jobs in this field vary widely between private industry and government. Most employers in private industry generally seek individuals with a master's degree in business administration or a related discipline. Some employers also require additional years of experience in the field in which the worker plans to consult, in addition to a master's degree. Some will hire workers with a bachelor's degree as a research analyst or associate. Research analysts usually need to pursue a master's degree in order to advance to a consulting position. Most government agencies hire people with a bachelor's degree and no pertinent work experience for entry-level management analyst positions.

Few universities or colleges offer formal programs of study in management consulting; however, many fields of study provide a suitable educational background for this occupation because of the wide range of areas addressed by management analysts. These include most academic programs in business and management, such as accounting and marketing, as well as economics, computer and information sciences, and engineering. In addition to the appropriate formal education, most entrants to this occupation have years of experience in management, human resources, information technology, or other specialties. Analysts also routinely attend conferences to keep abreast of current developments in their field.

Management analysts often work with minimal supervision, so they need to be self-motivated and disciplined. Analytical skills, the ability to get along with a wide range of people, strong oral and written communication skills, good judgment, time management skills, and creativity are other desirable qualities. The ability to work in teams also is an important attribute as consulting teams become more common.

As consultants gain experience, they often become solely responsible for a specific project, taking on more responsibility and managing their own hours. At the senior level, consultants may supervise lower level workers and become more involved in seeking out new business. Those with exceptional skills may eventually become a partner in the firm. Others with entrepreneurial ambition may open their own firm.

A high percentage of management consultants are self-employed, partly because business startup costs are low. Self-employed consultants also can share office space, administrative help, and other resources with other self-employed consultants or small consulting firms, thus reducing overhead costs. Because many small consulting firms fail each year for lack of managerial expertise and clients, persons interested in opening their own firm must have good organizational and marketing skills and several years of consulting experience.

The Institute of Management Consultants USA, Inc. (IMC USA) offers a wide range of professional development programs and resources, such as meetings and workshops, which can be helpful for management consultants. The IMC USA also offers the Certified Management Consultant (CMC) designation to those who meet minimum levels of education and experience, submit client reviews, and pass an interview and exam covering the IMC USA's Code of Ethics. Management consultants with a CMC designation must be recertified every 3 years. Certification is not mandatory for management consultants, but it may give a jobseeker a competitive advantage.

Job Outlook

Despite projected rapid employment growth, keen competition is expected for jobs as management analysts. Because analysts can come from such diverse educational backgrounds, the pool of applicants from which employers can draw is quite large. Furthermore, the independent and challenging nature of the work, combined with high earnings potential, makes this occupation attractive to many. Job opportunities are expected to be best for those with a graduate degree, industry expertise, and a talent for salesmanship and public relations.

Employment of management analysts is expected to grow faster than the average for all occupations through 2012, as industry and government increasingly rely on outside expertise to improve the performance of their organizations. Job growth is projected in very large consulting firms with international expertise and in smaller consulting firms that specialize in specific areas, such as biotechnology, healthcare, information technology, human resources, engineering, and marketing. Growth in the number of individual practitioners may be hindered, however, by increasing use of consulting teams, which permits examination of a variety of different issues and problems within an organization.

Employment growth of management analysts and consultants has been driven by a number of changes in the business environment that have forced firms to take a closer look at their operations. These changes include developments in information technology and the growth of electronic commerce. Traditional companies hire analysts to help design intranets or company Web sites, or establish online businesses. New Internet start-up companies hire analysts not only to design Web sites, but also to advise them in more traditional business practices, such as pricing strategies, marketing, and inventory and human resource management. In order to offer clients better quality and a wider variety of services, consulting firms are partnering with traditional computer software and technology firms. Also, many computer firms are developing consulting practices of their own in order to take advantage of this expanding market. Although information technology consulting should remain one of the fastest growing consulting areas, the volatility of the computer services industry necessitates that the most successful management analysts have knowledge of traditional business practices in addition to computer applications, systems integration, and Web design and management skills.

The growth of international business also has contributed to an increase in demand for management analysts. As U.S. firms expand their business abroad, many will hire management analysts to help them form the right strategy for entering the market; advise on legal matters pertaining to specific countries; or help with organizational, administrative, and other issues, especially if the U.S. company is involved in a partnership or merger with a local firm. These trends provide management analysts with more opportunities to travel or work abroad, but also require them to have a more comprehensive knowledge of international business and foreign cultures and languages.

Furthermore, as international and domestic markets have become more competitive, firms have needed to use resources more efficiently. Management analysts increasingly are sought to help reduce costs, streamline operations, and develop marketing strategies. As this process continues and businesses downsize, even more opportunities will be created for analysts to perform duties that previously were handled internally. Finally, management analysts also will be in greater demand in the public sector, as federal, state, and local government agencies seek ways to become more efficient.

Though management consultants are continually expanding their services, employment growth could be hampered by increasing competition for clients from occupations that do not traditionally perform consulting work, such as accountants, financial analysts, lawyers, and computer systems analysts. Furthermore, economic downturns also can have adverse effects on employment for some management consultants. In these times, businesses look to cut costs and consultants can be considered excess expense. On the other hand, some consultants might experience an increase in work during recessions because they advise businesses on how to cut costs and remain profitable.

Earnings

Salaries for management analysts vary widely by years of experience and education, geographic location, sector of expertise, and size of employer. Generally, management analysts employed in large firms or in metropolitan areas have the highest salaries. Median annual wage and salary earnings of management analysts in 2002 were $60,340. The middle 50 percent earned between $46,160 and $83,590. The lowest 10 percent earned less than $35,990, and the highest 10 percent earned more than $115,670. Median annual earnings in the industries employing the largest numbers of management analysts and consultants in 2002 were:

Management, scientific, and technical consulting services	$71,790
Computer systems design and related services	66,120
Federal government	65,480
Insurance carriers	51,780
State government	47,340

According to a 2002 survey by the Association of Management Consulting Firms, earnings—including bonuses and profit sharing—averaged $47,826 for research associates in member firms; $61,496 for entry-level consultants, $78,932 for management consultants, $112,716 for senior consultants, $168,998 for junior partners, and $254,817 for senior partners.

Salaried management analysts usually receive common benefits such as health and life insurance, a retirement plan, vacation, and sick leave, as well as less common benefits such as profit sharing and bonuses for outstanding work. In addition, all travel expenses usually are reimbursed by the employer. Self-employed consultants have to maintain their own office and provide their own benefits.

Related Occupations

Management analysts collect, review, and analyze data; make recommendations; and implement their ideas. Occupations with similar duties include accountants and auditors; budget analysts; cost estimators; financial analysts and personal financial advisors; operations research analysts; economists; and market and survey researchers. Some management analysts specialize in information technology and work with computers, as do computer systems analysts, database administrators, and computer scientists. Most management analysts also have managerial experience similar to that of administrative services managers; advertising, marketing, promotions, public relations, and sales managers; financial managers; human resources, training, and labor relations managers and specialists; and top executives.

Sources of Additional Information

Information about career opportunities in management consulting is available from:

- Association of Management Consulting Firms, 380 Lexington Ave., Suite 1700, New York, NY 10168. Internet: http://www.amcf.org

Information about the Certified Management Consultant designation can be obtained from:

- Institute of Management Consultants USA, Inc., 2025 M St. NW., Suite 800, Washington DC 20036. Internet: http://www.imcusa.org

Information on obtaining a management analyst position with the federal government is available from the Office of Personnel Management (OPM) through a telephone-based system. Consult your telephone directory under U.S. Government for a local number or call (703) 724-1850; Federal Relay Service: (800) 877-8339. The first number is not toll free, and charges may result. Information also is available from the OPM Internet site: http://www.usajobs.opm.gov.

Market and Survey Researchers

(O*NET 19-3021.00 and 19-3022.00)

Significant Points

- Strong demand is expected for market and survey researchers.
- A master's degree is the minimum requirement for many private sector jobs.
- Quantitative skills are critical.

Nature of the Work

Market, or marketing research analysts are concerned with the potential sales of a product or service. They analyze statistical data on past sales to predict future sales. They gather data on competitors and analyze prices, sales, and methods of marketing and distribution. Market research analysts devise methods and procedures for obtaining the data they need. They often design telephone, mail, or Internet surveys to assess consumer preferences. Some surveys are conducted as personal interviews by going door-to-door, leading focus group discussions, or setting up booths in public places such as shopping malls. Trained interviewers, under the market research analyst's direction, usually conduct the surveys.

After compiling the data, market research analysts evaluate them and make recommendations to their client or employer based upon their findings. They provide a company's management with information needed to make decisions on the promotion, distribution, design, and pricing of products or services. The information may also be used to determine the advisability of adding new lines of merchandise, opening new branches, or otherwise diversifying the company's operations. Market research analysts might also develop advertising brochures and commercials, sales plans, and product promotions such as rebates and giveaways.

Survey researchers design and conduct surveys for a variety of clients such as corporations, government agencies, political candidates, and service providers. They use surveys to collect information that is used for research, making fiscal or policy decisions, measuring policy effectiveness, and improving customer satisfaction. Analysts may conduct opinion research to determine public attitudes on various issues, which may help political or business leaders and others assess public support for their electoral prospects or social policies. Like market research analysts, survey researchers may use a variety of mediums to conduct surveys, such as the Internet, personal or telephone interviews, or mail questionnaires. They also may supervise interviewers who conduct surveys in person or over the telephone.

Survey researchers design surveys in many different formats, depending upon the scope of research and method of collection. Interview surveys, for example, are common because they can increase survey participation rates. Survey researchers may consult with economists, statisticians, market research analysts, or other data users in order to design surveys. They also may present survey results to clients.

Working Conditions

Market and survey researchers generally have structured work schedules. Some often work alone, writing reports, preparing statistical charts, and using computers, but they also may be an integral part of a research team. Market researchers who conduct personal interviews will have frequent contact with the public. Most work under pressure of deadlines and tight schedules, which may require overtime. Their routine may be interrupted by special requests for data, as well as by the need to attend meetings or conferences. Travel may be necessary.

Employment

Market and survey researchers held about a total of 155,000 jobs in 2002. Most of these jobs were held by market research analysts, who held 135,000 jobs. Private industry provided about 97 percent of salaried market research analyst jobs. Because of the applicability of market research to many industries, market research analysts are employed in most industries. The industries which employ the largest number of market research analysts are management, scientific, and technical consulting firms, insurance carriers, computer systems design and related firms, software publishers, securities and commodities brokers, and advertising and related firms.

Survey researchers held about 20,000 jobs in 2002. Survey researchers were mainly employed by professional, scientific, and technical services firms, including management, scientific and technical consulting firms, and scientific research and development firms; employment services, state government, and internet service providers and web search portals. A number of market and survey researchers combine a full-time job in government, academia, or business with part-time or consulting work in another setting. About 8 percent of market and survey researchers are self-employed.

Besides the jobs described above, many market and survey researchers held faculty positions in colleges and universities. Marketing faculties have flexible work schedules and may divide their time among teaching, research, consulting, and administration.

Training, Other Qualifications, and Advancement

A master's degree is the minimum requirement for many private sector market and survey research jobs, and for advancement to more responsible positions. Market and survey researchers may earn advanced degrees in business administration, marketing, statistics, communications, or some closely related discipline. Some schools help graduate students find internships or part-time employment in government agencies, consulting firms, financial institutions, or marketing research firms prior to graduation.

In addition to courses in business, marketing, and consumer behavior, prospective market and survey researchers should take other liberal arts and social science courses, including economics, psychology, English, and sociology. Because of the importance of quantitative skills to market and survey researchers, courses in mathematics, statistics, sampling theory and survey design, and computer science are extremely helpful.

Bachelor's degree holders who majored in marketing and related fields may qualify for many entry-level positions that might or might not be related to market and survey research. These positions include research assistant, administrative or management trainee, marketing interviewer, and salesperson, among others. Many businesses, research and consulting firms, and government agencies seek individuals who have strong computer and quantitative skills and can perform complex research. Many corporation and government executives have a strong background in marketing.

In addition to being required for most market and survey research jobs in business and industry, a master's degree is usually the minimum requirement for a job as an instructor in junior and community colleges. In most colleges and universities, however, a Ph.D. is necessary for appointment as an instructor. A Ph.D. and extensive publications in academic journals are required for a professorship, tenure, and promotion.

Aspiring market and survey researchers should gain experience gathering and analyzing data, conducting interviews or surveys, and writing reports on their findings while in college. This experience can prove invaluable later in obtaining a full-time position in the field, because much of the work, in the beginning, may center on these duties. With experience, market and survey researchers eventually are assigned their own research projects.

Those considering careers as market and survey researchers should be able to pay attention to details because much time is spent on precise data analysis. Patience and persistence are necessary qualities because market and survey researchers must spend long hours on independent study and problem solving. At the same time, they must work well with others, because they often oversee interviews of a wide variety of individuals. Communication skills are very important because market and survey researchers must be able to present their findings both orally and in writing, in a clear, concise manner.

Job Outlook

Employment of market and survey researchers is expected to grow faster than the average for all occupations through 2012. Many job openings are likely to result from the need to replace experienced workers who transfer to other occupations or who retire or leave the labor force for other reasons. Opportunities should be best for those with a master's or Ph.D. degree in marketing or a related field and strong quantitative skills.

Demand for market research analysts should be strong because of an increasingly competitive economy. Marketing research provides organizations valuable feedback from purchasers, allowing companies to evaluate consumer satisfaction and more effectively plan for the future. As companies seek to expand their market and as consumers become better informed, the need for marketing professionals will increase. As globalization of the marketplace continues, market researchers will also be increasingly utilized to analyze foreign markets and competition for goods and services.

Market research analysts should have opportunities in a wide range of employment settings, particularly in marketing research firms, as companies find it more profitable to contract for marketing research services rather than support their own marketing department. Increasingly, marketing research analysts are not only collecting and analyzing information, but are also helping the client implement their ideas and recommendations. Other organizations, including computer systems design companies, financial services organizations, healthcare institutions, advertising firms, manufacturing firms producing consumer goods, and insurance companies may offer job opportunities for market research analysts. Survey researchers will be needed to meet the growing demand for market and opinion research, as an increasingly competitive economy requires businesses to more effectively and efficiently allocate advertising funds.

Bachelor's degree holders may face competition for the limited number of market and survey research jobs for which they are eligible. However, they will qualify for a number of other positions, however, in which they can take advantage of their knowledge in conducting research, developing surveys, or analyzing data. Some graduates with bachelor's degrees will find jobs in industry and business as management or sales trainees or as administrative assistants. Bachelor's degree holders with good quantitative skills, including a strong background in mathematics, statistics, survey design, and computer science, may be hired by private firms as research assistants or interviewers.

Ph.D. degree holders in marketing and related fields should have a range of opportunities in industry and consulting firms. As in many other disciplines, however, Ph.D. holders are likely to face keen competition for tenured teaching positions in colleges and universities.

Earnings

Median annual earnings of market research analysts in 2002 were $53,810. The middle 50 percent earned between $38,760and $76,310. The lowest 10 percent earned less than $29,390, and the highest 10 percent earned more than $100,160. Median annual earnings in the industries employing the largest numbers of market research analysts in 2002 were as follows:

Management of companies and enterprises $56,750

Insurance carriers 46,700

Other professional, scientific, and technical
  services 46,380

Management, scientific, and technical
  consulting services 44,580

Median annual earnings of survey researchers in 2002 were $22,200. The middle 50 percent earned between $17,250 and $38,530. The lowest 10 percent earned less than $15,140, and the highest 10 percent earned more than $57,080. Median annual earnings of survey researchers in 2002 in other professional, scientific, and technical services were $19,610.

Related Occupations

Market and survey researchers do research to find out how well the market receives products or services. This may include planning, implementation, and analysis of surveys to determine people's needs and preferences. Other jobs using these skills include economists, psychologists, sociologists, statisticians, and urban and regional planners.

Sources of Additional Information

For information about careers and salaries in market and survey research, contact:

- Marketing Research Association, 1344 Silas Deane Hwy., Suite 306, Rocky Hill, CT 06067-0230. Internet: http://www.mra-net.org

- Council of American Survey Research Organizations, 3 Upper Devon, Port Jefferson, NY 11777. Internet: http://www.casro.org

Materials Engineers

(O*NET 17-2131.00)

Significant Points

- Overall, job opportunities in engineering are expected to be good, but will vary by specialty.

- A bachelor's degree is required for most entry-level jobs.

- Starting salaries are significantly higher than those of college graduates in other fields.

- Continuing education is critical to keep abreast of the latest technology.

Nature of the Work

Materials engineers are involved in the extraction, development, processing, and testing of the materials used to create a diversity of products, from computer chips and television screens to golf clubs and snow skis. They work with metals, ceramics, plastics, semiconductors, and combinations of materials called composites to create new materials that meet certain mechanical, electrical, and chemical requirements. They also are involved in selecting materials for new applications.

There are numerous new developments within materials engineering that make it possible to manipulate and use materials in various ways. For example, materials engineers have developed the ability to create and then study materials at an atomic level using advanced processes to replicate the characteristics of materials and their components with computers.

Most metallurgical engineers work in 1 of the 3 main branches of metallurgy—extractive or chemical, physical, and process. Extractive metallurgists are concerned with removing metals from ores and refining and alloying them to produce suitable inputs for a number of industrial processes. Physical metallurgists study the nature, structure, and physical properties of metals and their alloys to find the best methods of processing basic materials into final products. Process metallurgists develop and improve metalworking processes such as casting, forging, rolling, and drawing. Most materials engineers specialize in a particular material. For example, metallurgical engineers specialize in metals, while ceramic engineers develop ceramic materials and the processes for making ceramic materials into useful products. Ceramics include all nonmetallic, inorganic materials that generally require high temperatures in their processing. Ceramic engineers work on products as diverse as glassware, automobile and aircraft engine components, fiberoptic communication lines, tile, and electric insulators.

Working Conditions

Most engineers work in office buildings, laboratories, or industrial plants. Others may spend time outdoors at construction sites and oil and gas exploration and production sites, where they monitor or direct operations or solve onsite problems. Some engineers travel extensively to plants or worksites.

Many engineers work a standard 40-hour week. At times, deadlines or design standards may bring extra pressure to a job, sometimes requiring engineers to work longer hours.

Employment

Materials engineers held about 24,000 jobs in 2002. Because materials are building blocks for other goods, materials engineers are widely distributed among manufacturing industries. In fact, 68 percent of materials engineers worked in manufacturing industries, primarily computer and electronic products, transportation equipment, fabricated metal products, primary metal production, and machinery manufacturing. They also worked in services industries such as professional, scientific, and technical services. Most remaining materials engineers worked for federal and state governments.

Training, Other Qualifications, and Advancement

A bachelor's degree in engineering is required for almost all entry-level engineering jobs. College graduates with a degree in a physical science or mathematics occasionally may qualify for some engineering jobs, especially in specialties in high demand. Most engineering degrees are granted in electrical, electronics, mechanical, or civil engineering. However, engineers trained in one branch may work in related branches. For example, many aerospace engineers have training in mechanical engineering. This flexibility allows employers to meet staffing needs in new technologies and specialties in which engineers may be in short supply. It also allows engineers to shift to fields with better employment prospects or to those that more closely match their interests.

Most engineering programs involve a concentration of study in an engineering specialty, along with courses in both mathematics and science. Most programs include a design course, sometimes accompanied by a computer or laboratory class or both.

In addition to the standard engineering degree, many colleges offer 2- or 4-year degree programs in engineering technology. These programs, which usually include various hands-on laboratory classes that focus on current issues, prepare students for practical design and production work, rather than for jobs that require more theoretical and scientific knowledge. Graduates of 4-year technology programs may get jobs similar to those obtained by graduates with a bachelor's degree in engineering. Engineering technology graduates, however, are not qualified to register as professional engineers under the same terms as graduates with degrees in engineering. Some employers regard technology program graduates as having skills between those of a technician and an engineer.

Graduate training is essential for engineering faculty positions and many research and development programs, but is not required for the majority of entry-level engineering jobs. Many engineers obtain graduate degrees in engineering or business administration to learn new technology and broaden their education. Many high-level executives in government and industry began their careers as engineers.

About 340 colleges and universities offer bachelor's degree programs in engineering that are accredited by the Accreditation Board for Engineering and Technology (ABET), and about 240 colleges offer accredited bachelor's degree programs in engineering technology. ABET accreditation is based on an examination of an engineering program's student achievement, program improvement, faculty, curricular content, facilities, and institutional commitment. Although most institutions offer programs in the major branches of engineering, only a few offer programs in the smaller specialties. Also, programs of the same title may vary in content. For example, some programs emphasize industrial practices, preparing students for a job in industry, whereas others are more theoretical and are designed to prepare students for graduate work. Therefore, students should investigate curricula and check accreditations carefully before selecting a college.

Admissions requirements for undergraduate engineering schools include a solid background in mathematics (algebra, geometry, trigonometry, and calculus) and science (biology, chemistry, and physics), and courses in English, social studies, humanities, and computer and information technology. Bachelor's degree programs in engineering typically are designed to last 4 years, but many students find that it takes between 4 and 5 years to complete their studies. In a typical 4-year college curriculum, the first 2 years are spent studying mathematics, basic sciences, introductory engineering, humanities, and social sciences. In the last 2 years, most courses are in engineering, usually with a concentration in one branch. For example, the last 2 years of an aerospace program might include courses in fluid mechanics, heat transfer, applied aerodynamics, analytical mechanics, flight vehicle design, trajectory dynamics, and aerospace propulsion systems. Some programs offer a general engineering curriculum; students then specialize in graduate school or on the job.

Some engineering schools and 2-year colleges have agreements whereby the 2-year college provides the initial engineering education, and the engineering school automatically admits students for their last 2 years. In addition, a few engineering schools have arrangements whereby a student spends 3 years in a liberal arts college studying pre-engineering subjects and 2 years in an engineering school studying core subjects, and then receives a bachelor's degree from each school. Some colleges and universities offer 5-year master's degree programs. Some 5-year or even 6-year cooperative plans combine classroom study and practical work, permitting students to gain valuable experience and to finance part of their education.

All 50 states and the District of Columbia require licensure for engineers who offer their services directly to the public. Engineers who are licensed are called Professional Engineers (PE). This licensure generally requires a degree from an ABET-accredited engineering program, 4 years of relevant work experience, and successful completion of a state examination. Recent graduates can start the licensing process by taking the examination in two stages. The initial Fundamentals of Engineering (FE) examination can be taken upon graduation. Engineers who pass this examination commonly are called Engineers in Training (EIT) or Engineer Interns (EI). After acquiring suitable work experience, EITs can take the second examination, the Principles and Practice of Engineering exam. Several states have imposed mandatory continuing education requirements for relicensure. Most states recognize licensure from other states provided that the manner in which the initial license was obtained meets or exceeds their licensure requirements. Many civil, electrical, mechanical, and chemical engineers are licensed PEs.

Engineers should be creative, inquisitive, analytical, and detail-oriented. They should be able to work as part of a team and to communicate well, both orally and in writing.

Communication abilities are important because engineers often interact with specialists in a wide range of fields outside engineering.

Beginning engineering graduates usually work under the supervision of experienced engineers and, in large companies, also may receive formal classroom or seminar-type training. As new engineers gain knowledge and experience, they are assigned more difficult projects with greater independence to develop designs, solve problems, and make decisions. Engineers may advance to become technical specialists or to supervise a staff or team of engineers and technicians. Some may eventually become engineering managers or enter other managerial or sales jobs.

Job Outlook

Employment of materials engineers is expected to grow more slowly than the average for all occupations through 2012. Although many of the manufacturing industries in which materials engineers are concentrated are expected to experience declines in employment, more materials engineers will be needed to develop new materials for electronics, biotechnology, and plastics products. As manufacturing firms contract for their materials engineering needs, employment growth is expected in professional, scientific, and technical services industries. In addition to those arising from employment growth, job openings will result from the need to replace materials engineers who transfer to other occupations or leave the labor force.

Earnings

Median annual earnings of materials engineers were $62,590 in 2002. The middle 50 percent earned between $49,810 and $77,500. The lowest 10 percent earned less than $39,360, and the highest 10 percent earned more than $92,690.

According to a 2003 salary survey by the National Association of Colleges and Employers, bachelor's degree candidates in materials engineering received starting offers averaging $44,680 a year.

Related Occupations

Materials engineers apply the principles of physical science and mathematics in their work. Other workers who use scientific and mathematical principles include architects, except landscape and naval; engineering and natural sciences managers; computer and information systems managers; mathematicians; drafters; engineering technicians; sales engineers; science technicians; and physical and life scientists, including agricultural and food scientists, biological scientists, conservation scientists and foresters, atmospheric scientists, chemists and materials scientists, environmental scientists and geoscientists, and physicists and astronomers.

Sources of Additional Information

For information on careers, education, accreditation, and other topics related to materials engineers, contact:

- The Minerals, Metals, & Materials Society, 184 Thorn Hill Rd., Warrendale, PA 15086. Internet: http://www.tms.org

- ASM International, 9639 Kinsman Rd., Materials Park, OH 44073-0002. Internet: http://www.asm-intl.org

See the introduction to the section on engineers for information on working conditions, training requirements, and other sources of additional information.

Mechanical Engineers

(O*NET 17-2141.00)

Significant Points

- Overall, job opportunities in engineering are expected to be good, but will vary by specialty.

- A bachelor's degree is required for most entry-level jobs.

- Starting salaries are significantly higher than those of college graduates in other fields.

- Continuing education is critical to keep abreast of the latest technology.

Nature of the Work

Mechanical engineers research, develop, design, manufacture, and test tools, engines, machines, and other mechanical devices. They work on power-producing machines such as electric generators, internal combustion engines, and steam and gas turbines. They also develop power-using machines such as refrigeration and air-conditioning equipment, machine tools, material handling systems, elevators and escalators, industrial production equipment, and robots used in manufacturing. Mechanical engineers also design tools that other engineers need for their work. The field of nanotechnology, which involves the creation of high-performance materials and components by integrating atoms and molecules, is introducing entirely new principles to the design process.

Computers assist mechanical engineers by accurately and efficiently performing computations, and by permitting the modeling and simulation of new designs as well as facilitating changes to existing designs. Computer-Aided Design (CAD) and Computer-Aided Manufacturing (CAM) are used for design data processing and for turning the design into a product.

Mechanical engineers work in many industries, and their work varies by industry and function. Some specialize in energy systems; applied mechanics; automotive design; manufacturing; materials; plant engineering and maintenance; pressure vessels and piping; and heating, refrigeration, and air-conditioning systems. Mechanical engineering is one of the broadest engineering disciplines. Mechanical engineers may work in production operations in manufacturing or agriculture, maintenance, or technical sales; many are administrators or managers.

Working Conditions

Most engineers work in office buildings, laboratories, or industrial plants. Others may spend time outdoors at construction sites and oil and gas exploration and production sites, where they monitor or direct operations or solve onsite problems. Some engineers travel extensively to plants or worksites.

Many engineers work a standard 40-hour week. At times, deadlines or design standards may bring extra pressure to a job, sometimes requiring engineers to work longer hours.

Employment

Mechanical engineers held about 215,000 jobs in 2002. More than half of the jobs were in manufacturing—mostly in machinery, transportation equipment, computer and electronic products, and fabricated metal products manufacturing industries. Architectural, engineering, and related services, and the federal government provided many of the remaining jobs.

Training, Other Qualifications, and Advancement

A bachelor's degree in engineering is required for almost all entry-level engineering jobs. College graduates with a degree in a physical science or mathematics occasionally may qualify for some engineering jobs, especially in specialties in high demand. Most engineering degrees are granted in electrical, electronics, mechanical, or civil engineering. However, engineers trained in one branch may work in related branches. For example, many aerospace engineers have training in mechanical engineering. This flexibility allows employers to meet staffing needs in new technologies and specialties in which engineers may be in short supply. It also allows engineers to shift to fields with better employment prospects or to those that more closely match their interests.

Most engineering programs involve a concentration of study in an engineering specialty, along with courses in both mathematics and science. Most programs include a design course, sometimes accompanied by a computer or laboratory class or both.

In addition to the standard engineering degree, many colleges offer 2- or 4-year degree programs in engineering technology. These programs, which usually include various hands-on laboratory classes that focus on current issues, prepare students for practical design and production work, rather than for jobs that require more theoretical and scientific knowledge. Graduates of 4-year technology programs may get jobs similar to those obtained by graduates with a bachelor's degree in engineering. Engineering technology graduates, however, are not qualified to register as professional engineers under the same terms as graduates with degrees in engineering. Some employers regard technology program graduates as having skills between those of a technician and an engineer.

Graduate training is essential for engineering faculty positions and many research and development programs, but is not required for the majority of entry-level engineering jobs. Many engineers obtain graduate degrees in engineering or business administration to learn new technology and broaden their education. Many high-level executives in government and industry began their careers as engineers.

About 340 colleges and universities offer bachelor's degree programs in engineering that are accredited by the Accreditation Board for Engineering and Technology (ABET), and about 240 colleges offer accredited bachelor's degree programs in engineering technology. ABET accreditation is based on an examination of an engineering program's student achievement, program improvement, faculty, curricular content, facilities, and institutional commitment. Although most institutions offer programs in the major branches of engineering, only a few offer programs in the smaller specialties. Also, programs of the same title may vary in content. For example, some programs emphasize industrial practices, preparing students for a job in industry, whereas others are more theoretical and are designed to prepare students for graduate work. Therefore, students should investigate curricula and check accreditations carefully before selecting a college.

Admissions requirements for undergraduate engineering schools include a solid background in mathematics (algebra, geometry, trigonometry, and calculus) and science (biology, chemistry, and physics), and courses in English, social studies, humanities, and computer and information technology. Bachelor's degree programs in engineering typically are designed to last 4 years, but many students find that it takes between 4 and 5 years to complete their studies. In a typical 4-year college curriculum, the first 2 years are spent studying mathematics, basic sciences, introductory engineering, humanities, and social sciences. In the last 2 years, most courses are in engineering, usually with a concentration in one branch. For example, the last 2 years of an aerospace program might include courses in fluid mechanics, heat transfer, applied aerodynamics, analytical mechanics, flight vehicle design, trajectory dynamics, and aerospace propulsion systems. Some programs offer a general engineering curriculum; students then specialize in graduate school or on the job.

Some engineering schools and 2-year colleges have agreements whereby the 2-year college provides the initial engineering education, and the engineering school automatically admits students for their last 2 years. In addition, a few engineering schools have arrangements whereby a student spends 3 years in a liberal arts college studying

pre-engineering subjects and 2 years in an engineering school studying core subjects, and then receives a bachelor's degree from each school. Some colleges and universities offer 5-year master's degree programs. Some 5-year or even 6-year cooperative plans combine classroom study and practical work, permitting students to gain valuable experience and to finance part of their education.

All 50 states and the District of Columbia require licensure for engineers who offer their services directly to the public. Engineers who are licensed are called Professional Engineers (PE). This licensure generally requires a degree from an ABET-accredited engineering program, 4 years of relevant work experience, and successful completion of a state examination. Recent graduates can start the licensing process by taking the examination in two stages. The initial Fundamentals of Engineering (FE) examination can be taken upon graduation. Engineers who pass this examination commonly are called Engineers in Training (EIT) or Engineer Interns (EI). After acquiring suitable work experience, EITs can take the second examination, the Principles and Practice of Engineering exam. Several states have imposed mandatory continuing education requirements for relicensure. Most states recognize licensure from other states provided that the manner in which the initial license was obtained meets or exceeds their licensure requirements. Many civil, electrical, mechanical, and chemical engineers are licensed PEs.

Engineers should be creative, inquisitive, analytical, and detail-oriented. They should be able to work as part of a team and to communicate well, both orally and in writing. Communication abilities are important because engineers often interact with specialists in a wide range of fields outside engineering.

Beginning engineering graduates usually work under the supervision of experienced engineers and, in large companies, also may receive formal classroom or seminar-type training. As new engineers gain knowledge and experience, they are assigned more difficult projects with greater independence to develop designs, solve problems, and make decisions. Engineers may advance to become technical specialists or to supervise a staff or team of engineers and technicians. Some may eventually become engineering managers or enter other managerial or sales jobs.

Job Outlook

Employment of mechanical engineers is projected to grow more slowly than the average for all occupations though 2012. Although overall employment in manufacturing industries—where employment of mechanical engineers is concentrated—is expected to decrease slightly, employment of mechanical engineers in manufacturing should increase more rapidly as the demand for improved machinery and machine tools grows and as industrial machinery and processes become increasingly complex. Also, emerging technologies in biotechnology, materials science, and nanotechnology will create new job opportunities for mechanical engineers. Additional opportunities for mechanical engineers will arise because a degree in mechanical engineering often can be applied in other engineering specialties. In addition to job openings arising from growth, many openings should result from the need to replace workers who transfer to other occupations or leave the labor force.

Earnings

Median annual earnings of mechanical engineers were $62,880 in 2002. The middle 50 percent earned between $50,800 and $78,040. The lowest 10 percent earned less than $41,490, and the highest 10 percent earned more than $93,430. Median annual earnings in the industries employing the largest numbers of mechanical engineers in 2002 were:

Federal government $72,500

Architectural, engineering, and related
services 65,610

Navigational, measuring, electromedical, and
control instruments manufacturing 65,430

Aerospace products and parts manufacturing........65,160

Other general purpose machinery
manufacturing 55,850

According to a 2003 salary survey by the National Association of Colleges and Employers, bachelor's degree candidates in mechanical engineering received starting offers averaging $48,585 a year, master's degree candidates had offers averaging $54,565, and Ph.D. candidates were initially offered $69,904.

Related Occupations

Mechanical engineers apply the principles of physical science and mathematics in their work. Other workers who use scientific and mathematical principles include architects, except landscape and naval; engineering and natural sciences managers; computer and information systems managers; mathematicians; drafters; engineering technicians; sales engineers; science technicians; and physical and life scientists, including agricultural and food scientists, biological scientists, conservation scientists and foresters, atmospheric scientists, chemists and materials scientists, environmental scientists and geoscientists, and physicists and astronomers.

Sources of Additional Information

General information about mechanical engineers as well as information on careers, education, and training is available from:

● The American Society of Mechanical Engineers, 3 Park Ave., New York, NY 10016. Internet: http://www.asme.org

Information about heating, refrigeration, and air-conditioning engineering, a mechanical engineering specialty, is available from:

● American Society of Heating, Refrigerating, and Air-Conditioning Engineers, Inc., 1791 Tullie Circle NE., Atlanta, GA 30329. Internet: http://www.ashrae.org

Information about automotive engineering, a mechanical engineering specialty, is available from:

● Society of Automotive Engineers, 400 Commonwealth Dr., Warrendale, PA 15096-0001. Internet: http://www.sae.org

See the introduction to the section on engineers for information on working conditions, training requirements, and other sources of additional information.

Mathematicians

(O*NET 15-2021.00)

Significant Points

● A Ph.D. degree in mathematics usually is the minimum education needed, except in the federal government.

● Employment is expected to contract, reflecting the decline in the number of jobs with the title mathematician; competition will be keen for the limited number of jobs.

● Master's and Ph.D. degree holders with a strong background in mathematics and a related discipline, such as computer science or engineering, should have better employment opportunities in related occupations.

Nature of the Work

Mathematics is one of the oldest and most fundamental sciences. Mathematicians use mathematical theory, computational techniques, algorithms, and the latest computer technology to solve economic, scientific, engineering, physics, and business problems. The work of mathematicians falls into two broad classes—theoretical (pure) mathematics and applied mathematics. These classes, however, are not sharply defined, and often overlap.

Theoretical mathematicians advance mathematical knowledge by developing new principles and recognizing previously unknown relationships between existing principles of mathematics. Although these workers seek to increase basic knowledge without necessarily considering its practical use, such pure and abstract knowledge has been instrumental in producing or furthering many scientific and engineering achievements. Many theoretical mathematicians are employed as university faculty, and divide their time between teaching and conducting research.

Applied mathematicians, on the other hand, use theories and techniques, such as mathematical modeling and computational methods, to formulate and solve practical problems in business, government, and engineering and in the physical, life, and social sciences. For example, they may analyze the most efficient way to schedule airline routes between cities, the effect and safety of new drugs, the aerodynamic characteristics of an experimental automobile, or the cost-effectiveness of alternative manufacturing processes. Applied mathematicians working in industrial research and development may develop or enhance mathematical methods when solving a difficult problem. Some mathematicians, called cryptanalysts, analyze and decipher encryption systems designed to transmit military, political, financial, or law enforcement-related information in code.

Applied mathematicians start with a practical problem, envision the separate elements of the process under consideration, and then reduce the elements to mathematical variables. They often use computers to analyze relationships among the variables and solve complex problems by developing models with alternative solutions.

Much of the work in applied mathematics is done by individuals with titles other than mathematician. In fact, because mathematics is the foundation upon which so many other academic disciplines are built, the number of workers using mathematical techniques is much greater than the number formally designated as mathematicians. For example, engineers, computer scientists, physicists, and economists are among those who use mathematics extensively. Some professionals, including statisticians, actuaries, and operations research analysts, actually are specialists in a particular branch of mathematics. Frequently, applied mathematicians are required to collaborate with other workers in their organizations to achieve common solutions to problems.

Working Conditions

Mathematicians usually work in comfortable offices. They often are part of an interdisciplinary team that may include economists, engineers, computer scientists, physicists, technicians, and others. Deadlines, overtime work, special requests for information or analysis, and prolonged travel to attend seminars or conferences may be part of their jobs. Mathematicians who work in academia usually have a mix of teaching and research responsibilities. These mathematicians often conduct research alone, or are aided by graduate students interested in the topic being researched.

Employment

Mathematicians held about 2,900 jobs in 2002. In addition, about 20,000 persons held full-time mathematics faculty positions in colleges and universities in 2002, according to the American Mathematical Society.

Many nonfaculty mathematicians work for federal or state governments. The U.S. Department of Defense is the primary federal employer, accounting for about three-fourths of the mathematicians employed by the federal government. Most other mathematicians employed by the federal government work for the National Aeronautics and Space

Administration (NASA). In the private sector, major employers include insurance carriers, scientific research and development services, and management, scientific, and technical consulting services. Within manufacturing, the aerospace and pharmaceutical industries are the key employers. Some mathematicians also work for investment banks, insurance companies, and securities and commodity exchanges.

Training, Other Qualifications, and Advancement

A Ph.D. degree in mathematics usually is the minimum education needed for prospective mathematicians, except in the federal government. In the federal government, entry-level job candidates usually must have a 4-year degree with a major in mathematics or a 4-year degree with the equivalent of a mathematics major—24 semester hours of mathematics courses.

In private industry, candidates for mathematician jobs typically need a master's or Ph.D. degree. Most of the positions designated for mathematicians are in research and development laboratories, as part of technical teams. Research scientists in such positions engage either in basic research on pure mathematical principles or in applied research on developing or improving specific products or processes. The majority of those with a bachelor's or master's degree in mathematics who work in private industry do so not as mathematicians, but in related fields such as computer science, where they have titles such as computer programmer, systems analyst, or systems engineer.

A bachelor's degree in mathematics is offered by most colleges and universities. Mathematics courses usually required for this degree include calculus, differential equations, and linear and abstract algebra. Additional courses might include probability theory and statistics, mathematical analysis, numerical analysis, topology, discrete mathematics, and mathematical logic. Many colleges and universities urge or require students majoring in mathematics to take courses in a field that is closely related to mathematics, such as computer science, engineering, life science, physical science, or economics. A double major in mathematics and another related discipline is particularly desirable to many employers. High school students who are prospective college mathematics majors should take as many mathematics courses as possible while in high school.

In 2003, about 225 colleges and universities offered a master's degree as the highest degree in either pure or applied mathematics; about 200 offered a Ph.D. degree in pure or applied mathematics. In graduate school, students conduct research and take advanced courses, usually specializing in a subfield of mathematics.

For jobs in applied mathematics, training in the field in which the mathematics will be used is very important. Mathematics is used extensively in physics, actuarial science, statistics, engineering, and operations research. Computer science, business and industrial management, economics, finance, chemistry, geology, life sciences, and behavioral sciences are likewise dependent on applied mathematics. Mathematicians also should have substantial knowledge of computer programming, because most complex mathematical computation and much mathematical modeling are done on a computer.

Mathematicians need good reasoning ability and persistence in order to identify, analyze, and apply basic principles to technical problems. Communication skills are important, as mathematicians must be able to interact and discuss proposed solutions with people who may not have an extensive knowledge of mathematics.

Job Outlook

Competition is keen for the limited number of jobs as mathematicians. Employment of mathematicians is expected to decline through 2012, reflecting the decline in the number of jobs with the title mathematician. However, master's and Ph.D. degree holders with a strong background in mathematics and a related discipline, such as engineering or computer science, should have better opportunities. Many of these workers have job titles that reflect their occupation, such as systems analyst, rather than the title mathematician, reflecting their primary educational background.

Advancements in technology usually lead to expanding applications of mathematics, and more workers with knowledge of mathematics will be required in the future. However, jobs in industry and government often require advanced knowledge of related scientific disciplines in addition to mathematics. The most common fields in which mathematicians study and find work are computer science and software development, physics, engineering, and operations research. More mathematicians also are becoming involved in financial analysis. Mathematicians must compete for jobs, however, with people who have degrees in these other disciplines. The most successful jobseekers will be able to apply mathematical theory to real-world problems, and possess good communication, teamwork, and computer skills.

Private industry jobs require at least a master's degree in mathematics or in one of the related fields. Bachelor's degree holders in mathematics usually are not qualified for most jobs, and many seek advanced degrees in mathematics or a related discipline. However, bachelor's degree holders who meet state certification requirements may become primary or secondary school mathematics teachers.

Holders of a master's degree in mathematics will face very strong competition for jobs in theoretical research. Because the number of Ph.D. degrees awarded in mathematics continues to exceed the number of university positions available, many of these graduates will need to find employment in industry and government.

Earnings

Median annual earnings of mathematicians were $76,470 in 2002. The middle 50 percent earned between $56,160 and

$91,520. The lowest 10 percent had earnings of less than $38,930, while the highest 10 percent earned over $112,780.

According to a 2003 survey by the National Association of Colleges and Employers, starting salary offers averaged $40,512 a year for mathematics graduates with a bachelor's degree, and $42,348 for those with a master's degree. Doctoral degree candidates averaged $55,485.

In early 2003, the average annual salary for mathematicians employed by the federal government in supervisory, non-supervisory, and managerial positions was $80,877; that for mathematical statisticians was $83,472; and for cryptanalysts, the average was $78,662.

Related Occupations

Other occupations that require extensive knowledge of mathematics or, in some cases, a degree in mathematics include actuaries; statisticians; computer programmers; computer systems analysts, database administrators, and computer scientists; computer software engineers; and operations research analysts. A strong background in mathematics also facilitates employment as teachers—postsecondary; teachers—preschool, kindergarten, middle, elementary, and secondary; engineers; economists; market and survey researchers; financial analysts and personal financial advisors; and physicists and astronomers.

Sources of Additional Information

For more information about careers and training in mathematics, especially for doctoral-level employment, contact:

- American Mathematical Society, 201 Charles St., Providence, RI 02940. Internet: http://www.ams.org

For specific information on careers in applied mathematics, contact:

- Society for Industrial and Applied Mathematics, 3600 University City Science Center, Philadelphia, PA 19104-2688. Internet: http://www.siam.org

Information on obtaining a mathematician position with the federal government is available from the Office of Personnel Management (OPM) through a telephone-based system. Consult your telephone directory under U.S. government for a local number or call (703) 724-1850; Federal Relay Service: (800) 877-8339. The first number is not toll free, and charges may result. Information also is available from the OPM Internet site: http://www.usajobs.opm.gov.

Medical Assistants

(O*NET 31-9092.00)

Significant Points

- Some medical assistants are trained on the job, but many complete 1- or 2-year programs in vocational-technical high schools, postsecondary vocational schools, and community and junior colleges.

- Medical assistants is projected to be the fastest growing occupation over the 2002-12 period.

- Job prospects should be best for medical assistants with formal training or experience, particularly those with certification.

Nature of the Work

Medical assistants perform routine administrative and clinical tasks to keep the offices of physicians, podiatrists, chiropractors, and other health practitioners running smoothly. They should not be confused with physician assistants, who examine, diagnose, and treat patients under the direct supervision of a physician.

The duties of medical assistants vary from office to office, depending on the location and size of the practice and the practitioner's specialty. In small practices, medical assistants usually are "generalists," handling both administrative and clinical duties and reporting directly to an office manager, physician, or other health practitioner. Those in large practices tend to specialize in a particular area, under the supervision of department administrators.

Medical assistants perform many administrative duties, including answering telephones, greeting patients, updating and filing patients' medical records, filling out insurance forms, handling correspondence, scheduling appointments, arranging for hospital admission and laboratory services, and handling billing and bookkeeping.

Clinical duties vary according to state law and include taking medical histories and recording vital signs, explaining treatment procedures to patients, preparing patients for examination, and assisting the physician during the examination. Medical assistants collect and prepare laboratory specimens or perform basic laboratory tests on the premises, dispose of contaminated supplies, and sterilize medical instruments. They instruct patients about medications and special diets, prepare and administer medications as directed by a physician, authorize drug refills as directed, telephone prescriptions to a pharmacy, draw blood, prepare patients for x rays, take electrocardiograms, remove sutures, and change dressings.

Medical assistants also may arrange examining-room instruments and equipment, purchase and maintain supplies and equipment, and keep waiting and examining rooms neat and clean.

Assistants who specialize have additional duties. *Podiatric medical assistants* make castings of feet, expose and develop x rays, and assist podiatrists in surgery. *Ophthalmic medical assistants* help ophthalmologists provide eye care. They conduct diagnostic tests, measure and record vision, and test eye muscle function. They also show patients how to insert, remove, and care for contact lenses, and they apply eye dressings. Under the direction of the physician, ophthalmic medical assistants may administer eye medications. They also maintain optical and surgical instruments and may assist the ophthalmologist in surgery.

Working Conditions

Medical assistants work in well-lighted, clean environments. They constantly interact with other people and may have to handle several responsibilities at once.

Most full-time medical assistants work a regular 40-hour week. Some work part time, evenings, or weekends.

Employment

Medical assistants held about 365,000 jobs in 2002. Almost 60 percent worked in offices of physicians; about 14 percent worked in public and private hospitals, including inpatient and outpatient facilities; and almost 10 percent worked in offices of other health practitioners, such as chiropractors and podiatrists. The rest worked mostly in outpatient care centers, public and private educational services, other ambulatory healthcare services, state and local government agencies, medical and diagnostic laboratories, nursing care facilities, and employment services.

Training, Other Qualifications, and Advancement

Most employers prefer graduates of formal programs in medical assisting. Such programs are offered in vocational-technical high schools, postsecondary vocational schools, and community and junior colleges. Postsecondary programs usually last either 1 year, resulting in a certificate or diploma, or 2 years, resulting in an associate degree. Courses cover anatomy, physiology, and medical terminology, as well as typing, transcription, recordkeeping, accounting, and insurance processing. Students learn laboratory techniques, clinical and diagnostic procedures, pharmaceutical principles, the administration of medications, and first aid. They study office practices, patient relations, medical law, and ethics. Accredited programs include an internship that provides practical experience in physicians' offices, hospitals, or other healthcare facilities.

Two agencies recognized by the U.S. Department of Education accredit programs in medical assisting: The Commission on Accreditation of Allied Health Education Programs (CAAHEP) and the Accrediting Bureau of Health Education Schools (ABHES). In 2002, there were 495 medical assisting programs accredited by CAAHEP and about 170 accredited by ABHES. The Committee on Accreditation for Ophthalmic Medical Personnel approved 14 programs in ophthalmic medical assisting.

Formal training in medical assisting, while generally preferred, is not always required. Some medical assistants are trained on the job, although this practice is less common than in the past. Applicants usually need a high school diploma or the equivalent. Recommended high school courses include mathematics, health, biology, typing, bookkeeping, computers, and office skills. Volunteer experience in the healthcare field also is helpful.

Although medical assistants are not licensed, some states require them to take a test or a course before they can perform certain tasks, such as taking x rays. Employers prefer to hire experienced workers or certified applicants who have passed a national examination, indicating that the medical assistant meets certain standards of competence. The American Association of Medical Assistants awards the Certified Medical Assistant credential; the American Medical Technologists awards the Registered Medical Assistant credential; the American Society of Podiatric Medical Assistants awards the Podiatric Medical Assistant Certified credential; and the Joint Commission on Allied Health Personnel in Ophthalmology awards credentials at three levels: Certified Ophthalmic Assistant, Certified Ophthalmic Technician, and Certified Ophthalmic Medical Technologist.

Medical assistants deal with the public; therefore, they must be neat and well groomed and have a courteous, pleasant manner. Medical assistants must be able to put patients at ease and explain physicians' instructions. They must respect the confidential nature of medical information. Clinical duties require a reasonable level of manual dexterity and visual acuity.

Medical assistants may be able to advance to office manager. They may qualify for a variety of administrative support occupations or may teach medical assisting. With additional education, some enter other health occupations, such as nursing and medical technology.

Job Outlook

Employment of medical assistants is expected to grow much faster than the average for all occupations through the year 2012 as the health services industry expands because of technological advances in medicine, and a growing and aging population. Increasing utilization of medical assistants in the rapidly-growing healthcare industries will result in fast employment growth for the occupation. In fact, medical assistants is projected to be the fastest growing occupation over the 2002–12 period.

Employment growth will be driven by the increase in the number of group practices, clinics, and other healthcare facilities that need a high proportion of support personnel, particularly the flexible medical assistant who can handle both administrative and clinical duties. Medical assistants work primarily in outpatient settings, which are expected to exhibit much faster-than-average growth.

In view of the preference of many healthcare employers for trained personnel, job prospects should be best for medical assistants with formal training or experience, and particularly for those with certification.

Earnings

The earnings of medical assistants vary, depending on their experience, skill level, and location. Median annual earnings of medical assistants were $23,940 in 2002. The middle 50 percent earned between $20,260 and $28,410. The lowest 10 percent earned less than $17,640, and the highest 10 percent earned more than $34,130. Median annual earnings in the industries employing the largest numbers of medical assistants in 2002 were as follows:

General medical and surgical hospitals................$24,460

Offices of physicians 24,260

Outpatient care centers 23,980

Other ambulatory health care services 23,440

Offices of other health practitioners 21,620

Related Occupations

Workers in other medical support occupations include dental assistants, medical records and health information technicians, medical secretaries, occupational therapist assistants and aides, pharmacy aides, and physical therapist assistants and aides.

Sources of Additional Information

Information about career opportunities, educational programs in medical assisting accredited by the Commission on Accreditation of Allied Health Education Programs, and the Certified Medical Assistant exam is available from:

● American Association of Medical Assistants, 20 North Wacker Dr., Suite 1575, Chicago, IL 60606. Internet: http://www.aama-ntl.org

Information about career opportunities and the Registered Medical Assistant certification exam is available from:

● Registered Medical Assistants of American Medical Technologists, 710 Higgins Rd., Park Ridge, IL 60068-5765.

For a list of ABHES-accredited educational programs in medical assisting, contact:

● Accrediting Bureau of Health Education Schools, 7777 Leesburg Pike, Suite 314 N., Falls Church, VA 22043. Internet: http://www.abhes.org

Information about career opportunities, training programs, and the Certified Ophthalmic Assistant exam is available from:

● Joint Commission on Allied Health Personnel in Ophthalmology, 2025 Woodlane Dr., St. Paul, MN 55125-2998. Internet: http://www.jcahpo.org

Information about careers for podiatric assistants is available from:

● American Society of Podiatric Medical Assistants, 2124 S. Austin Blvd., Cicero, IL 60804. Internet: http://www.aspma.org

Medical Records and Health Information Technicians

(O*NET 29-2071.00)

Significant Points

- This is one of the few health occupations in which there is little or no direct contact with patients.

- Medical records and health information technicians entering the field usually have an associate degree; courses include anatomy, physiology, medical terminology, and computer science.

- Job prospects should be very good, particularly in offices of physicians.

Nature of the Work

Every time a patient receives healthcare, a record is maintained of the observations, medical or surgical interventions, and treatment outcomes. This record includes information that the patient provides concerning his or her symptoms and medical history, the results of examinations, reports of x rays and laboratory tests, diagnoses, and treatment plans. Medical records and health information technicians organize and evaluate these records for completeness and accuracy.

Technicians begin to assemble patients' health information by first making sure their initial medical charts are complete. They ensure that all forms are completed and properly identified and signed, and that all necessary information is in the computer. They regularly communicate with physicians or other healthcare professionals to clarify diagnoses or to obtain additional information.

Medical records and health information technicians assign a code to each diagnosis and procedure. They consult classification manuals and also rely on their knowledge of disease processes. Technicians then use computer software to assign the patient to one of several hundred "diagnosis-related groups," or DRGs. The DRG determines the amount for which the hospital will be reimbursed if the patient is covered by Medicare or other insurance programs using the DRG system. Technicians who specialize in coding are called health information coders, medical record coders, coder/abstractors, or coding specialists. In addition to the DRG system, coders use other coding systems, such as those geared towards ambulatory settings or long-term care.

Technicians also use computer programs to tabulate and analyze data to help improve patient care, to control costs, for use in legal actions, in response to surveys, or for use in research studies. Cancer registrars compile, maintain, and review records of cancer patients to provide information to physicians and for use in research studies.

Medical records and health information technicians' duties vary with the size of the facility. In large to medium-sized facilities, technicians may specialize in one aspect of health information, or supervise health information clerks and transcriptionists while a medical records and health information administrator manages the department. In small facilities, a credentialed medical records and health information technician sometimes manages the department.

Working Conditions

Medical records and health information technicians usually work a 40-hour week. Some overtime may be required. In hospitals—where health information departments often are open 24 hours a day, 7 days a week—technicians may work day, evening, and night shifts.

Medical records and health information technicians work in pleasant and comfortable offices. This is one of the few health occupations in which there is little or no direct contact with patients. Because accuracy is essential in their jobs, technicians must pay close attention to detail. Technicians who work at computer monitors for prolonged periods must guard against eyestrain and muscle pain.

Employment

Medical records and health information technicians held about 147,000 jobs in 2002. Thirty-seven percent of all jobs were in hospitals. The rest were mostly in offices of physicians, nursing care facilities, outpatient care centers, and home healthcare services. Insurance firms that deal in health matters employ a small number of health information technicians to tabulate and analyze health information. Public health departments also hire technicians to supervise data collection from healthcare institutions and to assist in research.

Training, Other Qualifications, and Advancement

Medical records and health information technicians entering the field usually have an associate degree from a community or junior college. In addition to general education, coursework includes medical terminology, anatomy and physiology, legal aspects of health information, coding and abstraction of data, statistics, database management, quality improvement methods, and computer science. Applicants can improve their chances of admission into a program by taking biology, chemistry, health, and computer science courses in high school.

Hospitals sometimes advance promising health information clerks to jobs as medical records and health information technicians, although this practice may be less common in the future. Advancement usually requires 2 to 4 years of job experience and completion of a hospital's in-house training program.

Most employers prefer to hire Registered Health Information Technicians (RHIT), who must pass a written examination offered by the American Health Information Management Association (AHIMA). To take the examination, a person must graduate from a 2-year associate degree program accredited by the Commission on Accreditation of Allied Health Education Programs (CAAHEP) of the American Medical Association. Technicians trained in non-CAAHEP-accredited programs, or on the job, are not eligible to take the examination. In 2003, CAAHEP accredited 182 programs for health information technicians. Technicians who specialize in coding may obtain voluntary certification.

Experienced medical records and health information technicians usually advance in one of two ways—by specializing or managing. Many senior technicians specialize in coding, particularly Medicare coding, or in cancer registry.

In large medical records and health information departments, experienced technicians may advance to section supervisor, overseeing the work of the coding, correspondence, or discharge sections, for example. Senior technicians with RHIT credentials may become director or assistant director of a medical records and health information department in a small facility. However, in larger institutions, the director is usually an administrator, with a bachelor's degree in medical records and health information administration.

Job Outlook

Job prospects should be very good. Employment of medical records and health information technicians is expected to grow much faster than the average for all occupations through 2012, due to rapid growth in the number of medical tests, treatments, and procedures that will be increasingly scrutinized by third-party payers, regulators, courts, and consumers.

Although employment growth in hospitals will not keep pace with growth in other healthcare industries, many new jobs will nevertheless be created. The fastest employment growth and a majority of the new jobs are expected in offices of physicians, due to increasing demand for detailed records, especially in large group practices. Rapid growth also is expected in nursing care facilities, home healthcare services, and outpatient care centers. Additional job openings will result from the need to replace technicians who retire or leave the occupation permanently.

Earnings

Median annual earnings of medical records and health information technicians were $23,890 in 2002. The middle 50 percent earned between $19,550 and $30,600. The lowest 10 percent earned less than $16,460, and the highest 10 percent earned more than $38,640. Median annual earnings in the industries employing the largest numbers of medical

records and health information technicians in 2002 were as follows:

Nursing care facilities	$25,160
General medical and surgical hospitals	24,910
Outpatient care centers	22,380
Offices of physicians	21,320

Related Occupations

Medical records and health information technicians need a strong clinical background to analyze the contents of medical records. Other workers who need knowledge of medical terminology, anatomy, and physiology, but have little or no direct contact with the patient, include medical secretaries and medical transcriptionists.

Sources of Additional Information

Information on careers in medical records and health information technology, including a list of programs accredited by the Commission on Accreditation of Allied Health Education Programs (CAAHEP), is available from:

- American Health Information Management Association, 233 N. Michigan Ave., Suite 2150, Chicago, IL 60601-5800. Internet: http://www.ahima.org

Medical Scientists

(O*NET 19-1041.00 and 19-1042.00)

Significant Points

- Epidemiologists typically require a master's degree in public health or, in some cases, a medical degree; other medical scientists need a Ph.D. degree in a biological science.

- Competition is expected for most positions.

- Most medical scientists work in research and development.

Nature of the Work

Medical scientists research human diseases in order to improve human health. Most medical scientists work in research and development. Some conduct basic research to advance knowledge of living organisms, including viruses, bacteria, and other infectious agents. Past research has resulted in the development of vaccines, medicines, and treatments for many diseases. Basic medical research continues to provide the building blocks necessary to develop solutions to human health problems. Medical scientists also engage in clinical investigation, technical writing, drug application review, patent examination, or related activities.

Medical scientists study biological systems to understand the causes of disease and other health problems and to develop treatments. They try to identify changes in a cell or chromosomes that signal the development of medical problems, such as different types of cancer. For example, a medical scientist involved in cancer research may formulate a combination of drugs that will lessen the effects of the disease. Medical scientists who are also physicians can administer these drugs to patients in clinical trials, monitor their reactions, and observe the results. Those who are not physicians normally collaborate with a physician who deals directly with patients. Medical scientists examine the results of clinical trials and, if necessary, adjust the dosage levels to reduce negative side effects or to try to induce even better results. In addition to developing treatments for health problems, medical scientists attempt to discover ways to prevent health problems, such as affirming the link between smoking and lung cancer, or between alcoholism and liver disease.

Many medical scientists work independently in private industry, university, or government laboratories, often exploring new areas of research or expanding on specialized research that they started in graduate school. Medical scientists working in colleges and universities, hospitals, and nonprofit medical research organizations typically submit grant proposals to obtain funding for their projects. Colleges and universities, private industry, and federal government agencies, such as the National Institutes of Health and the National Science Foundation, contribute to the support of scientists whose research proposals are determined to be financially feasible and have the potential to advance new ideas or processes.

Medical scientists who work in applied research or product development use knowledge provided by basic research to develop new drugs and medical treatments. They usually have less autonomy than basic researchers to choose the emphasis of their research, relying instead on market-driven directions based on the firm's products and goals. Medical scientists doing applied research and product development in private industry may be required to express their research plans or results to nonscientists who are in a position to veto or approve their ideas, and they must understand the impact of their work on business. Scientists increasingly work as part of teams, interacting with engineers, scientists of other disciplines, business managers, and technicians.

Medical scientists who conduct research usually work in laboratories and use electron microscopes, computers, thermal cyclers, or a wide variety of other equipment. Some may work directly with individual patients or larger groups as they administer drugs and monitor and observe the patients during clinical trials. Medical scientists who are also physicians may administer gene therapy to human patients, draw blood, excise tissue, or perform other invasive procedures.

Some medical scientists work in managerial, consulting, or administrative positions, usually after spending some time

doing research and learning about the firm, agency, or project. In the 1980s, swift advances in basic medical knowledge related to genetics and molecules spurred growth in the field of biotechnology. Medical scientists using this technology manipulate the genetic material of animals, attempting to make organisms more productive or resistant to disease. Research using biotechnology techniques, such as recombining DNA, has led to the discovery of important drugs, including human insulin and growth hormone. Many other substances not previously available in large quantities are now produced by biotechnological means; some may be useful in treating diseases such as Parkinson's or Alzheimer's. Today, many medical scientists are involved in the science of genetic engineering—isolating, identifying, and sequencing human genes and then determining their functionality. This work continues to lead to the discovery of the genes associated with specific diseases and inherited traits, such as certain types of cancer or obesity. These advances in biotechnology have opened up research opportunities in almost all areas of medical science.

Some medical scientists specialize in epidemiology. This branch of medical science investigates and describes the determinants of disease, disability, and other health outcomes and develops the means for prevention and control. Epidemiologists may study many different diseases such as tuberculosis, influenza, or cholera, often focusing on epidemics.

Epidemiologists can be separated into two groups, research and clinical. Research epidemiologists conduct basic and advanced research on infectious diseases that affect the entire body, such as AIDS or typhus—attempting to eradicate or control these diseases. Others may focus only on localized infections of the brain, lungs, or digestive tract, for example. Research epidemiologists work at colleges and universities, schools of public health, medical schools, and research and development services firms. For example, government agencies such as the Department of Defense may contract with a research firm's epidemiologists to evaluate the incidence of malaria in certain parts of the world. While some perform consulting services, other research epidemiologists may work as college and university faculty.

Clinical epidemiologists work primarily in consulting roles at hospitals, informing the medical staff of infectious outbreaks and providing containment solutions. These clinical epidemiologists sometimes are referred to as infection control professionals. Consequently, many epidemiologists in this specific area often are physicians. Epidemiologists who are not physicians often collaborate with physicians to find ways to contain diseases and outbreaks. In addition to traditional duties of studying and controlling diseases, clinical epidemiologists also may be required to develop standards and guidelines for the treatment and control of communicable diseases. Some clinical epidemiologists may work in outpatient settings.

Working Conditions

Medical scientists typically work regular hours in offices or laboratories and usually are not exposed to unsafe or unhealthy conditions. Those who work with dangerous organisms or toxic substances in the laboratory must follow strict safety procedures to avoid contamination. Medical scientists also spend time working in clinics and hospitals administering drugs and treatments to patients in clinical trials. On occasion, epidemiologists may be required to work evenings and weekends to attend meetings and hearings for medical investigations.

Some medical scientists depend on grant money to support their research. They may be under pressure to meet deadlines and to conform to rigid grant-writing specifications when preparing proposals to seek new or extended funding.

Employment

Medical scientists, including epidemiologists, held about 62,000 jobs in 2002. Medical scientists accounted for 58,000 of the total; epidemiologists, 3,900. In addition, many medical scientists held faculty positions in colleges and universities, but they are classified as college or university faculty.

Almost 30 percent of medical scientists were employed in scientific research and development services firms, another 24 percent worked in government, 14 percent in pharmaceutical and medicine manufacturing, 13 percent in private hospitals, and most of the remainder worked in private educational services and ambulatory health care services. About 1,000 were self-employed.

Among epidemiologists, nearly 45 percent were employed in government, another 20 percent worked in management, scientific, and technical consulting services firms, 14 percent in private hospitals, and 12 percent in scientific research and development services firms.

Training, Other Qualifications, and Advancement

A Ph.D. degree in a biological science is the minimum education required for most prospective medical scientists, except epidemiologists, because the work of medical scientists is almost entirely research oriented. A Ph.D. degree qualifies one to do research on basic life processes or on particular medical problems or diseases, and to analyze and interpret the results of experiments on patients. Some medical scientists obtain a medical degree instead of a Ph.D., but may not be licensed physicians because they have not taken the state licensing examination or completed a residency program, typically because they prefer research to clinical practice. Medical scientists who administer drug or gene therapy to human patients, or who otherwise interact medically with patients—drawing blood, excising tissue, or performing other invasive procedures—must be licensed physicians. To be licensed, physicians must graduate from an accredited medical school, pass a licensing examination, and complete 1 to 7 years of graduate medical education. It is particularly helpful for medical scientists to earn both Ph.D. and medical degrees.

Students planning careers as medical scientists should have a bachelor's degree in a biological science. In addition to required courses in chemistry and biology, undergraduates should study allied disciplines such as mathematics, physics, and computer science, or courses in their field of interest. Once they have completed undergraduate studies, they can then select a specialty area for their advanced degree, such as cytology, genomics, or pathology. In addition to formal education, medical scientists usually spend several years in a postdoctoral position before they apply for permanent jobs. Postdoctoral work provides valuable laboratory experience, including experience in specific processes and techniques such as gene splicing, which is transferable to other research projects. In some institutions, the postdoctoral position can lead to a permanent job.

Medical scientists should be able to work independently or as part of a team and be able to communicate clearly and concisely, both orally and in writing. Those in private industry, especially those who aspire to consulting and administrative positions, should possess strong communication skills so they can provide instruction and advice to physicians and other healthcare professionals.

The minimum educational requirement for epidemiology is a master's degree from a school of public health. Some jobs require a Ph.D. or medical degree, depending on the work performed. Epidemiologists who work in hospitals and healthcare centers often must have a medical degree with specific training in infectious diseases. Currently, 134 infectious disease training programs exist in 42 states. Some employees in research epidemiology positions are required to be licensed physicians, as they are required to administer drugs in clinical trials.

Epidemiologists who perform laboratory tests often require the knowledge and expertise of a licensed physician in order to administer drugs to patients in clinical trials. Epidemiologists who are not physicians frequently work closely with one.

Very few students select epidemiology for undergraduate study. Undergraduates, nonetheless, should study biological sciences and should have a solid background in chemistry, mathematics, and computer science. Once a student is prepared for graduate studies, he or she can choose a specialty within epidemiology. For example, those interested in studying environmental epidemiology should focus on environmental coursework, such as water pollution, air pollution, or pesticide use. The core work of environmental studies includes toxicology and molecular biology, and students may continue with advanced coursework in environmental or occupational epidemiology. Some epidemiologists are registered nurses and medical technologists seeking advancement.

Job Outlook

Employment of medical scientists is expected to grow faster than the average for all occupations through 2012. Despite projected rapid job growth for medical scientists, doctoral degree holders can expect to face considerable competition for basic research positions. The federal government funds much basic research and development, including many areas of medical research. Recent budget increases at the National Institutes of Health have led to large increases in federal basic research and development expenditures, with the number of grants awarded to researchers growing in number and dollar amount. At the same time, the number of newly trained medical scientists has continued to increase at least as fast as employment opportunities, so both new and established scientists have experienced greater difficulty winning and renewing research grants. If the number of advanced degrees awarded continues to grow unabated, as expected, this competitive situation is likely to persist.

Medical scientists enjoyed rapid gains in employment between the mid-1980s and mid-1990s, in part reflecting increased staffing requirements in new biotechnology companies. Employment growth should slow somewhat as increases in the number of new biotechnology firms slow and existing firms merge or are absorbed into larger ones. However, much of the basic medical research done in recent years has resulted in new knowledge, including the isolation and identification of new genes. Medical scientists will be needed to take this knowledge to the next stage, which is understanding how certain genes function within an entire organism, so that gene therapies can be developed to treat diseases. Even pharmaceutical and other firms not solely engaged in biotechnology are expected to increasingly use biotechnology techniques, thus creating employment for medical scientists.

Expected expansion in research related to health issues such as AIDS, cancer, and Alzheimer's disease also should result in employment growth. Although medical scientists greatly contributed to developing many vaccines and antibiotics, more medical research will be required to better understand these and other epidemics and to improve human health.

Opportunities in epidemiology also should be highly competitive, as the number of available positions remains limited. However, an increasing focus on monitoring patients at hospitals and healthcare centers to ensure positive patient outcomes will contribute to job growth. In addition, a heightened awareness of bioterrorism and infectious diseases such as West Nile Virus or SARS should also spur demand for these workers. As hospitals enhance their infection control programs, many will seek to boost the quality and quantity of their staff. Besides job openings due to employment growth, additional openings will result as workers leave the labor force or transfer to other occupations. Because employment of epidemiologists is somewhat tied to the healthcare industry, industry conditions will influence occupational demand.

Medical scientists and some epidemiologists are less likely to lose their jobs during recessions than are those in many other occupations because they are employed on long-term research projects. However, a recession could influence the amount of money allocated to new research and develop-ment efforts, particularly in areas of risky or innovative medical research. A recession also could limit the possibility of extension or renewal of existing projects.

Earnings

Median annual earnings of medical scientists, except epidemiologists, were $56,980 in 2002. The middle 50 percent earned between $40,180 and $82,720. The lowest 10 percent earned less than $29,980, and the highest 10 percent earned more than $114,640. Median annual earnings in the industries employing the largest numbers of medical scientists in 2002 were:

Pharmaceutical and medicine manufacturing	$72,330
Scientific research and development services	61,470
General medical and surgical hospitals	50,660
Colleges, universities, and professional schools	35,520

Median annual earnings of epidemiologists were $53,840 in 2002. The middle 50 percent earned between $44,900 and $66,510. The lowest 10 percent earned less than $35,910, and the highest 10 percent earned more than $85,930.

Related Occupations

Many other occupations deal with living organisms and require a level of training similar to that of medical scientists. These include biological scientists, agricultural and food scientists, and health occupations such as physicians and surgeons, dentists, and veterinarians.

Sources of Additional Information

For a brochure entitled *Is a Career in the Pharmaceutical Sciences Right for Me?*, contact:

● American Association of Pharmaceutical Scientists (AAPS), 2107 Wilson Blvd., Suite #700, Arlington, VA 22201.

For a career brochure entitled *A Million and One*, contact:

● American Society for Microbiology, Education Department, 1752 N St. NW, Washington, D.C. 20036-2804. Internet: http://www.asmusa.org

For information on infectious diseases training programs, contact:

● Infectious Diseases Society of America, Guide to Training Programs, 66 Canal Center Plaza, Suite # 600, Alexandria, VA 22314. Internet: http://www.idsociety.org

Information on obtaining a medical scientist position with the federal government is available from the Office of Personnel Management (OPM) through a telephone-based system. Consult your telephone directory under U.S. government for a local number or call (703) 724-1850; Federal Relay Service: (800) 877-8339. The first number is not toll free, and charges may result. Information also is available from the OPM Internet site: http://www.usajobs.opm.gov.

Medical Transcriptionists

(O*NET 31-9094.00)

Significant Points

- Job opportunities will be good.

- Employers prefer medical transcriptionists who have completed a postsecondary training program at a vocational school or community college.

- Many medical transcriptionists telecommute from home-based offices as employees or subcontractors for hospitals and transcription services or as self-employed, independent contractors.

- About 4 out of 10 worked in hospitals and another 3 out of 10 worked in offices of physicians.

Nature of the Work

Medical transcriptionists listen to dictated recordings made by physicians and other healthcare professionals and transcribe them into medical reports, correspondence, and other administrative material. They generally listen to recordings on a headset, using a foot pedal to pause the recording when necessary, and key the text into a personal computer or word processor, editing as necessary for grammar and clarity. The documents they produce include discharge summaries, history and physical examination reports, operative reports, consultation reports, autopsy reports, diagnostic imaging studies, progress notes, and referral letters. Medical transcriptionists return transcribed documents to the physicians or other healthcare professionals who dictated them for review and signature, or correction. These documents eventually become part of patients' permanent files.

To understand and accurately transcribe dictated reports into a format that is clear and comprehensible for the reader, medical transcriptionists must understand medical terminology, anatomy and physiology, diagnostic procedures, pharmacology, and treatment assessments. They also must be able to translate medical jargon and abbreviations into their expanded forms. To help identify terms appropriately, transcriptionists refer to standard medical reference materials—both printed and electronic; some of these are available over the Internet. Medical transcriptionists must comply with specific standards that apply to the style of medical records, in addition to the legal and ethical requirements involved with keeping patient information confidential.

Experienced transcriptionists spot mistakes or inconsistencies in a medical report and check to correct the information. Their ability to understand and correctly transcribe patient assessments and treatments reduces the chance of patients receiving ineffective or even harmful treatments and ensures high quality patient care.

Currently, most healthcare providers transmit dictation to medical transcriptionists using either digital or analog dictating equipment. The Internet has grown to be a popular mode for transmitting documentation. Many transcriptionists receive dictation over the Internet and are able to quickly return transcribed documents to clients for approval. Another emerging trend is the implementation of speech recognition technology, which electronically translates sound into text and creates drafts of reports. Reports are then formatted; edited for mistakes in translation, punctuation, or grammar; and checked for consistency and possible medical errors. Transcriptionists working in areas with standardized terminology, such as radiology or pathology, are more likely to encounter speech recognition technology. However, use of speech recognition technology will become more widespread as the technology becomes more sophisticated.

Medical transcriptionists who work in physicians' offices and clinics may have other office duties, such as receiving patients, scheduling appointments, answering the telephone, and handling incoming and outgoing mail. Medical secretaries may also transcribe as part of their jobs. Court reporters have similar duties, but with a different focus. They take verbatim reports of speeches, conversations, legal proceedings, meetings, and other events when written accounts of spoken words are necessary for correspondence, records, or legal proof.

Working Conditions

The majority of these workers are employed in comfortable settings, such as hospitals, physicians' offices, transcription service offices, clinics, laboratories, medical libraries, government medical facilities, or at home. Many medical transcriptionists telecommute from home-based offices as employees or subcontractors for hospitals and transcription services or as self-employed, independent contractors.

Work in this occupation presents hazards from sitting in the same position for long periods, and workers can suffer wrist, back, neck, or eye problems due to strain and risk repetitive motion injuries such as carpal tunnel syndrome. The pressure to be accurate and productive also can be stressful.

Many medical transcriptionists work a standard 40-hour week. Self-employed medical transcriptionists are more likely to work irregular hours—including part time, evenings, weekends, or on-call at any time.

Employment

Medical transcriptionists held about 101,000 jobs in 2002. About 4 out of 10 worked in hospitals and another 3 out of 10 worked in offices of physicians. Others worked for business support services, offices of other health practitioners, medical and diagnostic laboratories, outpatient care centers, and home healthcare services.

Training, Other Qualifications, and Advancement

Employers prefer to hire transcriptionists who have completed postsecondary training in medical transcription, offered by many vocational schools, community colleges, and distance-learning programs. Completion of a 2-year associate degree or 1-year certificate program—including coursework in anatomy, medical terminology, legal issues relating to healthcare documentation, and English grammar and punctuation—is highly recommended, but not always required. Many of these programs include supervised on-the-job experience. Some transcriptionists, especially those already familiar with medical terminology due to previous experience as a nurse or medical secretary, become proficient through on-the-job training.

The American Association for Medical Transcription (AAMT) awards the voluntary designation, Certified Medical Transcriptionist (CMT), to those who earn passing scores on written and practical examinations. As in many other fields, certification is recognized as a sign of competence. Because medical terminology is constantly evolving, medical transcriptionists are encouraged to regularly update their skills. Every 3 years, CMTs must earn continuing education credits to be recertified.

In addition to understanding medical terminology, transcriptionists must have good English grammar and punctuation skills, as well as proficiency with personal computers and word processing software. Normal hearing acuity and good listening skills also are necessary. Employers often require applicants to take pre-employment tests.

With experience, medical transcriptionists can advance to supervisory positions, home-based work, editing, consulting, or teaching. With additional education or training, some become medical records and health information technicians, medical coders, or medical records and health information administrators.

Job Outlook

Job opportunities will be good. Employment of medical transcriptionists is projected to grow faster than the average for all occupations through 2012. Demand for medical transcription services will be spurred by a growing and aging population. Older age groups receive proportionately greater numbers of medical tests, treatments, and procedures that require documentation. A high level of demand for transcription services also will be sustained by the continued need for electronic documentation that can be easily shared among providers, third-party payers, regulators, and consumers. Growing numbers of medical transcriptionists will be needed to amend patients' records, edit for grammar, and identify discrepancies in medical records.

Contracting out transcription work overseas and advancements in speech recognition technology are not expected to significantly reduce the need for well-trained medical transcriptionists domestically. Contracting out transcription work abroad—to countries such as India—has grown more popular as transmitting confidential health information over the Internet has become more secure; however, the demand for overseas transcription services is expected to supplement the demand for well-trained domestic medical transcriptionists. Speech-recognition technology allows physicians and other health professionals to dictate medical reports to a computer that immediately creates an electronic document. In spite of the advances in this technology, it has been difficult for the software to grasp and analyze the human voice and the English language with all its diversity. As a result, there will continue to be a need for skilled medical transcriptionists to identify and appropriately edit the inevitable errors created by speech recognition systems, and create a final document.

Hospitals will continue to employ a large percentage of medical transcriptionists, but job growth there will not be as fast as in other industries. Increasing demand for standardized records should result in rapid employment growth in offices of physicians or other health practitioners, especially in large group practices.

Earnings

Medical transcriptionists had median hourly earnings of $13.05 in 2002. The middle 50 percent earned between $10.87 and $15.63. The lowest 10 percent earned less than $9.27, and the highest 10 percent earned more than $17.97. Median hourly earnings in the industries employing the largest numbers of medical transcriptionists in 2002 were as follows:

General medical and surgical hospitals..................$13.20

Offices of physicians 13.00

Business support services.......................................12.42

Compensation methods for medical transcriptionists vary. Some are paid based on the number of hours they work or on the number of lines they transcribe. Others receive a base pay per hour with incentives for extra production. Employees of transcription services and independent contractors almost always receive production-based pay. Independent contractors earn more than transcriptionists who work for others but have higher expenses than their corporate counterparts, receive no benefits, and may face higher risk of termination than employed transcriptionists.

Related Occupations

A number of other workers type, record information, and process paperwork. Among these are Court reporters; human resources assistants, except payroll and timekeeping; receptionists and information clerks; and secretaries and administrative assistants. Other workers who provide medical support include medical assistants and medical records and health information technicians.

Sources of Additional Information

For information on a career as a medical transcriptionist, send a self-addressed, stamped envelope to:

- American Association for Medical Transcription, 100 Sycamore Ave., Modesto, CA 95354-0550. Internet: http://www.aamt.org

State employment service offices can provide information about job openings for medical transcriptionists.

Mining and Geological Engineers, Including Mining Safety Engineers

(O*NET 17-2151.00)

Significant Points

- Overall, job opportunities in engineering are expected to be good, but will vary by specialty.

- A bachelor's degree is required for most entry-level jobs.

- Starting salaries are significantly higher than those of college graduates in other fields.

- Continuing education is critical to keep abreast of the latest technology.

Nature of the Work

Mining and geological engineers find, extract, and prepare coal, metals, and minerals for use by manufacturing industries and utilities. They design open pit and underground mines, often using computers; supervise the construction of mine shafts and tunnels in underground operations; and devise methods for transporting minerals to processing plants. Mining engineers are responsible for the safe, economical, and environmentally sound operation of mines. Some mining engineers work with geologists and metallurgical engineers to locate and appraise new ore deposits. Others develop new mining equipment or direct mineral processing operations to separate minerals from the dirt, rock, and other materials with which they are mixed. Mining engineers frequently specialize in the mining of one mineral or metal, such as coal or gold. With increased emphasis on protecting the environment, many mining engineers work to solve problems related to land reclamation and water and air pollution.

Mining safety engineers use their knowledge of mine design and practices to ensure the safety of workers and to comply with state and federal safety regulations. They inspect walls and roof surfaces, test air samples, and examine mining equipment for compliance with safety practices.

Employment

Mining and geological engineers, including mining safety engineers, held about 5,200 jobs in 2002. While about 4 out of 10 mining engineers worked in the mining industry, over one-third worked in professional, scientific, and technical services firms, mostly providing consulting and other services to the mining industry. Most of the rest worked in state or federal government.

Mining engineers often are employed at the location of natural deposits, often near small communities, and sometimes outside the United States. Those in research and development, management, consulting, or sales, however, often are located in metropolitan areas.

Job Outlook

Despite a projected decline in employment, very good employment opportunities are expected in this small occupation. A significant number of mining engineers currently employed are approaching retirement age, which should create some job openings over the 2002-12 period. In addition, relatively few schools offer mining engineering programs, and the small number of graduates is not expected to increase.

Favorable job opportunities also may be available worldwide as mining operations around the world recruit graduates of U.S. mining engineering programs. As a result, some graduates should expect to travel frequently, or even live abroad.

Employment of mining and geological engineers, including mining safety engineers, is projected to decline through 2012. Most of the industries in which mining engineers are concentrated—such as coal, metal, and copper mining—are expected to experience declines in employment.

Earnings

Median annual earnings of mining and geological engineers, including mining safety engineers, were $61,770 in 2002. The middle 50 percent earned between $48,250 and $77,160. The lowest 10 percent earned less than $36,720, and the highest 10 percent earned more than $93,660.

According to a 2003 salary survey by the National Association of Colleges and Employers, bachelor's degree candidates in mining and mineral engineering (including geological) received starting offers averaging $44,326 a year.

Sources of Additional Information

For more information on careers, education, accreditation, and related topics for mining engineers, contact:

- The Society for Mining, Metallurgy, and Exploration, Inc., 8307 Shaffer Parkway, P.O. Box 277002, Littleton, CO 80127. Internet: http://www.smenet.org

See the introduction to the section on engineers for information on working conditions, training requirements, and other sources of additional information.

Nuclear Engineers

(O*NET 17-2161.00)

Significant Points

- Overall, job opportunities in engineering are expected to be good, but will vary by specialty.

- A bachelor's degree is required for most entry-level jobs.

- Starting salaries are significantly higher than those of college graduates in other fields.

- Continuing education is critical to keep abreast of the latest technology.

Nature of the Work

Nuclear engineers research and develop the processes, instruments, and systems used to derive benefits from nuclear energy and radiation. They design, develop, monitor, and operate nuclear plants used to generate power. They may work on the nuclear fuel cycle—the production, handling, and use of nuclear fuel and the safe disposal of waste produced by the generation of nuclear energy—or on the production of fusion energy. Some specialize in the development of nuclear power sources for spacecraft; others find industrial and medical uses for radioactive materials, such as equipment to diagnose and treat medical problems.

Working Conditions

Most engineers work in office buildings, laboratories, or industrial plants. Others may spend time outdoors at construction sites and oil and gas exploration and production sites, where they monitor or direct operations or solve onsite problems. Some engineers travel extensively to plants or worksites.

Many engineers work a standard 40-hour week. At times, deadlines or design standards may bring extra pressure to a job, sometimes requiring engineers to work longer hours.

Employment

Nuclear engineers held about 16,000 jobs in 2002. Almost half were employed in utilities, one-quarter in professional, scientific, and technical services firms, and 14 percent in the federal government. Many federally employed nuclear engineers were civilian employees of the U.S. Navy, and most of the rest worked for the U.S. Department of Energy.

Training, Other Qualifications, and Advancement

A bachelor's degree in engineering is required for almost all entry-level engineering jobs. College graduates with a degree in a physical science or mathematics occasionally may qualify for some engineering jobs, especially in specialties in high demand. Most engineering degrees are granted in electrical, electronics, mechanical, or civil engineering. However, engineers trained in one branch may work in related branches. For example, many aerospace engineers have training in mechanical engineering. This flexibility allows employers to meet staffing needs in new technologies and specialties in which engineers may be in short supply. It also allows engineers to shift to fields with better employment prospects or to those that more closely match their interests.

Most engineering programs involve a concentration of study in an engineering specialty, along with courses in both mathematics and science. Most programs include a design course, sometimes accompanied by a computer or laboratory class or both.

In addition to the standard engineering degree, many colleges offer 2- or 4-year degree programs in engineering technology. These programs, which usually include various hands-on laboratory classes that focus on current issues, prepare students for practical design and production work, rather than for jobs that require more theoretical and scientific knowledge. Graduates of 4-year technology programs may get jobs similar to those obtained by graduates with a bachelor's degree in engineering. Engineering technology graduates, however, are not qualified to register as professional engineers under the same terms as graduates with degrees in engineering. Some employers regard technology program graduates as having skills between those of a technician and an engineer.

Graduate training is essential for engineering faculty positions and many research and development programs, but is not required for the majority of entry-level engineering jobs. Many engineers obtain graduate degrees in engineering or business administration to learn new technology and broaden their education. Many high-level executives in government and industry began their careers as engineers.

About 340 colleges and universities offer bachelor's degree programs in engineering that are accredited by the Accreditation Board for Engineering and Technology (ABET), and about 240 colleges offer accredited bachelor's degree programs in engineering technology. ABET accreditation is based on an examination of an engineering program's student achievement, program improvement, faculty, curricular content, facilities, and institutional commitment. Although most institutions offer programs in the major branches of engineering, only a few offer programs in the smaller specialties. Also, programs of the same title may vary in content. For example, some programs emphasize industrial practices, preparing students for a job in industry, whereas others are more theoretical and are designed to prepare students for graduate work. Therefore, students should investigate curricula and check accreditations carefully before selecting a college.

Admissions requirements for undergraduate engineering schools include a solid background in mathematics (algebra, geometry, trigonometry, and calculus) and science (biology, chemistry, and physics), and courses in English, social studies, humanities, and computer and information technology. Bachelor's degree programs in engineering typically are designed to last 4 years, but many students find that it takes between 4 and 5 years to complete their studies. In a typical 4-year college curriculum, the first 2 years are spent studying mathematics, basic sciences, introductory engineering, humanities, and social sciences. In the last 2 years, most courses are in engineering, usually with a concentration in one branch. For example, the last 2 years of an aerospace program might include courses in fluid mechanics, heat transfer, applied aerodynamics, analytical mechanics, flight vehicle design, trajectory dynamics, and aerospace propulsion systems. Some programs offer a general engineering curriculum; students then specialize in graduate school or on the job.

Some engineering schools and 2-year colleges have agreements whereby the 2-year college provides the initial engineering education, and the engineering school automatically admits students for their last 2 years. In addition, a few engineering schools have arrangements whereby a student spends 3 years in a liberal arts college studying pre-engineering subjects and 2 years in an engineering school studying core subjects, and then receives a bachelor's degree from each school. Some colleges and universities offer 5-year master's degree programs. Some 5-year or even 6-year cooperative plans combine classroom study and practical work, permitting students to gain valuable experience and to finance part of their education.

All 50 states and the District of Columbia require licensure for engineers who offer their services directly to the public. Engineers who are licensed are called Professional Engineers (PE). This licensure generally requires a degree from an ABET-accredited engineering program, 4 years of relevant work experience, and successful completion of a state examination. Recent graduates can start the licensing process by taking the examination in two stages. The initial Fundamentals of Engineering (FE) examination can be taken upon graduation. Engineers who pass this examination commonly are called Engineers in Training (EIT) or Engineer Interns (EI). After acquiring suitable work experience, EITs can take the second examination, the Principles and Practice of Engineering exam. Several states have imposed mandatory continuing education requirements for relicensure. Most states recognize licensure from other states provided that the manner in which the initial license was obtained meets or exceeds their licensure requirements. Many civil, electrical, mechanical, and chemical engineers are licensed PEs.

Engineers should be creative, inquisitive, analytical, and detail-oriented. They should be able to work as part of a team and to communicate well, both orally and in writing. Communication abilities are important because engineers often interact with specialists in a wide range of fields outside engineering.

Beginning engineering graduates usually work under the supervision of experienced engineers and, in large companies, also may receive formal classroom or seminar-type training. As new engineers gain knowledge and experience, they are assigned more difficult projects with greater independence to develop designs, solve problems, and make decisions. Engineers may advance to become technical specialists or to supervise a staff or team of engineers and technicians. Some may eventually become engineering managers or enter other managerial or sales jobs.

Job Outlook

Good opportunities should exist for nuclear engineers because the small number of nuclear engineering graduates is likely to be in rough balance with the number of job openings. Because this is a small occupation, projected job growth will generate few openings; consequently, most openings will result from the need to replace nuclear engineers who transfer to other occupations or leave the labor force.

Little or no growth in employment of nuclear engineers is expected through 2012. Due to public concerns over the cost and safety of nuclear power, no commercial nuclear power plants have been built in the United States for many years. Nevertheless, nuclear engineers will be needed to operate existing plants. In addition, nuclear engineers may be needed to research and develop future nuclear power sources. They also will be needed to work in defense-related areas, to develop nuclear medical technology, and to improve and enforce waste management and safety standards.

Earnings

Median annual earnings of nuclear engineers were $81,350 in 2002. The middle 50 percent earned between $67,970 and $92,930. The lowest 10 percent earned less than $58,350, and the highest 10 percent earned more than $111,260. In the federal government, nuclear engineers in supervisory, nonsupervisory, and management positions earned an average of $73,769 a year in 2003.

According to a 2003 salary survey by the National Association of Colleges and Employers, bachelor's degree candidates in nuclear engineering received starting offers averaging $50,104 a year.

Related Occupations

Nuclear engineers apply the principles of physical science and mathematics in their work. Other workers who use scientific and mathematical principles include architects, except landscape and naval; engineering and natural sciences managers; computer and information systems managers; mathematicians; drafters; engineering technicians; sales engineers; science technicians; and physical and life scientists, including agricultural and food scientists, biological scientists, conservation scientists and foresters, atmospheric scientists, chemists and materials scientists, environmental scientists and geoscientists, and physicists and astronomers.

Sources of Additional Information

Information on careers and related topics for nuclear engineers is available from:

- American Nuclear Society, 555 North Kensington Ave., LaGrange Park, IL 60526. Internet: http://www.ans.org

See the introduction to the section on engineers for information on working conditions, training requirements, and other sources of additional information.

Nuclear Medicine Technologists

(O*NET 29-2033.00)

Significant Points

- Nuclear medicine technology programs range in length from 1 to 4 years and lead to a certificate, associate degree, or bachelor's degree.

- Faster-than-average growth will arise from an increase in the number of middle-aged and elderly persons, who are the primary users of diagnostic procedures.

Nature of the Work

Diagnostic imaging embraces several procedures that aid in diagnosing ailments, the most familiar being the x ray. Another increasingly common diagnostic imaging method, called magnetic resonance imaging (MRI), uses giant magnets and radio waves, rather than radiation, to create an image. Not all imaging technologies use ionizing radiation or radio waves, however: In nuclear medicine, radionuclides—unstable atoms that emit radiation spontaneously—are used to diagnose and treat disease. Radionuclides are purified and compounded to form radiopharmaceuticals. Nuclear medicine technologists administer radiopharmaceuticals to patients and then monitor the characteristics and functions of tissues or organs in which the drugs localize. Abnormal areas show higher- or lower-than-expected concentrations of radioactivity.

Nuclear medicine technologists operate cameras that detect and map the radioactive drug in a patient's body to create diagnostic images. After explaining test procedures to patients, technologists prepare a dosage of the radiopharmaceutical and administer it by mouth, injection, or other means. They position patients and start a gamma scintillation camera, or "scanner," which creates images of the distribution of a radiopharmaceutical as it localizes in, and emits signals from, the patient's body. The images are produced on a computer screen or on film for a physician to interpret.

When preparing radiopharmaceuticals, technologists adhere to safety standards that keep the radiation dose to workers and patients as low as possible. Technologists keep patient records and record the amount and type of radionuclides received, used, and discarded.

Radiologic technologists and technicians, diagnostic medical sonographers, and cardiovascular technologists and technicians also operate diagnostic imaging equipment, but their equipment creates images by means of a different technology.

Nuclear medicine technologists also perform radioimmunoassay studies that assess the behavior of a radioactive substance inside the body. For example, technologists may add radioactive substances to blood or serum to determine levels of hormones or of therapeutic drugs in the body. Some nuclear medicine studies, such as cardiac function studies, are processed with the aid of a computer.

Working Conditions

Nuclear medicine technologists generally work a 40-hour week, perhaps including evening or weekend hours in departments that operate on an extended schedule. Opportunities for part-time and shift work are also available. In addition, technologists in hospitals may have on-call duty on a rotational basis.

Because technologists are on their feet much of the day and may lift or turn disabled patients, physical stamina is important.

Although the potential for radiation exposure exists in this field, it is kept to a minimum by the use of shielded syringes, gloves, and other protective devices and by adherence to strict radiation safety guidelines. Technologists also wear badges that measure radiation levels. Because of safety programs, badge measurements rarely exceed established safety levels.

Employment

Nuclear medicine technologists held about 17,000 jobs in 2002. About two-thirds of all jobs were in hospitals. Most of the rest were in offices of physicians or in medical and diagnostic laboratories, including diagnostic imaging centers.

Training, Other Qualifications, and Advancement

Many employers and an increasing number of states require certification or licensure. Aspiring nuclear medicine technologists should check the requirements for the state in which they plan to work. Certification is available from the American Registry of Radiologic Technologists and from the Nuclear Medicine Technology Certification Board. Nuclear medicine technologists must meet the minimum federal standards on the administration of radioactive drugs and the operation of radiation detection equipment.

Nuclear medicine technology programs range in length from 1 to 4 years and lead to a certificate, associate degree, or bachelor's degree. Generally, certificate programs are offered in hospitals, associate degree programs in community colleges, and bachelor's degree programs in 4-year colleges and universities. Courses cover the physical sciences, biological effects of radiation exposure, radiation protection and procedures, the use of radiopharmaceuticals, imaging techniques, and computer applications.

One-year certificate programs are for health professionals—especially radiologic technologists and diagnostic medical sonographers—who wish to specialize in nuclear medicine. They also attract medical technologists, registered nurses, and others who wish to change fields or specialize. Others interested in the nuclear medicine technology field have three options: a 2-year certificate program, a 2-year associate degree program, or a 4-year bachelor's degree program.

The Joint Review Committee on Education Programs in Nuclear Medicine Technology accredits most formal training programs in nuclear medicine technology. In 2002, there were 92 accredited programs in the continental United States and Puerto Rico.

Nuclear medicine technologists should be sensitive to patients' physical and psychological needs. They must pay attention to detail, follow instructions, and work as part of a team. In addition, operating complicated equipment requires mechanical ability and manual dexterity.

Technologists may advance to supervisor, then to chief technologist, and, finally, to department administrator or director. Some technologists specialize in a clinical area such as nuclear cardiology or computer analysis or leave patient care to take positions in research laboratories. Some become instructors or directors in nuclear medicine technology programs, a step that usually requires a bachelor's or master's degree in nuclear medicine technology. Others leave the occupation to work as sales or training representatives for medical equipment and radiopharmaceutical manufacturing firms or as radiation safety officers in regulatory agencies or hospitals.

Job Outlook

Employment of nuclear medicine technologists is expected to grow faster than the average for all occupations through the year 2012. Growth will arise from an increase in the number of middle-aged and older persons, who are the primary users of diagnostic procedures, including nuclear medicine tests. However, the number of openings each year will be relatively low because the occupation is small. Technologists who are also trained in other diagnostic methods, such as radiologic technology or diagnostic medical sonography, will have the best prospects.

Technological innovations may increase the diagnostic uses of nuclear medicine. One example is the use of radiopharmaceuticals in combination with monoclonal antibodies to detect cancer at far earlier stages than is customary today and without resorting to surgery. Another is the use of radionuclides to examine the heart's ability to pump blood. Wider use of nuclear medical imaging to observe metabolic and biochemical changes for neurology, cardiology, and oncology procedures also will spur demand for nuclear medicine technologists.

Nonetheless, cost considerations will affect the speed with which new applications of nuclear medicine grow. Some promising nuclear medicine procedures, such as positron emission tomography, are extremely costly, and hospitals contemplating these procedures will have to consider equipment costs, reimbursement policies, and the number of potential users.

Earnings

Median annual earnings of nuclear medicine technologists were $48,750 in 2002. The middle 50 percent earned between $41,460 and $57,200. The lowest 10 percent earned less than $35,870, and the highest 10 percent earned more than $68,710. Median annual earnings of nuclear medicine technologists in 2002 were $48,210 in general medical and surgical hospitals.

Related Occupations

Nuclear medical technologists operate sophisticated equipment to help physicians and other health practitioners diagnose and treat patients. Cardiovascular technologists and technicians, clinical laboratory technologists and technicians, diagnostic medical sonographers, radiation therapists, Radiologic technologists and technicians, and respiratory therapists also perform similar functions.

Sources of Additional Information

Additional information on a career as a nuclear medicine technologist is available from:

- Society of Nuclear Medicine Technologists, 1850 Samuel Morse Dr., Reston, VA 20190-5316. Internet: http://www.snm.org

For career information, send a stamped, self-addressed, business-size envelope with your request to:

- American Society of Radiologic Technologists, 15000 Central Ave. SE., Albuquerque, NM 87123-3917. Telephone (toll-free): 800-444-2778. Internet: http://www.asrt.org

For a list of accredited programs in nuclear medicine technology, write to:

- Joint Review Committee on Educational Programs in Nuclear Medicine Technology, PMB 418, 1 2nd Ave. East, Suite C, Polson, MT 59860-2320. Internet: http://www.jrcnmt.org

Information on certification is available from:

- American Registry of Radiologic Technologists, 1255 Northland Dr., St. Paul, MN 55120-1155. Internet: http://www.arrt.org

- Nuclear Medicine Technology Certification Board, 2970 Clairmont Rd., Suite 935, Atlanta, GA 30329. Internet: http://www.nmtcb.org

Nursing, Psychiatric, and Home Health Aides

(O*NET 31-1011.00, 31-1012.00, and 31-1013.00)

Significant Points

- Most jobs are in nursing and residential care facilities, hospitals, and home healthcare services.

- Modest entry requirements, low pay, high physical and emotional demands, and lack of advancement opportunities characterize this occupation.

- Numerous job openings and excellent job opportunities are expected.

Nature of the Work

Nursing and psychiatric aides help care for physically or mentally ill, injured, disabled, or infirm individuals confined to hospitals, nursing care facilities, and mental health settings. Home health aides' duties are similar, but they work in patients' homes or residential care facilities.

Nursing aides, also known as nursing assistants, geriatric aides, unlicensed assistive personnel, or hospital attendants, perform routine tasks under the supervision of nursing and medical staff. They answer patients' call lights, deliver messages, serve meals, make beds, and help patients eat, dress, and bathe. Aides also may provide skin care to patients; take their temperatures, pulse rate, respiration rate, and blood pressure; and help patients get in and out of bed and walk. They also may escort patients to operating and examining rooms, keep patients' rooms neat, set up equipment, store and move supplies, or assist with some procedures. Aides observe patients' physical, mental, and emotional conditions and report any change to the nursing or medical staff.

Nursing aides employed in nursing care facilities often are the principal caregivers, having far more contact with residents than other members of the staff. Because some residents may stay in a nursing care facility for months or even years, aides develop ongoing relationships with them and interact with them in a positive, caring way.

Home health aides help elderly, convalescent, or disabled persons live in their own homes instead of in a health facility. Under the direction of nursing or medical staff, they provide health-related services, such as administering oral medications. Like nursing aides, home health aides may check patients' pulse rates, temperatures, and respiration rates; help with simple prescribed exercises; keep patients' rooms neat; and help patients move from bed, bathe, dress, and groom. Occasionally, they change nonsterile dressings, give massages and alcohol rubs, or assist with braces and artificial limbs. Experienced home health aides also may assist with medical equipment such as ventilators, which help patients breathe.

Most home health aides work with elderly or disabled persons who need more extensive care than family or friends can provide. Some help discharged hospital patients who have relatively short-term needs.

In home health agencies, a registered nurse, physical therapist, or social worker usually assigns specific duties and supervises home health aides, who keep records of the services they perform and record patients' condition and progress. They report changes in patients' conditions to the supervisor or case manager.

Psychiatric aides, also known as mental health assistants or psychiatric nursing assistants, care for mentally impaired or emotionally disturbed individuals. They work under a team that may include psychiatrists, psychologists, psychiatric nurses, social workers, and therapists. In addition to helping patients dress, bathe, groom, and eat, psychiatric aides socialize with them and lead them in educational and recreational activities. Psychiatric aides may play games such as cards with the patients, watch television with them, or participate in group activities, such as sports or field trips. They observe patients and report any physical or behavioral signs that might be important for the professional staff to know. They accompany patients to and from examinations and treatment. Because they have such close contact with patients, psychiatric aides can have a great deal of influence on their patients' outlook and treatment.

Working Conditions

Most full-time aides work about 40 hours a week, but because patients need care 24 hours a day, some aides work evenings, nights, weekends, and holidays. Many work part time. Aides spend many hours standing and walking, and they often face heavy workloads. Because they may have to move patients in and out of bed or help them stand or walk, aides must guard against back injury. Aides also may face hazards from minor infections and major diseases, such as hepatitis, but can avoid infections by following proper procedures.

Aides often have unpleasant duties, such as emptying bedpans and changing soiled bed linens. The patients they care for may be disoriented, irritable, or uncooperative. Psychiatric aides must be prepared to care for patients whose illness may cause violent behavior. While their work can be emotionally demanding, many aides gain satisfaction from assisting those in need.

Home health aides may go to the same patient's home for months or even years. However, most aides work with a number of different patients, each job lasting a few hours, days, or weeks. Home health aides often visit multiple patients on the same day.

Home health aides generally work alone, with periodic visits by their supervisor. They receive detailed instructions explaining when to visit patients and what services to perform. Aides are individually responsible for getting to patients' homes, and they may spend a good portion of the working day traveling from one patient to another. Because mechanical lifting devices available in institutional settings are seldom available in patients' homes, home health aides are particularly susceptible to injuries resulting from overexertion when they assist patients.

Employment

Nursing, psychiatric, and home health aides held about 2.0 million jobs in 2002. Nursing aides held the most jobs—approximately 1.4 million. Home health aides held roughly 580,000 jobs and psychiatric aides held about 59,000 jobs. Around 2 in 5 nursing aides worked in nursing care facilities, and about one-fourth worked in hospitals. Most home health aides (about one-third) were employed by home healthcare services. Others were employed in social assistance agencies, nursing and residential care facilities, and employment services. More than half of all psychiatric aides worked in hospitals, primarily in psychiatric and substance abuse hospitals—although some also worked in the psychiatric units of general medical and surgical hospitals. Others were employed in state government agencies; residential mental retardation, mental health, and substance abuse facilities; individual and family services; and outpatient care centers.

Training, Other Qualifications, and Advancement

In many cases, neither a high school diploma nor previous work experience is necessary for a job as a nursing, psychiatric, or home health aide. A few employers, however, require some training or experience. Hospitals may require experience as a nursing aide or home health aide. Nursing care facilities often hire inexperienced workers who must complete a minimum of 75 hours of mandatory training and pass a competency evaluation program within 4 months of their employment. Aides who complete the program are certified and placed on the state registry of nursing aides. Some states require psychiatric aides to complete a formal training program.

The federal government has guidelines for home health aides whose employers receive reimbursement from Medicare. Federal law requires home health aides to pass a competency test covering 12 areas: Communication skills; documentation of patient status and care provided; reading and recording vital signs; basic infection control procedures; basic body functions; maintenance of a healthy environment; emergency procedures; physical, emotional, and developmental characteristics of patients; personal hygiene and grooming; safe transfer techniques; normal range of motion and positioning; and basic nutrition.

A home health aide may receive training before taking the competency test. Federal law suggests at least 75 hours of classroom and practical training, supervised by a registered nurse. Training and testing programs may be offered by the employing agency, but must meet the standards of the Center for Medicare and Medicaid Services. Training programs vary with state regulations.

The National Association for Home Care offers national certification for home health aides. The certification is a voluntary demonstration that the individual has met industry standards.

Nursing aide training is offered in high schools, vocational-technical centers, some nursing care facilities, and some community colleges. Courses cover body mechanics, nutrition, anatomy and physiology, infection control, communication skills, and resident rights. Personal care skills, such as how to help patients bathe, eat, and groom, also are taught.

Some employers other than nursing care facilities provide classroom instruction for newly hired aides, while others rely exclusively on informal on-the-job instruction from a licensed nurse or an experienced aide. Such training may last several days to a few months. From time to time, aides also may attend lectures, workshops, and inservice training.

These occupations can offer individuals an entry into the world of work. The flexibility of night and weekend hours also provides high school and college students a chance to work during the school year.

Applicants should be tactful, patient, understanding, emotionally stable, and dependable and should have a desire to help people. They also should be able to work as part of a team, have good communication skills, and be willing to perform repetitive, routine tasks. Home health aides should be honest and discreet, because they work in private homes.

Aides must be in good health. A physical examination, including state-regulated tests such as those for tuberculosis, may be required.

Opportunities for advancement within these occupations are limited. To enter other health occupations, aides generally need additional formal training. Some employers and unions provide opportunities by simplifying the educational paths to advancement. Experience as an aide also can help individuals decide whether to pursue a career in the healthcare field.

Job Outlook

Numerous job openings for nursing, psychiatric, and home health aides will arise from a combination of fast employment growth and high replacement needs. High replacement needs in this large occupation reflect modest entry requirements, low pay, high physical and emotional demands, and lack of opportunities for advancement. For these same reasons, many people are unwilling to perform the kind of work required by the occupation. Therefore, persons who are interested in, and suited for, this work should have excellent job opportunities.

Overall employment of nursing, psychiatric, and home health aides is projected to grow faster than the average for all occupations through the year 2012, although individual occupational growth rates will vary. Employment of home health aides is expected to grow the fastest, as a result of both growing demand for home healthcare services from an aging population and efforts to contain healthcare costs by moving patients out of hospitals and nursing care facilities as quickly as possible. Consumer preference for care in the home and improvements in medical technologies for in-home treatment also will contribute to faster-than-average employment growth for home health aides.

Nursing aide employment will not grow as fast as home health aide employment, largely because nursing aides are concentrated in slower growing nursing care facilities. Nevertheless, employment of nursing aides is expected to grow faster than the average for all occupations in response to an increasing emphasis on rehabilitation and the long-term care needs of an increasing elderly population. Financial pressures on hospitals to discharge patients as soon as possible should produce more admissions to nursing care facilities. Modern medical technology also will increase the employment of nursing aides, because, as the technology saves and extends more lives, it increases the need for long-term care provided by aides.

Employment of psychiatric aides—the smallest of the three occupations—is expected to grow about as fast as the average for all occupations. The number of jobs for psychiatric aides in hospitals, where half of those in the occupation work, will grow slower than the average due to attempts to contain costs by limiting inpatient psychiatric treatment. Employment in other sectors will rise in response to growth in the number of older persons—many of whom will require mental health services, increasing public acceptance of formal treatment for substance abuse, and a lessening of the stigma attached to those receiving mental health care.

Earnings

Median hourly earnings of nursing aides, orderlies, and attendants were $9.59 in 2002. The middle 50 percent earned between $8.06 and $11.39 an hour. The lowest 10 percent earned less than $6.98, and the highest 10 percent earned more than $13.54 an hour. Median hourly earnings in the industries employing the largest numbers of nursing aides, orderlies, and attendants in 2002 were as follows:

Employment services	$11.38
Local government	10.33
General medical and surgical hospitals	10.09
Nursing care facilities	9.27
Community care facilities for the elderly	8.98

Nursing and psychiatric aides in hospitals generally receive at least 1 week's paid vacation after 1 year of service. Paid holidays and sick leave, hospital and medical benefits, extra pay for late-shift work, and pension plans also are available to many hospital, and some nursing care facility, employees.

Median hourly earnings of home health aides were $8.70 in 2002. The middle 50 percent earned between $7.54 and $10.37 an hour. The lowest 10 percent earned less than $6.56, and the highest 10 percent earned more than $12.34 an hour. Median hourly earnings in the industries employing the largest numbers of home health aides in 2002 were as follows:

Employment services	$9.21
Residential mental retardation, mental health, and substance abuse facilities	8.91
Home health care services	8.46
Community care facilities for the elderly	8.36
Individual and family services	8.20

Home health aides receive slight pay increases with experience and added responsibility. Usually, they are paid only for the time worked in the home; normally, they are not paid for travel time between jobs. Most employers hire only on-call hourly workers and provide no benefits.

Median hourly earnings of psychiatric aides were $11.04 in 2002. The middle 50 percent earned between $8.97 and $13.74 an hour. The lowest 10 percent earned less than $7.52, and the highest 10 percent earned more than $16.16 an hour. Median hourly earnings in the industries employing the largest numbers of psychiatric aides in 2002 were as follows:

State government	$13.14
Psychiatric and substance abuse hospitals	11.32
General medical and surgical hospitals	11.04

Related Occupations

Nursing, psychiatric, and home health aides help people who need routine care or treatment. So do childcare workers, medical assistants, occupational therapist assistants and aides, personal and home care aides, and physical therapist assistants and aides.

Sources of Additional Information

Information about employment opportunities may be obtained from local hospitals, nursing care facilities, home health-care agencies, psychiatric facilities, state boards of nursing, and local offices of the state employment service.

General information about training, referrals to state and local agencies about job opportunities, a list of relevant publications, and information on certification of home health aides are available from:

- National Association for Home Care, 228 7th St. SE, Washington, DC 2003. Internet: http://www.nahc.org

Occupational Health and Safety Specialists and Technicians

(O*NET 29-9011.00 and 29-9012.00)

Significant Points

- About 2 out of 5 worked in federal, state, and local government agencies that enforce rules on health and safety.

- Many employers, including the federal government, require 4-year college degrees in safety or a related field for some specialist positions.

- Projected average employment growth reflects a balance of continuing public demand for a safe and healthy work environment against the desire for smaller government and fewer regulations.

Nature of the Work

Occupational health and safety specialists and technicians, also known as occupational health and safety inspectors, industrial hygienists, environmental protection officers, or ergonomists, help prevent harm to workers, property, and the environment, as well as the general public. They promote occupational health and safety within organizations by developing safer, healthier, and more efficient ways of working.

Occupational health and safety specialists analyze work environments and design programs to control, eliminate, and prevent disease or injury caused by chemical, physical, and biological agents or ergonomic factors that involve the impact of equipment design on a worker's comfort or fatigue. They may conduct inspections and enforce adherence to laws, regulations, or employer policies governing worker health and safety.

Occupational health and safety technicians collect data on work environments for analysis by occupational health and safety specialists. Usually working under the supervision of specialists, they help implement and evaluate programs designed to limit risks to workers.

The specific responsibilities of occupational health and safety specialists and technicians vary by industry, work-place, and types of hazards affecting employees. In most settings, they initially focus on identifying hazardous conditions and practices. Sometimes they develop methods to predict hazards from experience, historical data, and other information sources. Then they identify potential hazards in systems, equipment, products, facilities, or processes planned for use in the future. After reviewing the causes or effects of hazards, they evaluate the probability and severity of accidents that may result. For example, they might uncover patterns in injury data that implicate a specific cause such as system failure, human error, incomplete or faulty decision making, or a weakness in existing policies or practices. Then they develop and help enforce a plan to eliminate hazards, conducting training sessions for management, supervisors, and workers on health and safety practices and regulations, as necessary. Lastly, they may check on the progress of the safety plan after its implementation. If improvements are not satisfactory, a new plan might be designed and put into practice.

Many occupational health and safety specialists examine and test machinery and equipment, such as lifting devices, machine guards, or scaffolding, to ensure the machinery and equipment meet appropriate safety regulations. They may check that personal protective equipment, such as masks, respirators, protective eyewear, or hardhats, is being used in workplaces according to regulations. They also check that dangerous materials are stored correctly. They test and identify work areas for potential accident and health hazards, such as toxic fumes and explosive gas-air mixtures, and may implement appropriate control measures, such as adjustments to ventilation systems. Their investigations might involve talking with workers and observing their work, as well as inspecting elements in their work environment, such as lighting, tools, and equipment.

To measure and control hazardous substances, such as the noise or radiation levels, occupational health and safety specialists and technicians prepare and calibrate scientific equipment. Samples of dust, gases, vapors, and other potentially toxic materials must be collected and handled properly to ensure safety and accurate test results.

If an accident occurs, occupational health and safety specialists help investigate unsafe working conditions, study possible causes, and recommend remedial action. Some occupational health and safety specialists and technicians assist with the rehabilitation of workers after accidents and injuries, and make sure they return to work successfully.

Frequent communication with management may be necessary to report on the status of occupational health and safety programs. Consultation with engineers or physicians also may be required.

Occupational health and safety specialists prepare reports including observations, analysis of contaminants, and recommendation for control and correction of hazards. Those who develop expertise in certain areas may develop occupational health and safety systems, including policies, procedures, and manuals.

Working Conditions

Occupational health and safety specialists and technicians work with many different people in a variety of environments. Their jobs often involve considerable fieldwork, and some travel frequently. Many occupational health and safety specialists and technicians work long and often irregular hours.

Occupational health and safety specialists and technicians may experience unpleasant, stressful, and dangerous working conditions. For example, health and safety inspectors are exposed to many of the same physically strenuous conditions and hazards as industrial employees, and the work may be performed in unpleasant, stressful, and dangerous working conditions. Health and safety inspectors may find themselves in adversarial roles when the organization or individual being inspected objects to the process or its consequences.

Employment

Occupational health and safety specialists and technicians held about 41,000 jobs in 2002, primarily in government agencies. Local governments employed 17 percent, state governments employed 14 percent, and the federal government—chiefly the Department of Labor—employed 6 percent. Other occupational health and safety specialists and technicians were employed in manufacturing firms; hospitals; educational services, including colleges, universities, and professional schools; employment services; management, scientific, and technical consulting services; management of companies and enterprises; electric power generation, transmission, and distribution; support activities for mining; scientific research and development services; and architectural, engineering, and related services.

Within the federal government, most jobs are as Occupational Safety and Health Administration (OSHA) inspectors, who enforce U.S. Department of Labor regulations that ensure adequate safety principles, practices, and techniques are applied in workplaces. Employers may be fined for violation of OSHA standards. Within the U.S. Department of Health and Human Services, occupational health and safety specialists working for the National Institute of Occupational Safety and Health (NIOSH) provide private companies with an avenue to evaluate the health and safety of their employees without the risk of being fined. Most large government agencies also employ occupational health and safety specialists and technicians who work to protect agency employees.

Most private companies either employ their own occupational health and safety personnel or contract with occupational health and safety professionals to ensure OSHA compliance.

Training, Other Qualifications, and Advancement

Requirements for becoming an occupational health and safety specialist or technician include a combination of education, experience, and passing scores on written examinations. Many employers, including the federal government, require a 4-year college degree in safety or a related field for some specialist positions. Experience as an occupational health and safety professional is also a prerequisite for many positions.

All occupational health and safety specialists and technicians are trained in the applicable laws or inspection procedures through some combination of classroom and on-the-job training. In general, people who want to enter this occupation should be responsible and like detailed work. Occupational health and safety specialists and technicians should be able to communicate well. Recommended high school courses include English, mathematics, chemistry, biology, and physics.

Certification is available through the Board of Certified Safety Professionals (BCSP) and the American Board of Industrial Hygiene (ABIH). The BCSP offers the Certified Safety Professional (CSP) credential, while the ABIH offers the Certified Industrial Hygienist (CIH) and Certified Associate Industrial Hygienist (CAIH) credentials. Also, the Council on Certification of Health, Environmental, and Safety Technologists, a joint effort between the BCSP and ABIH, awards the Occupational Health and Safety Technologist (OHST) credential. Requirements for the OHST credential are less stringent than those for the CSP, CIH, or CAIH credentials. Once education and experience requirements have been met, certification may be obtained through an examination. Continuing education is required for recertification. Although voluntary, many employers encourage certification.

Federal government occupational health and safety specialists and technicians whose job performance is satisfactory advance through their career ladder to a specified full-performance level. For positions above this level, usually supervisory positions, advancement is competitive and based on agency needs and individual merit. Advancement opportunities in state and local governments and the private sector are often similar to those in the federal government.

With additional experience or education, promotion to a managerial position is possible. Research or related teaching positions at the college level require advanced education.

Job Outlook

Employment of occupational health and safety specialists and technicians is expected to grow about as fast as the average for all occupations through 2012, reflecting a balance of continuing public demand for a safe and healthy work environment against the desire for smaller government and fewer regulations. Additional job openings will arise from the need to replace those who transfer to other occupations, retire, or leave the labor force for other reasons. In private industry, employment growth will reflect industry growth and the continuing self-enforcement of government and company regulations and policies.

Employment of occupational health and safety specialists and technicians is affected less by general economic fluctuations than employment in other occupations. Federal, state, and local governments, which employ about 2 out of 5 of all specialists and technicians, provide considerable job security.

Earnings

Median annual earnings of occupational health and safety specialists and technicians were $46,010 in 2002. The middle 50 percent earned between $34,280 and $58,230. The lowest 10 percent earned less than $25,080, and the highest 10 percent earned more than $71,450. Median annual earnings of occupational health and safety specialists and technicians in 2002 were $44,260 in state government and $42,430 in local government.

Most occupational health and safety specialists and technicians work for federal, state, and local governments or in large private firms, most of which generally offer more generous benefits than smaller firms.

Related Occupations

Occupational health and safety specialists and technicians ensure that laws and regulations are obeyed. Others who enforce laws and regulations include agricultural inspectors, construction and building inspectors, correctional officers, financial examiners, fire inspectors, police and detectives, and transportation inspectors.

Sources of Additional Information

Information about jobs in federal, state, and local government as well as in private industry is available from state employment service offices.

For information on a career as an industrial hygienist and a list of colleges and universities offering programs in industrial hygiene, contact:

● American Industrial Hygiene Association, 2700 Prosperity Ave., Suite 250, Fairfax, VA 22031. Internet: http://www.aiha.org

For information on the Certified Industrial Hygiene or Certified Associate Industrial Hygiene credential, contact:

● American Board of Industrial Hygiene, 6015 West St. Joseph Hwy., Suite 102, Lansing, MI 48917. Internet: http://www.abih.org

For more information on professions in safety and a list of colleges and universities offering safety and related degrees, including correspondence courses, contact:

● American Society of Safety Engineers, 1800 E Oakton St., Des Plaines, IL 60018. Internet: http://www.asse.org

For more information on professions in safety and the Certified Safety Professional credential, contact:

● Board of Certified Safety Professionals, 208 Burwash Ave., Savoy, IL 61874. Internet: http://www.bcsp.org

For information on the Occupational Health and Safety Technologist credential, contact:

● Council on Certification of Health, Environmental, and Safety Technologists, 208 Burwash Ave., Savoy, IL 61874. Internet: http://www.cchest.org

For additional career information, contact:

● U.S. Department of Health and Human Services, Center for Disease Control and Prevention, National Institute of Occupational Safety and Health, Hubert H. Humphrey Bldg., 200 Independence Ave. SW., Room 715H, Washington, DC 20201. Internet: http://www.cdc.gov/niosh

● U.S. Department of Labor, Occupational Safety and Health Administration, 200 Constitution Ave. NW, Washington, DC 20210. Internet: http://www.osha.gov

Information on obtaining positions as occupational health and safety specialists and technicians with the federal government is available from the Office of Personnel Management through a telephone-based system. Consult your telephone directory under U.S. government for a local number or call (703) 724-1850; Federal Relay Service: (800) 877-8339. The first number is not toll free, and charges may result. Information also is available from the Internet site: http://www.usajobs.opm.gov.

Occupational Therapist Assistants and Aides

(O*NET 31-2011.00 and 31-2012.00)

Significant Points

● Occupational therapist assistants generally must complete an associate degree or a certificate program; in contrast, occupational therapist aides usually receive most of their training on the job.

● Occupational therapists are expected to delegate more hands-on therapy work to occupational therapist assistants and aides.

● Employment is projected to increase much faster than the average, reflecting growth in the number of individuals with disabilities or limited function who require therapeutic services.

Nature of the Work

Occupational therapist assistants and aides work under the direction of occupational therapists to provide rehabilitative services to persons with mental, physical, emotional, or developmental impairments. The ultimate goal is to improve clients' quality of life and ability to perform daily activities. For example, occupational therapist assistants help injured workers re-enter the labor force by teaching them how to compensate for lost motor skills or help individuals with learning disabilities increase their independence.

Occupational therapist assistants help clients with rehabilitative activities and exercises outlined in a treatment plan developed in collaboration with an occupational therapist. Activities range from teaching the proper method of moving from a bed into a wheelchair to the best way to stretch and limber the muscles of the hand. Assistants monitor an individual's activities to make sure that they are performed correctly and to provide encouragement. They also record their client's progress for the occupational therapist. If the treatment is not having the intended effect, or the client is not improving as expected, the therapist may alter the treatment program in hopes of obtaining better results. In addition, occupational therapist assistants document the billing of the client's health insurance provider.

Occupational therapist aides typically prepare materials and assemble equipment used during treatment. They are responsible for a range of clerical tasks, including scheduling appointments, answering the telephone, restocking or ordering depleted supplies, and filling out insurance forms or other paperwork. Aides are not licensed, so the law does not allow them to perform as wide a range of tasks as occupational therapist assistants.

Working Conditions

The hours and days that occupational therapist assistants and aides work vary with the facility and with whether they are full- or part-time employees. Many outpatient therapy offices and clinics have evening and weekend hours, to help coincide with patients' personal schedules.

Occupational therapist assistants and aides need to have a moderate degree of strength, due to the physical exertion required in assisting patients with their treatment. For example, assistants and aides may need to lift patients. Constant kneeling, stooping, and standing for long periods also are part of the job.

Employment

Occupational therapist assistants and aides held about 27,000 jobs in 2002. Occupational therapist assistants held about 18,000 jobs, and occupational therapist aides held approximately 8,300. Over 30 percent of jobs for assistants and aides were in hospitals, 23 percent were in offices of other health practitioners (which includes offices of occupational therapists), and 18 percent were in nursing care

facilities. The rest were primarily in community care facilities for the elderly, home healthcare services, individual and family services, and state government agencies.

Training, Other Qualifications, and Advancement

An associate degree or a certificate from an accredited community college or technical school is generally required to qualify for occupational therapist assistant jobs. In contrast, occupational therapist aides usually receive most of their training on the job.

There were 161 accredited occupational therapist assistant programs in 2003. The first year of study typically involves an introduction to healthcare, basic medical terminology, anatomy, and physiology. In the second year, courses are more rigorous and usually include occupational therapist courses in areas such as mental health, adult physical disabilities, gerontology, and pediatrics. Students also must complete 16 weeks of supervised fieldwork in a clinic or community setting. Applicants to occupational therapist assistant programs can improve their chances of admission by taking high school courses in biology and health and by performing volunteer work in nursing care facilities, occupational or physical therapists' offices, or other healthcare settings.

Occupational therapist assistants are regulated in most states and must pass a national certification examination after they graduate. Those who pass the test are awarded the title "Certified Occupational Therapist Assistant."

Occupational therapist aides usually receive most of their training on the job. Qualified applicants must have a high school diploma, strong interpersonal skills, and a desire to help people in need. Applicants may increase their chances of getting a job by volunteering their services, thus displaying initiative and aptitude to the employer.

Assistants and aides must be responsible, patient, and willing to take directions and work as part of a team. Furthermore, they should be caring and want to help people who are not able to help themselves.

Job Outlook

Employment of occupational therapist assistants and aides is expected to grow much faster than the average for all occupations through 2012. The impact of proposed federal legislation imposing limits on reimbursement for therapy services may adversely affect the job market for occupational therapist assistants and aides in the near term. However, over the long run, demand for occupational therapist assistants and aides will continue to rise, due to growth in the number of individuals with disabilities or limited function. Job growth will result from an aging population, including the baby-boom generation, which will need more occupational therapy services. Increasing demand also will result from advances in medicine that allow more people with critical problems to survive and then need rehabilitative therapy. Third-party payers, concerned with rising healthcare costs, are expected to encourage occupational therapists to delegate more hands-on therapy work to occupational therapist assistants and aides. By having assistants and aides work more closely with clients under the guidance of a therapist, the cost of therapy should decline.

Earnings

Median annual earnings of occupational therapist assistants were $36,660 in 2002. The middle 50 percent earned between $31,090 and $43,030. The lowest 10 percent earned less than $25,600, and the highest 10 percent earned more than $48,480.

Median annual earnings of occupational therapist aides were $22,040 in 2002. The middle 50 percent earned between $18,040 and $29,130. The lowest 10 percent earned less than $15,400, and the highest 10 percent earned more than $38,170.

Related Occupations

Occupational therapist assistants and aides work under the supervision and direction of occupational therapists. Other workers in the healthcare field who work under similar supervision include dental assistants, medical assistants, pharmacy aides, pharmacy technicians, and physical therapist assistants and aides.

Sources of Additional Information

For information on a career as an occupational therapist assistant or aide, and a list of accredited programs, contact:

- American Occupational Therapy Association, 4720 Montgomery Lane, Bethesda, MD 20824-1220. Internet: http://www.aota.org

Occupational Therapists

(O*NET 29-1122.00)

Significant Points

- Employment is projected to increase faster than the average, as rapid growth in the number of middle-aged and elderly individuals increases the demand for therapeutic services.

- A bachelor's degree in occupational therapy is the minimum educational requirement; beginning in 2007, however, a master's degree or higher will be required.

- Occupational therapists are increasingly taking on supervisory roles.

- More than a quarter of occupational therapists work part time.

Nature of the Work

Occupational therapists (OTs) help people improve their ability to perform tasks in their daily living and working environments. They work with individuals who have conditions that are mentally, physically, developmentally, or emotionally disabling. They also help them to develop, recover, or maintain daily living and work skills. Occupational therapists help clients not only to improve their basic motor functions and reasoning abilities, but also to compensate for permanent loss of function. Their goal is to help clients have independent, productive, and satisfying lives.

Occupational therapists assist clients in performing activities of all types, ranging from using a computer to caring for daily needs such as dressing, cooking, and eating. Physical exercises may be used to increase strength and dexterity, while other activities may be chosen to improve visual acuity and the ability to discern patterns. For example, a client with short-term memory loss might be encouraged to make lists to aid recall, and a person with coordination problems might be assigned exercises to improve hand-eye coordination. Occupational therapists also use computer programs to help clients improve decisionmaking, abstract-reasoning, problem-solving, and perceptual skills, as well as memory, sequencing, and coordination—all of which are important for independent living.

Therapists instruct those with permanent disabilities, such as spinal cord injuries, cerebral palsy, or muscular dystrophy, in the use of adaptive equipment, including wheelchairs, splints, and aids for eating and dressing. They also design or make special equipment needed at home or at work. Therapists develop computer-aided adaptive equipment and teach clients with severe limitations how to use that equipment in order to communicate better and control various aspects of their environment.

Some occupational therapists treat individuals whose ability to function in a work environment has been impaired. These practitioners arrange employment, evaluate the work environment, plan work activities, and assess the client's progress. Therapists also may collaborate with the client and the employer to modify the work environment so that the work can be successfully completed.

Occupational therapists may work exclusively with individuals in a particular age group or with particular disabilities. In schools, for example, they evaluate children's abilities, recommend and provide therapy, modify classroom equipment, and help children participate as fully as possible in school programs and activities. Occupational therapy also is beneficial to the elderly population. Therapists help the elderly lead more productive, active, and independent lives through a variety of methods, including the use of adaptive equipment.

Occupational therapists in mental-health settings treat individuals who are mentally ill, mentally retarded, or emotionally disturbed. To treat these problems, therapists choose activities that help people learn to engage in and cope with daily life. Activities include time management skills, budgeting, shopping, homemaking, and the use of public transportation. Occupational therapists also may work with individuals who are dealing with alcoholism, drug abuse, depression, eating disorders, or stress-related disorders.

Assessing and recording a client's activities and progress is an important part of an occupational therapist's job. Accurate records are essential for evaluating clients, for billing, and for reporting to physicians and other healthcare providers.

Working Conditions

Occupational therapists in hospitals and other healthcare and community settings usually work a 40-hour week. Those in schools may participate in meetings and other activities during and after the school day. In 2002, more than a quarter of occupational therapists worked part time.

In large rehabilitation centers, therapists may work in spacious rooms equipped with machines, tools, and other devices generating noise. The work can be tiring, because therapists are on their feet much of the time. Those providing home healthcare services may spend time driving from appointment to appointment. Therapists also face hazards such as back strain from lifting and moving clients and equipment.

Therapists increasingly are taking on supervisory roles. Due to rising healthcare costs, third-party payers are beginning to encourage occupational therapist assistants and aides to take more hands-on responsibility. By having assistants and aides work more closely with clients under the guidance of a therapist, the cost of therapy should decline.

Employment

Occupational therapists held about 82,000 jobs in 2002. About 1 in 10 occupational therapists held more than one job. The largest number of jobs was in hospitals. Other major employers were offices of other health practitioners (which includes offices of occupational therapists), public and private educational services, and nursing care facilities. Some occupational therapists were employed by home healthcare services, outpatient care centers, offices of physicians, individual and family services, community care facilities for the elderly, and government agencies.

A small number of occupational therapists were self-employed in private practice. These practitioners saw clients referred by physicians or other health professionals or provided contract or consulting services to nursing care facilities, schools, adult daycare programs, and home healthcare agencies.

Training, Other Qualifications, and Advancement

Currently, a bachelor's degree in occupational therapy is the minimum requirement for entry into this field. Beginning in 2007, however, a master's degree or higher will be the minimum educational requirement. As a result, students in bachelor's-level programs should complete their coursework and fieldwork before 2007. All states, Puerto Rico, and the District of Columbia regulate the practice of occupational therapy. To obtain a license, applicants must graduate from an accredited educational program and pass a national certification examination. Those who pass the exam are awarded the title "Occupational Therapist Registered (OTR)."

In 2003, entry-level education was offered in 38 bachelor's degree programs, 3 postbaccalaureate certificate programs for students with a degree other than occupational therapy, and 86 entry-level master's degree programs. There were 48 programs that offered a combined bachelor's and master's degree and 5 offered an entry-level doctoral degree. Most schools have full-time programs, although a growing number also offer weekend or part-time programs.

Occupational therapy coursework includes physical, biological, and behavioral sciences and the application of occupational therapy theory and skills. Completion of 6 months of supervised fieldwork also is required.

Persons considering this profession should take high school courses in biology, chemistry, physics, health, art, and the social sciences. College admissions offices also look favorably at paid or volunteer experience in the healthcare field.

Occupational therapists need patience and strong interpersonal skills to inspire trust and respect in their clients. Ingenuity and imagination in adapting activities to individual needs are assets. Those working in home healthcare services must be able to adapt to a variety of settings.

Job Outlook

Employment of occupational therapists is expected to increase faster than the average for all occupations through 2012. The impact of proposed federal legislation imposing limits on reimbursement for therapy services may adversely affect the job market for occupational therapists in the near term. However, over the long run, the demand for occupational therapists should continue to rise as a result of growth in the number of individuals with disabilities or limited function who require therapy services. The baby-boom generation's movement into middle age, a period when the incidence of heart attack and stroke increases, will spur the demand for therapeutic services. Growth in the population 75 years and older—an age group that suffers from high incidences of disabling conditions—also will increase the demand for therapeutic services. In addition, medical advances now enable more patients with critical problems to survive—patients who ultimately may need extensive therapy.

Hospitals will continue to employ a large number of occupational therapists to provide therapy services to acutely ill inpatients. Hospitals also will need occupational therapists to staff their outpatient rehabilitation programs.

Employment growth in schools will result from the expansion of the school-age population and extended services for disabled students. Therapists will be needed to help children with disabilities prepare to enter special education programs.

Earnings

Median annual earnings of occupational therapists were $51,990 in 2002. The middle 50 percent earned between $42,910 and $61,620. The lowest 10 percent earned less than $35,130, and the highest 10 percent earned more than $74,390. Median annual earnings in the industries employing the largest numbers of occupational therapists in 2002 were as follows:

Offices of other health practitioners $53,660
Nursing care facilities..53,930
General medical and surgical hospitals..................53,210
Elementary and secondary schools 45,740

Related Occupations

Occupational therapists use specialized knowledge to help individuals perform daily living skills and achieve maximum independence. Other workers performing similar duties include audiologists, chiropractors, physical therapists, recreational therapists, rehabilitation counselors, respiratory therapists, and speech-language pathologists.

Sources of Additional Information

For more information on occupational therapy as a career, contact:

- American Occupational Therapy Association, 4720 Montgomery Lane, Bethesda, MD 20824-1220. Internet: http://www.aota.org

Operations Research Analysts

(O*NET 15-2031.00 and 15-2041.00)

Significant Points

- Employers generally prefer applicants with at least a master's degree in operations research or a closely related field, such as computer science, engineering, business, mathematics, information systems, or management science.

- Employment growth is projected to be slower than average, reflecting slow growth in the number of jobs with the title "operations research analyst."

- Individuals with a master's or Ph.D. degree in management science or operations research should have good job opportunities as operations research analysts or in closely related occupations, such as systems analysts, computer scientists, or management analysts.

Nature of the Work

Operations research and *management science* are terms that are used interchangeably to describe the discipline of applying advanced analytical techniques to help make better decisions and to solve problems. The procedures of operations research have given effective assistance during wartime missions, such as deploying radar, searching for enemy submarines, and getting supplies where they were most needed. New analytical methods have been developed and numerous peacetime applications have emerged, leading to the use of operations research in many industries and occupations.

The prevalence of operations research in the nation's economy reflects the growing complexity of managing large organizations that require the effective use of money, materials, equipment, and people. Operations research analysts help determine better ways to coordinate these elements by applying analytical methods from mathematics, science, and engineering. They solve problems in different ways and propose alternative solutions to management, which then chooses the course of action that best meets the organization's goals. In general, operations research analysts may be concerned with diverse issues such as top-level strategy, planning, forecasting, resource allocation, performance measurement, scheduling, the design of production facilities and systems, supply chain management, pricing, transportation and distribution, and the analysis of large databases.

The duties of the operations research analyst vary according to the structure and management philosophy of the employer or client. Some firms centralize operations research in one department; others use operations research in each division. Operations research analysts also may work closely with senior managers to identify and solve a variety of problems. Some organizations contract operations research services with a consulting firm. Economists, systems analysts, mathematicians, industrial engineers, and others may apply operations research techniques to address problems in their respective fields.

Regardless of the type or structure of the client organization, operations research in its classical role entails a similar set of procedures in carrying out analysis to support management's quest to improve performance. Managers begin the process by describing the symptoms of a problem to the analyst, who then formally defines the problem. For example, an operations research analyst for an auto manufacturer may be asked to determine the best inventory level for each of the parts needed on a production line and to ascertain the optimal number of windshields to be kept in inventory. Too many windshields would be wasteful and expensive, while too few could result in an unintended halt in production.

Operations research analysts study such problems, breaking them into their components. Analysts then gather information about each of the components from a variety of sources. To determine the most efficient amount of inventory to be kept on hand, for example, operations research analysts might talk with engineers about production levels, discuss purchasing arrangements with buyers, and examine storage-cost data provided by the accounting department.

With the relevant information in hand, the analyst is ready to select the most appropriate analytical technique. Analysts can use any of several techniques, including simulation, linear and nonlinear programming, dynamic programming, queuing and other stochastic-process models, Markov decision processes, econometric methods, data envelopment analysis, neural networks, expert systems, decision analysis, and the analytic hierarchy process. Nearly all of these techniques, however, involve the construction of a mathematical model that attempts to describe the system being studied. The use of models enables the analyst to assign values to the different components and clarify the relationships among them. The values can be altered to examine what may happen to the system under different circumstances.

In most cases, the computer program developed to solve the model must be modified and run repeatedly to obtain different solutions. A model for airline flight scheduling, for example, might include variables for the cities to be connected, the amount of fuel required to fly the routes, projected levels of passenger demand, varying ticket and fuel prices, pilot scheduling, and maintenance costs. By locating the right combination of values for the variable, the analyst is able to produce the best flight schedule consistent with particular assumptions.

Upon concluding the analysis, the operations research analyst presents management with recommendations based on the results. Additional computer runs to consider different assumptions may be needed before the analyst presents the final recommendation. Once management reaches a decision, the analyst usually works with others in the organization to ensure the plan's successful implementation.

Working Conditions

Operations research analysts generally work regular hours in an office environment. Because they work on projects that are of immediate interest to top management, operations research analysts often are under pressure to meet deadlines and work more than a 40-hour week.

Employment

Operations research analysts held about 61,700 jobs in 2002. Major employers include telecommunication companies, aerospace manufacturers, computer systems design firms, financial institutions, insurance carriers, engineering

and management services firms, and federal and state governments. More than 4 out of 5 operations research analysts in the federal government work for the Department of Defense, and many in private industry work directly or indirectly on national defense. About 1 out of 5 analysts works in architectural, engineering, or related services; computer systems design and related services; management, scientific, and technical consulting services; and scientific research and development firms that offer consulting services in the field of operations research.

Training, Other Qualifications, and Advancement

Employers generally prefer applicants with at least a master's degree in operations research or a closely related field, such as computer science, engineering, business, mathematics, information systems, or management science, coupled with a bachelor's degree in computer science or a quantitative discipline, such as economics, mathematics, or statistics. Dual graduate degrees in operations research and computer science are especially attractive to employers. Operations research analysts also must be able to think logically and work well with people, and employers prefer workers with good oral and written communication skills.

In addition to supporting formal education in one manner or another, employers often sponsor training for experienced workers, helping them keep up with new developments in operations research techniques and computer science. Some analysts attend advanced university classes on these subjects at their employer's expense.

Because computers are the most important tools for performing in-depth analysis, training and experience in programming are required. Operations research analysts typically need to be proficient in database collection and management, programming, and the development and use of sophisticated software packages.

Beginning analysts usually perform routine work under the supervision of more experienced analysts. As the novices gain knowledge and experience, they are assigned more complex tasks and given greater autonomy to design models and solve problems. Operations research analysts advance by assuming positions as technical specialists or supervisors. The skills acquired by operations research analysts are useful for a variety of higher level management jobs, so experienced analysts may leave the field to assume nontechnical managerial or administrative positions. Operations research analysts with significant experience may become consultants, and some may even open their own consulting practice.

Job Outlook

Employment of operations research analysts is expected to grow more slowly than the average for all occupations through 2012, reflecting slow growth in the number of jobs with the title "operations research analyst." Job opportunities in operations research should be good, however, because organizations throughout the economy will strive to improve their productivity, effectiveness, and competitiveness and because of the extensive availability of data, computers, and software. Many jobs in operations research have other titles, such as "operations analyst," "management analyst," "systems analyst," and "policy analyst." Individuals who hold a master's or Ph.D. degree in operations research, management science, or a closely related field should find good job opportunities because the number of openings generated by employment growth and the need to replace those leaving the occupation are expected to exceed the number of persons graduating with those credentials.

Organizations face pressure today from growing domestic and international competition and must work to make their operations as effective as possible. As a result, businesses will increasingly rely on operations research analysts to optimize profits by improving productivity and reducing costs. As new technology is introduced into the marketplace, operations research analysts will be needed to determine how to utilize the technology in the best way.

Opportunities for operations research analysts exist in almost every industry because of the diversity of applications for their work. However, opportunities should be especially good in highly competitive industries, such as manufacturing, transportation, telecommunications, and finance. As businesses and government agencies continue to contract out jobs to cut costs, many operations research analysts also will find opportunities as consultants, either working for a consulting firm or setting up their own practice. Opportunities in the military will exist as well, but will depend on the size of future military budgets. As the military develops new weapons systems and strategies, military leaders will rely on operations research analysts to test and evaluate their accuracy and effectiveness.

Earnings

Median annual earnings of operations research analysts were $56,920 in 2002. The middle 50 percent earned between $43,220 and $74,460. The lowest 10 percent had earnings of less than $34,140, while the highest 10 percent earned more than $92,430.

The average annual salary for operations research analysts in the federal government in nonsupervisory, supervisory, and managerial positions was $83,740 in 2003.

Related Occupations

Operations research analysts apply advanced analytical methods to large, complicated problems. Workers in other occupations that stress advanced analysis include computer systems analysts, database administrators, and computer scientists; computer programmers; engineers; mathematicians; statisticians; economists; and market and survey researchers. Because its goal is improved organizational effectiveness, operations research also is closely allied to managerial occu-

pations, such as computer and information systems managers, and management analysts.

Sources of Additional Information

Information on career opportunities for operations research analysts is available from:

- Institute for Operations Research and Management Science, 901 Elkridge Landing Rd., Suite 400, Linthicum, MD 21090. Internet: http://www.informs.org

For information on operations research careers in the Armed Forces and the U.S. Department of Defense, contact:

- Military Operations Research Society, 1703 N. Beauregard St., Suite 450, Alexandria, VA 22311. Internet: http://www.mors.org

Information on obtaining an operations research analyst position with the federal government is available from the Office of Personnel Management (OPM) through a telephone-based system. Consult your telephone directory under U.S. government for a local number or call (703) 724-1850; Federal Relay Service: (800) 877-8339. The first number is not toll free, and charges may result. Information also is available from the OPM Internet site: http://www.usajobs.opm.gov.

Ophthalmic Laboratory Technicians

(O*NET 51-9083.01 and 51-9083.02)

Significant Points

- Nearly all ophthalmic laboratory technicians learn their skills on the job.

- Employment is expected to grow more slowly than the average, reflecting the increasing use of automated machinery.

- Only a limited number of job openings will be created each year, because the occupation is small.

Nature of the Work

Ophthalmic laboratory technicians—also known as manufacturing opticians, optical mechanics, or optical goods workers—make prescription eyeglass or contact lenses. Prescription lenses are curved in such a way that light is correctly focused onto the retina of the patient's eye, improving his or her vision. Some ophthalmic laboratory technicians manufacture lenses for other optical instruments, such as telescopes and binoculars. Ophthalmic laboratory technicians cut, grind, edge, and finish lenses according to specifications provided by dispensing opticians, optometrists, or ophthalmologists and may insert lenses into frames to produce finished glasses. Although some lenses still are produced by hand, technicians are increasingly using automated equipment to make lenses.

Ophthalmic laboratory technicians should not be confused with workers in other vision care occupations. Ophthalmologists and optometrists are "eye doctors" who examine eyes, diagnose and treat vision problems, and prescribe corrective lenses. Ophthalmologists are physicians who perform eye surgery. Dispensing opticians, who also may do the work of ophthalmic laboratory technicians, help patients select frames and lenses, and adjust finished eyeglasses.

Ophthalmic laboratory technicians read prescription specifications, select standard glass or plastic lens blanks, and then mark them to indicate where the curves specified on the prescription should be ground. They place the lens in the lens grinder, set the dials for the prescribed curvature, and start the machine. After a minute or so, the lens is ready to be "finished" by a machine that rotates it against a fine abrasive, to grind it and smooth out rough edges. The lens is then placed in a polishing machine with an even finer abrasive, to polish it to a smooth, bright finish.

Next, the technician examines the lens through a lensometer, an instrument similar in shape to a microscope, to make sure that the degree and placement of the curve are correct. The technician then cuts the lenses and bevels the edges to fit the frame, dips each lens into dye if the prescription calls for tinted or coated lenses, polishes the edges, and assembles the lenses and frame parts into a finished pair of glasses.

In small laboratories, technicians usually handle every phase of the operation. In large ones, in which virtually every phase of the operation is automated, technicians may be responsible for operating computerized equipment. Technicians also inspect the final product for quality and accuracy.

Working Conditions

Ophthalmic laboratory technicians work in relatively clean and well-lighted laboratories and have limited contact with the public. Their surroundings are relatively quiet despite the humming of machines. At times, technicians wear goggles to protect their eyes, and they may spend a great deal of time standing.

Most ophthalmic laboratory technicians work a 5-day, 40-hour week, which may include weekends, evenings, or, occasionally, some overtime. Some work part time.

Ophthalmic laboratory technicians need to take precautions against the hazards associated with cutting glass, handling chemicals, and working near machinery.

Employment

Ophthalmic laboratory technicians held about 33,000 jobs in 2002. Around 34 percent were in health and personal care stores, such as optical goods stores that manufacture and sell

prescription glasses and contact lenses. About 29 percent were in medical equipment and supplies manufacturing, working for ophthalmic goods manufacturers that produce eyewear and contact lenses for sale by retail stores, as well as by ophthalmologists and optometrists. Most of the rest were in offices of other health practitioners, professional and commercial equipment and supplies merchant wholesalers, office of physicians, employment services, or in commercial and service industry machine manufacturing firms that produce lenses for other optical instruments, such as telescopes and binoculars.

Training, Other Qualifications, and Advancement

Nearly all ophthalmic laboratory technicians learn their skills on the job. Employers filling trainee jobs prefer applicants who are high school graduates. Courses in science, mathematics, and computers are valuable; manual dexterity and the ability to do precision work are essential.

Technician trainees producing lenses by hand start on simple tasks, such as marking or blocking lenses for grinding, and then progress to grinding, cutting, edging, and beveling lenses, and, finally, to assembling the eyeglasses. Depending on individual aptitude, it may take up to 6 months to become proficient in all phases of the work.

Technicians using automated systems will find computer skills valuable. Training is completed on the job and varies in duration, depending on the type of machinery and the worker's aptitude.

A very small number of ophthalmic laboratory technicians learn their trade in the Armed Forces or in the few programs in optical technology offered by vocational-technical institutes or trade schools. These programs have classes in optical theory, surfacing and lens finishing, and the reading and applying of prescriptions. Programs vary in length from 6 months to 1 year and award certificates or diplomas.

Ophthalmic laboratory technicians can become supervisors and managers. Some become dispensing opticians, although further education or training generally is required in that occupation.

Job Outlook

Overall employment of ophthalmic laboratory technicians is expected to grow more slowly than the average for all occupations through the year 2012, reflecting the increasing use of automated machinery. Most job openings will arise from the need to replace technicians who transfer to other occupations or who leave the labor force. Only a limited number of job openings will be created each year, because the occupation is small.

Demographic trends make it likely that many more Americans will need vision care in the years ahead. Not only will the population grow, but also, the proportion of middle-aged and older adults is projected to increase rapidly. Middle age is a time when many people use corrective lenses for the first time, and elderly persons usually require more vision care than others.

Fashion also influences demand. Frames come in a variety of styles and colors, encouraging people to buy more than one pair. Demand is expected to grow as well in response to the availability of new technologies that improve the quality and look of corrective lenses, such as antireflective coatings and bifocal lenses without the line that is visible in traditional bifocals.

Earnings

Median hourly earnings of ophthalmic laboratory technicians were $10.46 in 2002. The middle 50 percent earned between $8.73 and $13.05 an hour. The lowest 10 percent earned less than $7.56, and the highest 10 percent earned more than $16.40 an hour. In 2002, median hourly earnings of ophthalmic laboratory technicians were $10.68 in medical equipment and supplies manufacturing and $10.15 in health and personal care stores.

Related Occupations

Workers in other precision production occupations include dental laboratory technicians; opticians, dispensing; orthotists and prosthetists; and precision instrument and equipment repairers.

Sources of Additional Information

For a list of accredited programs in ophthalmic laboratory technology, contact:

- Commission on Opticianry Accreditation, P.O. Box 3073, Merrifield, VA 22116-3073.

State employment service offices can provide information about job openings for ophthalmic laboratory technicians.

Opticians, Dispensing

(O*NET 29-2081.00)

Significant Points

- Most dispensing opticians receive training on the job or through apprenticeships lasting 2 or more years; twenty-one states require a license.

- Projected employment growth reflects steady demand for corrective lenses and eyeglass frames that are in fashion.

- The number of job openings will be limited because the occupation is small.

Nature of the Work

Dispensing opticians fit eyeglasses and contact lenses, following prescriptions written by ophthalmologists or optometrists.

Dispensing opticians examine written prescriptions to determine the specifications of lenses. They recommend eyeglass frames, lenses, and lens coatings after considering the prescription and the customer's occupation, habits, and facial features. Dispensing opticians measure clients' eyes, including the distance between the centers of the pupils and the distance between the surface and the lens. For customers without prescriptions, dispensing opticians may use a lensometer to record eyeglass measurements. They also may obtain a customer's previous record or verify a prescription with the examining optometrist or ophthalmologist.

Dispensing opticians prepare work orders that give ophthalmic laboratory technicians information needed to grind and insert lenses into a frame. The work order includes prescriptions for lenses and information on their size, material, color, and style. Some dispensing opticians grind and insert lenses themselves. After the glasses are made, dispensing opticians verify that the lenses have been ground to specifications. Then they may reshape or bend the frame, by hand or using pliers, so that the eyeglasses fit the customer properly and comfortably. Some also fix, adjust, and refit broken frames. They instruct clients about adapting to, wearing, or caring for eyeglasses.

Some dispensing opticians specialize in fitting contacts, artificial eyes, or cosmetic shells to cover blemished eyes. To fit contact lenses, dispensing opticians measure the shape and size of the eye, select the type of contact lens material, and prepare work orders specifying the prescription and lens size. Fitting contact lenses requires considerable skill, care, and patience. Dispensing opticians observe customers' eyes, corneas, lids, and contact lenses with special instruments and microscopes. During several visits, opticians show customers how to insert, remove, and care for their contacts. Opticians do all this to ensure that the fit is correct.

Dispensing opticians keep records on customers' prescriptions, work orders, and payments; track inventory and sales; and perform other administrative duties.

Working Conditions

Dispensing opticians work indoors in attractive, well-lighted, and well-ventilated surroundings. They may work in medical offices or small stores where customers are served one at a time. Some work in large stores where several dispensing opticians serve a number of customers at once. Opticians spend a lot of time on their feet. If they prepare lenses, they need to take precautions against the hazards associated with glass cutting, chemicals, and machinery.

Most dispensing opticians work a 40-hour week, although some work longer hours. Those in retail stores may work evenings and weekends. Some work part time.

Employment

Dispensing opticians held about 63,000 jobs in 2002. About 2 out of 5 worked in health and personal care stores, including optical goods stores. Many of these stores offer one-stop shopping. Customers may have their eyes examined, choose frames, and have glasses made on the spot. Another 2 out of 5 dispensing opticians worked in offices of physicians or other health practitioners for ophthalmologists or optometrists who sell glasses directly to patients. Some work in optical departments of department stores or other general merchandise stores, such as warehouse clubs and superstores.

Training, Other Qualifications, and Advancement

Employers usually hire individuals with no background as an optician or those who have worked as ophthalmic laboratory technicians. The employers then provide the required training. Most dispensing opticians receive training on the job or through apprenticeships lasting 2 or more years. Some employers, however, seek people with postsecondary training in the field.

Knowledge of physics, basic anatomy, algebra, geometry, and mechanical drawing is particularly valuable, because training usually includes instruction in optical mathematics, optical physics, and the use of precision measuring instruments and other machinery and tools. Dispensing opticians deal directly with the public, so they should be tactful, pleasant, and communicate well. Manual dexterity and the ability to do precision work are essential.

Large employers usually offer structured apprenticeship programs; small employers provide more informal, on-the-job training. In the 21 states that require dispensing opticians to be licensed, individuals without postsecondary training work from 2 to 4 years as apprentices. Apprenticeship or formal training is offered in most states as well.

Apprentices receive technical training and learn office management and sales. Under the supervision of an experienced optician, optometrist, or ophthalmologist, apprentices work directly with patients, fitting eyeglasses and contact lenses. In states requiring licensure, information about apprenticeships and licensing procedures is available from the state board of occupational licensing.

Formal training in the field is offered in community colleges and a few colleges and universities. In 2002, the Commission on Opticianry Accreditation accredited 22 programs that awarded 2-year associate degrees. There also are shorter programs of 1 year or less. Some states that offer a license to dispensing opticians allow graduates to take the licensure exam immediately upon graduation; others require a few months to a year of experience.

Dispensing opticians may apply to the American Board of Opticianry (ABO) and the National Contact Lens Examiners (NCLE) for certification of their skills. Certification must be renewed every 3 years through continuing education. Those licensed in states where licensing renewal requirements include continuing education credits may use proof of their renewed state license to meet the recertification requirements of the ABO. Likewise, the NCLE will accept proof of renewal from any state that has contact lens requirements.

Many experienced dispensing opticians open their own optical stores. Others become managers of optical stores or sales representatives for wholesalers or manufacturers of eyeglasses or lenses.

Job Outlook

Employment of dispensing opticians is expected to increase about as fast as the average for all occupations through 2012 as demand grows for corrective lenses. The number of middle-aged and elderly persons is projected to increase rapidly. Middle age is a time when many individuals use corrective lenses for the first time, and elderly persons generally require more vision care than others.

Fashion, too, influences demand. Frames come in a growing variety of styles and colors—encouraging people to buy more than one pair. Demand also is expected to grow in response to the availability of new technologies that improve the quality and look of corrective lenses, such as antireflective coatings and bifocal lenses without the line that is visible in old-style bifocals. Improvements in bifocal, extended-wear, and disposable contact lenses also will spur demand.

The need to replace those who leave the occupation will result in additional job openings. Nevertheless, the number of job openings will be limited because the occupation is small. Dispensing opticians are vulnerable to changes in the business cycle, because eyewear purchases often can be deferred for a time.

Earnings

Median annual earnings of dispensing opticians were $25,600 in 2002. The middle 50 percent earned between $19,960 and $33,530. The lowest 10 percent earned less than $16,310, and the highest 10 percent earned more than $43,490. Median annual earnings in the industries employing the largest numbers of dispensing opticians in 2002 were as follows:

Offices of physicians $28,250

Health and personal care stores.............................. 25,860

Offices of other health practitioners 24,900

Related Occupations

Other workers who deal with customers and perform delicate work include jewelers and precious stone and metal workers, locksmiths and safe repairers, orthotists and prosthetists, and precision instrument and equipment repairers.

Sources of Additional Information

For general information about opticians and a list of home-study programs, seminars, and review materials, contact:

- National Academy of Opticianry, 8401 Corporate Dr., Suite 605, Landover, MD 20785. Telephone (toll-free): 800-229-4828. Internet: http://www.nao.org

For a list of accredited programs in opticianry, contact:

- Commission on Opticianry Accreditation, P.O. Box 3073, Merrifield, VA 22116-3073.

To learn about voluntary certification for opticians who fit eyeglasses, as well as a list of state licensing boards for opticians, contact:

- American Board of Opticianry, 6506 Loisdale Rd., Suite 209, Springfield, VA 22150. Internet: http://www.abo.org

For information on voluntary certification for dispensing opticians who fit contact lenses, contact:

- National Contact Lens Examiners, 6506 Loisdale Rd., Suite 209, Springfield, VA 22150. Internet: http://www.abo.org

Optometrists

(O*NET 29-1041.00)

Significant Points

- Licensed optometrists must earn a Doctor of Optometry degree from an accredited optometry school and pass a written and a clinical state board examination.

- Admission to optometry school is competitive.

- Optometrists usually remain in practice until they retire, so relatively few job openings arise from the need to replace those who leave the occupation.

Nature of the Work

Optometrists, also known as *doctors of optometry,* or *ODs,* provide most primary vision care. They examine people's eyes to diagnose vision problems and eye diseases, and they test patients' visual acuity, depth and color perception, and ability to focus and coordinate the eyes. Optometrists prescribe eyeglasses and contact lenses and provide vision therapy and low-vision rehabilitation. Optometrists analyze test results and develop a treatment plan. They administer drugs to patients to aid in the diagnosis of vision problems and prescribe drugs to treat some eye diseases. Optometrists often provide preoperative and postoperative care to cataract patients, as well as patients who have had laser vision correction or other eye surgery. They also diagnose conditions due to systemic diseases such as diabetes and high blood pressure, referring patients to other health practitioners as needed.

Optometrists should not be confused with ophthalmologists or dispensing opticians. Ophthalmologists are physicians who perform eye surgery, and diagnose and treat eye diseases and injuries. Like optometrists, they also examine eyes and prescribe eyeglasses and contact lenses. Dispensing opticians fit and adjust eyeglasses and, in some states, may fit contact lenses according to prescriptions written by ophthalmologists or optometrists.

Most optometrists are in general practice. Some specialize in work with the elderly, children, or partially sighted persons who need specialized visual devices. Others develop and implement ways to protect workers' eyes from on-the-job strain or injury. Some specialize in contact lenses, sports vision, or vision therapy. A few teach optometry, perform research, or consult.

Most optometrists are private practitioners who also handle the business aspects of running an office, such as developing a patient base, hiring employees, keeping records, and ordering equipment and supplies. Optometrists who operate franchise optical stores also may have some of these duties.

Working Conditions

Optometrists work in places—usually their own offices—that are clean, well lighted, and comfortable. Most full-time optometrists work about 40 hours a week. Many work weekends and evenings to suit the needs of patients. Emergency calls, once uncommon, have increased with the passage of therapeutic-drug laws expanding optometrists' ability to prescribe medications.

Employment

Optometrists held about 32,000 jobs in 2002. The number of jobs is greater than the number of practicing optometrists because some optometrists hold two or more jobs. For example, an optometrist may have a private practice, but also work in another practice, in a clinic, or in a vision care center. According to the American Optometric Association, about two-thirds of practicing optometrists are in private practice. Although many optometrists practice alone, a growing number are in a partnership or group practice.

Salaried jobs for optometrists were primarily in offices of other health practitioners, including optometrists; offices of physicians, including ophthalmologists; or health and personal care stores, including optical goods stores. A small number of salaried jobs for optometrists were in hospitals; the federal government; or outpatient care centers, including health maintenance organizations. Almost a third of optometrists were self-employed.

Training, Other Qualifications, and Advancement

All states and the District of Columbia require that optometrists be licensed. Applicants for a license must have a Doctor of Optometry degree from an accredited optometry school and pass both a written and a clinical state board examination. In many states, applicants can substitute the examinations of the National Board of Examiners in Optometry, usually taken during the student's academic career, for part or all of the written examination. Licenses are renewed every 1 to 3 years, and, in all states, continuing education credits are needed for renewal.

The Doctor of Optometry degree requires the completion of a 4-year program at an accredited optometry school, preceded by at least 3 years of preoptometric study at an accredited college or university. Most optometry students hold a bachelor's or higher degree. In 2002, 17 U.S. schools and colleges of optometry held an accredited status with the Accreditation Council on Optometric Education of the American Optometric Association.

Requirements for admission to schools of optometry include courses in English, mathematics, physics, chemistry, and biology. A few schools also require or recommend courses in psychology, history, sociology, speech, or business. Since a strong background in science is important, many applicants to optometry school major in a science such as biology or chemistry, while other applicants major in another subject and take many science courses as well. Applicants must take the Optometry Admissions Test, which measures academic ability and scientific comprehension. Most applicants take the test after their sophomore or junior year, allowing them an opportunity to take the test again and raise their score. A small number of applicants are accepted to optometry school after 3 years of college and complete their bachelor's degree while attending optometry school. Admission to optometry school is competitive.

Optometry programs include classroom and laboratory study of health and visual sciences, as well as clinical training in the diagnosis and treatment of eye disorders. Courses in pharmacology, optics, vision science, biochemistry, and systemic disease are included.

Business ability, self-discipline, and the ability to deal tactfully with patients are important for success. The work of optometrists requires attention to detail and manual dexterity.

Optometrists wishing to teach or do research may study for a master's or Ph.D. degree in visual science, physiological optics, neurophysiology, public health, health administration, health information and communication, or health education. One-year postgraduate clinical residency programs are available for optometrists who wish to specialize in family practice optometry, pediatric optometry, geriatric optometry, vision therapy, contact lenses, hospital-based optometry, primary care optometry, or ocular disease.

Job Outlook

Employment of optometrists is expected to grow about as fast as the average for all occupations through 2012, in response to the vision care needs of a growing and aging population. As baby boomers age, they will be more likely to visit optometrists and ophthalmologists because of the onset of vision problems in middle age, including those resulting from the extensive use of computers. The demand for optometric services also will increase because of growth in the oldest age group, with its increased likelihood of cataracts, glaucoma, diabetes, and hypertension. Greater recognition of the importance of vision care, rising personal incomes, and growth in employee vision care plans will spur employment growth, as well.

Employment of optometrists would grow more rapidly were it not for anticipated productivity gains that will allow each optometrist to see more patients. These expected gains stem from greater use of optometric assistants and other support personnel, who will reduce the amount of time optometrists need with each patient. Also, laser surgery that can correct some vision problems is available, but expensive. Optometrists will still be needed to perform preoperative and postoperative care for laser surgery; however, patients who successfully undergo this surgery may not require optometrists to prescribe glasses or contacts for several years.

In addition to growth, the need to replace optometrists who leave the occupation will create employment opportunities. Relatively few opportunities from this source are expected, however, because optometrists usually continue to practice until they retire; few transfer to other occupations.

Earnings

Median annual earnings of salaried optometrists were $86,090 in 2002. The middle 50 percent earned between $62,030 and $115,550. Median annual earnings of salaried optometrists in 2002 were $87,070 in offices of other health practitioners. Salaried optometrists tend to earn more initially than do optometrists who set up their own independent practice. In the long run, however, those in private practice usually earn more.

According to the American Optometric Association, median net annual income for all optometrists, including the self-employed, was $110,000 in 2002. The middle 50 percent earned between $82,500 and $156,500.

Related Occupations

Other workers who apply scientific knowledge to prevent, diagnose, and treat disorders and injuries are chiropractors, dentists, physicians and surgeons, podiatrists, and veterinarians.

Sources of Additional Information

For information on optometry as a career and a list of accredited optometric educational institutions, contact:

* Association of Schools and Colleges of Optometry, 6110 Executive Blvd., Suite 510, Rockville, MD 20852. Internet: http://www.opted.org

Additional career information is available from:

• American Optometric Association, Educational Services, 243 North Lindbergh Blvd., St. Louis, MO 63141-7881. Internet: http://www.aoanet.org

The Board of Optometry in each state can supply information on licensing requirements.

For information on specific admission requirements and sources of financial aid, contact the admissions officers of individual optometry schools.

Paralegals and Legal Assistants

(O*NET 23-2011.00)

Significant Points

- While some paralegals train on the job, employers increasingly prefer graduates of postsecondary paralegal education programs; college graduates who have taken some paralegal courses are especially in demand in some markets.

- Paralegals are projected to grow faster than average, as law offices try to reduce costs by assigning them tasks formerly carried out by lawyers.

- Paralegals are employed by law firms, corporate legal departments, and various government offices and they may specialize in many different areas of the law.

Nature of the Work

While lawyers assume ultimate responsibility for legal work, they often delegate many of their tasks to paralegals. In fact, paralegals—also called legal assistants—continue to assume a growing range of tasks in the nation's legal offices and perform many of the same tasks as lawyers. Nevertheless, they are still explicitly prohibited from carrying out duties which are considered to be the practice of law, such as setting legal fees, giving legal advice, and presenting cases in court.

One of a paralegal's most important tasks is helping lawyers prepare for closings, hearings, trials, and corporate meetings. Paralegals investigate the facts of cases and ensure that all relevant information is considered. They also identify appropriate laws, judicial decisions, legal articles, and other materials that are relevant to assigned cases. After they analyze and organize the information, paralegals may prepare written reports that attorneys use in determining how cases should be handled. Should attorneys decide to file lawsuits on behalf of clients, paralegals may help prepare the legal arguments, draft pleadings and motions to be filed with the court, obtain affidavits, and assist attorneys during trials. Paralegals also organize and track files of all important case documents and make them available and easily accessible to attorneys.

In addition to this preparatory work, paralegals also perform a number of other vital functions. For example, they help draft contracts, mortgages, separation agreements, and trust instruments. They also may assist in preparing tax returns and planning estates. Some paralegals coordinate the activities of other law office employees and maintain financial office records. Various additional tasks may differ, depending on the employer.

Paralegals are found in all types of organizations, but most are employed by law firms, corporate legal departments, and various government offices. In these organizations, they can work in many different areas of the law, including litigation, personal injury, corporate law, criminal law, employee benefits, intellectual property, labor law, bankruptcy, immigration, family law, and real estate. As the law has become more complex, paralegals have responded by becoming more specialized. Within specialties, functions often are broken down further so that paralegals may deal with a specific area. For example, paralegals specializing in labor law may deal exclusively with employee benefits.

The duties of paralegals also differ widely based on the type of organization in which they are employed. Paralegals who work for corporations often assist attorneys with employee contracts, shareholder agreements, stock-option plans, and employee benefit plans. They also may help prepare and file annual financial reports, maintain corporate minute books and record resolutions, and prepare forms to secure loans for the corporation. Paralegals often monitor and review government regulations to ensure that the corporation is aware of new requirements and it operates within the law.

The duties of paralegals who work in the public sector usually vary within each agency. In general, they analyze legal material for internal use, maintain reference files, conduct research for attorneys, and collect and analyze evidence for agency hearings. They may then prepare informative or explanatory material on laws, agency regulations, and agency policy for general use by the agency and the public. Paralegals employed in community legal-service projects help the poor, the aged, and others in need of legal assistance. They file forms, conduct research, prepare documents, and when authorized by law, may represent clients at administrative hearings.

Paralegals in small and medium-sized law firms usually perform a variety of duties that require a general knowledge of the law. For example, they may research judicial decisions on improper police arrests or help prepare a mortgage contract. Paralegals employed by large law firms, government agencies, and corporations, however, are more likely to specialize in one aspect of the law.

Computer use and technical knowledge has become essential to paralegal work. Computer software packages and the Internet are increasingly used to search legal literature stored in computer databases and on CD-ROM. In litigation involving many supporting documents, paralegals may use computer databases to retrieve, organize, and index various materials. Imaging software allows paralegals to scan documents directly into a database, while billing programs help them to track hours billed to clients. Computer software packages also may be used to perform tax computations and explore the consequences of possible tax strategies for clients.

Working Conditions

Paralegals employed by corporations and government usually work a standard 40-hour week. Although most paralegals work year round, some are temporarily employed during busy times of the year, then released when the workload diminishes. Paralegals who work for law firms sometimes work very long hours when they are under pressure to meet deadlines. Some law firms reward such loyalty with bonuses and additional time off.

These workers handle many routine assignments, particularly when they are inexperienced. As they gain experience, paralegals usually assume more varied tasks with additional responsibility. Paralegals do most of their work at desks in offices and law libraries. Occasionally, they travel to gather information and perform other duties.

Employment

Paralegals and legal assistants held about 200,000 jobs in 2002. Private law firms employed 7 out of 10 paralegals and legal assistants; most of the remainder worked for corporate legal departments and various levels of government. Within the federal government, the U.S. Department of Justice is the largest employer, followed by the Social Security Administration and the U.S. Department of Treasury. A small number of paralegals own their own businesses and work as freelance legal assistants, contracting their services to attorneys or corporate legal departments.

Training, Other Qualifications, and Advancement

There are several ways to become a paralegal. The most common is through a community college paralegal program that leads to an associate's degree. The other common method of entry, mainly for those who have a college degree, is through a certification program that leads to a certification in paralegal studies. A small number of schools also offer bachelor's and master's degrees in paralegal studies. Some employers train paralegals on the job, hiring college graduates with no legal experience or promoting experienced legal secretaries. Other entrants have experience in a technical field that is useful to law firms, such as a background in tax preparation for tax and estate practice, criminal justice, or nursing or health administration for personal injury practice.

Formal paralegal training programs are offered by an estimated 600 colleges and universities, law schools, and proprietary schools. Approximately 250 paralegal programs are approved by the American Bar Association (ABA). Although this approval is neither required nor sought by many programs, graduation from an ABA-approved program can enhance one's employment opportunities. The requirements for admission to these programs vary. Some require certain college courses or a bachelor's degree; others accept high school graduates or those with legal experience; and a few schools require standardized tests and personal interviews.

Paralegal programs include 2-year associate's degree programs, 4-year bachelor's degree programs, and certificate programs that can take only a few months to complete. Most certificate programs provide intensive paralegal training for individuals who already hold college degrees, while associate's and bachelor's degree programs usually combine paralegal training with courses in other academic subjects. The quality of paralegal training programs varies; the better programs usually include job placement. Programs increasingly include courses introducing students to the legal applications of computers, including how to perform legal research using the Internet. Many paralegal training programs include an internship in which students gain practical experience by working for several months in a private law firm, office of a public defender or attorney general, bank, corporate legal department, legal-aid organization, or government agency. Experience gained in internships is an asset when seeking a job after graduation. Prospective students should examine the experiences of recent graduates before enrolling in those programs.

Although most employers do not require certification, earning a voluntary certificate from a professional society may offer advantages in the labor market. The National Association of Legal Assistants, for example, has established standards for certification requiring various combinations of education and experience. Paralegals who meet these standards are eligible to take a 2-day examination, given three times each year at several regional testing centers. Those who pass this examination may use the designation Certified Legal Assistant (CLA). In addition, the Paralegal Advanced Competency Exam, established in 1996 and administered through the National Federation of Paralegal Associations, offers professional recognition to paralegals with a bachelor's degree and at least 2 years of experience. Those who pass this examination may use the designation Registered Paralegal (RP).

Paralegals must be able to document and present their findings and opinions to their supervising attorney. They need to understand legal terminology and have good research and investigative skills. Familiarity with the operation and applications of computers in legal research and litigation support also is increasingly important. Paralegals should stay informed of new developments in the laws that affect their area of practice. Participation in continuing legal education seminars allows paralegals to maintain and expand their legal knowledge.

Because paralegals frequently deal with the public, they should be courteous and uphold the ethical standards of the legal profession. The National Association of Legal Assistants, the National Federation of Paralegal Associations, and a few states have established ethical guidelines for paralegals to follow.

Paralegals usually are given more responsibilities and less supervision as they gain work experience. Experienced paralegals who work in large law firms, corporate legal departments, and government agencies may supervise and delegate assignments to other paralegals and clerical staff. Advancement opportunities also include promotion to managerial and other law-related positions within the firm or corporate legal department. However, some paralegals find it easier to move to another law firm when seeking increased responsibility or advancement.

Job Outlook

Paralegals and legal assistants are projected to grow faster than the average for all occupations through 2012. Some employment growth stems from law firms and other employers with legal staffs increasingly hiring paralegals to lower the cost and increase the availability and efficiency of legal services. The majority of job openings for paralegals in the future will be new jobs created by employment growth, but additional job openings will arise as people leave the occupation. Despite projections of fast employment growth, competition for jobs should continue as many people seek to go into this profession; however, highly skilled, formally trained paralegals have excellent employment potential.

Private law firms will continue to be the largest employers of paralegals, but a growing array of other organizations, such as corporate legal departments, insurance companies, real estate and title insurance firms, and banks hire paralegals. Corporations, in particular, are boosting their in-house legal departments to cut costs. Demand for paralegals also is expected to grow as an increasing population requires legal services, especially in areas such as intellectual property, healthcare, international, elder issues, criminal, and environmental law. The growth of prepaid legal plans also should contribute to the demand for legal services. Paralegal employment is expected to increase as organizations presently employing paralegals assign them a growing range of tasks, and as paralegals are increasingly employed in small and medium-sized establishments. A growing number of experienced paralegals are expected to establish their own businesses.

Job opportunities for paralegals will expand in the public sector as well. Community legal-service programs, which provide assistance to the poor, aged, minorities, and middle-income families, will employ additional paralegals to minimize expenses and serve the most people. Federal, state, and local government agencies, consumer organizations, and the courts also should continue to hire paralegals in increasing numbers.

To a limited extent, paralegal jobs are affected by the business cycle. During recessions, demand declines for some discretionary legal services, such as planning estates, drafting wills, and handling real estate transactions. Corporations are less inclined to initiate certain types of litigation when falling sales and profits lead to fiscal belt tightening. As a result, full-time paralegals employed in offices adversely affected by a recession may be laid off or have their work hours reduced. On the other hand, during recessions, corporations and individuals are more likely to face other problems that require legal assistance, such as bankruptcies, foreclosures, and divorces. Paralegals, who provide many of the same legal services as lawyers at a lower cost, tend to fare relatively better in difficult economic conditions.

Earnings

Earnings of paralegals and legal assistants vary greatly. Salaries depend on education, training, experience, type and size of employer, and geographic location of the job. In general, paralegals who work for large law firms or in large metropolitan areas earn more than those who work for smaller firms or in less populated regions. In addition to a salary, many paralegals receive bonuses. In 2002, full-time, wage and salary paralegals and legal assistants had median annual earnings, including bonuses, of $37,950. The middle 50 percent earned between $30,020 and $48,760. The top 10 percent earned more than $61,150, while the bottom 10 percent earned less than $24,470. Median annual earnings in the industries employing the largest numbers of paralegals in 2002 were as follows:

Federal government $53,770

Legal services 36,780

Local government 36,030

State government..34,750

Related Occupations

Several other occupations call for a specialized understanding of the law and the legal system, but do not require the extensive training of a lawyer. These include law clerks; title examiners, abstractors, and searchers; claims adjusters, appraisers, examiners, and investigators; and occupational health and safety specialists and technicians.

Sources of Additional Information

General information on a career as a paralegal can be obtained from:

- Standing Committee on Legal Assistants, American Bar Association, 541 N. Fairbanks Ct., Chicago, IL 60611. Internet: http://www.abanet.org

For information on the Certified Legal Assistant exam, schools that offer training programs in a specific state, and standards and guidelines for paralegals, contact:

- National Association of Legal Assistants, Inc., 1516 South Boston St., Suite 200, Tulsa, OK 74119. Internet: http://www.nala.org

Information on a career as a paralegal, schools that offer training programs, job postings for paralegals, the Paralegal Advanced Competency Exam, and local paralegal associations can be obtained from:

- National Federation of Paralegal Associations, P.O. Box 33108, Kansas City, MO 64114. Internet: http://www.paralegals.org

Information on paralegal training programs, including the pamphlet "How to Choose a Paralegal Education Program," may be obtained from:

- American Association for Paralegal Education, 407 Wekiva Springs Road, Suite 241, Longwood, FL 32779. Internet: http://www.aafpe.org

Information on obtaining a position as a paralegal specialist with the federal government is available from the Office of Personnel Management (OPM) through a telephone-based system. Consult your telephone directory under U.S. government for a local number or call (703) 724-1850; Federal Relay Service: (800) 877-8339. The first number is not toll free, and charges may result. Information also is available from the OPM Internet site: http://www.usajobs.opm.gov.

Pharmacists

(O*NET 29-1051.00)

Significant Points

- Pharmacists are becoming more involved in drug therapy decisionmaking and patient counseling.

- A license is required; one must graduate from an accredited college of pharmacy and pass a state examination.

- Very good employment opportunities are expected.

- Earnings are very high, but some pharmacists work long hours, nights, weekends, and holidays.

Nature of the Work

Pharmacists dispense drugs prescribed by physicians and other health practitioners and provide information to patients about medications and their use. They advise physicians and other health practitioners on the selection, dosages, interactions, and side effects of medications. Pharmacists also monitor the health and progress of patients in response to drug therapy to ensure safe and effective use of medication. Pharmacists must understand the use, clinical effects, and composition of drugs, including their chemical, biological, and physical properties. Compounding—the actual mixing of ingredients to form powders, tablets, capsules, ointments, and solutions—is a small part of a pharmacist's practice, because most medicines are produced by pharmaceutical companies in a standard dosage and drug delivery form. Traditionally, most pharmacists work in a community setting, such as a retail drugstore, or in a healthcare facility, such as a hospital, nursing home, mental health institution, or neighborhood health clinic.

Pharmacists in community and retail pharmacies counsel patients and answer questions about prescription drugs, including questions regarding possible side effects or interactions among various drugs. They provide information about over-the-counter drugs and make recommendations after talking with the patient. They also may give advice about diet, exercise, or stress management, or about durable medical equipment and home healthcare supplies. They also may complete third-party insurance forms and other paperwork. Those who own or manage community pharmacies may sell non-health-related merchandise, hire and supervise personnel, and oversee the general operation of the pharmacy. Some community pharmacists provide specialized services to help patients manage conditions such as diabetes, asthma, smoking cessation, or high blood pressure. Some community pharmacists are also certified to administer vaccinations.

Pharmacists in healthcare facilities dispense medications and advise the medical staff on the selection and effects of drugs. They may make sterile solutions and buy medical supplies. They also assess, plan, and monitor drug programs or regimens. They counsel patients on the use of drugs while in the hospital, and on their use at home when the patients are discharged. Pharmacists also may evaluate drug use patterns and outcomes for patients in hospitals or managed care organizations.

Pharmacists who work in home healthcare monitor drug therapy and prepare infusions—solutions that are injected into patients—and other medications for use in the home.

Some pharmacists specialize in specific drug therapy areas, such as intravenous nutrition support, oncology (cancer), nuclear pharmacy (used for chemotherapy), geriatric pharmacy, and psychopharmacotherapy (the treatment of mental disorders with drugs).

Most pharmacists keep confidential computerized records of patients' drug therapies to ensure that harmful drug interactions do not occur. Pharmacists are responsible for the accuracy of every prescription that is filled, but they often rely upon pharmacy technicians and pharmacy aides to assist them in the dispensing process. Thus, the pharmacist may delegate prescription-filling and administrative tasks and supervise their completion. They also frequently oversee pharmacy students serving as interns in preparation for graduation and licensure.

Increasingly, pharmacists pursue nontraditional pharmacy work. Some are involved in research for pharmaceutical manufacturers, developing new drugs and therapies and testing their effects on people. Others work in marketing or sales, providing expertise to clients on a drug's use, effectiveness, and possible side effects. Some pharmacists also work for health insurance companies, developing pharmacy benefit packages and carrying out cost-benefit analyses on certain drugs. Other pharmacists work for the government and pharmacy associations. Finally, some pharmacists are employed full time or part time as college faculty, teaching classes and performing research in a wide range of areas.

Working Conditions

Pharmacists work in clean, well-lighted, and well-ventilated areas. Many pharmacists spend most of their workday on their feet. When working with sterile or potentially dangerous pharmaceutical products, pharmacists wear gloves and masks and work with other special protective equipment. Many community and hospital pharmacies are open for extended hours or around the clock, so pharmacists may work evenings, nights, weekends, and holidays. Consultant pharmacists may travel to nursing homes or other facilities to monitor patients' drug therapy.

About 19 percent of pharmacists worked part time in 2002. Most full-time salaried pharmacists worked about 40 hours a week. Some, including many self-employed pharmacists, worked more than 50 hours a week.

Employment

Pharmacists held about 230,000 jobs in 2002. About 62 percent work in community pharmacies that are either independently owned or part of a drugstore chain, grocery store, department store, or mass merchandiser. Most community pharmacists are salaried employees, but some are self-employed owners. About 22 percent of salaried pharmacists work in hospitals, and others work in clinics, mail-order pharmacies, pharmaceutical wholesalers, home healthcare agencies, or the federal government.

Training, Other Qualifications, and Advancement

A license to practice pharmacy is required in all states, the District of Columbia, and U.S. territories. To obtain a license, one must graduate from a college of pharmacy accredited by the American Council on Pharmaceutical Education (ACPE) and pass an examination. All states except California require the North American Pharmacist Licensure Exam (NAPLEX) and the Multistate Pharmacy Jurisprudence Exam (MPJE), both administered by the National Association of Boards of Pharmacy. California has its own pharmacist licensure exam. In addition to the NAPLEX and MPJE, some states require additional exams unique to their state. All states except California currently grant a license without extensive re-examination to qualified pharmacists already licensed by another state. In Florida, reexamination is not required if a pharmacist passed the NAPLEX and MPJE within 12 years of his or her application for license transfer. Many pharmacists are licensed to practice in more than one state. States may require continuing education for license renewal. Persons interested in a career as a pharmacist should check with state boards of pharmacy for details on examination requirements and license transfer procedures.

In 2002, 85 colleges of pharmacy were accredited to confer degrees by the American Council on Pharmaceutical Education. Pharmacy programs grant the degree of Doctor of Pharmacy (Pharm.D.), which requires at least 6 years of postsecondary study and the passing of the licensure examination of a state board of pharmacy. Courses offered at colleges of pharmacy are designed to teach students how to dispense prescriptions and communicate with patients and other health care providers about drug information and

patient care. Students also learn professional ethics.. In addition to classroom study, students in the Pharm.D. program are provided in-depth exposure to and active participation in a variety of pharmacy practice settings under the supervision of licensed pharmacists. The Pharm.D. degree has replaced the Bachelor of Pharmacy (B.Pharm.) degree, which is no longer offered to new students and will cease to be awarded after 2005.

The Pharm.D. is a 4-year program that requires at least 2 years of college study prior to admittance, although most applicants have 3 years prior to entering the program. Entry requirements usually include courses in mathematics and natural sciences, such as chemistry, biology, and physics, as well as courses in the humanities and social sciences. Approximately half of all colleges require the applicant to take the Pharmacy College Admissions Test (PCAT).

In 2003, the American Association of Colleges of Pharmacy (AACP) launched the Pharmacy College Application Service, known as PharmCAS, for students interested in applying to schools and colleges of pharmacy. This centralized service allows applicants to use a single Web-based application and one set of transcripts to apply to multiple Pharm.D. degree programs. A total of 43 pharmacy programs participated in 2003.

In the 2002-03 academic year, 66 colleges of pharmacy awarded the master of science degree or the Ph.D. degree. Both the master's and Ph.D. degrees are awarded after completion of a Pharm.D. degree. These degrees are designed for those who want more laboratory and research experience. Many master's and Ph.D. degree holders do research for a drug company or teach at a university. Other options for pharmacy graduates who are interested in further training include 1- or 2-year residency programs or fellowships. Pharmacy residencies are postgraduate training programs in pharmacy practice, and usually require the completion of a research study. Pharmacy fellowships are highly individualized programs designed to prepare participants to work in research laboratories. Some pharmacists who run their own pharmacy obtain a master's degree in business administration (MBA).

Areas of graduate study include pharmaceutics and pharmaceutical chemistry (physical and chemical properties of drugs and dosage forms), pharmacology (effects of drugs on the body), and pharmacy administration.

Prospective pharmacists should have scientific aptitude, good communication skills, and a desire to help others. They also must be conscientious and pay close attention to detail, because the decisions they make affect human lives.

In community pharmacies, pharmacists usually begin at the staff level. In independent pharmacies, after they gain experience and secure the necessary capital, some become owners or part owners of pharmacies. Pharmacists in chain drugstores may be promoted to pharmacy supervisor or manager at the store level, then to manager at the district or regional level, and later to an executive position within the chain's headquarters.

Hospital pharmacists may advance to supervisory or administrative positions. Pharmacists in the pharmaceutical industry may advance in marketing, sales, research, quality control, production, packaging, or other areas.

Job Outlook

Very good employment opportunities are expected for pharmacists over the 2002-12 period because the number of degrees granted in pharmacy is expected to be less than the number of job openings created by employment growth and the need to replace pharmacists who retire or otherwise leave the occupation. Recently, enrollments in pharmacy programs are rising as more students are attracted by high salaries and good job prospects. Despite this increase in enrollments, pharmacist jobs should still be more numerous than those seeking employment.

Employment of pharmacists is expected to grow faster than the average for all occupations through the year 2012, due to the increased pharmaceutical needs of a growing elderly population and increased use of medications. The growing numbers of middle-aged and elderly people—who, on average, use more prescription drugs than do younger people—will continue to spur demand for pharmacists in all employment settings. Other factors likely to increase the demand for pharmacists include scientific advances that will make more drug products available, new developments in genome research and medication distribution systems, increasingly sophisticated consumers seeking more information about drugs, and coverage of prescription drugs by a greater number of health insurance plans and by Medicare.

Community pharmacies are taking steps to manage increasing prescription volume. Automation of drug dispensing and greater employment of pharmacy technicians and pharmacy aides will help these establishments to dispense more prescriptions.

With its emphasis on cost control, managed care encourages the use of lower cost prescription drug distributors, such as mail-order firms and online pharmacies, for purchases of certain medications. Prescriptions ordered through the mail via the Internet are filled in a central location and shipped to the patient at a lower cost. Mail-order and online pharmacies typically use automated technology to dispense medication and employ fewer pharmacists. If the utilization of mail-order pharmacies increases rapidly, job growth among pharmacists could be limited.

Employment of pharmacists will not grow as fast in hospitals as in other industries, as hospitals reduce inpatient stays, downsize, and consolidate departments. The increase in outpatient surgeries means more patients are discharged and purchase medications through retail, supermarket, or mail-order pharmacies, rather than through the hospital. An aging population means more pharmacy services are required in nursing homes, assisted living facilities, and home care settings, where the most rapid job growth among pharmacists is expected.

New opportunities are emerging for pharmacists in managed-care organizations, where they may analyze trends and patterns in medication use for their populations of patients, and for pharmacists trained in research, disease management, and pharmacoeconomics—determining the costs and benefits of different drug therapies. Pharmacists also will have opportunities to work in research and development as well as sales and marketing for pharmaceutical manufacturing firms. New breakthroughs in biotechnology will increase the potential for drugs to treat diseases and expand the opportunities for pharmacists to conduct research and sell medications.

Job opportunities for pharmacists in patient care will arise as cost-conscious insurers and health systems continue to emphasize the role of pharmacists in primary and preventive health services. Health insurance companies realize that the expense of using medication to treat diseases and various health conditions often is considerably less than the potential costs for patients whose conditions go untreated. Pharmacists also can reduce the expenses resulting from unexpected complications due to allergic reactions or medication interactions.

Earnings

Median annual wage and salary earnings of pharmacists in 2002 were $77,050. The middle 50 percent earned between $66,210 and $87,250 a year. The lowest 10 percent earned less than $54,110, and the highest 10 percent earned more than $94,570 a year. Median annual earnings in the industries employing the largest numbers of pharmacists in 2002 were as follows:

Grocery stores $78,270

Health and personal care stores.............................76,800

General medical and surgical hospitals..................76,620

Related Occupations

Pharmacy technicians and pharmacy aides also work in pharmacies. Persons in other professions who may work with pharmaceutical compounds include biological scientists, medical scientists, and chemists and materials scientists. Increasingly, pharmacists are involved in patient care and therapy, work that they have in common with physicians and surgeons.

Sources of Additional Information

For information on pharmacy as a career, preprofessional and professional requirements, programs offered by colleges of pharmacy, and student financial aid, contact:

● American Association of Colleges of Pharmacy, 1426 Prince St., Alexandria, VA 22314. Internet: http://www.aacp.org

General information on careers in pharmacy is available from:

- American Society of Health-System Pharmacists, 7272 Wisconsin Ave., Bethesda, MD 20814. Internet: http://www.ashp.org

- National Association of Chain Drug Stores, 413 N. Lee St., P.O. Box 1417-D49, Alexandria, VA 22313-1480. Internet: http://www.nacds.org

Information on the North American Pharmacist Licensure Exam (NAPLEX) and the Multistate Pharmacy Jurisprudence Exam (MPJE) is available from:

- National Association of Boards of Pharmacy, 700 Busse Hwy., Park Ridge, IL 60068. Internet: http://www.nabp.net

State licensure requirements are available from each state's Board of Pharmacy. Information on specific college entrance requirements, curriculums, and financial aid is available from any college of pharmacy.

Pharmacy Aides

(O*NET 31-9095.00)

Significant Points

- Many pharmacy aides work evenings, weekends, and holidays.

- Eighty percent of jobs are in retail pharmacies.

- Job opportunities are expected to be good, especially for those with related work experience.

Nature of the Work

Pharmacy aides help licensed pharmacists with administrative duties in running a pharmacy. Aides often are clerks or cashiers who primarily answer telephones, handle money, stock shelves, and perform other clerical duties. They work closely with pharmacy technicians. *Pharmacy technicians* usually perform more complex tasks than do aides, although, in some states, the duties and titles of the jobs overlap. Aides refer any questions regarding prescriptions, drug information, or health matters to a pharmacist.

Aides have several important duties that help the pharmacy to function smoothly. They may establish and maintain patient profiles, prepare insurance claim forms, and stock and take inventory of prescription and over-the-counter medications. Accurate recordkeeping is necessary to help avert a potentially dangerous drug interaction. Because many people have medical insurance to help pay for the prescription, it is essential that pharmacy aides efficiently and correctly correspond with the third-party insurance providers to obtain payment. Pharmacy aides also maintain the inventory and inform the supervisor of stock needs so that the pharmacy has the vital medications for those who need them. Some also clean pharmacy equipment, help with the maintenance of equipment and supplies, and manage the cash register.

Working Conditions

Pharmacy aides work in clean, organized, well-lighted, and well-ventilated areas. Most of their workday is spent on their feet. They may be required to lift heavy boxes or to use stepladders to retrieve supplies from high shelves.

Aides work the same hours that pharmacists work. These include evenings, nights, weekends, and some holidays. Because some hospital and retail pharmacies are open 24 hours a day, aides may work varying shifts. There are many opportunities for part-time work in both retail and hospital settings.

Employment

Pharmacy aides held about 60,000 jobs in 2002. About 80 percent work in retail pharmacies either independently owned or part of a drug store chain, grocery store, department store, or mass retailer; the vast majority of these are in drug stores. About 1 in 10 work in hospitals, and the rest work in mail-order pharmacies, clinics, and pharmaceutical wholesalers.

Training, Other Qualifications, and Advancement

Most pharmacy aides receive informal on-the-job training, but employers favor those with at least a high school diploma. Prospective pharmacy aides with experience working as a cashier may have an advantage when applying for jobs. Employers also prefer applicants with strong customer service and communication skills and experience managing inventories and using a computer. Aides entering the field need strong spelling, reading, and mathematics skills.

Successful pharmacy aides are organized, dedicated, friendly, and responsible. They should be willing and able to take directions. Candidates interested in becoming pharmacy aides cannot have prior records of drug or substance abuse. Strong interpersonal and communication skills are needed because there is a lot of interaction with patients, coworkers, and healthcare professionals. Teamwork is very important because aides are often required to work with technicians and pharmacists.

Pharmacy aides almost always are trained on the job. They may begin by observing a more experienced worker. After they become familiar with the store's equipment, policies, and procedures, they begin to work on their own. Once they become experienced workers, they are not likely to receive additional training, except when new equipment is introduced or when policies or procedures change.

To become a pharmacy aide, one should be able to perform repetitive work accurately. Aides need good basic mathematics skills and good manual dexterity. Because they deal constantly with the public, pharmacy aides should be neat in appearance and able to deal pleasantly and tactfully with customers. Some employers may prefer people with experience typing, handling money, or operating specialized equipment, including computers.

Advancement usually is limited, although some aides may decide to become pharmacy technicians or to enroll in pharmacy school to become pharmacists.

Job Outlook

Job opportunities for full-time and part-time work are expected to be good, especially for aides with related work experience in pharmacies, or as cashiers or stock clerks in other retail settings. Job openings will be created by employment growth and by the need to replace workers who transfer to other occupations or leave the labor force.

Employment of pharmacy aides is expected to grow about as fast as the average for all occupations through 2012 due to the increased use of medication in treating patients. In addition, a greater number of middle-aged and elderly people—who, on average, use more prescription drugs than do younger people—will spur demand for aides in all practice settings.

Cost-conscious insurers, pharmacies, and health systems will continue to employ aides. As a result, pharmacy aides will assume some responsibility for routine tasks previously performed by pharmacists and pharmacy technicians, thereby giving pharmacists more time to interact with patients and affording technicians more time to prepare medications. The number of pharmacy aides will not grow as fast as those of pharmacists and pharmacy technicians, however, because of legal limitations regarding their duties. Many smaller pharmacies that can afford only a small staff will favor pharmacy technicians because of their more extensive training and job skills.

Earnings

Median hourly wage and salary earnings of pharmacy aides were $8.86 in 2002. The middle 50 percent earned between $7.41 and $11.00; the lowest 10 percent earned less than $6.36, and the highest 10 percent earned more than $13.71. Median hourly earnings of pharmacy aides were $8.33 in health and personal care stores, $11.77 in general medical and surgical hospitals, and $9.08 in grocery stores in 2002.

Related Occupations

The work of pharmacy aides is closely related to that of pharmacy technicians, cashiers, and stock clerks and order fillers. Workers in other medical support occupations include dental assistants, licensed practical and licensed vocational nurses, medical transcriptionists, medical records and health information technicians, occupational therapist assistants and aides, physical therapist assistants and aides, and surgical technologists.

Sources of Additional Information

For information on employment opportunities, contact local employers or local offices of the state employment service.

Pharmacy Technicians

(O*NET 29-2052.00)

Significant Points

- Job opportunities are expected to be good, especially for those with certification or previous work experience.

- Many technicians work evenings, weekends, and holidays.

- Two-thirds of all jobs are in retail pharmacies.

Nature of the Work

Pharmacy technicians help licensed pharmacists provide medication and other healthcare products to patients. Technicians usually perform routine tasks to help prepare prescribed medication for patients, such as counting tablets and labeling bottles. Technicians refer any questions regarding prescriptions, drug information, or health matters to a *pharmacist*.

Pharmacy aides work closely with pharmacy technicians. They are often clerks or cashiers who primarily answer telephones, handle money, stock shelves, and perform other clerical duties. Pharmacy technicians usually perform more complex tasks than do pharmacy aides, although, in some states, their duties and job titles overlap.

Pharmacy technicians who work in retail or mail-order pharmacies have varying responsibilities, depending on state rules and regulations. Technicians receive written prescriptions or requests for prescription refills from patients. They also may receive prescriptions sent electronically from the doctor's office. They must verify that the information on the prescription is complete and accurate. To prepare the prescription, technicians must retrieve, count, pour, weigh, measure, and sometimes mix the medication. Then, they prepare the prescription labels, select the type of prescription container, and affix the prescription and auxiliary labels to the container. Once the prescription is filled, technicians price and file the prescription, which must be checked by a pharmacist before it is given to a patient. Technicians may establish and maintain patient profiles, prepare insurance claim forms, and stock and take inventory of prescription and over-the-counter medications.

In hospitals, nursing homes, and assisted-living facilities, technicians have added responsibilities. They read patient charts and prepare and deliver the medicine to patients. The pharmacist must check the order before it is delivered to the patient. The technician then copies the information about the prescribed medication onto the patient's profile. Technicians also may assemble a 24-hour supply of medicine for every patient. They package and label each dose separately. The package is then placed in the medicine cabinet of each patient until the supervising pharmacist checks it for accuracy. It is then given to the patient.

Working Conditions

Pharmacy technicians work in clean, organized, well-lighted, and well-ventilated areas. Most of their workday is spent on their feet. They may be required to lift heavy boxes or to use stepladders to retrieve supplies from high shelves.

Technicians work the same hours that pharmacists work. These may include evenings, nights, weekends, and holidays. Because some hospital and retail pharmacies are open 24 hours a day, technicians may work varying shifts. As their seniority increases, technicians often have increased control over the hours they work. There are many opportunities for part-time work in both retail and hospital settings.

Employment

Pharmacy technicians held about 211,000 jobs in 2002. Two-thirds of all jobs were in retail pharmacies, either independently owned or part of a drugstore chain, grocery store, department store, or mass retailer. About 22 percent of jobs were in hospitals and a small proportion was in mail-order and Internet pharmacies, clinics, pharmaceutical wholesalers, and the federal government.

Training, Other Qualifications, and Advancement

Although most pharmacy technicians receive informal on-the-job training, employers favor those who have completed formal training and certification. However, there are currently few state and no federal requirements for formal training or certification of pharmacy technicians. Employers who have neither the time nor money to give on-the-job training often seek formally educated pharmacy technicians. Formal education programs and certification emphasize the technician's interest in and dedication to the work. In addition to the military, some hospitals, proprietary schools, vocational or technical colleges, and community colleges offer formal education programs.

Formal pharmacy technician education programs require classroom and laboratory work in a variety of areas, including medical and pharmaceutical terminology, pharmaceutical calculations, pharmacy recordkeeping, pharmaceutical techniques, and pharmacy law and ethics. Technicians also are required to learn medication names, actions, uses, and doses. Many training programs include internships, in which students gain hands-on experience in actual pharmacies. Students receive a diploma, a certificate, or an associate degree, depending on the program.

Prospective pharmacy technicians with experience working as an aide in a community pharmacy or volunteering in a hospital may have an advantage. Employers also prefer applicants with strong customer service and communication skills and with experience managing inventories, counting, measuring, and using computers. Technicians entering the field need strong mathematics, spelling, and reading skills. A background in chemistry, English, and health education also may be beneficial. Some technicians are hired without formal training, but under the condition that they obtain certification within a specified period to retain employment.

The Pharmacy Technician Certification Board administers the National Pharmacy Technician Certification Examination. This exam is voluntary in most states and displays the competency of the individual to act as a pharmacy technician. However, more states and employers are requiring certification as reliance on pharmacy technicians grows. Eligible candidates must have a high school diploma or GED and no felony convictions, and those who pass the exam earn the title of Certified Pharmacy Technician (CPhT). The exam is offered several times per year at various locations nationally. Employers, often pharmacists, know that individuals who pass the exam have a standardized body of knowledge and skills. Many employers will also reimburse the costs of the exam as an incentive for certification.

Certified technicians must be recertified every 2 years. Technicians must complete 20 contact hours of pharmacy-related topics within the 2-year certification period to become eligible for recertification. Contact hours are awarded for on-the-job training, attending lectures, and college coursework. At least 1 contact hour must be in pharmacy law. Contact hours can be earned from several different sources, including pharmacy associations, pharmacy colleges, and pharmacy technician training programs. Up to 10 contact hours can be earned when the technician is employed under the direct supervision and instruction of a pharmacist.

Successful pharmacy technicians are alert, observant, organized, dedicated, and responsible. They should be willing and able to take directions. They must enjoy precise work—details are sometimes a matter of life and death. Although a pharmacist must check and approve all their work, they should be able to work on their own without constant instruction from the pharmacist. Candidates interested in becoming pharmacy technicians cannot have prior records of drug or substance abuse.

Strong interpersonal and communication skills are needed because there is a lot of interaction with patients, coworkers, and healthcare professionals. Teamwork is very important because technicians are often required to work with pharmacists, aides, and other technicians.

Job Outlook

Good job opportunities are expected for full-time and part-time work, especially for technicians with formal training or previous experience. Job openings for pharmacy technicians will result from the expansion of retail pharmacies and other employment settings, and from the need to replace workers who transfer to other occupations or leave the labor force.

Employment of pharmacy technicians is expected to grow faster than the average for all occupations through 2012 due to the increased pharmaceutical needs of a larger and older population, and to the greater use of medication. The increased number of middle-aged and elderly people—who, on average, use more prescription drugs than do younger people—will spur demand for technicians in all practice settings. With advances in science, more medications are becoming available to treat more conditions.

Cost-conscious insurers, pharmacies, and health systems will continue to emphasize the role of technicians. As a result, pharmacy technicians will assume responsibility for more routine tasks previously performed by pharmacists. Pharmacy technicians also will need to learn and master new pharmacy technology as it surfaces. For example, robotic machines are used to dispense medicine into containers; technicians must oversee the machines, stock the bins, and label the containers. Thus, while automation is increasingly incorporated into the job, it will not necessarily reduce the need for technicians.

Almost all states have legislated the maximum number of technicians who can safely work under a pharmacist at one time. In some states, technicians have assumed more medication dispensing duties as pharmacists have become more involved in patient care, resulting in more technicians per pharmacist. Changes in these laws could directly affect employment.

Earnings

Median hourly earnings of wage and salary pharmacy technicians in 2002 were $10.70. The middle 50 percent earned between $8.74 and $13.19; the lowest 10 percent earned less than $7.44, and the highest 10 percent earned more than $15.82. Median hourly earnings in the industries employing the largest numbers of pharmacy technicians in 2002 were as follows:

General medical and surgical hospitals	$12.32
Grocery stores	11.34
Drugs and druggists' sundries merchant wholesalers	10.60
Health and personal care stores	9.70
Department stores	9.69

Certified technicians may earn more. Shift differentials for working evenings or weekends also can increase earnings. Some technicians belong to unions representing hospital or grocery store workers.

Related Occupations

This occupation is most closely related to pharmacists and pharmacy aides. Workers in other medical support occupations include dental assistants, licensed practical and licensed vocational nurses, medical transcriptionists, medical records and health information technicians, occupational therapist assistants and aides, physical therapist assistants and aides, and surgical technologists.

Sources of Additional Information

For information on the Certified Pharmacy Technician designation, contact:

- Pharmacy Technician Certification Board, 2215 Constitution Ave. NW, Washington, DC 20037. Internet: http://www.ptcb.org

For a list of accredited pharmacy technician training programs, contact:

- American Society of Health-System Pharmacists, 7272 Wisconsin Ave., Bethesda, MD 20814. Internet: http://www.ashp.org

Photographers

(O*NET 27-4021.01 and 27-4021.02)

Significant Points

- Competition for jobs is expected to be keen because the work is attractive to many people.

- Technical expertise, a "good eye," imagination, and creativity are essential.

- More than half of all photographers are self-employed; the most successful are able to adapt to rapidly changing technologies and are adept at operating a business.

Nature of the Work

Photographers produce and preserve images that paint a picture, tell a story, or record an event. To create commercial quality photographs, photographers need both technical expertise and creativity. Producing a successful picture requires choosing and presenting a subject to achieve a particular effect, and selecting the appropriate equipment. For example, photographers may enhance the subject's appearance with natural or artificial light, use a particular lens depending on the desired range or level of detail, or draw attention to a particular aspect of the subject by blurring the background.

Today, many cameras adjust settings such as shutter speed and aperture automatically. They also let the photographer adjust these settings manually, allowing greater creative and technical control over the picture-taking process. In addition to automatic and manual cameras, photographers use an array of film, lenses, and equipment—from filters, tripods, and flash attachments to specially constructed lighting equipment.

Photographers use either a traditional camera that records images on silver halide film that is developed into prints or a digital camera that electronically records images. Some photographers send their film to laboratories for processing. Color film requires expensive equipment and exacting conditions for correct processing and printing. Other photographers, especially those who use black and white film or who require special effects, prefer to develop and print their own photographs. Photographers who do their own film developing must have the technical skill to operate a fully equipped darkroom or the appropriate computer software to process prints digitally.

Recent advances in electronic technology now make it possible for the professional photographer to develop and scan standard 35mm or other types of film and use flatbed scanners and photofinishing laboratories to produce computer-readable, digital images from film. After converting the film to a digital image, photographers can edit and electronically transmit images using a method as simple as e-mail or as advanced as a satellite phone. This makes it easier and faster to shoot, develop, and transmit pictures from remote locations.

Using computers and specialized software, photographers also can manipulate and enhance the scanned or digital image to create a desired effect. Images can be stored on portable memory devices including compact disks (CDs) or on new types of smaller "mini pocket" storage devices such as flash disks, which are small memory cards used in digital cameras. Digital technology also allows the production of larger, more colorful, and more accurate prints or images for use in advertising, photographic art, and scientific research. Some photographers use this technology to create electronic portfolios as well. Because much photography now involves the use of computer technology, photographers must have hands-on knowledge of computer editing software.

Some photographers specialize in areas such as portrait, commercial and industrial, scientific, news, or fine arts photography. *Portrait photographers* take pictures of individuals or groups of people and often work in their own studios. Some specialize in weddings, religious ceremonies, or school photographs and may work on location. Portrait photographers who are business owners arrange for advertising, schedule appointments, set and adjust equipment, develop and retouch negatives, and mount and frame pictures. They also purchase supplies, keep records, bill customers, and may hire and train employees.

Commercial and industrial photographers take pictures of various subjects, such as buildings, models, merchandise, artifacts, and landscapes. These photographs are used in a variety of media, including books, reports, advertisements, and catalogs. Industrial photographers often take pictures of equipment, machinery, products, workers, and company officials. The pictures are used for various purposes—for example, analysis of engineering projects, publicity, or records of equipment development or deployment, such as placement of an offshore rig. This photography frequently is done on location.

Scientific photographers take images of a variety of subjects to illustrate or record scientific or medical data or phenomena, using knowledge of scientific procedures. They typically possess additional knowledge in areas such as engineering, medicine, biology, or chemistry.

News photographers, also called *photojournalists*, photograph newsworthy people, places, and sporting, political, and community events for newspapers, journals, magazines, or television. Some news photographers are salaried staff; others are self-employed and are known as freelance photographers.

Fine arts photographers sell their photographs as fine artwork. In addition to technical proficiency, fine arts photographers need artistic talent and creativity.

Self-employed, or freelance, photographers may license the use of their photographs through stock photo agencies or contract with clients or agencies to provide photographs as necessary. Stock agencies grant magazines and other customers the right to purchase the use of photographs, and, in turn, pay the photographer on a commission basis. Stock photo agencies require an application from the photographer and a sizable portfolio. Once accepted, a large number of new submissions usually is required from the photographer each year.

Working Conditions

Working conditions for photographers vary considerably. Photographers employed in government and advertising agencies usually work a 5-day, 40-hour week. On the other hand, news photographers often work long, irregular hours and must be available to work on short notice. Many photographers work part-time or variable schedules.

Portrait photographers usually work in their own studios but also may travel to take photographs at the client's location, such as a school, a company office, or a private home. News and commercial photographers frequently travel locally, stay overnight on assignments, or travel to distant places for long periods.

Some photographers work in uncomfortable or even dangerous surroundings, especially news photographers covering accidents, natural disasters, civil unrest, or military conflicts. Many photographers must wait long hours in all kinds of weather for an event to take place and stand or walk for long periods while carrying heavy equipment. News photographers often work under strict deadlines.

Self-employment allows for greater autonomy, freedom of expression, and flexible scheduling. However, income can be uncertain and the continuous, time-consuming search for new clients can be stressful. Some self-employed photographers hire assistants who help seek out new business.

Employment

Photographers held about 130,000 jobs in 2002. More than half were self-employed, a much higher proportion than the average for all occupations. Some self-employed photographers have contracts with advertising agencies, magazines, or others to do individual projects at a predetermined fee, while others operate portrait studios or provide photographs to stock photo agencies.

Most salaried photographers work in portrait or commercial photography studios. Newspapers, magazines, television broadcasters, and advertising agencies employ most of the others. Most photographers work in metropolitan areas.

Training, Other Qualifications, and Advancement

Employers usually seek applicants with a "good eye," imagination, and creativity, as well as a good technical understanding of photography. Entry-level positions in photojournalism or in industrial or scientific photography generally require a college degree in journalism or photography. Freelance and portrait photographers need technical proficiency, whether gained through a degree program, vocational training, or extensive work experience.

Many universities, community and junior colleges, vocational-technical institutes, and private trade and technical schools offer photography courses. Basic courses in photography cover equipment, processes, and techniques. Bachelor's degree programs, especially those including business courses, provide a well-rounded education. Art schools offer useful training in design and composition.

Individuals interested in photography should subscribe to photographic newsletters and magazines, join camera clubs, and seek summer or part-time employment in camera stores, newspapers, or photo studios.

Photographers may start out as assistants to experienced photographers. Assistants learn to mix chemicals, develop film, and print photographs, and acquire the other skills necessary to run a portrait or commercial photography business. Freelance photographers also should develop an individual style of photography in order to differentiate themselves from the competition. Some photographers enter the field by submitting unsolicited photographs to magazines and to art directors at advertising agencies. For freelance photographers, a good portfolio of their work is critical.

Photographers need good eyesight, artistic ability, and good hand-eye coordination. They should be patient, accurate, and detail-oriented. Photographers should be able to work well with others, as they frequently deal with clients, graphic designers, or advertising and publishing specialists. Increasingly, photographers need to know how to use computer software programs and applications that allow them to prepare and edit images.

Portrait photographers need the ability to help people relax in front of the camera. Commercial and fine arts photographers must be imaginative and original. News photographers not only must be good with a camera, but also must understand the story behind an event so that their pictures match the story. They must be decisive in recognizing a potentially good photograph and act quickly to capture it.

Photographers who operate their own businesses, or freelance, need business skills as well as talent. These individuals must know how to prepare a business plan; submit bids; write contracts; market their work; hire models, if needed; get permission to shoot on locations that normally are not open to the public; obtain releases to use photographs of people; license and price photographs; secure copyright protection for their work; and keep financial records. Knowledge of licensing and copyright laws as well as contract negotiation procedures is especially important for self-employed photographers, in order to protect their rights and their work.

After several years of experience, magazine and news photographers may advance to photography or picture editor positions. Some photographers teach at technical schools, film schools, or universities.

Job Outlook

Photographers can expect keen competition for job openings because the work is attractive to many people. The number of individuals interested in positions as commercial and news photographers usually is much greater than the number of openings. Those who succeed in landing a salaried job or attracting enough work to earn a living by freelancing are likely to be the most creative, able to adapt to rapidly changing technologies, and adept at operating a business. Related work experience, job-related training, or some unique skill or talent—such as a background in computers or electronics—also are beneficial to prospective photographers.

Employment of photographers is expected to increase about as fast as the average for all occupations through 2012. Demand for portrait photographers should increase as the population grows. As the number of electronic versions of magazines, journals, and newspapers increases on the Internet, commercial photographers will be needed to provide digital images.

Job growth, however, will be constrained somewhat by the widespread use of digital photography and the falling price of digital equipment. Besides increasing photographers' productivity, improvements in digital technology reduce barriers of entry into this profession and allow more individual consumers and businesses to produce, store, and access photographic images on their own. Declines in the newspaper industry also will reduce demand for photographers to provide still images for print.

Earnings

Median annual earnings of salaried photographers were $24,040 in 2002. The middle 50 percent earned between $17,740 and $34,910. The lowest 10 percent earned less than $14,640, and the highest 10 percent earned more than

$49,920. Median annual earnings in the industries employing the largest numbers of salaried photographers were $15.12 for newspapers and periodicals and $10.51 for other professional or scientific services.

Salaried photographers—more of whom work full time—tend to earn more than those who are self-employed. Because most freelance and portrait photographers purchase their own equipment, they incur considerable expense acquiring and maintaining cameras and accessories. Unlike news and commercial photographers, few fine arts photographers are successful enough to support themselves solely through their art.

Related Occupations

Other occupations requiring artistic talent and creativity include architects, except landscape and naval; artists and related workers; designers; news analysts, reporters, and correspondents; and television, video, and motion picture camera operators and editors.

Sources of Additional Information

Career information on photography is available from:

- Professional Photographers of America, Inc., 229 Peachtree St. NE., Suite 2200, Atlanta, GA 30303.

- National Press Photographers Association, Inc., 3200 Croasdaile Dr., Suite 306, Durham, NC 27705. Internet: http://www.nppa.org

Photographic Process Workers and Processing Machine Operators

(O*NET 51-9131.01, 51-9131.02, 51-9131.03, 51-9131.04, and 51-9132.00)

Significant Points

- Little or no employment growth is expected as digital photography becomes commonplace.

- Most receive on-the-job training from their companies, manufacturers' representatives, and experienced workers.

- Job opportunities will be best for individuals with experience using computers and digital technology.

Nature of the Work

Both amateur and professional photographers rely heavily on photographic process workers and processing machine operators to develop film, make prints or slides, and do related tasks, such as enlarging or retouching photographs. *Photographic processing machine operators* operate various machines, such as mounting presses and motion picture film printing, photographic printing, and film developing machines. *Photographic process workers* perform more delicate tasks, such as retouching photographic negatives and prints to emphasize or correct specific features.

Photographic processing machine operators often have specialized jobs. *Film process technicians* operate machines that develop exposed photographic film or sensitized paper in a series of chemical and water baths to produce negative or positive images. First, technicians mix developing and fixing solutions, following a formula. They then load the film in the machine, which immerses the exposed film in a developer solution. This brings out the latent image. The next steps include immersing the negative in a stop-bath to halt the developer action, transferring it to a hyposolution to fix the image, and then immersing it in water to remove the chemicals. The technician then dries the film. In some cases, these steps are performed by hand.

Color printer operators control equipment that produces color prints from negatives. These workers read customer instructions to determine processing requirements. They load film into color printing equipment, examine negatives to determine equipment control settings, set controls, and produce a specified number of prints. Finally, they inspect the finished prints for defects, remove any that are found, and insert the processed negatives and prints into an envelope for return to the customer.

Photographic process workers, sometimes known as *digital imaging technicians*, use computer images of conventional negatives and specialized computer software to vary the contrast of images, remove unwanted background, or combine features from different photographs. Although computers and digital technology are replacing much manual work, some photographic process workers, especially those who work in portrait studios, still perform many specialized tasks by hand directly on the photo or negative. *Airbrush artists* restore damaged and faded photographs, and may color or shade drawings to create photographic likenesses using an airbrush. *Photographic retouchers* alter photographic negatives, prints, or images to accentuate the subject. *Colorists* apply oil colors to portrait photographs to create natural, lifelike appearances. *Photographic spotters* remove imperfections on photographic prints and images.

Working Conditions

Photographic process workers and processing machine operators generally spend their work hours in clean, appropriately lighted, well-ventilated, and air-conditioned offices, photofinishing laboratories, or 1-hour minilabs. In recent years, more commercial photographic processing has been done on computers than in darkrooms, and this trend is expected to continue.

Some photographic process workers and processing machine operators are exposed to the chemicals and fumes associated with developing and printing. These workers must wear rubber gloves and aprons and take precautions against these hazards. Those who use computers for extended periods may experience back pain, eyestrain, or fatigue.

Photographic processing machine operators must do repetitive work at a rapid pace without any loss of accuracy. Photographic process workers do detailed tasks, such as airbrushing and spotting, which can contribute to eye fatigue.

Many photo laboratory employees work a 40-hour week, including evenings and weekends, and may work overtime during peak seasons. Almost one-fourth work part time.

Employment

Photographic process workers held about 28,000 jobs in 2002. Almost one in four photographic process workers were employed in photofinishing laboratories and 1-hour minilabs. More than one in six worked for portrait studios or commercial laboratories that specialize in processing the work of professional photographers for advertising and other industries. An additional one in six were employed by general merchandise stores, and one in ten in the printing, publishing, and motion picture industries.

Photographic processing machine operators held about 54,000 jobs in 2002. About four in ten worked in retail establishments, primarily in general merchandise stores and drug stores. About three in ten worked in photofinishing laboratories and 1-hour minilabs. Small numbers were employed in the printing industry and in portrait studios and commercial laboratories that process the work of professional photographers.

Employment fluctuates somewhat over the course of the year. Typically, employment peaks during school graduation and summer vacation periods, and again during the winter holiday season.

Training, Other Qualifications, and Advancement

Most photographic process workers and processing machine operators receive on-the-job training from their companies, manufacturers' representatives, and experienced workers. New employees gradually learn to use the machines and chemicals that develop and print film.

Employers prefer applicants who are high school graduates or those who have some experience in the field. Familiarity with computers is essential for photographic processing machine operators. The ability to perform simple mathematical calculations also is helpful. Photography courses that include instruction in film processing are valuable preparation. Such courses are available through high schools, vocational-technical institutes, private trade schools, and colleges and universities.

On-the-job training in photographic processing occupations can range from just a few hours for print machine operators to several months for photographic processing workers such as airbrush artists and colorists. Some workers attend periodic training seminars to maintain a high level of skill. Manual dexterity, good hand-eye coordination, and good vision, including normal color perception, are important qualifications for photographic process workers.

Photographic process machine workers can sometimes advance from jobs as machine operators to supervisory positions in laboratories or to management positions within retail stores.

Job Outlook

Slower than average growth is expected for photographic process workers and processing machine operators through the year 2012. Most openings will result from replacement needs, which are higher for machine operators than for photographic process workers.

In recent years, the use of digital cameras, which use electronic memory rather than film to record images, has grown rapidly among professional photographers and advanced amateurs. As the cost of digital photography drops, the use of such cameras will become more widespread among amateur photographers, reducing the demand for traditional photographic processing machine operators. However, conventional cameras, which use film to record images, are expected to continue to be the camera of choice among most casual photographers. Population growth and the popularity of amateur and family photography will contribute to a continuing need for photographic processing machine operators to process the film used in conventional cameras, including increasingly sophisticated disposable cameras. This need will prevent what otherwise would be even slower growth in the number of these workers.

Digital photography also will reduce demand for photographic process workers. Using digital cameras and technology, consumers who have a personal computer and the proper software will be able to download and view pictures on their computer, as well as manipulate, correct, and retouch their own photographs. No matter what improvements occur in camera technology, though, some photographic processing tasks will still require skillful manual treatment. Moreover, not all consumers will want to invest in the software. Job opportunities will be best for individuals with experience using computers and digital technology.

Earnings

Earnings of photographic process workers vary greatly depending on skill level, experience, and geographic location. Median hourly earnings for photographic process workers were $9.72 in 2002. The middle 50 percent earned between $7.84 and $13.08. The lowest 10 percent earned less than $6.79, and the highest 10 percent earned more than $17.43. Median hourly earnings were $9.75 in photofinishing laboratories, the largest employer of photographic process workers.

Median hourly earning for photographic processing machine operators were $9.05 in 2002. The middle 50 percent earned between $7.53 and $11.63. The lowest 10 percent earned less than $6.53, and the highest 10 percent earned more than $15.60. Median hourly earnings in the two industries employing the largest numbers of photographic processing machine operators were $10.15 in photofinishing laboratories and $7.20 in health and personal care stores.

Related Occupations

Photographic process workers and processing machine operators need specialized knowledge of the photo developing process. Other workers who apply specialized technical knowledge include clinical laboratory technologists and technicians, computer operators, jewelers and precious stone and metal workers, prepress technicians and workers, printing machine operators, and science technicians.

Sources of Additional Information

For information about employment opportunities in photographic laboratories and schools that offer degrees in photographic technology, contact:

- Photo Marketing Association International, 3000 Picture Place, Jackson, MI 49201.

Physical Therapist Assistants and Aides

(O*NET 31-2021.00 and 31-2022.00)

Significant Points

- Employment in the occupation is projected to increase much faster than the average, reflecting the growing number of individuals with disabilities or limited function and the increasing use of physical therapist assistants to reduce the cost of therapeutic services.

- Physical therapist assistants generally have an associate degree, but physical therapist aides usually learn skills on the job.

- Almost three-fourths of all jobs were in hospitals or offices of physical therapists.

Nature of the Work

Physical therapist assistants and aides perform components of physical therapy procedures and related tasks selected by a supervising physical therapist. These workers assist physical therapists in providing services that help improve mobility, relieve pain, and prevent or limit permanent physical disabilities of patients suffering from injuries or disease. Patients include accident victims and individuals with disabling conditions such as low-back pain, arthritis, heart disease, fractures, head injuries, and cerebral palsy.

Physical therapist assistants perform a variety of tasks. Components of treatment procedures performed by these workers, under the direction and supervision of physical therapists, involve exercises, massages, electrical stimulation, paraffin baths, hot and cold packs, traction, and ultrasound. Physical therapist assistants record the patient's responses to treatment and report the outcome of each treatment to the physical therapist.

Physical therapist aides help make therapy sessions productive, under the direct supervision of a physical therapist or physical therapist assistant. They usually are responsible for keeping the treatment area clean and organized and for preparing for each patient's therapy. When patients need assistance moving to or from a treatment area, aides push them in a wheelchair or provide them with a shoulder to lean on. Because they are not licensed, aides do not perform the clinical tasks of a physical therapist assistant.

The duties of aides include some clerical tasks, such as ordering depleted supplies, answering the phone, and filling out insurance forms and other paperwork. The extent to which an aide or an assistant performs clerical tasks depends on the size and location of the facility.

Working Conditions

The hours and days that physical therapist assistants and aides work vary with the facility and with whether they are full- or part-time employees. Many outpatient physical therapy offices and clinics have evening and weekend hours, to help coincide with patients' personal schedules.

Physical therapist assistants and aides need a moderate degree of strength because of the physical exertion required in assisting patients with their treatment. In some cases, assistants and aides need to lift patients. Constant kneeling, stooping, and standing for long periods also are part of the job.

Employment

Physical therapist assistants and aides held about 87,000 jobs in 2002. Physical therapist assistants held about 50,000 jobs, physical therapist aides approximately 37,000. Both work alongside physical therapists in a variety of settings. Almost three-fourths of all jobs were in hospitals or in offices of other health practitioners (which includes offices of physical therapists). Others worked primarily in nursing care facilities, offices of physicians, home healthcare services, and outpatient care centers.

Training, Other Qualifications, and Advancement

Physical therapist aides are trained on the job, but physical therapist assistants typically earn an associate degree from an accredited physical therapist assistant program. Not all states require licensure or registration in order for the physical therapist assistant to practice. The states that require licensure stipulate specific educational and examination criteria. Complete information on practice acts and regulations can be obtained from the state licensing boards. Additional requirements may include certification in cardiopulmonary resuscitation (CPR) and other first aid and a minimum number of hours of clinical experience.

According to the American Physical Therapy Association, there were 245 accredited physical therapist assistant programs in the United States as of 2003. Accredited physical therapist assistant programs are designed to last 2 years, or 4 semesters, and culminate in an associate degree. Programs are divided into academic study and hands-on clinical experience. Academic course work includes algebra, anatomy and physiology, biology, chemistry, and psychology. Many programs require that students complete a semester of anatomy and physiology and have certifications in CPR and other first aid even before they begin their clinical field experience. Both educators and prospective employers view clinical experience as integral to ensuring that students understand the responsibilities of a physical therapist assistant.

Employers typically require physical therapist aides to have a high school diploma, strong interpersonal skills, and a desire to assist people in need. Most employers provide clinical on-the-job training.

Job Outlook

Employment of physical therapist assistants and aides is expected to grow much faster than the average through the year 2012. The impact of proposed federal legislation imposing limits on reimbursement for therapy services may adversely affect the short-term job outlook for physical therapist assistants and aides. However, over the long run, demand for physical therapist assistants and aides will continue to rise, in accordance with growth in the number of individuals with disabilities or limited function. The growing elderly population is particularly vulnerable to chronic and debilitating conditions that require therapeutic services. These patients often need additional assistance in their treatment, making the roles of assistants and aides vital. The large baby-boom generation is entering the prime age for heart attacks and strokes, further increasing the demand for cardiac and physical rehabilitation. In addition, future medical developments should permit an increased percentage of trauma victims to survive, creating added demand for therapy services.

Physical therapists are expected to increasingly utilize assistants to reduce the cost of physical therapy services. Once a patient is evaluated and a treatment plan is designed by the physical therapist, the physical therapist assistant can provide many aspects of treatment, as prescribed by the therapist.

Earnings

Median annual earnings of physical therapist assistants were $36,080 in 2002. The middle 50 percent earned between $30,260 and $42,780. The lowest 10 percent earned less than $23,530, and the highest 10 percent earned more than $48,910. Median annual earnings of physical therapist assistants in 2002 were $35,870 in general medical and surgical hospitals and $35,750 in offices of other health practitioners.

Median annual earnings of physical therapist aides were $20,670 in 2002. The middle 50 percent earned between $17,430 and $24,560. The lowest 10 percent earned less than $15,290, and the highest 10 percent earned more than $29,990. Median annual earnings of physical therapist aides in 2002 were $20,690 in general medical and surgical hospitals and $19,840 in offices of other health practitioners.

Related Occupations

Physical therapist assistants and aides work under the supervision of physical therapists. Other workers in the healthcare field who work under similar supervision include dental assistants, medical assistants, occupational therapist assistants and aides, pharmacy aides, and pharmacy technicians.

Sources of Additional Information

Career information on physical therapist assistants and a list of schools offering accredited programs can be obtained from:

● The American Physical Therapy Association, 1111 North Fairfax St., Alexandria, VA 22314-1488. Internet: http://www.apta.org

Physical Therapists

(O*NET 29-1123.00)

Significant Points

● Employment is expected to increase faster than the average, as growth in the number of individuals with disabilities or limited function spurs demand for therapy services.

● After graduating from an accredited physical therapist educational program, therapists must pass a licensure exam before they can practice.

- About two-thirds of physical therapists work either in hospitals or in offices of physical therapists.

Nature of the Work

Physical therapists (PTs) provide services that help restore function, improve mobility, relieve pain, and prevent or limit permanent physical disabilities of patients suffering from injuries or disease. They restore, maintain, and promote overall fitness and health. Their patients include accident victims and individuals with disabling conditions such as low-back pain, arthritis, heart disease, fractures, head injuries, and cerebral palsy.

Therapists examine patients' medical histories and then test and measure the patients' strength, range of motion, balance and coordination, posture, muscle performance, respiration, and motor function. They also determine patients' ability to be independent and reintegrate into the community or workplace after injury or illness. Next, physical therapists develop treatment plans describing a treatment strategy, its purpose, and its anticipated outcome. Physical therapist assistants, under the direction and supervision of a physical therapist, may be involved in implementing treatment plans with patients. Physical therapist aides perform routine support tasks, as directed by the therapist.

Treatment often includes exercise for patients who have been immobilized and lack flexibility, strength, or endurance. Physical therapists encourage patients to use their own muscles to increase their flexibility and range of motion before finally advancing to other exercises that improve strength, balance, coordination, and endurance. The goal is to improve how an individual functions at work and at home.

Physical therapists also use electrical stimulation, hot packs or cold compresses, and ultrasound to relieve pain and reduce swelling. They may use traction or deep-tissue massage to relieve pain. Therapists also teach patients to use assistive and adaptive devices, such as crutches, prostheses, and wheelchairs. They also may show patients exercises to do at home to expedite their recovery.

As treatment continues, physical therapists document the patient's progress, conduct periodic examinations, and modify treatments when necessary. Besides tracking the patient's progress, such documentation identifies areas requiring more or less attention.

Physical therapists often consult and practice with a variety of other professionals, such as physicians, dentists, nurses, educators, social workers, occupational therapists, speech-language pathologists, and audiologists.

Some physical therapists treat a wide range of ailments; others specialize in areas such as pediatrics, geriatrics, orthopedics, sports medicine, neurology, and cardiopulmonary physical therapy.

Working Conditions

Physical therapists practice in hospitals, clinics, and private offices that have specially equipped facilities, or they treat patients in hospital rooms, homes, or schools.

In 2002, most full-time physical therapists worked a 40-hour week; some worked evenings and weekends to fit their patients' schedules. More than 1 in 5 physical therapists worked part time. The job can be physically demanding because therapists often have to stoop, kneel, crouch, lift, and stand for long periods. In addition, physical therapists move heavy equipment and lift patients or help them turn, stand, or walk.

Employment

Physical therapists held about 137,000 jobs in 2002. The number of jobs is greater than the number of practicing physical therapists, because some physical therapists hold two or more jobs. For example, some may work in a private practice, but also work part time in another healthcare facility.

About two-thirds of jobs for physical therapists were either in hospitals or in offices of other health practitioners (which includes offices of physical therapists). Other jobs were in home healthcare services, nursing care facilities, outpatient care centers, and offices of physicians.

Some physical therapists were self-employed in private practices, seeing individual patients and contracting to provide services in hospitals, rehabilitation centers, nursing care facilities, home healthcare agencies, adult daycare programs, and schools. Physical therapists also teach in academic institutions and conduct research.

Training, Other Qualifications, and Advancement

All states require physical therapists to pass a licensure exam before they can practice, after graduating from an accredited physical therapist educational program.

According to the American Physical Therapy Association, there were 203 accredited physical therapist programs in 2003. Of the accredited programs, 113 offered master's degrees, and 90 offered doctoral degrees. All physical therapist programs seeking accreditation are required to offer degrees at the master's degree level and above, in accordance with the Commission on Accreditation in Physical Therapy Education.

Physical therapist programs start with basic science courses such as biology, chemistry, and physics and then introduce specialized courses, including biomechanics, neuroanatomy, human growth and development, manifestations of disease, examination techniques, and therapeutic procedures. Besides getting classroom and laboratory instruction, students receive supervised clinical experience. Among the courses that are useful when one applies to a physical therapist educational program are anatomy, biology, chemistry, social science, mathematics, and physics. Before granting admission, many professional education programs require experience as a volunteer in a physical therapy department of a hospital or clinic.

Physical therapists should have strong interpersonal skills in order to be able to educate patients about their physical therapy treatments. PTs also should be compassionate and possess a desire to help patients. Similar traits are needed to interact with the patient's family.

Physical therapists are expected to continue their professional development by participating in continuing education courses and workshops. In fact, a number of states require continuing education as a condition of maintaining one's licensure.

Job Outlook

Employment of physical therapists is expected to grow faster than the average for all occupations through 2012. The impact of proposed federal legislation imposing limits on reimbursement for therapy services may adversely affect the short-term job outlook for physical therapists. However, over the long run, the demand for physical therapists should continue to rise as growth in the number of individuals with disabilities or limited function spurs demand for therapy services. The growing elderly population is particularly vulnerable to chronic and debilitating conditions that require therapeutic services. Also, the baby-boom generation is entering the prime age for heart attacks and strokes, increasing the demand for cardiac and physical rehabilitation. Further, young people will need physical therapy as technological advances save the lives of a larger proportion of newborns with severe birth defects.

Future medical developments also should permit a higher percentage of trauma victims to survive, creating additional demand for rehabilitative care. In addition, growth may result from advances in medical technology that could permit the treatment of more disabling conditions.

Widespread interest in health promotion also should increase demand for physical therapy services. A growing number of employers are using physical therapists to evaluate worksites, develop exercise programs, and teach safe work habits to employees in the hope of reducing injuries.

Earnings

Median annual earnings of physical therapists were $57,330 in 2002. The middle 50 percent earned between $48,480 and $70.050. The lowest 10 percent earned less than $40,200, and the highest 10 percent earned more than $86,260. Median annual earnings in the industries employing the largest numbers of physical therapists in 2002 were as follows:

Home health care services $62,480

Offices of other health practitioners 58,510

Offices of physicians 57,640

Nursing care facilities 57,570

General medical and surgical hospitals 57,200

Related Occupations

Physical therapists rehabilitate persons with physical disabilities. Others who work in the rehabilitation field include audiologists, chiropractors, occupational therapists, recreational therapists, rehabilitation counselors, respiratory therapists, and speech-language pathologists.

Sources of Additional Information

Additional career information and a list of accredited educational programs in physical therapy are available from:

- American Physical Therapy Association, 1111 North Fairfax St., Alexandria, VA 22314-1488. Internet: http://www.apta.org

Physician Assistants

(O*NET 29-1071.00)

Significant Points

- The typical physician assistant program lasts about 2 years and requires at least 2 years of college and some healthcare experience for admission.
- Most applicants to physician assistant programs hold a bachelor's or master's degree.
- Job opportunities should be good, particularly in rural and inner city clinics.
- Earnings are high.

Nature of the Work

Physician assistants (PAs) provide healthcare services under the supervision of physicians. They should not be confused with medical assistants, who perform routine clinical and clerical tasks. PAs are formally trained to provide diagnostic, therapeutic, and preventive healthcare services, as delegated by a physician. Working as members of the healthcare team, they take medical histories, examine and treat patients, order and interpret laboratory tests and x rays, make diagnoses, and prescribe medications. They also treat minor injuries, by suturing, splinting, and casting. PAs record progress notes, instruct and counsel patients, and order or carry out therapy. In 47 states and the District of Columbia, physician assistants may prescribe medications. PAs also may have managerial duties. Some order medical and laboratory supplies and equipment and may supervise technicians and assistants.

Physician assistants work under the supervision of a physician. However, PAs may be the principal care providers in rural or inner city clinics, where a physician is present for only 1 or 2 days each week. In such cases, the PA confers with the supervising physician and other medical professionals as needed or as required by law. PAs also may make house calls or go to hospitals and nursing care facilities to check on patients, after which they report back to the physician.

The duties of physician assistants are determined by the supervising physician and by state law. Aspiring PAs should investigate the laws and regulations in the states in which they wish to practice.

Many PAs work in primary care specialties, such as general internal medicine, pediatrics, and family medicine. Others specialty areas include general and thoracic surgery, emergency medicine, orthopedics, and geriatrics. PAs specializing in surgery provide preoperative and postoperative care and may work as first or second assistants during major surgery.

Working Conditions

Although PAs usually work in a comfortable, well-lighted environment, those in surgery often stand for long periods, and others do considerable walking. Schedules vary according to the practice setting, and often depend on the hours of the supervising physician. The workweek of hospital-based PAs may include weekends, nights, or early morning hospital rounds to visit patients. These workers also may be on call. PAs in clinics usually work a 40-hour week.

Employment

Physician assistants held about 63,000 jobs in 2002. The number of jobs is greater than the number of practicing PAs because some hold two or more jobs. For example, some PAs work with a supervising physician, but also work in another practice, clinic, or hospital. According to the American Academy of Physician Assistants, almost 90 percent of certified PAs were in clinical practice in 2003.

More than half of jobs for PAs were in the offices of physicians or other health practitioners. About a quarter were in hospitals. The rest were mostly in outpatient care centers, the federal government, educational services, and employment services.

Training, Other Qualifications, and Advancement

All states require that new PAs complete an accredited, formal education program. In 2002 there were about 133 accredited or provisionally accredited education programs for physician assistants. Sixty-eight of these programs offered a master's degree, and the rest offered either a bachelor's degree or an associate degree. Most PA graduates have at least a bachelor's degree.

Admission requirements vary, but many programs require 2 years of college and some work experience in the healthcare field. Students should take courses in biology, English, chemistry, mathematics, psychology, and the social sciences. Most applicants to PA programs hold a bachelor's or master's degree. Many PAs have backgrounds as registered nurses, while others come from varied backgrounds, including military corpsman/medics and allied health occupations such as respiratory therapists, physical therapists, and emergency medical technicians and paramedics.

PA programs usually last at least 2 years and are full time. Most programs are in schools of allied health, academic health centers, medical schools, or 4-year colleges; a few are in community colleges, the military, or hospitals. Many accredited PA programs have clinical teaching affiliations with medical schools.

PA education includes classroom instruction in biochemistry, pathology, human anatomy, physiology, microbiology, clinical pharmacology, clinical medicine, geriatric and home healthcare, disease prevention, and medical ethics. Students obtain supervised clinical training in several areas, including primary care medicine, inpatient medicine, surgery, obstetrics and gynecology, geriatrics, emergency medicine, psychiatry, and pediatrics. Sometimes, PA students serve one or more of these "rotations" under the supervision of a physician who is seeking to hire a PA. The rotations often lead to permanent employment.

All states and the District of Columbia have legislation governing the qualifications or practice of physician assistants. All jurisdictions require physician assistants to pass the Physician Assistants National Certifying Examination, administered by the National Commission on Certification of Physician Assistants (NCCPA) and open to graduates of accredited PA education programs. Only those successfully completing the examination may use the credential "Physician Assistant-Certified." In order to remain certified, PAs must complete 100 hours of continuing medical education every 2 years. Every 6 years, they must pass a recertification examination or complete an alternative program combining learning experiences and a take-home examination.

Some PAs pursue additional education in a specialty such as surgery, neonatology, or emergency medicine. PA postgraduate residency training programs are available in areas such as internal medicine, rural primary care, emergency medicine, surgery, pediatrics, neonatology, and occupational medicine. Candidates must be graduates of an accredited program and be certified by the NCCPA.

Physician assistants need leadership skills, self-confidence, and emotional stability. They must be willing to continue studying throughout their career to keep up with medical advances.

As they attain greater clinical knowledge and experience, PAs can advance to added responsibilities and higher earnings. However, by the very nature of the profession, clinically practicing PAs always are supervised by physicians.

Job Outlook

Employment of PAs is expected to grow much faster than the average for all occupations through the year 2012, due to anticipated expansion of the health services industry and an emphasis on cost containment, resulting in increasing utilization of PAs by physicians and healthcare institutions.

Physicians and institutions are expected to employ more PAs to provide primary care and to assist with medical and surgical procedures because PAs are cost-effective and productive members of the healthcare team. Physician assistants can relieve physicians of routine duties and procedures. Telemedicine—using technology to facilitate interactive consultations between physicians and physician assistants—also will expand the use of physician assistants. Job opportunities for PAs should be good, particularly in rural and inner city clinics, because those settings have difficulty attracting physicians.

Besides the traditional office-based setting, PAs should find a growing number of jobs in institutional settings such as hospitals, academic medical centers, public clinics, and prisons. Additional PAs may be needed to augment medical staffing in inpatient teaching hospital settings as the number of hours physician residents are permitted to work is reduced, encouraging hospitals to use PAs to supply some physician resident services. Opportunities will be best in states that allow PAs a wider scope of practice.

Earnings

Median annual earnings of physician assistants were $64,670 in 2002. The middle 50 percent earned between $49,640 and $77,280. The lowest 10 percent earned less than $35,410, and the highest 10 percent earned more than $90,350. Median annual earnings of physician assistants in 2002 were $65,910 in general medical and surgical hospitals and $64,170 in offices of physicians.

According to the American Academy of Physician Assistants, median income for physician assistants in full-time clinical practice in 2003 was about $72,457; median income for first-year graduates was about $63,437. Income varies by specialty, practice setting, geographical location, and years of experience.

Related Occupations

Other health workers who provide direct patient care that requires a similar level of skill and training include audiologists, occupational therapists, physical therapists, and speech-language pathologists.

Sources of Additional Information

For information on a career as a physician assistant, contact:

- American Academy of Physician Assistants Information Center, 950 North Washington St., Alexandria, VA 22314-1552. Internet: http://www.aapa.org

For a list of accredited programs and a catalog of individual PA training programs, contact:

- Association of Physician Assistant Programs, 950 North Washington St., Alexandria, VA 22314-1552. Internet: http://www.apap.org

For eligibility requirements and a description of the Physician Assistant National Certifying Examination, contact:

- National Commission on Certification of Physician Assistants, Inc., 6849–B Peachtree Dunwoody Rd., Atlanta, GA 30328. Internet: http://www.nccpa.net

Power Plant Operators, Distributors, and Dispatchers

(O*NET 51-8011.00, 51-8012.00, 51-8013.01, and 51-8013.02)

Significant Points

- Most entry-level workers start as helpers or laborers, and several years of training and experience are required to become fully qualified.

- Applicants are expected to encounter keen competition for jobs.

- Opportunities will be best for operators with training in computers and automated equipment.

Nature of the Work

Electricity is vital for most everyday activities. From the moment you flip the first switch each morning, you are connecting to a huge network of people, electric lines, and generating equipment. Power plant operators control the machinery that generates electricity. Power plant distributors and dispatchers control the flow of electricity from the power plant, over a network of transmission lines, to industrial plants and substations, and, finally, over distribution lines to residential users.

Power plant operators control and monitor boilers, turbines, generators, and auxiliary equipment in power-generating plants. Operators distribute power demands among generators, combine the current from several generators, and monitor instruments to maintain voltage and regulate electricity flows from the plant. When power requirements change, these workers start or stop generators and connect or disconnect them from circuits. They often use computers to keep records of switching operations and loads on generators, lines, and transformers. Operators also may use computers to prepare reports of unusual incidents, malfunctioning equipment, or maintenance performed during their shift.

Operators in plants with automated control systems work mainly in a central control room and usually are called *control room operators* and *control room operator trainees* or *assistants*. In older plants, the controls for the equipment are not centralized, and *switchboard operators* control the flow of electricity from a central point, whereas *auxiliary equipment operators* work throughout the plant, operating and monitoring valves, switches, and gauges.

The Nuclear Regulatory Commission (NRC) licenses operators of nuclear power plants. *Reactor operators* are authorized to control equipment that affects the power of the reactor in a nuclear power plant. In addition, an NRC-licensed *senior reactor operator* must be on duty during each shift to act as the plant supervisor and supervise the operation of all controls in the control room.

Power distributors and dispatchers, also called *load dispatchers* or *systems operators*, control the flow of electricity through transmission lines to industrial plants and substations that supply residential electric needs. They monitor and operate current converters, voltage transformers, and circuit breakers. Dispatchers also monitor other distribution equipment and record readings at a pilot board—a map of the transmission grid system showing the status of transmission circuits and connections with substations and industrial plants.

Dispatchers also anticipate power needs, such as those caused by changes in the weather. They call control room operators to start or stop boilers and generators, to bring production into balance with needs. Dispatchers handle emergencies such as transformer or transmission line failures and route current around affected areas. In substations, they also operate and monitor equipment that increases or decreases voltage, and they operate switchboard levers to control the flow of electricity in and out of the substations.

Working Conditions

Because electricity is provided around the clock, operators, distributors, and dispatchers usually work one of three daily 8-hour shifts or one of two 12-hour shifts on a rotating basis. Shift assignments may change periodically, so that all operators can share duty on less desirable shifts. Work on rotating shifts can be stressful and fatiguing, because of the constant change in living and sleeping patterns. Operators, distributors, and dispatchers who work in control rooms generally sit or stand at a control station. This work is not physically strenuous, but it does require constant attention. Operators who work outside the control room may be exposed to danger from electric shock, falls, and burns.

Nuclear power plant operators are subject to random drug and alcohol tests, as are most workers at such plants.

Employment

Power plant operators, distributors, and dispatchers held about 51,000 jobs in 2002. Jobs were located throughout the country. About 86 percent of jobs were in utility companies and government agencies that produced electricity. Others worked for manufacturing establishments that produced electricity for their own use.

Training, Other Qualifications, and Advancement

Employers seek high school graduates for entry-level operator, distributor, and dispatcher positions. Candidates with strong mathematics and science skills are preferred. College-level courses or prior experience in a mechanical or technical job may be helpful. With computers now used to keep records, generate reports, and track maintenance, employers are increasingly requiring computer proficiency. Most entry-level workers start as helpers or laborers. Depending on the results of aptitude tests, their own preferences, and the availability of openings, workers may be assigned to train for one of many utility positions.

Workers selected for training as a fossil-fueled power plant operator or distributor undergo extensive on-the-job and classroom instruction. Several years of training and experience are required to become a fully qualified control room operator or power plant distributor. With further training and experience, workers may advance to shift supervisor. Utilities generally promote from within; therefore, opportunities to advance by moving to another employer are limited.

Extensive training and experience are necessary to pass the NRC examinations for reactor operators and senior reactor operators. To maintain their license, licensed reactor operators must pass an annual practical plant operation exam and a biennial written exam administered by their employers. Training may include simulator and on-the-job training, classroom instruction, and individual study. Entrants to nuclear power plant operator trainee jobs must have strong mathematics and science skills. Experience in other power plants or with Navy nuclear propulsion plants also is helpful. With further training and experience, reactor operators may advance to senior reactor operator positions.

In addition to receiving preliminary training as a power plant operator, distributor, or dispatcher, most workers are given periodic refresher training—frequently in the case of nuclear power plant operators. Refresher training usually is taken on plant simulators designed specifically to replicate procedures and situations that might be encountered at the trainee's plant.

Job Outlook

People who want to become power plant operators, distributors, and dispatchers are expected to encounter keen competition for these high-paying jobs. Declining employment and very low replacement needs in the occupation will result in few job opportunities. The slow pace of construction of new plants also will limit opportunities for power plant operators, distributors, and dispatchers. In addition, the increasing use of automatic controls and more computerized equipment should boost productivity and decrease the demand for operators. As a result, individuals with training in computers and automated equipment will have the best job prospects.

A decline in employment of power plant operators, distributors, and dispatchers is expected through the year 2012, as the utilities industry continues to restructure in response to deregulation and increasing competition. The Energy Policy Act of 1992 continues to have an impact on the organization of the industry. The Act aims at increasing competition in power-generating utilities by allowing independent producers to sell power directly to industrial and other wholesale customers. Consequently, utilities, which historically operated as regulated local monopolies, are restructuring their operations in order to reduce costs and compete effectively; as a result, the number of jobs is decreasing.

Earnings

Median annual earnings of power plant operators were $49,920 in 2002. The middle 50 percent earned between $40,090 and $58,690. The lowest 10 percent earned less than $31,290, and the highest 10 percent earned more than $67,950. Median annual earnings of power plant operators in 2002 were $52,410 in electric power generation, transmission, and distribution and $44,200 in local government.

Median annual earnings of nuclear power reactor operators were $61,060 in 2002. The middle 50 percent earned between $53,060 and $70,580. The lowest 10 percent earned less than $48,060, and the highest 10 percent earned more than $79,880.

Median annual earnings of power distributors and dispatchers were $54,120 in 2002. The middle 50 percent earned between $43,750 and $65,390. The lowest 10 percent earned less than $34,640, and the highest 10 percent earned more than $75,420.

Related Occupations

Other workers who monitor and operate plant and system equipment include chemical plant and system operators; petroleum pump system operators, refinery operators, and gaugers; stationary engineers and boiler operators; and water and liquid waste treatment plant and system operators.

Sources of Additional Information

For information about employment opportunities, contact local electric utility companies, locals of unions, and state employment service offices.

For general information about power plant operators, nuclear power reactor operators, and power plant distributors and dispatchers, contact:

- American Public Power Association, 2301 M St. NW, Washington, DC 20037-1484. Internet: http://www.appanet.org

- nternational Brotherhood of Electrical Workers, 1125 15th St. NW, Washington, DC 20005.

Precision Instrument and Equipment Repairers

(O*NET 49-9061.00, 49-9063.01, 49-9063.02, 49-9063.03, 49-9063.04, 49-9064.00, and 49-9069.99)

Significant Points

- Training requirements include a high school diploma and, in some cases, postsecondary education, coupled with significant on-the-job training.

- Good opportunities are expected for most types of jobs.

- Overall employment is expected to grow more slowly than average, but projected growth varies by detailed occupation.

- About 1 out of 5 is self-employed.

Nature of the Work

Repairing and maintaining watches, cameras, musical instruments, medical equipment, and other precision instruments requires a high level of skill and attention to detail. For example, some devices contain tiny gears that must be manufactured to within one one-hundredth of a millimeter of design specifications, and other devices contain sophisticated electronic controls.

Camera and photographic equipment repairers work through a series of steps in fixing a camera. The first step is determining whether a repair should be attempted, because many inexpensive cameras cost more to repair than to replace. Of the problems for which repair seems worthwhile, the most complicated or expensive are referred back to the manufacturer. If the repairers decide to proceed with the job themselves, they diagnose the problem, often by disassembling numerous small parts in order to reach the source. They then make needed adjustments or replace a defective part. Many problems are caused by the electronic circuits used in many cameras, which require an understanding of electronics. Camera repairers also maintain cameras by removing and replacing broken or worn parts and cleaning and lubricating gears and springs. Because many of the components and parts involved are extremely small, repairers must have a great deal of manual dexterity. Frequently, older camera parts are no longer available, requiring repairers to build replacement parts or to strip junked cameras. When machining new parts, workers often use a small lathe, a grinding wheel, and other metalworking tools.

Camera repairers also repair the increasingly popular digital cameras. Repairs on such cameras are similar to those for most modern cameras, but, because digital cameras have no film to wind, they have fewer moving parts.

Watch and clock repairers work almost exclusively on expensive and antique timepieces, as moderately priced timepieces are cheaper to replace than to repair. Electrically powered clocks and quartz watches and clocks function with almost no moving parts, limiting necessary maintenance to replacing the battery. Many expensive timepieces still employ old-style mechanical movements and a manual or automatic winding mechanism. This type of timepiece must be regularly adjusted and maintained. Repair and maintenance work on a mechanical timepiece requires using handtools to disassemble many fine gears and components. Each part is inspected for signs of wear. Some gears or springs may need to be replaced or machined. Exterior portions of the watch may require polishing and buffing. Specialized machines are used to clean all of the parts with ultrasonic waves and a series of baths in cleaning agents. Reassembling a watch requires lubricating key parts.

As with older cameras, replacement parts are frequently unavailable for antique watches or clocks. In such cases, watch repairers must machine their own parts. They employ small lathes and other machines in creating tiny parts.

Musical instrument repairers and tuners combine their love of music with a highly skilled craft. Musical instrument repairers and tuners, often referred to as technicians, work in four specialties: Band instruments, pianos and organs, violins, and guitars.

Band instrument repairers, brass and wind instrument repairers, and percussion instrument repairers focus on woodwind, brass, reed, and percussion instruments damaged through deterioration or by accident. They move mechanical parts or play scales to find problems. They may unscrew and remove rod pins, keys, worn cork pads, and pistons and remove soldered parts using gas torches. They repair dents in metal and wood using filling techniques or a mallet. These repairers use gas torches, grinding wheels, lathes, shears, mallets, and small handtools and are skilled in metalworking and woodworking. Percussion instrument repairers often must install new drumheads, which are cut from animal skin.

Violin repairers and guitar repairers adjust and repair stringed instruments. Some repairers work on both stringed and band instruments. Initially, repairers play and inspect the instrument to find any defects. They replace or repair cracked or broken sections and damaged parts. They also restring the instruments and repair damage to their finish.

Piano tuners and repairers use similar techniques, skills, and tools. Most workers in this group are piano tuners, tuning and making minor repairs. Tuning involves tightening and loosening different strings to achieve the proper tone or pitch. Because pianos are difficult to transport, tuners normally make house calls. Some repairers specialize in restoring older pianos. Restoration is complicated work, often involving replacing many of the more than 12,000 parts in some pianos. With proper maintenance and restoration, pianos often survive more than 100 years.

Pipe organ repairers do work similar to that of piano repairers, but on a larger scale. Additionally, they assemble new organs. Because pipe organs are too large to transport, they must be assembled onsite. Even with repairers working in teams or with assistants, the organ assembly process can take several weeks or even months, depending upon the size of the organ.

Medical equipment repairers and *other precision instrument and equipment repairers* maintain, adjust, calibrate, and repair electronic, electromechanical, and hydraulic equipment. They use various tools, including multimeters, specialized software, and computers designed to communicate with specific pieces of hardware. Some of their tools are specialized, such as equipment designed to simulate water or air pressure. These repairers use handtools, soldering irons, and other electronic tools to repair and adjust the equipment. Faulty circuit boards and other parts are normally removed and replaced. Medical equipment and other precision instrument repairers must maintain careful, detailed logs of all maintenance and repair on each piece of equipment.

Medical equipment repairers, often called *biomedical equipment technicians*, work on medical equipment such as defibrillators, heart monitors, medical imaging equipment (x rays, CAT scanners, and ultrasound equipment), and electric wheelchairs.

Other precision instrument and equipment repairers service, repair, and replace a wide range of equipment associated with automated or instrument-controlled manufacturing processes. A precision instrument repairer working at an electric powerplant, for example, would repair and maintain instruments that monitor the operation of the plant, such as pressure and temperature gauges. Replacement parts are not always available, so repairers sometimes machine or fabricate a new part. Preventive maintenance involves regular lubrication, cleaning, and adjustment of many measuring devices.

Working Conditions

Camera, watch, and musical instrument repairers work under fairly similar solitary, low-stress conditions with minimal supervision. A quiet, well-lighted workshop or repair shop is typical, while a few of these repairers travel to the instrument being repaired, such as a piano, organ, or grandfather clock.

Medical equipment and precision instrument and equipment repairers normally work daytime hours, but are often expected to be on call. But, like other hospital and factory employees, some repairers work irregular hours. Precision instrument repairers work under a wide array of conditions, from hot, dirty, noisy factories to air-conditioned workshops to outdoor fieldwork. Attention to safety is essential, as the work sometimes involves dangerous machinery or toxic chemicals. Due to the individual nature of the work, supervision is fairly minimal.

Employment

Precision instrument and equipment repairers held 64,000 jobs in 2002. Medical equipment repairers often work for hospitals or wholesale equipment suppliers, while precision instrument repairers, all other, often work for manufacturing companies and durable goods wholesalers. About 1 out of 5 precision instrument and equipment repairers was self-employed—they may own jewelry, camera, medical equipment, or music stores. The following tabulation presents employment by detailed occupation:

Medical equipment repairers	29,000
Camera and photographic equipment repairers	6,900
Musical instrument repairers and tuners	6,200
Watch repairers	4,800
All other precision instrument and equipment repairers	17,000

Training, Other Qualifications, and Advancement

Most employers require at least a high school diploma for beginning precision instrument and equipment repairers. Many employers prefer applicants with some postsecondary education. Much training takes place on the job. The ability to read and understand technical manuals is important. Necessary physical qualities include good fine motor skills and vision. Also, precision equipment repairers must be able to pay close attention to details, enjoy problem solving, and have the desire to disassemble machines to see how they work. Most precision equipment repairers must be able to work alone with minimal supervision.

The educational background required for camera and photographic equipment repairers varies, but some knowledge of electronics is necessary. Some workers complete postsecondary training, such as an associate degree, in this field. The job requires the ability to read an electronic schematic diagram and comprehend other technical information, in addition to good manual dexterity. New employees are trained on the job in two stages over about a year. First, they assist a senior repairer for about 6 months. Then, they refine their skills by performing repairs on their own for an additional 6 months. Finally, repairers continually hone and improve their skills by attending manufacturer-sponsored seminars on the specifics of particular models.

Training also varies for watch and clock repairers. Several associations, including the American Watchmakers-Clockmakers Institute (AWI) and the National Association of Watch and Clock Collectors, offer certifications. Some certifications can be completed in a few months; some require simply passing an examination; and the most demanding certifications require 3,000 hours, over 2 years, of classroom time in technical institutes or colleges. Clock repairers generally require less training than do watch repairers because watches have smaller components and require greater precision. Some repairers opt to learn through assisting a master watch repairer. Nevertheless, developing proficiency in watch or clock repair requires several years of education and experience.

For musical instrument repairers and tuners, employers prefer people with post-high school training in music repair technology. According to a Piano Technicians Guild membership survey, the overwhelming majority of respondents had completed at least some college work; most had a bachelor's or higher degree, although not always in music repair technology. Almost all repairers have a strong musical background. A basic ability to play the instruments being repaired is helpful, but not always required. A few technical schools and colleges offer courses in instrument repair, and correspondence courses also are common. Graduates of these programs normally receive additional training on the job, working with an experienced repairer. A few musical instrument repairers and tuners begin learning their trade on the job as assistants or apprentices. Trainees perform a variety of tasks around the shop. Full qualification usually requires 2 to 5 years of training and practice.

Medical equipment repairers are trained in a similar manner. An associate degree in electronics or medical technology is helpful, but not always required. The required training varies by specialty. On-the-job training, for those with a background in electronics, is more common for workers repairing less critical equipment such as hospital beds or electric wheelchairs. An associate or even a bachelor's degree, often in medical technology or engineering, and a passing grade on a certification exam is likely to be required of persons repairing more critical equipment such as CAT scanners and defibrillators. Some repairers are trained in the military. New repairers begin by observing and assisting an experienced worker over a period of 3 to 6 months. Gradually, they begin working independently, while still under close supervision.

Educational requirements for other precision instrument and equipment repair jobs also vary, but include a high school diploma, with a focus on mathematics and science courses. Most employers require an associate or sometimes a bachelor's degree in instrumentation and control, electronics, or a related engineering field, as repairers need to understand blueprints, electrical schematic diagrams, and electrical, hydraulic, and electromechanical systems. In addition to formal education, a year or two of on-the-job training is required before a repairer is considered fully qualified. Some advancement opportunities exist, but many supervisory positions require a bachelor's degree.

Job Outlook

Good opportunities are expected for most types of precision instrument and equipment repairer jobs. Overall employment growth is projected to be slower than the average for all occupations over the 2002-12 period. However, projected growth varies by detailed occupation.

Job growth among medical equipment repairers should be about as fast as the average for all occupations over the projected period. The rapidly expanding healthcare industry and elderly population should spark demand for increasingly sophisticated medical equipment and, in turn, create good employment opportunities in this occupation.

On the other hand, employment of musical instrument repairers is expected to increase more slowly than the average. Replacement needs will provide the most job opportunities as many repairers and tuners are expected to retire. While an increase in the number of school-age children involved with music should spur demand for repairers, music must compete with other extracurricular activities and interests. Without new musicians, there will be a slump in instrument rentals, purchases, and repairs. Because training in the repair of musical instruments is difficult to obtain—there are only a few schools that offer training programs, and few experienced workers are willing to take on apprentices—opportunities should be good for those who receive training.

Employment of camera and photographic equipment repairers is expected to decline. The popularity of inexpensive cameras adversely affects employment in this occupation, as most point-and-shoot cameras are cheaper to replace than repair. The rapid technological progress in digital cameras also has hurt the job prospects of repairers. When a digital camera breaks, not only is replacing the camera often not much more expensive, but the new model is also far more advanced.

Employment of watch repairers is expected to increase more slowly than the average. Over the past few decades, changes in technology, including the invention of digital and quartz watches that need few repairs, caused a significant decline in the demand for watch repairers. In recent years, this trend was somewhat reversed, as the growing popularity of expensive mechanical watches increased the need for watch repairers. While the demand for watch repairers has risen, however, few new repairers have entered the field. The small number of entrants, coupled with the fact that a large proportion of watch and clock repairers are approaching retirement age, should result in very good job opportunities in this field.

The projected slower-than-average employment growth of other precision instrument and equipment repairers reflects the expected lack of employment growth in manufacturing and other industries in which they are employed. Nevertheless, good employment opportunities are expected for these precision instrument and equipment repairers due to the relatively small number of people entering the occupation and the need to replace repairers who retire.

Earnings

The following tabulation shows median hourly earnings for various precision instrument and equipment repairers in 2002. Earnings ranged from less than $7.59 for the lowest 10 percent of watch repairers, to more than $30.68 for the highest 10 percent of precision instrument and equipment repairers, all other. Median hourly earnings of all precision instrument and equipment repairers by occupation are:

Precision instrument and equipment repairers, all other	$21.20
Medical equipment repairers	17.49
Camera and photographic equipment repairers	15.09
Musical instrument repairers and tuners	14.15
Watch repairers	12.77

Earnings within the different occupations vary significantly, depending upon skill levels. For example, a watch and clock repairer may simply change batteries and replace worn wrist straps, while highly skilled watch and clock repairers, with years of training and experience, may rebuild and replace worn parts. According to a survey by the American Watchmakers-Clockmakers Institute, the median annual earnings of highly skilled watch and clock repairers were about $42,500 in 2001.

Related Occupations

Many precision instrument and equipment repairers work with precision mechanical and electronic equipment. Other workers who repair precision mechanical and electronic equipment include computer, automated teller, and office machine repairers and coin, vending, and amusement machine servicers and repairers. Other workers who make precision items include dental laboratory technicians and ophthalmic laboratory technicians. Some precision instrument and equipment repairers work with a wide array of industrial equipment. Their work environment and responsibilities are similar to those of industrial machinery installation, maintenance, and repair workers. Much of the work of watch repairers is similar to that of jewelers and precious stone and metal workers. Camera repairers' work is similar to that of electronic home entertainment equipment installers and repairers; both occupations work with consumer electronics that are based around a circuit board, but that also involve numerous moving mechanical parts.

Sources of Additional Information

For more information about camera repair careers, contact:

- National Association of Photographic Equipment Technicians (NAPET), 3000 Picture Pl., Jackson, MI 49201.

For information on musical instrument repair, including schools offering training, contact:

- National Association of Professional Band Instrument Repair Technicians (NAPBIRT), P.O. Box 51, Normal, IL 61761. Internet: http://www.napbirt.org

For additional information on piano tuning and repairwork, contact:

- Piano Technicians Guild, 3930 Washington St., Kansas City, MO 64111-2963. Internet: http://www.ptg.org

For information about training, mentoring programs, employers, and schools with programs in precision instrumentation, automation, and control, contact:

● ISA-The Instrumentation, Systems, and Automation Society, 67 Alexander Dr., P.O. Box 12277, Research Triangle Park, NC 27709. Internet: http://www.isa.org

For information about watch and clock repair and a list of schools with related programs of study, contact:

● American Watchmakers-Clockmakers Institute (AWI), 701 Enterprise Dr., Harrison, OH 45030-1696. Internet: http://www.awi-net.org

For information about medical equipment technicians and a list of schools with related programs of study, contact:

● Association for the Advancement of Medical Instrumentation (AAMI), 1110 North Glebe Rd., Arlington, VA 22201-4795. Internet: http://www.aami.org

Prepress Technicians and Workers

(O*NET 51-5022.01, 51-5022.02, 51-5022.03, 51-5022.04, 51-5022.05, 51-5022.06, 51-5022.07, 51-5022.08, and 51-5022.09)

Significant Points

● Most workers train on the job; some complete formal graphics arts programs or other postsecondary programs in printing technology.

● Most employers prefer to hire workers with experience in the printing industry.

● Employment is projected to decline as the increased use of computers in typesetting and page layout eliminates many prepress jobs.

Nature of the Work

The printing process has three stages—prepress, press, and binding or postpress. In small print shops, *job printers* may be responsible for all three stages. They do the composition and page layout of the material received from the customer, check proofs for errors and print clarity and correct mistakes, print the job, and attach each copy's pages together. In most printing firms, however, each of the stages is the responsibility of a specialized group of workers. *Prepress technicians and workers* are responsible for the first stage, preparing the material for printing presses. They perform a variety of tasks involved with transforming text and pictures into finished pages and making printing plates of the pages.

Typesetting and page layout have been greatly affected by technological changes over the years and, today, advances in computer software and printing technology continue to change prepress work. The old "hot type" method of text composition—in which molten lead was used to create individual letters, which were placed in frames to produce paragraphs and full pages of text—has become rare. Its successor, phototypesetting or "cold type" technology, is still used for

some composition work, but it, in turn, is being rapidly replaced by computerized digital imaging technology. Customers today are able to provide printers with pages of material that look like the desired finished product they want printed and bound in volume. Using a process called "desktop publishing," customers are increasingly using their own computers to do much of the typesetting and page layout work formerly done by prepress technicians. Many regular customers employ workers called desktop publishers to do this work. Other customers employ in-house graphic designers who do desktop publishing as part of their work, or send the work out to freelance graphic designers. It is increasingly common for prepress technicians or other printing workers to receive files from the customer on a computer disk or submitted by e-mail, that contains typeset material already laid out in pages.

The printing industry is doing more prepress work using complete "digital imaging." Using this technology, prepress technicians called "preflight technicians" take material received on computer disks from customers, check it for completeness, and format it into pages using electronic page layout systems; even though the pages may already be laid out, they still may have to be formatted to fit the dimensions of the paper stock to be used. When color printing is required, the technicians use digital color page-makeup systems to electronically produce an image of the printed pages, then use off-press color proofing systems to print a copy, or "proof," of the pages as they will appear when printed. The technician then has the proofs delivered or mailed to the customer for a final check. Once the customer gives the "OK to print," technicians use laser "imagesetters" to expose digital images of the pages directly onto thin aluminum printing plates.

Some customers continue to provide material to printers that is more suitable for cold type prepress technology. Cold type processing, which describes any of a variety of methods to create a printing plate without molten lead, has traditionally used "phototypesetting" to prepare text and pictures for printing. Although this method has many variations, all use photography to create images on paper. The images are assembled into page format and rephotographed to create film negatives from which the actual printing plates are made.

In one common form of phototypesetting, printed text received from the customer must first be entered into a computer programmed to hyphenate, space, and create columns of text. Typesetters or data entry clerks may do the keyboarding of text at the printing establishment. The coded text then is transferred to a typesetting machine, which uses photography, a cathode-ray tube, or a laser to create an image on typesetting paper or film. Once it has been developed, the paper or film is sent to a lithographer who makes the actual printing plate.

With traditional photolithographic processes, the material to be printed is arranged and typeset, and then passed on to workers who further prepare it for the presses. *Camera operators* start the process of making a lithographic plate by photographing and developing film negatives or positives of the material to be printed. They adjust light and expose film for a specified length of time, and then develop the film in a series of chemical baths. They may load exposed film in machines that automatically develop and fix the image. The lithographic printing process requires that images be made up of tiny dots coming together to form a picture. Photographs cannot be printed without them. When normal "continuous-tone" photographs need to be reproduced, camera operators use halftone cameras to separate the photograph into an image containing the dots of varying sizes corresponding to the values of the original photograph.

Color separation photography is more complex. In this process, camera operators produce four-color separation negatives from a continuous-tone color print or transparency. Because this is a complicated and time-consuming process, most of this separation work is instead being done electronically on scanners. *Scanner operators* use computerized equipment to capture photographs or art as digital data, or to create film negatives or positives of photographs or art. The computer controls the color separation of the scanning process and, with the help of the operator, corrects for mistakes or compensates for deficiencies in the original color print or transparency. Each scan produces a dotted image, or halftone, of the original in 1 of 4 primary printing colors—yellow, magenta, cyan, and black. The images are used to produce printing plates that print each of these colors, with transparent colored inks, one at a time. Superimposition of the images on the photos produces "secondary" color combinations of red, green, blue, and black that approximate the colors and hues of the original photograph.

Where this process is still being used, *film strippers* cut the film of text and images to the required size and arrange and tape the negatives onto "flats"—or layout sheets used by platemakers to make press plates. When completed, flats resemble large film negatives of the text in its final form. Platemakers use a photographic process to make printing plates. The flat is placed on top of a thin metal plate coated with a light-sensitive resin. Exposure to ultraviolet light activates the chemical in parts of the plate not protected by the film's dark areas. The plate then is developed in a solution that removes the unexposed nonimage area, exposing bare metal. The chemical on areas of the plate exposed to the light hardens and becomes water repellent. The hardened parts of the plate form the text and images to be printed.

During the printing process, the plate is first covered with a thin coat of water. The water adheres only to the bare metal nonimage areas, and is repelled by the hardened areas that were exposed to light. Next, the plate comes in contact with a rubber roller covered with oil-based ink. Because oil and water do not mix, the ink is repelled by the water-coated area and sticks to the hardened areas. The ink covering the hardened text is transferred to paper.

Working Conditions

Prepress technicians and workers usually work in clean, air-conditioned areas with little noise. Some workers may develop eyestrain from working in front of a video display terminal, or musculoskeletal problems such as backaches. Platemakers, who still work with toxic chemicals, face the hazard of skin irritations. Workers often are subject to stress and the pressures of short deadlines and tight work schedules.

Prepress employees usually work an 8-hour day. Some workers—particularly those employed by newspapers—work night shifts, weekends, and holidays.

Employment

Prepress technicians and workers overall held about 148,000 jobs in 2002. Of these, approximately 56,000 were employed as job printers; the remainder was employed as prepress technicians and other prepress workers. Most prepress jobs are found in the printing industry, while newspaper publishing employs the second largest number of prepress technicians and workers.

The printing and publishing industries are two of the most geographically dispersed in the United States, and prepress jobs are found throughout the country. However, jobs are concentrated in large metropolitan cities such as New York; Chicago; Los Angeles; Philadelphia; Washington, DC; and Dallas.

Training, Other Qualifications, and Advancement

Traditionally, prepress technicians and workers started as helpers and were trained on the job, the length of training varying by occupation. Some jobs required years of experience performing the detailed handwork to become skillful enough to perform even difficult tasks quickly. Instead of painstakingly taping pieces of photographic negatives to flats, today's prepress technicians increasingly use computer software skills to electronically modify and lay out the material; in some cases, the first time the material appears on paper is when the final product rolls off the printing press. As this digital imaging technology increasingly replaces cold type print technology, persons seeking to enter prepress technician jobs will require formal graphic communications training in the various types of computer software used in digital imaging.

Postsecondary graphic communications programs are available from a variety of sources. For beginners, 2-year associate degree programs offered by community and junior colleges and technical schools, and some 4-year bachelor's degree programs in graphic design colleges teach the latest prepress skills and allow students to practice applying them. However, bachelor's programs usually are intended for students who may eventually move into management positions in printing or design jobs. Community and junior colleges, 4-year colleges and universities, vocational-technical institutes, industry-sponsored update and retraining programs, and private trade and technical schools all also offer prepress-related courses for workers who do not wish to enroll in a degree program. Many workers with experience in other printing jobs take a few college graphic communications courses to upgrade their skills and qualify for prepress jobs. Prepress training designed to train skilled workers already employed in the printing industry also is offered through unions in the printing industry. Many employers view individuals with a combination of experience in the printing industry and formal training in the new digital technology as the best candidates for prepress jobs. The experience of these applicants in printing press operator or other jobs provides them with an understanding of how printing plants operate, familiarizes them with basic prepress functions, and demonstrates their reliability and interest in advancing in the industry.

Employers prefer workers with good communication skills, both oral and written, for prepress jobs. Prepress technicians and workers should be able to deal courteously with people because, when prepress problems arise, they sometimes have to contact the customer to resolve them. Also, in small shops, they may take customer orders. Persons interested in working for firms using advanced printing technology need to know the basics of electronics and computers. Mathematical skills also are essential for operating many of the software packages used to run modern, computerized prepress equipment. At times, prepress personnel may have to perform computations in order to estimate job costs.

Prepress technicians and workers need good manual dexterity, and they must be able to pay attention to detail and work independently. Good eyesight, including visual acuity, depth perception, field of view, color vision, and the ability to focus quickly, also are assets. Artistic ability is often a plus. Employers also seek persons who possess an even temperament and an ability to adapt, important qualities for workers who often must meet deadlines and learn how to use new software or operate new equipment.

Job Outlook

Overall employment of prepress technicians and workers is expected to decline through 2012. The number of job printers, however, is expected to grow, though at a rate slower than average. Demand for printed material should continue to grow, spurred by rising levels of personal income, increasing school enrollments, higher levels of educational attainment, and expanding markets. But increased use of computers in desktop publishing will contribute to the elimination of many jobs for prepress technicians.

Technological advances will have a varying effect on employment among the prepress occupations. This reflects the increasing proportion of page layout and design that will be performed using computers. Thus, the need for preflight technicians will remain strong. However, most prepress technicians and workers such as pasteup, composition and typesetting, photoengraving, platemaking, film stripping, and camera operator occupations are expected to experience declines as handwork becomes automated. Computer software that allows office workers to specify text typeface and style, and to format pages at a desktop computer terminal, already has eliminated most typesetting and composition jobs; more jobs will disappear in the years ahead.

Job prospects also will vary by industry. Changes in technology have shifted many prepress functions away from the traditional printing plants into advertising and public relations agencies, graphic design firms, and large corporations. Many companies are turning to in-house desktop publishing as page layout and graphic design capabilities of computer software have improved and become less expensive and more user-friendly. Some firms are finding it more profitable to prepare their own newsletters and other reports than to send them out to trade shops. At newspapers, writers and editors also are doing more composition using publishing software.

Some new jobs for prepress technicians and workers are expected to emerge in commercial printing establishments. New equipment should reduce the time needed to complete a printing job, and allow commercial printers to make inroads into new markets that require fast turnaround. Because small establishments predominate, commercial printing should provide the best opportunities for inexperienced workers who want to gain a good background in all facets of printing.

Employers in the printing industry prefer to hire workers experienced in all facets of printing. Among persons without experience, however, opportunities should be best for those with computer backgrounds who have completed postsecondary programs in printing technology or graphic communications. Many employers prefer graduates of these programs because the comprehensive training that they receive helps them to learn the printing process and to adapt more rapidly to new processes and techniques.

Earnings

Median hourly earnings of prepress technicians and workers were $14.98 in 2002. The middle 50 percent earned between $11.25 and $19.68 an hour. The lowest 10 percent earned less than $8.68, and the highest 10 percent earned more than $24.36 an hour.

For job printers, median hourly earnings were $14.47 in 2002. The middle 50 percent earned between $10.98 and $18.91 an hour. The lowest 10 percent earned less than $8.59, while the highest 10 percent earned more than $23.06 an hour.

Median hourly earnings in commercial printing, the industry employing the largest number of prepress technicians and workers, were $16.05 in 2002, while the figure for these workers in the newspaper, periodical, and book publishing industry was $13.07 an hour. For job printers, median hourly earnings in commercial printing in 2002 were $14.84, while in the newspaper, periodical, and book publishing industry median hourly earnings were $13.98.

Wage rates for prepress technicians and workers vary according to occupation, level of experience, training, location, size of firm, and union membership status.

Related Occupations

Prepress technicians and workers use artistic skills in their work. These skills also are essential for artists and related workers, graphic designers, and desktop publishers. Moreover, many of the skills used in Web site design also are employed in prepress technology.

In addition to typesetters, other workers who operate machines equipped with keyboards include data entry and information processing workers. Prepress technicians' work also is tied in closely with that of printing machine operators, including job printers.

Sources of Additional Information

Details about training programs may be obtained from local employers such as newspapers and printing shops, or from local offices of the state employment service.

For information on careers and training in printing and the graphic arts, write to:

- Printing Industries of America, 100 Daingerfield Rd., Alexandria, VA 22314. Internet: http://www.gain.net

- Graphic Communications Council, 1899 Preston White Dr., Reston, VA 20191. Internet: http://www.teched.vt.edu/gcc

- Graphic Communications International Union, 1900 L St. NW, Washington, DC 20036. Internet: http://www.gciu.org

- Graphic Arts Technical Foundation, 200 Deer Run Rd., Sewickley, PA 15143. Internet: http://www.gatf.org

Radio and Telecommunications Equipment Installers and Repairers

(O*NET 49-2021.00, 49-2022.01, 49-2022.02, 49-2022.03, 49-2022.04, and 49-2022.05)

Significant Points

- Employment is projected to decline.

- Applicants with electronics training and computer skills should have the best opportunities.

- Weekend and holiday hours are common; repairers may be on call around the clock in case of emergencies.

Nature of the Work

Telephones and radios depend on a variety of equipment to transmit communications signals. Electronic switches route telephone signals to their destinations. Switchboards direct telephone calls within a single location or organization. Radio transmitters and receivers relay signals from wireless phones and radios to their destinations. Newer telecommunications equipment is computerized and can communicate a variety of information, including data, graphics, and video. The workers who set up and maintain this sophisticated equipment are radio and telecommunications equipment installers and repairers.

Central office installers set up switches, cables, and other equipment in central offices. These locations are the hubs of a telecommunications network—they contain the switches and routers that direct packets of information to their destinations. Although most telephone lines connecting houses to central offices and switching stations are still copper, the lines connecting these central hubs are fiber optic. Fiber optic lines have led to a revolution in switching equipment. The greatly increased transmission capacity of each line has allowed a few fiber optic lines to replace many copper lines. Packet switching equipment is evolving rapidly, ever increasing the amount of information that a single fiber optic line can carry. These switches and routers have the ability to transmit, process, amplify, and direct a massive amount of information. Installing and maintaining this equipment requires a high level of technical knowledge.

The increasing reliability of telephone switches and routers has simplified maintenance. New telephone switches are self-monitoring and alert repairers to malfunctions. Some switches allow repairers to diagnose and correct problems from remote locations. When faced with a malfunction, the repairer may refer to manufacturers' manuals that provide maintenance instructions.

When problems with telecommunications equipment arise, telecommunications equipment repairers diagnose the source of the problem by testing each of the different parts of the equipment, which requires an understanding of how the software and hardware interact. Repairers often use spectrum and/or network analyzers to locate the problem. A network analyzer sends a signal through the equipment to detect any distortion in the signal. The nature of the signal distortion often directs the repairer to the source of the problem. To fix the equipment, repairers may use small handtools, including pliers and screwdrivers, to remove and replace defective components such as circuit boards or wiring. Newer equipment is easier to repair because whole boards and parts are designed to be quickly removed and replaced. Repairers also may install updated software or programs that maintain existing software.

PBX installers and repairers set up private branch exchange (PBX) switchboards, which relay incoming, outgoing, and interoffice calls within a single location or organization. To install switches and switchboards, installers first connect the equipment to power lines and communications cables and install frames and supports. They test the connections to ensure that adequate power is available and that the communication links function. They also install equipment such as power systems, alarms, and telephone sets. New switches and switchboards are computerized; workers install software or program the equipment to provide specific features. For example, as a cost-cutting feature, an installer may program a PBX switchboard to route calls over different lines at different times of the day. However, other workers, such as computer support specialists generally handle complex programming. Finally, the installer performs tests to verify that the newly installed equipment functions properly. If a problem arises, PBX repairers determine whether it is located within the PBX system or originates in the telephone lines maintained by the local phone company.

Due to rapidly developing technologies, PBX installers must adapt and learn new technologies. Instead of installing PBX systems, many companies are choosing to install voice-over Internet protocol (VoIP) systems. VoIP systems operate like a PBX system, but they use a company's computer wiring to run Internet access, network applications, and telephone communications. Specialized phones have their own Internet protocol (IP) addresses. The phones can be plugged into any port in the system and still use the same number.

Station installers and repairers, telephone—commonly known as *telephone installers and repairers* or *telecommunications service technicians*—install and repair telephone wiring and equipment on customers' premises. They install telephone or digital subscriber line (DSL) service by connecting customers' telephone wires to outside service lines. These lines run on telephone poles or in underground conduits. The installer may climb poles or ladders to make the connections. Once the connection is made, the line is tested. When a maintenance problem occurs, repairers test the customers' lines to determine if the problem is located in the customers' premises or in the outside service lines. When onsite procedures fail to resolve installation or maintenance problems, repairers may request support from their technical service center. Line installers and repairers install the wires and cables that connect customers with central offices.

Radio mechanics install and maintain radio transmitting and receiving equipment. This includes stationary equipment mounted on transmission towers and mobile equipment, such as radio communications systems in service and emergency vehicles. Radio mechanics do not work on cellular communications towers and equipment. Newer radio equipment is self-monitoring and may alert mechanics to potential malfunctions. When malfunctions occur, these mechanics examine equipment for damaged components and loose or broken wires. They use electrical measuring instruments to monitor signal strength, transmission capacity, interference, and signal delay, as well as handtools to replace defective components and parts and to adjust equipment so that it performs within required specifications.

Working Conditions

Radio and telecommunications equipment installers and repairers generally work in clean, well-lighted, air-conditioned surroundings, such as a telephone company's central office, a customer's PBX location, or an electronic repair shop or service center. Telephone installers and repairers work on rooftops, ladders, and telephone poles. Telephone and PBX installers must travel to a customer's location. Radio mechanics may maintain equipment located on the tops of transmissions towers. While working outdoors, these workers are subject to a variety of weather conditions.

Nearly all radio and telecommunications equipment installers and repairers work full time. Many work regular business hours to meet the demand for repair services during the workday. Schedules are more irregular at companies that need repair services 24 hours a day or where installation and maintenance must take place after business hours. At these locations, mechanics work a variety of shifts, including weekend and holiday hours. Repairers may be on call around the clock, in case of emergencies, and may have to work overtime.

The work of most repairers involves lifting, reaching, stooping, crouching, and crawling. Adherence to safety precautions is important in order to guard against work hazards. These hazards include falls, minor burns, electrical shock, and contact with hazardous materials.

Employment

Radio and telecommunications equipment installers and repairers held about 226,000 jobs in 2002. About 219,000 were telecommunications equipment installers and repairers, except line installers, mostly working in the telecommunications industry, and the rest were radio mechanics. Radio mechanics worked in electronic and precision equipment repair and maintenance, telecommunications, electronics and appliance stores, and many other industries.

Training, Other Qualifications, and Advancement

Most employers seek applicants with postsecondary training in electronics and a familiarity with computers. Training sources include 2- and 4-year college programs in electronics or communications, trade schools, and equipment and software manufacturers. Military experience with communications equipment is valued by many employers. Many equipment repairers begin working in telecommunications companies as line-installers or telephone installers, before moving up to the job of central office installer and other more complex work.

Newly hired repairers usually receive some training from their employers. This may include formal classroom training in electronics, communications systems, or software and informal hands-on training assisting an experienced repairer. Large companies may send repairers to outside training sessions to keep them informed about new equipment and service procedures. As networks have become more sophisticated—often including equipment from a variety of companies—the knowledge needed for installation and maintenance also has increased.

Telecommunications equipment companies provide much of the training on specific equipment. With the rapid advances in switches, routers, and other equipment, repairers need to continually take courses and work to obtain manufacturers' certifications on the latest technology.

Repairers must be able to distinguish colors, because wires are color-coded, and they must be able to hear distinctions in the various tones on a telephone system. For positions that require climbing poles and towers, workers must be in good physical shape. Repairers who handle assignments alone at a customer's site must be able to work without close supervision. For workers who frequently contact customers, a pleasant personality, neat appearance, and good communications skills also are important.

Experienced repairers with advanced training may become specialists or troubleshooters who help other repairers diagnose difficult problems, or may work with engineers in designing equipment and developing maintenance procedures. Because of their familiarity with equipment, repairers are particularly well qualified to become manufacturers' sales workers. Workers with leadership ability also may become maintenance supervisors or service managers. Some experienced workers open their own repair services or shops, or become wholesalers or retailers of electronic equipment.

Job Outlook

Employment of radio and telecommunications equipment installers and repairers is expected to decline through 2012. Although the need for installation work will remain as companies seek to upgrade their telecommunications networks, there will be a declining need for maintenance work—performed by telecommunications equipment installers and repairers, except line installers—because of increasingly reliable self-monitoring and self-diagnosing equipment and because installation of higher capacity equipment will reduce the amount of equipment needed. The replacement of two-way radio systems with wireless systems, especially in service vehicles, will eliminate the need in many companies for onsite radio mechanics. The increased reliability of wireless equipment and the use of self-monitoring systems also will continue to lessen the need for radio mechanics. Applicants with electronics training and computer skills should have the best opportunities for radio and telecommunications equipment installer and repairer jobs.

Job opportunities will vary by specialty. For example, opportunities should be available for central office and PBX installers and repairers experienced in current technology, as the growing popularity of VoIP, expanded multimedia offerings such as video on demand, and other telecommunications services continue to place additional demand on telecommunications networks. These new services require high data transfer rates, which can be achieved only by installing new optical switching and routing equipment. Extending high-speed communications from central offices to customers also will require the installation of more advanced switching and routing equipment. Whereas increased reliability and automation of switching equipment will limit opportunities, these effects will be somewhat offset by the demand for installation and upgrading of switching equipment.

Station installers and repairers can expect keen competition. Prewired buildings and the increasing reliability of telephone equipment will reduce the need for installation and maintenance of customers' telephones. Upgrading internal lines in businesses and the wiring of new homes and businesses with fiber optic lines should offset some of these losses. As cellular telephones have increased in popularity, the number of pay phones is declining, which also will adversely affect employment of station installers and repairers as pay phone installation and maintenance is one of their major functions.

Earnings

In 2002, median hourly earnings of telecommunications equipment installers and repairers, except line installers were $22.78. The middle 50 percent earned between $18.07 and $26.38. The bottom 10 percent earned less than $13.27, whereas the top 10 percent earned more than $29.09. Median hourly earnings in the wired telecommunications carriers (telephone) industry were $24.07 in 2002.

Median hourly earnings of radio mechanics in 2002 were $17.42. The middle 50 percent earned between $13.17 and $22.78. The bottom 10 percent earned less than $10.34, whereas the top 10 percent earned more than $28.38.

Related Occupations

Related occupations that involve work with electronic equipment include broadcast and sound engineering technicians and radio operators; computer, automated teller, and office machine repairers; electronic home entertainment equipment installers and repairers; and electrical and electronics installers and repairers. Line installers and repairers also set up and install telecommunications equipment. Engineering technicians also may repair electronic equipment as part of their duties.

Sources of Additional Information

For information on career and training opportunities, contact:

- International Brotherhood of Electrical Workers, Telecommunications Department, 1125 15th St. NW., Room 807, Washington, DC 20005. Internet: http://www.ibew.org

- Communications Workers of America, 501 3rd St. NW, Washington, DC 20001.

For information on careers and schools, contact:

- Electronics Technicians Association International, 5 Depot St., Greencastle, IN 46135.

For information on training and professional certifications for those already employed by cable telecommunications firms, contact:

● Society of Cable Telecommunications Engineers, Certification Department, 140 Phillips Rd., Exton, PA 19341-1318. Internet: http://www.scte.org

Radiologic Technologists and Technicians

(O*NET 29-2034.01)

Significant Points

- Formal training programs in radiography range in length from 1 to 4 years and lead to a certificate, associate degree, or bachelor's degree.

- Although hospitals will remain the primary employer, a greater number of new jobs will be found in physicians' offices and diagnostic imaging centers.

- Job opportunities are expected to be favorable; some employers report difficulty hiring sufficient numbers of radiologic technologists and technicians.

Nature of the Work

Radiologic technologists and technicians take X rays and administer nonradioactive materials into patients' bloodstreams for diagnostic purposes. Some specialize in diagnostic imaging technologies, such as computerized tomography (CT) and magnetic resonance imaging (MRI).

In addition to radiologic technologists and technicians, others who conduct diagnostic imaging procedures include cardiovascular technologists and technicians, diagnostic medical sonographers, and nuclear medicine technologists.

Radiologic technologists and technicians, also referred to as *radiographers*, produce X-ray films (radiographs) of parts of the human body for use in diagnosing medical problems. They prepare patients for radiologic examinations by explaining the procedure, removing articles such as jewelry, through which X rays cannot pass, and positioning patients so that the parts of the body can be appropriately radiographed. To prevent unnecessary radiation exposure, these workers surround the exposed area with radiation protection devices, such as lead shields, or limit the size of the X-ray beam. Radiographers position radiographic equipment at the correct angle and height over the appropriate area of a patient's body. Using instruments similar to a measuring tape, they may measure the thickness of the section to be radiographed and set controls on the X-ray machine to produce radiographs of the appropriate density, detail, and contrast. They place the X-ray film under the part of the patient's body to be examined and make the exposure. They then remove the film and develop it.

Experienced radiographers may perform more complex imaging procedures. For fluoroscopies, radiographers prepare a solution of contrast medium for the patient to drink, allowing the radiologist (a physician who interprets radiographs) to see soft tissues in the body. Some radiographers, called *CT technologists,* operate CT scanners to produce cross-sectional images of patients. Radiographers who operate machines that use strong magnets and radio waves, rather than radiation, to create an image are called *MRI technologists.*

Radiologic technologists and technicians must follow physicians' orders precisely and conform to regulations concerning the use of radiation to protect themselves, their patients, and their coworkers from unnecessary exposure.

In addition to preparing patients and operating equipment, radiologic technologists and technicians keep patient records and adjust and maintain equipment. They also may prepare work schedules, evaluate equipment purchases, or manage a radiology department.

Working Conditions

Most full-time radiologic technologists and technicians work about 40 hours a week; they may have evening, weekend, or on-call hours. Opportunities for part-time and shift work also are available.

Because technologists and technicians are on their feet for long periods and may lift or turn disabled patients, physical stamina is important. Technologists and technicians work at diagnostic machines, but may also perform some procedures at patients' bedsides. Some travel to patients in large vans equipped with sophisticated diagnostic equipment.

Although radiation hazards exist in this occupation, they are minimized by the use of lead aprons, gloves, and other shielding devices, as well as by instruments monitoring radiation exposure. Technologists and technicians wear badges measuring radiation levels in the radiation area, and detailed records are kept on their cumulative lifetime dose.

Employment

Radiologic technologists and technicians held about 174,100 jobs in 2002. Almost 1 in 5 worked part time. About half of all jobs were in hospitals. Most of the rest were in offices of physicians; medical and diagnostic laboratories, including diagnostic imaging centers; and outpatient care centers.

Training, Other Qualifications, and Advancement

Preparation for this profession is offered in hospitals, colleges and universities, vocational-technical institutes, and the U.S. Armed Forces. Hospitals, which employ most radiologic technologists and technicians, prefer to hire those with formal training.

Formal training programs in radiography range in length from 1 to 4 years and lead to a certificate, associate degree, or bachelor's degree. Two-year associate degree programs are most prevalent.

Some 1-year certificate programs are available for experienced radiographers or individuals from other health occupations, such as medical technologists and registered nurses, who want to change fields or specialize in CT or MRI. A bachelor's or master's degree in one of the radiologic technologies is desirable for supervisory, administrative, or teaching positions.

The Joint Review Committee on Education in Radiologic Technology accredits most formal training programs for the field. The committee accredited 587 radiography programs in 2003. Radiography programs require, at a minimum, a high school diploma or the equivalent. High school courses in mathematics, physics, chemistry, and biology are helpful. The programs provide both classroom and clinical instruction in anatomy and physiology, patient care procedures, radiation physics, radiation protection, principles of imaging, medical terminology, positioning of patients, medical ethics, radiobiology, and pathology.

federal legislation protects the public from the hazards of unnecessary exposure to medical and dental radiation by ensuring operators of radiologic equipment are properly trained. Under this legislation, the federal government sets voluntary standards that the states, in turn, may use for accrediting training programs and certifying individuals who engage in medical or dental radiography.

In 2003, about 38 states licensed radiologic technologists and technicians. Voluntary registration is offered by the American Registry of Radiologic Technologists. To be eligible for registration, technologists generally must have graduated from an accredited program and pass an examination. Many employers prefer to hire registered radiographers. To be recertified, radiographers must complete 24 hours of continuing education every other year.

Radiologic technologists and technicians should be sensitive to patients' physical and psychological needs. They must pay attention to detail, follow instructions, and work as part of a team. In addition, operating complicated equipment requires mechanical ability and manual dexterity.

With experience and additional training, staff technologists may become specialists, performing CT scanning, angiography, and magnetic resonance imaging. Experienced technologists also may be promoted to supervisor, chief radiologic technologist, and, ultimately, department administrator or director. Depending on the institution, courses or a master's degree in business or health administration may be necessary for the director's position. Some technologists progress by leaving the occupation to become instructors or directors in radiologic technology programs; others take jobs as sales representatives or instructors with equipment manufacturers.

Job Outlook

Job opportunities are expected to be favorable. Some employers report difficulty hiring sufficient numbers of radiologic technologists and technicians. Imbalances between the demand for, and supply of, qualified workers should spur efforts to attract and retain qualified radiologic technologists and technicians. As an example of such efforts, employers may provide more flexible training programs or improve compensation and working conditions.

Radiologic technologists who also are experienced in more complex diagnostic imaging procedures, such as CT or MRI, will have better employment opportunities, as employers seek to control costs by using multiskilled employees.

Employment of radiologic technologists and technicians is expected to grow faster than the average for all occupations through 2012, as the population grows and ages, increasing the demand for diagnostic imaging. Although healthcare providers are enthusiastic about the clinical benefits of new technologies, the extent to which they are adopted depends largely on cost and reimbursement considerations. For example, digital imaging technology can improve quality and efficiency, but remains expensive. Some promising new technologies may not come into widespread use because they are too expensive and third-party payers may not be willing to pay for their use.

Hospitals will remain the principal employer of radiologic technologists and technicians. However, a greater number of new jobs will be found in offices of physicians and diagnostic imaging centers. Health facilities such as these are expected to grow rapidly through 2012, due to the strong shift toward outpatient care, encouraged by third-party payers and made possible by technological advances that permit more procedures to be performed outside the hospital. Some job openings also will arise from the need to replace technologists and technicians who leave the occupation.

Earnings

Median annual earnings of radiologic technologists and technicians were $38,970 in 2002. The middle 50 percent earned between $32,370 and $46,510. The lowest 10 percent earned less than $27,190, and the highest 10 percent earned more than $55,430. Median annual earnings in the industries employing the largest numbers of radiologic technologists and technicians in 2002 were as follows:

Medical and diagnostic laboratories $42,470

General medical and surgical hospitals..................39,580

Offices of physicians 36,490

Related Occupations

Radiologic technologists and technicians operate sophisticated equipment to help physicians, dentists, and other health practitioners diagnose and treat patients. Workers in related occupations include cardiovascular technologists and technicians, clinical laboratory technologists and technicians, diagnostic medical sonographers, nuclear medicine technologists, radiation therapists, and respiratory therapists.

Sources of Additional Information

For career information, send a stamped, self-addressed business-size envelope with your request to:

- American Society of Radiologic Technologists, 15000 Central Ave. SE., Albuquerque, NM 87123-3917. Telephone (toll-free): 800-444-2778. Internet: http://www.asrt.org

For the current list of accredited education programs in radiography, write to:

- Joint Review Committee on Education in Radiologic Technology, 20 N. Wacker Dr., Suite 900, Chicago, IL 60606-2901. Internet: http://www.jrcert.org

For information on certification, contact:

- American Registry of Radiologic Technologists, 1255 Northland Dr., St. Paul, MN 55120-1155. Internet: http://www.arrt.org

Registered Nurses

(O*NET 29-1111.00)

Significant Points

- Registered nurses constitute the largest healthcare occupation, with 2.3 million jobs.

- More new jobs are expected to be created for registered nurses than for any other occupation.

- Job opportunities are expected to be very good.

- The three major educational paths to registered nursing are a bachelor's degree, an associate degree, and a diploma.

Nature of the Work

Registered nurses (RNs) work to promote health, prevent disease, and help patients cope with illness. They are advocates and health educators for patients, families, and communities. When providing direct patient care, they observe, assess, and record symptoms, reactions, and progress in patients; assist physicians during surgeries, treatments, and examinations; administer medications; and assist in convalescence and rehabilitation. RNs also develop and manage nursing care plans, instruct patients and their families in proper care, and help individuals and groups take steps to improve or maintain their health. While state laws govern the tasks that RNs may perform, it is usually the work setting that determines their daily job duties.

Hospital nurses form the largest group of nurses. Most are staff nurses, who provide bedside nursing care and carry out medical regimens. They also may supervise licensed practical nurses and nursing aides. Hospital nurses usually are assigned to one department, such as surgery, maternity, pediatrics, the emergency room, intensive care, or the treatment of cancer patients. Some may rotate among departments.

Office nurses care for outpatients in physicians' offices, clinics, ambulatory surgical centers, and emergency medical centers. They prepare patients for, and assist with, examinations; administer injections and medications; dress wounds and incisions; assist with minor surgery; and maintain records. Some also perform routine laboratory and office work.

Nursing care facility nurses manage care for residents with conditions ranging from a fracture to Alzheimer's disease. Although they often spend much of their time on administrative and supervisory tasks, RNs also assess residents' health, develop treatment plans, supervise licensed practical nurses and nursing aides, and perform invasive procedures, such as starting intravenous fluids. They also work in specialty-care departments, such as long-term rehabilitation units for patients with strokes and head injuries.

Home health nurses provide nursing services to patients at home. RNs assess patients' home environments and instruct patients and their families. Home health nurses care for a broad range of patients, such as those recovering from illnesses and accidents, cancer, and childbirth. They must be able to work independently and may supervise home health aides.

Public health nurses work in government and private agencies, including clinics, schools, retirement communities, and other community settings. They focus on populations, working with individuals, groups, and families to improve the overall health of communities. They also work with communities to help plan and implement programs. Public health nurses instruct individuals, families, and other groups regarding health issues such as preventive care, nutrition, and childcare. They arrange for immunizations, blood pressure testing, and other health screening. These nurses also work with community leaders, teachers, parents, and physicians in community health education.

Occupational health nurses, also called *industrial nurses*, provide nursing care at worksites to employees, customers, and others with injuries and illnesses. They give emergency care, prepare accident reports, and arrange for further care if necessary. They also offer health counseling, conduct health examinations and inoculations, and assess work environments to identify potential or actual health problems.

Head nurses or *nurse supervisors* direct nursing activities, primarily in hospitals. They plan work schedules and assign duties to nurses and aides, provide or arrange for training, and visit patients to observe nurses and to ensure that the patients receive proper care. They also may ensure that records are maintained and equipment and supplies are ordered.

At the advanced level, *nurse practitioners* provide basic, primary healthcare. They diagnose and treat common acute illnesses and injuries. Nurse practitioners also can prescribe medications—but certification and licensing requirements vary by state. Other advanced practice nurses include *clinical nurse specialists, certified registered nurse anesthetists,* and *certified nurse midwives.* Advanced practice nurses must meet educational and clinical practice requirements beyond the basic nursing education and licensing required of all RNs.

Working Conditions

Most nurses work in well-lighted, comfortable healthcare facilities. Home health and public health nurses travel to patients' homes, schools, community centers, and other sites. Nurses may spend considerable time walking and standing. Patients in hospitals and nursing care facilities require 24-hour care; consequently, nurses in these institutions may work nights, weekends, and holidays. RNs also may be on call—available to work on short notice. Office, occupational health, and public health nurses are more likely to work regular business hours. More than 1 in 5 RNs worked part time in 2002 and nearly 1 in 10 held more than one job.

Nursing has its hazards, especially in hospitals, nursing care facilities, and clinics, in all three of which nurses may care for individuals with infectious diseases. Nurses must observe rigid standardized guidelines to guard against disease and other dangers, such as those posed by radiation, accidental needle sticks, chemicals used to sterilize instruments, and anesthetics. In addition, they are vulnerable to back injury when moving patients, shocks from electrical equipment, and hazards posed by compressed gases.

Employment

As the largest healthcare occupation, registered nurses held about 2.3 million jobs in 2002. Almost 3 out of 5 jobs were in hospitals, in inpatient and outpatient departments. Others worked in offices of physicians, nursing care facilities, home healthcare services, employment services, government agencies, and outpatient care centers. The remainder worked mostly in social assistance agencies and educational services, public and private. About 1 in 5 RNs worked part time.

Training, Other Qualifications, and Advancement

In all states and the District of Columbia, students must graduate from an approved nursing program and pass a national licensing examination in order to obtain a nursing license. Nurses may be licensed in more than one state, either by examination, by the endorsement of a license issued by another state, or through a multi-state licensing agreement. All states require periodic renewal of licenses, which may involve continuing education.

There are three major educational paths to registered nursing: a bachelor's of science degree in nursing (BSN), an associate degree in Nursing (ADN), and a diploma. BSN programs, offered by colleges and universities, take about 4 years to complete. In 2002, 678 nursing programs offered degrees at the bachelor's level. ADN programs, offered by community and junior colleges, take about 2 to 3 years to complete. About 700 RN programs in 2002 were at the ADN level. Diploma programs, administered in hospitals, last about 3 years. Only a small and declining number of programs offer diplomas. Generally, licensed graduates of any of the three types of educational programs qualify for entry-level positions as staff nurses.

Many ADN- and diploma-educated nurses later enter bachelor's programs to prepare for a broader scope of nursing practice. Often, they can find a staff nurse position and then take advantage of tuition reimbursement benefits to work toward a BSN by completing one of many RN-to-BSN programs.

Accelerated BSN programs also are available for individuals who have a bachelor's or higher degree in another field and who are interested in moving into nursing. In 2002, more than 110 of these programs were available. Accelerated BSN programs last 12 to 18 months and provide the fastest route to a BSN for individuals who already hold a degree. Accelerated master's degree programs in nursing also are available and take about 3 years to complete.

Individuals considering nursing should carefully weigh the advantages and disadvantages of enrolling in a BSN program, because, if they do, their advancement opportunities usually are broader. In fact, some career paths are open only to nurses with bachelor's or advanced degrees. A bachelor's degree often is necessary for administrative positions and is a prerequisite for admission to graduate nursing programs in research, consulting, teaching, or a clinical specialization.

Nursing education includes classroom instruction and supervised clinical experience in hospitals and other healthcare facilities. Students take courses in anatomy, physiology, microbiology, chemistry, nutrition, psychology and other behavioral sciences, and nursing. Course work also includes the liberal arts.

Supervised clinical experience is provided in hospital departments such as pediatrics, psychiatry, maternity, and surgery. A growing number of programs include clinical experience in nursing care facilities, public health departments, home health agencies, and ambulatory clinics.

Nurses should be caring, sympathetic, responsible, and detail oriented. They must be able to direct or supervise others, correctly assess patients' conditions, and determine when consultation is required. They need emotional stability to cope with human suffering, emergencies, and other stresses.

Experience and good performance can lead to promotion to more responsible positions. In management, nurses can advance to assistant head nurse or head nurse and, from there, to assistant director, director, and vice president.

Increasingly, management-level nursing positions require a graduate or an advanced degree in nursing or health services administration. They also require leadership, negotiation skills, and good judgment. Graduate programs preparing executive-level nurses usually last about 2 years.

Within patient care, nurses can move into a nursing specialty such as clinical nurse specialist, nurse practitioner, certified nurse midwife, or certified registered nurse anesthetist. These positions require about 2 years of graduate education leading to a master's degree.

Some nurses move into the business side of health care. Their nursing expertise and experience on a healthcare team equip them with the ability to manage ambulatory, acute, home health, and chronic care services. Employers—including hospitals, insurance companies, pharmaceutical manufacturers, and managed care organizations, among others—need RNs for health planning and development, marketing, consulting, policy development, and quality assurance. Other nurses work as college and university faculty or conduct research.

Job Outlook

Job opportunities for RNs are expected to be very good. Employment of registered nurses is expected to grow faster than the average for all occupations through 2012, and because the occupation is very large, many new jobs will result. In fact, more new jobs are expected be created for RNs than for any other occupation. Thousands of job openings also will result from the need to replace experienced nurses who leave the occupation, especially as the median age of the registered nurse population continues to rise.

Faster-than-average growth will be driven by technological advances in patient care, which permit a greater number of medical problems to be treated, and an increasing emphasis on preventive care. In addition, the number of older people, who are much more likely than younger people to need nursing care, is projected to grow rapidly.

Employers in some parts of the country are reporting difficulty in attracting and retaining an adequate number of RNs, due primarily to an aging RN workforce and insufficient nursing school enrollments. Imbalances between the supply of, and demand for, qualified workers should spur efforts to attract and retain qualified RNs. For example, employers may restructure workloads, improve compensation and working conditions, and subsidize training or continuing education.

Employment in hospitals, the largest sector, is expected to grow more slowly than in most other healthcare sectors. While the intensity of nursing care is likely to increase, requiring more nurses per patient, the number of inpatients (those who remain in the hospital for more than 24 hours) is not likely to increase much. Patients are being discharged earlier and more procedures are being done on an outpatient basis, both inside and outside hospitals. Rapid growth is expected in hospital outpatient facilities, such as those providing same-day surgery, rehabilitation, and chemotherapy.

An increasing proportion of sophisticated procedures, which once were performed only in hospitals, are being performed in physicians' offices and in outpatient care centers, such as freestanding ambulatory surgical and emergency centers. Accordingly, employment is expected to grow faster than average in these places as healthcare in general expands.

Employment in nursing care facilities is expected to grow faster than average due to increases in the number of elderly, many of whom require long-term care. In addition, the financial pressure on hospitals to discharge patients as soon as possible should produce more admissions to nursing care facilities. Job growth also is expected in units that provide specialized long-term rehabilitation for stroke and head injury patients, as well as units that treat Alzheimer's victims.

Employment in home healthcare is expected to increase rapidly in response to the growing number of older persons with functional disabilities, consumer preference for care in the home, and technological advances that make it possible to bring increasingly complex treatments into the home. The type of care demanded will require nurses who are able to perform complex procedures.

In evolving integrated healthcare networks, nurses may rotate among various employment settings. Because jobs in traditional hospital nursing positions are no longer the only option, RNs will need to be flexible. Opportunities should be excellent, particularly for nurses with advanced education and training.

Earnings

Median annual earnings of registered nurses were $48,090 in 2002. The middle 50 percent earned between $40,140 and $57,490. The lowest 10 percent earned less than $33,970, and the highest 10 percent earned more than $69,670. Median annual earnings in the industries employing the largest numbers of registered nurses in 2002 were as follows:

Employment services	$55,980
General medical and surgical hospitals	49,190
Home health care services	45,890
Offices of physicians	44,870
Nursing care facilities	43,850

Many employers offer flexible work schedules, childcare, educational benefits, and bonuses.

Related Occupations

Workers in other healthcare occupations with responsibilities and duties related to those of registered nurses are emergency medical technicians and paramedics, occupational therapists, physical therapists, physician assistants, respiratory therapists, and social workers.

Sources of Additional Information

For information on a career as a registered nurse and nursing education, contact:

- National League for Nursing, 61 Broadway, New York, NY 10006. Internet: http://www.nln.org

For a list of BSN, graduate, and accelerated nursing programs, contact:

- American Association of Colleges of Nursing, 1 Dupont Circle NW., Suite 530, Washington, DC 20036. Internet: http://www.aacn.nche.edu

Information on registered nurses also is available from:

- American Nurses Association, 600 Maryland Ave. SW, Washington, DC 20024-2571. Internet: http://www.nursingworld.org

Respiratory Therapists

(O*NET 29-1126.00 and 29-2054.00)

Significant Points

- An associate degree has become the general requirement for entry into this field.

- Hospitals will continue to employ the vast majority of respiratory therapists, but a growing number of therapists will work in other settings.

- Job opportunities will be very good, especially for therapists with cardiopulmonary care skills or experience working with newborns and infants.

Nature of the Work

Respiratory therapists and *respiratory therapy technicians*—also known as respiratory care practitioners—evaluate, treat, and care for patients with breathing or other cardiopulmonary disorders. Respiratory therapists, practicing under physician direction, assume primary responsibility for all respiratory care therapeutic treatments and diagnostic procedures, including the supervision of respiratory therapy technicians. Respiratory therapy technicians follow specific, well-defined respiratory care procedures, under the direction of respiratory therapists and physicians. In clinical practice, many of the daily duties of therapists and technicians overlap, although therapists generally have greater responsibility than technicians. For example, respiratory therapists will primarily consult with physicians and other healthcare staff to help develop and modify individual patient care plans. Respiratory therapists are also more likely to provide complex therapy requiring considerable independent judgment, such as caring for patients on life support in hospital inten-

sive care units. In this statement, the term *respiratory therapists* includes both respiratory therapists and respiratory therapy technicians.

To evaluate patients, respiratory therapists interview them, perform limited physical examinations, and conduct diagnostic tests. For example, respiratory therapists test patients' breathing capacity and determine the concentration of oxygen and other gases in patients' blood. They also measure patients' pH, which indicates the acidity or alkalinity level of the blood. To evaluate a patient's lung capacity, respiratory therapists have the patient breathe into an instrument that measures the volume and flow of oxygen during inhalation and exhalation. By comparing the reading with the norm for the patient's age, height, weight, and sex, respiratory therapists can provide information that helps determine whether the patient has any lung deficiencies. To analyze oxygen, carbon dioxide, and pH levels, therapists draw an arterial blood sample, place it in a blood gas analyzer, and relay the results to a physician. Physicians rely on data provided by respiratory therapists to make treatment decisions.

Respiratory therapists treat all types of patients, ranging from premature infants whose lungs are not fully developed to elderly people whose lungs are diseased. Respiratory therapists provide temporary relief to patients with chronic asthma or emphysema, as well as emergency care to patients who are victims of a heart attack, stroke, drowning, or shock.

To treat patients, respiratory therapists use oxygen or oxygen mixtures, chest physiotherapy, and aerosol medications. When a patient has difficulty getting enough oxygen into their blood, therapists increase the patient's concentration of oxygen by placing an oxygen mask or nasal cannula on a patient and set the oxygen flow at the level prescribed by a physician. Therapists also connect patients who cannot breathe on their own to ventilators that deliver pressurized oxygen into the lungs. The therapists insert a tube into the patient's trachea, or windpipe; connect the tube to the ventilator; and set the rate, volume, and oxygen concentration of the oxygen mixture entering the patient's lungs.

Therapists perform regular checks on patients and equipment. If the patient appears to be having difficulty, or if the oxygen, carbon dioxide, or pH level of the blood is abnormal, therapists change the ventilator setting according to the doctor's orders or check the equipment for mechanical problems. In home care, therapists teach patients and their families to use ventilators and other life-support systems. In addition, therapists visit patients several times a month to inspect and clean equipment and to ensure its proper use. Therapists also make emergency visits if equipment problems arise.

Respiratory therapists perform chest physiotherapy on patients to remove mucus from their lungs and make it easier for them to breathe. For example, during surgery, anesthesia depresses respiration, so chest physiotherapy may be prescribed to help get the patient's lungs back to normal and to prevent congestion. Chest physiotherapy also helps patients suffering from lung diseases, such as cystic fibrosis, that cause mucus to collect in the lungs. Therapists place patients in positions that help drain mucus, and then they thump and vibrate the patients' rib cages and instruct the patients to cough.

Respiratory therapists also administer aerosols—liquid medications suspended in a gas that forms a mist which is inhaled—and teach patients how to inhale the aerosol properly to ensure its effectiveness.

In some hospitals, therapists perform tasks that fall outside their traditional role. Therapists' tasks are expanding into cardiopulmonary procedures such as taking electrocardiograms and administering stress tests, as well as other areas—for example, drawing blood samples from patients. Therapists also keep records of materials used and charges to patients.

Working Conditions

Respiratory therapists generally work between 35 and 40 hours a week. Because hospitals operate around the clock, therapists may work evenings, nights, or weekends. They spend long periods standing and walking between patients' rooms. In an emergency, therapists work under a great deal of stress. Respiratory therapists employed in home healthcare must travel frequently to the homes of patients.

Respiratory therapists are trained to work with gases stored under pressure that can be hazardous. Adherence to safety precautions and regular maintenance and testing of equipment minimize the risk of injury. As in many other health occupations, respiratory therapists run a risk of catching an infectious disease, but carefully following proper procedures minimizes this risk.

Employment

Respiratory therapists held about 112,000 jobs in 2002. More than 4 out of 5 jobs were in hospital departments of respiratory care, anesthesiology, or pulmonary medicine. Most of the remaining jobs were found in offices of physicians or other health practitioners, consumer goods rental firms that supply respiratory equipment for home use, nursing care facilities, and home healthcare services. Holding a second job is relatively common for respiratory therapists. About 17 percent held another job, compared with 5 percent of workers in all occupations.

Training, Other Qualifications, and Advancement

Formal training is necessary for entry into this field. Training is offered at the postsecondary level by colleges and universities, medical schools, vocational-technical institutes, and the Armed Forces. An associate degree has become the general requirement for entry into this field. Most programs award associate or bachelor's degrees and prepare graduates for jobs as advanced respiratory therapists. Other programs award associate degrees or certificates and lead to jobs as entry-level respiratory therapists. According to the Commission on Accreditation of Allied Health Education Programs (CAAHEP), 59 entry-level and 319 advanced respiratory therapy programs are presently accredited in the United States, including Puerto Rico.

Areas of study in respiratory therapy programs include human anatomy and physiology, pathophysiology, chemistry, physics, microbiology, pharmacology, and mathematics. Other courses deal with therapeutic and diagnostic procedures and tests, equipment, patient assessment, cardiopulmonary resuscitation, application of clinical practice guidelines, patient care outside of hospitals, cardiac and pulmonary rehabilitation, respiratory health promotion and disease prevention, and medical recordkeeping and reimbursement.

More than 40 states license respiratory care personnel. Aspiring respiratory care practitioners should check on licensure requirements with the board of respiratory care examiners for the state in which they plan to work. Also, most employers require respiratory therapists to maintain a cardiopulmonary resuscitation (CPR) certification.

The National Board for Respiratory Care (NBRC) offers voluntary certification and registration to graduates of programs accredited by CAAHEP or the Committee on Accreditation for Respiratory Care (CoARC). Two credentials are awarded to respiratory therapists who satisfy the requirements: Registered Respiratory Therapist (RRT) and Certified Respiratory Therapist (CRT). Graduates from accredited programs in respiratory therapy may take the CRT examination. CRTs who meet education and experience requirements can take two separate examinations leading to the award of the RRT credential. The CRT examination is the standard in the states requiring licensure.

Most employers require applicants for entry-level or generalist positions to hold the CRT or at least be eligible to take the certification examination. Supervisory positions and intensive-care specialties usually require the RRT or RRT eligibility.

Therapists should be sensitive to patients' physical and psychological needs. Respiratory care practitioners must pay attention to detail, follow instructions, and work as part of a team. In addition, operating advanced equipment requires proficiency with computers.

High school students interested in a career in respiratory care should take courses in health, biology, mathematics, chemistry, and physics. Respiratory care involves basic mathematical problem solving and an understanding of chemical and physical principles. For example, respiratory care workers must be able to compute dosages of medication and calculate gas concentrations.

Respiratory therapists advance in clinical practice by moving from general care to care of critical patients who have significant problems in other organ systems, such as the heart or kidneys. Respiratory therapists, especially those with 4-year degrees, may also advance to supervisory or managerial positions in a respiratory therapy department. Respiratory therapists in home healthcare and equipment rental firms may become branch managers. Some respiratory therapists advance by moving into teaching positions.

Job Outlook

Job opportunities are expected to be very good, especially for respiratory therapists with cardiopulmonary care skills or experience working with infants. Employment of respiratory therapists is expected to increase faster than the average for all occupations through the year 2012, because of substantial growth in numbers of the middle-aged and elderly population—a development that will heighten the incidence of cardiopulmonary disease.

Older Americans suffer most from respiratory ailments and cardiopulmonary diseases such as pneumonia, chronic bronchitis, emphysema, and heart disease. As their numbers increase, the need for respiratory therapists will increase as well. In addition, advances in treating victims of heart attacks, accident victims, and premature infants (many of whom are dependent on a ventilator during part of their treatment) will increase the demand for the services of respiratory care practitioners.

Although hospitals will continue to employ the vast majority of therapists, a growing number can expect to work outside of hospitals in home healthcare services, offices of physicians or other health practitioners, or consumer goods rental firms.

Earnings

Median annual earnings of respiratory therapists were $40,220 in 2002. The middle 50 percent earned between $34,430 and $46,130. The lowest 10 percent earned less than $30,270, and the highest 10 percent earned more than $54,030. In general medical and surgical hospitals, median annual earnings of respiratory therapists were $40,390 in 2002.

Median annual earnings of respiratory therapy technicians were $34,130 in 2002. The middle 50 percent earned between $28,460 and $41,140. The lowest 10 percent earned less than $23,230, and the highest 10 percent earned more than $47,800. Median annual earnings of respiratory therapy technicians employed in general medical and surgical hospitals were $34,210 in 2002.

Related Occupations

Under the supervision of a physician, respiratory therapists administer respiratory care and life support to patients with heart and lung difficulties. Other workers who care for, treat, or train people to improve their physical condition include registered nurses, occupational therapists, physical therapists, and radiation therapists.

Sources of Additional Information

Information concerning a career in respiratory care is available from:

● American Association for Respiratory Care, 11030 Ables Ln., Dallas, TX 75229-4593. Internet: http://www.aarc.org

For a list of accredited educational programs for respiratory care practitioners, contact:

● Commission on Accreditation for Allied Health Education Programs, 39 East Wacker Dr., Chicago, IL 60601. Internet: http://www.caahep.org

● Committee on Accreditation for Respiratory Care, 1248 Harwood Rd., Bedford, TX 76021-4244.

Information on gaining credentials in respiratory care and a list of state licensing agencies can be obtained from:

● National Board for Respiratory Care, Inc., 8310 Nieman Rd., Lenexa, KS 66214-1579. Internet: http://www.nbrc.org

Sales Engineers

(O*NET 41-9031.00)

Significant Points

● A bachelor's degree in engineering is required; many sales engineers have previous work experience in an engineering specialty.

● Projected employment growth stems from the increasing number and technical nature of products to be sold.

● More job opportunities are expected in independent agencies.

● Earnings are based on a combination of salary and commission.

Nature of the Work

Many products and services, especially those purchased by large companies and institutions, are highly complex. Sales engineers, using their engineering skills, help customers determine which products or services provided by the sales engineer's employer best suit their needs. Sales engineers—who also may be called manufacturers' agents, sales representatives, or technical sales support workers—often work with both the customer and the production, engineering, or research and development departments of their company, or of independent firms, to determine how products and services could be designed or modified to best suit the customer's needs. They also may advise the customer on how to best utilize the products or services being provided.

Selling, of course, is an important part of the job. Sales engineers use their technical skills to demonstrate to potential customers how and why the products or services they are selling would suit the customer better than competitors' products. Often, there may not be a directly competitive product. In these cases, the job of the sales engineer is to demonstrate to the customer the usefulness of the product or service—for example, how much money new production machinery would save.

Most sales engineers have a bachelor's degree in engineering and some have previous work experience in an engineering specialty. Engineers apply the theories and principles of science and mathematics to technical problems. Their work is the link between scientific discoveries and commercial applications. Many sales engineers specialize in an area related to an engineering specialty. For example, sales engineers selling chemical products may have chemical engineering backgrounds, while those selling electrical products may have degrees in electrical engineering.

Many of the job duties of sales engineers are similar to those of other salespersons. They must interest the client in purchasing their products, many of which are durable manufactured products such as turbines. Sales engineers are often teamed with other salespersons who concentrate on the marketing and sales, enabling the sales engineer to concentrate on the technical aspects of the job. By working as a sales team, each member is able to utilize his or her strengths and knowledge.

Sales engineers tend to employ selling techniques that are different from those used by most other sales workers. They may use a "consultative" style; that is, they focus on the client's problem and show how it could be solved or mitigated with their product or service. This selling style differs from the "benefits and features" method, whereby the product is described and the customer is left to decide how the product would be useful.

In addition to maintaining current clients and attracting new ones, sales engineers help clients solve any problems that arise when the product is installed, and may continue to serve as a liaison between the client and their company. In addition, using their familiarity with client needs, sales engineers may help identify and develop new products.

Sales engineers may work directly for manufacturers or service providers, or in small independent firms. In an independent firm, they may sell complimentary products from several different suppliers and be paid on a commission basis.

Working Conditions

Many sales engineers work more than 40 hours per week to meet sales goals and their clients' needs. Selling can be stressful because sales engineers' income and job security often directly depend on their success in sales and customer service.

Some sales engineers have large territories and travel extensively. Because sales regions may cover several states, sales engineers may be away from home for several days or even weeks at a time. Others work near their "home base" and travel mostly by automobile. International travel, to secure contracts with foreign customers, is becoming more important.

Although the hours may be long and are often irregular, many sales engineers have the freedom to determine their own schedule. Consequently, they often can arrange their appointments so that they can have time off when they want it. However, most independent sales workers do not earn any income while on vacation.

Employment

Sales engineers held about 82,000 jobs in 2002. About 32 percent were employed in the manufacturing industries and another 28 percent were employed in wholesale trade. Unlike workers in many other sales occupations, very few sales engineers are self-employed.

Training, Other Qualifications, and Advancement

A bachelor's degree in engineering is usually required to become a sales engineer. However, some workers with previous experience in sales combined with technical experience or training sometimes hold the title of sales engineer. Also, workers who have a degree in a science, such as chemistry, or even a degree in business with little or no previous sales experience, may be termed sales engineers.

Admissions requirements for undergraduate engineering schools include a solid background in mathematics (algebra, geometry, trigonometry, and calculus), physical sciences (biology, chemistry, and physics), and courses in English, social studies, humanities, and computer science. University programs vary in content. For example, some programs emphasize industrial practices, preparing students for a job in industry, whereas others are more theoretical and prepare students for graduate school. Therefore, students should investigate curriculums and check accreditations carefully before making a selection. Once a university has been selected, a student must choose an area of engineering in which to specialize. Some programs offer a general engineering curriculum; students then specialize in graduate school or on the job. Most engineering degrees are granted in electrical, mechanical, or civil engineering. However, engineers trained in one branch may work in related branches.

Many sales engineers first worked as engineers. For some, the engineering experience was necessary to obtain the technical background needed to effectively sell their employers' products or services. Others moved into the occupation because it offered better earnings and advancement potential or because they were looking for a new challenge.

New graduates with engineering degrees may need sales experience and training to obtain employment directly as a sales engineer. This may involve teaming with a sales mentor who is familiar with the business practices, customers, and company procedures and culture. After the training period has been completed, the sales engineer may continue to partner with someone who lacks technical skills, yet excels in the art of sales.

Promotion may include a higher commission rate, larger sales territory, or elevation to the position of supervisor or marketing manager. In other cases, sales engineers may leave their companies and form an independent firm that may offer higher commissions and more freedom. Independent firms tend to be small, although relatively few sales engineers are self-employed.

It is important for sales engineers to continue their education throughout their careers because much of their value to their employers depends on their knowledge of the latest technology. Sales engineers in high-technology areas, such as information technology or advanced electronics, may find that technical knowledge can become obsolete rapidly.

Job Outlook

Employment of sales engineers is expected to grow about as fast as the average for all occupations through the year 2012. Projected employment growth stems from the increasing variety and number of goods to be sold. Competitive pressures and advancing technology will force companies to improve and update product designs more frequently and to optimize their manufacturing and sales processes. In addition to new positions created as companies expand their sales force, some openings will arise each year from the need to replace sales workers who transfer to other occupations or leave the labor force.

Manufacturers are expected to continue contracting out more of their sales functions to independent sales agencies in an attempt to control their costs. This should mean more job opportunities for sales engineers in independent agencies and for self-employed independent sales engineers.

Employment opportunities and earnings may fluctuate from year to year because sales are affected by changing economic conditions, legislative issues, and consumer preferences. Prospects will be best for those with the appropriate knowledge or technical expertise, as well as the personal traits necessary for successful sales work.

Earnings

Compensation varies significantly by the type of firm and product sold. Most employers use a combination of salary and commission or salary plus bonus. Commissions usually are based on the amount of sales, whereas bonuses may depend on individual performance, on the performance of all sales workers in the group or district, or on the company's performance. Earnings from commissions and bonuses may vary greatly from year to year, depending on sales ability, the demand for the company's products or services, and the overall economy.

Median annual earnings of sales engineers, including commissions, were $63,660 in 2002. The middle 50 percent earned between $48,650 and $84,880 a year. The lowest 10 percent earned less than $37,430, and the highest 10 percent earned more than $108,080 a year. Median annual earnings employed by firms in the computer systems design and related services industry in 2002 were $77,100; earnings for sales engineers in the professional and commercial equipment and supplies merchant wholesalers industry were $53,170.

In addition to their earnings, sales engineers who work for manufacturers are usually reimbursed for expenses such as transportation, meals, hotels, and customer entertainment. In addition to typical benefits, sales engineers often get personal use of a company car and frequent-flyer mileage. Some companies offer incentives such as free vacation trips or gifts for outstanding performance. Sales engineers who work in independent firms may have higher but less stable earnings and, often, relatively few benefits.

Related Occupations

Sales engineers must have sales ability and knowledge of the products they sell, as well as technical and analytical skills. Other occupations that require similar skills include advertising, marketing, promotions, public relations, and sales managers; engineers; insurance sales agents; purchasing managers, buyers, and purchasing agents; real estate brokers and sales agents; sales representatives, wholesale and manufacturing; and securities, commodities, and financial services sales agents.

Sources of Additional Information

Information on careers for manufacturers' representatives and agents is available from:

- Manufacturers' Agents National Association, P.O. Box 3467, Laguna Hills, CA 92654-3467. Internet: http://www.manaonline.org

- Manufacturers' Representatives Educational Research Foundation, P.O. Box 247, Geneva, IL 60134. Internet: http://www.mrerf.org

Science Technicians

(O*NET 19-4011.01, 19-4011.02, 19-4021.00, 19-4031.00, 19-4041.01, 19-4041.02, 19-4051.01, 19-4051.02, and 19-4091.00)

Significant Points

- Science technicians in production jobs can be employed on day, evening, or night shifts.

- Many employers prefer applicants who have at least 2 years of specialized training or an associate degree.

- Job opportunities are expected to be best for graduates of applied science technology programs.

- Job growth will be concentrated in pharmaceutical manufacturing, chemical manufacturing, and biotechnological research and development firms.

Nature of the Work

Science technicians use the principles and theories of science and mathematics to solve problems in research and development and to help invent and improve products and processes. However, their jobs are more practically oriented than those of scientists. Technicians set up, operate, and maintain laboratory instruments, monitor experiments, make observations, calculate and record results, and often develop conclusions. They must keep detailed logs of all of their work-related activities. Those who work in production monitor manufacturing processes and may be involved in ensuring quality by testing products for proper proportions of ingredients, for purity, or for strength and durability.

As laboratory instrumentation and procedures have become more complex in recent years, the role of science technicians in research and development has expanded. In addition to performing routine tasks, many technicians also develop and adapt laboratory procedures to achieve the best results, interpret data, and devise solutions to problems, under the direction of scientists. Moreover, technicians must master the laboratory equipment so that they can adjust settings when necessary and recognize when equipment is malfunctioning.

The increasing use of robotics to perform many routine tasks has freed technicians to operate more sophisticated laboratory equipment. Science technicians make extensive use of computers, computer-interfaced equipment, robotics, and high-technology industrial applications, such as biological engineering.

Most science technicians specialize, learning skills and working in the same disciplines in which scientists work. Occupational titles, therefore, tend to follow the same structure as those for scientists. *Agricultural technicians* work with agricultural scientists in food, fiber, and animal research, production, and processing. Some conduct tests and experiments to improve the yield and quality of crops or to increase the resistance of plants and animals to disease, insects, or other hazards. Other agricultural technicians do animal breeding and nutrition work. *Food science technicians* assist food scientists and technologists in research and development, production technology, and quality control. For example, food science technicians may conduct tests on food additives and preservatives to ensure FDA compliance on factors such as color, texture, and nutrients. They analyze, record, and compile test results; order supplies to maintain laboratory inventory; and clean and sterilize laboratory equipment.

Biological technicians work with biologists studying living organisms. Many assist scientists who conduct medical research—helping to find a cure for cancer or AIDS, for example. Those who work in pharmaceutical companies help develop and manufacture medicinal and pharmaceutical preparations. Those working in the field of microbiology generally work as lab assistants, studying living organisms and infectious agents. Biological technicians also analyze organic substances, such as blood, food, and drugs, and some examine evidence in a forensic science laboratory. Biological technicians working in biotechnology labs use the knowledge and techniques gained from basic research by scientists, including gene splicing and recombinant DNA, and apply them in product development.

Chemical technicians work with chemists and chemical engineers, developing and using chemicals and related products and equipment. Generally, there are two types of chemical technicians—research and development technicians who work in experimental laboratories, and process control technicians who work in manufacturing or other industrial plants. Many research and development chemical technicians conduct a variety of laboratory procedures, from routine process control to complex research projects. For example, they may collect and analyze samples of air and water to monitor pollution levels or produce compounds through complex organic synthesis. Most process technicians work in manufacturing, where they test packaging for design, integrity of materials, and environmental acceptability. Often, process technicians who work in plants also focus on quality assurance: there, they monitor product quality or production processes and develop new production techniques. A few work in shipping to provide technical support and expertise for these functions.

Environmental science and protection technicians perform laboratory and field tests to monitor environmental resources and determine the contaminants and sources of pollution. They may collect samples for testing or be involved in abating, controlling, or remediating sources of environmental pollutants. Some are responsible for waste management operations, control and management of hazardous materials inventory, or general activities involving regulatory compliance.

Forensic science technicians investigate crimes by collecting and analyzing physical evidence. Often, they specialize in areas such as DNA analysis or firearm examination, performing tests on weapons or substances such as fiber, hair, tissue, or body fluids to determine significance to the investigation. They also prepare reports to document their findings and the laboratory techniques used, and may provide information and expert opinion to investigators. When criminal cases come to trial, forensic science technicians often provide testimony, as expert witnesses, on specific laboratory findings by identifying and classifying substances, materials, and other evidence collected at the crime scene.

Forest and conservation technicians compile data on the size, content, and condition of forest land tracts. These workers usually work in a forest under the supervision of a forester, conducting specific tasks such as measuring timber, supervising harvesting operations, assisting in roadbuilding operations, and locating property lines and features. They also may gather basic information, such as species and population of trees, disease and insect damage, tree seedling mortality, and conditions that may cause fire danger. Forest and conservation technicians also train and lead forest and conservation workers in seasonal activities, such as planting tree seedlings, putting out forest fires, and maintaining recreational facilities.

Geological and petroleum technicians measure and record physical and geologic conditions in oil or gas wells, using advanced instruments lowered into wells or by analysis of the mud from wells. In oil and gas exploration, these technicians collect and examine geological data or test geological samples to determine petroleum and mineral and element composition using scanning electron microscopes. Some petroleum technicians, called *scouts*, collect information about oil and gas well drilling operations, geological and geophysical prospecting, and land or lease contracts.

Nuclear technicians operate nuclear test and research equipment, monitor radiation, and assist nuclear engineers and physicists in research. Some also operate remote control equipment to manipulate radioactive materials or materials to be exposed to radioactivity.

Other science technicians collect weather information or assist oceanographers.

Working Conditions

Science technicians work under a wide variety of conditions. Most work indoors, usually in laboratories, and have regular hours. Some occasionally work irregular hours to monitor experiments that cannot be completed during regular working hours. Production technicians often work in 8-hour shifts around the clock. Others, such as agricultural, forest and conservation, geological and petroleum, and environmental science and protection technicians, perform much of their work outdoors, sometimes in remote locations.

Some science technicians may be exposed to hazards from equipment, chemicals, or toxic materials. Chemical technicians sometimes work with toxic chemicals or radioactive isotopes, nuclear technicians may be exposed to radiation, and biological technicians sometimes work with disease-causing organisms or radioactive agents. Forensic science technicians often are exposed to human body fluids and firearms. However, these working conditions pose little risk, if proper safety procedures are followed. For forensic science technicians, collecting evidence from crime scenes can be distressing and unpleasant.

Employment

Science technicians held about 208,000 jobs in 2002. As indicated by the following tabulation, chemical and biological technicians accounted for over half of all jobs:

Chemical technicians 69,000

Biological technicians 48,000

Environmental science and protection
   technicians, including health 28,000

Agricultural and food science technicians 20,000

Forest and conservation technicians.....................19,000

Geological and petroleum technicians 11,000

Forensic science technicians 8,400

Nuclear technicians 5,700

Chemical technicians held jobs in a wide range of manufacturing and service industries, but were concentrated in chemical manufacturing, where they held 26,000 jobs. About 17,000 worked in professional, scientific, or technical services firms; about 17,000 biological technicians also worked in professional, scientific, or technical services firms. Most other biological technicians worked in pharmaceutical and medicine manufacturing or for federal, state, or local governments. Significant numbers of environmental science and protection technicians also worked for state and local governments and professional, scientific, and technical services firms. Almost two-thirds of forest and conservation technicians held jobs in the federal government; another 20 percent worked for state governments. Around 22 percent of agricultural and food science technicians worked for food processing companies; most of the rest worked for scientific research and development services firms and state governments. Over one-fifth of all geological and petroleum technicians worked for oil and gas extraction companies, and forensic science technicians worked primarily for state and local governments.

Training, Other Qualifications, and Advancement

There are several ways to qualify for a job as a science technician. Many employers prefer applicants who have at least 2 years of specialized training or an associate degree in applied science or science-related technology. Because employers' preferences vary, however, some science technicians have a bachelor's degree in chemistry, biology, or forensic science, or have taken several science and math courses at 4-year colleges.

Many technical and community colleges offer associate degrees in a specific technology or a more general education in science and mathematics. A number of 2-year associate degree programs are designed to provide easy transfer to a 4-year college or university, if desired. Technical institutes usually offer technician training, but provide less theory and general education than do technical or community colleges. The length of programs at technical institutes varies, although 1-year certificate programs and 2-year associate degree programs are common.

More than 20 colleges or universities offer a bachelor's degree program in forensic science; more than 10 additional schools offer a bachelor's of science in chemistry, biochemistry, or genetic engineering with an emphasis on forensic science; a few additional schools offer a bachelor's of science degree with an emphasis in a specialty area, such as criminalistics, pathology, jurisprudence, odontology, toxicology, or forensic accounting. In contrast to some other science technician positions that require only a 2-year degree, a

4-year degree in forensics science is usually necessary to work in the field. Knowledge and understanding of legal procedures also can be helpful. Forestry and conservation technicians can choose from more than 20 associate degree programs in forest technology accredited by the Society of American Foresters.

Most chemical process technicians have a 2-year degree, usually an associate degree in process technology, although in some cases a high school diploma is sufficient. They usually receive additional on-the- job training. Entry-level workers whose college training encompasses extensive hands-on experience with a variety of diagnostic laboratory equipment usually require less on-the-job training. Those with a high school diploma typically begin work as trainees under the direct supervision of a more experienced process technician. Many with only a high school diploma eventually earn a 2-year degree in process technology, often paid for by their employer.

Some schools offer cooperative-education or internship programs, allowing students the opportunity to work at a local company or other workplace while attending classes in alternate terms. Participation in such programs can significantly enhance a student's employment prospects.

Persons interested in careers as science technicians should take as many high school science and math courses as possible. Science courses taken beyond high school, in an associate or bachelor's degree program, should be laboratory oriented, with an emphasis on bench skills. A solid background in applied basic chemistry, physics, and math is vital. Because computers often are used in research and development laboratories, technicians should have strong computer skills. Communication skills also are important; technicians often are required to report their findings both orally and in writing. Additionally, technicians should be able to work well with others, because teamwork is common. Organizational ability, an eye for detail, and skill in interpreting scientific results also are important. High mechanical aptitude, attention to detail, and analytical thinking are all important characteristics of science technicians.

Prospective science technicians can acquire good career preparation through 2-year formal training programs that combine the teaching of scientific principles and theory with practical hands-on application in a laboratory setting with up-to-date equipment. Graduates of 4-year bachelor's degree programs in science who have considerable experience in laboratory-based courses, have completed internships, or have held summer jobs in laboratories also are well qualified for science technician positions and are preferred by some employers. However, those with a bachelor's degree who accept technician jobs generally cannot find employment that uses their advanced academic education.

Technicians usually begin work as trainees in routine positions, under the direct supervision of a scientist or a more experienced technician. Job candidates whose training or educational background encompasses extensive hands-on experience with a variety of laboratory equipment, including computers and related equipment, usually require a short period of on-the-job training. As they gain experience, technicians take on more responsibility and carry out assignments under only general supervision, and some eventually become supervisors. However, technicians employed at universities often have their fortunes tied to those of particular professors; when professors retire or leave, these technicians face uncertain employment prospects.

Job Outlook

Overall employment of science technicians is expected to increase about as fast as the average for all occupations through the year 2012. Continued growth of scientific and medical research, particularly research related to biotechnology, as well as the development and production of technical products, should stimulate demand for science technicians in many industries. The increase in the number of biological technicians will be about as fast as average, as the growing number of agricultural and medicinal products developed using biotechnology techniques will boost demand for these workers. Also, stronger competition among pharmaceutical companies and an aging population are expected to contribute to the need for innovative and improved drugs, further spurring demand for biological technicians. Fastest employment growth of biological technicians should occur in the pharmaceutical and medicine manufacturing industry and in scientific research and development services firms.

Job growth for chemical technicians is projected to grow more slowly than average. The chemical manufacturing industry, the major employer of chemical technicians, will experience a decline in overall employment as companies downsize and turn to outside contractors to provide specialized services. Job opportunities are expected to be more plentiful in pharmaceutical and medicine manufacturing as the public continues to demand newer and better pharmaceuticals. To meet this demand, pharmaceutical manufacturing firms are expected to continue to devote money to research and development, either through in-house teams, or, increasingly, by contracting to scientific research and development services firms, spurring employment growth of chemical technicians in that industry. An increasing focus on quality assurance will require a greater number of process technicians, further stimulating demand for these workers.

Employment of environmental science and protection technicians should grow much faster than average to help regulate waste products; to collect air, water, and soil samples for measuring levels of pollutants; to monitor compliance with environmental regulations; and to clean up contaminated sites.

There will be limited demand for forest and conservation technicians at the federal and state government levels, leading to slower-than-average growth, due to general downsizing and reductions in timber harvesting on federal lands. However, increased emphasis on specific conservation issues, such as environmental protection, water resources preservation, and control of exotic and invasive pests, may provide some employment opportunities.

Employment of agricultural and food science technicians should grow more slowly than average, mainly due to limited growth in agriculture and the food processing industry. However, research will still be necessary, particularly biotechnological research in the private sector, as it becomes increasingly important to balance greater agricultural output with protection and preservation of soil, water, and the ecosystem. Specifically, research will be needed to combat insects and diseases as they continue to adapt to pesticides and as soil fertility and water quality continue to need improvement.

Jobs for forensic science technicians are expected to increase about as fast as average. Crime scene technicians who work for state Public Safety Departments may experience favorable employment prospects if the number of qualified applicants remains low.

Little or no growth in employment of geological and petroleum technicians is expected because employment in the oil and gas extraction and mining industries, among the largest employers of geological and petroleum technicians, is expected to decline. Job opportunities will be more favorable in professional, scientific, and technical services firms, as geological and petroleum technicians will be needed to consult companies regarding environmental policy and federal government mandates, such as those requiring lower sulfur emissions.

Job opportunities are expected to be best for graduates of applied science technology programs who are well trained on equipment used in industrial and government laboratories and production facilities. As the instrumentation and techniques used in industrial research, development, and production become increasingly more complex, employers are seeking individuals with highly developed technical and communication skills.

Along with opportunities created by growth, many job openings should arise from the need to replace technicians who retire or leave the labor force for other reasons. During periods of economic recession, layoffs of science technicians may occur.

Earnings

Median hourly earnings of science technicians in 2002 were as follows:

Nuclear technicians	$28.84
Forensic science technicians	19.73
Geological and petroleum technicians	18.96
Chemical technicians	18.00
Environmental science and protection technicians, including health	16.98
Biological technicians	15.73
Forest and conservation technicians	14.90
Agricultural and food science technicians	13.74

In 2003, the average annual salary in nonsupervisory, supervisory, and managerial positions in the federal government was $30,440 for biological science technicians; $44,068 for physical science technicians; $55,374 for geodetic technicians; $40,781 for hydrologic technicians; and $52,585 for meteorological technicians.

Related Occupations

Other technicians who apply scientific principles at a level usually acquired in 2-year associate degree programs include engineering technicians, broadcast and sound engineering technicians and radio operators, drafters, and health technologists and technicians, especially clinical laboratory technologists and technicians, diagnostic medical sonographers, and radiologic technologists and technicians.

Sources of Additional Information

For information about a career as a chemical technician, contact:

● American Chemical Society, Education Division, Career Publications, 1155 16th St. NW, Washington, DC 20036. Internet: http://www.acs.org

For career information and a list of undergraduate, graduate, and doctoral programs in forensic sciences, contact:

● American Academy of Forensic Sciences, P.O. Box 669, Colorado Springs, CO 80901. Internet: http://www.aafs.org

For general education information on forestry technicians and lists of schools offering education in forestry, send a self-addressed, stamped business envelope to:

● Society of American Foresters, 5400 Grosvenor Ln., Bethesda, MD 20814. Internet: http://www.safnet.org

Semiconductor Processors

(O*NET 51-9141.00)

Significant Points

● Employment is expected to decline over the next 10 years because of rising imports of computer chips and increasing automation of fabrication plants in this country.

● An associate degree in a relevant curriculum is increasingly required.

Nature of the Work

Electronic semiconductors—also known as computer chips, microchips, or integrated circuits—are the miniature but powerful brains of high-technology equipment. Semiconductors are composed of a myriad of tiny aluminum or copper lines and electric switches, which manipulate the flow of electrical current. Semiconductor processors are responsible for many of the steps necessary in the manufacture of each semiconductor that goes into personal computers, missile guidance systems, and a host of other electronic equipment.

Semiconductor processors manufacture semiconductors in disks of varying sizes, generally eight to twelve inches wide. These disks, called wafers, are thin slices of silicon on which the circuitry of the microchips is layered. Each wafer is eventually cut into dozens or scores of individual chips.

Semiconductor processors make wafers by means of photolithography, a printing process for creating patterns from photographic images. Operating automated equipment, workers imprint precise microscopic patterns of the circuitry on the wafers, etch out the patterns with acids, and replace the patterns with metals that conduct electricity. Then, the wafers receive a chemical bath to make them smooth, and the imprint process begins again on a new layer with the next pattern. Wafers usually have from 8 to 20 such layers of microscopic, three-dimensional circuitry.

Semiconductors are produced in semiconductor-fabricating plants, or "fabs." Within fabs, the manufacture and cutting of wafers to create semiconductors takes place in "cleanrooms"—production areas that must be kept free of any airborne matter, because the least bit of dust can damage a semiconductor. All semiconductor processors working in cleanrooms—both operators and technicians—must wear special lightweight outer garments known as "bunny suits." These garments fit over clothing to prevent lint and other particles from contaminating semiconductor-processing worksites.

Operators, who make up the majority of the workers in cleanrooms, start and monitor the sophisticated equipment that performs the various tasks during the many steps of the semiconductor production sequence. They spend a great deal of time at computer terminals, monitoring the operation of the equipment to ensure that each of the tasks in the production of the wafer is performed correctly. Operators also may transfer wafer carriers from one development station to the next; in newer fabs, the lifting of heavy wafer carriers and the constant monitoring for quality control are increasingly being automated.

Once begun, the production of semiconductor wafers is continuous. Operators work to the pace of the machinery that has largely automated the production process. Operators are responsible for keeping the automated machinery within proper operating parameters.

Technicians account for a smaller percentage of the workers in cleanrooms, but they troubleshoot production problems and make equipment adjustments and repairs. They also take the lead in assuring quality control and in maintaining equipment. To keep equipment repairs to a minimum, technicians perform diagnostic analyses and run computations. For example, technicians may determine if a flaw in a chip is due to contamination, and peculiar to that wafer, or if the flaw is inherent in the manufacturing process.

Working Conditions

The work pace in cleanrooms is deliberately slow. Limited movement keeps the air in cleanrooms as free as possible of dust and other particles, which can destroy semiconductors during their production. Because the machinery sets operators' rate of work in the largely automated production process, workers maintain an easygoing pace. Although workers spend some time alone monitoring equipment, operators and technicians spend much of their time working in teams.

Technicians are on their feet most of the day, walking through the cleanroom to oversee production activities. Operators spend a great deal of time sitting or standing at workstations, monitoring computer readouts and gauges. Sometimes, they must retrieve wafers from one station and take them to another.

The temperature in the cleanrooms must be kept within a narrow range: usually, it is set at a comfortable 72 degrees Fahrenheit. Although bunny suits cover virtually the entire body, except perhaps the eyes (over which workers wear protective glasses), their lightweight fabric keeps the temperature inside fairly comfortable as well. Entry and exit of workers in bunny suits from the cleanroom are controlled to minimize contamination, and workers must be reclothed in a clean suit and decontaminated each time they return to the cleanroom.

Several highly toxic chemicals are used at various points in the process of manufacturing semiconductors. Workers who are exposed to such chemicals can be harmed. However, semiconductor fabrication plants are designed with safeguards to ensure that these chemicals are handled, used, and disposed of without exposure to workers or the surrounding environment. Toxic chemicals are applied to wafers by computer-controlled machine tools in sealed chambers and there is normally little risk of workers coming into contact with them.

Semiconductor-fabricating plants operate around the clock. For this reason, night and weekend work is common. In some plants, workers maintain standard 8-hour shifts, 5 days a week. In other plants, employees are on duty for 12-hour shifts to minimize the disruption of cleanroom operations brought about by changes in shift. In some plants, managers allow workers to alternate schedules, thereby distributing the "graveyard" shift equitably.

Employment

Electronic semiconductor processors held approximately 46,000 jobs in 2002. Nearly all of them were employed in facilities that manufacture semiconductors and other electronic components and accessories, though a small percentage worked in plants that primarily manufacture computers and office equipment.

Training, Other Qualifications, and Advancement

People interested in becoming semiconductor processors—either operators or technicians—need a solid background in mathematics and the physical sciences. In addition to applying these disciplines to the complex manufacturing processes performed in fabs, math and science knowledge are essentials for pursuing higher education in semiconductor technology—and knowledge of both subjects is one of the best ways to advance in the semiconductor fabricating field.

Semiconductor processor workers must also be able to think analytically and critically to anticipate problems and avoid costly mistakes. Communication skills also are vital, as workers must be able to convey their thoughts and ideas both orally and in writing.

A high school diploma or equivalent is the minimum requirement for entry-level operator jobs in semiconductor fabrication plants. However, employers increasingly prefer persons who have completed associate degree programs for semiconductor processor jobs. While completion of a 1-year certificate program in semiconductor technology offered by some community colleges is an asset for most processor jobs, technicians must have at least an associate degree in electronics technology or a related field.

Degree or certificate candidates who get hands-on training while attending school look even more attractive to prospective employers. Semiconductor technology programs in a growing number of community colleges include an internship at a semiconductor fabricating plant; many students in these programs already hold full- or part-time jobs in the industry and work toward degrees in semiconductor technology in their spare time to update their skills or qualify for promotion to technician jobs. In addition, to ensure that operators and technicians keep their skills current, many employers provide 40 hours of formal training annually. Some employers also provide financial assistance to employees who want to earn associate and bachelor's degrees.

Summer and part-time employment provide another option for getting started in the field for those who live near a semiconductor processing plant. Students often are hired to work during the summer, and some students are allowed to continue working part time during the school year. Students in summer and part-time semiconductor processor jobs learn what education they need to prosper in the field. They also gain valuable experience that may lead to full-time employment after graduation.

Some semiconductor processing technicians transfer to sales engineer jobs with suppliers of the machines that manufacture the semiconductors or become field support personnel.

Job Outlook

Between 2002 and 2012, employment of semiconductor processors is projected to decline. The two main reasons for this reversal are much higher productivity and rising imports. Companies are upgrading many of their older fabs to make larger 12" wafers, which produce twice as many chips as fabs making 8" wafers. These plants also are more automated, allowing them to sharply increase production with the same number of workers. A number of domestic companies also are building more fabs overseas, where costs are lower. In addition, imports of semiconductors from non-U.S. companies are on the rise and should continue to increase throughout the decade. Besides the creation of new jobs, additional openings will result from the need to replace workers who leave the occupation.

Despite the expected decline in employment of semiconductor processors, the demand for semiconductor chips remains very high stemming from the many existing and future applications for semiconductors in computers, appliances, machinery, biotechnology, vehicles, cell phones and other telecommunications devices, and other equipment. Moreover, the advent of the new 64-bit microchip is expected to provide the power of computer servers or workstations, onto desktop computers and open up a wealth of new applications, particularly in medical devices.

Industry development of semiconductors made from better materials means that semiconductors will become even smaller, more powerful, and more durable. For example, the industry has begun producing a new generation of microchips made with copper rather than aluminum wires, which will better conduct electricity. Also, technology to develop chips based on plastic, rather than on silicon, will make computers durable enough to be used in a variety of applications in which they could not easily have been used previously.

Job prospects will be best for people with postsecondary education in electronics or semiconductor technology.

Earnings

Median hourly earnings of electronic semiconductor processors were $13.14 in 2002. The middle 50 percent earned between $10.76 and $16.39 an hour. The lowest 10 percent earned less than $9.28, and the top 10 percent earned more than $20.35 an hour.

Technicians with an associate degree in electronics or semiconductor technology generally start at higher salaries than those with less education. Between a fourth and a half of all electronic semiconductor processors belong to a union, considerably higher than the rate for all occupations.

Related Occupations

Electronic semiconductor processors do production work that resembles the work of precision assemblers and fabricators of electrical and electronic equipment. Also, many electronic semiconductor processors have academic training in semiconductor technology, which emphasizes scientific and engineering principles. Other occupations that require some college or postsecondary vocational training emphasizing such principles are engineering technicians, electrical and electronics engineers, and science technicians.

Sources of Additional Information

For more information on semiconductor processor careers, contact:

- Semiconductor Industry Association, 181 Metro Dr., Suite 450, San Jose, CA 95110. Internet: http://www.semichips.org

- Maricopa Advanced Technology Education Center (MATEC), 2323 West 14th St., Suite 540, Tempe, AZ 85281. Internet: http://matec.org/ops/career.shtml

Speech-Language Pathologists

(O*NET 29-1127.00)

Significant Points

- Employment of speech-language pathologists is expected to grow rapidly because the expanding population in older age groups is prone to medical conditions that result in speech, language, and swallowing problems.

- About half worked in educational services, and most others were employed by healthcare and social assistance facilities.

- A master's degree in speech-language pathology is the standard credential.

Nature of the Work

Speech-language pathologists, sometimes called *speech therapists*, assess, diagnose, treat, and help to prevent speech, language, cognitive, communication, voice, swallowing, fluency, and other related disorders.

Speech-language pathologists work with people who cannot make speech sounds, or cannot make them clearly; those with speech rhythm and fluency problems, such as stuttering; people with voice quality problems, such as inappropriate pitch or harsh voice; those with problems understanding and producing language; those who wish to improve their communication skills by modifying an accent; those with cognitive communication impairments, such as attention, memory, and problem solving disorders; and those with hearing loss who use hearing aids or cochlear implants in order to develop auditory skills and improve communication. They also work with people who have swallowing difficulties.

Speech and language difficulties can result from a variety of causes including stroke, brain injury or deterioration, developmental delays, cerebral palsy, cleft palate, voice pathology, mental retardation, hearing impairment, or emotional problems. Problems can be congenital, developmental, or acquired. Speech-language pathologists use written and oral tests, as well as special instruments, to diagnose the nature and extent of impairment and to record and analyze speech, language, and swallowing irregularities. Speech-language pathologists develop an individualized plan of care, tailored to each patient's needs. For individuals with little or no speech capability, speech-language pathologists may select augmentative or alternative communication methods, including automated devices and sign language, and teach their use. They teach these individuals how to make sounds, improve their voices, or increase their language skills to communicate more effectively. Speech-language pathologists help patients develop, or recover, reliable communication skills so patients can fulfill their educational, vocational, and social roles.

Most speech-language pathologists provide direct clinical services to individuals with communication or swallowing disorders. In speech and language clinics, they may independently develop and carry out treatment programs. In medical facilities, they may work with physicians, social workers, psychologists, and other therapists. Speech-language pathologists in schools develop individual or group programs, counsel parents, and may assist teachers with classroom activities.

Speech-language pathologists keep records on the initial evaluation, progress, and discharge of clients. This helps pinpoint problems, tracks client progress, and justifies the cost of treatment when applying for reimbursement. They counsel individuals and their families concerning communication disorders and how to cope with the stress and misunderstanding that often accompany them. They also work with family members to recognize and change behavior patterns that impede communication and treatment and show them communication-enhancing techniques to use at home.

Some speech-language pathologists conduct research on how people communicate. Others design and develop equipment or techniques for diagnosing and treating speech problems.

Working Conditions

Speech-language pathologists usually work at a desk or table in clean comfortable surroundings. In medical settings, they may work at the patient's bedside and assist in positioning the patient. In school settings they may participate in classroom activities. While the job is not physically demanding, it requires attention to detail and intense concentration. The emotional needs of clients and their families may be demanding. Most full-time speech-language pathologists work between 35 and 40 hours per week; some work part time. Those who work on a contract basis may spend a substantial amount of time traveling between facilities.

Employment

Speech-language pathologists held about 94,000 jobs in 2002. About half of jobs were in educational services, including preschools, elementary and secondary schools, and colleges and universities. Others were in hospitals; offices of other health practitioners, including speech-language pathologists; nursing care facilities; home healthcare services; individual and family services; outpatient care centers; child day care services; or other facilities.

A few speech-language pathologists are self-employed in private practice. They contract to provide services in schools, offices of physicians, hospitals, or nursing care facilities, or work as consultants to industry.

Training, Other Qualifications, and Advancement

Of the 46 states that regulate licensing, almost all require a master's degree or equivalent. A passing score on a national examination on speech-language pathology offered through the Praxis Series of the Educational Testing Service is needed, as well. Other requirements are 300 to 375 hours of supervised clinical experience and 9 months of postgraduate professional clinical experience. Thirty-eight states have continuing education requirements for licensure renewal. Medicaid, Medicare, and private health insurers generally require a practitioner to be licensed to qualify for reimbursement.

About 233 colleges and universities offer graduate programs in speech-language pathology. Courses cover anatomy and physiology of the areas of the body involved in speech, language, swallowing, and hearing; the development of normal speech, language, swallowing, and hearing; the nature of disorders; acoustics; and psychological aspects of communication. Graduate students also learn to evaluate and treat speech, language, swallowing, and hearing disorders and receive supervised clinical training in communication disorders.

Speech-language pathologists can acquire the Certificate of Clinical Competence in Speech-Language Pathology (CCC-SLP) offered by the American Speech-Language-Hearing Association. To earn a CCC, a person must have a graduate degree and 375 hours of supervised clinical experience, complete a 36-week postgraduate clinical fellowship, and pass the Praxis Series examination in speech-language pathology administered by the Educational Testing Service (ETS).

Speech-language pathologists should be able to effectively communicate diagnostic test results, diagnoses, and proposed treatment in a manner easily understood by their clients. They must be able to approach problems objectively and provide support to clients and their families. Because a client's progress may be slow, patience, compassion, and good listening skills are necessary.

Job Outlook

Employment of speech-language pathologists is expected to grow faster than the average for all occupations through the year 2012. Members of the baby boom generation are now entering middle age, when the possibility of neurological disorders and associated speech, language, swallowing, and hearing impairments increases. Medical advances are also improving the survival rate of premature infants and trauma and stroke victims, who then need assessment and possible treatment. Many states now require that all newborns be screened for hearing loss and receive appropriate early intervention services.

In health services facilities, the impact of proposed federal legislation imposing limits on reimbursement for therapy services may adversely affect the short-term job outlook for therapy providers. However, over the long run, the demand for therapists should continue to rise as growth in the number of individuals with disabilities or limited function spurs demand for therapy services.

Employment in educational services will increase along with growth in elementary and secondary school enrollments, including enrollment of special education students. Federal law guarantees special education and related services to all eligible children with disabilities. Greater awareness of the importance of early identification and diagnosis of speech, language, swallowing, and hearing disorders will also increase employment.

The number of speech-language pathologists in private practice will rise due to the increasing use of contract services by hospitals, schools, and nursing care facilities. In addition to job openings stemming from employment growth, a number of openings for speech-language pathologists will arise from the need to replace those who leave the occupation.

Earnings

Median annual earnings of speech-language pathologists were $49,450 in 2002. The middle 50 percent earned between $39,930 and $60,190. The lowest 10 percent earned less than $32,580, and the highest 10 percent earned more than $74,010. Median annual earnings in the industries employing the largest numbers of speech-language pathologists in 2002 were as follows:

Offices of other health practitioners	$53,090
General medical and surgical hospitals	52,940
Elementary and secondary schools	46,060

According to a 2003 survey by the American Speech-Language-Hearing Association, the median annual salary for full-time certified speech-language pathologists who worked on a calendar-year basis, generally 11 or 12 months annually, was $48,000. For those who worked on an academic-year basis, usually 9 or 10 months annually, the median annual salary was $44,800. Certified speech-language pathologists who worked 25 or fewer hours per week had a median hourly salary of $40.00. Starting salaries for certified speech-language pathologists with one to three years experience were $42,000 for those who worked on a calendar-year basis and $37,000 for those who worked on an academic-year basis.

Related Occupations

Speech-language pathologists specialize in the prevention, diagnosis, and treatment of speech and language problems. Workers in related occupations include audiologists, occupational therapists, optometrists, physical therapists, psychologists, recreational therapists, and rehabilitation counselors.

Sources of Additional Information

State licensing boards can provide information on licensure requirements. State departments of education can supply information on certification requirements for those who wish to work in public schools.

General information on careers in speech-language pathology is available from:

- American Speech-Language-Hearing Association, 10801 Rockville Pike, Rockville, MD 20852. Internet: http://www.asha.org

Stationary Engineers and Boiler Operators

(O*NET 51-8021.01 and 51-8021.02)

Significant Points

- Applicants may face competition for jobs; opportunities will be best for workers with training in computerized controls and instrumentation.

- Stationary engineers and boiler operators usually acquire their skills through a formal apprenticeship program, or on-the-job training supplemented by courses at a trade or technical school.

- Most states and cities have licensing requirements.

Nature of the Work

Heating, air-conditioning, refrigeration, and ventilation systems keep large buildings and other commercial facilities comfortable all year long. Industrial plants often have facilities to provide electrical power, steam, or other services. Stationary engineers and boiler operators operate and maintain these systems, which include boilers, air-conditioning and refrigeration equipment, diesel engines, turbines, generators, pumps, condensers, and compressors. The equipment that stationary engineers and boiler operators control is sim-ilar to equipment operated by locomotive or marine engineers, except that it is not in a moving vehicle.

Stationary engineers and boiler operators start up, regulate, repair, and shut down equipment. They ensure that the equipment operates safely, economically, and within established limits by monitoring meters, gauges, and computerized controls. Stationary engineers and boiler operators control equipment manually and, if necessary, make adjustments. They also record relevant events and facts concerning the operation and maintenance of the equipment in a log. With regard to steam boilers, for example, they observe, control, and record the steam pressure, temperature, water level, chemistry, power output, fuel consumption, and emissions from the vessel. They watch and listen to machinery and routinely check safety devices, identifying and correcting any trouble that develops. They use hand and power tools to perform repairs and maintenance ranging from a complete overhaul to replacing defective valves, gaskets, or bearings. Service, troubleshooting, repair, and monitoring of modern systems require the use of sophisticated electrical and electronic test equipment.

Stationary engineers typically use computers to operate the mechanical, electrical, and fire safety systems of new buildings and plants. Engineers monitor, adjust, and diagnose these systems from a central location, using a computer linked into the buildings' communications network.

Routine maintenance, such as lubricating moving parts, replacing filters, and removing soot and corrosion that can reduce the boiler's operating efficiency, is a regular part of the work of stationary engineers and boiler operators. They test the water in the boiler and add chemicals to prevent corrosion and harmful deposits. In most facilities, stationary engineers are responsible for the maintenance and balancing of air systems, as well as hydronic systems that heat or cool buildings by circulating fluid (as water or vapor) in a closed system of pipes. They also may check the air quality of the ventilation system and make adjustments to keep the operation of the boiler within mandated guidelines.

In a large building or industrial plant, a stationary engineer may be in charge of all mechanical systems in the building. Engineers may supervise the work of assistant stationary engineers, turbine operators, boiler tenders, and air-conditioning and refrigeration operators and mechanics. Most stationary engineers perform other maintenance duties, such as carpentry, plumbing, locksmithing, and electrical repairs. In a small building or industrial plant, there may be only one stationary engineer.

Working Conditions

Stationary engineers and boiler operators generally have steady, year-round employment. The average workweek is 40 hours. In facilities that operate around the clock, engineers and operators usually work one of three daily 8-hour shifts on a rotating basis. Weekend and holiday work often is required.

Engine rooms, power plants, boiler rooms, mechanical rooms, and electrical rooms usually are clean and well lighted. Even under the most favorable conditions, however, some stationary engineers and boiler operators are exposed to high temperatures, dust, dirt, and high noise levels from the equipment. General maintenance duties also may require contact with oil, grease, or smoke. Workers spend much of the time on their feet. They may also have to crawl inside boilers and work in crouching or kneeling positions to inspect, clean, or repair equipment.

Stationary engineers and boiler operators work around hazardous machinery, such as low and high pressure boilers and electrical equipment. They must follow procedures to guard against burns, electric shock, noise, moving parts, and exposure to hazardous materials, such as asbestos or certain chemicals.

Employment

Stationary engineers and boiler operators held about 55,000 jobs in 2002. Jobs were dispersed throughout a variety of industries. The majority of jobs were in state and local government facilities; hospitals; educational services; manufacturing firms, such as pulp, paper, and paperboard mills; and electric power generation, transmission and distribution facilities. Other jobs were in architectural, engineering, and related services; traveler accommodation (hotels); and lessors of real estate (apartment and commercial buildings). Some were employed as contractors to a building or plant.

Stationary engineers and boiler operators worked throughout the country, generally in the more heavily populated areas in which large industrial and commercial establishments are located.

Training, Other Qualifications, and Advancement

Stationary engineers and boiler operators usually acquire their skills through a formal apprenticeship program, or on-the-job training supplemented by courses at a trade or technical school. In addition, valuable experience can be obtained in the Navy or the merchant marine, because marine engineering plants are similar to many stationary power and heating plants. Most employers prefer to hire persons with at least a high school diploma or the equivalent, due to the increasing complexity of the equipment with which engineers and operators now work. Many Stationary engineers and boiler operators have some form of continuing education including college. Mechanical aptitude, manual dexterity, and good physical condition also are important.

The International Union of Operating Engineers sponsors apprenticeship programs and is the principal union for Stationary engineers and boiler operators. In selecting apprentices, most local labor-management apprenticeship committees prefer applicants with education or training in mathematics, computers, mechanical drawing, machine shop practice, physics, and chemistry. An apprenticeship usually lasts 4 years and includes 8,000 hours of on-the-job training. In addition, apprentices receive 600 hours of classroom instruction in subjects such as boiler design and operation, elementary physics, pneumatics, refrigeration, air-conditioning, electricity, and electronics.

Those who acquire their skills on the job usually start as boiler tenders or helpers to experienced stationary engineers and boiler operators. This practical experience may be supplemented by postsecondary vocational training in computerized controls and instrumentation. However, becoming an engineer or operator without completing a formal apprenticeship program usually requires many years of work experience.

Most large and some small employers encourage and pay for skill-improvement training for their employees. Training almost always is provided when new equipment is introduced or when regulations concerning some aspect of the workers' duties change.

Most states and cities have licensing requirements for Stationary engineers and boiler operators. Applicants usually must be at least 18 years of age, reside for a specified period in the state or locality, meet experience requirements, and pass a written examination. A stationary engineer or boiler operator who moves from one state or city to another may have to pass an examination for a new license due to regional differences in licensing requirements.

There are several classes of stationary engineer licenses. Each class specifies the type and size of equipment the engineer can operate without supervision. A licensed first-class stationary engineer is qualified to run a large facility, supervise others, and operate equipment of all types and capacities. An applicant for this license may be required to have a high school education, apprenticeship or on-the-job training, and several years of experience. Licenses below first class limit the types or capacities of equipment the engineer may operate without supervision.

Stationary engineers and boiler operators advance by being placed in charge of larger, more powerful, or more varied equipment. Generally, engineers advance to these jobs as they obtain higher class licenses. Some stationary engineers and boiler operators advance to boiler inspectors, chief plant engineers, building and plant superintendents, or building managers. A few obtain jobs as examining engineers or technical instructors.

Job Outlook

Applicants may face competition for jobs as stationary engineers and boiler operators. Employment opportunities will be best for those with apprenticeship training or vocational school courses covering systems that are operated by computerized controls and instrumentation.

Employment of stationary engineers and boiler operators is expected to show little or no growth through the year 2012. Continuing commercial and industrial development will increase the amount of equipment to be operated and maintained. However, automated systems and computerized controls are making newly installed equipment more efficient, thus reducing the number of jobs needed for its operation. Furthermore, relatively few job openings will arise from the need to replace experienced workers who transfer to other occupations or leave the labor force. The low replacement rate in this occupation reflects its high wages.

Earnings

Median annual earnings of Stationary engineers and boiler operators were $43,240 in 2002. The middle 50 percent earned between $33,860 and $54,550. The lowest 10 percent earned less than $26,340, and the highest 10 percent earned more than $65,290. Median annual earnings of Stationary engineers and boiler operators in 2002 were $48,450 in local government and $40,800 in general medical and surgical hospitals.

Related Occupations

Workers who monitor and operate stationary machinery include chemical plant and system operators; gas plant operators; petroleum pump system operators, refinery operators, and gaugers; power plant operators, distributors, and dispatchers; and water and liquid waste treatment plant and system operators. Other workers who maintain the equipment and machinery in a building or plant are industrial machinery installation, repair, and maintenance workers, as well as millwrights.

Sources of Additional Information

Information about apprenticeships, vocational training, and work opportunities is available from state employment service offices, locals of the International Union of Operating Engineers, vocational schools, and state and local licensing agencies.

Specific questions about this occupation should be addressed to:

- International Union of Operating Engineers, 1125 17th St. NW, Washington, DC 20036. Internet: http://www.iuoe.org

- National Association of Power Engineers, Inc., 1 Springfield St., Chicopee, MA 01013.

- Building Owners and Managers Institute International, 1521 Ritchie Hwy., Arnold, MD 21012. Internet: http://www.bomi-edu.org

Statisticians

(O*NET 15-2041.00)

Significant Points

- Many individuals with degrees in statistics enter jobs that do not have the title statistician.

- A master's degree in statistics or mathematics is the minimum educational requirement for most jobs with this title.

- Although little or no change is expected in employment of statisticians over the 2000-10 period, job opportunities should remain favorable for individuals with statistical degrees.

Nature of the Work

Statistics is the scientific application of mathematical principles to the collection, analysis, and presentation of numerical data. Statisticians contribute to scientific inquiry by applying their mathematical knowledge to the design of surveys and experiments; collection, processing, and analysis of data; and interpretation of the results. Statisticians often apply their knowledge of statistical methods to a variety of subject areas, such as biology, economics, engineering, medicine, public health, psychology, marketing, education, and sports. Many applications cannot occur without the use of statistical techniques, such as designing experiments to gain federal approval of a newly manufactured drug.

One technique that is especially useful to statisticians is sampling—obtaining information about a population of people or group of things by surveying a small portion of the total. For example, to determine the size of the audience for particular programs, television-rating services survey only a few thousand families, rather than all viewers. Statisticians decide where and how to gather the data, determine the type and size of the sample group, and develop the survey questionnaire or reporting form. They also prepare instructions for workers who will collect and tabulate the data. Finally, statisticians analyze, interpret, and summarize the data using computer software.

In business and industry, statisticians play an important role in quality control and product development and improvement. In an automobile company, for example, statisticians might design experiments to determine the failure time of engines exposed to extreme weather conditions by running individual engines until failure and breakdown. Working for a pharmaceutical company, statisticians might develop and evaluate the results of clinical trials to determine the safety and effectiveness of new medications. And at a computer software firm, statisticians might help construct new statistical software packages to analyze data more accurately and efficiently. In addition to product development and testing, some statisticians also are involved in deciding what products to manufacture, how much to charge for them, and to whom the products should be marketed. Statisticians also may manage assets and liabilities, determining the risks and returns of certain investments.

Numerous statisticians also are employed by nearly every government agency. Some government statisticians develop surveys that measure population growth, consumer prices, or unemployment. Other statisticians work for scientific, environmental, and agricultural agencies and may help to determine the amount of pesticides in drinking water, the number of endangered species living in a particular area, or the number of people afflicted with a particular disease. Other statisticians are employed in national defense agencies, determining the accuracy of new weapons and defense strategies.

Because statistical specialists are used in so many work areas, specialists who use statistics often have different professional designations. For example, a person using statistical methods on economic data may have the title econometrician, while statisticians in public health and medicine may hold titles such as biostatistician, biometrician, or epidemiologist.

Working Conditions

Statisticians usually work regular hours in comfortable offices. Some statisticians travel to provide advice on research projects, supervise and set up surveys, or gather statistical data. Some may have duties that vary widely, such as designing experiments or performing fieldwork in various communities. Statisticians who work in academia generally have a mix of teaching and research responsibilities.

Employment

Statisticians held about 19,000 jobs in 2000. One-fifth of these jobs were in the federal government, where statisticians were concentrated in the Departments of Commerce, Agriculture, and Health and Human Services. Most of the remaining jobs were in private industry, especially in the research and testing services and management and public relations industries. In addition, many professionals with a background in statistics were among the 20,000 full-time mathematics faculty in colleges and universities in 2000, according to the American Mathematical Society.

Training, Other Qualifications, and Advancement

Although more employment opportunities are becoming available to well-qualified statisticians with bachelor's degrees, a master's degree in statistics or mathematics is usually the minimum educational requirement for most statistician jobs. Research and academic positions in institutions of higher education, for example, require a graduate degree, usually a doctorate, in statistics. Beginning positions in industrial research often require a master's degree combined with several years of experience.

The training required for employment as an entry-level statistician in the federal government, however, is a bachelor's degree, including at least 15 semester hours of statistics or a combination of 15 hours of mathematics and statistics, if at least 6 semester hours are in statistics. Qualifying as a mathematical statistician in the federal government requires 24 semester hours of mathematics and statistics with a minimum of 6 semester hours in statistics and 12 semester hours in an area of advanced mathematics, such as calculus, differential equations, or vector analysis.

About 80 colleges and universities offered bachelor's degrees in statistics in 2000. Many other schools also offered degrees in mathematics, operations research, and other fields that included a sufficient number of courses in statistics to qualify graduates for some beginning positions in the. Required subjects for statistics majors include differential and integral calculus, statistical methods, mathematical modeling, and probability theory. Additional courses that undergraduates should take include linear algebra, design and analysis of experiments, applied multivariate analysis, and mathematical statistics.

In 2000, approximately 110 universities offered a master's degree program in statistics, and about 60 offered a doctoral degree program. Many other schools also offered graduate-level courses in applied statistics for students majoring in biology, business, economics, education, engineering, psychology, and other fields. Acceptance into graduate statistics programs does not require an undergraduate degree in statistics, although good training in mathematics is essential.

Because computers are used extensively for statistical applications, a strong background in computer science is highly recommended. For positions involving quality and productivity improvement, training in engineering or physical science is useful. A background in biological, chemical, or health science is important for positions involving the preparation and testing of pharmaceutical or agricultural products. Courses in economics and business administration are helpful for many jobs in market research, business analysis, and forecasting.

Good communications skills are important for prospective statisticians in industry, where they often need to explain technical matters to persons without statistical expertise. An understanding of business and the economy also is valuable for those who plan to work in private industry.

Beginning statisticians generally are supervised by an experienced statistician. With experience, they may advance to positions with more technical responsibility and, in some cases, supervisory duties. However, opportunities for promotion increase with advanced degrees. Master's and Ph.D. degree holders usually enjoy independence in their work and become qualified to engage in research, develop statistical methods, or, after a number of years of experience in a particular area, become statistical consultants.

Job Outlook

Little or no change is expected in employment of statisticians over the 2000-10 period. However, job opportunities should remain favorable for individuals with statistical degrees, although many of these positions will not carry the explicit job title statistician. This is especially true of jobs that involve the analysis and interpretation of data from other disciplines such as economics, biological science, psychology, or engineering. In addition to the limited number of jobs resulting from growth, a number of openings will become available as statisticians retire, transfer to other occupations, or leave the workforce for other reasons.

Among graduates with a bachelor's or master's degree in statistics, those with a strong background in an allied field, such as finance, engineering, or computer science, should have the best prospects of finding jobs related to their field of study. Federal agencies will hire statisticians in many fields, including demography, agriculture, consumer and producer surveys, Social Security, healthcare, and environmental quality. Competition for entry-level positions in the federal government is expected to be strong for those just meeting the minimum qualification standards for statisticians, because the federal government is one of the few employers that considers a bachelor's degree to be an adequate entry-level qualification. Those who meet state certification requirements may become high school statistics teachers.

Manufacturing firms will hire statisticians with master's and doctoral degrees for quality control of various products, including pharmaceuticals, motor vehicles, chemicals, and food. For example, pharmaceutical firms employ statisticians to assess the safety and effectiveness of new drugs. To address global product competition, motor vehicle manufacturers will need statisticians to improve the quality of automobiles, trucks, and their components by developing and testing new designs. Statisticians with knowledge of engineering and the physical sciences will find jobs in research and development, working with teams of scientists and engineers to help improve design and production processes to ensure consistent quality of newly developed products. Many statisticians also will find opportunities developing statistical software for computer software manufacturing firms.

Business firms will rely heavily on workers with a background in statistics to forecast sales, analyze business conditions, and help solve management problems in order to maximize profits. In addition, consulting firms increasingly will offer sophisticated statistical services to other businesses. Because of the widespread use of computers in this field, statisticians in all industries should have good computer programming skills and knowledge of statistical software.

Earnings

Median annual earnings of statisticians were $51,990 in 2000. The middle 50 percent earned between $37,160 and $69,220. The lowest 10 percent had earnings of less than $28,430, while the highest 10 percent earned more than $86,660.

The average annual salary for statisticians in the federal government in nonsupervisory, supervisory, and managerial positions was $68,900 in 2001, while mathematical statisticians averaged $76,530. According to a 2001 survey by the National Association of Colleges and Employers, starting salary offers for mathematics/statistics graduates with a bachelor's degree averaged $46,466 a year.

Related Occupations

People in numerous occupations work with statistics. Among these are actuaries; mathematicians; operations research analysts; computer systems analysts, database administrators, and computer scientists; computer programmers; computer software engineers; engineers; economists and market and survey researchers; and financial analysts and personal financial advisors.

Sources of Additional Information

For information about career opportunities in statistics, contact:

- American Statistical Association, 1429 Duke St., Alexandria, VA 22314. Internet: http://www.amstat.org

For more information on doctoral-level careers and training in mathematics, a field closely related to statistics, contact:

- American Mathematical Society, 201 Charles St., Providence, RI 02940. Internet: http://www.ams.org

Surgical Technologists

(O*NET 29-2055.00)

Significant Points

- Training programs last 9 to 24 months and lead to a certificate, diploma, or associate degree.

- Job opportunities are expected to be favorable.

- Hospitals will continue to be the primary employer, although much faster employment growth is expected in offices of physicians and in outpatient care centers, including ambulatory surgical centers.

Nature of the Work

Surgical technologists, also called scrubs and surgical or operating room technicians, assist in surgical operations under the supervision of surgeons, registered nurses, or other surgical personnel. Surgical technologists are members of operating room teams, which most commonly include surgeons, anesthesiologists, and circulating nurses. Before an operation, surgical technologists help prepare the operating room by setting up surgical instruments and equipment, sterile drapes, and sterile solutions. They assemble both sterile and nonsterile equipment, as well as adjust and check it to ensure it is working properly. Technologists also get patients ready for surgery by washing, shaving, and disinfecting incision sites. They transport patients to the operating room, help position them on the operating table, and cover them with sterile surgical "drapes." Technologists also observe patients' vital signs, check charts, and assist the surgical team with putting on sterile gowns and gloves.

During surgery, technologists pass instruments and other sterile supplies to surgeons and surgeon assistants. They may hold retractors, cut sutures, and help count sponges, needles, supplies, and instruments. Surgical technologists help prepare, care for, and dispose of specimens taken for laboratory analysis and help apply dressings. Some operate sterilizers, lights, or suction machines, and help operate diagnostic equipment.

After an operation, surgical technologists may help transfer patients to the recovery room and clean and restock the operating room.

Working Conditions

Surgical technologists work in clean, well-lighted, cool environments. They must stand for long periods and remain alert during operations. At times they may be exposed to communicable diseases and unpleasant sights, odors, and materials.

Most surgical technologists work a regular 40-hour week, although they may be on call or work nights, weekends and holidays on a rotating basis.

Employment

Surgical technologists held about 72,000 jobs in 2002. About three-quarters of jobs for surgical technologists were in hospitals, mainly in operating and delivery rooms. Other jobs were in offices of physicians or dentists who perform outpatient surgery and in outpatient care centers, including ambulatory surgical centers. A few, known as private scrubs, are employed directly by surgeons who have special surgical teams, like those for liver transplants.

Training, Other Qualifications, and Advancement

Surgical technologists receive their training in formal programs offered by community and junior colleges, vocational schools, universities, hospitals, and the military. In 2002, the Commission on Accreditation of Allied Health Education Programs (CAAHEP) recognized 361 accredited programs. High school graduation normally is required for admission. Programs last 9 to 24 months and lead to a certificate, diploma, or associate degree.

Programs provide classroom education and supervised clinical experience. Students take courses in anatomy, physiology, microbiology, pharmacology, professional ethics, and medical terminology. Other studies cover the care and safety of patients during surgery, sterile techniques, and surgical procedures. Students also learn to sterilize instruments; prevent and control infection; and handle special drugs, solutions, supplies, and equipment.

Most employers prefer to hire certified technologists. Technologists may obtain voluntary professional certification from the Liaison Council on Certification for the Surgical Technologist by graduating from a CAAHEP-accredited program and passing a national certification examination. They may then use the Certified Surgical Technologist (CST) designation. Continuing education or reexamination is required to maintain certification, which must be renewed every 4 years.

Certification may also be obtained from the National Center for Competency Testing. To qualify to take the exam, candidates follow one of three paths: complete an accredited training program, undergo a 2-year hospital on-the-job training program, or acquire seven years of experience working in the field. After passing the exam, individuals may use the designation Tech in Surgery-Certified, TS-C (NCCT). This certification may be renewed every 5 years through either continuing education or reexamination.

Surgical technologists need manual dexterity to handle instruments quickly. They also must be conscientious, orderly, and emotionally stable to handle the demands of the operating room environment. Technologists must respond quickly and know procedures well to have instruments ready for surgeons without having to be told. They are expected to keep abreast of new developments in the field. Recommended high school courses include health, biology, chemistry, and mathematics.

Technologists advance by specializing in a particular area of surgery, such as neurosurgery or open heart surgery. They also may work as circulating technologists. A circulating technologist is the "unsterile" member of the surgical team who prepares patients; helps with anesthesia; obtains and opens packages for the "sterile" persons to remove the sterile contents during the procedure; interviews the patient before surgery; keeps a written account of the surgical procedure; and answers the surgeon's questions about the patient during the surgery. With additional training, some technologists advance to first assistants, who help with retracting, sponging, suturing, cauterizing bleeders, and closing and treating wounds. Some surgical technologists manage central supply departments in hospitals, or take positions with insurance companies, sterile supply services, and operating equipment firms.

Job Outlook

Job opportunities are expected to be favorable. Employment of surgical technologists is expected to grow faster than the average for all occupations through the year 2012 as the volume of surgery increases. The number of surgical procedures is expected to rise as the population grows and ages. As members of the baby boom generation approach retirement age, the over-50 population, who generally require more surgical procedures, will account for a larger portion of the general population. Technological advances, such as fiber optics and laser technology, will also permit new surgical procedures to be performed.

Hospitals will continue to be the primary employer of surgical technologists, although much faster employment growth is expected in offices of physicians and in outpatient care centers, including ambulatory surgical centers.

Earnings

Median annual earnings of surgical technologists were $31,210 in 2002. The middle 50 percent earned between $26,000 and $36,740. The lowest 10 percent earned less than $21,920, and the highest 10 percent earned more than $43,470. Median annual earnings of surgical technologists in 2002 were $33,790 in offices of physicians and $30,590 in general medical and surgical hospitals.

Related Occupations

Other health occupations requiring approximately 1 year of training after high school include dental assistants, licensed practical and licensed vocational nurses, clinical laboratory technicians, and medical assistants.

Sources of Additional Information

For additional information on a career as a surgical technologist and a list of CAAHEP-accredited programs, contact:

- Association of Surgical Technologists, 7108-C South Alton Way, Centennial, CO 80112. Internet: http://www.ast.org

For information on becoming a Certified Surgical Technologist, contact:

- Liaison Council on Certification for the Surgical Technologist, 128 S. Tejon St., Suite 301, Colorado Springs, CO 80903. Internet: http://www.lcc-st.org

For information on becoming a Tech in Surgery-Certified, contact:

- National Center for Competency Testing, 7007 College Blvd., Suite 250, Overland Park, KS 66211.

Surveyors, Cartographers, Photogrammetrists, and Surveying Technicians

(O*NET 17-1021.00, 17-1022.00, 17-3031.01, and 17-3031.02)

Significant Points

- Almost 2 out of 3 jobs were in architectural, engineering, and related services.
- Opportunities will be best for surveyors, cartographers, and photogrammetrists who have at least a bachelor's degree and strong technical skills.
- Computer skills enhance employment opportunities.

Nature of the Work

Several different types of workers are responsible for measuring and mapping the earth's surface. Traditional *land surveyors* establish official land, air space, and water boundaries. They write descriptions of land for deeds, leases, and other legal documents; define airspace for airports; and measure construction and mineral sites. Other surveyors provide data relevant to the shape, contour, location, elevation, or dimension of land or land features. *Cartographers* compile geographic, political, and cultural information and prepare maps of large areas. *Photogrammetrists* measure and analyze aerial photographs that are subsequently used to prepare detailed maps and drawings. *Surveying technicians* assist land surveyors by operating survey instruments and collecting information in the field and by performing computations and computer-aided drafting in offices. *Mapping technicians* calculate mapmaking information from field notes. They also draw topographical maps and verify their accuracy.

Land surveyors manage survey parties who measure distances, directions, and angles between points and elevations of points, lines, and contours on, above, and below the earth's surface. They plan the fieldwork, select known survey reference points, and determine the precise location of important features in the survey area. Surveyors research legal records, look for evidence of previous boundaries, and analyze the data to determine the location of boundary lines. They also record the results of surveys, verify the accuracy of data, and prepare plots, maps, and reports. Surveyors who establish boundaries must be licensed by the state in which they work. Known as professional land surveyors, they are sometimes called to provide expert testimony in court cases concerning matters pertaining to surveying.

A survey party gathers the information needed by the land surveyor. A typical survey party consists of a party chief and one or more surveying technicians and helpers. The party chief, who may be either a land surveyor or a senior surveying technician, leads day-to-day work activities. Surveying technicians assist the party chief by adjusting and operating surveying instruments, such as the theodolite (used to measure horizontal and vertical angles) and electronic distance-measuring equipment. Surveying technicians or assistants position and hold the vertical rods, or targets, that the theodolite operator sights on to measure angles, distances, or elevations. In addition, they may hold measuring tapes, if electronic distance-measuring equipment is not used. Surveying technicians compile notes, make sketches, and enter the data obtained from surveying instruments into computers. Survey parties also may include laborers or helpers who perform less skilled duties, such as clearing brush from sight lines, driving stakes, or carrying equipment.

New technology is changing the nature of the work of surveyors and surveying technicians. On larger projects, surveyors are increasingly using the Global Positioning System (GPS), a satellite system that locates points on the earth to a high degree of precision by using radio signals transmitted via satellites. To use this system, a surveyor places a satellite signal receiver—a small instrument mounted on a tripod—on a desired point. The receiver simultaneously collects information from several satellites to establish a precise position. The receiver also can be placed in a vehicle for tracing out road systems. Because receivers now come in different sizes and shapes, and because the cost of receivers has fallen, much more surveying work can be done with GPS. Surveyors then must interpret and check the results produced by the new technology.

Cartographers measure, map, and chart the earth's surface. Their work involves everything from performing geographical research and compiling data to actually producing maps. Cartographers collect, analyze, and interpret both spatial data—such as latitude, longitude, elevation, and distance—and nonspatial data—for example, population density, land-use patterns, annual precipitation levels, and demographic characteristics. They prepare maps in either digital or graphic form, using information provided by geodetic surveys, aerial photographs, and satellite data. *Photogrammetrists* prepare detailed maps and drawings from aerial photographs, usually of areas that are inaccessible, difficult, or less cost efficient to survey by other methods. *Map editors* develop and verify the contents of maps, using aerial photographs and other reference sources. Some states require photogrammetrists to be licensed as professional land surveyors.

Some surveyors perform specialized functions closer to those of cartographers than to those of traditional surveyors. For example, *geodetic surveyors* use high-accuracy techniques, including satellite observations (remote sensing), to measure large areas of the earth's surface. *Geophysical prospecting surveyors* mark sites for subsurface exploration, usually in relation to petroleum. *Marine or hydrographic surveyors* survey harbors, rivers, and other bodies of water to determine shorelines, the topography of the bottom, water depth, and other features.

The work of surveyors and cartographers is changing because of advancements in technology, including not only the GPS, but also new earth resources data satellites, improved aerial photography, and geographic information systems (GIS)—computerized data banks of spatial data, along with the hardware, software, and staff needed to use them. These systems are capable of assembling, integrating, analyzing, and displaying data identified according to location. A GIS typically is used to handle maps which combine information that is useful for environmental studies, geology, engineering, planning, business marketing, and other

disciplines. As more of these systems are developed, a new type of mapping scientist is emerging from the older specialties of photogrammetrist and cartographer: the *geographic information specialist* combines the functions of mapping science and surveying into a broader field concerned with the collection and analysis of geographic data.

Working Conditions

Surveyors usually work an 8-hour day, 5 days a week, and may spend a lot of time outdoors. Sometimes they work longer hours during the summer, when weather and light conditions are most suitable for fieldwork. Seasonal demands for longer hours are related to demand for specific surveying services. Home purchases traditionally are related to the start and end of the school year; construction is related to the materials to be used (unlike wood framing, concrete and asphalt are restricted by outside temperatures); and aerial photography is most effective when the leaves are off the trees.

Land surveyors and technicians engage in active, sometimes strenuous, work. They often stand for long periods, walk considerable distances, and climb hills with heavy packs of instruments and other equipment. They also can be exposed to all types of weather. Traveling often is part of the job, and land surveyors and technicians may commute long distances, stay away from home overnight, or temporarily relocate near a survey site.

Although surveyors can spend considerable time indoors, planning surveys, analyzing data, and preparing reports and maps, cartographers and photogrammetrists spend virtually all of their time in offices and seldom visit the sites they are mapping.

Employment

Surveyors, cartographers, photogrammetrists, and surveying technicians held about 124,000 jobs in 2002. Architectural, engineering, and related services firms—including firms that provided surveying and mapping services to other industries on a contract basis—provided about two-thirds of jobs for these workers. Federal, state, and local governmental agencies provided almost 1 in 6 jobs. Major federal government employers are the U.S. Geological Survey (USGS), the Bureau of Land Management (BLM), the Army Corps of Engineers, the Forest Service (USFS), the National Oceanic and Atmospheric Administration (NOAA), the National Imagery and Mapping Agency (NIMA), and the Federal Emergency Management Agency (FEMA). Most surveyors in state and local government work for highway departments and urban planning and redevelopment agencies. Construction firms, mining and oil and gas extraction companies, and utilities also employ surveyors, cartographers, photogrammetrists, and surveying technicians. Only a small number were self-employed in 2002.

Training, Other Qualifications, and Advancement

Most people prepare for a career as a licensed surveyor by combining postsecondary school courses in surveying with extensive on-the-job training. However, as technology advances, a 4-year college degree is increasingly becoming a prerequisite. About 50 universities now offer 4-year programs leading to a B.S. degree in surveying. Junior and community colleges, technical institutes, and vocational schools offer 1-, 2-, and 3-year programs in both surveying and surveying technology.

All 50 states and all U.S. territories (Puerto Rico, Guam, the Mariana Islands, and the Virgin Islands) license land surveyors. For licensure, most state licensing boards require that individuals pass a written examination given by the National Council of Examiners for Engineering and Surveying. Most states also require surveyors to pass a written examination prepared by the state licensing board. In addition, candidates must meet varying standards of formal education and work experience in the field.

In the past, many with little formal training in surveying started as members of survey crews and worked their way up to become licensed surveyors. However, because of advancing technology and rising licensing standards, formal education requirements are increasing. Specific requirements vary among states. Generally, the quickest route to licensure is a combination of 4 years of college, up to 4 years of experience under the supervision of an experienced surveyor (a few states do not require any such experience), and passing the licensing examinations. An increasing number of states require a bachelor's degree in surveying or in a closely related field, such as civil engineering or forestry (with courses in surveying), regardless of the number of years of experience. Many states also have a continuing education requirement.

High school students interested in surveying should take courses in algebra, geometry, trigonometry, drafting, mechanical drawing, and computer science. High school graduates with no formal training in surveying usually start as apprentices. Beginners with postsecondary school training in surveying usually can start as technicians or assistants. With on-the-job experience and formal training in surveying—either in an institutional program or from a correspondence school—workers may advance to senior survey technician, then to party chief, and, in some cases, to licensed surveyor (depending on state licensing requirements).

The National Society of Professional Surveyors, a member organization of the American Congress on Surveying and Mapping, has a voluntary certification program for surveying technicians. Technicians are certified at four levels requiring progressive amounts of experience, in addition to the passing of written examinations. Although not required for state licensure, many employers require certification for promotion to positions with greater responsibilities.

Surveyors should have the ability to visualize objects, distances, sizes, and abstract forms. They must work with precision and accuracy, because mistakes can be costly. Members of a survey party must be in good physical condition, because they work outdoors and often carry equipment over difficult terrain. They need good eyesight, coordination, and hearing to communicate verbally and manually (using hand signals). Surveying is a cooperative operation, so good interpersonal skills and the ability to work as part of a team are important. Good office skills also are essential, because surveyors must be able to research old deeds and other legal papers and prepare reports that document their work.

Cartographers and photogrammetrists usually have a bachelor's degree in a field such as engineering, forestry, geography, or a physical science. Although it is possible to enter these positions through previous experience as a photogrammetric or cartographic technician, nowadays most cartographic and photogrammetric technicians have had some specialized postsecondary school training. With the development of GIS, cartographers and photogrammetrists need additional education and stronger technical skills—including more experience with computers—than in the past.

The American Society for Photogrammetry and Remote Sensing has a voluntary certification program for photogrammetrists. To qualify for this professional distinction, individuals must meet work experience standards and pass an oral or a written examination.

Job Outlook

Overall employment of surveyors, cartographers, photogrammetrists, and surveying technicians is expected to grow about as fast as the average for all occupations through the year 2012. The widespread availability and use of advanced technologies, such as GPS, GIS, and remote sensing, will continue to increase both the accuracy and productivity of these workers, resulting in modest overall growth in employment. However, job openings will continue to result from the need to replace workers who transfer to other occupations or who leave the labor force altogether.

Employment of surveying and mapping technicians is expected to grow faster than the average for all occupations through 2012. The short training period needed to learn to operate the equipment, the current lack of any formal testing or licensing, the growing demand for people to do basic GIS-related data-entry work, and relatively lower wages all encourage demand for these technicians. However, many persons possess the basic skills needed to qualify for the jobs that are available, so competition for job openings may result.

As technologies become more complex, opportunities will be best for surveyors, cartographers, and photogrammetrists who have at least a bachelor's degree and strong technical skills. Increasing demand for geographic data, as opposed to traditional surveying services, will mean better opportunities for cartographers and photogrammetrists who are involved in the development and use of geographic and land information systems. New technologies, such as GPS and GIS, also may enhance employment opportunities for surveyors, as well as for those surveying technicians who have the educational background and who have acquired technical skills that enable them to work with the new systems. At the same time, upgraded licensing requirements will continue to limit opportunities for professional advancement for those without bachelor's degrees.

Opportunities for surveyors, cartographers, and photogrammetrists should remain concentrated in architectural, engineering, and related services firms. However, nontraditional areas, such as urban planning, emergency preparedness, and natural resource exploration and mapping, also should provide employment growth, particularly with regard to producing maps for the management of emergencies and updating maps with the newly available technology. Continued growth in construction through 2012 will require surveyors to lay out streets, shopping centers, housing developments, factories, office buildings, and recreation areas, while setting aside flood plains, wetlands, wildlife habitats, and environmentally sensitive areas for protection. However, employment may fluctuate from year to year along with construction activity or with mapping needs for land and resource management.

Earnings

Median annual earnings of cartographers and photogrammetrists were $42,870 in 2002. The middle 50 percent earned between $32,580 and $55,610. The lowest 10 percent earned less than $25,810 and the highest 10 percent earned more than $69,320.

Median annual earnings of surveyors were $39,970 in 2002. The middle 50 percent earned between $29,320 and $53,440. The lowest 10 percent earned less than $22,260, and the highest 10 percent earned more than $67,700. Median hourly earnings of surveyors employed in architectural, engineering, and related services were $38,370 in 2002.

Median annual earnings of surveying and mapping technicians were $29,230 in 2002. The middle 50 percent earned between $22,640 and $39,070 in 2002. The lowest 10 percent earned less than $18,490, and the highest 10 percent earned more than $48,970. Median annual earnings of surveying and mapping technicians employed in architectural, engineering, and related services were $27,130 in 2002, while those employed by local governments had median annual earnings of $33,680.

In 2003, land surveyors in nonsupervisory, supervisory, and managerial positions in the federal government earned an average salary of $62,980; cartographers, $67,989; geodetic technicians, $55,374; surveying technicians, $33,316; and cartographic technicians, $43,517.

Related Occupations

Surveying is related to the work of civil engineers, architects, and landscape architects because an accurate survey is the first step in land development and construction projects. Cartography and geodetic surveying are related to the work of environmental scientists and geoscientists, who study the earth's internal composition, surface, and atmosphere. Cartography also is related to the work of geographers and urban and regional planners, who study and decide how the earth's surface is to be used.

Sources of Additional Information

For career information on surveyors, cartographers, photogrammetrists, and surveying technicians, contact:

- The American Congress on Surveying and Mapping, Suite #403, 6 Montgomery Village Ave., Gaithersburg, MD 20879. Internet: http://www.acsm.net

Information about career opportunities, licensure requirements, and the surveying technician certification program is available from:

- National Society of Professional Surveyors, Suite #403, 6 Montgomery Village Ave., Gaithersburg, MD 20879. Internet: http://www.acsm.net/nsps

For information on a career as a geodetic surveyor, contact:

- American Association of Geodetic Surveying (AAGS), Suite #403, 6 Montgomery Village Ave., Gaithersburg, MD 20879. Internet: http://www.acsm.net/aags

General information on careers in photogrammetry and remote sensing is available from:

- ASPRS: The Imaging and Geospatial Information Society, 5410 Grosvenor Ln., Suite 210, Bethesda, MD 20814-2160. Internet: http://www.asprs.org

Television, Video, and Motion Picture Camera Operators and Editors

(O*NET 27-4031.00 and 27-4032.00)

Significant Points

- Workers acquire their skills through on-the-job or formal postsecondary training.

- Technical expertise, a "good eye," imagination, and creativity are essential.

- Keen competition for job openings is expected, because many talented peopled are attracted to the field.

- About one in five camera operators are self-employed.

Nature of the Work

Television, video, and motion picture camera operators produce images that tell a story, inform or entertain an audience, or record an event. *Film and video editors* edit soundtracks, film, and video for the motion picture, cable, and broadcast television industries. Some camera operators do their own editing.

Making commercial-quality movies and video programs requires technical expertise and creativity. Producing successful images requires choosing and presenting interesting material, selecting appropriate equipment, and applying a good eye and steady hand to assure smooth, natural movement of the camera.

Camera operators use television, video, or motion picture cameras to shoot a wide range of material, including television series, studio programs, news and sporting events, music videos, motion pictures, documentaries, and training sessions. Some camera operators film or videotape private ceremonies and special events. Those who record images on videotape are often called *videographers*. Many are employed by independent television stations, local affiliates, large cable and television networks, or smaller, independent production companies. *Studio camera operators* work in a broadcast studio and usually videotape their subjects from a fixed position. *News camera operators*, also called *electronic news gathering (ENG) operators*, work as part of a reporting team, following newsworthy events as they unfold. To capture live events, they must anticipate the action and act quickly. ENG operators may need to edit raw footage on the spot for relay to a television affiliate for broadcast.

Camera operators employed in the entertainment field use motion picture cameras to film movies, television programs, and commercials. Those who film motion pictures are also known as *cinematographers*. Some specialize in filming cartoons or special effects. They may be an integral part of the action, using cameras in any of several different mounts. For example, the camera operator can be stationary and shoot whatever passes in front of the lens, or the camera can be mounted on a track, with the camera operator responsible for shooting the scene from different angles or directions. More recently, the introduction of digital cameras has enhanced the number of angles and the clarity that a camera operator can provide. Other camera operators sit on cranes and follow the action while crane operators move them into position. *Steadicam operators* mount a harness and carry the camera on their shoulders to provide a clear picture while they move about the action. Camera operators who work in the entertainment field often meet with directors, actors, editors, and camera assistants to discuss ways of filming, editing, and improving scenes.

Working Conditions

Working conditions for camera operators and editors vary considerably. Those employed in government, television and cable networks, and advertising agencies usually work a 5-day, 40-hour week. By contrast, ENG operators often work long, irregular hours and must be available to work on short notice. Camera operators and editors working in motion picture production also may work long, irregular hours.

ENG operators and those who cover major events, such as conventions or sporting events, frequently travel locally, stay overnight on assignments, or travel to distant places for longer periods. Camera operators filming television programs or motion pictures may travel to film on location.

Some camera operators—especially ENG operators covering accidents, natural disasters, civil unrest, or military conflicts—work in uncomfortable or even dangerous surroundings. Many camera operators must wait long hours in all kinds of weather for an event to take place and must stand or walk for long periods while carrying heavy equipment. ENG operators often work under strict deadlines.

Employment

Television, video, and motion picture camera operators held about 28,000 jobs in 2002, and film and video editors held about 19,000. About 1 in 5 camera operators were self-employed. Some self-employed camera operators contracted with television networks, documentary or independent filmmakers, advertising agencies, or trade show or convention sponsors to work on individual projects for a predetermined fee, often at a daily rate.

Most of the salaried camera operators were employed by television broadcasting stations or motion picture studios. More than half of the salaried film and video editors worked for motion picture studios. Most camera operators and editors worked in large metropolitan areas.

Training, Other Qualifications, and Advancement

Employers usually seek applicants with a "good eye," imagination, and creativity, as well as a good technical understanding of how the camera operates. Television, video, and motion picture camera operators and editors usually acquire their skills through on-the-job training or formal postsecondary training at vocational schools, colleges, universities, or photographic institutes. Formal education may be required for some positions.

Many universities, community and junior colleges, vocational-technical institutes, and private trade and technical schools offer courses in camera operation and videography. Basic courses cover equipment, processes, and techniques. Bachelor's degree programs, especially those including business courses, provide a well-rounded education.

Individuals interested in camera operations should subscribe to videographic newsletters and magazines, join clubs, and seek summer or part-time employment in cable and television networks, motion picture studios, or camera and video stores.

Camera operators in entry-level jobs learn to set up lights, cameras, and other equipment. They may receive routine assignments requiring adjustments to their cameras or decisions on what subject matter to capture. Camera operators in the film and television industries usually are hired for a project on the basis of recommendations from individuals such as producers, directors of photography, and camera assistants from previous projects or through interviews with the producer. ENG and studio camera operators who work for television affiliates usually start in small markets to gain experience.

Camera operators need good eyesight, artistic ability, and hand-eye coordination. They should be patient, accurate, and detail oriented. Camera operators also should have good communication skills and, if needed, the ability to hold a camera by hand for extended periods.

Camera operators who run their own businesses, or freelance, need business skills as well as talent. These individuals must know how to submit bids, write contracts, get permission to shoot on locations that normally are not open to the public, obtain releases to use film or tape of people, price their services, secure copyright protection for their work, and keep financial records.

With increased experience, operators may advance to more demanding assignments or to positions with larger or network television stations. Advancement for ENG operators may mean moving to larger media markets. Other camera operators and editors may become directors of photography for movie studios, advertising agencies, or television programs. Some teach at technical schools, film schools, or universities.

Job Outlook

Television, video, and motion picture camera operators and editors can expect keen competition for job openings because the work is attractive to many people. The number of individuals interested in positions as videographers and movie camera operators usually is much greater than the number of openings. Those who succeed in landing a salaried job or attracting enough work to earn a living by freelancing are likely to be the most creative, highly motivated, able to adapt to rapidly changing technologies, and adept at operating a business. Related work experience or job-related training also can benefit prospective camera operators.

Employment of camera operators and editors is expected to grow about as fast as the average for all occupations through 2012. Rapid expansion of the entertainment market, especially motion picture production and distribution, will spur growth of camera operators. In addition, computer and Internet services will provide new outlets for interactive productions. Growth will be tempered, however, by the increased off-shore production of motion pictures. Camera operators will be needed to film made-for-the-Internet broadcasts, such as live music videos, digital movies, sports features, and general information or entertainment pro-gramming. These images can be delivered directly into the home either on compact discs or over the Internet. Job growth also is expected in radio and television broadcasting.

Earnings

Median annual earnings for television, video, and motion picture camera operators were $32,720 in 2002. The middle 50 percent earned between $20,610 and $51,000. The lowest 10 percent earned less than $14,710, and the highest 10 percent earned more than $65,070. Median annual earnings were $46,540 in the motion picture and video industries and $25,830 in radio and television broadcasting.

Median annual earnings for film and video editors were $38,270 in 2002. The middle 50 percent earned between $26,780 and $55,300. The lowest 10 percent earned less than $20,030, and the highest 10 percent earned more than $78,070. Median annual earnings were $41,440 in the motion picture and video industries, which employ the largest numbers of film and video editors.

Many camera operators who work in film or video are freelancers whose earnings tend to fluctuate each year. Because most freelance camera operators purchase their own equipment, they incur considerable expense acquiring and maintaining cameras and accessories. Some camera operators belong to unions, including the International Alliance of Theatrical Stage Employees and the National Association of Broadcast Employees and Technicians.

Related Occupations

Related arts and media occupations include artists and related workers, broadcast and sound engineering technicians and radio operators, designers, and photographers.

Sources of Additional Information

Information about career and employment opportunities for camera operators and film and video editors is available from local offices of state employment service agencies, local offices of the relevant trade unions, and local television and film production companies that employ these workers.

Tool and Die Makers

(O*NET 51-4111.00)

Significant Points

- Most tool and die makers train for 4 or 5 years in apprenticeships or postsecondary programs; employers typically recommend apprenticeship training.

- Jobseekers with the appropriate skills and background should enjoy excellent opportunities and very high earnings.

Nature of the Work

Tool and die makers are among the most highly skilled workers in manufacturing. These workers produce tools, dies, and special guiding and holding devices that enable machines to manufacture a variety of products we use daily—from clothing and furniture to heavy equipment and parts for aircraft.

Toolmakers craft precision tools and machines that are used to cut, shape, and form metal and other materials. They also produce jigs and fixtures (devices that hold metal while it is bored, stamped, or drilled) and gauges and other measuring devices. Die makers construct metal forms (dies) that are used to shape metal in stamping and forging operations. They also make metal molds for diecasting and for molding plastics, ceramics, and composite materials. Some tool and die makers craft prototypes of parts, and then determine how best to manufacture the part. In addition to developing, designing, and producing new tools and dies, these workers also may repair worn or damaged tools, dies, gauges, jigs, and fixtures.

To perform these functions, tool and die makers employ many types of machine tools and precision measuring instruments. They also must be familiar with the machining properties, such as hardness and heat tolerance, of a wide variety of common metals and alloys. As a result, tool and die makers are knowledgeable in machining operations, mathematics, and blueprint reading. In fact, tool and die makers often are considered highly specialized machinists. The main difference between tool and die makers and machinists is that machinists normally make a single part during the production process, while tool and die makers make parts and machines used in the production process.

Working from blueprints, tool and die makers first must plan the sequence of operations necessary to manufacture the tool or die. Next, they measure and mark the pieces of metal that will be cut to form parts of the final product. At this point, tool and die makers cut, drill, or bore the part as required, checking to ensure that the final product meets specifications. Finally, these workers assemble the parts and perform finishing jobs such as filing, grinding, and polishing surfaces.

Modern technology has changed the ways in which tool and die makers perform their jobs. Today, for example, these workers often use computer-aided design (CAD) to develop products and parts. Specifications entered into computer programs can be used to electronically develop drawings for the required tools and dies. Numerical tool and process control programmers use computer-aided manufacturing (CAM) programs to convert electronic drawings into computer programs that contain instructions for a sequence of cutting tool operations. Once these programs are developed, computer numerically controlled (CNC) machines follow the set of instructions contained in the program to produce the part. Computer-controlled machine tool operators or machinists normally operate CNC machines; however, tool and die makers are trained in both operating CNC machines and writing CNC programs, and they may perform either task. CNC programs are stored electronically for future use, saving time and increasing worker productivity.

After machining the parts, tool and die makers carefully check the accuracy of the parts using many tools, including coordinate measuring machines (CMM), which use software and sensor arms to compare the dimensions of the part to electronic blueprints. Next, they assemble the different parts into a functioning machine. They file, grind, shim, and adjust the different parts to properly fit them together. Finally, the tool and die makers set up a test run using the tools or dies they have made to make sure that the manufactured parts meet specifications. If problems occur, they compensate by adjusting the tools or dies.

Working Conditions

Tool and die makers usually work in toolrooms. These areas are quieter than the production floor because there are fewer machines in use at one time. They also are generally kept clean and cool to minimize heat-related expansion of metal workpieces and to accommodate the growing number of computer-operated machines. To minimize the exposure of workers to moving parts, machines have guards and shields. Most computer-controlled machines are totally enclosed, minimizing the exposure of workers to noise, dust, and the lubricants used to cool workpieces during machining. Tool and die makers also must follow safety rules and wear protective equipment, such as safety glasses to shield against bits of flying metal, earplugs to protect against noise, and gloves and masks to reduce exposure to hazardous lubricants and cleaners. These workers also need stamina because they often spend much of the day on their feet and may do moderately heavy lifting.

Companies employing tool and die makers have traditionally operated only one shift per day. Overtime and weekend work are common, especially during peak production periods.

Employment

Tool and die makers held about 109,000 jobs in 2002. Most worked in industries that manufacture metalworking machinery, transportation equipment (such as motor vehicle parts and aerospace products), and fabricated metal products, as well as plastics product manufacturing. Although they are found throughout the country, jobs are most plentiful in the Midwest, Northeast, and West, where many of the metalworking industries are located.

Training, Other Qualifications, and Advancement

Most tool and die makers learn their trade through 4 or 5 years of education and training in formal apprenticeships or postsecondary programs. Apprenticeship programs include a mix of classroom instruction and job experience and often require 10,400 hours, or about 5 years to complete. According to most employers these apprenticeship programs are the best way to learn all aspects of tool and die making. A growing number of tool and die makers receive most of their formal classroom training from community and technical colleges, sometimes in conjunction with an apprenticeship program.

Even after completing their apprenticeship, tool and die makers still need years of experience to become highly skilled. Most specialize in making certain types of tools, molds, or dies.

Tool and die maker trainees learn to operate milling machines, lathes, grinders, wire electrical discharge machines, and other machine tools. They also learn to use handtools for fitting and assembling gauges, and other mechanical and metal-forming equipment. In addition, they study metalworking processes, such as heat treating and plating. Classroom training usually consists of mechanical drawing, tool designing, tool programming, blueprint reading, and mathematics courses, including algebra, geometry, trigonometry, and basic statistics. Tool and die makers increasingly must have good computer skills to work with CAD technology, CNC machine tools, and computerized measuring machines.

Workers who become tool and die makers without completing formal apprenticeships generally acquire their skills through a combination of informal on-the-job training and classroom instruction at a vocational school or community college. They often begin as machine operators and gradually take on more difficult assignments. Many machinists become tool and die makers.

Because tools and dies must meet strict specifications—precision to one ten-thousandth of an inch is common—the work of tool and die makers requires skill with precision measuring devices and a high degree of patience and attention to detail. Good eyesight is essential. Persons entering this occupation also should be mechanically inclined, able to work and solve problems independently, and capable of doing work that requires concentration and physical effort.

There are several ways for skilled workers to advance. Some move into supervisory and administrative positions in their firms; many obtain their college degree and go into engineering or tool design; and some may start their own shops.

Job Outlook

Applicants with the appropriate skills and background should enjoy excellent opportunities for tool and die maker jobs. The number of workers receiving training in this occupation is expected to continue to be fewer than the number of openings created each year by tool and die makers who retire or transfer to other occupations. As more of these highly skilled workers retire, employers in certain parts of the country report difficulty attracting well-trained applicants. A major factor limiting the number of people entering the occupation is that many young people who have the

educational and personal qualifications necessary to learn tool and die making may prefer to attend college or may not wish to enter production-related occupations.

Despite expected excellent employment opportunities, little or no growth in employment of tool and die makers is projected over the 2002-12 period because advancements in automation, including CNC machine tools and computer-aided design, should improve worker productivity, thus limiting employment. On the other hand, tool and die makers play a key role in building and maintaining advanced automated manufacturing equipment. As firms invest in new equipment, modify production techniques, and implement product design changes more rapidly, they will continue to rely heavily on skilled tool and die makers for retooling.

Earnings

Median hourly earnings of tool and die makers were $20.54 in 2002. The middle 50 percent earned between $16.33 and $25.64. The lowest 10 percent had earnings of less than $12.97, while the top 10 percent earned more than $30.74. Median hourly earnings in the manufacturing industries employing the largest numbers of tool and die makers in 2002 are shown below.

Motor vehicle parts manufacturing	$25.64
Metalworking machinery manufacturing	20.02
Forging and stamping	19.97
Plastics product manufacturing	19.79

Related Occupations

The occupations most closely related to the work of tool and die makers are other machining occupations. These include machinists; computer-control programmers and operators; and machine setters, operators, and tenders—metal and plastic. Another occupation that requires precision and skill in working with metal is welding, soldering, and brazing workers.

Like tool and die makers, assemblers and fabricators assemble complex machinery. When measuring parts, tool and die makers use some of the same tools and equipment that inspectors, testers, sorters, samplers, and weighers use in their jobs.

Sources of Additional Information

For career information and to have inquiries on training and employment referred to member companies, contact:

● Precision Machine Products Association, 6700 West Snowville Rd., Brecksville, OH 44141-3292. Internet: http://www.pmpa.org

For lists of schools and employers with tool and die apprenticeship and training programs, contact:

● National Tooling and Machining Association, 9300 Livingston Rd., Ft. Washington, MD 20744. Internet: http://www.ntma.org

For information on careers, education and training, earnings, and apprenticeship opportunities in metalworking, contact:

- Precision Metalforming Association Educational Foundation, 6363 Oak Tree Blvd., Independence, OH 44131-2500. Internet: http://www.pmaef.org

Veterinary Technologists and Technicians

(O*NET 29-2056.00)

Significant Points

- Animal lovers get satisfaction in this occupation, but aspects of the work can sometimes be unpleasant and physically and emotionally demanding.

- Entrants generally complete a 2-year or 4-year veterinary technology program, and must pass a state examination.

- Employment is expected to grow much faster than average.

Nature of the Work

Owners of pets and other animals today expect state-of-the-art veterinary care. To provide this service, veterinarians use the skills of veterinary technologists and technicians, who perform many of the same duties for a veterinarian that a nurse would for a physician, including routine laboratory and clinical procedures. Although specific job duties vary by employer, there often is little difference between the tasks done by technicians and by technologists, despite some differences in formal education and training. As a result, most workers in this occupation are called technicians.

Veterinary technologists and technicians typically conduct clinical work in a private practice under the supervision of a veterinarian—often performing various medical tests along with treating and diagnosing medical conditions and diseases in animals. For example, they may perform laboratory tests such as urinalysis and blood counts, assist with dental prophylaxis, prepare tissue samples, take blood samples, or assist veterinarians in a variety of tests and analyses in which they often utilize various items of medical equipment, such as test tubes and diagnostic equipment. While most of these duties are performed in a laboratory setting, many tasks are not. For example, some veterinary technicians obtain and record patient case histories, expose and develop x-rays, and provide specialized nursing care. Additionally, experienced veterinary technicians may discuss a pet's condition with its owners and train new clinic personnel. Veterinary technologists and technicians assisting small-animal practitioners usually care for companion animals, such as cats and dogs, but can perform a variety of duties with mice, rats, sheep, pigs, cattle, monkeys, birds, fish, and frogs. Very few veterinary technologists work in mixed animal practices where they care for both small companion animals and larger, nondomestic animals.

In addition to working in private clinics and animal hospitals, veterinary technologists and technicians also may work in research facilities. There, they may administer medications orally or topically, prepare samples for laboratory examinations, and record information on genealogy, diet, weight, medications, food intake, and clinical signs of pain and distress. Some may be required to sterilize laboratory and surgical equipment and provide routine postoperative care. At research facilities, veterinary technologists typically work under the guidance of veterinarians, physicians, and other laboratory technicians. Some veterinary technologists vaccinate newly admitted animals and occasionally are required to euthanize seriously ill, severely injured, or unwanted animals.

While the goal of most veterinary technologists and technicians goal is to promote animal health, some contribute to human health as well. Veterinary technologists occasionally assist veterinarians as they work with other scientists in medical-related fields such as gene therapy and cloning. Some find opportunities in biomedical research, wildlife medicine, the military, livestock management, or pharmaceutical sales.

Working Conditions

People who love animals get satisfaction from working with and helping them. However, some of the work may be unpleasant, physically and emotionally demanding, and sometimes dangerous. Veterinary technicians sometimes must clean cages and lift, hold, or restrain animals, risking exposure to bites or scratches. These workers must take precautions when treating animals with germicides or insecticides. The work setting can be noisy.

Veterinary technologists and technicians who witness abused animals or who euthanize unwanted, aged, or hopelessly injured animals may experience emotional stress. Those working for humane societies and animal shelters often deal with the public, some of whom might react with hostility to any implication that the owners are neglecting or abusing their pets. Such workers must maintain a calm and professional demeanor while they enforce the laws regarding animal care. In some animal hospitals, research facilities, and animal shelters, a veterinary technician is on duty 24 hours a day, which means some may work night shifts. Most full-time veterinary technologists and technicians work about 40 hours a week, while some work 50 or more hours a week.

Employment

Veterinary technologists and technicians held about 53,000 jobs in 2002. Most worked in veterinary services. The remainder worked in boarding kennels, animal shelters, stables, grooming shops, zoos, and local, state, and federal agencies.

Training, Other Qualifications, and Advancement

There are primarily two levels of education and training for entry to this occupation—a 2-year program for veterinary technicians and a 4-year program for veterinary technologists. Most entry-level veterinary technicians have a 2-year degree, usually an associate degree, from an accredited community college program in veterinary technology, in which courses are taught in clinical and laboratory settings using live animals. A few colleges offer veterinary technology programs that are longer and that may culminate in a 4-year bachelor's degree in veterinary technology. These 4-year colleges, in addition to some vocational schools, also offer 2-year programs in laboratory animal science.

In 2003, more than 80 veterinary technology programs in 41 states were accredited by the American Veterinary Medical Association (AVMA). Graduation from an AVMA-accredited veterinary technology program allows students to take the credentialing exam in any state in the country. Each state regulates veterinary technicians and technologists differently; however, all states require them to pass a credentialing exam following coursework. Passing the state exam assures the public that the technician or technologist has sufficient knowledge to work in a veterinary clinic or hospital. Candidates are tested for competency through an examination that includes oral, written, and practical portions. This process is regulated by the state Board of Veterinary Examiners, or the appropriate state agency. Depending on the state, candidates may become registered, licensed, or certified. Most states, however, use the National Veterinary Technician (NVT) exam. Prospects usually can have their passing scores transferred from one state to another, so long as both states utilize the same exam.

Employers recommend American Association for Laboratory Animal Science (AALAS) certification for those seeking employment in a research facility. AALAS offers certification for three levels of technician competence, with a focus on three principle areas—animal husbandry and welfare, facility administration and management, and animal health. Those who wish to become certified must satisfy a combination of education and experience requirements prior to taking an exam. Work experience must be directly related to the maintenance, health, and well-being of laboratory animals and must be gained in a laboratory animal facility as defined by AALAS. Candidates who meet the necessary criteria can begin pursuing the desired certification, based on their qualifications. The lowest level of certification is Animal Laboratory Assistant Technician (ALAT); the second level is Laboratory Animal Technician (LAT); and the highest level of certification is Laboratory Animal Technologist (LATG). The examination consists of multiple-choice questions and is longer and more difficult for higher levels of certification.

Persons interested in careers as veterinary technologists and technicians should take as many high school science, biology, and math courses as possible. Science courses taken beyond high school, in an associate or bachelor's degree program, should emphasize practical skills in a clinical or laboratory setting. Because veterinary technologists and technicians often deal with pet owners, communication skills are very important. Additionally, technologists and technicians should be able to work well with others, because teamwork with veterinarians is common. Organizational ability and the ability to pay attention to detail also are important.

Technologists and technicians usually begin work as trainees in routine positions under the direct supervision of a veterinarian. Entry-level workers whose training or educational background encompasses extensive hands-on experience with a variety of laboratory equipment, including diagnostic and medical equipment, usually require a shorter period of on-the-job training. As they gain experience, technologists and technicians take on more responsibility and carry out more assignments under only general veterinary supervision, and some eventually may become supervisors.

Job Outlook

Employment of veterinary technologists and technicians is expected to grow much faster than the average for all occupations through the year 2012. Job openings also will stem from the need to replace veterinary technologists and technicians who leave the occupation over the 2002-12 period. Keen competition is expected for veterinary technologist and technician jobs in zoos, due to expected slow growth in zoo capacity, low turnover among workers, the limited number of positions, and the fact that the occupation attracts many candidates.

Pet owners are becoming more affluent and more willing to pay for advanced care because many of them consider their pet to be part of the family, spurring employment growth for veterinary technologists and technicians. The number of dogs as pets, which also drives employment growth, is expected to increase more slowly during the projection period than in the previous decade. However, the rapidly growing number of cats as pets is expected to boost the demand for feline medicine, offsetting any reduced demand for veterinary care for dogs. The availability of advanced veterinary services, such as preventive dental care and surgical procedures, may provide opportunities for workers specializing in those areas. Biomedical facilities, diagnostic laboratories, wildlife facilities, humane societies, animal control facilities, drug or food manufacturing companies, and food safety inspection facilities will provide more jobs for veterinary technologists and technicians. Furthermore, demand for these workers will stem from the desire to replace veterinary assistants with more highly skilled technicians and technologists in animal clinics and hospitals, shelters, kennels, and humane societies.

Employment of veterinary technicians and technologists is relatively stable during periods of economic recession. Layoffs are less likely to occur among veterinary technologists and technicians than in some other occupations because animals will continue to require medical care.

Earnings

Median annual earnings of veterinary technologists and technicians were $22,950 in 2002. The middle 50 percent earned between $19,210 and $27,890. The bottom 10 percent earned less than $16,170, and the top 10 percent earned more than $33,750.

Related Occupations

Others who work extensively with animals include animal care and service workers. Like veterinary technologists and technicians, they must have patience and feel comfortable with animals. However, the level of training required for these occupations is less than that needed by veterinary technologists and technicians. Veterinarians also work extensively with animals. They prevent, diagnose, and treat diseases, disorders, and injuries in animals.

Sources of Additional Information

For information on certification as a laboratory animal technician or technologist, contact:

- American Association for Laboratory Animal Science, 9190 Crestwyn Hills Dr., Memphis, TN 38125. Internet: http://www.aalas.org

For information on careers in veterinary medicine and a listing of AVMA-accredited veterinary technology programs, contact:

- American Veterinary Medical Association, 1931 N. Meacham Rd., Suite 100, Schaumburg, IL 60173-4360. Internet: http://www.avma.org

For information on veterinary technology programs, contact:

- Association of American Veterinary Medical Colleges, 1101 Vermont Ave. NW., Suite 710, Washington, DC 20005. Internet: http://www.aavmc.org

For information on becoming a veterinary technician, contact:

- National Association of Veterinary Technicians in America, P.O. Box 224, Battle Ground, IN 47920. Internet: http://www.navta.net

Water and Liquid Waste Treatment Plant and System Operators

(O*NET 51-8031.00)

Significant Points

- Employment is concentrated in local government and private water, sewage, and other systems utilities.

- The completion of an associate degree or 1-year certificate program is increasingly becoming an asset.

- Operators must pass exams certifying that they are capable of overseeing various treatment processes.

- Job prospects will be good for qualified individuals because the number of applicants in this field is normally low.

Nature of the Work

Clean water is essential for everyday life. *Water treatment plant and system operators* treat water so that it is safe to drink. *Liquid waste treatment plant and system operators*, also known as wastewater treatment plant and system operators, remove harmful pollutants from domestic and industrial liquid waste so that it is safe to return to the environment.

Water is pumped from wells, rivers, streams, and reservoirs to water treatment plants, where it is treated and distributed to customers. Liquid waste travels through customers' sewer pipes to liquid waste treatment plants, where it is either treated and returned to streams, rivers, and oceans or reused for irrigation and landscaping. Operators in both types of plants control equipment and processes that remove or destroy harmful materials, chemical compounds, and microorganisms from the water. They also control pumps, valves, and other equipment that moves the water or liquid waste through the various treatment processes, after which they dispose of the removed waste materials.

Operators read, interpret, and adjust meters and gauges to make sure that plant equipment and processes are working properly. Operators operate chemical-feeding devices, take samples of the water or liquid waste, perform chemical and biological laboratory analyses, and adjust the amounts of chemicals, such as chlorine, in the water. They use a variety of instruments to sample and measure water quality and common hand and power tools to make repairs. Operators also make minor repairs to valves, pumps, and other equipment.

Water and liquid waste treatment plant and system operators increasingly rely on computers to help monitor equipment, store the results of sampling, make process-control decisions, schedule and record maintenance activities, and produce reports. When equipment malfunctions, operators also may use computers to determine the cause of the malfunction and seek its solution.

Occasionally, operators must work during emergencies. A heavy rainstorm, for example, may cause large amounts of liquid waste to flow into sewers, exceeding a plant's treatment capacity. Emergencies also can be caused by conditions inside a plant, such as chlorine gas leaks or oxygen deficiencies. To handle these conditions, operators are trained to make an emergency management response and use special safety equipment and procedures to protect public health and the facility. During these periods, operators may work under extreme pressure to correct problems as quickly as possible. Because working conditions may be dangerous, operators must be extremely cautious.

The specific duties of plant operators depend on the type and size of plant. In smaller plants, one operator may control all of the machinery, perform tests, keep records, handle complaints, and perform repairs and maintenance. A few operators may handle both a water treatment and a liquid waste treatment plant. In larger plants with many employees, operators may be more specialized and monitor only one process. The staff also may include chemists, engineers, laboratory technicians, mechanics, helpers, supervisors, and a superintendent.

Water pollution standards have become increasingly stringent since the adoption of two major federal environmental statutes: the Clean Water Act of 1972, which implemented a national system of regulation on the discharge of pollutants; and the Safe Drinking Water Act of 1974, which established standards for drinking water. Industrial facilities sending their wastes to municipal treatment plants must meet certain minimum standards to ensure that the wastes have been adequately pretreated and will not damage municipal treatment facilities. Municipal water treatment plants also must meet stringent drinking water standards. The list of contaminants regulated by these statutes has grown over time. As a result, plant operators must be familiar with the guidelines established by federal regulations and how they affect their plant. In addition to knowing and understanding the federal regulations, operators must be aware of any guidelines imposed by the state or locality in which the plant operates.

Working Conditions

Water and liquid waste treatment plant and system operators work both indoors and outdoors and may be exposed to noise from machinery and to unpleasant odors. Operators' work is physically demanding and often is performed in unclean locations. Operators must pay close attention to safety procedures, due to the presence of hazardous conditions, such as slippery walkways, dangerous gases, and malfunctioning equipment. Plants operate 24 hours a day, 7 days a week; therefore, operators work one of three 8-hour shifts, including weekends and holidays, on a rotational basis. Operators may be required to work overtime.

Employment

Water and liquid waste treatment plant and system operators held about 99,000 jobs in 2002. About 3 in 4 operators worked for local governments. Others worked primarily for private water, sewage, and other systems utilities, and for private waste treatment and disposal companies. Private firms are increasingly providing operation and management services to local governments on a contract basis.

Water and liquid waste treatment plant and system operators were employed throughout the country, but most jobs were in larger towns and cities. Although nearly all operators worked full time, those in small towns may work only part time at the treatment plant, with the remainder of their time spent handling other municipal duties.

Training, Other Qualifications, and Advancement

A high school diploma usually is required for an individual to become a water or liquid waste treatment plant operator. Operators need mechanical aptitude and should be competent in basic mathematics, chemistry, and biology. They must have the ability to apply data to formulas prescribing treatment requirements, flow levels, and concentration levels. Some basic familiarity with computers also is necessary because of the trend toward computer-controlled equipment and more sophisticated instrumentation. Certain positions—particularly in larger cities and towns—are covered by civil service regulations. Applicants for these positions may be required to pass a written examination testing their mathematics skills, mechanical aptitude, and general intelligence.

The completion of an associate degree or a 1-year certificate program in water quality and liquid waste treatment technology increases an applicant's chances for employment and promotion because plants are becoming more complex. Offered throughout the country, these programs provide a good general knowledge of water and liquid waste treatment processes, as well as basic preparation for becoming an operator.

Trainees usually start as attendants or operators-in-training and learn their skills on the job under the direction of an experienced operator. They learn by observing and doing routine tasks such as recording meter readings, taking samples of liquid waste and sludge, and performing simple maintenance and repair work on pumps, electric motors, valves, and other plant equipment. Larger treatment plants generally combine this on-the-job training with formal classroom or self-paced study programs.

The Safe Drinking Water Act Amendments of 1996, enforced by the U.S. Environmental Protection Agency, specify national minimum standards for certification and recertification of operators of community and nontransient, noncommunity water systems. As a result, operators must pass an examination to certify that they are capable of overseeing liquid waste treatment plant operations. There are different levels of certification, depending on the operator's experience and training. Higher certification levels qualify the operator for a wider variety of treatment processes. Certification requirements vary by state and by size of treatment plants. Although relocation may mean having to become certified in a new jurisdiction, many states accept other states' certifications.

Most state drinking water and water pollution control agencies offer courses to improve operators' skills and knowledge. The courses cover principles of treatment processes and process control, laboratory procedures, maintenance, management skills, collection systems, safety, chlorination, sedimentation, biological treatment, sludge treatment and disposal, and flow measurements. Some operators take correspondence courses on subjects related to water and liquid waste treatment, and some employers pay part of the tuition for related college courses in science or engineering.

As operators are promoted, they become responsible for more complex treatment processes. Some operators are promoted to plant supervisor or superintendent; others advance by transferring to a larger facility. Postsecondary training in water and liquid waste treatment, coupled with increasingly responsible experience as an operator, may be sufficient to qualify a worker for becoming superintendent of a small plant, where a superintendent also serves as an operator. However, educational requirements are rising as larger, more complex treatment plants are built to meet new drinking water and water pollution control standards. With each promotion, the operator must have greater knowledge of federal, state, and local regulations. Superintendents of large plants generally need an engineering or a science degree.

A few operators get jobs as technicians with state drinking water or water pollution control agencies. In that capacity, they monitor and provide technical assistance to plants throughout the state. Vocational-technical school or community college training generally is preferred for technician jobs. Experienced operators may transfer to related jobs with industrial liquid waste treatment plants, water or liquid waste treatment equipment and chemical companies, engineering consulting firms, or vocational-technical schools.

Job Outlook

Employment of water and liquid waste treatment plant and system operators is expected to grow about as fast as the average for all occupations through the year 2012. Job prospects will be good for qualified individuals because the number of applicants in this field is normally low, due primarily to the unclean and physically demanding nature of the work.

The increasing population and growth of the economy are expected to boost demand for essential water and liquid waste treatment services. As new plants are constructed to meet this demand, employment of water and liquid waste treatment plant and system operators will increase. In addition, many job openings will occur as experienced operators leave the labor force or transfer to other occupations.

Local governments are the largest employers of water and liquid waste treatment plant and system operators. However, federal certification requirements have increased utilities' reliance on private firms specializing in the operation and management of water and liquid waste treatment facilities. As a result, employment in privately owned facilities will grow faster than the average.

Earnings

Median annual earnings of water and liquid waste treatment plant and system operators were $33,390 in 2002. The middle 50 percent earned between $25,790 and $42,490. The lowest 10 percent earned less than $20,220, and the highest 10 percent earned more than $52,110. Median annual earnings of water and liquid waste treatment plant and systems operators in 2002 were $33,210 in local government and $32,190 in water, sewage, and other systems.

In addition to their annual salaries, water and liquid waste treatment plant and system operators usually receive benefits that may include health and life insurance, a retirement plan, and educational reimbursement for job-related courses.

Related Occupations

Other workers whose main activity consists of operating a system of machinery to process or produce materials include chemical plant and system operators; gas plant operators; petroleum pump system operators, refinery operators, and gaugers; power plant operators, distributors, and dispatchers; and stationary engineers and boiler operators.

Sources of Additional Information

For information on employment opportunities, contact state or local water pollution control agencies, state water and liquid waste operator associations, state environmental training centers, or local offices of the state employment service.

For information on certification, contact:

- Association of Boards of Certification, 208 Fifth St., Ames, IA 50010-6259. Internet: http://www.abccert.org

For educational information related to a career as a water or liquid waste treatment plant and system operator, contact:

- American Water Works Association, 6666 West Quincy Ave., Denver, CO 80235. Internet: http://www.awwa.org
- Water Environment Federation, 601 Wythe St., Alexandria, VA 22314-1994. Internet: http://www.wef.org

Section Two

THE QUICK JOB SEARCH

Seven Steps to Getting a Good Job in Less Time

The Complete Text of a Results-Oriented Booklet by Michael Farr

Millions of job seekers have found better jobs faster using the techniques in The Quick Job Search. So can you! The Quick Job Search covers the essential steps proven to cut job search time in half and is used widely by job search programs throughout North America. Topics include how to identify your key skills, define and research your ideal job, write a great resume quickly, use the most effective job search methods, get more interviews, answer tough interview questions in three steps, and much more.

While it is a section in this book, The Quick Job Search is available as a separate booklet and in an expanded form as Seven Steps to Getting a Job Fast.

◆

The Quick Job Search Is Short, But It May Be All You Need

While *The Quick Job Search* is short, it covers the basics on how to explore career options and conduct an effective job search. While these topics can seem complex, I have found some simple truths about job searches:

★ If you are going to work, you might as well define what you really want to do and are good at.

★ If you are looking for a job, you might as well use techniques that will reduce the time it takes to find one—and that help you get a better job than you might otherwise.

That's what I emphasize in this little book.

Trust Me—Do the Worksheets. I know you will resist completing the worksheets. But trust me, they are worth your time. Doing them will give you a better sense of what you are good at, what you want to do, and how to go about getting it. You will also most likely get more interviews and present yourself better. Is this worth giving up a night of TV? Yes, I think so.

Once you finish this minibook and its activities, you will have spent more time planning your career than most people do. And you will know more than the average job seeker about finding a job.

Why Such a Short Book? I've taught job seeking skills for many years, and I've written longer and more detailed books than this one. Yet I have often been asked to tell someone, in a few minutes or hours, the most important things they should do in their career planning or job search. Instructors and counselors also ask the same question because they have only a short time to spend with folks they're trying to help. I've given this a lot of thought, and the seven topics in this minibook are the ones I think are most important to know.

This minibook is short enough to scan in a morning and conduct a more effective job search that afternoon. Doing all the activities would take more time but would prepare you far better. Of course, you can learn more about all of the topics it covers, but this little book may be all you need.

Y ou can't just read about getting a job. The best way to get a job is to go out and get interviews! And the best way to get interviews is to make a job out of getting a job.

After many years of experience, I have identified just seven basic things you need to do that make a big difference in your job search. Each will be covered and expanded on in this minibook.

1. Identify your key skills.

2. Define your ideal job.

3. Learn the two most effective job search methods.

4. Write a superior resume.

5. Organize your time to get two interviews a day.

6. Dramatically improve your interviewing skills.

7. Follow up on all leads.

We all have thousands of skills. Consider the many skills required to do even a simple thing like ride a bike or bake a cake. But, of all the skills you have, employers want to know those key skills you have for the job they need done. You must clearly identify these key skills, and then emphasize them in interviews.

Step 1

Identify Your Key Skills and Develop a "Skills Language" to Describe Yourself

One employer survey found that about 90 percent of the people interviewed by the employers did not present the skills they had to do the job they sought. They could not answer the basic question "Why should I hire you?"

Knowing and describing your skills are essential to doing well in interviews. This same knowledge is important in deciding what type of job you will enjoy and do well. For these reasons, I consider identifying your skills a necessary part of a successful career plan or job search.

The Three Types of Skills

Most people think of their "skills" as job-related skills, such as using a computer. But we all have other types of skills that are important for success on a job—and that are important to employers. The triangle at right presents skills in three groups, and I think that this is a very useful way to consider skills for our purposes.

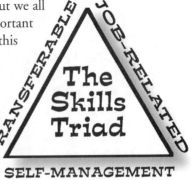

The Skills Triad

Let's review these three types of skills—self-management, transferable, and job-related—and identify those that are most important to you.

Self-Management Skills

Write down three things about yourself that you think make you a good worker.

YOUR "GOOD WORKER" TRAITS

1. _____

2. _____

3. _____

You just wrote down the most important things for an employer to know about you! They describe your basic personality and your ability to adapt to new environments. They are some of the most important skills to emphasize in interviews, yet most job seekers don't realize their importance—and don't mention them.

Review the Self-Management Skills Checklist that follows and put a check mark beside any skills you have. The key self-management skills listed first cover abilities that employers find particularly important. If one or more of the key self-management skills apply to you, mentioning them in interviews can help you greatly.

SELF-MANAGEMENT SKILLS CHECKLIST

Check Your Key Self-Management Skills—Employers Value These Highly

_____ accept supervision	_____ good attendance	_____ productive
_____ get along with coworkers	_____ hard worker	_____ punctual
_____ get things done on time	_____ honest	

Check Your Other Self-Management Skills

_____ able to coordinate	_____ enthusiastic	_____ learn quickly
_____ ambitious	_____ expressive	_____ loyal
_____ assertive	_____ flexible	_____ mature
_____ capable	_____ formal	_____ methodical
_____ cheerful	_____ friendly	_____ modest
_____ competent	_____ good-natured	_____ motivated
_____ complete assignments	_____ helpful	_____ natural
_____ conscientious	_____ humble	_____ open-minded
_____ creative	_____ imaginative	_____ optimistic
_____ dependable	_____ independent	_____ original
_____ discreet	_____ industrious	_____ patient
_____ eager	_____ informal	_____ persistent
_____ efficient	_____ intelligent	_____ physically strong
_____ energetic	_____ intuitive	_____ practice new skills

(continued)

(continued)

_____ reliable	_____ solve problems	_____ thrifty
_____ resourceful	_____ spontaneous	_____ trustworthy
_____ responsible	_____ steady	_____ versatile
_____ self-confident	_____ tactful	_____ well-organized
_____ sense of humor	_____ take pride in work	
_____ sincere	_____ tenacious	

List Your Other Self-Management Skills

_____

_____

After you are done with the list, circle the five skills you feel are most important and list them in the box that follows.

YOUR TOP FIVE SELF-MANAGEMENT SKILLS

1. _____

2. _____

3. _____

4. _____

5. _____

N o t e

When thinking about their skills, some people find it helpful to complete the Essential Job Search Data Worksheet that starts on page 314. It organizes skills and accomplishments from previous jobs and other life experiences. Take a look at it and decide whether to complete it now or later.

Transferable Skills

We all have skills that can transfer from one job or career to another. For example, the ability to organize events could be used in a variety of jobs and may be essential for success in certain occupations. Your mission is to find a job that requires the skills you have and enjoy using.

In the following list, put a check mark beside the skills you have. You may have used them in a previous job or in some non-work setting.

Quip

It's not bragging if it's true. Using your new skills language may be uncomfortable at first, but employers need to learn about your skills. So practice saying positive things about the skills you have for the job. If you don't, who will?

TRANSFERABLE SKILLS CHECKLIST

Check Your Key Transferable Skills—Employers Value These Highly

_____ computer skills	_____ manage people	_____ organize/manage projects
_____ negotiate	_____ meet deadlines	_____ public speaking
_____ manage money, budgets	_____ meet the public	_____ written communication

Check Your Skills for Working with Things

_____ assemble things	_____ good with hands	_____ use complex equipment
_____ build things	_____ observe/inspect things	_____ use computers
_____ construct/repair things	_____ operate tools, machines	
_____ drive, operate vehicles	_____ repair things	

Check Your Skills for Working with Data

_____ analyze data	_____ compile	_____ manage money
_____ audit records	_____ count	_____ observe/inspect
_____ budget	_____ detail-oriented	_____ record facts
_____ calculate/compute	_____ evaluate	_____ research
_____ check for accuracy	_____ investigate	_____ synthesize
_____ classify things	_____ keep financial records	_____ take inventory
_____ compare	_____ locate information	

Check Your Skills for Working with People

_____ administer	_____ instruct others	_____ pleasant
_____ advise	_____ interview people	_____ sensitive
_____ care for	_____ kind	_____ sociable
_____ coach	_____ listen	_____ supervise
_____ confront others	_____ negotiate	_____ tactful
_____ counsel people	_____ outgoing	_____ tolerant
_____ demonstrate	_____ patient	_____ tough
_____ diplomatic	_____ perceptive	_____ trusting
_____ help others	_____ persuade	_____ understanding

(continued)

Check Your Skills for Working with Words/Ideas

_____ articulate

_____ communicate verbally

_____ correspond with others

_____ create new ideas

_____ design

_____ edit

_____ ingenious

_____ inventive

_____ library or Internet research

_____ logical

_____ public speaking

_____ remember information

_____ write clearly

Check Your Leadership Skills

_____ arrange social functions

_____ competitive

_____ decisive

_____ delegate

_____ direct others

_____ explain things to others

_____ influence others

_____ initiate new tasks

_____ make decisions

_____ manage or direct others

_____ mediate problems

_____ motivate people

_____ negotiate agreements

_____ plan events

_____ results-oriented

_____ risk-taker

_____ run meetings

_____ self-confident

_____ self-motivate

_____ solve problems

Check Your Creative/Artistic Skills

_____ artistic

_____ dance, body movement

_____ drawing, art

_____ expressive

_____ perform, act

_____ present artistic ideas

List Your Other Transferable Skills

_____

_____

When you are finished, circle the five transferable skills you feel are most important for you to use in your next job and list them in the box below.

YOUR TOP FIVE TRANSFERABLE SKILLS

1. _____

2. _____

3. _____

4. _____

5. _____

Job-Related Skills

Job content or job-related skills are those you need to do a particular occupation. A carpenter, for example, needs to know how to use various tools. Before you select job-related skills to emphasize, you must first have a clear idea of the jobs you want. So let's put off developing your job-related skills list until you have defined the job you want. That topic is covered next.

Complete the worksheet that follows after you have read "Step 2: Define Your Ideal Job."

Quip

It's a hassle, but... Completing the Essential Job Search Data Worksheet that starts on page 314 will help you define what you are good at—and remember examples of when you did things well. This information will help you define your ideal job and will be of great value in interviews. Look at the worksheet now, and promise to do it tonight.

YOUR TOP FIVE JOB-RELATED SKILLS

1. _____
2. _____
3. _____
4. _____
5. _____

Step 2

Define Your Ideal Job (You Can Compromise on It Later If Needed)

Too many people look for a job without clearly knowing what they are looking for. Before you go out seeking *a* job, I suggest that you first define exactly what you want—*the* job.

Most people think that a job objective is the same as a job title, but it isn't. You need to consider other elements of what makes a job satisfying for you. Then, later, you can decide what that job is called and what industry it might be in.

EIGHT FACTORS TO CONSIDER IN DEFINING YOUR IDEAL JOB

As you try to define your ideal job, consider the following eight important questions. Once you know what you want, your task then becomes finding a position that is as close to your ideal job as possible.

1. **What skills do you want to use?** From the skills lists in Step 1, select the top five skills that you enjoy using and most want to use in your next job. _____

_____

_____

(continued)

(continued)

2. **What type of special knowledge do you have?** Perhaps you know how to fix radios, keep accounting records, or cook food. Write down the things you know from schooling, training, hobbies, family experiences, and other sources. One or more of these knowledges could make you a very special applicant in the right setting. _____

_____

_____

3. **With what types of people do you prefer to work?** Do you like to work in competition with others, or do you prefer hardworking folks, creative personalities, or some other types? _____

_____

_____

4. **What type of work environment do you prefer?** Do you want to work inside, outside, in a quiet place, a busy place, a clean place, or have a window with a nice view? List the types of things that are most important to you. _____

_____

_____

5. **Where do you want your next job to be located—in what city or region?** Near a bus line? Close to a childcare center? If you are open to living and working anywhere, what would your ideal community be like? _____

_____

_____

6. **How much money do you hope to make in your next job?** Many people will take less money if they like a job in other ways—or if they quickly need a job to survive. Think about the minimum you would take as well as what you would eventually like to earn. Your next job will probably pay somewhere in between. _____

_____

_____

7. **How much responsibility are you willing to accept?** Usually, the more money you want to make, the more responsibility you must accept. Do you want to work by yourself, be part of a group, or be in charge? If so, at what level? _____

_____

_____

8. **What things are important or have meaning to you?** Do you have important values you would prefer to include as a basis of the work you do? For example, some people want to work to help others, clean up our environment, build things, make machines work, gain power or prestige, or care for animals or plants. Think about what is important to you and how you might include this in your next job.

_____

_____

Is It Possible to Find Your Ideal Job?

Can you find a job that meets all the criteria you just defined? Perhaps. Some people do. The harder you look, the more likely you are to find it. But you will likely need to compromise, so it is useful to know what is *most* important to include in your next job. Go back over your responses to the eight factors and mark those few things that you would most like to have or include in your ideal job. Then write a brief outline of this ideal job below. Don't worry about a job title, or whether you have the experience, or other practical matters yet.

MY IDEAL JOB WOULD BE

Explore Specific Job Titles and Industries

You might find your ideal job in an occupation you haven't considered yet. And, even if you are sure of the occupation you want, it may be in an industry that's not familiar to you. This combination of occupation and industry forms the basis for your job search, and you should consider a variety of options.

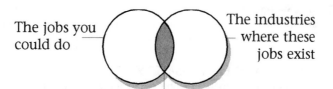

The jobs you could do — The industries where these jobs exist

Your ideal job exists in the overlap of those jobs that interest you most *and* of those industries that best meet your needs and interests!

REVIEW THE TOP JOBS IN THE WORKFORCE

There are thousands of job titles, and many jobs are highly specialized, employing just a few people. While one of these more specialized jobs may be just what you want, most work falls within more general job titles that employ large numbers of people.

The list of job titles that follows was developed by the U.S. Department of Labor. It contains approximately 270 major jobs that employ about 88 percent of the U.S. workforce.

The job titles are organized within 14 major groupings called interest areas, presented in all capital letters and bold type. These groupings will help you quickly identify fields most likely to interest you. Job titles are presented in regular type within these groupings.

(continued)

(continued)

Begin with the interest areas that appeal to you most, and underline any job title that interests you. (Don't worry for now about whether you have the experience or credentials to do these jobs.) Then quickly review the remaining interest areas, underlining any job titles there that interest you. Note that some job titles are listed more than once because they fit into more than one interest area. When you have gone through all 14 interest areas, go back and circle the 5 to 10 job titles that interest you most. These are the ones you will want to research in more detail.

1. **ARTS, ENTERTAINMENT, AND MEDIA**—Actors, Producers, and Directors; Announcers; Artists and Related Workers; Athletes, Coaches, Umpires, and Related Workers; Barbers, Cosmetologists, and Other Personal Appearance Workers; Broadcast and Sound Engineering Technicians and Radio Operators; Dancers and Choreographers; Demonstrators, Product Promoters, and Models; Designers; Desktop Publishers; Interpreters and Translators; Musicians, Singers, and Related Workers; News Analysts, Reporters, and Correspondents; Photographers; Prepress Technicians and Workers; Public Relations Specialists; Recreation and Fitness Workers; Television, Video, and Motion Picture Camera Operators and Editors; Writers and Editors

2. **SCIENCE, MATH, AND ENGINEERING**—Actuaries; Aerospace Engineers; Agricultural and Food Scientists; Agricultural Engineers; Architects, Except Landscape and Naval; Atmospheric Scientists; Biological Scientists; Biomedical Engineers; Chemical Engineers; Chemists and Materials Scientists; Civil Engineers; Computer and Information Systems Managers; Computer Hardware Engineers; Computer Programmers; Computer Software Engineers; Computer Support Specialists and Systems Administrators; Computer Systems Analysts, Database Administrators, and Computer Scientists; Computer-Control Programmers and Operators; Conservation Scientists and Foresters; Construction and Building Inspectors; Drafters; Economists; Electrical and Electronics Engineers, Except Computer; Engineering and Natural Sciences Managers; Engineering Technicians; Engineers; Environmental Engineers; Environmental Scientists and Geoscientists; Industrial Engineers, Including Health and Safety; Landscape Architects; Market and Survey Researchers; Materials Engineers; Mathematicians; Mechanical Engineers; Medical Scientists; Mining and Geological Engineers, Including Mining Safety Engineers; Nuclear Engineers; Operations Research Analysts; Petroleum Engineers; Photographers; Physicists and Astronomers; Psychologists; Sales Engineers; Science Technicians; Social Scientists, Other; Surveyors, Cartographers, Photogrammetrists, and Surveying Technicians; Urban and Regional Planners

3. **PLANTS AND ANIMALS**—Agricultural Workers; Animal Care and Service Workers; Farmers, Ranchers, and Agricultural Managers; Fishers and Fishing Vessel Operators; Forest, Conservation, and Logging Workers; Grounds Maintenance Workers; Pest Control Workers; Science Technicians; Veterinarians; Veterinary Technologists and Technicians

4. **LAW, LAW ENFORCEMENT, AND PUBLIC SAFETY**—Correctional Officers; Emergency Medical Technicians and Paramedics; Firefighting Occupations; Job Opportunities in the Armed Forces; Judges, Magistrates, and Other Judicial Workers; Lawyers; Occupational Health and Safety Specialists and Technicians; Paralegals and Legal Assistants; Police and Detectives; Private Detectives and Investigators; Science Technicians; Security Guards and Gaming Surveillance Officers

5. **MECHANICS, INSTALLERS, AND REPAIRERS**—Aircraft and Avionics Equipment Mechanics and Service Technicians; Automotive Body and Related Repairers; Automotive Service Technicians and Mechanics; Coin, Vending, and Amusement Machine Servicers and Repairers; Computer, Automated Teller, and Office Machine Repairers; Diesel Service Technicians and Mechanics; Electrical and Electronics Installers and Repairers; Electronic Home Entertainment Equipment Installers and Repairers; Elevator Installers and Repairers; Heating, Air-Conditioning, and Refrigeration Mechanics and Installers; Heavy Vehicle and Mobile Equipment Service Technicians and Mechanics; Home Appliance Repairers; Industrial Machinery Installation, Repair, and Maintenance Workers, Except Millwrights; Line Installers and Repairers; Maintenance and Repair Workers, General; Millwrights; Ophthalmic Laboratory Technicians; Painting and Coating Workers, Except Construction and Maintenance; Precision Instrument and Equipment Repairers; Radio and Telecommunications Equipment Installers and Repairers; Small Engine Mechanics

6. **CONSTRUCTION, MINING, AND DRILLING**—Boilermakers; Brickmasons, Blockmasons, and Stonemasons; Carpenters; Carpet, Floor, and Tile Installers and Finishers; Cement Masons, Concrete Finishers, Segmental Pavers, and Terrazzo Workers; Construction Equipment Operators; Construction Laborers; Construction Managers; Drywall Installers, Ceiling Tile Installers, and Tapers; Electricians; Glaziers; Hazardous Materials Removal Workers; Insulation Workers; Material Moving Occupations; Painters and Paperhangers; Pipelayers,

Plumbers, Pipefitters, and Steamfitters; Plasterers and Stucco Masons; Roofers; Sheet Metal Workers; Structural and Reinforcing Iron and Metal Workers

7. **TRANSPORTATION**—Air Traffic Controllers; Aircraft Pilots and Flight Engineers; Bus Drivers; Material Moving Occupations; Rail Transportation Occupations; Taxi Drivers and Chauffeurs; Truck Drivers and Driver/Sales Workers; Water Transportation Occupations

8. **INDUSTRIAL PRODUCTION**—Assemblers and Fabricators; Bookbinders and Bindery Workers; Computer-Control Programmers and Operators; Dental Laboratory Technicians; Food-Processing Occupations; Forest, Conservation, and Logging Workers; Industrial Production Managers; Inspectors, Testers, Sorters, Samplers, and Weighers; Jewelers and Precious Stone and Metal Workers; Machine Setters, Operators, and Tenders—Metal and Plastic; Machinists; Material Moving Occupations; Ophthalmic Laboratory Technicians; Painting and Coating Workers, Except Construction and Maintenance; Photographic Process Workers and Processing Machine Operators; Power Plant Operators, Distributors, and Dispatchers; Prepress Technicians and Workers; Printing Machine Operators; Semiconductor Processors; Stationary Engineers and Boiler Operators; Textile, Apparel, and Furnishings Occupations; Tool and Die Makers; Water and Liquid Waste Treatment Plant and System Operators; Water Transportation Occupations; Welding, Soldering, and Brazing Workers; Woodworkers

9. **BUSINESS DETAIL**—Administrative Services Managers; Bill and Account Collectors; Billing and Posting Clerks and Machine Operators; Bookkeeping, Accounting, and Auditing Clerks; Brokerage Clerks; Cargo and Freight Agents; Cashiers; Communications Equipment Operators; Computer Operators; Computer, Automated Teller, and Office Machine Repairers; Counter and Rental Clerks; Couriers and Messengers; Court Reporters; Credit Authorizers, Checkers, and Clerks; Customer Service Representatives; Data Entry and Information Processing Workers; Dispatchers; File Clerks; Financial Clerks; Gaming Cage Workers; Human Resources Assistants, Except Payroll and Timekeeping; Information and Record Clerks; Interviewers; Material Recording, Scheduling, Dispatching, and Distributing Occupations; Medical Records and Health Information Technicians; Medical Transcriptionists; Meter Readers, Utilities; Office and Administrative Support Worker Supervisors and Managers; Office Clerks, General; Order Clerks; Payroll and Timekeeping Clerks; Postal Service Workers; Prepress Technicians and Workers; Procurement Clerks; Production, Planning, and Expediting Clerks; Receptionists and Information Clerks; Reservation and Transportation Ticket Agents and Travel Clerks; Secretaries and Administrative Assistants; Shipping, Receiving, and Traffic Clerks; Stock Clerks and Order Fillers; Tellers; Weighers, Measurers, Checkers, and Samplers, Recordkeeping

10. **SALES AND MARKETING**—Advertising, Marketing, Promotions, Public Relations, and Sales Managers; Demonstrators, Product Promoters, and Models; Insurance Sales Agents; Material Recording, Scheduling, Dispatching, and Distributing Occupations; Real Estate Brokers and Sales Agents; Retail Salespersons; Sales Representatives, Wholesale and Manufacturing; Sales Worker Supervisors; Securities, Commodities, and Financial Services Sales Agents; Stock Clerks and Order Fillers; Travel Agents

11. **RECREATION, TRAVEL, AND OTHER PERSONAL SERVICES**—Barbers, Cosmetologists, and Other Personal Appearance Workers; Building Cleaning Workers; Chefs, Cooks, and Food Preparation Workers; Flight Attendants; Food and Beverage Serving and Related Workers; Food Service Managers; Food-Processing Occupations; Gaming Services Occupations; Hotel, Motel, and Resort Desk Clerks; Information and Record Clerks; Lodging Managers; Material Moving Occupations; Personal and Home Care Aides; Recreation and Fitness Workers; Reservation and Transportation Ticket Agents and Travel Clerks; Textile, Apparel, and Furnishings Occupations

12. **EDUCATION AND SOCIAL SERVICE**—Archivists, Curators, and Museum Technicians; Childcare Workers; Clergy; Conservation Scientists and Foresters; Counselors; Education Administrators; Financial Analysts and Personal Financial Advisors; Information and Record Clerks; Instructional Coordinators; Librarians; Library Assistants, Clerical; Library Technicians; Probation Officers and Correctional Treatment Specialists; Protestant Ministers; Psychologists; Rabbis; Roman Catholic Priests; Social and Human Service Assistants; Social Workers; Teacher Assistants

13. **GENERAL MANAGEMENT AND SUPPORT**—Accountants and Auditors; Advertising, Marketing, Promotions, Public Relations, and Sales Managers; Budget Analysts; Claims Adjusters, Appraisers, Examiners and Investigators; Cost Estimators; Financial Analysts and Personal Financial Advisors; Financial Managers; Funeral Directors; Human Resources, Training, and Labor Relations Managers and Specialists; Insurance Underwriters;

(continued)

(continued)

Loan Counselors and Officers; Management Analysts; Market and Survey Researchers; Property, Real Estate, and Community Association Managers; Purchasing Managers, Buyers, and Purchasing Agents; Tax Examiners, Collectors, and Revenue Agents; Top Executives

14. **MEDICAL AND HEALTH SERVICES**—Audiologists; Cardiovascular Technologists and Technicians; Chiropractors; Clinical Laboratory Technologists and Technicians; Dental Assistants; Dental Hygienists; Dentists; Diagnostic Medical Sonographers; Dietitians and Nutritionists; Licensed Practical and Licensed Vocational Nurses; Medical and Health Services Managers; Medical Assistants; Nuclear Medicine Technologists; Nursing, Psychiatric, and Home Health Aides; Occupational Therapist Assistants and Aides; Occupational Therapists; Opticians, Dispensing; Optometrists; Pharmacists; Pharmacy Aides; Pharmacy Technicians; Physical Therapist Assistants and Aides; Physical Therapists; Physician Assistants; Physicians and Surgeons; Podiatrists; Radiologic Technologists and Technicians; Recreational Therapists; Registered Nurses; Respiratory Therapists; Speech-Language Pathologists; Surgical Technologists

---

Thorough descriptions for the job titles in the preceding list can be found in this book. You can also find these job descriptions on the Internet at http://www.bls.gov/oco/.

The Guide for Occupational Exploration, Third Edition, provides more information on the interest areas used in the list. This book is published by JIST Works and also describes about 1,000 major jobs, arranged within groupings of related jobs.

Finally, "A Short List of Additional Resources" at the end of this minibook will give you resources for more job information.

CONSIDER MAJOR INDUSTRIES

The *Career Guide to Industries,* another book by the U.S. Department of Labor, gives very helpful reviews for the major industries mentioned in the list below. Organized in groups of related industries, this list covers about 75 percent of the nation's workforce. Many libraries and bookstores carry the *Career Guide to Industries,* or you can find the information on the Internet at http://www.bls.gov/oco/cg/.

Underline industries that interest you, and then learn more about the opportunities they present. Note that some industries pay more than others, often for the same skills or jobs, so you should explore a variety of industry options.

Agriculture, Mining, and Construction: agriculture, forestry, and fishing; construction; mining; oil and gas extraction.

Manufacturing: aerospace product and parts manufacturing; apparel manufacturing; chemical manufacturing, except pharmaceutical and medicine manufacturing; computer and electronic product manufacturing; food manufacturing; motor vehicle and parts manufacturing; pharmaceutical and medicine manufacturing; printing; steel manufacturing; textile mills and products.

Trade: automobile dealers; clothing, accessory, and general merchandise stores; grocery stores; wholesale trade.

Transportation and Utilities: air transportation; truck transportation and warehousing; utilities.

Information: broadcasting; motion picture and video industries; publishing, except software; software publishers; telecommunications.

Financial Activities: banking; insurance; securities, commodities, and other investments.

Professional and Business Services: advertising and public relations services; computer systems design and related services; employment services; management, scientific, and technical consulting services.

Education and Health Services: child daycare services; educational services; health services; social assistance, except child day care.

Leisure and Hospitality: arts, entertainment, and recreation; food services and drinking places; hotels and other accommodations.

Government: federal government, excluding the postal service; state and local government, except education and health.

YOUR TOP JOBS AND INDUSTRIES WORKSHEET

Go back over the lists of job titles and industries. For items 1 and 2 below, list the jobs that interest you most. Then select the industries that interest you most, and list them below in item 3. These are the jobs and industries you should research most carefully. Your ideal job is likely to be found in some combination of these jobs and industries, or in more specialized but related jobs and industries.

1. The 5 job titles that interest you most _____

_____

_____

_____

_____

2. The 5 next most interesting job titles _____

_____

_____

_____

_____

3. The industries that interest you most _____

_____

_____

_____

_____

And, Now, We Return to Job-Related Skills

Back on page 283, I suggested that you should first define the job you want and then identify key job-related skills you have that support your ability to do it. These are the job-related skills to emphasize in interviews.

So, now that you have determined your ideal job, you can pinpoint the job-related skills it requires. If you haven't done so, complete the Essential Job Search Data Worksheet on pages 314–318. It will give you specific skills and accomplishments to highlight.

Yes, completing that worksheet requires time, but doing so will help you clearly define key skills to emphasize in interviews, when what you say matters so much. People who complete that worksheet will do better in their interviews than those who don't.

After you complete the Essential Job Search Data Worksheet, go back to page 283 and write in Your Top Five Job-Related Skills. Include there the job-related skills you have that you would most like to use in your next job.

Use the Most Effective Methods to Reduce Your Job Search Time

Employer surveys found that most employers don't advertise their job openings. They hire people they know, people who find out about the jobs through word of mouth, and people who happen to be in the right place at the right time. While luck plays a part, you can increase your "luck" in finding job openings.

Let's look at the job search methods that people use. The U.S. Department of Labor conducts a regular survey of unemployed people actively looking for work. The survey results are presented below.

Percentage of Unemployed Using Various Job Search Methods

- Contacted employer directly: 64.5%
- Sent out resumes/filled out applications: 48.3%
- Contacted public employment agency: 20.4%
- Placed or answered help wanted ads: 14.5%
- Contacted friends or relatives: 13.5%
- Contacted private employment agency: 6.6%
- Used other active search methods: 4.4%
- Contacted school employment center: 2.3%
- Checked union or professional registers: 1.5%

Source: U.S. Department of Labor, Current Population Survey

This section covers a number of job search methods. Most of the material is presented as information, with a few interactive activities. While each topic is short and reasonably interesting, taking a break now and then will help you absorb it all.

What Job Search Methods Work Best?

The survey shows that most people use more than one job search technique. For example, one person might read want ads, fill out applications, and ask friends for job leads. Others might send out resumes, contact everyone they know from professional contacts, and sign up at employment agencies.

But the survey covered only nine job search methods and, on those, asked only whether the job seeker did or did not use each method. The survey did not cover the Internet, nor did it ask whether a method worked in getting job offers.

Unfortunately, there hasn't been much recent research on the effectiveness of various job search methods. Most of what we know is based on older research and the observations of people who work with job seekers. I'll share what we do know about the effectiveness of job search methods in the content that follows.

Getting the Most Out of Less-Effective Job Search Methods

The truth is that every job search method works for some people. But experience and research show that some methods are more effective than others are. Your task in the job search is to spend more of your time using more effective methods—and increase the effectiveness of all the methods you use.

Quip

Your job search objective. Almost everyone finds a job eventually, so your objective should be to find a good job in less time. The job search methods I emphasize in this minibook will help you do just that.

So let's start by looking at some traditional job search methods and how you can increase their effectiveness. Only about one-third of all job seekers get their jobs using one of these methods, but you should consider using them.

Help Wanted Ads

Most jobs are never advertised, and only about 15 percent of all people get their jobs through the want ads. Everyone who reads the paper knows about these openings, so competition is fierce. The Internet also lists many job openings. But, as with want ads, enormous numbers of people view these postings. Some people do get jobs this way, so go ahead and apply. Just be sure to spend most of your time using more effective methods.

Filling Out Applications

Most employers require job seekers to complete an application form. But applications are designed to collect negative information—and employers use applications to screen people out. If, for example, your training or work history is not the best, you will often never get an interview, even if you can do the job.

Completing applications is a more effective approach for young job seekers than for adults. The reason is that there is a shortage of workers for the relatively low-paying and entry-level jobs youth typically seek. As a result, employers are more willing to accept a lack of experience or lack of job skills in youth. Even so, you will get better results by filling out the application if asked to do so and then requesting an interview with the person in charge.

When you complete an application, make it neat and error-free, and do not include anything that could get you screened out. If necessary, leave a problem section blank. It can always be explained after you get an interview.

Employment Agencies

There are three types of employment agencies. One is operated by the government and is free. The others are run as for-profit businesses and charge a fee to either you or an employer. There are advantages and disadvantages to using each.

The government employment service and one-stop centers. Each state has a network of local offices to pay unemployment compensation, provide job leads, and offer other services—at no charge to you or to employers. The service's name varies by state, and it may be called "Job Service," "Department of Labor," "Unemployment Office," "Workforce Development," or another name. Many states have "One-Stop Centers" that provide employment counseling, reference books, computerized career information, job listings, and other resources.

An Internet site at www.careeronestop.org uses will give you information on the programs provided by the government employment service, plus links to other useful sites. Another Internet site called America's Job Bank, at www.ajb.dni.us, allows visitors to see all jobs listed with the government employment service and to search for jobs by region and other criteria.

The government employment service lists only 5 to 10 percent of the available openings nationally, and only about 6 percent of all job seekers get their jobs there. Even so, visit your local office early in your job search. Find out if you qualify for unemployment compensation and learn more about its services. Look into it—the price is right.

Private employment agencies. Private employment agencies are businesses that charge a fee either to you or to the employer who hires you. You will often see their ads in the help wanted section of the newspaper, and many have Web sites. Fees can be from less than one month's pay to 15 percent or more of your annual salary.

Be careful about using fee-based employment agencies. Recent research indicates that more people use and benefit from fee-based agencies than in the past. But realize that relatively few people who register with private agencies get a job through them.

If you use them, ask for interviews where the employer pays the fee. Do not sign an exclusive agreement or be pressured into accepting a job, and continue to actively look for your own leads. You can find these agencies in the phone book's yellow pages, and a government-run Web site at www.ajb.dni.us lists many of them as well.

Temporary agencies. Temporary agencies offer jobs lasting from several days to many months. They charge the employer a bit more than your salary, and then pay you and keep the difference. You pay no direct fee to the agency. Many private employment agencies now provide temporary jobs as well.

Temp agencies have grown rapidly for good reason. They provide employers with short-term help, and employers often use them to find people they may want to hire later. Temp agencies can help you survive between jobs and get experience in different work settings; working for a temp agency may lead to a regular job. They provide a very good option while you look for long-term work, and you may get a job offer while working in a temp job.

School and Employment Services

Contacting a school employment center is one of the job search methods included in the survey presented earlier. Only a small percentage of respondents said they used this option. This is probably because few had the service available.

If you are a student or graduate, find out about these services. Some schools provide free career counseling, resume-writing help, referrals to job openings, career interest tests, reference materials, and other services. Special career programs work with veterans, people with disabilities, welfare recipients, union members, professional groups, and many others. So check out these services and consider using them.

Mailing Resumes and Posting Them on the Internet

Many job search "experts" used to suggest that sending out lots of resumes was a great technique. That advice probably helped sell their resume books, but mailing resumes to people you do not know was never an effective approach. Every so often this would work, but a 95-percent failure rate and few interviews were the more common outcomes, and still are.

While mailing your resume to strangers doesn't make much sense, posting it on the Internet might because

1. It doesn't take much time.

2. Many employers have the potential of finding your resume.

But job searching on the Internet also has its limitations, just like other methods. I'll cover resumes in more detail later and provide tips on using the Internet throughout this minibook.

The Two Job Search Methods That Work Best

The fact is that most jobs are not advertised, so how do *you* find them? The same way that about two-thirds of all job seekers do: networking with people you know (which I call warm contacts) and making direct contacts with an employer (which I call cold contacts). Both of these methods are based on the most important job search rule of all:

THE MOST IMPORTANT JOB SEARCH RULE
DON'T WAIT UNTIL THE JOB OPENS BEFORE CONTACTING THE EMPLOYER!

Employers fill most jobs with people they have met before jobs formally "open." So the trick is to meet people who can hire you before a job is available! Instead of saying, "Do you have any jobs open?" say, "I realize you may not have any openings now, but I would still like to talk to you about the possibility of future openings."

Method 1: Develop a Network of Contacts in Five Easy Stages

One study found that 40 percent of all people located their jobs through a lead provided by a friend, a relative, or an acquaintance. That makes people you know the number one source of job leads—more effective than all the traditional methods combined!

Developing and using your contacts is called "networking," and here's how it works:

1. **Make lists of people you know.** Make a thorough list of anyone you are friendly with. Then make a separate list of all your relatives. These two lists alone often add up to 25 to 100 people or more. Next, think of other groups of people that you have something in common with, such as former coworkers or classmates, members of your social or sports groups, members of your professional association, former employers, and members of your religious group. You may not know many of these people personally or well, but most will help you if you ask them.

2. **Contact them in a systematic way.** Next, contact each of these people. Obviously, some people will be more helpful than others, but any one of them might help you find a job lead.

3. **Present yourself well.** Begin with your friends and relatives. Call and tell them you are looking for a job and need their help. Be as clear as possible about the type of employment you want and the skills and qualifications you have. Look at the sample JIST Card and phone script later in this minibook for good presentation ideas.

4. **Ask them for leads.** It is possible that your contacts will know of a job opening that might interest you. If so, get the details and get right on it! More likely, however, they will not, so you should ask each person these three questions:

◆

The Three Magic Networking Questions

- ◆ *Do you know of any openings for a person with my skills?* If the answer is no (which it usually is), then ask…
- ◆ *Do you know of someone else who might know of such an opening?* If your contact does, get that name and ask for another one. If he or she doesn't, ask…
- ◆ *Do you know of anyone who might know of someone else who might know?* Another good way to ask this is "Do you know someone who knows lots of people?" If all else fails, this will usually get you a name.

◆

5. **Contact these referrals and ask them the same questions.** With each original contact, you can extend your network of acquaintances by hundreds of people. Eventually, one of these people will hire you or refer you to someone who will!

If you are persistent in following these five steps, networking may be the only job search method you need. It works.

Method 2: Contact Employers Directly

It takes more courage, but making direct contact with employers is a very effective job search technique. I call these "cold contacts" because people you don't know in advance will need to "warm up" to your inquiries. Two basic techniques for making cold contacts follow.

Use the yellow pages to find potential employers. Begin by looking at the index in your phone book's yellow pages. For each entry, ask yourself, "Would an organization of this kind need a person with my skills?" If you answer yes, then that organization or business type is a possible target. You can also rate "yes" entries based on your interest, writing an A next to those that seem very interesting, a B next to those that you are not sure of, and a C next to those that aren't interesting at all.

Next, select a type of organization that got a "yes" response, such as "hotels," and turn to that section of the yellow pages. Call each hotel listed and ask to speak to the person who is most likely to hire or supervise you. A sample telephone script is included later in this section to give you ideas about what to say.

You can easily adapt this approach to the Internet by using sites like www.yellowpages.com to get contacts anywhere in the world.

Drop in without an appointment. You can also walk into a business or organization that interests you and ask to speak to the person in charge. Particularly effective in small businesses, dropping in also works surprisingly well in larger ones. Remember to ask for an interview even if there are no openings now. If your timing is inconvenient, ask for a better time to come back for an interview.

Most Jobs Are with Small Employers

Businesses and organizations with 250 or fewer employees employ about 70 percent of all U.S. workers. They are also the source for as much as 80 percent of the new jobs created each year. They are simply too important to overlook in your job search! Many of them don't have personnel departments, making direct contacts even easier and more effective.

JIST Cards®—An Effective Mini Resume

Look at the sample cards that follow—they are JIST Cards, and they get results. Computer printed or even neatly written on a 3-by-5–inch card, JIST Cards include the essential information employers want to know.

JIST Cards have been used by thousands of job search programs and millions of people. Employers like their direct and timesaving format, and they have been proven as an effective tool to get job leads. Attach one to your resume. Give them to friends, relatives, and other contacts and ask them to pass them along to others who might know of an opening. Enclose them in thank-you notes after an interview. Leave one with employers as a business card. However you get them in circulation, you may be surprised at how well they work.

Sandra Zaremba

Home phone: (219) 232-7608
E-mail: SKZ1128@aol.com

Position: General Office/Clerical

Over two years' work experience, plus one year of training in office practices. Familiar with a variety of computer programs, including word processing, spreadsheets, accounting, and some database and graphic design programs. Am Internet literate and word-process 70 wpm accurately. Can post general ledger and handle payables, receivables, and most accounting tasks. Responsible for daily deposits averaging more than $200,000 monthly. Good interpersonal skills. Can meet strict deadlines and handle pressure well.

Willing to work any hours.

Organized, honest, reliable, and hard working.

```
                    Jonathan McLaughlin
            Answering machine: (509) 674-8736
                 Cell phone: (509) 541-0981
                    jonmcl@fauxmail.com
Objective: Electronics-installation, maintenance, and sales

Skills: Four years of work experience, plus two years advanced
training in electronics. AS degree in Electronics Engineering
Technology. Managed a $500,000/year business while going to school
full time, with grades in the top 25%. Familiar with all major
electronics diagnostic and repair equipment. Hands-on experience
with medical, consumer,communications, business, and industrial
electronics equipment and applications. Good problem-solving and
communication skills. Customer service oriented.

Willing to do what it takes to get the job done.

Self-motivated, dependable, learn quickly.
```

You can easily create JIST Cards on a computer and print them on card stock you can buy at any office supply store. Or have a few hundred printed cheaply by a local quick print shop. While they are often done as 3-by-5 cards, they can be printed in any size or format.

Use the Phone to Get Job Leads

Once you have created your JIST Card, you can use it as the basis for a phone "script" to make warm or cold calls. Revise your JIST Card content so that it sounds natural when spoken, and then edit it until you can read it out loud in about 30 seconds. Use the sample phone script that follows to help you write your own.

"Hello, my name is Pam Nykanen. I am interested in a position in hotel management. I have four years' experience in sales, catering, and accounting with a 300-room hotel. I also have an associate degree in hotel management, plus one year of experience with the Bradey Culinary Institute. During my employment, I helped double revenues from meetings and conferences and increased bar revenues by 46 percent. I have good problem-solving skills and am good with people. I am also well-organized, hard working, and detail-oriented. When may I come in for an interview?"

Once you have your script, make some practice calls to warm or cold contacts. If making cold calls, contact the person most likely to supervise you. Then present your script just as you practiced it, without stopping.

While it doesn't work every time, most people, with practice, can get one or more interviews in an hour by making such calls.

While the sample script assumes you are calling someone you don't know, it can be changed for warm contacts and referrals. Making cold calls takes courage—but works very well for many who are willing to do it.

Quip
Dialing for dollars. The phone can get you more interviews per hour than any other job search tool. But it won't work unless you use it actively.

Quip
Overcome phone phobia! Making cold calls takes guts, but job search programs find that most people can get one or more interviews an hour using cold calls. Start by calling people you know and people they refer you to. Then try calls to businesses that don't sound very interesting. As you get better, call more desirable targets.

Using the Internet in Your Job Search

I provide Internet-related tips throughout this minibook, but the Internet deserves a separate section, so here it is.

The Internet has limitations as a job search tool. While many have used it to get job leads, it has not worked well for far more. Too many assume they can simply add their resume to resume databases, and employers will line up to hire them. Just like the older approach of sending out lots of resumes, good things sometimes happen, but not often.

I recommend two points that apply to all job search methods, including using the Internet:

♦ It is unwise to rely on just one or two methods in conducting your job search.

♦ It is essential that you use an active rather than a passive approach in your job search.

Tips to Increase Your Internet Effectiveness

I encourage you to use the Internet in your job search but suggest you use it along with other techniques, including direct contacts with employers. The following suggestions can increase the effectiveness of using the Internet in your job search.

Be as specific as possible in the job you seek. This is important in using any job search method and even more so in using the Internet. The Internet is enormous, so it is essential to be as focused as possible in what you are looking for. Narrow your job title or titles to be as specific as possible. Limit your search to specific industries or areas of specialization.

Have reasonable expectations. Success on the Internet is more likely if you understand its limitations. For example, employers trying to find someone with skills in high demand, such as network engineers or nurses, are more likely to use the Internet to recruit job candidates.

Quip

If the Internet is new to you, I recommend a book titled Cyberspace Job Search Kit by Mary Nemnich and Fred Jandt. It covers the basics plus lots of advice on using the Internet for career planning and job seeking.

Limit your geographic options. If you don't want to move, or would move but only to certain areas, state this preference on your resume and restrict your search to those areas. Many Internet sites allow you to view only those jobs that meet your location criteria.

Create an electronic resume. With few exceptions, resumes submitted on the Internet end up as simple text files with no graphic elements. Employers search databases of many resumes for those that include key words or meet other searchable criteria. So create a simple text resume for Internet use and include on it words likely to be used by employers searching for someone with your abilities. See the resume on page 306 for an example.

Get your resume into the major resume databases. Most Internet employment sites let you add your resume for free, and then charge employers to advertise openings or to search for candidates. These easy-to-use sites often provide all sorts of useful information for job seekers.

Make direct contacts. Visit Web sites of organizations that interest you and learn more about them. Some will post openings, allow you to apply online, or even provide access to staff who can answer your questions. Even if they don't, you can always e-mail a request for the name of the person in charge of the area that interests you and then communicate with that person directly.

Network. You can network online, too, to get names and e-mail addresses of potential employer contacts or other people who might know of someone with a job opening. Look at interest groups, professional association sites, alumni sites, chat rooms, and employer sites—just some of the many creative ways to network with and to interact with people via the Internet.

Useful Internet Sites

Thousands of Internet sites provide information on careers or education. Many have links to other sites that they recommend. Service providers such as America Online (www.aol.com) and the Microsoft Network (www.msn.com) have career information and job listings plus links to other sites. Larger portal sites offer links to recommended career-related sites—Lycos (www.lycos.com) and Yahoo (www.yahoo.com) are just a couple of these portals. These major career-specific sites can get you started:

- The Riley Guide at www.rileyguide.com
- America's Job Bank at www.ajb.dni.us
- careerbuilder.com at www.careerbuilder.com
- Monster.com at www.monster.com
- The JIST site at www.jist.com

Step 4

Write a Simple Resume Now and a Better One Later

Sending out resumes and waiting for responses is not an effective job-seeking technique. But, many employers *will* ask you for one, and a resume can be a useful tool in your job search. I suggest that you begin with a simple resume you can complete quickly. I've seen too many people spend weeks working on their resume when they could have been out getting interviews instead. If you want a "better" resume, you can work on it on weekends and evenings. So let's begin with the basics.

Tips for Creating a Superior Resume

The following tips make sense for any resume format:

Write it yourself. It's okay to look at other resumes for ideas, but write yours yourself. It will force you to organize your thoughts and background.

Make it error-free. One spelling or grammar error will create a negative impressionist (see what I mean?). Get someone else to review your final draft for any errors. Then review it again because these rascals have a way of slipping in.

Make it look good. Poor copy quality, cheap paper, bad type quality, or anything else that creates a poor appearance will turn off employers to even the best resume content. Get professional help with design and printing if necessary. Many professional resume writers and even print shops offer writing and desktop design services if you need help.

Be brief, be relevant. Many good resumes fit on one page, and few justify more than two. Include only the most important points. Use short sentences and action words. If it doesn't relate to and support the job objective, cut it!

> ### Quip
>
> *Most jobs are never advertised because employers don't need to advertise or don't want to. Employers trust people referred to them by someone they know far more than they trust strangers. And most jobs are filled by referrals and people that the employer knows, eliminating the need to advertise. So, your job search must involve more than looking at ads.*

Be honest. Don't overstate your qualifications. If you end up getting a job you can't handle, who does it help? And a lie can result in your being fired later.

Be positive. Emphasize your accomplishments and results. A resume is no place to be too humble or to display your faults.

Be specific. Instead of saying, "I am good with people," say, "I supervised four people in the warehouse and increased productivity by 30 percent." Use numbers whenever possible, such as the number of people served, percent sales increase, or dollars saved.

You should also know that everyone feels that he or she is a resume expert. Whatever you do, someone will tell you that it's wrong. Remember that a resume is simply a job search tool. You should never delay or slow down your job search because your resume is not "good enough." The best approach is to create a simple and acceptable resume as quickly as possible and then use it. As time permits, create a better one if you feel you must.

> **Quip**
>
> *Avoid the resume pile.* Resume experts often suggest that a "dynamite" resume will jump out of the pile. This is old-fashioned advice. It assumes that you are applying to large organizations and for advertised jobs. Today, most jobs are with small employers and are not advertised. My advice is to avoid joining that stack of resumes in the first place by looking for openings that others overlook.

Chronological Resumes

Most resumes use a chronological format where the most recent experience is listed first, followed by each previous job. This arrangement works fine for someone with work experience in several similar jobs, but not as well for those with limited experience or for career changers.

Look at the two resumes for Judith Jones that follow. Both use the chronological approach. The first resume would work fine for most job search needs—and it could be completed in about an hour. Notice that the second one includes some improvements. The first resume is good, but most employers would like the additional positive information in the improved resume.

Basic Chronological Resume Example

Judith J. Jones

115 South Hawthorne Avenue
Chicago, Illinois 66204
(312) 653-9217 (home)
email: jj@earthlink.com

Leaves lots of options open by not using one job title.

JOB OBJECTIVE

Desire a position in the office management, accounting, or administrative assistant area. Prefer a position requiring responsibility and a variety of tasks.

EDUCATION AND TRAINING

Acme Business College, Lincoln, Illinois
Graduate of a one-year business program.

U.S. Army
Financial procedures, accounting functions.

John Adams High School, South Bend, Indiana
Diploma, business education.

Other: Continuing education classes and workshops in business communication, computer spreadsheet and database programs, scheduling systems, and customer relations.

Emphasis on all related education is important, because it helps overcome her lack of "work" experience.

Everything supports her job objective

EXPERIENCE

2001-present—Claims Processor, Blue Spear Insurance Co., Wilmette, Illinois. Handle customer medical claims, develop management reports based on spreadsheets I created, exceed productivity goals.

2000-2001—Returned to school to upgrade my business and computer skills. Took courses in advanced accounting, spreadsheet and database programs, office management, human relations, and new office techniques.

1998-2000—E4, U.S. Army. Assigned to various stations as a specialist in finance operations. Promoted prior to honorable discharge.

1996-1998—Sandy's Boutique, Wilmette, Illinois. Responsible for counter sales, display design, cash register and other tasks.

1994-1996—Held part-time and summer jobs throughout high school.

Uses her education in this section to add credentials

PERSONAL

I am reliable, hard working, and good with people.

Improved Chronological Resume Example

Judith J. Jones

115 South Hawthorne Avenue • Chicago, Illinois 66204
(312) 653-9217 (home)
email: jj@earthlink.com

Adds lots of details to reinforce skills throughout.

More details here.

JOB OBJECTIVE

Seeking position requiring excellent business management skills in an office environment. Position should require a variety of tasks, including office management, word processing, and spreadsheet and database program use.

EDUCATION AND TRAINING

Acme Business College, Lincoln, Illinois.
Completed one-year program in Professional Office Management. Grades in top 30 percent of my class. Courses included word processing, accounting theory and systems, advanced spreadsheet and database programs, time management, and basic supervision.

John Adams High School, South Bend, Indiana.
Graduated with emphasis on business courses. Excellent grades in all business topics and won top award for word-processing speed and accuracy.

Other: Continuing education programs at my own expense, including business communications, customer relations, computer applications, sales techniques, and others.

Uses numbers to reinforce results.

EXPERIENCE

2001-present—Claims Processor, Blue Spear Insurance Company, Wilmette, Illinois. Handle 50 complex medical insurance claims per day, almost 20 percent above department average. Created a spreadsheet report process that decreased department labor costs by over $30,000 a year (one position). Received two merit raises for performance.

2000-2001—Returned to business school to gain advanced skills in accounting, office management, sales and human resources. Computer courses included word processing and graphics design, accounting and spreadsheet software, and database and networking applications. Grades in top 30 percent of class.

1998-2000—Finance Specialist (E4), U.S. Army. Responsible for the systematic processing of over 200 invoices per day from commercial vendors. Trained and supervised eight employees. Devised internal system allowing 15 percent increase in invoices processed with a decrease in personnel. Managed department with a budget equivalent of over $350,000 a year. Honorable discharge.

1996-1998—Sales Associate promoted to Assistant Manager, Sandy's Boutique, Wilmette, Illinois. Made direct sales and supervised four employees. Managed daily cash balances and deposits, made purchasing and inventory decisions, and handled all management functions during owner's absence. Sales increased 26 percent and profits doubled during my tenure.

1994-1996—Held various part-time and summer jobs through high school while maintaining good grades. Earned enough to pay all personal expenses, including car and car insurance. Learned to deal with customers, meet deadlines, work hard, handle multiple priorities, and develop other skills.

SPECIAL SKILLS AND ABILITIES

Quickly learn new computer applications and am experienced with a number of business software applications. Have excellent interpersonal, written, and oral communication and math skills. Accept supervision well, am able to supervise others, and work well as a team member. Like to get things done and have an excellent attendance record.

Tips for Writing a Simple Chronological Resume

Follow these tips for writing a basic chronological resume.

Name. Use your formal name rather than a nickname if it sounds more professional.

Address and contact information. Avoid abbreviations in your address and include your ZIP code. If you may move, use a friend's address or include a forwarding address. Most employers will not write to you, so you must provide reliable phone numbers and other contact options. Always include your area code in your phone number because you never know where your resume might travel. If you don't have an answering machine, get one—and leave it on whenever you leave home. Make sure your voice message presents you in a professional way. Include alternative ways to reach you, like a cell phone, beeper, and e-mail address.

Job objective. You should almost always have one, even if it is general. In the sample resumes, notice how Judy keeps her options open with her broad job objective. Writing "secretary" or "clerical" might limit her from being considered for jobs she might take.

Education and training. Include any training or education you've had that supports your job objective. If you did not finish a formal degree or program, list what you did complete and emphasize accomplishments. If your experience is not strong, add details here like related courses and extracurricular activities. In the two examples, Judy puts her business schooling in both the education and experience sections. Doing this fills a job gap and allows her to present her training as equal to work experience.

Previous experience. Include the basics like employer name, job title, dates employed, and responsibilities—but emphasize things like specific skills, results, accomplishments, and superior performance.

Personal data. Do not include irrelevant details like height, weight, and marital status—doing so is considered very old-fashioned. But you can include information like hobbies or leisure activities in a special section that directly supports your job objective. The first sample includes a "Personal" section in which Judy lists some of her strengths, which are often not included in a resume.

References. You do not need to list references since employers will ask for them if they want them. If your references are particularly good, you can mention this somewhere—the last section is often a good place. List your references on a separate page and give it to employers who ask. Ask your references what they will say about you and, if positive, if they would write you a letter of recommendation to give to employers.

Tips for an Improved Chronological Resume

Once you have a simple, errorless, and eye-pleasing resume, get on with your job search. There is no reason to delay! If you want to create a better resume in your spare time (evenings or weekends), try these additional tips.

> ## Quip
>
> *Skip the negatives. Remember that a resume can get you screened out, but it is up to you to get the interview and the job. So, cut out anything negative in your resume!*

Job objective. A poorly written job objective can limit the jobs an employer might consider you for. Think of the skills you have and the types of jobs you want to do; describe them in general terms. Instead of using a narrow job title like "restaurant manager," you might write "manage a small to mid-sized business."

Education and training. New graduates should emphasize their recent training and education more than those with a few years of related work experience would. A more detailed education and training section might include specific courses you took, and activities or accomplishments that support your job objective or reinforce your key skills. Include other details that reflect how hard you work, such as working your way through school or handling family responsibilities.

Skills and accomplishments. Include things that support your ability to do well in the job you seek now. Even small things count. Maybe your attendance was perfect, you met a tight deadline, or you did the work of others during vacations. Be specific and include numbers—even if you have to estimate them. The improved chronological resume example features a "Special Skills and Abilities" section and more accomplishments and skills. Notice the impact of the numbers to reinforce results.

Job titles. Past job titles may not accurately reflect what you did. For example, your job title may have been "cashier," but you also opened the store, trained new staff, and covered for the boss on vacations. Perhaps "head cashier and assistant manager" would be more accurate. Check with your previous employer if you are not sure.

Promotions. If you were promoted or got good evaluations, say so—"cashier, promoted to assistant manager," for example. A promotion to a more responsible job can be handled as a separate job if doing so results in a stronger resume.

Gaps in employment and other problem areas. Employee turnover is expensive, so few employers want to hire people who won't stay or who won't work out. Gaps in employment, jobs held for short periods, or a lack of direction in the jobs you've held are all things that concern employers. So consider your situation and try to give an explanation of a problem area. Here are a few examples:

> 2001—Continued my education at…

> 2004—Traveled extensively throughout the United States.

> 2000 to present—Self-employed barn painter and widget maker.

> 2003—Had first child, took year off before returning to work.

Use entire years to avoid displaying an employment gap you can't explain easily. For example "2002 to 2003" can cover a few months of unemployment at the beginning of 2002.

Skills and Combination Resumes

The functional or "skills" resume emphasizes your most important skills, supported by specific examples of how you have used them. This approach allows you to use any part of your life history to support your ability to do the job you want.

While a skills resume can be very effective, it requires more work to create one. And some employers don't like them because they can hide a job seeker's faults (such as job gaps, lack of formal education, or little related work experience) better than a chronological resume. Still, a skills resume may make sense for you.

Look over the sample resumes that follow for ideas. Notice that one resume includes elements of a skills *and* a chronological resume. This so-called "combination" resume makes sense if your previous job history or education and training are positive.

More Resume Examples

Find resume layout and presentation ideas in the four samples that follow.

The chronological resume sample on page 303 focuses on accomplishments through the use of numbers. While Maria's resume does not say so, it is obvious that she works hard and that she gets results.

The skills resume on page 304 is for a recent high school graduate whose only paid work experience was at a fast-food place!

The combination resume on page 305 emphasizes Mary Beth's relevant education and transferable skills because she has no work experience in the field. The resume was submitted by professional resume writer Janet L. Beckstrom of Flint, Michigan (e-mail wordcrafter@voyager.net).

The electronic resume on page 306 is appropriate for scanning or e-mail submission. It has a plain format that is easily read by scanners. It also has lots of key words that increase its chances of being selected when an employer searches a database. The resume is based on one from *Cyberspace Resume Kit* by Mary Nemnich and Fred Jandt and published by JIST Works.

Quip

A resume is not the most effective tool for getting interviews. A better approach is to make direct contact with those who hire or supervise people with your skills and ask them for an interview, even if no openings exist now. Then send a resume.

Chronological Resume Emphasizes Results

A simple chronological format with few but carefully chosen words. It has an effective summary at the beginning, and every word supports her job objective.

She emphasizes results!

Maria Marquez

4141 Beachway Road
Redondo Beach, California 90277

Messages: (213) 432-2279
E-mail: mmarq@msn.net

Objective: Management Position in a Major Hotel

Summary of Experience: Four years' experience in sales, catering, banquet services, and guest relations in 300-room hotel. <u>Doubled sales revenues</u> from conferences and meetings. <u>Increased dining room and bar revenues by 44%.</u> <u>Won prestigious national and local awards</u> for increased productivity and services.

Experience:
Park Regency Hotel, Los Angeles, California
Assistant Manager
1999 to Present
- Oversee a staff of 36 including dining room and bar, housekeeping, and public relations operations.
- Introduced new menus and increased dining room revenues by 44% Gourmet America awarded us their first place Hotel Haute Cuisine award as a result of my efforts.
- Attracted 28% more diners with the first revival of Big Band Cocktail Dances in the Los Angeles area.

Notice her use of numbers to increase impact of statements.

Kingsmont Hotel, Redondo Beach, California
Sales and Public Relations
1997 to 1999
- Doubled revenues per month from conferences and meetings.
- Redecorated meeting rooms and updated sound and visual media equipment. Careful scheduling resulted in no lost revenue during this time.
- Instituted staff reward program, which resulted in an upgrade from B- to AAA+ in the *Car and Travel Handbook*.

Bullets here and above increase readability and emphasis.

Education: Associate Degree in Hotel Management from Henfield College of San Francisco. One-year certification program with the Boileau Culinary Institute, where I won the Grand Prize Scholarship.

While Maria had only a few years of related work experience, she used this resume to help her land a very responsible job in a large resort hotel.

Skills Resume for Someone with Limited Work Experience

A skills resume where each skill directly supports the job objective of this recent high school graduate with very limited work experience.

Lisa M. Rhodes
813 Lava Court • Denver, Colorado 81613
Home: (413) 643-2173 (leave message)
Cell phone: (413) 442-1659
Email: lrhodes@netcom.net

Position Desired
Sales-oriented position in a retail sales or distribution business.

Support for the skills comes from all life activities: school, clubs, part-time jobs.

key skills

Skills and Abilities

Communications
Good written and verbal presentation skills. Use proper grammar and have a good speaking voice.

Interpersonal
Able to get along well with coworkers and accept supervision. Received positive evaluations from previous supervisors.

Flexible
Willing to try new things and am interested in improving efficiency on assigned tasks.

← Good emphasis on adaptive skills.

Attention to Detail
Concerned with quality. My work is typically orderly and attractive. Like to see things completed correctly and on time.

Hard Working
Throughout high school, worked long hours in strenuous activities while attending school full-time. Often handled as many as 65 hours a week in school and other structured activities, while maintaining above-average grades.

Very strong statement.

Customer Contacts
Routinely handled as many as 500 customer contacts a day (10,000 per month) in a busy retail outlet. Averaged lower than a .001% complaint rate and was given the "Employee of the Month" award in my second month of employment. Received two merit increases. Never absent or late.

Good use of numbers

Cash Sales
Handled over $2,000 a day ($40,000 a month) in cash sales. Balanced register and prepared daily sales summary and deposits.

Reliable
Excellent attendance record, trusted to deliver daily cash deposits totaling over $40,000 a month.

Education
Franklin High School. Took advanced English and other classes. Member of award-winning band. Excellent attendance record. Superior communication skills. Graduated in top 30% of class.

Other
Active gymnastics competitor for four years. This taught me discipline, teamwork, how to follow instructions, and hard work. I am ambitious, outgoing, reliable, and willing to work.

Lisa's resume makes it clear that she is talented and hard working.

Combination Resume for a Career Changer

Writer's comments: This client was finishing computer programming school and had no work experience in the field. After listing the topics covered in the course, I summarized her employment experience, specifying that she earned promotions quickly. This **Mary Beth Kurzak** *would be attractive to any employer.*

2188 Huron River Drive • Ann Arbor, MI 48104 • 734-555-4912 • e-mail: mbkurzak@fauxmail.com

Profile

➤ Strong educational preparation with practical applications in computer/internet programming.
➤ Highly motivated to excel in new career.
➤ A fast learner, as evidenced by success in accelerated training program.
➤ Self-directed, independent worker with proven ability to meet deadlines and work under pressure.
➤ Maintain team perspective with ability to build positive working relationships and foster open communication.

Education/Training

ADVANCED TECHNOLOGY CENTER • Dearborn, MI   xxxx-Present
Pursuing Certification in **Internet/Information Technology**   *Anticipated completion:* Aug. xxxx
An accelerated program focusing on computer and internet programming.
Highlights of Training:

Important to include specific things learned

- Networking Concepts	- Client Server	- UNIX
- Programming Concepts	- Visual Basic	- IIS
- Programming in Java/Java Script	- C/C++	- VB/ASP
- Web Authoring Using HTML	- Oracle	- CGI
- Photoshop	- DHTML, XML	- Perl

Highlights of Experience and Abilities

Customer Service

Experiences selected to support job objective

➤ Determined member eligibility and verified policy benefits.
➤ Responded to customer questions; interpreted and explained complex insurance concepts.
➤ Collaborated with health care providers regarding billing and claim procedures.

Leadership
➤ Creatively supervised 30 employees, many of whom were significantly older.
➤ Motivated employees and improved working conditions, resulting in greater camaraderie.
➤ Trained coworkers in various technical and nontechnical processes.

Analytical/Troubleshooting
➤ Investigated and resolved computer system errors.
➤ Researched discrepancies in claims and identified appropriate actions.
➤ Compiled and analyzed claims statistics.

Administrative Support and Accounting
➤ Managed and processed medical, mental health and substance abuse claims.
➤ Oversaw accounts receivable; reconciled receipts and prepared bank deposits.
➤ Coordinated 50+ line switchboard; routed calls as appropriate.

Employment History

MEDICAL SERVICES PLUS [Contracted by Health Solutions - Southfield, MI]   xxxx-xxxx
Promoted within eight months of hire.
Claims Supervisor / Claims Adjudicator

HANSEN AGENCY OF MICHIGAN • Ann Arbor, MI   xxxx-xxxx
Earned two promotions in one year.
Claims Adjudicator / Accounting Clerk / Receptionist

FORD WILLOW RUN TRANSMISSION PLANT • Ypsilanti, MI   Summer xxxx
Temporary Production Worker

PEARL HARBOR MEMORIAL MUSEUM • Pearl Harbor, HI   xxxx-xxxx
Assistant Crew Manager

References available on request

Submitted by Janet L. Beckstrom

Electronic Resume

RICHARD JONES

3456 Generic Street

Potomac MD 11721

Phone messages: (301) 927-1189

E-mail: richj@riverview.com

Format to be scanned or e-mailed. No bold, bullets, or italics.

SUMMARY OF SKILLS

Lots of key words to help get selected by computer searches by employers.

Rigger, maintenance mechanic (carpentry, electrical, plumbing, painting), work leader. Read schematic diagrams. Flooring (wood, linoleum, carpet, ceramic and vinyl tile). Plumbing (pipes, fixtures, fire systems). Certified crane and forklift operator, work planner, inspector.

++

EXPERIENCE *Includes results statements and numbers below*

Total of nine years in the trades—apprentice to work leader.

* MAINTENANCE MECHANIC LEADER, Smithsonian Institution, Washington, DC, April 2001 to present: Promoted to supervise nine staff in all trades, including plumbing, painting, electrical, carpentry, drywall, flooring. Prioritize and schedule work. Inspect and approve completed jobs. Responsible for annual budget of $750,000 and assuring that all work done to museum standards and building codes.

* RIGGER / MAINTENANCE MECHANIC, Smithsonian Institution, February 1998 to April 2001: Built and set up exhibits. Operated cranes, rollers, forklifts, and rigged mechanical and hydraulic systems to safely move huge, priceless museum exhibits. Worked with other trades in carpentry, plumbing, painting, electrical and flooring to construct exhibits.

* RIGGER APPRENTICE, Portsmouth Naval Shipyard, Portsmouth, NH, August 1996 to January 1998: Qualified signalman for cranes. Moved and positioned heavy machines and structural parts for shipbuilding. Responsible for safe operation of over $2,000,000 of equipment on a daily basis, with no injury or accidents. Used cranes, skids, rollers, jacks, forklifts and other equipment.

++

TRAINING AND EDUCATION

HS graduate, top 50% of class.

Additional training in residential electricity, drywall, HV/AC, and refrigeration systems. Certified in heavy crane operation, forklift, regulated waste disposal, industrial blueprints.

Use the information from your completed Essential Job Search Data Worksheet to write your resume.

Step 5

Redefine What Counts As an Interview, Then Get 2 a Day

The average job seeker gets about 5 interviews a month—fewer than 2 a week. Yet many job seekers use the methods in this minibook to get 2 interviews a day. Getting 2 interviews a day equals 10 a week and 40 a month. That's 800 percent more interviews than the average job seeker gets. Who do you think will get a job offer quicker?

But getting 2 interviews a day is nearly impossible unless you redefine what counts as an interview. If you define an interview in a different way, getting 2 a day is quite possible.

THE NEW DEFINITION OF AN INTERVIEW

AN INTERVIEW IS ANY FACE-TO-FACE CONTACT WITH SOMEONE WHO HAS THE AUTHORITY TO HIRE OR SUPERVISE A PERSON WITH YOUR SKILLS—EVEN IF NO OPENING EXISTS AT THE TIME YOU INTERVIEW.

If you use this new definition, it becomes *much* easier to get interviews. You can now interview with all sorts of potential employers, not just those who have job openings now. While most other job seekers look for advertised or actual openings, you can get interviews before a job opens up or before it is advertised and widely known. You will be considered for jobs that may soon be created but that others will not know about. And, of course, you can also interview for existing openings like everyone else does.

Spending as much time as possible on your job search and setting a job search schedule are important parts of this step.

Make Your Search a Full-Time Job

Job seekers average fewer than 15 hours a week looking for work. On average, unemployment lasts three or more months, with some people out of work far longer (older workers and higher earners, for example). My many years of experience with job seekers indicate that the more time you spend on your job search each week, the less time you will likely remain unemployed.

Of course, using the more effective job search methods presented in this minibook also helps. Many job search programs that teach job seekers my basic approach of using more effective methods and spending more time looking have proven to cut in half the average time needed to find a job. More importantly, many job seekers also find better jobs using these methods.

So, if you are unemployed and looking for a full-time job, you should plan to look on a full-time basis. It just makes sense to do so, although many do not, or they start out well but quickly get discouraged. Most job seekers simply don't have a structured plan—they have no idea what they are going to do next Thursday. The plan that follows will show you how to structure your job search like a job.

Decide How Much Time You Will Spend Looking for Work Each Week and Day

First and most importantly, decide how many hours you are willing to spend each week on your job search. You should spend a minimum of 25 hours a week on hard-core job search activities with no goofing around. Let me walk you through a simple but effective process to set a job search schedule for each week.

PLAN YOUR JOB SEARCH WEEK

1. How many hours are you willing to spend each week looking for a job? _____

2. Which days of the week will you spend looking for a job? _____

_____

3. How many hours will you look each day? _____

4. At what times will you begin and end your job search on each of these days? _____

_____

Create a Specific Daily Job Search Schedule

Having a specific daily schedule is essential because most job seekers find it hard to stay productive each day. The sample daily schedule that follows is the result of years of research into what schedule gets the best results. I tested many schedules in job search programs I ran, and this particular schedule worked best. So use the sample daily schedule for ideas on creating your own, but I urge you to consider using one like this. Why? Because it works.

A Sample Daily Schedule That Works

Time	Activity
7 a.m.	Get up, shower, dress, eat breakfast.
8–8:15 a.m.	Organize work space, review schedule for today's interviews and promised follow-ups, check e-mail, update schedule as needed.
8:15–9 a.m.	Review old leads for follow-up needed today; develop new leads from want ads, yellow pages, the Internet, warm contact lists, and other sources; complete daily contact list.
9–10 a.m.	Make phone calls and set up interviews.
10–10:15 a.m.	Take a break.
10:15–11 a.m.	Make more phone calls, set up more interviews.
11 a.m.–Noon	Send follow-up notes and do other "office" activities as needed.
Noon–1 p.m.	Lunch break, relax.
1–3 p.m.	Go on interviews, make cold contacts in the field.
Evening	Read job search books, make calls to warm contacts not reachable during the day, work on a "better" resume, spend time with friends and family, exercise, relax.

Do It Now: Get a Daily Planner and Write Down Your Job Search Schedule

This is important: If you are not accustomed to using a daily schedule book or electronic planner, promise yourself to get a good one tomorrow. Choose one that allows plenty of space for each day's plan on an hourly basis, plus room for daily to-do listings. Write in your daily schedule in advance; then add interviews as they come. Get used to carrying it with you and use it!

Step 6

Dramatically Improve Your Interviewing Skills

Interviews are where the job search action is. You have to get them; then you have to do well in them. According to surveys of employers, most job seekers do not effectively present the skills they have to do the job. Even worse, most job seekers can't answer one or more problem questions.

This lack of performance in interviews is one reason why employers will often hire a job seeker who does well in the interview over someone with better credentials. The good news is that you can do simple things to dramatically improve your interviewing skills. This section will emphasize interviewing tips and techniques that make the most difference.

Your First Impression May Be the Only One You Make

Some research suggests that if the interviewer forms a negative impression in the first five minutes of an interview, your chances of getting a job offer approach zero. But I know from experience that many job seekers can create a lasting negative impression in seconds. Since a positive first impression is so important, here are some suggestions to help you get off to a good start.

Dress and groom like the interviewer is likely to be dressed—but cleaner! Employer surveys find that almost half of all people's dress or grooming creates an initial negative impression. So this is a big problem. If necessary, get advice on your interviewing outfits from someone who dresses well. Pay close attention to your grooming too—little things do count.

Be early. Leave in plenty of time to be a few minutes early to an interview.

Be friendly and respectful with the receptionist. Doing otherwise will often get back to the interviewer and result in a quick rejection.

Follow the interviewer's lead in the first few minutes. It's often informal small talk but very important for that person to see how you interact. This is a good time to make a positive comment on the organization or even something you see in the office.

Do some homework on the organization before you go. You can often get information on a business and on industry trends from the Internet or a library.

Make a good impression before you arrive. Your resume, e-mails, applications, and other written correspondence create an impression before the interview, so make them professional and error-free.

A Traditional Interview Is Not a Friendly Exchange

In a traditional interview situation, there is a job opening, and you will be one of several applicants for it. In this setting, the employer's task is to eliminate all applicants but one. The interviewer's questions are designed to elicit information that can be used to screen you out. And your objective is to avoid getting screened out. It's hardly an open and honest interaction, is it?

This illustrates yet another advantage of setting up interviews before an opening exists. This eliminates the stress of a traditional interview. Employers are not trying to screen you out, and you are not trying to keep them from finding out stuff about you.

Having said that, knowing how to answer questions that might be asked in a traditional interview is good preparation for any interview you face.

How to Answer Tough Interview Questions

Your answers to a few key problem questions may determine if you get a job offer. There are simply too many possible interview questions to cover one by one. Instead, the 10 basic questions below cover variations of most other interview questions. So, if you can learn to answer these 10 questions well, you will know how to answer most others.

Top 10 Problem Interview Questions

1. Why should I hire you?

2. Why don't you tell me about yourself?

3. What are your major strengths?

4. What are your major weaknesses?

5. What sort of pay do you expect to receive?

6. How does your previous experience relate to the jobs we have here?

7. What are your plans for the future?

8. What will your former employer (or references) say about you?

9. Why are you looking for this type of position, and why here?

10. Why don't you tell me about your personal situation?

The Three-Step Process for Answering Interview Questions

I know this might seem too simple, but the three-step process is easy to remember and can help you create a good answer to most interview questions. The technique has worked for thousands of people, so consider trying it. The three steps are

1. Understand what is really being asked.

2. Answer the question briefly.

3. Answer the real concern.

Step 1. Understand what is really being asked. Most questions are designed to find out about your self-management skills and personality, but interviewers are rarely this blunt. The employer's *real* question is often one or more of the following:

- ◆ Can I depend on you?

- ◆ Are you easy to get along with?

- ◆ Are you a good worker?

- ◆ Do you have the experience and training to do the job if we hire you?

- ◆ Are you likely to stay on the job for a reasonable period of time and be productive?

Ultimately, if you don't convince the employer that you will stay and be a good worker, it won't matter if you have the best credentials—he or she won't hire you.

Step 2. Answer the question briefly. Present the facts of your particular work experience, but...

♦ Present them as advantages, not disadvantages.

Many interview questions encourage you to provide negative information. One classic question I included in my list of Top 10 Problem Interview Questions was "What are your major weaknesses?" This is obviously a trick question, and many people are just not prepared for it.

A good response is to mention something that is not very damaging, such as *"I have been told that I am a perfectionist, sometimes not delegating as effectively as I might."* But your answer is not complete until you continue with Step 3.

Step 3. Answer the real concern by presenting your related skills.

♦ Base your answer on the key skills you have that support the job, and give examples to support these skills.

For example, an employer might say to a recent graduate, "We were looking for someone with more experience in this field. Why should we consider you?" Here is one possible answer:

"I'm sure there are people who have more experience, but I do have more than six years of work experience, including three years of advanced training and hands-on experience using the latest methods and techniques. Because my training is recent, I am open to new ideas and am used to working hard and learning quickly."

In the previous example (about your need to delegate), a good skills statement might be

"I've been working on this problem and have learned to let my staff do more, making sure that they have good training and supervision. I've found that their performance improves, and it frees me up to do other things."

Whatever your situation, learn to answer questions that present you well. It's essential to communicate your skills during an interview, and the three-step process can help you answer problem questions and dramatically improve your responses. It works!

The Most Important Interview Question of All: "Why Should I Hire You?"

This is the most important question of all to answer well. Do you have a convincing argument why someone should hire you over someone else? If you don't, you probably won't get that job you really want. So think carefully about why someone *should* hire you and practice your response. Then, make sure you communicate this in the interview, even if the interviewer never asks the question in a clear way.

Tips on Negotiating Pay—How to Earn a Thousand Dollars a Minute

Remember these few essential ideas when it comes time to negotiate your pay.

THE ONLY TIME TO NEGOTIATE IS AFTER YOU HAVE BEEN OFFERED THE JOB.

Employers want to know how much you want to be paid so that they can eliminate you from consideration. They figure if you want too much, you won't be happy with their job and won't stay. And if you will take too little, they may think you don't have enough experience. So *never* discuss your salary expectations until an employer offers you the job.

IF PRESSED, SPEAK IN TERMS OF WIDE PAY RANGES.

If you are pushed to reveal your pay expectations early in an interview, ask the interviewer what the normal pay range is for this job. Interviewers will often tell you, and you can say that you would consider offers in this range.

If you are forced to be more specific, speak in terms of a wide pay range. For example, if you figure that the company will likely pay from $20,000 to $25,000 a year, say that you would consider "any fair offer in the low to mid-twenties." This statement covers the employer's range *and goes a bit higher*. If all else fails, tell the interviewer that you would consider any reasonable offer.

For this to work, you must know in advance what the job is likely to pay. You can get this information by asking people who do similar work, or from a variety of books and Internet sources of career information.

SALARY NEGOTIATION RULE
THE ONE WHO NAMES A SPECIFIC NUMBER FIRST, LOSES.

Don't Say "No" Too Quickly

Never, ever turn down a job offer during an interview! Instead, thank the interviewer for the offer and ask to consider the offer overnight. You can turn it down tomorrow, saying how much you appreciate the offer and asking to be considered for other jobs that pay better or whatever.

But this is no time to be playing games. If you want the job, you should say so. And it is okay to ask for additional pay or other concessions. But if you simply can't accept the offer, say why and ask the interviewer to keep you in mind for future opportunities. You just never know.

Step 7

Follow Up on All Contacts

It's a fact: People who follow up with potential employers and with others in their network get jobs faster than those who do not. Here are a few rules to guide you in your job search.

Rules for Effective Follow-Up

- Send a thank-you note or e-mail to every person who helps you in your job search.
- Send the note within 24 hours after speaking with the person.
- Enclose JIST Cards with thank-you notes and all other correspondence.
- Develop a system to keep following up with good contacts.

Thank-You Notes Make a Difference

While thank-you notes can be e-mailed, most people appreciate and are more impressed by a mailed note. Here are some tips about mailed thank-you notes that you can easily adapt to e-mail use.

Thank-you notes can be handwritten or typed on quality paper and matching envelopes. Keep them simple, neat, and error-free. And make sure to include a few copies of your JIST Cards. Here is an example of a simple thank-you note.

2244 Riverwood Avenue
Philadelphia, PA 17963
April 16, XXXX

Ms. Helen A. Colcord
Henderson & Associates, Inc.
1801 Washington Blvd., Suite 1201
Philadelphia, PA 17993

Dear Ms. Colcord:

Thank you for sharing your time with me so generously today. I really appreciated seeing your state-of-the-art computer equipment.

Your advice has already proved helpful. I have an appointment to meet with Mr. Robert Hopper on Friday. As you anticipated, he does intend to add more computer operators in the next few months.

In case you think of someone else who might need a person like me, I'm enclosing another JIST Card. I will let you know how the interview with Mr. Hopper goes.

Sincerely,

William Henderson

William Henderson

Use Job Lead Cards to Help Organize Follow-Ups

If you use contact management software, use it to schedule follow-up activities. But the simple paper system I describe here can work very well or can be adapted for setting up your contact management software.

Use a simple 3-by-5–inch card to record essential information about each person in your network. Buy a 3-by-5–inch card file box and tabs for each day of the month. File the cards under the date you want to contact the person, and the rest is easy.

I've found that staying in touch with a good contact every other week can pay off big. Here's a sample card to give you ideas about creating your own.

Organization: Mutual Health Insurance
Contact person: Anna Tomey
Phone number: (555) 555-2211
Source of lead: Aunt Ruth
Notes: 4/10 called. Anna on vacation. Call back 4/15. 4/15 Interview set 4/20 at 1:30. 4/20 Anna showed me around. They use the same computers we used in school. Sent thank-you note and JIST Card. Call back 5/1. 5/1 Second interview 5/8 at 9 a.m.

In Closing

You won't get a job offer because someone knocks on your door and offers one. Job seeking does involve luck, but you are more likely to get lucky if you are out getting interviews.

I'll close this minibook with a few final tips:

- Approach your job search as if it were a job itself. Create and stick to a daily schedule, and spend at least 25 hours a week looking.

- Follow up on each lead you generate and ask each one for referrals.

- Set out each day to schedule at least two interviews, and use the new definition of an interview, which includes talking to businesses that don't have an opening now.

- Send out lots of thank-you notes and JIST Cards.

- When you want the job, tell the employer that you want it and why the company should hire you over someone else.

Don't get discouraged. There are lots of jobs out there, and someone needs an employee with your skills—your job is to find that someone.

I wish you luck in your job search and your life.

ESSENTIAL JOB SEARCH DATA WORKSHEET

Take some time to complete this worksheet carefully. It will help you write your resume and answer interview questions. You can also photocopy it and take it with you to help complete applications and as a reference throughout your job search. Use an erasable pen or pencil to allow for corrections. Whenever possible, emphasize skills and accomplishments that support your ability to do the job you want. Use extra sheets as needed.

Your name _____

Date completed _____

Job objective _____

Key Accomplishments

List three accomplishments that best prove your ability to do the kind of job you want.

1. _____

2. _____

3. _____

Education and Training

Name of high school(s); years attended _____

_____

Subjects related to job objective _____

_____

Related extracurricular activities/hobbies/leisure activities_____

_____

Accomplishments/things you did well _____

_____

Specific things you can do as a result _____

_____

Schools you attended after high school; years attended; degrees/certificates earned _____

_____

Courses related to job objective _____

_____

Related extracurricular activities/hobbies/leisure activities_____

_____

Accomplishments/things you did well _____

_____

Specific things you can do as a result _____

_____

Other Training

Include formal or informal learning, workshops, military training, things you learned on the job or from hobbies—anything that will help support your job objective. Include specific dates, certificates earned, or other details as needed. _____

_____

_____

_____

Work and Volunteer History

List your most recent job first, followed by each previous job. Military experience, unpaid or volunteer work, and work in a family business should be included here, too. If needed, use additional sheets to cover *all* significant paid or unpaid work experiences. Emphasize details that will help support your new job objective! Include numbers to support what you did: the number of people served over one or more years,

(continued)

the number of transactions processed, percentage of sales increased, total inventory value you were responsible for, payroll of the staff you supervised, total budget responsible for, and so on. Emphasize results you achieved, using numbers to support them whenever possible. Mentioning these things on your resume and in an interview will help you get the job you want!

Job 1

Dates employed _____

Name of organization _____

Supervisor's name and job title _____

Address _____

_____

Phone number/e-mail address/Web site _____

_____

What did you accomplish and do well? _____

_____

Things you learned, skills you developed or used _____

_____

Raises, promotions, positive evaluations, awards _____

_____

Computer software, hardware, and other equipment you used _____

_____

Other details that might support your job objective _____

_____

Job 2

Dates employed _____

Name of organization _____

Supervisor's name and job title _____

Address _____

_____

Phone number/e-mail address/Web site _____

_____

What did you accomplish and do well? _____

_____

Things you learned, skills you developed or used _____

_____

Raises, promotions, positive evaluations, awards _____

_____

Computer software, hardware, and other equipment you used _____

_____

Other details that might support your job objective _____

_____

Job 3

Dates employed _____

Name of organization _____

Supervisor's name and job title _____

Address _____

_____

Phone number/e-mail address/Web site _____

_____

What did you accomplish and do well? _____

_____

Things you learned, skills you developed or used _____

_____

Raises, promotions, positive evaluations, awards _____

_____

Computer software, hardware, and other equipment you used _____

_____

Other details that might support your job objective _____

_____

References

Think of people who know your work well and will say positive things about your work and character. Past supervisors are best. Contact them and tell them what type of job you want and your qualifications, and ask what they will say about you if contacted by a potential employer. Some employers will not provide references by phone, so ask them for a letter of reference for you in advance. If a past employer may say negative things, negotiate what they will say or get written references from others you worked with there.

(continued)

(continued)

Reference name _____

Position or title _____

Relationship to you _____

Contact information (complete address, phone number, e-mail address) _____

_____

Reference name _____

Position or title _____

Relationship to you _____

Contact information (complete address, phone number, e-mail address) _____

_____

_____

Reference name _____

Position or title _____

Relationship to you _____

Contact information (complete address, phone number, e-mail address) _____

_____

_____

A Short List of Additional Resources

Thousands of books and uncounted Internet sites provide information on career subjects. Space limitations do not permit me to describe the many good resources available, so I list here some of the most useful ones. Because this is my list, I've included books I've written or that JIST publishes. You should be able to find these and many other resources at libraries, bookstores, and Web book-selling sites, such as www.jist.com and www.amazon.com.

Resumes and Cover Letter Books

My books. I'm told that *The Quick Resume & Cover Letter Book* is now one of the top-selling resume books at various large bookstore chains. It is very simple to follow, is inexpensive, has good design, and has good sample resumes written by professional resume writers. *America's Top Resumes for America's Top Jobs* includes a wonderfully diverse collection of resumes covering most major jobs and life situations, plus brief but helpful resume-writing advice. With its helpful worksheets and expert samples, *Same-Day Resume* can help you write a great resume quickly so you can get on with your job search.

Other books published by JIST. The following titles include many sample resumes written by professional resume writers, as well as good advice: *Cover Letter Magic,* by Enelow and Kursmark; *Cyberspace Resume Kit,* Nemnich and Jandt; *The Edge Resume & Job Search Strategy,* Corbin and Wright; *Federal Resume Guidebook,* Troutman; *Expert Resumes for Computer and Web Jobs,* Enelow and Kursmark; *Expert Resumes for Teachers and Educators,* Enelow and Kursmark; *Gallery of Best Cover Letters,* Noble; *Gallery of Best Resumes,* Noble; and *Resume Magic,* Whitcomb.

Job Search Books

My books. *The Very Quick Job Search—Get a Better Job in Half the Time* is a thorough book with detailed advice and a "quick" section of key tips you can finish in a few hours. *The Quick Interview & Salary Negotiation Book* also has a section of quick tips likely to make the biggest difference in your job search, as well as sections with more detailed information on problem questions and other topics. *Getting the Job You Really Want* includes many in-the-book activities and good career decision-making and job search advice.

Other books published by JIST. Titles include *Career Success Is Color-Blind*, Stevenson; *Cyberspace Job Search Kit*, Nemnich and Jandt; *Inside Secrets of Finding a Teaching Job*, Warner and Bryan; and *Job Search Handbook for People with Disabilities*, Ryan.

Books with Information on Jobs

Primary references. The *Occupational Outlook Handbook* is the source of job titles listed in this minibook. Published by the U.S. Department of Labor and updated every other year, the *OOH* covers about 88 percent of the workforce. A book titled the *O*NET Dictionary of Occupational Titles* has descriptions for over 1,100 jobs based on the O*NET (for Occupational Information Network) database developed by the Department of Labor. The *Enhanced Occupational Outlook Handbook* includes the *OOH* descriptions plus more than 7,000 additional descriptions of related jobs from the O*NET and other sources. The *Guide for Occupational Exploration*, Third Edition, allows you to explore major jobs based on your interests. All of these books are available from JIST.

Other books published by JIST. Here are a few good books that include job descriptions and helpful details on career options: *America's 101 Fastest Growing Jobs*; *America's Top 101 Jobs for College Graduates*; *America's Top 101 Jobs for People Without a Four-Year Degree*; *America's Top 101 Computer and Technical Jobs*; *America's Top Medical, Education & Human Services Jobs*; *America's Top White-Collar Jobs*; *Best Jobs for the 21st Century* (plus versions for people with and without degrees); *Career Guide to America's Top Industries*; and *Guide to America's Federal Jobs*.

Internet Resources

If the Internet is new to you, I recommend a book titled *Cyberspace Job Search Kit* by Mary Nemnich and Fred Jandt. It covers the basics plus offers advice on using the Internet for career planning and job seeking. *Best Career and Education Web Sites* by Rachel Singer Gordon and Anne Wolfinger gives excellent reviews of the most helpful sites and ideas on how to use them. The *Occupational Outlook Handbook*'s job descriptions also include Internet addresses. And www.jist.com lists recommended sites for career, education, and related topics, along with comments on each.

Be aware that some sites provide poor advice, so ask your librarian, instructor, or counselor for suggestions on those best for your needs.

Other Resources

Libraries. Most libraries have the books mentioned here, as well as many other resources. Many also provide Internet access so that you can research online information. Ask the librarian for help finding what you need.

People. People who hold the jobs that interest you are one of the best career information sources. Ask them what they like and don't like about their work, how they got started, and the education or training needed. Most people are helpful and will give advice you can't get any other way.

Career counseling. A good vocational counselor can help you explore career options. Take advantage of this service if it is available to you! Also consider a career-planning course or program, which will encourage you to be more thorough in your thinking.

Sample Resumes for Some of America's Top Computer and Technical Jobs

If you read the previous information in this section, you know that I believe that resumes are an overrated job search tool. Even so, you will probably need one, and you should have a good one.

Unlike some career authors, I do not preach that there is only one right way to do a resume. I encourage you to be an individual and to do what you think will work well for you. But I also know that some resumes are clearly better than others. The following pages contain several resumes that you can use as examples when preparing your own resume.

The resumes have these points in common:

- Each is for an occupation described in this book. The resumes are arranged in alphabetical order by job title.

- Each resume is particularly good in some way.

- Each resume was written by a professional resume writer who is a member of one or more professional associations, including the Professional Association of Resume Writers (www.parw.com) or the National Resume Writers' Association (www.nrwa.com). These writers are highly qualified and hold various credentials. Most are willing to provide help (for a fee) and welcome your contacting them (although this is not a personal endorsement).

The resumes are from the following five books, all available from JIST Publishing:

- *America's Top Resumes for America's Top Jobs,* Second Edition, by Michael Farr with Louise M. Kursmark

- *Best Resumes for College Students and New Grads,* by Louise M. Kursmark

- *Expert Resumes for Computer and Web Jobs,* by Wendy S. Enelow and Louise M. Kursmark

- *Expert Resumes for Health Care Careers,* by Wendy S. Enelow and Louise M. Kursmark

- *Gallery of Best Resumes,* Third Edition, by David F. Noble

Contact Information for Resume Contributors

The following professional resume writers contributed resumes to this section. Their names are listed in alphabetical order. Each entry indicates which resume that person contributed.

Janet L. Beckstrom, CPRW
Owner, Word Crafter
1717 Montclair Ave.
Flint, MI 48503
Phone: (810) 232-9257
Toll-free: (800) 351-9818
Fax: (810) 232-9257
E-mail: wordcrafter@voyager.net
Resume on page 334

Diane Burns, CPRW, CCM
Career Marketing Techniques
Columbia, MD
Phone: (410) 884-0213
E-mail: dianecprw@aol.com
Web site: www.polishedresumes.com
Resume on page 326

(Ms.) Freddie Cheek, M.S.Ed., CPRW, CWDP, CCM, CRW

Cheek & Cristantello Career Connections
4511 Harlem Rd., Ste. 3
Amherst, NY 14226
Phone: (716) 839-3635
Fax: (716) 831-9320
E-mail: fscheek@adelphia.net
Web site: www.CheekandCristantello.com
Resume on page 329

Daniel J. Dorotik, Jr., NCRW

100PercentResumes
9803 Clinton Ave.
Lubbock, TX 79424
Phone: (806) 783-9900
Fax: (214) 722-1510
E-mail: dan@100percentresumes.com
Web site: www.100percentresumes.com
Resume on page 325

Rosemarie Ginsberg, CPRW, CEIP

Employment Recruiter
Creative Staffing Associates, Inc.
15 Michael Rd.
Framingham, MA 01701
Phone: (508) 877-5100
Fax: (508) 877-3511
E-mail: csadirecthire@aol.com
Web site: www.creativeresumesnjobs.com
Resume on page 331

Peter Hill, CPRW

Distinctive Resumes
Honolulu, HI
Phone: (808) 306-3920
E-mail: distinctiveresumes@yahoo.com
Web site: www.peterhill.biz
Resume on page 322

Nancy Karvonen, CPRW, CCM, IJCTC, CEIP

Executive Director, A Better Word & Resume
4490 County Rd. HH
Orland, CA 95963
Phone: (209) 745-5107
Toll-free: (877) 973-7863
Fax: (209) 745-7114
E-mail: careers@aresumecoach.com
Web site: www.aresumecoach.com
Resume on page 332

Jeanne Knight, JCTC

Career and Job Search Coach
P.O. Box 828
Melrose, MA 02176
Phone: (617) 968-7747
E-mail: Jeanne@careerdesigns.biz
Web site: www.careerdesigns.biz
Resume on page 328

Ann Stewart, CPRW

Advantage Services
Roanoke, TX
E-mail: ASresume@aol.com
Resume on page 324

Deanna Verbouwens

Ace in the Hole Resume Writing & Career Services
14 Mitchell Ct.
Hicksville, NY 11801
Phone: (516) 942-5986
E-mail: verbouwens@yahoo.com and info@aceinthehole.net
Web site: www.aceinthehole.net
Resume on page 327

Computer and Information Systems Managers

DAVID KENT

5555 Kalanianaole Hwy. • Honolulu, Hawaii 00000
808-555-5555 • dkent@islandemail.com

COMPUTER AND INFORMATION SYSTEMS MANAGER
Administrative Intranets/Public Web Sites/Software Engineering

7+ years of Web planning, development, and administration experience. Thorough knowledge and effective execution of state-of-the-art Internet and intranet systems technology. Proven communication and presentation skills. Easily introduce technical information to project participants and to the public. Project management expertise spans single and multi-institutional organizations, and academia.

- Information and Reporting Systems
- Real-Time Database Management Systems
- IT/Web-Based Media Support
- Scientific Document/Media Support
- Science Communication
- Web/Database Servers
- Project Quality Control
- Content Development

Specializing in the development and implementation of automated and paperless systems for data collection; procedures reporting; information submission, storage, and retrieval; and formal report and Web content production.

RELEVANT EXPERIENCE

RESEARCH CORPORATION OF THE UNIVERSITY OF HAWAII, Honolulu, 1998–Present

Computer and Information Systems Manager (1/2000–Present)
Marine Bioproducts Engineering Center (MarBEC)

Supervise Information and Reporting System (IRS) software development team of up to 8 (2 faculty and 6 students). Establish IRS content management and administrative procedures. Provide comprehensive annual report preparation support, including research updates and timely production and delivery. Plan and meet marketing, IT, and AV requirements of MarBEC-sponsored meetings and symposiums.

- Designed and developed proprietary IRS software, securing $500,000 in additional funding. Anticipated time savings of 40%–60% in annual report content preparation, 80%–90% in research-related Web content publishing. Has potential to save NSF $2.2 million of ERC annual expenditures if fully deployed.
- Completed special project: Culture Collection (CC) database management system resulting in real-time online availability of CC content.
- Delivered Beta version of Annual report Volume II reporting system 8 weeks ahead of schedule. Delivered full system version 1.01 on schedule and within budget.
- Presented several successful Web development and software engineering multimedia seminars: PowerPoint site visit presentations; ERC annual meeting IRS demonstrations; IRS demo to University Information and Computing Sciences (ICS) Department.
- Assisted with planning and production of Fourth Asia-Pacific Marine Biotechnology Conference (produced proceedings and coordinated AV requirements) and Microalgae Production for the Aquaculture Industry Workshop (produced workshop video).

Database/Web Development Specialist (7/1999–1/2000)
MarBEC

Coordinated planning, development, and implementation of Relational Database Management System (RDMS), including time frame for deliverables. Maintained and estimated budgets for subcontracted work and personal assistant. Created Internet and intranet content/applications in support of internal and external activities. Trained users at multiple sites. Developed related standards, policies, and procedures.

DAVID KENT—COMPUTER AND INFORMATION SYSTEMS MANAGER
Page 2

Computer Specialist III (6/1998–6/1999)
NOAA National Marine Fisheries Service (NMFS) Honolulu Laboratory

Coordinated NMFS Honolulu Laboratory, PIAO, WPCFIN, and Coast Watch Web sites to comply with NOAA standards. Collaborated to develop and implement standards for these and other sub-webs. Established and chaired laboratory's Web committee. Established laboratory's Web presence. Identified, obtained, and published Web site material.

- Designed and developed intranet and Internet Web sites in 6 months, 10 weeks ahead of schedule. Conceptualized and built from scratch NOAA R/V *Townsend Cromwell* student connection outreach Web site.

CHESAPEAKE BAY RESEARCH CONSORTIUM, Annapolis, Maryland, 1995–1998

Environmental Management Fellow
EPA Chesapeake Bay Program (CBP) Office

Worked closely and in coordination with CBP management committee members and other federal, state, and university staff to provide means of publishing and maintaining CBP Web site material.

- Established notable Web presence through coding, designing, and administering intranet and Internet World Wide Web sites. Co-authored CBP *Web Document Guidance.*

_____**TECHNICAL EXPERTISE** _____

HARDWARE: Intel-Based Systems • Macintosh • UNIX • Digital Imaging Devices • Telecommunications • Local Area Networks

SOFTWARE: Operating Systems • HTML • Database/Spreadsheet • Microsoft Project 2000 • Graphics Packages • File Manipulations • E-mail Editors • GIS • FTP • Word Processors • Directory Manipulations • Multimedia Digital Imaging

PROGRAMMING AND CODING PROFICIENCIES/FAMILIARITIES: HTML Editors • XHTML • CSS • JavaScript • Dynamic HTML • SQL • CGI Scripting • Visual Basic • DOM • COM • ColdFusion Markup Language • DTDs • XML • XSL • XSLT

_____ **ADDITIONAL TRAINING** _____

Troubleshooting and Maintaining the Macintosh • XML Certification • Web Process and Project Management • Web Site Development and Design • Brochure, Catalog Ad, Newsletter, and Report Design • Graphics and Animation Creation • Data and Information Presentation • Windows-Based Environment Programming

_____ **EDUCATION** _____

Bachelor of Science—Oceanography (Mathematics Emphasis), 1992
Humboldt State University, Arcata, California

Computer Programmers

BRENT D. BOATMAN

1836 Tameria Drive, Dallas, TX 75234 · (214) 251-3415 · bboatman@texas.net

Game Programmer		
C/C++	Open GL	Nintendo 64
Win32 API	3D Graphics	Nintendo Dolphin
MFC	AI	Sega Dreamcast
DirectX SDK	Console Development	Sony PlayStation 2
Assembly		Microsoft X-Box

PROFESSIONAL EXPERIENCE

1998 – 2000   **Koala Game Studio · Dallas, Texas**
Developer and publisher of entertainment software
Console Game Programmer

- ◆ Participated as a graphics programmer on a cross-functional development team that published a highly successful leading-edge sports game for Nintendo 64 and Sega Dreamcast. Recognized for strong individual contribution and emerging technical leadership.
- ◆ Represented company on team partnered with Microsoft that successfully resolved software incompatibility issues inhibiting game's development.
- ◆ Currently creating leading-edge graphics technology for next-generation platforms (Sony PlayStation 2, Microsoft X-Box, Nintendo Dolphin).

Manager's Comments: "very hard worker" … "goes above and beyond to meet schedule" … "instrumental in Nintendo 64/Sega Dreamcast versions of game" … "very high-quality work."

1997 – 1998   **University of North Texas · Denton, Texas**
Computer Science Department
Student Intern

- ◆ Helped design and code an educational game under a research grant; incorporated graphics, sound, and network play into game.
- ◆ Assisted professor in innovative computer game development lab.

EDUCATION   **University of North Texas · Denton, Texas**
Bachelor of Science, 1998
Major: Computer Science
Minor: Mathematics

Attended PlayStation 2 Developers' Conference, 2000

Computer Software Engineers

RICHARD LEVINSON

0000 Preston Avenue ◆ Houston, TX 77000 ◆ (281) 000-0000 ◆ myname@aol.com

Career Target: Software Programmer / Software Engineer

PROFILE

Talented software programmer with BBA degree, strong educational background in programming, and experience using cutting-edge development tools. Articulate and professional communication skills, including formal presentations and technical documentation. Productive in both team-based and self-managed projects; dedicated to maintaining up-to-date industry knowledge and IT skills.

Knowledge & Skill Areas:

- Software Development Lifecycle
- Object-Oriented Programming
- Problem Analysis & Resolution
- Web Site Design & Development

- Requirements Gathering & Analysis
- Technical & End User Documentation
- Software Testing & Troubleshooting
- Project Teamwork & Communications

TECHNICAL SUMMARY

Languages: Java, C, C++, JSP, ASP, Rational, HTML, SQL, Unified Process
Operating Systems: Linux, Windows XP/2000/9x
Object-Oriented Design: UML, Design Patterns

EDUCATION

TEXAS UNIVERSITY, Houston, TX
Bachelor of Business Administration in Computer Science, 2002

- ◆ Earned place on President's List for 3 semesters (4.0 GPA)
- ◆ Member, Golden Key National Honor Society & Honors Fraternity
- ◆ Selected for listing in *Who's Who Among Students in American Universities and Colleges*

Relevant Coursework:

- Software Engineering
- Project Management
- Database Design

- Systems Engineering
- Differential Equations
- Classical / Modern Physics

- Calculus I, II, III
- Logic Circuits
- Systems Analysis

Project Highlights:

- ◆ **Software Engineering**—Served as Design Team Leader and member of Programming group for semester-long project involving development of software for actual implementation within Texas University Recreation Center. Determined requirements, created "look and feel" for user interface, and maintained explicit written documentation.

- ◆ **Systems Engineering**—Teamed with group of 4 in conceptualizing and designing client-server application to interconnect POS and inventory systems for retail outlet, delivering class presentation that highlighted specifications and projected $2 million in cost savings.

COMMUNITY COLLEGE, Houston, Texas
- ◆ 3.96 GPA / Concentration in Computer Science coursework

EXPERIENCE

DATAFRAME CONCEPTS, L.L.C., Houston, TX   2000–Present
Software Developer

- ◆ Worked with small team of developers to brainstorm and implement ideas for shipping/receiving software representing leading-edge concept within transportation industry.

- ◆ Planned and initiated redesign of existing standalone application, utilizing object-oriented design/programming and Java in creating thin-client GUI for new distributed system.

- ◆ Collaborated with marketing director in strategies to further business growth, including Web site enhancement that drove 65% increase in visitor interest for product offering.

* References and additional information will gladly be provided upon request.

Computer Systems Analysts, Database Administrators, and Computer Scientists

Myra C. Landers

1256 GEYERS LANE, ELLICOTT CITY, MD 21046 — 301.555.5555 — MCL@HOTMAIL.COM

Network Administrator / Systems Analyst

Tech Profile

- ▶ PC Hardware & Software Configurations
- ▶ DOS
- ▶ LAN/WAN
- ▶ Windows NT Workstation (4.0 & 5.0)
- ▶ ADP
- ▶ Microsoft Products

Awards

- ▶ Received a number of notable awards for excellence in managing computer operations, professionalism, and team leadership. Please inquire as to the nature of the awards.

Profile

- ▶ Expert knowledge of all Microsoft products.
- ▶ Microsoft Certified Professional, NT Workstation 4.0, April 2000.
- ▶ Ten years' direct experience supervising critical computer operations.
- ▶ Troubleshoot operations, processes, and networks; determine accurate and timely solutions. Apply quality assurance measures.

Experience

UNITED STATES ARMY, 1993 to 2001   *Top Secret Clearance*
Network Administrator/Systems Analyst, Germany   **1996 to Present**

- ▶ Supervise two personnel supporting critical computer requirements and ongoing operations. Effectively manage daily operations in a network with 50 computers, two servers (40 offices), and 250 clients.
- ▶ Implement upgrades and policies regarding network security. Excellent ability to research and figure new ways to make applications run smoother. Skilled problem solver. Provide quality service to all customers. React quickly and thoughtfully to ADP problems, applying an experienced knowledge of computer systems to ensure minimal computer problems/downtime. Keep all automation systems free from viruses. Analyze problems/glitches and recommend or implement viable working solutions.
- ▶ Maintain a comprehensive, working knowledge of Windows NT 4.0 Server Workstation and Exchange Server 5.0. Proficient knowledge of PC server hardware and software configurations and LAN/WAN networking.
- ▶ Start new accounts for secure Internet access. Manage and issue PKI email encryption software to best secure military email.
- ▶ Selected by senior management to co-lead a diverse team in providing daily customer service and network administration. Instrumental in getting a new server on-line.

SPECIFIC PROJECT

- ▶ Developed a system policy and implemented network security upgrading software, ensuring compatibility with the fast-paced civilian sector, which was running dual operating systems. Ensured the DOS-based programs operated correctly, then installed more server-based software and services enabling server-based administration of the network, significantly enhancing initial response time to the client.

Power Generation Section, Team Leader, Kentucky   **1993 to 1996**

- ▶ Supervised a team of six mechanics. Performed direct support, maintenance, repair, overhauling, and rebuilding of power generation equipment.
- ▶ Trained, guided, and offered assistance to a team of mechanics to ensure full mission capability at all times. Reviewed operator's equipment licenses.
- ▶ Conducted troubleshooting of mechanical, electrical, and hydraulic systems and determined faults.
- ▶ Prepared status reports for senior management on equipment and parts tracking. Managed inventory and parts tracking databases. Administered quality control measures.

Education and Training

- ▶ AA in Computer Science, Central Texas College, 1995
- ▶ Microsoft NT Server 4.0 Core Technologies, New Horizons, 1999 (Certificate of Training)
- ▶ Internetworking Using MS TCP/IP, New Horizons, 1999 (Certificate of Training)
- ▶ Primary Leadership Development Course, U.S. Army, 1995
- ▶ Power Generation Management, U.S. Army, 1993

Designers

Aimeé Kufari

555 Henry Street ● Apartment 5A ● Brooklyn, New York ● 55555 ● 646.555.5555

Profile

A creative graphic design/illustration professional with more than seven years of proven talent; expert in designing graphics and illustrations for textbooks, catalogs, magazines and Web pages coupled with an amazing understanding of composition and color usage. Excellent project management skills. Ability to establish rapport with individuals at all levels, analyze needs and develop appropriate materials within project scope.

Areas of Expertise

Illustration ● Graphic Design ● Color Correcting ● Logo Design ● Brochure, Magazine and Newsletter Design

Computer Experience

Adobe Photoshop ● Adobe Illustrator ● InDesign ● Dimensions ● Streamline ● QuarkXPress
Microsoft Word, Excel and PowerPoint ● Mac and PC operating systems

Professional Experience

McGraw-Hill, School Division, 2001 to Present
Senior Designer: Produce artwork; design textbook covers and packaging for all educational CD-ROMs for grades K through 6; maintain total responsibility for color correcting, batching and scaling raw digital images. Primary liaison between department manager and junior designers; ensure that all assignments are completed within project scope.

Accessory Collaboration Network, 2000
Illustrator: Created illustrations of messenger bags, backpacks and tote bags for publication in nation-wide catalog.

Global Business Techniques, 1998 to 1999
Art Director: Designed corporate identity and branding image; developed business cards, letterhead and envelopes. Created all brochures; mini-magazines; newsletters; and trade-show, convention and corporate event banners and promotional giveaways: T-shirts, pins and postcards.

Hofstra University, 1994 to 1998
Art Designer: Designed and implemented all university publications, advertisements and brochures, including but not limited to student handbooks and course catalogs, *New York Times* magazine advertisements, posters for university club-sponsored events, invitations for faculty and staff university and alumni affairs and various departmental newsletters.

Freelance Design Experience

Two Side Advantage: Designed all marketing materials, including Website (www.twosidedvantage.isp), T-shirts, posters, bumper stickers, pins and print flyers promoting tours, documentaries and appearances.

U.S. Pastry Chefs: Solely responsible for design and implementation of the corporate identity and branding image, including brochures, newsletters, business cards and letterhead.

Jackie's Chocolate: Developed logo, business cards, letterhead, indoor displays and store-front signs; major contributor responsible for the design of all retail chocolate boxes.

Audio Vision: Created corporate identity, responsible for the design and implementation of a variety of magazine and trade publication advertisements.

Friendly Automotive: Designed logo and corporate image; created artwork for all marketing materials, including pamphlets and brochures; and cdesigned direct-mail campaign postcards, T-shirts and coupon books.

Business Concepts of New York: Developed business cards, letterhead and envelopes for all corporate divisions.

Super 5678 Tattoo: Designed outside store-front sign, in-shop displays, business cards, T-shirts and print advertisements for various publications, including the *Village Voice*.

Education

New York Institute of Technology, Bachelor of Fine Arts, Graphic Design, 1994

Industrial Engineers, Including Health and Safety

SEAN L. STEEPER

17 Woodcliff Road   Home: 333-333-3333
Westboro, MA 01581   slsteeper@hotmail.com

INDUSTRIAL ENGINEER
New Product Design • Manufacturing Process Redesign • Project Management

EDUCATION

University of Massachusetts ~ Amherst, MA
B.S. Industrial Engineering ~ Graduated with Honors ~ May 2003

RELEVANT COURSEWORK

Engineering Design • Systems Engineering • Computer Integrated Manufacturing • Production Systems
Production Engineering • Operations Research • Oral and Visual Communications
Industrial Psychology • Ergonomics • Quality Management

ACADEMIC PROJECTS

- Researched and recommended alternative methods for coating coronary stents for a leading manufacturer of cardiovascular products. Designed and manufactured prototype for spray-coating each stent, as opposed to the current practice of dipping them, which resulted in a 25% reduction in defects.
- Designed a facility and assembly-line layout to optimize production for an electronics products company.
- Generated a comprehensive Safety and Development Plan for a medical devices company.
- Created an ergonomically efficient material-handling trolley.

ENGINEERING EXPERIENCE

ABC Cardiovascular, Amherst, MA   5/02–10/02
Industrial Engineer, Co–Op

- Designed, developed, and implemented a unique device for facilitating the movement of coronary stent and catheter products from one workstation to another, resulting in a 20% decrease in scrapped product.
- Revised and simplified the Standard Operating Procedure for a label-printing machine that included detailed, easy-to-follow troubleshooting procedures and digital photographs.
- Analyzed production reports associated with a crimping machine and successfully identified one product that was consistently more prone to defects than others. Recommended machine adjustments to alleviate defects.
- Optimized floor space by rearranging and redesigning four production cells within a tightly constricted space.
- Member of a team to prepare for a critical FDA audit. Ensured machines were fully validated and safety guards were properly and securely in place.

ADDITIONAL EXPERIENCE

Albright Roofing and Painting, Framingham, MA   9/03–Present
Construction Laborer—Contribute to roofing and home painting projects.

Dunmore Plastering, Southboro, MA   Summers 01 and 03
Plasters Foreman—Organized and monitored building materials and inventory levels.

Independently Employed, Amherst, MA   1/99–5/01
Agricultural Contractor—Performed agricultural contract work for farmers.

Licensed Practical and Licensed Vocational Nurses

MICHELLE R. BROWN, LPN

428 Walden Avenue • Syracuse, New York 13135 • (315) 555-8328

LICENSED PRACTICAL NURSE
Patient Care and Education / Supervision / Nursing Recruitment / Quality Improvement

Professional Profile:

Over 10 years' experience providing knowledgeable, compassionate, and professional care to patients of all ages and medical conditions. Gained specialized experience working with patients who have sustained traumatic brain injuries and spinal-cord injuries. Provided professional and high-quality patient care in a high-stress, rapidly changing environment while always addressing the patients' health needs, personal concerns, and safety. Identified opportunities to instruct patients and caregivers to promote wellness and healthful follow-up care. Supervised healthcare staff and enhanced productivity and efficiency. Demonstrated skills in public speaking.

Summary:
- Assisted in problem-solving related to staffing, supplies, and resident care.
- Ensured that resident care standards were maintained and the rights of residents and preferences in care and treatment were respected.
- Gained experience in a variety of medical units, including Traumatic Brain Injury and Spinal Cord Rehabilitation, Orthopedics, Internal Medicine, Family Medicine, Telemetry, Ambulatory Surgery, OT / PT / Speech Therapy, and Hemodialysis and Peritoneal Dialysis.
- Instructed patients and family members in safety issues, infection control, wound and injury care, disease and pain management, nutrition, and general wellness.
- Performed diagnostic testing and utilized a variety of test equipment.
- Conveyed a friendly, caring, and positive attitude to patients and their caregivers.
- Served as Team Leader with responsibility for delegating patient-care assignments, documenting treatment and progress, communicating with physicians and other healthcare professionals, and overseeing medication administration.
- Managed such office duties as scheduling, filing, faxing, data entry, typing, answering telephones, and communicating with vendors and insurance companies.
- Utilized computer skills in Microsoft Word, Access, and Excel; and Meditech to update patient information and prepare billing.
- Drew blood and performed extensive laboratory work.
- Demonstrated ability to interact well with people of all ages and backgrounds.

Education:

Cazenovia College, Cazenovia, New York
Associate in Applied Science — Nursing　　　　　　　　　　　　　2001
Graduated with Distinction　3.38 GPA

Syracuse Vocational Technical Center, Syracuse, New York
Licensed Practical Nurse　　　　　　　　　　　　　　　　　　1991

Professional development training in:
Hemodialysis and Peritoneal Dialysis	Orthopedics and Telemetry	EKG Testing
Venipuncture and IV Insertion	Isolation Techniques	Infection Control
Splint Application and Removal	CVP Flushing, Care, and Use	PCA Pumps
Safe Drug Administration	Computerized Medicine Cart	PICC Lines

Licensed Practical and Licensed Vocational Nurses, continued

Michelle R. Brown   **Page Two**

Licensure:

New York State Licensed Practical Nurse, #135847-1

Clinical Experience:

Fillmore Medical Center — Medical / Surgical and Psychiatric
Children's Hospital — Pediatrics
Sisters of Charity — Oncology
Lancaster Hospital — Medical / Surgical, Maternity, and Geriatrics
Syracuse General — Medical / Surgical

Work Experience:

Aurora Senior Healthcare, Syracuse, New York   2002–Present
LPN Supervisor
Monitor and supervise the personal-care services provided by 12 Resident Assistants. Oversee the administration of medications and treatments and manage the storage and distribution of controlled-substance medications. Ensure a safe and healthful work environment and make certain that quality standards are maintained. Promote the policy and procedures of Aurora Senior Healthcare. Identify and report unusual symptoms, daily needs, and progress of residents. Maintain accurate documentation in case notes, medication administration records, change-of-shift reports, and treatment records.
➤ *Received Nursing Department Achievement Award.*

Fillmore Medical Center, Syracuse, New York   1991–2001
Senior Licensed Practical Nurse
Provided the full range of nursing care. Collected patient data, both objective and subjective, and entered information into kardex/ppc. Prepared progress notes and updated charts. Administered medication orally; topically; and by pump, catheter, tube, and PICC line. Treated patients with chest, oral, nasal, and tracheal tubes. Assisted with burn treatments, wound care, suture and staple care, and decubitus ulcer care. Handled narcotics and controlled substances with responsibility for keys and documentation. Provided pre- and post-op care and pain-management therapy.
➤ *Received Certificate of Merit from the Department of Rehabilitation Medicine.*
➤ *Collaborated with therapists to rearrange patients' schedules to ensure proper morning care and nutrition.*
➤ *Assisted in the creation of therapeutic pass questionnaire to document problems during home visits.*
➤ *Received Certificate of Recognition for outstanding work with brain-injury and spinal-cord-injury patients.*
➤ *Served on Quality Improvement Committee.*

Sisters of Charity, Syracuse, New York   1987–1989
Certified Nursing Assistant

Garden Terrace Nursing Home, Syracuse, New York   1986–1987
Certified Nursing Assistant

Photographers

Margo L. Kramer

2520 Main Street • Townsville, MA 01583 • 508/555-1234 • pixperfect@cs.com

Objective

To apply photography education along with freelance and internship experience in a studio or fine-arts institution.

Education

Bachelor of Fine Arts, May 2002   The Art Institute of Boston, Boston, MA
    Photography major
    Portfolio scholarship award for Rail Series, 1999

Internships

The Image Maker, Boston, MA   A non-profit photography gallery
    Assistant to Director during auction and member selection for exhibits. Independently built and maintained an accurate mailing list.

The Art of Life, Inc., Boston, MA   A custom black-and-white photofinishing, matting, and framing studio
    Applied photography techniques to assist with retouching/spotting of finished fine-art photographs for gallery inventory and professional darkroom clients. Acquired experience and became proficient in matting and framing fine-art photographs. Utilizing computer skills, scanned photographs, and entered pertinent data relative to individual photographs into database, creating a foundation for the existing photographic database.

Exhibits

Gallery 601, "Behind the Scenes Portfolio"
Equinox Grille, "Mixed Media"
Water Street Café, "Thanksgiving Parade"
Kougeaus Gallery, "Waiting" (from "Rails" series; selected photography)
First Impression Gallery, "Student Exhibit"

Publications

Old House Interiors ....Stylist/Photo Assistant, "Bates Mansion 2001"
Gallery Guide ....Advertisement for Kougeaus Gallery Exhibition
Art Institute of Boston ....Awards Brochure, "Connections"

Additional

Experienced with medium-format photography and digital photography for portraits, documentaries, and special events, including weddings, birthdays, anniversaries. Additional experience includes extensive knowledge of textures and patterns for visual display.

Funded education working in local restaurant and as freelance photographer, stylist, and garden planner.

Portfolio available   www.margosart.com/portfolio

TAMURA YAMAGUCHI

400 Woodruff Lane
Oakwood, Kansas 66022

tyamaguchi@southernbell.net
(883) 109-9743

DIGITAL PRE-PRESS OPERATOR

PROFESSIONAL PROFILE

Talented print production specialist with impressive experience in digital imaging pre-press operations. Fast, accurate, and willing to work long hours to meet deadlines. Communicate with customers and vendors. Develop customer awareness of color and file format preparation.

SOFTWARE PACKAGES

- Illustrator
- Photoshop
- PageMaker
- FrameMaker
- QuarkXpress
- FileMaker Pro
- Acrobat Distiller and Exchange
- Preps
- Trapwise
- PressTouch
- PowerPoint Mac & PC

WORKFLOW

- Delta Workstation
- Scitex PS and PS Ripping

EQUIPMENT

- AgfaSelect Set 7000
- AgfaAvantra 44 Imagesetter
- Creo Platesetter and Lodum (CTP) Output

FILE MANAGEMENT

- Manual Trapping
- Print Files to Disk
- Color Manipulation
- Troubleshooting Postscript and PDF Files
- Pre-Flight for Digital Imaging

VALUE OFFERED

Premier Printing, Inc., Oakwood, Kansas   2000–Present
Senior Desktop Operator

Produce complex metallic-on-metallic printing for one of state's largest sheetfed printing firms, serving software clients.

- Print Scitex workflow to Brisque Workstation, rip and trap, and impose files with Preps.
- Print ICF file to Brisque and output Iris 43 wide-digital Dylux or Iris4Print for Kodak approval.

Oakwood Printing Inc., Oakwood, Kansas   1999–2000
Desktop Operator

Accomplished digital pre-press operation for commercial printing firm.

- Reproduced jobs on Delta Workstation, ripped and trapped, imposed file with Signastation, and output with Epson Digital Dylux.
- Implemented Delta Workflow and directed to plate.

(Continued)

TAMURA YAMAGUCHI
PAGE TWO

VALUE OFFERED (CONTINUED)

MidWest Lithographer, Oakwood, Kansas   1997–1999
Digital Imaging Technician/Lead

Led crew in digital pre-press for one of oldest printing companies in Kansas.

- Instrumental in setting up on-site processing team at Cisco.
- Completed and uploaded complex rush FTP website project in 3 hours. Instructed client on file preparation.

AMP Graphic Services, Kansas City, Kansas   1993–1997
Pre-Press Foreman
Oversaw 3 shifts for turnkey and fulfillment house utilizing web press. As qualified digital pre-press operator, prepared files for digital printing.

- Collected data and created 3000-record FileMaker Pro database for easy archival and retrieval of complete job histories including photos.
- Set company production record for 3-day turnaround of 8-book set of 50,000 prints to Europe. Worked crews in 3 shifts to finish 750 plates within 24 hours.
- Directed, trained, and evaluated desktop operator, stripper, proofer, and plater.
- Coordinated daily operations with pressroom foreman.
- Wrote and instituted detailed procedures in compliance with ISO Certification.

Advanced Publishing, Ltd., Tokyo, Japan   1986–1993
Production Manager/Photographer/Graphic Artist

Rapidly progressed from graphic artist to production manager for this fast-paced firm. Published monthly and weekly architectural publications within tight time frames.

- Supervised 9-person production team consisting of graphic designers, artists, and photographers.
- Produced business cards, letterhead, 4-color brochures, and flyers for commercial-art customers.
- Interacted with customers to correct errors and identify potential color and preparation problems.

SPECIALIZED TRAINING

University of Wisconsin—Madison, Wisconsin

First Institute of Art & Design—Tokyo, Japan

- Graphic Arts • Graphic Design • Delta System • Color Production
- Applescript • Commercial Photography
- Fingerprint Press Device Calibration to Ensure Color Accuracy

Respiratory Therapists

ANGELA P. CARDOVA, CRT

1834 Highlands Dr.   248-555-3729
Novi, MI 48375   cardova@msn.com

PROFILE

✓ Over 8 years as Respiratory Therapist.
✓ Adult and pediatric care provider at emergency, critical, and subacute levels. Strong patient-assessment skills.
✓ Additional experience in home-care settings.

HIGHLIGHTS OF CLINICAL SKILLS

✓ Basic respiratory therapy
✓ Ventilator set-up and management (including high-frequency oscillator ventilators)
✓ Nasal CPAP therapy
✓ Arterial blood gas sampling and analysis

✓ Oxygen therapy
✓ Pulmonary function testing
✓ Extubation
✓ Weaning
✓ Protocol-driven therapy

CERTIFICATIONS

✓ Certified Respiratory Therapist/Registry-eligible (NBRC)   ✓ BCLS (American Heart Assoc.)

EMPLOYMENT HISTORY

Respiratory Therapist: MERCY HOSPITAL • Livonia, Michigan   2002–Present
• Set up respiratory and related equipment in homes of recently discharged patients. Equipment includes:
   ✓ Oxygen concentrator   ✓ Nebulizer compressor   ✓ Air compressor
   ✓ Liquid oxygen   ✓ Apnea monitor   ✓ Suction machine
   ✓ Oxygen conserving device   ✓ Ultrasonic nebulizer   ✓ CPAP fitting and set-up
• Perform respiratory assessments.
• Verify health benefits; maintain familiarity with Medicare guidelines.

Polysomnography Technician: OAKDALE HEALTH SYSTEM • Ypsilanti, Michigan   2001–2002
• Prepared for and monitored patients during sleep studies for evaluation of obstructive sleep apnea and other sleeping disorders.

Respiratory Therapist
HALMARK HOME HEALTH CARE CENTERS • Centerline, Michigan   1998–1999
ST. JOSEPH MERCY HOSPITAL • Ann Arbor, Michigan   1995–1998

EDUCATION

AAS in Respiratory Care: GRAND VALLEY STATE UNIVERSITY • Grand Rapids, Michigan   1995
Certified Medical Assistant Program: CLEARY COLLEGE • Ypsilanti, Michigan   1990

ACCOMPLISHMENTS

✓ Collaborated with other students to reactivate Zeta Phi Beta Sorority chapter at Grand Valley State University. Served as Chapter President for one year.

References available on request.

Section Three

Important Trends in Jobs and Industries

In putting this section together, my objective was to give you a quick review of major labor market trends. To accomplish that, I included three excellent articles that originally appeared in U.S. Department of Labor publications.

The first article is "Tomorrow's Jobs." It provides a superb—and short—review of the major trends that *will* affect your career in the years to come. Read it for ideas on selecting a career path for the long term.

The second article is "Employment Trends in Major Industries." While you may not have thought much about it, the industry you work in is just as important as your occupational choice. This great article will help you learn about the major trends affecting various industries.

The third article, "Training for Techies," covers a multitude of education and training options that can lead to jobs in computer-related and technical fields. Its charts and real-world examples show you that you may already have the training you need to get a job in your chosen field.

Tomorrow's Jobs

Comments

This article, with minor changes, comes from the *Occupational Outlook Handbook* and was written by the U.S. Department of Labor staff. The material provides a good review of major labor market trends, including trends for broad types of occupations and industries.

Much of this article uses 2002 data, the most recent available at press time. By the time it is carefully collected and analyzed, the data used by the Department of Labor is typically several years old. Since labor market trends tend to be gradual, this delay does not affect the material's usefulness.

You may notice that some job titles in this article differ from those used elsewhere in *America's Top 101 Computer and Technical Jobs.* This is not an error. The material that follows uses a different set of occupations than I used in choosing the jobs this book describes.

Making informed career decisions requires reliable information about opportunities in the future. Opportunities result from the relationships between the population, labor force, and the demand for goods and services.

Population ultimately limits the size of the labor force—individuals working or looking for work—which constrains how much can be produced. Demand for various goods and services determines employment in the industries providing them. Occupational employment opportunities, in turn, result from demand for skills needed within specific industries. Opportunities for medical assistants and other health-care occupations, for example, have surged in response to rapid growth in demand for health services.

Examining the past and projecting changes in these relationships is the foundation of the Occupational Outlook Program. This chapter presents highlights of Bureau of Labor Statistics projections of the labor force and occupational and industry employment that can help guide your career plans.

Population

Population trends affect employment opportunities in a number of ways. Changes in population influence the demand for goods and services. For example, a growing and aging population has increased the demand for health services. Equally important, population changes produce corresponding changes in the size and demographic composition of the labor force.

The U.S. population is expected to increase by 24 million over the 2002–12 period, at a slower rate of growth than during both the 1992–2002 and 1982–92 periods (Chart 1). Continued growth will mean more consumers of goods and services, spurring demand for workers in a wide range of occupations and industries. The effects of population growth on various occupations will differ. The differences are partially accounted for by the age distribution of the future population.

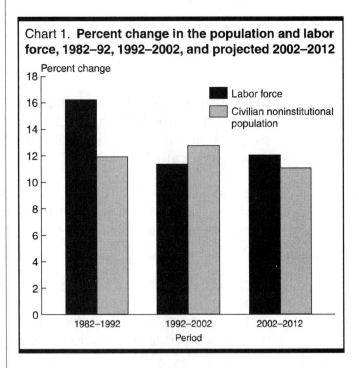

Chart 1. **Percent change in the population and labor force, 1982–92, 1992–2002, and projected 2002–2012**

The youth population, aged 16 to 24, will grow 7 percent over the 2002–12 period. As the baby boomers continue to age, the group aged 55 to 64 will increase by 43.6 percent or 11.5 million persons, more than any other group. Those aged 35 to 44 will decrease in size, reflecting the birth dearth following the baby boom generation.

Minorities and immigrants will constitute a larger share of the U.S. population in 2012. The number of Hispanics is projected to continue to grow much faster than those of all other racial and ethnic groups.

Labor Force

Population is the single most important factor in determining the size and composition of the labor force—that is, people who are either working or looking for work. The civilian labor force is projected to increase by 17.4 million, or 12 percent, to 162.3 million over the 2002–12 period.

The U.S. workforce will become more diverse by 2012. White, non-Hispanic persons will continue to make up a decreasing share of the labor force, falling from 71.3 percent in 2002 to 65.5 percent in 2012 (Chart 2). However, despite relatively slow growth, white, non-Hispanics will remain the largest group in the labor force in 2012. Hispanics are projected to account for an increasing share of the labor force by 2012, growing from 12.4 to 14.7 percent. By 2012, Hispanics will constitute a larger proportion of the labor force than will blacks, whose share will grow from 11.4 percent to 12.2 percent. Asians will continue to be the fastest growing of the four labor force groups.

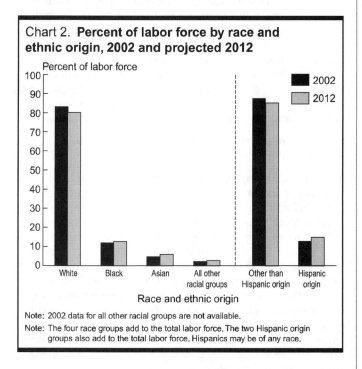

Chart 2. **Percent of labor force by race and ethnic origin, 2002 and projected 2012**

Note: 2002 data for all other racial groups are not available.

Note: The four race groups add to the total labor force. The two Hispanic origin groups also add to the total labor force. Hispanics may be of any race.

The numbers of men and women in the labor force will grow, but the number of women will grow at a faster rate than the number of men. The male labor force is projected to grow by 10 percent from 2002 to 2012, compared with 14.3 percent for women. As a result, men's share of the labor force is expected to decrease from 53.5 to 52.5 percent, while women's share is expected to increase from 46.5 to 47.5 percent.

The youth labor force, aged 16 to 24, is expected to slightly decrease its share of the labor force to 15 percent by 2012. The primary working age group, between 25 and 54 years

old, is projected to decline from 70.2 percent of the labor force in 2002 to 65.9 percent by 2012. Workers 55 and older, on the other hand, are projected to increase from 14.3 percent to 19.1 percent of the labor force between 2002 and 2012, due to the aging of the baby-boom generation (Chart 3).

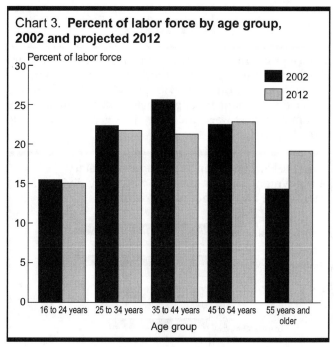

Chart 3. **Percent of labor force by age group, 2002 and projected 2012**

Employment

Total employment is expected to increase from 144 million in 2002 to 165 million in 2012, or by 14.8 percent. The 21 million jobs that will be added by 2012 will not be evenly distributed across major industrial and occupational groups. Changes in consumer demand, technology, and many other factors will contribute to the continually changing employment structure in the U.S. economy.

The following two sections examine projected employment change from both industrial and occupational perspectives. The industrial profile is discussed in terms of primary wage and salary employment. Primary employment excludes secondary jobs for those who hold multiple jobs. The exception is employment in agriculture, which includes self-employed and unpaid family workers in addition to wage and salary workers.

The occupational profile is viewed in terms of total employment—including primary and secondary jobs for wage and salary, self-employed, and unpaid family workers. Of the nearly 144 million jobs in the U.S. economy in 2002, wage and salary workers accounted for 132 million; self-employed workers accounted for 11.5 million; and unpaid family workers accounted for about 140,000. Secondary employment accounted for 1.7 million jobs. Self-employed workers held 9 out of 10 secondary jobs; wage and salary workers held most of the remainder.

★ ★ ★ ★ ★ ★ ★ ★ ★ ★

Industry

Service-providing industries. The long-term shift from goods-producing to service-providing employment is expected to continue. Service-providing industries are expected to account for approximately 20.8 million of the 21.6 million new wage and salary jobs generated over the 2002–12 period (Chart 4).

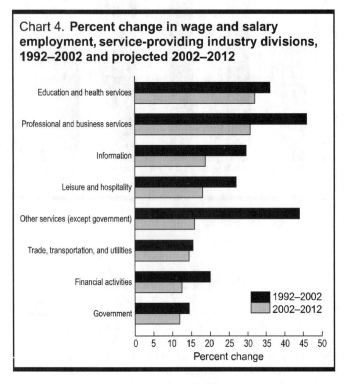

Chart 4. Percent change in wage and salary employment, service-providing industry divisions, 1992–2002 and projected 2002–2012

Education and health services. This industry supersector is projected to grow faster—31.8 percent—and add more jobs than any other industry supersector. About 1 out of every 4 new jobs created in the U.S. economy will be in either the healthcare and social assistance or private educational services sectors.

Healthcare and social assistance—including private hospitals, nursing and residential care facilities, and individual and family services—will grow by 32.4 percent and add 4.4 million new jobs. Employment growth will be driven by increasing demand for healthcare and social assistance because of an aging population and longer life expectancies. Also, as more women enter the labor force, demand for childcare services is expected to grow.

Private educational services will grow by 28.7 percent and add 759,000 new jobs through 2012. Rising student enrollments at all levels of education will create demand for educational services.

Professional and business services. This group will grow by 30.4 percent and add nearly 5 million new jobs. This industry supersector includes some of the fastest growing industries in the U.S. economy.

Employment in administrative and support and waste management and remediation services will grow by 37 percent and add 2.8 million new jobs to the economy by 2012. The fastest growing industry in this sector will be employment services, which will grow by 54.3 percent and will contribute almost two-thirds of all new jobs in administrative and support and waste management and remediation services. Employment services ranks among the fastest growing industries in the nation and is expected to be among those that provide the most new jobs.

Employment in professional, scientific, and technical services will grow by 27.8 percent and add 1.9 million new jobs by 2012. Employment in computer systems design and related services will grow by 54.6 percent and add more than one-third of all new jobs in professional, scientific, and technical services. Employment growth will be driven by the increasing reliance of businesses on information technology and the continuing importance of maintaining system and network security. Management, scientific, and technical consulting services also will grow very rapidly, by 55.4 percent, spurred by the increased use of new technology and computer software and the growing complexity of business.

Management of companies and enterprises will grow by 11.4 percent and add 195,000 new jobs.

Information. Employment in the information supersector is expected to increase by 18.5 percent, adding 632,000 jobs by 2012. Information contains some of the fast growing computer-related industries such as software publishers; Internet publishing and broadcasting; and Internet service providers, Web search portals, and data processing services. Employment in these industries is expected to grow by 67.9 percent, 41.1 percent, and 48.2 percent, respectively. The information supersector also includes telecommunications; broadcasting; and newspaper, periodical, book, and directory publishers. Increased demand for residential and business land-line and wireless services, cable service, high-speed Internet connections, and software will fuel job growth among these industries.

Leisure and hospitality. Overall employment will grow by 17.8 percent. Arts, entertainment, and recreation will grow by 28 percent and add 497,000 new jobs by 2012. Most of these new job openings will come from the amusement, gambling, and recreation sector. Job growth will stem from public participation in arts, entertainment, and recreation activities—reflecting increasing incomes, leisure time, and awareness of the health benefits of physical fitness.

Accommodation and food services is expected to grow by 16.1 percent and add 1.6 million new jobs through 2012.

Job growth will be concentrated in food services and drinking places, reflecting increases in population, dual-income families, and dining sophistication.

Trade, transportation, and utilities. Overall employment in this industry supersector will grow by 14.1 percent between 2002 and 2012. Transportation and warehousing is expected to increase by 914,000 jobs, or by 21.7 percent, through 2012. Truck transportation will grow by 20.5 percent, adding 275,000 new jobs, while rail and water transportation are both projected to decline. The warehousing and storage and the couriers and messengers industries are projected to grow rapidly at 28.6 percent and 41.7 percent, respectively. Demand for truck transportation and warehousing services will expand as many manufacturers concentrate on their core competencies and contract out their product transportation and storage functions.

Employment in retail trade is expected to increase by 13.8 percent, from 15 million to 17.1 million. Increases in population, personal income, and leisure time will contribute to employment growth in this industry, as consumers demand more goods. Wholesale trade is expected to increase by 11.3 percent, growing from 5.6 million to 6.3 million jobs.

Employment in utilities is projected to decrease by 5.7 percent through 2012. Despite increased output, employment in electric power generation, transmission, and distribution and natural gas distribution is expected to decline through 2012 due to improved technology that increases worker productivity. However, employment in water, sewage, and other systems is expected to increase 46.4 percent by 2012. Jobs are not easily eliminated by technological gains in this industry because water treatment and waste disposal are very labor-intensive activities.

Financial activities. Employment is projected to grow 12.3 percent over the 2002–12 period. Real estate and rental and leasing is expected to grow by 18.4 percent and add 374,000 jobs by 2012. Growth will be due, in part, to increased demand for housing as the population grows. The fastest growing industry in the financial activities supersector will be commercial and industrial machinery and equipment rental and leasing, which will grow by 39.8 percent.

Finance and insurance is expected to increase by 590,000 jobs, or 10.2 percent, by 2012. Employment in securities, commodity contracts, and other financial investments and related activities is expected to grow 15.5 percent by 2012, reflecting the increased number of baby boomers in their peak savings years, the growth of tax-favorable retirement plans, and the globalization of the securities markets. Employment in credit intermediation and related services, including banks, will grow by 10.9 percent and add about half of all new jobs within finance and insurance. Insurance carriers and related activities is expected to grow by 7.5 percent and add 168,000 new jobs by 2012. The number of jobs within agencies, brokerages, and other insurance-related activities is expected to grow about 14.5 percent as many insurance carriers downsize their sales staffs and as agents set up their own businesses.

Government. Between 2002 and 2012, government employment, including that in public education and hospitals, is expected to increase by 11.8 percent, from 21.5 million to 24 million jobs. Growth in government employment will be fueled by growth in state and local educational services and the shift of responsibilities from the federal government to the state and local governments. Local government educational services is projected to increase 17.5 percent, adding over 1.3 million jobs. State government educational services also is projected to grow 17.5 percent, adding 388,000 jobs. Federal government employment, including the Postal Service, is expected to increase by less than 1 percent as the federal government continues to contract out many government jobs to private companies.

Other services (except government). Employment will grow by 15.7 percent. More than 4 out of 10 new jobs in this supersector will be in religious organizations, which are expected to grow by 24.4 percent. Personal care services will be the fastest growing industry at 27.6 percent. Also included among other services is private household employment, which is expected to decrease 7.2 percent.

Goods-producing industries. Employment in the goods-producing industries has been relatively stagnant since the early 1980s. Overall, this sector is expected to grow 3.3 percent over the 2002–12 period. Although employment is expected to increase more slowly than in the service providing industries, projected growth among goods-producing industries varies considerably (Chart 5).

Construction. Employment in construction is expected to increase by 15.1 percent, from 6.7 million to 7.7 million. Demand for new housing and an increase in road, bridge, and tunnel construction will account for the bulk of job growth in this supersector.

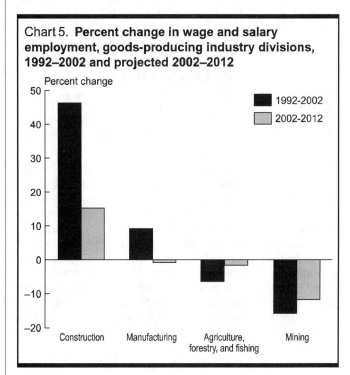

Chart 5. **Percent change in wage and salary employment, goods-producing industry divisions, 1992–2002 and projected 2002–2012**

Manufacturing. Employment change in manufacturing will vary by individual industry, but overall employment in this supersector will decline by 1 percent, or 157,000 jobs. For example, employment in plastics and rubber products manufacturing and machinery manufacturing is expected to grow by 138,000 and 120,000 jobs, respectively. Due to an aging population and increasing life expectancies, pharmaceutical and medicine manufacturing is expected to grow by 23.2 percent and add 68,000 jobs through 2012. However, productivity gains, job automation, and international competition will adversely affect employment in many other manufacturing industries. Employment in textile mills and apparel manufacturing will decline by 136,000 and 245,000 jobs, respectively. Employment in computer and electronic product manufacturing also will decline by 189,000 jobs through 2012.

Agriculture, forestry, fishing, and hunting. Overall employment in agriculture, forestry, fishing, and hunting is expected to decrease by 2 percent. Employment is expected to continue to decline due to advancements in technology. The only industry within this supersector expected to grow is support activities for agriculture and forestry, which includes farm labor contractors and farm management services. This industry is expected to grow by 18.4 percent and add 17,000 new jobs.

Mining. Employment in mining is expected to decrease 11.8 percent, or by some 60,000 jobs, by 2012. Employment in coal mining and metal ore mining is expected to decline by 30.2 percent and 38.8 percent, respectively. Employment in oil and gas extraction also is projected to decline by 27.8 percent through 2012. Employment decreases in these industries are attributable mainly to technology gains that boost worker productivity, growing international competition, restricted access to federal lands, and strict environmental regulations that require cleaning of burning fuels.

Occupation

Expansion of service-providing industries is expected to continue, creating demand for many occupations. However, projected job growth varies among major occupational groups (Chart 6).

Professional and related occupations. Professional and related occupations will grow the fastest and add more new jobs than any other major occupational group. Over the 2002–12 period, a 23.3-percent increase in the number of professional and related jobs is projected, a gain of 6.5 million. Professional and related workers perform a wide variety of duties and are employed throughout private industry and government. About three-quarters of the job growth will come from three groups of professional occupations—computer and mathematical occupations, healthcare practitioners and technical occupations, and education, training, and library occupations—which will add 4.9 million jobs combined.

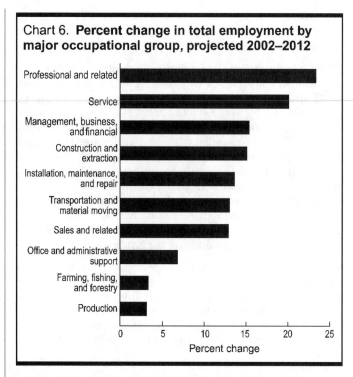

Chart 6. **Percent change in total employment by major occupational group, projected 2002–2012**

Service occupations. Service workers perform services for the public. Employment in service occupations is projected to increase by 5.3 million, or 20.1 percent, the second largest numerical gain and second highest rate of growth among the major occupational groups. Food preparation and serving related occupations are expected to add the most jobs among the service occupations, 1.6 million by 2012. However, healthcare support occupations are expected to grow the fastest, 34.5 percent, adding 1.1 million new jobs.

Management, business, and financial occupations. Workers in management, business, and financial occupations plan and direct the activities of business, government, and other organizations. Their employment is expected to increase by 2.4 million, or 15.4 percent, by 2012. Among managers, the numbers of computer and information systems managers and of preschool and childcare center/program educational administrators will grow the fastest, by 36.1 percent and 32 percent, respectively. General and operations managers will add the most new jobs, 376,000, by 2012. Farmers and ranchers are the only workers in this major occupational group whose numbers are expected to decline, losing 238,000 jobs. Among business and financial occupations, accountants and auditors and management analysts will add the most jobs, 381,000 combined. Management analysts also will be one of the fastest growing occupations in this group, along with personal financial advisors, with job increases of 30.4 percent and 34.6 percent, respectively.

Construction and extraction occupations. Construction and extraction workers construct new residential and commercial buildings and also work in mines, quarries, and oil and gas fields. Employment of these workers is expected to grow 15 percent, adding 1.1 million new jobs. Construction trades and related workers will account for more than three-fourths of these new jobs, 857,000, by 2012. Many extraction occupations will decline, reflecting overall employment losses in the mining and oil and gas extraction industries.

Installation, maintenance, and repair occupations. Workers in installation, maintenance, and repair occupations install new equipment and maintain and repair older equipment. These occupations will add 776,000 jobs by 2012, growing by 13.6 percent. Automotive service technicians and mechanics and general maintenance and repair workers will account for more than 4 in 10 new installation, maintenance, and repair jobs. The fastest growth rate will be among heating, air-conditioning, and refrigeration mechanics and installers, an occupation that is expected to grow 31.8 percent over the 2002–12 period.

Transportation and material moving occupations. Transportation and material moving workers transport people and materials by land, sea, or air. The number of these workers should grow 13.1 percent, accounting for 1.3 million additional jobs by 2012. Among transportation occupations, motor vehicle operators will add the most jobs, 760,000. Rail transportation occupations are the only group in which employment is projected to decline, by 5.4 percent, through 2012. Material moving occupations will grow 8.9 percent and will add 422,000 jobs.

Sales and related occupations. Sales and related workers transfer goods and services among businesses and consumers. Sales and related occupations are expected to add 2 million new jobs by 2012, growing by 12.9 percent. The majority of these jobs will be among retail salespersons and cashiers, occupations that will add more than 1 million jobs combined.

Office and administrative support occupations. Office and administrative support workers perform the day-to-day activities of the office, such as preparing and filing documents, dealing with the public, and distributing information. Employment in these occupations is expected to grow by 6.8 percent, adding 1.6 million new jobs by 2012. Customer service representatives will add the most new jobs, 460,000. Desktop publishers will be among the fastest growing occupations in this group, increasing by 29.2 percent over the decade. Office and administrative support occupations account for 11 of the 20 occupations with the largest employment declines.

Farming, fishing, and forestry occupations. Farming, fishing, and forestry workers cultivate plants, breed and raise livestock, and catch animals. These occupations will grow 3.3 percent and add 35,000 new jobs by 2012. Agricultural workers, including farmworkers and laborers, accounted for the overwhelming majority of new jobs in this group. The numbers of both fishing and logging workers are expected to decline, by 26.8 percent and 3.2 percent, respectively.

Production occupations. Production workers are employed mainly in manufacturing, where they assemble goods and operate plants. Production occupations will have the slowest job growth among the major occupational groups, 3.2 percent, adding 354,000 jobs by 2012. Jobs will be created

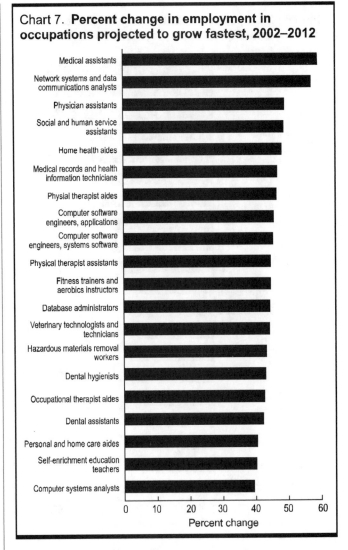

Chart 7. **Percent change in employment in occupations projected to grow fastest, 2002–2012**

for many production occupations, including food processing workers; machinists; and welders, cutters, solderers, and brazers. Textile, apparel, and furnishings occupations, as well as assemblers and fabricators, will account for much of the job losses among production occupations.

Among all occupations in the economy, computer and healthcare occupations are expected to grow the fastest over the projection period (Chart 7). In fact, healthcare occupations make up 10 of the 20 fastest growing occupations, while computer occupations account for 5 out of the 20 fastest growing occupations in the economy. In addition to high growth rates, these 15 computer and healthcare occupations combined will add more than 1.5 million new jobs. High growth rates among computer and healthcare occupations reflect projected rapid growth in the computer and data processing and health services industries.

The 20 occupations listed in Chart 8 will account for more than one-third of all new jobs, 8 million combined, over the 2002–12 period. The occupations with the largest numerical increases cover a wider range of occupational categories than do those occupations with the fastest growth rates.

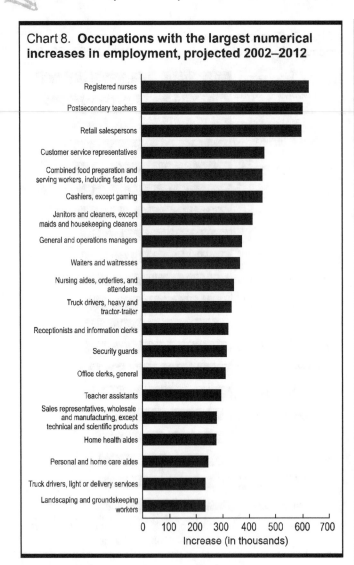

Chart 8. Occupations with the largest numerical increases in employment, projected 2002–2012

Registered nurses
Postsecondary teachers
Retail salespersons
Customer service representatives
Combined food preparation and serving workers, including fast food
Cashiers, except gaming
Janitors and cleaners, except maids and housekeeping cleaners
General and operations managers
Waiters and waitresses
Nursing aides, orderlies, and attendants
Truck drivers, heavy and tractor-trailer
Receptionists and information clerks
Security guards
Office clerks, general
Teacher assistants
Sales representatives, wholesale and manufacturing, except technical and scientific products
Home health aides
Personal and home care aides
Truck drivers, light or delivery services
Landscaping and groundskeeping workers

Increase (in thousands)

Health occupations will account for some of these increases in employment, as well as occupations in education, sales, transportation, office and administrative support, and food service. Many of these occupations are very large and will create more new jobs than will those with high growth rates. Only 2 out of the 20 fastest growing occupations—home health aides and personal and home care aides—also are projected to be among the 20 occupations with the largest numerical increases in employment.

Declining occupational employment stems from declining industry employment, technological advancements, changes in business practices, and other factors. For example, increased productivity and farm consolidations are expected to result in a decline of 238,000 farmers and ranchers over the 2002–12 period (Chart 9). The majority of the 20 occupations with the largest numerical decreases are office and administrative support and production occupations, which are affected by increasing plant and factory automation and the implementation of office technology that reduces the needs for these workers. For example, employment of word processors and typists is expected to decline due to the proliferation of personal computers, which allows other workers to perform duties formerly assigned to word processors and typists.

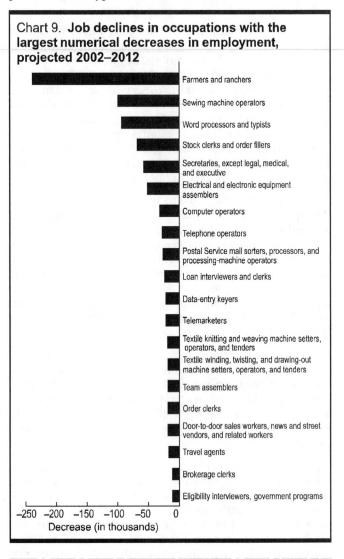

Chart 9. Job declines in occupations with the largest numerical decreases in employment, projected 2002–2012

Farmers and ranchers
Sewing machine operators
Word processors and typists
Stock clerks and order fillers
Secretaries, except legal, medical, and executive
Electrical and electronic equipment assemblers
Computer operators
Telephone operators
Postal Service mail sorters, processors, and processing-machine operators
Loan interviewers and clerks
Data-entry keyers
Telemarketers
Textile knitting and weaving machine setters, operators, and tenders
Textile winding, twisting, and drawing-out machine setters, operators, and tenders
Team assemblers
Order clerks
Door-to-door sales workers, news and street vendors, and related workers
Travel agents
Brokerage clerks
Eligibility interviewers, government programs

Decrease (in thousands)

Education and Training

Education is essential in getting a high-paying job. In fact, for all but 1 of the 50 highest paying occupations, a college degree or higher is the most significant source of education or training. Air traffic controllers is the only occupation of the 50 highest paying for which this is not the case.

Among the 20 fastest growing occupations, a bachelor's or associate degree is the most significant source of education or training for 10 of them—network systems and data communications analysts; physician assistants; medical records and health information technicians; computer software engineers, applications; computer software engineers, systems software; physical therapist assistants; database administrators; veterinary technologists and technicians; dental hygienists; and computer systems analysts. On-the-job training is the most significant source of education or training for another 8 of the 20 fastest growing occupations—medical assistants, social and human service assistants, home health aides, physical therapist aides, hazardous materials removal workers, occupational therapist aides, dental assistants, and personal and home care aides. In contrast, on-the-job training is the most significant source of education or training for 17 of the 20 occupations with the largest numerical increases; 3 of these 20 occupations—registered nurses, postsecondary teachers, and general and operations managers—have an associate or higher degree as the most significant source of education or training. On-the-job training also is the most significant source of education or training for 19 of the 20 occupations with the largest numerical decreases; one of these 20 occupations—travel agents—has a postsecondary vocational award as the most significant source of education or training.

Total Job Openings

Job openings stem from both employment growth and replacement needs (Chart 10). Replacement needs arise as workers leave occupations. Some transfer to other occupations while others retire, return to school, or quit to assume household responsibilities. Replacement needs are projected to account for 60 percent of the approximately 56 million job openings between 2002 and 2012. Thus, even occupations projected to experience little or no growth or to decline in employment still may offer many job openings.

Professional and related occupations are projected to grow faster and add more jobs than any other major occupational group, with 6.5 million new jobs by 2012. Three-fourths of the job growth in professional and related occupations is expected among computer and mathematical occupations; healthcare practitioners and technical occupations; and education, training, and library occupations. With 5.3 million job openings due to replacement needs, professional and related occupations are the only major group projected to generate more openings from job growth than from replacement needs.

Service occupations are projected to have the largest number of total job openings, 13 million, reflecting high replacement needs. A large number of replacements will be necessary as young workers leave food preparation and service occupations. Replacement needs generally are greatest in the largest occupations and in those with relatively low pay or limited training requirements.

Office automation will significantly affect many individual office and administrative support occupations. Overall, these occupations are projected to grow more slowly than average, while some are projected to decline. Office and administrative support occupations are projected to create 7.5 million job openings over the 2002–12 period, ranking third behind service and professional and related occupations.

Farming, fishing, and forestry occupations are projected to have the fewest job openings, approximately 335,000. Because job growth is expected to be slow and levels of retirement and job turnover high, more than 85 percent of these projected job openings are due to replacement needs.

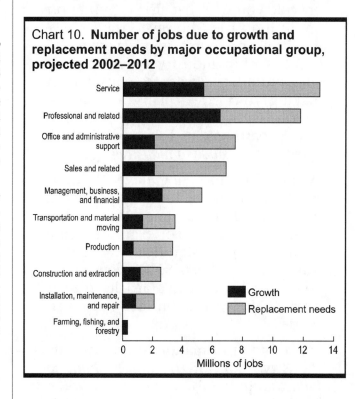

Chart 10. **Number of jobs due to growth and replacement needs by major occupational group, projected 2002–2012**

Employment Trends in Major Industries

Comments

While hundreds of specialized industries exist, about 75 percent of all workers are employed in just 42 major ones. Space limitations do not allow us to provide you with detailed information on all industries; however, the following article presents a good overview of trends within industry types. It gives you important facts to consider in making your career plans. The article comes, with minor changes, from a U.S. Department of Labor publication titled *Career Guide to Industries*.

While you may not have thought much about it, the industry you work in will often be as important as the career you choose. For example, some industries pay significantly higher wages than others. So, if you found your way back to this article, read it over carefully and consider the possibilities.

For more information on a specific industry, look for the *Career Guide to Industries* in your library. A more widely available version of the same book is published by JIST under the title *Career Guide to America's Top Industries*. It is available through bookstores and many libraries. Here are the industries covered in the *Career Guide to Industries*:

Agriculture, Mining, and Construction
Agriculture, Forestry, and Fishing
Construction
Mining
Oil and Gas Extraction
Manufacturing
Aerospace Product and Parts Manufacturing
Apparel Manufacturing
Chemical Manufacturing, Except Pharmaceutical and Medicine Manufacturing
Computer and Electronic Product Manufacturing
Food Manufacturing
Motor Vehicle and Parts Manufacturing
Pharmaceutical and Medicine Manufacturing
Printing
Steel Manufacturing
Textile Mills and Products
Trade
Automobile Dealers
Clothing, Accessory, and General Merchandise Stores
Grocery Stores
Wholesale Trade
Transportation and Utilities
Air Transportation
Truck Transportation and Warehousing
Utilities
Information
Broadcasting
Motion Picture and Video Industries
Publishing, Except Software
Software Publishers
Telecommunications
Financial Activities
Banking
Insurance
Securities, Commodities, and Other Investments
Professional and Business Services
Advertising and Public Relations Services
Computer Systems Design and Related Services
Employment Services
Management, Scientific, and Technical Consulting Services
Education and Health Services
Child Daycare Services
Educational Services
Health Services
Social Assistance, Except Child Daycare
Leisure and Hospitality
Arts, Entertainment, and Recreation
Food Services and Drinking Places
Hotels and Other Accommodations
Government
Federal Government, Excluding the Postal Service
State and Local Government, Excluding Education and Hospitals

Overview

The U.S. economy is comprised of industries with diverse characteristics. For each industry covered in the Department of Labor's publication *Career Guide to Industries,* detailed information is provided about specific characteristics: The nature of the industry, working conditions, employment, occupational composition, training and advancement requirements, earnings, and job outlook. This chapter provides an overview of these characteristics and the outlook for the various industries and economy as a whole.

Nature of the Industry

Industries are defined by the processes they use to produce goods and services. Workers in the United States produce and provide a wide variety of products and services and as a result, the types of industries in the U.S. economy range widely—from agriculture, forestry, and fishing to aerospace manufacturing. Although many of these industries are related, each industry has a unique combination of occupations, production techniques, inputs and outputs, and business characteristics. Understanding the nature of the industry is important, because it is this unique combination that determines working conditions, educational requirements, and the job outlook for each of the industries discussed in the *Career Guide.*

Industries consist of many different places of work, called *establishments,* which range from large factories and office complexes employing thousands of workers to small businesses employing only a few workers. Not to be confused with companies, which are legal entities, establishments are physical locations in which people work, such as the branch office of a bank. Thus, a company may have more than one establishment. Establishments that use the same or similar processes to produce goods or services are organized together into *industries.* Industries are, in turn, organized together into *industry groups.* These are further organized into industry subsectors and then ultimately into *industry sectors.* For the purposes of labor market analysis, the Bureau of Labor Statistics organized industry sectors into *industry supersectors* and then divided the supersectors into two broad groups: *Goods-producing industries* (natural resources and mining; construction; and manufacturing) and *service-providing industries* (trade, transportation, and utilities; information; financial activities; professional and business services; education and health services; leisure and hospitality; other services; and public administration).

Each industry subsector is made up of a number of industry groups, which are, as mentioned, determined by differences in production processes. An easily recognized example of these distinctions is in the food manufacturing subsector, which is made up of industry groups that produce meat products, preserved fruits and vegetables, bakery items, and dairy products, among others. Each of these industry groups requires workers with varying skills and employs unique production techniques. Another example of these distinc-

tions is found in utilities, which employs workers in establishments that provide electricity, natural gas, and water.

There were almost 7.8 million private business establishments in the United States in 2002. The average size of these establishments varies widely across industries.

Most establishments in the construction, wholesale trade, retail trade, finance and insurance, real estate and rental and leasing, and professional, scientific, and technical services industries are small, averaging fewer than 15 employees per establishment. however, wide differences within industries can exist. Hospitals, for example, employ an average of 712.4 workers, while physicians' offices employ an average of 9.3. Similarly, although there is an average of 13.3 employees per establishment for all of retail trade, department stores employ an average of 166.5 people.

Business establishments in the United States are predominantly small; 59.6 percent of all establishments employed fewer than 5 workers in 2002. However, the medium-sized to large establishments employ a greater proportion of all workers. For example, establishments that employed 50 or more workers accounted for only 4.7 percent of all establishments, yet employed 57.4 percent of all workers. The large establishments—those with more than 500 workers—accounted for only 0.2 percent of all establishments, but employed 18.2 percent of all workers. Table 1 presents the percent distribution of employment according to establishment size.

TABLE 1

Percent distribution of establishments and employment in all private industries by establishment size, March 2002

Establishment size (number of workers)	Establishments	Employment
Total	100.0	100.0
1 to 4	59.6	6.6
5 to 9	16.9	8.2
10 to 19	11.1	10.9
20 to 49	7.7	17.0
50 to 99	2.6	13.3
100 to 249	1.5	16.4
250 to 499	0.4	9.5
500 to 999	0.1	7.0
1,000 or more	0.1	11.2

Establishment size can play a role in the characteristics of each job. Large establishments generally offer workers greater occupational mobility and advancement potential, whereas small establishments may provide their employees with broader experience by requiring them to assume a wider range of responsibilities. Also, small establishments are distributed throughout the nation; every locality has a few small businesses. Large establishments, in contrast, employ more workers and are less common, but they play a much more prominent role in the economies of the areas in which they are located.

Working Conditions

Just as the goods and services produced in each industry are different, working conditions vary significantly among industries. In some industries, the work setting is quiet, temperature-controlled, and virtually hazard free; while other industries are characterized by noisy, uncomfortable, and sometimes dangerous work environments. Some industries require long workweeks and shift work; in many industries, standard 40-hour workweeks are common. Still other industries can be seasonal, requiring long hours during busy periods and abbreviated schedules during slower months. Production processes, establishment size, and the physical location of work usually determine these varying conditions.

One of the most telling indicators of working conditions is an industry's injury and illness rate. Overexertion, being struck by an object, and falls on the same level are among the most common incidents causing work-related injury or illness. In 2002, approximately 4.7 million nonfatal injuries and illnesses were reported throughout private industry. Among major industry divisions, manufacturing had the highest rate of injury and illness—7.2 cases for every 100 full-time workers—while finance, insurance, and real estate had the lowest rate—1.7 cases. About 5,500 work-related fatalities were reported in 2002; the most common events resulting in fatal injuries were transportation incidents, contact with objects and equipment, assaults and violent acts, and falls.

Work schedules are another important reflection of working conditions, and the operational requirements of each industry lead to large differences in hours worked and in part-time versus full-time status. In food services and drinking places, for example, 37.9 percent of employees worked part time in 2002 compared with only 1.3 percent in mining. Table 2 presents industries having relatively high and low percentages of part-time workers.

TABLE 2

Part-time workers as a percent of total employment, selected industries, 2002

Industry	Percent part-time
All industries	15.8
Many part-time workers	
Food services and drinking places	37.9
Grocery stores	30.1
Clothing, accessory, and general merchandise stores	29.2
Child day care services	29.1
Arts, entertainment, and recreation	28.1
Motion picture and video industries	24.8
Social assistance, except child day care	21.8
Educational services	21.1
Few part-time workers	
Chemical manufacturing, except drugs	3.1
Pharmaceutical and medicine manufacturing	3.1
Computer and electronic product manufacturing	2.6
Utilities	2.5
Aerospace product and parts manufacturing	2.1
Motor vehicle and parts manufacturing	1.8
Steel manufacturing	1.8
Mining	1.3

The low proportion of part-time workers in some manufacturing industries often reflects the continuous nature of the production processes that makes it difficult to adapt the volume of production to short-term fluctuations in product demand. Once begun, it is costly to halt these processes; machinery must be tended and materials must be moved continuously. For example, the chemical manufacturing industry produces many different chemical products through controlled chemical reactions. These processes require chemical operators to monitor and adjust the flow of materials into and out of the line of production. Because production may continue 24 hours a day, 7 days a week, under the watchful eyes of chemical operators who work in shifts, full-time workers are more likely to be employed. Retail trade and service industries, on the other hand, have seasonal cycles marked by various events that affect the hours worked, such as school openings or important holidays. During busy times of the year, longer hours are common, whereas slack periods lead to cutbacks in work hours and shorter workweeks. Jobs in these industries are generally appealing to students and others who desire flexible, part-time schedules.

Employment

The total number of jobs in the United States in 2002 was 144 million. This included 11.4 million self-employed workers, 140,000 unpaid workers in family businesses, and 132.3 million wage and salary workers—including primary and secondary job holders. The total number of jobs is projected to increase to 165.3 million by 2012, and wage and salary jobs are projected to account for more than 153.8 million of them.

As shown in Table 3, although wage and salary jobs are the vast majority of all jobs, they are not evenly divided among the various industries. The education and health services industry supersector is the largest source of employment, with about 26 million workers in 2002. The trade, transportation, and utilities supersector is next largest, followed by professional and business services, employing 25.5 million and 16 million workers, respectively. Wage and salary employment ranged from only 122,500 in oil and gas extraction to 12.5 million in educational services. Three industries—educational services, health services, and food services and drinking places—together accounted for 33.5 million jobs, or one quarter of the nation's wage and salary employment.

TABLE 3

Wage and salary employment in selected industries, 2002, and projected change, 2002-12
(Employment in thousands)

Industry	2002 Employment	2002 Percent distribution	2012 Employment	2012 Percent distribution	2002-12 Percent change	2002-12 Employment change
All industries	132,279	100.0	153,883	100.0	16.3	21,603
Goods-producing industries	23,766	18.0	24,539	15.9	3.2	772
Natural resources and mining	1,728	1.3	1,644	1.1	-4.9	-84
Agriculture, forestry, fishing, and hunting	1,216	0.9	1,192	0.8	-1.9	-24
Oil and gas extraction	123	0.1	88	0.1	-27.8	-34
Mining	212	0.2	180	0.1	-15.0	-32
Construction	6,732	5.1	7,745	5.0	15.1	1,014
Manufacturing	15,307	11.6	15,149	9.8	-1.0	-157
Aerospace product and parts manufacturing	468	0.4	386	0.3	-17.6	-83
Apparel manufacturing	358	0.3	112	0.1	-68.6	-245
Chemical manufacturing, except drugs	636	0.5	530	0.3	-16.7	-106
Computer and electronic product manufacturing	1,521	1.1	1,333	0.9	-12.4	-189
Food manufacturing	1,525	1.2	1,597	1.0	4.7	72
Motor vehicle and parts manufacturing	1,152	0.9	1,181	0.8	2.6	29
Pharmaceutical and medicine manufacturing	293	0.2	361	0.2	23.2	68
Printing	710	0.5	734	0.5	3.3	24
Steel manufacturing	170	0.1	136	0.1	-20.0	-34
Textile mills and products	489	0.4	338	0.2	-31.0	-152
Service-providing industries	108,513	82.0	129,344	84.1	19.2	20,831
Trade, transportation, and utilities	25,493	19.3	29,093	18.9	14.1	3,600
Automobile dealers	1,250	0.9	1,408	0.9	12.6	158
Clothing, accessory, and general merchandise stores	4,129	3.1	4,473	2.9	8.3	344
Grocery stores	2,478	1.9	2,611	1.7	5.4	133
Wholesale trade	5,641	4.3	6,279	4.1	11.3	638
Air transportation	559	0.4	626	0.4	12.0	67
Truck transportation and warehousing	1,853	1.4	2,274	1.5	22.7	422
Utilities	600	0.5	565	0.4	-5.7	-34
Information	3,420	2.6	4,052	2.6	18.5	632
Broadcasting	334	0.3	362	0.2	8.5	28
Motion picture and video industries	360	0.3	472	0.3	31.1	112
Publishing, except software	714	0.5	703	0.5	-1.5	-11
Software publishers	256	0.2	430	0.3	67.9	174
Telecommunications	1,201	0.9	1,281	0.8	6.7	80

(continued)

TABLE 3 (CONTINUED)

Wage and salary employment in selected industries, 2002, and projected change, 2002-12

(Employment in thousands)

Industry	2002 Employment	2002 Percent distribution	2012 Employment	2012 Percent distribution	2002-12 Percent change	2002-12 Employment change
Financial activities	5,815	4.4	6,405	4.2	10.1	590
Banking	1,761	1.3	1,873	1.2	6.4	112
Insurance	2,223	1.7	2,391	1.6	7.5	168
Securities, commodities, and other investments	801	0.6	925	0.6	15.5	124
Professional and business services	16,010	12.1	20,876	13.6	30.4	4,866
Advertising and public relations services	442	0.3	525	0.3	18.9	84
Computer systems design and related services	1,163	0.9	1,798	1.2	54.6	635
Employment services	3,249	2.5	5,012	3.3	54.3	1,764
Management, scientific, and technical consulting services	732	0.6	1,137	0.7	55.4	406
Education and health services	26,060	19.7	32,935	21.4	26.4	6,875
Child day care services	734	0.6	1,050	0.7	43.1	316
Educational services	12,527	9.5	15,016	9.8	19.9	2,489
Health services	12,524	9.5	16,025	10.4	28.0	3,501
Social assistance, except child day care	1,269	1.0	1,867	1.2	47.1	597
Leisure and hospitality	11,969	9.0	14,104	9.2	17.8	2,135
Arts, entertainment, and recreation	1,778	1.3	2,275	1.5	28.0	497
Food services and drinking places	8,412	6.4	9,749	6.3	15.9	1,337
Hotels and other accommodations	1,780	1.3	2,080	1.4	16.9	301
Public administration	9,774	7.4	10,582	6.9	8.3	808
Federal Government, excluding the postal service	1,922	1.5	1,972	1.3	2.6	50
State and local government, except education and health	7,851	5.9	8,610	5.6	9.7	759

NOTE: May not add to totals due to omission of industries not covered in the *Career Guide*.

Although workers of all ages are employed in each industry, certain industries tend to possess workers of distinct age groups. For the previously mentioned reasons, retail trade employs a relatively high proportion of younger workers to fill part-time and temporary positions. The manufacturing sector, on the other hand, has a relatively high median age because many jobs in the sector require a number of years to learn and perfect specialized skills that do not easily transfer to other firms. Also, manufacturing employment has been declining, providing fewer opportunities for younger workers to get jobs. As a result, one-fourth of the workers in retail trade were 24 years of age or younger in 2002, compared with only 8.4 percent of workers in manufacturing. Table 4 contrasts the age distribution of workers in all industries with the distributions in five very different industries.

Employment in some industries is concentrated in one region of the country. Such industries often are located near a source of raw or unfinished materials upon which the industry relies. For example, oil and gas extraction jobs are concentrated in Texas, Louisiana, and Oklahoma; many textile mills and products manufacturing jobs are found in North Carolina, South Carolina, and Georgia; and a significant proportion of motor vehicle manufacturing jobs are located in Michigan and Ohio. On the other hand, some industries—such as grocery stores and educational services—have jobs distributed throughout the nation, reflecting the general population density.

TABLE 4

Percent distribution of wage and salary workers by age group, selected industries, 2002

| Industry | Age group | | | |
	16 to 24	25 to 44	45 to 64	65 and older
All industries	15	48	34	3
Computer systems design and related services	7	68	25	1
Educational services	10	43	44	3
Food services and drinking places	45	39	15	2
Telecommunications	10	58	32	1
Utilities	6	47	45	2

Occupations in the Industry

The occupations found in each industry depend on the types of services provided or goods produced. For example, because construction companies require skilled trades workers to build and renovate buildings, these companies employ large numbers of carpenters, electricians, plumbers, painters, and sheet metal workers. Other occupations common to construction include construction equipment operators and mechanics, installers, and repairers. Retail trade, on the other hand, displays and sells manufactured goods to consumers. As a result, retail trade employs numerous sales clerks and other workers, including more than three-fourths of all cashiers. Table 5 shows the industry sectors and the occupational groups that predominate in each.

TABLE 5

Industry sectors and their largest occupational group, 2002

Industry sector	Largest occupational group	Percent of industry wage and salary jobs
Agriculture, forestry, fishing, and hunting	Farming, fishing, and forestry occupations	61.1
Mining	Construction and extraction occupations	33.3
Construction	Construction and extraction occupations	66.2
Manufacturing	Production occupations	52.1
Wholesale trade	Sales and related occupations	24.7
Retail trade	Sales and related occupations	52.5
Transportation and warehousing	Transportation and material moving occupations	56.0
Utilities	Installation, maintenance, and repair occupations	25.6
Information	Professional and related occupations	29.1
Finance and insurance	Office and administrative support occupations	51.4
Real estate and rental and leasing	Sales and related occupations	22.7
Professional, scientific, and technical services	Professional and related occupations	42.6
Management of companies and enterprises	Office and administrative support occupations	33.6
Administrative and support and waste management and remediation services	Office and administrative support occupations	23.2
Educational services, private	Professional and related occupations	59.6
Health care and social assistance	Professional and related occupations	42.6
Arts, entertainment, and recreation	Service occupations	57.2
Accommodation and food services	Service occupations	84.0
Government	Professional and related occupations	43.7

The nation's occupational distribution clearly is influenced by its industrial structure, yet there are many occupations, such as general manager or secretary, that are found in all industries. In fact, some of the largest occupations in the U.S. economy are dispersed across many industries. For example, the office and administrative support occupational group is among the largest in the nation since nearly every industry relies on administrative support workers. (See Table 6.) Other large occupational groups include professional and related occupations, service occupations, management, business, and financial occupations, and sales and related occupations.

TABLE 6

Total employment and projected change by broad occupational group, 2002-12

(Employment in thousands)

Occupational group	Employment, 2002	Percent change, 2002-12
Total, all occupations	144,014	14.8
Professional and related occupations	27,687	23.3
Service occupations	26,569	20.1
Office and administrative support occupations....................	23,851	6.8
Management, business, and financial occupations.................	15,501	15.4
Sales and related occupations	15,260	12.9
Production occupations	11,258	3.2
Transportation and material moving occupations...................	9,828	13.1
Construction and extraction occupations	7,292	15.0
Installation, maintenance, and repair occupations	5,696	13.6
Farming, fishing, and forestry occupations.............................	1,072	3.3

Training and Advancement

Workers prepare for employment in many ways, but the most fundamental form of job training in the United States is a high school education. Fully 88 percent of the nation's workforce possessed a high school diploma or its equivalent in 2002. However, many occupations require more training, so growing numbers of workers pursue additional training or education after high school. In 2002, 28.7 percent of the nation's workforce reported having completed some college or an associate's degree as their highest level of education, while an additional 28.7 percent continued in their studies and attained a bachelor's or higher degree. In addition to these types of formal education, other sources of qualifying

training include formal company provided training, apprenticeships, informal on-the-job training, correspondence courses, the Armed Forces vocational training, and non-work-related training.

The unique combination of training required to succeed in each industry is determined largely by the industry's production process and the mix of occupations it requires. For example, manufacturing employs many machine operators who generally need little formal education after high school, but sometimes complete considerable on-the-job training. In contrast, educational services employs many types of teachers, most of whom require a bachelor's or higher degree. Training requirements by industry sector are shown in table 7.

Persons with no more than a high school diploma accounted for about 65.4 percent of all workers in agriculture, forestry, fishing, and hunting; 64.7 percent in construction; 63.3 percent in accommodation and food services; 56.9

TABLE 7

Percent distribution of workers by highest grade completed or degree received, by industry sector, 2002

Industry sector	High school diploma or less	Some college or associate's degree	Bachelor's or higher degree
All industries	42.5	28.7	28.7
Agriculture, forestry, fishing, and hunting..........................	65.4	21.2	13.4
Mining	57.0	23.5	19.5
Construction	64.7	25.1	10.2
Manufacturing	52.9	25.7	21.4
Wholesale trade	44.8	27.9	27.3
Retail trade............................	52.7	31.1	16.1
Transportation and warehousing.........................	52.9	32.1	15.1
Utilities..................................	39.8	35.3	25.0
Information	27.6	33.0	39.3
Finance and insurance...........	26.1	32.0	41.9
Real estate and rental and leasing	38.9	31.5	29.6
Professional, scientific, and technical services.................	15.3	24.3	60.4
Administrative and support and waste management and remediation services	54.9	27.3	17.9
Educational services, private ..	18.9	19.5	61.6
Health care and social assistance	31.9	34.4	33.7
Arts, entertainment, and recreation.............................	41.4	30.7	27.8
Accommodation and food services.................................	63.3	26.4	10.3
Government...........................	25.6	36.7	37.8

percent in mining; 52.9 percent in manufacturing; and 52.7 in retail trade. On the other hand, those who had acquired a bachelor's or higher degree accounted for 61.6 percent of all workers in educational services, private; 60.4 percent in professional, scientific, and technical services; 41.9 percent in finance and insurance; 39.3 percent in information; and 37.8 percent in government.

Education and training also are important factors in the variety of advancement paths found in different industries. Each industry has some unique advancement paths, but workers who complete additional on-the-job training or education generally help their chances of being promoted. In much of the manufacturing sector, for example, production workers who receive training in management and computer skills increase their likelihood of being promoted to supervisory positions. Other factors that impact advancement include the size of the establishments, institutionalized career tracks, and the mix of occupations. As a result, persons who seek jobs in particular industries should be aware of how these advancement paths and other factors may later shape their careers.

Earnings

Like other characteristics, earnings differ by industry, the result of a highly complicated process that reflects a number of factors. For example, earnings may vary due to the nature of occupations in the industry, average hours worked, geographical location, workers' average age, educational requirements, industry profits, and union penetration of the workforce. In general, wages are highest in metropolitan areas to compensate for the higher cost of living. Also, as would be expected, industries that employ a large proportion of unskilled minimum-wage or part time workers tend to have lower earnings.

The difference in earnings of all wage and salary workers in computer systems design and related services, which averaged $1,112 a week in 2002, and those in food service and drinking places, where the weekly average was $359, provide a good illustration of how various factors can affect earnings. The difference is so large primarily because computer systems design and related services establishments employ more highly skilled full-time workers, while food service and drinking places employ many lower-skilled part-time workers. In addition, many workers in food service and drinking places are able to supplement their low wages with money they receive as tips, which is not included in the industry wages data. Table 8 highlights the industries with the highest and lowest average weekly earnings.

Employee benefits, once a minor addition to wages and salaries, continue to grow in diversity and cost. In addition to traditional benefits—including paid vacations, life and health insurance, and pensions—many employers now offer various benefits to accommodate the needs of a changing labor force. Such benefits include childcare, employee assistance programs that provide counseling for personal problems, and wellness programs that encourage exercise, stress management, and self-improvement. Benefits vary among occupational groups, full- and part-time workers, public and private sector workers, regions, unionized and nonunionized workers, and small and large establishments. Data indicate that full-time workers and those in medium-sized and large establishments—those with 100 or more workers—receive better benefits than do part-time workers and those in smaller establishments.

TABLE 8

Average weekly earnings of production or nonsupervisory workers on private nonfarm payrolls, selected industries, 2002

Industry	Earnings
All industries	$610
Industries with high earnings	
Computer systems design and related services	1,112
Management, scientific, and technical consulting services	992
Securities, commodities, and other investments	971
Aerospace product and parts manufacturing	952
Pharmaceutical and medicine manufacturing	940
Software publishers	921
Computer and electronic product manufacturing	859
Telecommunications	836
Industries with low earnings	
Textile mills and products	446
Grocery stores	424
Clothing, accessory, and general merchandise stores	418
Hotels and other accommodations	410
Agriculture, forestry, fishing, and hunting	376
Food services and drinking places	359
Apparel manufacturing	348
Child day care services	348

Union penetration of the workforce varies widely by industry, and it also may play a role in earnings and benefits. In 2002, about 14.5 percent of workers throughout the nation were union members or covered by union contracts. As Table 9 demonstrates, union affiliation of workers varies widely by industry. Almost 45 percent of the workers in air transportation were union members, the highest rate of all the industries, followed by 38.5 percent in educational services and

36.9 percent in steel manufacturing. Industries with the lowest unionization rate include software publishers, 0 percent; food services and drinking places, 1.8 percent; and computer systems design and related services, 1.9 percent.

TABLE 9

Union members and other workers covered by union contracts as a percent of total employment, selected industries, 2002

Industry	Percent union members or covered by union contract
All industries	14.5
Industries with high unionization rates	
Air transportation	44.8
Educational services	38.5
Steel manufacturing	36.9
Government	35.2
Motor vehicle and parts manufacturing	32.3
Industries with low unionization rates	
Banking	2.1
Advertising and public relations services......	2.0
Computer systems design and related services	1.9
Food services and drinking places	1.8
Software publishers.......................................	0.0

Outlook

Total employment in the United States is projected to increase by about 15 percent over the 2002-12 period. Employment growth, however, is only one source of job openings. The total number of openings in any industry also depends on the industry's current employment level and its need to replace workers who leave their jobs. Throughout the economy, in fact, replacement needs will create more job openings than will employment growth. Employment size is a major determinant of job openings—larger industries generally have larger numbers of workers who must be replaced and provide more openings. The occupational composition of an industry is another factor. Industries with high concentrations of professional, technical, and other jobs that require more formal education—occupations in which workers tend to leave their jobs less frequently—generally have fewer openings resulting from replacement needs. On the other hand, more replacement openings generally occur in industries with high concentrations of service, laborer, and other jobs that require little formal education and have lower wages because workers in these jobs are more likely to leave their occupations.

Employment growth is determined largely by changes in the demand for the goods and services provided by an industry, worker productivity, and foreign competition. Each industry is affected by a different set of variables that determines the number and composition of jobs that will be available. Even within an industry, employment may grow at different rates in different occupations. For example, changes in technology, production methods, and business practices in an industry might eliminate some jobs while creating others. Some industries may be growing rapidly overall, yet opportunities for workers in occupations that are adversely affected by technological change could be stagnant or even declining. Similarly, employment of some occupations may be declining in the economy as a whole, yet may be increasing in a rapidly growing industry.

As shown in Table 3, employment growth rates over the next decade will vary widely among industries. Employment in goods-producing industries is expected to increase as growth in construction is partially offset by declining employment in agriculture, forestry, fishing, and hunting; mining; and manufacturing. Growth in construction employment will stem from new factory construction as existing facilities are modernized; from new school construction, reflecting growth in the school-age population; and from infrastructure improvements, such as road and bridge construction. Employment in mining is expected to decline due to labor-saving technology and continued reliance on foreign sources of energy.

Manufacturing employment will decrease slightly—employment declines in apparel manufacturing, computer and electronic product manufacturing, and textile mills and products manufacturing will be partially offset by employment gains in food manufacturing and pharmaceutical and medicine manufacturing. Apparel manufacturing is projected to lose about 245,000 jobs over the 2002-12 period—more than any other manufacturing industry—due primarily to increasing imports replacing domestic products. Employment growth in food manufacturing is expected, as a growing and ever-more-diverse population increase the demand for manufactured food products. Employment growth in pharmaceutical and medicine manufacturing is expected as sales of pharmaceuticals increase with growth in the population, particularly among the elderly, and with the introduction of new medicines to the market. Both food and pharmaceutical and medicine manufacturing also have growing export markets.

Growth in overall employment will result primarily from growth in service-providing industries over the 2002-12 period, almost all of which are expected to have increasing employment. Rising employment in service-providing industries is expected to occur predominantly in health services and educational services—the two largest industries—as well as in employment services, food services and drinking places, state and local government, and wholesale trade. When combined, these sectors will account for almost half of all new wage and salary jobs across the nation.

Health services will account for the most new wage and salary jobs, about 3.5 million over the 2002-12 period. Population growth, advances in medical technologies that increase the number of treatable diseases, and a growing share of the population in older age groups will drive employment growth. Offices of physicians, the largest health services industry group, is expected to account for about 770,000 of these new jobs as patients seek more healthcare outside of the traditional inpatient hospital setting.

Educational services is expected to grow by nearly 20 percent over the 2002-12 period, adding about 2.5 million new jobs. A growing emphasis on improving education and making it available to more children and young adults will be the primary factors contributing to employment growth. Employment growth at all levels of education is expected, particularly at the postsecondary level, as children of the baby boomers continue to reach college age and as more adults pursue continuing education to enhance or update their skills.

Employment in one of the nation's fastest-growing industries—employment services—is expected to increase by more than 50 percent, adding another 1.8 million jobs over the 2002-12 period. Employment will increase, particularly in temporary help services and professional employer organizations, as businesses seek new ways to make their workforces more specialized and responsive to changes in demand.

The food services and drinking places industry is expected to add more than 1.3 million new jobs over the 2002-12 projection period. Increases in population, dual-income families, and dining sophistication will contribute to job growth. In addition, the increasing diversity of the population will contribute to job growth in food service and drinking places that offer a wider variety of ethnic foods and drinks.

Almost 760,000 new jobs are expected to arise in state and local government, adding almost 10 percent over the 2002-12 period. Job growth will result primarily from growth in the population and its demand for public services. Additional job growth will result as state and local governments continue to receive greater responsibility for administering federally funded programs from the federal government.

Wholesale trade is expected to add almost 640,000 new jobs over the coming decade, reflecting growth both in trade and in the overall economy. Most new jobs will be in durable goods merchant wholesalers, such as professional and commercial equipment and supplies; electrical and electronic goods; and furniture and home furnishing. However, industry consolidation and the growth of electronic commerce using the Internet are expected to limit job growth to 11 percent over the 2002-12 period, less than the 15 percent projected for all industries.

Continual changes in the economy have far-reaching and complex effects on employment. Jobseekers should be aware of these changes, keeping alert for developments that can affect job opportunities in industries and the variety of occupations that are found in each industry. For more detailed information on specific occupations, consult the 2004-05 edition of the *Occupational Outlook Handbook*, which provides information on more than 275 occupations.

Training for Techies: Career Preparation in Information Technology

Maria and Spencer are both in their early twenties. Maria recently completed her bachelor's degree in English; Spencer dropped out of college after a few semesters. If asked to speculate on Maria's and Spencer's occupations, perhaps you would guess writer and waiter.

But it might surprise you to learn that Maria is a computer systems analyst and Spencer is a computer programmer. While majoring in English, Maria took several computer-related courses and gained experience working in a computer lab. Spencer, although not formally enrolled in a degree program, took courses at a community college and earned certification in a programming language. Both benefited from the flexible training requirements for individuals hoping to work in information technology, often identified as IT.

The Bureau of Labor Statistics (BLS) projects that 8 of the 10 fastest-growing occupations between 2000 and 2010 will be computer related. For this reason, future jobseekers need to know about the variety of ways to prepare for a career in information technology. Following a discussion of how these workers are defined, this article focuses on the available training, which ranges from certificates to advanced degrees.

What Is an Information Technology Worker?

The information technology workforce is defined differently by trade organizations and government sources.

The Information Technology Association of America defines an information technology worker by using the eight career clusters developed by the National Workforce Center for Emerging Technologies. Those career clusters include programming and software engineering, technical support,

enterprise systems, database development and administration, Web development and administration, network design and administration, digital media, and technical writing. According to its latest study, "Bouncing Back: Jobs, Skills, and the Continuing Demand for IT Workers," the Association notes that 92 percent of all information technology workers are in non-information technology companies, 80 percent of them in small companies outside the information technology industry.

The U.S. Department of Commerce identifies the information technology workforce more broadly. In its report on information technology, "Digital Economy 2002," the Department defines workers in information technology occupations as those who design, manufacture, operate, maintain, and repair information technology products and provide related services across all industries.

For purposes of this article, information technology workers are considered to be those employed in 12 computer-related Standard Occupational Classification System (SOC) occupations. These occupations are

- Computer and information systems managers
- Computer programmers
- Computer and information scientists
- Computer systems analysts
- Computer hardware engineers
- Computer software engineers, applications
- Computer software engineers, systems software
- Computer support specialists
- Database administrators
- Network and computer systems administrators
- Network systems and data communications analysts
- All other computer specialists, a residual category of workers

Using this definition, BLS data show that about 3.3 million information technology workers were employed in the United States in 2000. However, that number excludes marketing and sales workers employed by information technology companies.

What Type of Training Do I Need?

As Maria's and Spencer's backgrounds suggest, there is considerable interest in the topic of education and training required for information technology workers. This interest stems from the U.S. economy's demand for such workers and a presumption that the current educational system is not producing enough of them for the workforce. Rita Caldwell, director of the National Science Foundation, notes that there are many pathways for becoming an information technology worker. Training ranges from a few months for certification to 6 years for a doctoral degree.

BLS data show that in 2001, most information technology workers—almost 70 percent—had a bachelor's or higher degree, although the number who had some college but no degree is rapidly increasing and accounted for almost 16 percent of these workers. (See Chart 1.) In fact, anecdotal information suggests that many people attend community colleges not to earn degrees but to take computer-related courses in hopes of getting a job or as a way to retrain and update their skills. And according to the National Science Foundation, two-thirds of workers who had a bachelor's degree and worked in a computer-related occupation in 1999 had majored in subjects other than computer and information sciences. (See Chart 2.)

Clearly, earning a postsecondary degree in a computer-related field is not the only way to prepare for a job in information technology. But learning the technical skills necessary to work in these occupations remains paramount. Specialized certification and degree programs—associate, bachelor's, and graduate-level ones—are the primary ways workers train for information technology occupations.

Certification

Technical or professional certification demonstrates that an individual has achieved a level of competency in a particular field. There are various certifications available for information technology workers. Spencer, for example, earned certification that qualified him for a computer programming job. Product vendors and industry organizations offer different types of certification, providing a training niche that is expected to continue.

Chart 1
Distribution of workers in computer-related occupations by highest level of educational attainment, 2001

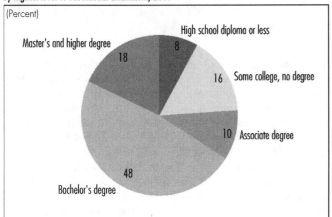

Growth of certification. According to the Information Technology Association of America's study on the information technology workforce, the significance of certification has grown in each of its job categories in the last year. Kenneth Bartlett, project director for the National Research Center for Career and Technical Education, says that as of August 2002, there were almost 100 vendors and organizations offering more than 670 separate certifications in information technology.

And these certifications are growing more popular. Data from the U.S. Department of Education's National Center for Education Statistics show that the number of awards of less than 1 year granted in computer and information sciences grew almost 400 percent between 1990 and 2000.

When international trends are considered, the impact of certification is even more dramatic. In his 2000 report, "The Certification System in Information Technology," author Clifford Adelman describes a "parallel universe" outside conventional educational routes for potential information technology workers to develop skills. The report notes that, by early 2000, about 1.6 million people worldwide had earned roughly 2.4 million information technology certifications.

Vendor and organization certification. Product vendors and software firms—including Microsoft, Cisco, and Oracle—offer certification and may require individuals who work with their products to be certified. And industry organizations, such as the Institute for the Certification of Computing Professionals, offer voluntary certification. The Institute's certification is available to those who have a college degree and at least 2 years of experience and have passed a series of examinations.

Vendor certification evolved from the difficulty employers had finding skilled workers to fill the rising number of high-tech jobs created by the Internet boom in the mid- to late 1990s. Because certification is faster, cheaper, and more focused than traditional educational tracks, vendor certification soon emerged as a solution to the problem of worker shortages.

As of May 2002, Microsoft Corporation had issued more than 1.2 million certifications to individuals classified as Microsoft Certified Professionals. One example of the rapid growth in vendor certification is the increase in the number of Microsoft Certified Systems Engineer awards over the last few years: 35,000 in fall 1997; 280,000 by June 2000; and almost 463,000 by July 2002.

Future of certification. Certification has become an increasingly important standard in the information technology industry in the last decade. However, it has also become more controversial. Although it enables workers to demonstrate a specific set of skills, some employers say that certification is not a viable substitute for practical experience. Others prefer that workers have formal education and practical experience, predicting that certifications will diminish in importance. But as the following example illustrates, certification should continue to play a role in training information technology workers.

Chart 2
Field of study distribution for all degree holders in computer-related occupations, 1999

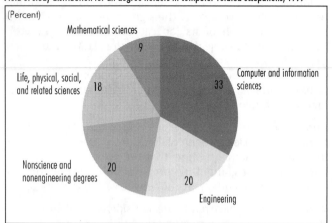

(Percent)

Mathematical sciences 9

Life, physical, social, and related sciences 18

Computer and information sciences 33

Nonscience and nonengineering degrees 20

Engineering 20

Source: National Science Foundation. 1999 SESTAT Integrated Data System. The SESTAT Web site is sestat.nsf.gov.

The growing importance of network security in information technology has led to an increased demand for computer security professionals. Someone who wants to work in information security can get one of a variety of certifications instead of a 2- or 4-year degree. Employers interested in securing their organizations' computer networks seek individuals with expertise in information security, which a specialized certification presumably demonstrates.

In an era in which new technology may become obsolete in a few years, acquiring skills quickly is important to both employers and workers.

Degrees

Many employers of information technology workers require applicants to have a degree, which they perceive as proof of a worker's ability to think logically. And there are plenty of options for students interested in earning a degree in information technology. According to the National Center for Education Statistics, computer and information sciences include computer programming, data processing, information science and systems, computer systems analysis, and computer science.

But, as mentioned previously, most information technology workers who have a degree do not have one in a computer field. Some, like Maria, studied subjects completely unrelated to information technology and gained computer knowledge through other coursework and related experience. Associate, bachelor's, and graduate degree programs have different focuses in training workers for information technology jobs.

Chart 3
Degrees awarded in computer and information sciences, 1989-90 to 1999-2000

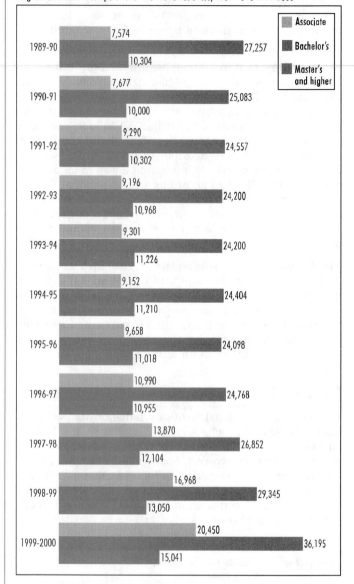

Legend: Associate, Bachelor's, Master's and higher

Year	Associate	Bachelor's	Master's and higher
1989-90	7,574	27,257	10,304
1990-91	7,677	25,083	10,000
1991-92	9,290	24,557	10,302
1992-93	9,196	24,200	10,968
1993-94	9,301	24,200	11,226
1994-95	9,152	24,404	11,210
1995-96	9,658	24,098	11,018
1996-97	10,990	24,768	10,955
1997-98	13,870	26,852	12,104
1998-99	16,968	29,345	13,050
1999-2000	20,450	36,195	15,041

Source: U.S. Department of Education, National Center for Education Statistics

Associate degrees. The associate degree is an increasingly attractive option for information technology workers. Most community colleges and many independent technical institutes and proprietary schools offer an associate degree in computer science or related information technology fields. Because many of these programs are designed to meet the needs of local businesses, they are more occupation-specific than are those of a 4-year degree. Some jobs may be better suited to the level of training these programs offer. Many students who earn an associate degree seek employment as computer support specialists or as computer programmers.

There has been a steady rise in the number of associate degrees granted in the computer and information sciences over the last decade, from fewer than 8,000 in 1990 to more than 20,000 in 2000. (See Chart 3.) Furthermore, the number of associate degrees conferred in the business information and data processing services doubled from about 7,000 in 1991 to nearly 14,000 in 2000.

Bachelor's degrees. As previously indicated, most information technology workers have at least a bachelor's degree. In his report for the National Research Center for Career and Technical Education, "The Perceived Influence of Industry-Sponsored Credentials," Kenneth Bartlett points out that employers still prefer a 4-year college degree as preparation for information technology jobs. And in a tight job market, preference for a bachelor's degree rises as employers attempt to differentiate among potential jobseekers. But the degree concentration and relevant experience required may vary by occupation.

For computer software engineers, most employers prefer that applicants have at least a bachelor's degree and broad knowledge and experience with computer systems and technologies. The usual degree concentrations for applications software engineers are computer science and software engineering; for systems software engineers, usual concentrations are computer science and computer information systems.

There is no universally accepted way to prepare for a job as a systems analyst or database administrator, network administrator, or network systems and data communications analyst. However, most employers place a premium on some formal college education; a bachelor's degree is a prerequisite for many jobs. Some workers in these occupations have a degree in either computer science, mathematics, or information systems.

The number of bachelor's degrees awarded in computer science rose between 1990 and 2000. However, an increasing number of people in the information technology workforce had a non-computer-related degree. Chart 4 shows that for bachelor's degree holders in computer-related occupations in 1999, more than half the workers had studied something other than the computer and information sciences. Large numbers of workers did have degrees in related fields, such as engineering and math. According to the National Center for Education Statistics, for example, the number of bachelor's degrees conferred in management information systems rose dramatically: from 4,700 in 1991 to almost 15,000 in 2000.

The lack of emphasis on computer-related bachelor's degrees in information technology occupations points to an important trend for prospective information technology workers. Employers still demand technical skills, but "soft" skills—including the ability to communicate effectively, both orally and in writing—also are important for these jobseekers to have. Knowing how to write a computer program or administer a database is critical, but ability to interact with other computer specialists, clients, customers, and users continues to gain importance.

The need for multidimensional workers in information technology means that employers prefer workers who have business skills and acumen, along with relevant and up-to-date technical expertise. Thus, it is not surprising that increasing numbers of information technology workers do not have computer-related degrees. National Science Foundation data illustrate this point: In 1995, roughly 18 percent of computer scientists either had a nonscience or nonengineering degree or had a degree in the life, physical, social, and related sciences. But by 1999, the number of computer scientists with a degree in those concentrations had nearly doubled, growing to 35 percent.

Graduate degrees. Graduate degrees are preferred for some of the more complex jobs in software engineering and database administration. According to the National Center for Education Statistics, the number of master's degrees conferred in computer and information sciences rose sharply between 1990 and 2000, while the number of doctoral degrees in computer science grew slightly.

Many computer and information systems mangers have a master's degree in business administration (MBA) with technology as a core component. This so-called techno-MBA degree differs from a traditional MBA because of its heavy emphasis on information technology in addition to the standard business curriculum. And because computer and information systems managers make not only technology decisions but also business decisions for their organizations, techno-MBA programs are becoming increasingly popular.

Information technology workers interested in becoming a computer or information scientist usually need a doctoral degree in computer science or computer engineering because of the highly innovative and technical nature of the work. Some computer and information systems managers may have a doctoral degree in a computer-related field, demonstrating thorough technical knowledge.

Flexible Pathways

The discussion about career preparation for information technology occupations reveals that there is no universal education and training requirement for jobseekers in information technology. A computer-related degree may be the easiest and most direct route to take, but it is by no means the only one. There is a variety of ways in which workers can demonstrate the computer knowledge and skills necessary to get a job in one of several computer-related occupations. Practical experience, although difficult to measure and quantify, is important and allows jobseekers flexibility—especially for those who do not have a computer-related degree.

Information technology workers must continually acquire new skills to remain in this dynamic field. To this end, the role of community colleges in educating and retraining information technology workers should continue to grow in the coming years. A May 2000 Urban Institute report, "The Role of Community Colleges in Expanding the Supply of

Chart 4
Distribution of bachelor's degree holders in computer-related occupations by field of study, 1999

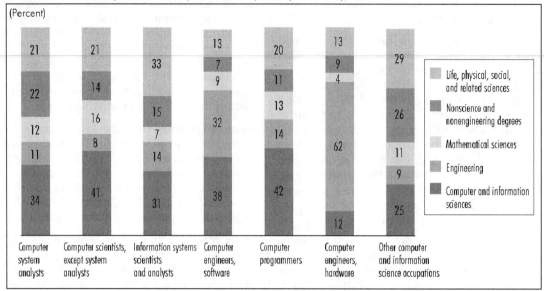

Source: National Science Foundation. 1999 SEST AT Integrated Data System. The SEST AT Web site is sestat.nsf.gov.

Information Technology Workers," says that these schools conduct a large amount of information technology training and contribute to retraining both veteran workers and those from other fields.

Technology changes at such a rapid pace that retraining and updating information technology skills is essential, even for workers already in their jobs. The emphasis on nondegree programs, such as employer training and self-study, also will rise in importance. And just as colleges and universities are increasingly using distance education as an efficient and cost-saving measure, organizations are using it to train and retrain their employees in information technology.

There are several ways that individuals may prepare to become an information technology worker. At first glance, the tracks that Maria and Spencer took to get jobs in their respective computer-related occupations might seem unorthodox. Yet with rapidly changing technology and increasingly flexible training requirements, the routes they took should remain commonplace.

For More Information

The following organizations provide information for computer-related careers:

Association for Computing Machinery (ACM)
1515 Broadway
New York, NY 10036-5701
(800) 342-6626
(212) 869-7440
www.acm.org

IEEE Computer Society
Headquarters Office
1730 Massachusetts Ave. NW
Washington, DC 20036-1992
(800) 678-4333
(202) 371-0101
www.computer.org

National Workforce Center for Emerging Technologies
3000 Landerholm Circle SE
Bellevue, WA 98007
(425) 564-4215
www.nwcet.org

Information about the designation of Certified Computing Professional is available from

Institute for Certification of Computer Professionals (ICCP)
2200 E. Devon Ave., Suite 247
Des Plaines, IL 60018
(800) U-GET-CCP (843-8227)
www.iccp.org

Information about training leading to a CompTIA certification is available from

Computing Technology Industry Association (CompTIA)
1815 S. Myers Rd., Suite 300
Oakbrook Terrace, IL 60181-5228
(630) 268-1818
www.comptia.org

For information about training for Microsoft certification, contact

> Microsoft Corporation
> One Microsoft Way
> Redmond, WA 98052-6399
> (800) 636-7544
> **www.microsoft.com/train_cert**

Information about training for Oracle certification is available from

> Oracle Corporation
> 500 Oracle Parkway
> Redwood Shores, CA 94065
> (800) 529-0165
> **education.oracle.com**

For information about training for Cisco certification, contact

> Cisco Systems, Inc.
> 170 W. Tasman Dr.
> San Jose, CA 95134
> (800) 829-6387
> **www.cisco.com/warp/public/10/ wwtraining**

Information about training for Novell certification is available from

> Novell, Inc.
> 2211 N. First St.
> San Jose, CA 95131
> (800) 233-3382
> **education.novell.com**

From the Occupational Outlook Quarterly *by the U.S. Department of Labor. Written by Roger Moncarz, an economist in the Office of Occupational Statistics and Employment Projections, BLS.*

O*NET Dictionary of Occupational Titles,
Third Edition

Based on data from the U.S. Department of Labor
Developed under the direction of Michael Farr with
database work by Laurence Shatkin, Ph.D.

JIST was the first publisher to use the Department of Labor's O*NET data, which was developed to replace the *Dictionary of Occupational Titles*. This reference includes descriptions of the more than 1,100 jobs in the latest O*NET database and is the only printed source of this information!

ISBN 1-56370-962-7 / Order Code LP-J9627 / **$39.95** Softcover
ISBN 1-56370-963-5 / Order Code LP-J9635 / **$49.95** Hardcover

Career Guide to America's Top Industries,
Sixth Edition

U.S. Department of Labor

This information-packed review of 42 top industries discusses careers from an industry perspective and covers employment trends, earnings, types of jobs available, working conditions, training required, and more. Helps the reader see that choosing the right industry is as important as choosing the right occupation.

This valuable companion reference to the *Occupational Outlook Handbook* includes cross-references to jobs listed there.

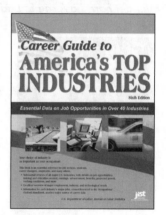

ISBN 1-59357-032-5 / Order Code LP-J0325 / **$13.95**

Best Jobs for the 21ˢᵗ Century, Third Edition

Michael Farr with database work by Laurence Shatkin, Ph.D.

This data-packed reference is ideal for students, teachers, working people, and anyone interested in career planning and job advancement. It contains 65 lists of jobs with the best pay, fastest growth, and most openings in numerous categories.

The second part of the book describes more than 500 jobs with fast growth, many openings, or high pay—all based on the latest O*NET data from the U.S. Department of Labor.

ISBN 1-56370-961-9 / Order Code LP-J9619 / **$19.95**